# BRINK™

## OFFICIAL GAME GUIDE

# FOREWORD

## Hail, Reader

About three years ago, we sat down to write the very first pitch document for *Brink*. It started off as a very blank piece of paper. We joked that it would be much easier if we could just leap into the future, buy the official strategy guide, and thus instantly comprehend every detail of *Brink*'s world: game design, gameplay, the maps, the weapons, the abilities, and the sights, sounds, and smells of the Ark.

While we had to make do the old fashioned way, you've now got the entire world of *Brink* at your fingertips. With simple flips of your powerful thumb, you can feast upon every particular of it, allowing you to formulate cunning tactics, stratagems, and ruses; to delve deep within the murky secret interiors of the gameplay; to raise an inquisitive eyebrow at the plot and backstory twists; and to devise expertly efficient routes through the maps and missions.

Our goal for *Brink* always was to create a game accessible enough to be enjoyed by players who'd never (or only momentarily) tried online multi-player, but still with the depth of gameplay and infinite replay possibilities to reward constant revisiting and experimentation. Easy to play, hard to master, endlessly rewarding, these were our watchwords. Also, SHOOTYBANG and RUNRUNRUN. Those were also our watchwords. And "topiary." I'll be honest; we're not 100% sure what a watchword is. But this guide will tell you, along with many other things.

I cannot even indicate with my outstretched arms how enormously cool it is to see this finished book. It represents such an insane amount of work, both by our team at Splash Damage and the good people at Prima. Kudos to 'em all—their dedication and smarts and general awesomeness are now laid out for you, right within these pages.

We hope you enjoy this book, and enjoy exploring *Brink*. See you online!

Ed "BongoBoy" Stern
Lead Writer, *Brink*

# CONTENTS

# A HISTORY OF THE ARK

## The Last Refuge of Humanity

### Briefing

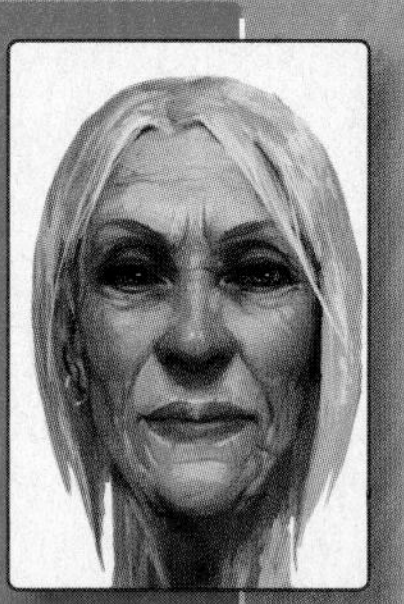

Welcome to the Ark. Originally conceived as a model of sustainable living, reconceived as a luxury resort when the funding ran out, and finally repurposed as a floating refugee camp and last bastion of humanity in a ruined world, the Ark and its inhabitants exist in a precarious balance. Resources are in short supply, suspicions and conspiracy theories run rampant, and the Ark's inhabitants are choosing sides. There are two sides to the story of the Ark, and neither one is telling the whole truth about their motivations to fight. Will you battle on the side of order to preserve the status quo, or on the side of anarchy to redistribute resources and carve your own place in a new society?

*Brink* takes place in the year 2045 on an artificial mid-ocean habitat called the Ark. The Ark is not a single structure; it's an archipelago of man-made floating structures, some several acres in area. It was originally built as an experimental self-sufficient habitat, but the rapid rise of the Earth's oceans has cut the Ark off from all outside contact, leaving it a last refuge for survivors.

Crammed with the original Founders (and their descendents) as well as tens of thousands of refugee "Guests," the Ark exists in total isolation from the rest of the world. Despite the Ark's supposed sustainability, the increasing demand for resources outpaces the Ark's ever shorter supply. The delicate balance of power between the Ark's competing social factions is about to explode into civil war. You must choose whether to side with the Resistance to escape the Ark, or join Security and preserve it.

### Phase 1: Ark City

In the 2010s, amid rising concerns at the rate of climate change, an international consortium set about constructing a floating city called the Ark. Inspired by cutting-edge architectural and environmental concepts, the Ark was originally intended to be a totally self-sufficient living laboratory that would prove the principle of ecologically sustainable development. The original design was a high-minded manifesto for a better life.

The colossal scale of the project meant construction moved at a snail's pace while the fundamental structures of the Ark were established—with artificial atolls as temporary foundations and colossal pontoons as permanent bases. Early construction had to be largely in steel, using existing naval engineering techniques. Entire Bulk Oil Carrier hulls were up-ended and recycled as foundations. One structure was sponsored by an international charity devoted to publicizing the possibilities of cheap, recycled materials and was consequently made out of intermodal shipping containers. The result was practical and colorful, but looked more like a steampunk vertical slum than a clean and futuristic vision of the future. The reality of Ark development did not meet the public's expectation of the clean, high-tech vision of the future promised by the Ark's planners. Consequently, funding dried up and the Ark Consortium was forced to re-conceptualize.

## ↘ Phase 2: Luxury at Sea

The project was reconceived as a dual-purpose experimental habitat and luxury eco-tourism resort. From the rusty shipyard atmosphere of the Ark site rose the stunning Ark Tower. This radical surge in progress was made possible by the development of Arkoral, an architectural building material derived from genetically modified coral. Ark scientists developed further electro-deposition techniques to grow new watertight hulls by passing current through metal mesh screens, causing calcium and silicon compounds to accumulate into a watertight wall.

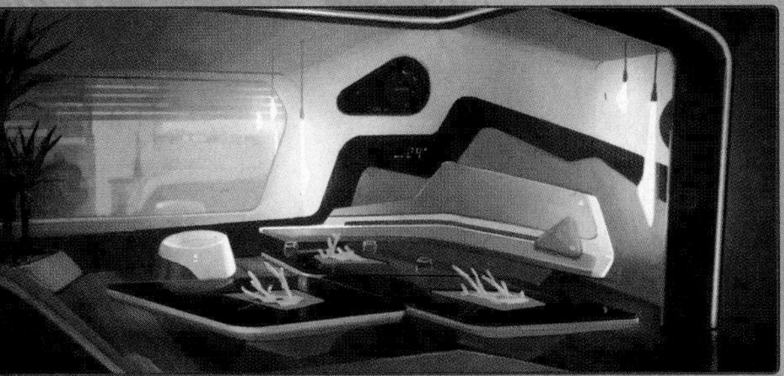

The reinvention of the Ark as a "ten star hotel" was a mixed blessing for the project. Although this repurposing was denounced by some original consortium members as a betrayal of the project's original goals, the new luxury resort incarnation of the Ark attracted huge publicity and endless celebrity visits, and generated much-needed further financing. There was some resentment of the well-heeled celebrity "guests" by the established research and administration crew, but the newcomers brought badly needed financial stability. However perfunctory their visits, even if their stays lasted no longer than their photo ops, their wealth kept the Ark project afloat and growing.

## ↘ Phase 3: The Ark, The Answer

By the late 2030s, global warming was a reality. The sea was rising. Coastal and littoral regions were increasingly inundated, water tables were contaminated by marine salination, entire populations had to be evacuated and re-housed. Increasingly scarce resources exacerbated social tensions in almost every nation. As steel costs skyrocketed, the emphasis of the Ark shifted again to a research and development facility, developing sustainable (and highly marketable) technologies that would help humanity survive a globally warmed future. Additional islands were added to the Ark complex to serve as experimental science labs.

Whatever the original visionary theories, the Ark had to work in practice. The Ark's population swelled to include the ranks of mechanical and electronic engineers, civil and naval architects, materials experts, and construction workers that it needed to expand.

The Ark was only ever intended to sustain a limited population—a few thousand at most. Other than the Ark Consortium headquarters, there was a small permanent administration staff, a long-term temporary army of construction workers, and a rotating population of several hundred visiting scholars, scientists, and students on a variety of sponsored scholarships, bursaries, and internships mainly dealing in marine biology, waste management, construction techniques, resource conservation etc.

However, the catastrophic sudden sea rises in the 2030s caused a sudden influx of refugees, many of them highly qualified scientists, but all in desperate need. Almost overnight, the Ark's population increased a hundredfold. New islands were constructed in extreme haste to house the Ark's new guests. Even so, many had to be turned away, and one hastily constructed refugee Accommodation Island capsized and sank with terrible loss of life.

So long as the Ark remains self-sufficient, the current status quo can endure. But rumors are beginning to spread: that the Ark is running low on key resources, that it no longer has the spare parts to maintain or repair key facilities, that the water desalination plants are failing, that soon there will have to be a violent struggle for control of the strategic pelgos.

## Phase 4: Guests of the Ark

In many ways the current Ark started in 2038. Before then it was a science project and luxury resort. Suddenly it was a crowded city, a nation, cut off from the rest of the world. The Ark's Guests were the world in miniature. They came from every conceivable racial, national, and social group. Some were unlettered peasant farmers and fishermen, some emeritus professors, some billionaires whose paper wealth was suddenly meaningless.

The psychological trauma of their arrival cannot be overstated. Common to many was a simultaneous exultation at survival, along with a vast sorrow as their sudden loss of family, wealth, privilege, and status proved traumatic, let alone the memory and knowledge of their home cities' inundation beneath the advancing seas. Even for the most practical, they had to not only adjust to a new lifestyle, they had to create it. The Ark's sudden growth demanded an entirely new way of living. Every resource had to be rationed, all waste had to be recycled, amenities and utilities had to be improvised. Many of the "uneducated" new arrivals proved vastly more adept at Ark life, possessing proven survival and improvisation skills. Life in the early days of the new Ark required vast resources of pragmatism and practical ability: things had to be made to work, right away. Professional scientists, accustomed to more controlled, less chaotic environments, often became demoralized and unproductive.

It is a common cause of resentment among the present Guest community that it was actually the Guests' expertise and effort that ensured the survival of the Ark. It is widely believed that the original Founder community was paralyzed with shock, incapable of helping itself or its new expanded population. The early days of the new Ark were chaotic, and many mistakes were made. Things are better now, but major tensions remain.

## How the Ark Works

The Ark's precise location is a secret. Initially located off the coast of San Francisco, Ark was moved away from the mainland to promote exclusivity during its time as a luxury resort. Its final, permanent location is somewhere in the middle of the Pacific Ocean.

Ark is made up of an archipelago of artificial islands we call pelgos. All the Ark pelgos make up the artificial archipelago that is the Ark. Each pelgo is constructed on the "Floating Spar" principle: most of its mass is under the sea's surface and incorporates a ballast control section that keeps the pelgo both buoyant and stable. Most previous marine engineering projects such as oil drilling rigs were made of steel, which rusts away at sea. But the Ark's pelgos are made from Arkoral.

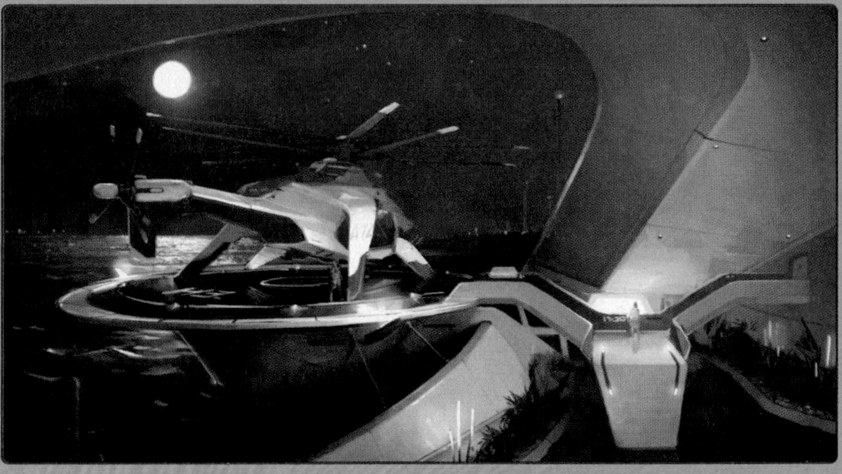

Arkoral is a genetically modified form of coral specially developed by Ark scientists for use as a next-generation construction material. It's as strong as concrete, but whiter and lighter. And unlike concrete or cement, Arkoral doesn't give off greenhouse gases as it sets; instead, it actually captures C02!

Ark is protected from the open ocean by a perimeter seawall: a series of wavefarms and breakwater ramps that dispel incoming waves and harness their energy for use by Ark. Farthest from the Ark, belts of surface wavefarms absorb some of the wave energy before it gets to the seawall sections. Then the main breakwater stops ocean waves breaking over the inner pelgos. It's not a continuous or tall fortress wall rising up above the surface of the sea; it's made up of many sections of inclined ramp, with much of its bulk hidden underwater. The inclined ramp sections absorb and harness the kinetic energy of incoming waves both by bobbing up and down (powering hydraulic compression generators) and also by funnelling incoming wave impulses toward underwater turbine generators.

A clean, efficient monorail service allows people, equipment, and cargo to be moved easily around the Ark. Boats and other floating craft are also common, but even within the Ark's perimeter breakwater, waves can get rough when the wind is high.

To power all Ark's services and systems, Ark engineers had to develop as many different clean, renewable energy sources as possible. Arrays of next-generation solar panels convert the sun's rays into electrical energy, banks of wind turbines placed to windward harness the powerful sea breezes, and smaller rooftop turbines can provide enough power for individual houses. The Ark's perimeter breakwater is like one enormous generator, powered by the endless energy of the ocean waves. Below the surface waves, the sea itself is moving, pushed by enormously powerful ocean currents. The Ark has huge banks of underwater turbines that can harness that energy: The Ark's revolutionary Ocean Thermal Energy Conversion (OTEC) plant uses the difference in temperature between surface and deep ocean water to power a heat engine. Day and night, the OTEC plant steadily generates vital power for heating and lighting; a vital byproduct of the OTEC plant is clean drinking water.

## Ark Timeline

**2005:** Construction begins offshore. This version of the Ark is intended as a proof of concept: using existing technologies to build a self-sustaining floating city.

**2010:** The resulting collection of floating ship hulls, cargo containers, and repurposed materials looks more like an industrial zone than a utopian eco-village, and funding quickly dries up.

**2013:** Ark construction halted.

**2015:** New investors reconceive the Ark as a floating luxury resort that relies on high-tech innovations to achieve a sustainable lifestyle for wealthy residents. The Ark is moved away from the mainland to avoid shipping lanes and flight paths.

**2017:** Perimeter seawall construction begins at the Ark's permanent mid-ocean location.

**2020:** Infrastructure construction is completed—power generation, food production, and recycling systems are all complete and online; research labs are up and running; and primary residential areas have been built.

**2025:** Rising sea levels and mainland blight prompt the first waves of refugees to arrive at the Ark. Initially housed in tidy container conversions, their numbers soon outpace the construction resources of the Ark, and more shambolic accommodations are adopted. Ark society is already forming divisions.

**2027:** Earlobe ID chips become compulsory for all Ark Guests.

**2030:** Amid a sharp increase in refugee arrivals, the Ark loses all contact with the outside world. Two distinct factions coalesce in Ark society as shelter and resources become scarce and austerity measures become essential.

**2035:** A Resistance movement emerges. Underground activists begin to organize, questioning the status quo of the Ark's social structure and resource allocation. An accident at the desalination facility and failing technology at the Ocean Thermal Energy Conversion plant mean that water and power supplies are increasingly unreliable and unpredictable.

**2038:** Water rationing begins, accompanied by increased Security presence. Resistance activism responds accordingly.

**2039:** Resistance cells begin to actively raid the Upper Ark, and skirmishes ensue.

**2045:** As sickness ravages the slums of the Lower Ark, the Upper Ark institutes a quarantine lockdown. Society on the Ark has reached a breaking point, and the battle is beginning.

Ark has extensive kelp and fish farms, many marked out by their own wind/solar farm pylons rising from the waters. Back when the OTEC plant was working, the warm upwellings were exploited to attract fish/increase kelp growth. The Ark is researching Integrated Multi-Trophic Aquaculture: where the wastes of one species are recycled as the foods for another. The Ark can farm everything from microalgae and beneficial cyano-bacteria like Spirulina to tasty seaweeds and fish, and can even raise tanks of freshwater fish. The heat from the heat exchangers allows cold water food species like lobster to be farmed, even in tropical waters.

Ark must grow all of its own food. In addition to the kelp beds and fisheries under the sea, the Ark also boasts vertical farms, greenhouses, and bioreactors. Ark is a floating farm that relies on desalinated water to keep everything alive and growing.

Ark is pioneering new desalination technology, combined with a holistic recycling philosophy. The Arks' main recycling pelgo uses a combination of sunlight, phytoplankton, and microalgae to break down organic waste into reusable nutrients and clean water.

## Ark Society

Despite all the lofty goals of the Ark in all its phases, the reality of climate change and overpopulation have proved to be a great strain on the theoretical tenets of the Ark: self-sustaining and unsinkable it may be, but current circumstances are testing that to the limit. Despite having the facilities to create an endless supply of power, water, and food, the Ark's isolation makes it a constant struggle to keep essential systems running—in fact, many of these systems are irreparably broken, exacerbating the social tensions inherent in living on an overcrowded island. Power, water, food, and supplies are all rationed, and Ark Guests feel the shortages much more than the Founders do.

The original Ark project was only supposed to support a few thousand engineers, scientists, and celebrity backers. This original development consisted only of what ended up being the Upper Ark: Founders' Tower, the Resort, the Airport, a few science labs, factories, and professional dorms; some factory and R&D labs with associated wind and solar farms; and an old cargo facility. When throngs of Guests begin arriving in the 2020s, accommodations had to be constructed; this is the origin of the Lower Ark. The cargo facility was relocated and metastasized into Container City, and soon the Guest dorms and then Container City slums and tied-together ship slums were added. At its peak population, the Ark supported 45,000 inhabitants. The population density of the Ark is sharply divided, with a mere 3,000 Founders living permanently in the Founders' Tower/Resort Villas of the "Upper" Upper Ark. About 7,000 technically skilled people live in the dorms and labs in the "Lower" Upper Ark. Of the remaining 35,000 Guests, only 5,000-9,000 are in the nicer Guest Dorms ("Upper" Lower Ark), while the rest live in close quarters in Container City and the ship slums ("Lower" Lower Ark)

Due to the scarcity of farmed food, most people on the Ark eat primarily kelp and krill and very occasionally fish (although usually as an unappetising unidentifiable protein), all of which makes people very hungry for steak. Rumors persist that the idle rich may resort to unsavory measures to satisfy their cravings for richer protein—some Guest disappearances can't be explained by disease or accident.

Some of the more intrepid residents have attempted to hunt for additional food supplies, but this is no easy task. From its early days offshore, the Ark has maintained a population of seagulls that remained with the Ark when it was towed farther out to sea; they are a constant raucous reminder that the Ark is an ocean island. These seagulls are smart and hard to catch, although occasionally they get caught in the windfarm turbines. However, trying to collect the gulls is a perilous business and may result in even more protein being deposited.

Fishing, too, provides its share of complications. Ark requires an extensive fishing trawler fleet to feed its population, but Security has to accompany every ship. Hardline Conspiracist Resistance think that Security insist on this to prevent people escaping to freedom. Security retort that the Resistance keep mutinying, stealing Ark's precious trawlers, and forcing the crews to sail to their doom.

These factors are at the heart of the divisions in Ark society, and tensions may soon boil over into outright conflict. Political factions on the Ark are becoming more organized, and with two charismatic leaders in charge, the situation will inevitable come to a head.

HISTORY OF THE ARK
CHARACTER CREATION
GAMEPLAY
WEAPONS DETAIL
CAMPAIGN & FREEPLAY MAPS
CHALLENGES
APPENDICES

# Factions: Resistance vs. Security

One of the greatest social tensions in the Ark is that of status, and whether it should be purely meritocratic or based on previous pre-Deluge society. Many high-profile near-celebrity scientists were initially welcomed as honored guests, but proved to have no usable skills. Their pre-Deluge status became increasingly irrelevant, as they proved time and time again that they could not contribute to the new community. Many Founders are of the opinion that though it may not be fair, the Ark is theirs. They didn't have to take so many Guests aboard, but they did. They should not now have to surrender their own possessions and positions merely because their Guests have become demanding. Others are not as harsh in their beliefs, but believe that adherence to pre-Deluge status is all that can hold the community together.

The Ark currently has a delicate balance of power—no one faction predominates, although the Founders have a much easier life than the Guests. The Guests do all the work, but are dependent on the Founders for employment (not to mention power, heat, light, and food). The Founders feel they have done enough to give the Guests a home, and any requests for additional resources should be earned. However, the Founders depend on the Guests to keep the Ark running—the thousand menial jobs that keep the Ark alive all have to be performed by Guests. Captain Mokoena's Security protects the status quo.

The Resistance's aims are various and somewhat incoherent. Some want to overturn the power structure entirely, some merely to gain better political representation and more equal distribution of the Ark's resources. Some are insistent that the priority must be to re-establish contact with the outside world, reasoning that there's no way the seas rose high enough to destroy all human life. Brother Chen has managed to keep the various strands of dissent united under his leadership. So far.

While the factions strongly distrust one another, there are some honorable and upright people on both sides (and some dangerous thugs as well). There is no clear right vs. wrong; both factions fight for the way of life that they deem necessary to ensure the future of the Ark and the survival of humanity. Despite motivations both noble and ignoble on both sides, neither faction's leader is being entirely honest with their men (although they have all sorts of reasons why such deception is necessary).

## The Political Spectrum

Although the political divisions on the Ark are complex, with widely varying motivations for any given individual's beliefs, the political spectrum on the Ark can be broadly classified. The debate over the fate of humanity is a polarizing one, as is the tension between advocates of social order and of revolution.

### Catastrophist vs Conspiracist

The Ark's authorities claim that the Ark is the only vestige of human civilization left. Catastrophists on the Ark believe this claim that no other humans survive. Conspiracists suspect there might be other enclaves of humanity.

Hardline Catastrophists believe that all other civilization on Earth perished due to global warming, and that only the Ark remains. They think there might be a few humans left, but they're probably desperate raiders who want to steal the Ark's precious resources.

Moderate Catastrophists believe that some other civilized societies may have survived, but very few and it's not worth expending resources looking for them. If they exist, they'll make contact via radio, so why not just sit tight and make the best of things.

Moderate Conspiracists suspect that they're being lied to and think that more efforts should be made to contact the outside world. They don't believe the official version of how the world is, but they're not sure what's actually going on.

Hardline Conspiracists believe absolutely that the rest of the world is carrying on fine, that global warming never happened, and that Ark is a prison, holding them captive against their will.

### Authoritarian vs Anarchist

The distribution of resources is a constant issue on the Ark, and there are two prevailing philosophies on how to optimize their allocation. Authoritarians believe that there must be a central body that determines how resources are divided, while the Anarchists believe that sharing all resources equally is the only way forward.

Hardline Authoritarians believe in a strict social order: resources are limited and everyone needs to know their place and stick to it. They believe that the Founders have a right to the lion's share of resources, and the Guests are lucky to be on the Ark at all.

Moderate Authoritarians believe that some social order is necessary, and that the Ark's needs are probably best served by the existing status quo (although it could do with some rebalancing or mild reform).

Moderate Anarchists believe that the status quo is unfair and want a fairer distribution of resources, with the Founders getting less and the Guests getting more.

Hardline Anarchists believe the entire Ark project is an oppressive oligarchy and must be overthrown at all costs.

## Founders

The Founders, many of whom can take credit for the very existence of the Ark, live in the quieter enclaves of the Upper Ark. They are the ones who started building the Ark, who guided it through its various stages of development, and who ultimately made the decision to allow Guests to take refuge on their visionary island. The Founders lived on the Ark in self-imposed, ideologically motivated isolation before the Guests arrived, and the Founders were ill prepared for the harsh realities the Guests brought with them. Although they often relied on the ingenuity and practical skills of the Guests, most Founders still believe that they are the benefactors of humanity, and that the Guests survive thanks to the Founders' largesse. This disparity in lifestyle between the Founders and the Guests is a constant source of resentment, so the Founders are rarely seen outside the Upper Ark and tend to avoid interaction with the Guests, leaving that duty to their Security forces.

### Ishmael

Ishmael is the mysterious older woman who is never seen but often heard. Ishmael appears to have been one of the original Founders of the Ark project—her involvement likely predates the Ark's construction. She's smart, dry, wry, and commanding, and she knows much more about the Ark than anyone else. She looks back on the idealistic vision of eco-sustainable living as a naive youthful dream, but has an equally skeptical view about the current armed posturing taking place on the Ark.

## The Resistance

The Resistance, like many political movements, only looks united from the outside. Members of the Resistance range from earnest fighters for social justice to career criminals ready to exploit the unrest for their own profit. The majority of Resistance fighters, however, are reasonable and humane people who feel reluctantly forced to action by the unreasonable actions of others. Led by Brother Chen, the Resistance wants to eliminate the distinction between Founders and Guests, and to distribute Ark resources equally among all inhabitants.

### Brother Chen

**Full Name:** "Brother" Joe Peng Chen

**Born:** 1985

**Age in 2045:** 60 (although still vigorous, so could be in his 50s)

**Position:** Head of the Resistance

**Ethnicity:** Chinese

Chen, with his younger brother, helped build the Ark. Steve Chen died in an Arkoral-pouring accident, and is buried within the support wall of Founders' Tower. Joe Chen still feels his loss keenly.

Chen's background as a construction worker and labor organizer has given him both a passionate concern for the fate of the working man and inspirational leadership skills. Chen is dedicated to improving the fate of the Guest population. He is respected and trusted among them. He suspects that neither the Founders nor Security are telling the truth about the Ark's predicament and wants to know the truth.

Despite his current role opposing authority, Chen harbors a secret: he was originally a sort of policeman, violently suppressing worker unrest. Back in China, before he went to work abroad as a marine engineer, he was conscripted into the militia and ordered to participate in a violent crackdown on worker unrest and dissent. He still remembers the shock down his arm when he fractured a man's skull with a police baton. His lasting hatred and distrust of authority is driven by what he did himself and what he saw done by a regime he supported.

Although he likes to play up his Honest Joe image, which keeps him acceptable to both refugee Guests and the Founders, Chen is wilier than he appears.

Chen and Security's leader Captain Mokoena aren't so dissimilar. Chen is more ambitious and self-regarding, but he has a similar sense of duty and the ability to ignore the better angels of his nature and persuade himself that he's doing the right thing. But he's a politician, prone to all the weaknesses that even the most selfless and idealistic politicians fall into. After a while, it seems like it's impossible for politicians to distinguish between the interests of those they represent, and their own career. The nobler your end, the grubbier the means you end up justifying.

### Nechayev

Nechayev is a Resistance fighter with some valuable skills, who has landed himself in prison. Because Nechayev is a pilot, the Resistance needs to keep him safe, in case any of the Conspiricists' plans to leave the Ark ever come to fruition. Thus, Brother Chen considers it a Resistance imperative to extract Nechayev from his present predicament.

## Security

As the refugee numbers swelled, the demand for a peace-keeping body was self-evident. Equally inevitable, as resources became increasingly scarce, was the tendency for questionable methods to crop up in the Security forces' operations. Like any police force, Ark's Security force attracted exactly the right and precisely the wrong sort of people. The selection process for Security officers moved too quickly for careful screening to occur, so selfless altruists with necessary skills find themselves working side by side with power-hungry mercenaries out for personal gain. Captain Mokoena, the Ark's Head of Security, uses any tools at his disposal to maintain balance and order on the Ark.

### Captain Mokoena

**Full Name:** Captain Clinton Mokoena

**Born:** 1992

**Age in 2045:** 53

**Position:** Head of Security

**Ethnicity:** Sub-Saharan African

Captain Mokoena is the head of Security, having succeeded the Ark's original Security Chief McCaffrey after the latter's accidental death in 2035. He is a forceful advocate of law and order, and believes that the Resistance are fantasists set on destroying the fragile balance of life on Ark necessary to keep everyone fed and alive.

Many of the Ark Security Section's original staff were former armed forces or paramilitary contractors. Mokoena's background was in law enforcement and disaster management. Mokoena grew up amid civil strife and turmoil, which has left him with a hatred of chaos, disorder, and what humans will do to each other to save themselves.

He has seen nations, societies, and populations destroyed by the rising sea, and he sincerely believes that the Ark is all that's left of the human race. He believes social order is only possible with the consent of the policed and that ultimately no society can survive without social justice. However, he is convinced that desperate times call for desperate measures; the Ark is in a permanent state of emergency, and some civil liberties must be curtailed. He is resolutely opposed to Resistance members who would disrupt or destroy the Ark's social order to find human life elsewhere. Mokoena's secret? He did bad things to get on the Ark.

Contrary to the belief in some corners of the Resistance, Mokoena is no implacable fascist dictator; in fact, he seems to be an honorable, noble man who has compromised his principles after being asked to do the impossible by ignorant and unrealistic bosses. He may do disagreeable things, but he has his reasons, and strives to do the right thing. Mokena is occasionally driven to extreme actions, sometimes against his better instincts, because he feels forced to defend the bad against the worse. In his mind, he's a good man doing bad things, an honest man talking himself out of doing what his conscience tells him.

An honest sense of duty can lead good men to do terrible things.

# CHARACTER CREATION

## Brinktroduction

This chapter guides you through creating your own, unique member of the Resistance and Security forces. This reveals all of the different variables to choose from during character creation, the augmentations you can select, the unlockables given out as your character gains ranks and experience (XP), and the various outfits and important abilities you can earn. Don't start leveling up your character until you've read through this chapter!

**Points? In order to make sense of the "points" mentioned throughout this and the Weapons chapter, cross-reference the different sections. For example, a landmine can inflict 175 points. But that information isn't useful until you check the number of points each body type has: Light = 120, Medium = 140, and Heavy = 180. So now you know that a landmine will dispatch Light and Medium enemies, but a Heavy enemy can survive one. Just!**

 **NOTE**

## Character Selection

Before your experience aboard the Ark pelgo can begin, you must select a character. This menu lets you cycle through your previously created characters, or create a new one (up to a maximum of 10). Your character's Rank, Level, Ability Points, XP, and the total characters you've created are displayed here.

**Save the Ark, Escape the Ark: At this point, you can decide which Campaign to start first: playing as either the Resistance or Security. Although the character you create wears the garb of the faction you've chosen, you can swap sides at any time; you're actually ranking up a single character with unlockable attire and weaponry from both factions.**

 **TIP**

### Creating and Customizing

**The checklist below shows every possible appearance change you can customize, both as Resistance or Security characters. The character level in which the customization becomes available is also noted. "Special Unlock" indicates that the item is a pre-order unlock, or otherwise specific unlock normally unavailable through regular gameplay.**

 **TIP**

Once you've completed your character's initial creation, whenever you want to change anything about him, simply access the Characters & Weapons menu option. Whenever anything new is available, this menu will pulse. Within the menu, you can choose the following options:

**Appearance:** Customize the clothing, hair, and face paint of your character. Your facial features, tattoos, and scars are permanent and cannot be changed.

**Weapons:** Choose the two firearms your character carries at the start of each mission from this menu. Consult the Weapons chapter for further details.

**Abilities:** You can expend Level Credits (one per level, to a maximum of 20) to choose an ability. These are covered later in this chapter.

**Preferred Class:** This enables you to choose the type of character you wish to begin a mission as. This is useful, because you won't then need to locate a Command Post to switch classes, and can reach Core Objectives more quickly.

**Character Selection:** Go back and pick a different, or new, character to play as.

## Character Appearance Checklist

### Archetypes

This cannot be changed once selected!

The Look

Initially available

The Geezer

Initially available

The Nose

Initially available

The Chin

Initially available

The Sensei

Initially available

The Smooth

Initially available

The Bruiser

Initially available

The Psycho

Initially available

The Young

Initially available

The Sour

Initially available

The Veteran

Initially available

The Suave

Initially available

## ↘ Head

The following appearance changes apply to your head only.

### Resistance Face Gear

These cover up or partially hide scars, tattoos, and paint.

The Goggles

Unlocked at Level 11

The Hockey Mask

Unlocked at Level 9

The Sweat

Unlocked at Level 12

The Grin

Special Unlock

The Firestarter

Unlocked at Level 6

The Anger

Unlocked at Level 20

The Fortress

Unlocked at Level 18

The Cannibal

Unlocked at Level 13

The Voice

Unlocked at Level 15

The Dude

Unlocked at Level 0

### Security Face Gear

These cover up or partially hide scars, tattoos, and paint.

The Look

Unlocked at Level 11

The Bouncer

Unlocked at Level 15

The Bug

Unlocked at Level 1

The Cop Glasses

Unlocked at Level 12

The Unit

Unlocked at Level 2

The Good Cop

Unlocked at Level 0

The Jesse

Unlocked at Level 17

The Sloani

Special Unlock

The Eel

Unlocked at Level 13

The Freak

Unlocked at Level 20

The Shield

Unlocked at Level 4

### Resistance Face Paint

This is daubed onto the face, and can be washed off.

White Skull Face Paint

Unlocked at Level 0

Headshot Face Paint

Unlocked at Level 4

Clown Face Paint

Unlocked at Level 19

Voodoo Face Paint

Unlocked at Level 16

Tribal Face Paint

Unlocked at Level 12

Hand Print Face Paint

Unlocked at Level 9

### Security Face Paint

This is daubed onto the face, and can be washed off.

Adhesive Bandages

Unlocked at Level 0

Barbarian Face Paint

Unlocked at Level 12

War Paint

Unlocked at Level 4

Camo. Face Paint

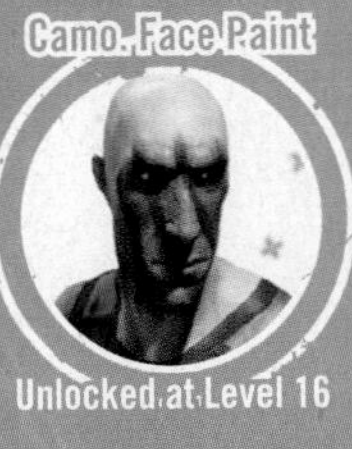

Unlocked at Level 16

Broken Nose

Unlocked at Level 9

Dirty Face

Unlocked at Level 19

## Facial Hair

Grow or shave this fluff between missions

The Disgrace

Resistance only. Unlocked at Level 17

The Beardy

Unlocked at Level 8

The Beatnik

Unlocked at Level 16

The Chinny

Unlocked at Level 8

The Chops

Unlocked at Level 16

The Goatee

Unlocked at Level 8

The Wrestler

Unlocked at Level 16

The Plait

Unlocked at Level 8

The Stubble
Unlocked at Level 0

The P.I.
Unlocked at Level 8

The Trimmed
Unlocked at Level 16

The Wolf
Unlocked at Level 16

## Resistance Hair & Head Gear

This mainly covers your hair, and a few cover your face.

The Dude

Unlocked at Level 11

DOOM Bandana

Special Unlock

Fallout Bandana

Special Unlock

The G

Unlocked at Level 2

The Safety

Unlocked at Level 10

The Shemagh

Unlocked at Level 17

The Spikes

Unlocked at Level 17

The Fortress

Unlocked at Level 18

The Dreads

Unlocked at Level 14

The Mohawk

Unlocked at Level 3

The Rasta

Unlocked at Level 10

The Scruff

Unlocked at Level 4

The Spiky Big Hair

Unlocked at Level 14

The Spiky Hair

Unlocked at Level 14

The Stripes

Unlocked at Level 10

The Receding

Unlocked at Level 0

The Buzz Cut

Unlocked at Level 0

The Corn Rows

Unlocked at Level 3

The Cropped

Unlocked at Level 0

The Dreadlocks

Unlocked at Level 0

The Fin
Unlocked at Level 3

The Tighten-Up
Unlocked at Level 0

The Tendril Afro
Unlocked at Level 3

The Natural
Unlocked at Level 10

## Security Hair & Head Gear

This mainly covers your hair, and a few cover your face.

The Beret
Unlocked at Level 12

The Cap

Unlocked at Level 17

The Jesse

Unlocked at Level 6

UAC Beanie Cap

Special Unlock

Vault-Tec Beanie Cap
Special Unlock

The Bomb
Unlocked at Level 18

The Tank
Unlocked at Level 0

The Flat Top
Unlocked at Level 3

The Dreads and Cap
Unlocked at Level 14

The Military Mohawk
Unlocked at Level 10

The Ponytail
Unlocked at Level 10

The Fashion
Unlocked at Level 14

The Receding
Unlocked at Level 0

The Buzz Cut
Unlocked at Level 0

The Corn Rows
Unlocked at Level 3

The Cropped
Unlocked at Level 0

The Dreadlocks
Unlocked at Level 0

The Fin
Unlocked at Level 3

The Tighten-Up
Unlocked at Level 0

The Tendril Afro
Unlocked at Level 3

The Natural
Unlocked at Level 10

## Tattoos & Scars

These can only be chosen once, and are permanent!

Kirituhi Half Face Tattoo
Unlocked at Level 0

Kirituhi Full Face Tattoo
Unlocked at Level 0

El Salvadorean Face Tattoo
Unlocked at Level 0

Crosstacean Face Tattoo
Unlocked at Level 0

Mayan Face Tattoo
Unlocked at Level 0

Kirituhi Lip Tattoo
Unlocked at Level 0

Deadeye Knife Scar
Unlocked at Level 0

Windscreen Scar
Unlocked at Level 0

Surgical Staples
Unlocked at Level 0

Tribal Eye Tattoo
Unlocked at Level 0

Ritual Scars
Unlocked at Level 0

Acid Burn Scar
Unlocked at Level 0

Stitched Scars
Unlocked at Level 0

Rough Acne Scars
Unlocked at Level 0

Glasgow Smile Scar
Unlocked at Level 0

# Full Body

The following appearance changes apply to your entire mass.

## Body Tattoo

These can only be chosen once, and are permanent!

Yakuza Tattoo
Unlocked at Level 0

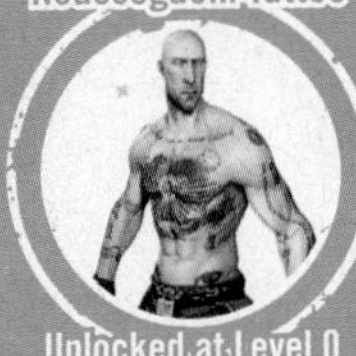
Nedosegaem Tattoo
Unlocked at Level 0

El Salvadorean Tattoo
Unlocked at Level 0

Samoan Tattoo
Unlocked at Level 0

Kirituhi Tattoo
Unlocked at Level 0

Crosstacean Tattoo
Unlocked at Level 0

Regimental Tattoo
Unlocked at Level 0

Runic Tattoo
Unlocked at Level 0

Biker Flames Tattoo
Unlocked at Level 0

Borneo Tattoo
Unlocked at Level 0

Devil Skull Tattoo
Unlocked at Level 0

The Sword Victim
Unlocked at Level 0

Tortured Soul Tattoo
Special Unlock

Hellspawn Tattoo
Special Unlock

Vault 101 Tattoo
Special Unlock

Dog Tag Tattoo
Special Unlock

## Body Type

Body type governs your speed, the weapons you can carry, and the environment you can maneuver over. These differences are not superficial, but can be changed between missions.

Heavy
Unlocked at Level 5

Medium
Unlocked at Level 0

Light
Unlocked at Level 7

## Resistance Shirts

These can be changed. Jackets usually hide some or all of this type of under-clothing.

Tattered Vest
Unlocked at Level 10

Tattered Shirt
Unlocked at Level 0

Forearm Bandages
Unlocked at Level 0

Vest
Unlocked at Level 0

String Vest
Unlocked at Level 13

Long-Sleeve Shirt
Unlocked at Level 19

Screaming Soul Shirt
Special Unlock

Vault Boy Shirt
Special Unlock

## Security Shirts

These can be changed. Jackets usually hide some or all of this type of under-clothing.

Muscle Vest
Unlocked at Level 0

Shirt & Sweatband
Unlocked at Level 0

Bouncer Shirt
Unlocked at Level 15

Muscle Shirt
Unlocked at Level 0

Stab Vest
Unlocked at Level 19

The Eel Shirt
Unlocked at Level 13

UAC Body Armor Shirt
Special Unlock

Vault Boy Shirt
Special Unlock

## Resistance Jackets

These can be changed. Jackets usually hide any shirts you may be wearing.

The Anger

Unlocked at Level 20

The Boiler Suit
Unlocked at Level 9

The G
Unlocked at Level 2

The Dude

Unlocked at Level 11

The Straps
Unlocked at Level 0

The Fortress

Unlocked at Level 18

The Lost
Unlocked at Level 13

The Voice

Unlocked at Level 15

The Warrior

Unlocked at Level 1

The Wasted

Unlocked at Level 4

The Firestarter

Unlocked at Level 6

## Security Jackets

These can be changed. Jackets usually hide any shirts you may be wearing.

The Bomb

Unlocked at Level 18

The Bouncer
Unlocked at Level 15

The Bug

Unlocked at Level 1

The Jesse

Unlocked at Level 6

The Tank
Unlocked at Level 0

The Tank Vest
Unlocked at Level 0

The Unit
Unlocked at Level 2

The Eel
Unlocked at Level 13

The Freak

Unlocked at Level 20

The Good Cop
Unlocked at Level 9

The Look
Unlocked at Level 11

The Shield
Unlocked at Level 4

## Resistance Pants

Change these whenever you wish.

The Anger

Unlocked at Level 20

The Boiler Suit

Unlocked at Level 9

The Firestarter

Unlocked at Level 6

The G

Unlocked at Level 2

The Sweat
Unlocked at Level 12

The Dude

Unlocked at Level 11

The Fortress

Unlocked at Level 18

The Lost

Unlocked at Level 13

The Voice

Unlocked at Level 15

The Warrior

Unlocked at Level 1

The Wasted

Unlocked at Level 4

## Security Pants

Change these whenever you wish.

The Bomb

Unlocked at Level 18

The Bouncer

Unlocked at Level 15

The Bug

Unlocked at Level 1

The Jesse

Unlocked at Level 6

The Tank

Unlocked at Level 0

The Unit

Unlocked at Level 2

The Eel

Unlocked at Level 13

The Freak
Unlocked at Level 20

The Good Cop

Unlocked at Level 9

The Look
Unlocked at Level 11

The Shield

Unlocked at Level 4

# Abilities

Abilities are unique and important skills that you choose for your character through a series of purchases via Level Credits:

You receive one Level Credit each time you level up thanks to Experience (XP) gain, to a maximum of 20.

You have the same number of Level Credits as you do levels, although you can sell your abilities to start over at any time. The penalty you pay is to drop a level. Why do this? To purchase abilities more suited to your style of play, and to remove abilities you don't find yourself using or needing.

Abilities are also ranked from 1 to 5. You can only purchase an ability when you are that rank, or higher. You receive an additional rank every five levels. So, a Rank 3 ability can be purchased when you are Level 10 or higher. Every ability costs one Level Credit, no matter what rank it is.

**Classes? Special abilities? Supply meter? What now? All of these terms are discussed in the Training videos. Please watch them (more than once) for additional beneficial information. Find further information regarding classes in the Gameplay chapter of this guide.**

 NOTE

**Mapping: Be sure to check the Abilities menu because certain abilities (basically the ones allowing you to throw or place grenades, armor, or other items) can be mapped to a specific directional pad or keyboard command. Do this, and the ability becomes a lot more useful!**

 TIP

**Remember! Certain special abilities or "buffs" that you give to your teammates only last a certain time, so don't just inject or throw helpful items into your friends. Use these abilities as the situation dictates.**

 CAUTION

## Universal Abilities

### Battle Hardened

Rank 1

Battle Hardened permanently increases your Life meter by one pip, allowing you to withstand a small amount of additional damage. This is recommended, because an increase in health is always welcome; it's like having the benefits of a Health Command Post on top of any other bonuses (including taking the post itself, because this gives you yet another pip!).

### Combat Intuition

Rank 1

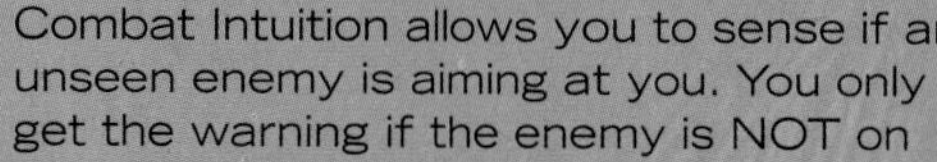

Combat Intuition allows you to sense if an unseen enemy is aiming at you. You only get the warning if the enemy is NOT on your radar, and if their crosshairs are directly on you. Useful if you're primarily a sniper or like to camp and use the map.

### Grenade Shooting

Rank 1

Grenade Shooting allows you to shoot down your own Frag Grenades mid-flight, giving you more control over when and where they will explode (if your aim is right). Consult the nearby information box for advice on using this fantastic alternative to grenade "cooking."

#### You'll Never Cook Again: Granade Shooting

Grenade Shooting is essentially an alternative to grenade cooking, but it requires a bit of skill. Once perfected, there's never a need to cook again.

To "cook" a grenade, you hold it for a few seconds before you throw, and the grenade explodes on impact instead of hitting the ground and detonating later, usually after enemies flee the area.

To "shoot" a grenade, aim high, tap (do not hold) "throw," then immediately aim back down toward the horizon. Wait for the grenade to "fall" into your aim, and fire (rapid fire/spread weapons are easier to hit with, obviously). You don't have to be incredibly accurate here—there is a forgiving aim on the grenade for just your shots.

This also allows a few mind tricks. Enemies may see the full fuse time on the grenade, and think you've been a fool for not cooking it. They may then decide they have enough time to run across it. This is the perfect time to prematurely explode the grenade.

**Grenade Damage: Frag grenades knock you down and inflict damage. The grenade indicator appears on your screen to warn when you're near an unexploded enemy grenade, and let you take evasive action.**

 TIP

### Sense of Perspective

Rank 1

Sense of Perspective snaps your view to a third-person perspective while you capture Command Posts or build/repair stationary objectives as an Engineer. Instead of being able to move while doing these lengthy actions, you can spin your camera around to watch for enemies from all angles. As the Engineer uses this more often, it may be wise to choose this if you're primarily this class. Additional vision comes at the expense of the ability to step around an objective to hide from enemy fire.

### Sprinting Grenade

Rank 1

Sprinting Grenade lets you cook and throw grenades without interrupting your sprint. This is extremely beneficial for those who want to be more adept and flexible during combat.

### Sprinting Reload
Rank 1

Sprinting Reload lets you reload your weapons while sprinting. Like Sprinting Grenade, this is a firm favorite among those who primarily rely on their carried weapons.

### Supply Max Increase

Rank 1

Supply Max Increase permanently increases your Supply meter by one pip, which allows you one additional use of special abilities before you must wait for a recharge. This is recommended, because an extra pip on your Supply meter (bottom left HUD on your screen) allows you to take advantage of your class's special ability; this is like having the benefits of a Supply Command Post on top of any other bonuses (including taking the post itself, because this gives you yet another pip!).

### Resupply Rate Increase
Rank 3

Resupply Rate Increase boosts the recharge rate of your Supply meter for all classes, shaving several seconds off the normal recharge rate for each pip. The exact amount of the increase is 20 percent compared to normal, and should be used with Supply Max Increase. This is obviously handy, because anything that gives you more time to use a special ability is beneficial.

### Silent Running

Rank 4

Silent Running makes you move completely silently. Normally, your movement noise makes you appear on an enemy's radar from a large distance, but with this, you will not appear at all until you're within striking distance. This reduces the volume of sound produced by footsteps, clothing, and equipment by 80 percent and stops you from appearing on the radar unless you fire or are seen. It is great for a more stealthy character—maybe an Operative or Light Body Type—although it is applicable to anyone.

### Downed Fire
Rank 5

Downed Fire lets you shoot even when you're incapacitated, but only with your backup weapon, and only after an initial delay of three seconds. If you purchase this, it will also reduce how much damage you can take while incapacitated before being killed outright. You will have almost no health while incapacitated, making it easy for enemies to finish you, so it's less likely that a Medic will be able to revive you. However, during the panic of firefights, this can be a true irritation to the enemy, and an especially satisfying way to dispatch a foe you almost defeated! It is also tactically beneficial, because your final shots may stop an objective from being completed. This can be nullified by an enemy Operative using the Comms Hack Ability on a downed foe.

## Soldier Abilities

### Standard Soldier Kit
Rank Auto

Soldiers complete destruction objectives using an HE Charge, and can resupply their teammates' ammo, as well as their own. Soldiers also carry Molotov Cocktails by default, giving them more grenade power than any other class. These are your special abilities, which cannot be sold. Remember you can plant a charge on any "buildable" objective, such as a door, gate, barricade, or stairs. Don't forget to rearm your teammates (and yourself), too!

**HE Charges: Both friendly and enemy HE Charges can kill you. When HE Charges are placed, a countdown timer appears in the top right of your HUD, you'll hear a countdown in the last five seconds, and if you're really close you can hear the HE Charge itself beeping. Keep an eye and ear on the HE Charge, and keep clear when it's about to explode.**

TIP

### Molotov Cocktail
Rank Auto

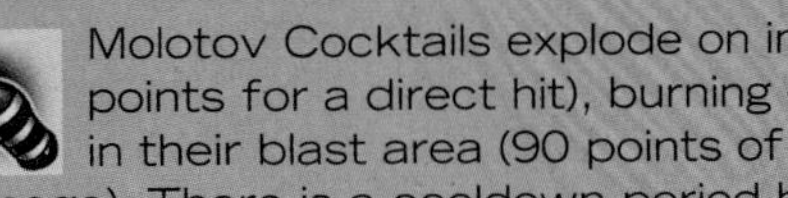

Molotov Cocktails explode on impact (110 points for a direct hit), burning everything in their blast area (90 points of splash damage). There is a cooldown period between successive uses. This is a part of the Standard Soldier Kit, and can be re-mapped in the Abilities menu. These quick, lethal weapons are recommended when charging a enemy fortification. This cannot be sold.

### Armor Piercing Ammo
Rank 2

Armor Piercing Ammo upgrades the ammunition you supply yourself with, making it 100% effective against enemies who have the Extra Kevlar buff. However you cannot supply your teammates with the upgraded ammo, only yourself. This negates the Extra Kevlar buff 100 percent, which is excellent, but only against opponents who have (and use) the "Extra Kevlar" Rank 2 Ability. If this isn't being used, there's no bonuses to having this. When Kevlar-coated enemies receive fire, you'll see sparks.

### Grenade Mastery
Rank 2

Grenade Mastery speeds up your grenade recharge timer (reducing cooldown by 0.3 seconds), allowing you to throw standard Frag Grenades more often, as long as you remain a Soldier, Note, this does not affect the cooldown period of specialty grenades. This is a good choice if you're specializing in other abilities related to your Frag Grenades (and only those).

### Flashbang Grenades

Rank 2

Flashbang Grenades temporarily blind enemy players who see them detonate. Teammates who see them will only see a brief flash, unless you are playing in a Friendly Fire–enabled match, in which case they can be blinded too. The blindness lasts for eight seconds and there is a cooldown period between successive uses. When these are used by your forces, you should quickly take down blinded enemies. When they're used against you, continue moving (ideally into cover), or circling around quickly and stay active so you don't simply wait for death.

**Learn the layout of the maps so you can move about them blindly, by timing how long it takes you to walk, run, and sprint down every corridor. This minimizes the problems Flashbangs inflict. Also keep firing once a Flashbang erupts, as brief enemy stats can be seen to help situate you.**

TIP

### Scavenge

Rank 2

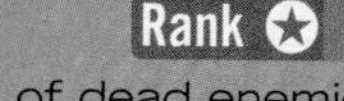

Scavenge the equipment of dead enemies by interacting with them to refill your Supply meter. This is great if you're using close-assault weaponry, but not so much if you're tagging from range (although snipers can help you collect equipment). Remember this serves to refill your Supply meter only.

### Kevlar Vest

Rank 3

Kevlar Vest increases your damage resistance while you are a Soldier. Only 90 percent of a weapon's damage is applied to you; the rest is dissipated. Enemies equipped with Armor Piercing rounds can still do full damage to you. Usually, this is an obvious choice, although the Extra Kevlar Ability that kindly Engineers can administer to you renders this useless. When you receive enemy fire, the enemy sees sparks; a sure-fire giveaway that you're wearing Kevlar!

### Extra Magazine

Rank 3

Extra Magazine allows you to increase the total ammo capacity of your teammates (or yourself) by an extra magazine's worth (one extra magazine). Subsequent resupply by Soldiers will fill up ammo to the increased limit. This is almost always an excellent option, for any of your team that uses up a load of bullets. For weapons with higher capacities (such as the Kross SMG), this may not be necessary; but that may mean you're not killing enough foes!

### Frag Blast

Rank 4

Frag Blast increases the blast radius of your Frag Grenades (by 20 percent compared to normal), but not their damage. This bonus does not apply to Grenade Launcher ammunition, only standard Frags. If you're using Frags and the associated abilities (Grenade Shooting, Grenade Damage, Grenade Mastery, Sprinting Grenade), this is another vital improvement to take.

### Grenade Damage

Rank 4

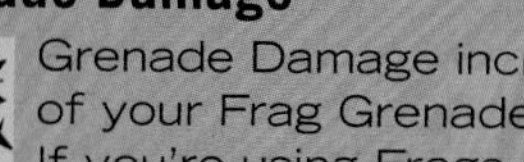

Grenade Damage increases the damage of your Frag Grenades by 20 percent. If you're using Frags and the associated abilities (Grenade Shooting, Frag Blast, Grenade Mastery, Sprinting Grenade), this is another vital improvement to take.

### Satchel Charges

Rank 5

Satchel Charges are remote-control bombs plantable on any flat surface. You can place up to three and detonate them simultaneously or individually. Detonate them individually by looking directly at the one you want to blow up and activating them, or detonate all three simultaneously (with the ability selected). Satchel Charges can be shot, destroyed with Frag Grenades or gunfire, or disabled by EMP Grenades. Unlike landmines, Satchel Charges are visible to enemies and don't have to be spotted by Operatives, so try not to plant them in obvious places. They inflict 160 points of damage. In general, throughout the Campaign and Freeplay chapters of this guide, there are locations that are flagged as optimal for "mine" placement. These are just as suitable for Satchel Charges. With these, and an Engineer with mines, you can really cover and defend a location!

## Medic Abilities

### Standard Medic Kit

Rank Auto

Medics can buff their teammates' health one pip above the normal maximum, and return incapacitated teammates to action by throwing them a Revive Syringe. They can also Heal and Revive Escort Objective VIPs. These are your special abilities, which cannot be sold. Remember your primary role is to keep the rest of your team, and particularly those more involved in gunfights, as healthy as possible. Buffing the health of every team member should be your initial task every time.

### Adrenaline Boost

Rank 2

Adrenaline Boost lets you buff a teammate so they ignore all damage for five seconds. When the effect (indicated by a yellow outline) wears off, they'll receive the damage they ignored, all at once. There is a long cooldown (60 seconds) before you can re-use the ability, and you can't self-administer it. This is useful when a heroic teammate is about to make a sacrificial dash to deliver an item, knock out defenses, or other selfless, but tactically vital act: Administer it then.

## Increase Supplies

Rank 2

Increase Supplies increases the length of your Supply meter by one pip, but only as long as you remain a Medic. Like extra goodies? Then take this ability, which is handy because it effectively gives you more items to buff to your teammates, turning you into a more effective team player.

## Metabolism

Rank 2

Metabolism lets you make a teammate's health regenerate at a faster rate than normal (twice as fast). The effect remains until they die. You cannot administer this buff to yourself. The value this gives your team cannot be underestimated; imagine seven teammates with quicker regeneration, and a fellow Medic administering this to you. A worthwhile investment.

## Transfer Supplies

Rank 2

Transfer Supplies lets you refill a teammate's Supply meter at the cost of your own. If you select this ability you see interaction prompts on teammates who are low on supplies. Mark this down in the "selfless" column of your online acts; you must fully understand that to be truly beneficial, a Medic is the classic "helper" character. Then refill a friend who is about to assault an enemy compound or defenses, or who has savaged his own Supply meter.

## Speed Boost

Rank 3

Speed Boost lets you increase a teammate's sprint speed (10 percent quicker than normal) for 15 seconds. You cannot administer this buff to yourself. This is incredibly helpful for Light Body Types (who move fast anyway) who are carrying a vital item to a location, or need to quickly outflank the enemy. However, this is also handy to jab into your Heavy, tank-like Soldiers who become much more lithe in the combat zone.

## Improved Increase Supplies

Rank 3

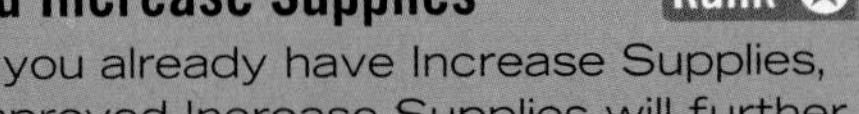

If you already have Increase Supplies, Improved Increase Supplies will further increase your Supply meter, but only as long as you remain a Medic. This makes you the ultimate team player, and your teammates will fully benefit from (but possibly not fully acknowledge) your adeptness in helping others.

## Improved Life Buff

Rank 4

Improved Life Buff lets you increase a teammate's health by two pips, instead of the normal one pip. Need to craft a team of super heroes who can shrug off enemy fire? Buff them with this, and with other bonuses (such as the Health Command Post), they become extremely tough!

## Self Resurrection

Rank 4

Self Resurrection allows you to Revive yourself (100 health upon resurrection) when incapacitated. There is a very long cooldown period (120 seconds) between successive uses. This is handy in situations when the enemy thinks you're dead (or no longer a threat), and you can leap up behind them, or close to an important objective. This also helps you stay close to the combat zone and your more battle-hardened teammates, who you're trying to continuously augment.

## Lazarus Grenade

Rank 5

The Lazarus Grenade is an experimental pharmaceutical aerosol bomb, letting you revive all incapacitated teammates (with a health of 1) within its healing cloud. There is a 60-second cooldown period between successive uses. Learn the width of the cloud by playing some friendly matches, and then follow your team into narrower objective locations and frighten the opposition with your life-giving prowess!

# Engineer Abilities

## Standard Engineer Kit

Rank Auto

Engineers can complete construction and repair objectives, disarm enemy HE Charges, remove enemy Hack Boxes, and buff their teammates' weapon damage (by 18 percent). They can plant landmines that are hidden from the enemy, and also defuse them. These are your special abilities, which cannot be sold. Remember your primary role is to reinforce the objectives you're instructed to defend, take down enemies with the placement of mines and turrets, and buff your entire team's firearms to increase their potency. Note that the "wrench" icon appears in many Secondary Objectives; you'll be busy!

**Weapon Buff: As an Engineer, you can increase the damage of your team's weapons. If you have sufficient supplies and are near enough to buff a teammate's weapons, you'll see a prompt over them. The weapon buff increases the damage done by both a player's primary and secondary weapons and lasts until the player is incapacitated. Buffing teammates' weapons earns you a lot of XP. You can buff your own weapon damage if you have sufficient supplies too. Watch out for the telltale golden shimmer of a buffed weapon. If you can see an enemy has a buffed weapon and you don't, you may decide not to get into a duel with them.**

TIP

## Landmine

Rank Auto

Part of the Standard Engineer Kit, this lets you plant a mine on flat surfaces. Plant a new one, and the old one is removed. Your mine's status is shown in the HUD at bottom left. Enemies can't see these mines unless their Operatives spot them. You can re-map the mine in the Abilities menu. The mine inflicts 175 damage to an enemy when they step off it. However, if a foe stays on a mine, it can be defused by an enemy Engineer.

The Campaign and Freeplay chapters have information on the optimal places to set mines and turrets, both as Resistance and Security forces. Consult that to figure out the best choices before you engage the enemy.

 TIP

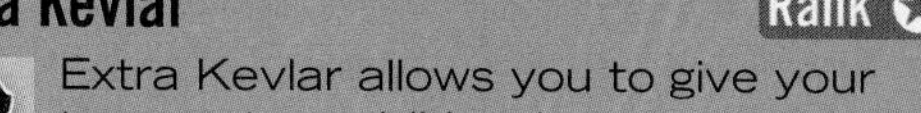

### Extra Kevlar — Rank 2

Extra Kevlar allows you to give your teammates additional armor protection that lasts until they die or change class. All damage received is reduced by 10 percent. You cannot administer this buff to yourself, or to a Soldier who already has the Kevlar Vest Ability. The fact that you can't self-administer, and certain Soldiers are unable to utilize this, lessens the otherwise stellar effectiveness of this ability. Note that Armor Piercing Ammo ignores this ability entirely.

### Gear Head — Rank 2

Gear Head increases how fast you can build and repair turrets, deploy mines, and build MG Nests. Upgrading and repairing is 30 percent faster. Building and deploying takes 80 percent of the usual time. Setting defenses is an Engineer's primary function, so this is incredibly helpful if you're constantly placing turrets and mines in combat-heavy locations, and didn't have time to plan ahead.

### Light Turret — Rank 2

This lets you plant a light turret on flat surfaces. It only scans a small area, but once it acquires a target, it will turn 360 degrees to track it. Its status is shown on the HUD at bottom left: if it's damaged, any friendly Engineer can repair it. If you place a new turret, the old one will disappear. It inflicts 10 damage per shot. This is an excellent choice, because it's another offensive weapon that distracts the enemy and slows them down. Remember to fix any friendly turret you come across!

### Nerves of Steel — Rank 2

Nerves of Steel increases the speed at which you disarm enemy explosives by 30 percent. This is another primary focus for this class, and therefore an almost essential purchase, unless your foes aren't the mine-laying kind.

### Command Post Upgrade — Rank 3

Command Post Upgrade allows you to upgrade any Health or Supply Command Post to double its effect on the entire team. This is accomplished by accessing the Command Post wheel for an extended time. During this process, a progress meter appears on screen. This upgrade is what the "Engineer Advantage" flag throughout the Campaign and Freeplay chapters of this guide refers to: The effects are huge, long-lasting, and team-wide. This is also why Engineers are excellent for sending off to capture Command Posts, because they can upgrade them at the same time.

### Medium Turret — Rank 3

This lets you plant a more powerful auto-turret that will detect and fire at any enemies. You cannot purchase this ability without first purchasing Light Turret. Damage is still 10 per shot, but the rate-of-fire increases by 33 percent. Once again, this is an essential purchase when your objectives are primarily defensive.

### Extra Landmine — Rank 4

Extra Landmine allows you to have two mines active at once; you simply place two, and when you try to place a third, the first one is erased. Need to cover more than one exit? Then this is another excellent purchase.

Landmines: Landmines are armed when an enemy steps on them but explode only when the enemy moves off them. If the enemy keeps his nerve and doesn't move, an Engineer on the same team may come and defuse it for him. Enemy landmines are invisible until spotted by a friendly Operative. Once a landmine has been spotted, an Engineer can defuse it from a safe distance, or it can be destroyed with Frag Grenades or gunfire.

 TIP

### Improved Weapon Buff — Rank 4

Improved Weapon Buff allows you to further increase your teammates' weapon damage: by 31 percent (which includes the original weapon buff increase). Augmenting your entire team's firearms by an even more impressive amount is a real help, and is extremely useful as long as your teammates wait around for you to get to them!

### Gatling Turret — Rank 5

This lets you plant a Gatling auto-turret that can detect and fire at any enemies. You cannot purchase this ability without first purchasing Light Turret and Medium Turret. Damage is still 10 per shot, but the rate-of-fire increases by 58 percent. These are the finest turrets you can buy and the ultimate in defensive deterrents. As with all turrets, they require repairing when damaged by enemy fire, but are excellent at cutting down attackers.

Turrets: Enemy turrets automatically detect and fire at you if you're within range. You can try to destroy an enemy turret with Frag Grenades or gunfire, or avoid it entirely. Each Engineer can have only one turret operational on a map at a time. Turrets that have merely been damaged, not entirely destroyed, can be repaired by Engineers. An Engineer can see the health of his turret and whether it is firing at an enemy.

 TIP

## Operative Abilities

### Standard Operative Kit
Rank Auto

Operatives can complete hack objectives, spot enemy landmines by Iron Sighting over them, and disguise themselves as downed enemies. Operatives are generally loners, but have abilities that can help the team remotely, which is reason for having at least one on your team at all times.

**Operatives In Disguise: Operatives can use the bodies of downed enemies to disguise themselves. If you see yourself on the battlefield, that's not you, it's an Operative in disguise! Disguised Operatives only lose their disguise if they fire a weapon, attempt to capture a Command Post, attempt an objective, are incapacitated, or are hit by an enemy Homing Beacon. Operatives take a short time to disguise themselves, and are vulnerable while doing so.**

TIP

### Comms Hack
Rank 2

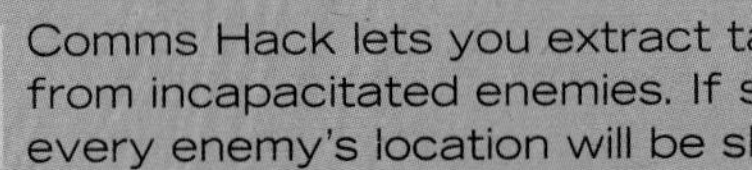

Comms Hack lets you extract tactical intel from incapacitated enemies. If successful, every enemy's location will be shown on your and your teammate's radars, giving your team a huge advantage. The effect only lasts for five seconds and has a 20-second cooldown afterward. This is useful when you aren't playing solo matches, and as long as you announce to your teammates when the intel is about to be released, If your team is using the radar to its fullest, this is a recommended ability. Comms Hacking an incapacitated enemy prevents them from using the Downed Fire Ability.

### Firewall Command Post
Rank 2

Firewall Command Post makes it take 25 percent longer for an enemy to capture your team's Health or Supply Command Post. Do this by accessing the Command Post wheel for an extended period of time. During this process, a progress meter appears onscreen. This is what the "Operative Advantage" flag throughout the Campaign and Freeplay chapters of this guide refers to. The effects are long-lasting and help everyone. This is also why Operatives are excellent for sending off to capture Command Posts, because they can install a Firewall at the same time. Also beware if you're trying to capture a Firewalled Command Post: Watch your back...the Operative may still be close.

### Homing Beacon
Rank 2

Homing Beacon allows you to place a red outline on an enemy for six seconds by Iron Sighting on them. The ability can be used while in disguise. This allows the enemy to be seen by all your teammates, even through walls. Homing Beacon also lets you reveal enemy Operatives in disguise. This is helpful if an Operative spots a particularly troublesome foe, or one about to complete an objective, and you can't immediately engage him. Be careful: enemy Operatives can do the same to you!

### Sticky Bomb
Rank 2

Sticky Bomb lets you throw a powerful grenade (500 points of damage to the target, and 120 to enemies within the radius of the explosion) which sticks to any enemy it touches and can only be removed by their teammates. Enemies can destroy the grenade by shooting at it while it's still on the ground. There is a 20-second cooldown between successive uses. This is your most powerful mobile offensive weapon, and it's great for removing foes close to one another. Avoid stepping on or being caught by these, and if you do, flee to a death on your own or allow your teammates to remove the grenade from you, instead of causing everyone to be wounded by the splash damage.

**You can destroy a Sticky Bomb with gunfire or a Frag Grenade before it can get stuck to you. If you do get stuck with a Sticky Bomb and no friendly teammate is nearby to remove it for you, you might as well head toward the enemy and try to catch them in the imminent explosion. Operatives can only have one Sticky Bomb in the world at once. Skillful Operatives throw their Sticky Bomb directly at an enemy, giving them no chance to avoid being stuck.**

TIP

### Caltrop Grenades

Rank 3

Caltrop Grenades scatter sharp spikes that damage enemies who cross over them, unless they move slowly (either by slowing down or by using Iron Sights). The caltrops will not hurt teammates, and remain in the world for the length of the ability's cooldown period (30 seconds). Damage is calculated at five points per spike, to a maximum of 25 damage per second; more damage is dealt if the enemy is running at speeds faster than your movement with Iron Sights. Think of these as less-damaging but more-annoying mines: In general, throughout the Campaign and Freeplay chapters of this guide, locations that are flagged as optimal for "mine" placement are as just as suitable for Caltrop Grenades.

### Hack Turret

Rank 3

Hack Turret lets you reprogram an enemy turret to become a friendly turret, owned by you. Approach the enemy turret from behind to improve your chances of hacking it. This is useful if the turret is close to the enemy, within their defenses, or you're outflanking them. It is also another reason why it is important for Engineers to constantly check on their automated ordnance.

### Control Turret

Rank 4

Control Turret allows you to take remote first person control of friendly turrets. To initiate remote control, first place the device on the turret, and then interact with it from a distance. That distance should involve hiding where you won't be shot, and the control process can be annoying and distracting for the enemy as they deal with your interception; hopefully while your teammates get on with winning the match. Keep track of the turret's status on your HUD, and control it from anywhere on the map. However, the turret may overheat if fired continuously.

### Cortex Bomb

Rank 4

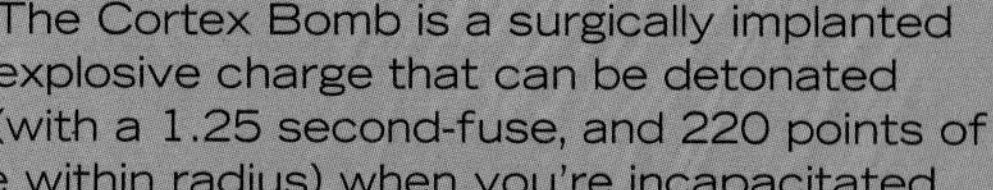

The Cortex Bomb is a surgically implanted explosive charge that can be detonated (with a 1.25 second-fuse, and 220 points of damage within radius) when you're incapacitated, eliminating any nearby enemies. This is extremely satisfying, and can be the final insult after you wound a foe who thought they'd shot you using the Downed Fire Ability. This isn't as helpful if your team's Medics are on the ball. If you can catch a foe (ideally someone attempting an objective) with this, so much the better. You hear a telltale sound just before the Cortex Bomb detonates, but it's wise to approach incapacitated Operatives with extreme caution. The Operative cannot survive triggering their Cortex Bomb.

### EMP Grenade

Rank 5

EMP Grenades temporarily disable enemy turrets, mines, and radars. They also slow down the progress of enemy hacks and HE Charges (hack speed and HE timer rate reduced by 50 percent). EMP Grenades even temporarily stop enemy-held Command Posts from giving beneficial effects to their team. Anything affected by an EMP Grenade will emit sparks until the EMP wears off. There is a 30-second cooldown period between successive uses. The disabling duration varies depending on the electrical item in question:

Delay: 1 second for Sticky Grenades.

Delay: 10 seconds for turrets, Command Posts, Cortex Bombs, mines, Satchel Charges, PDAs, Hack Boxes, and radar.

Delay: 30 seconds on a Soldier's Demo Charge.

Naturally, this is a match-winning ability, and can also be used to slow down Maintenance Bots. Hacking is fraught at the best of times, so lob in an EMP Grenade to make it significantly worse. Remember that this weapon can be re-mapped in the Abilities menu.

## Body Types

### Light, Medium, and Heavy

In the full-figure Appearance menu, a specific menu, called "Body Type," has a significant effect on the general physique and maneuverability of your character in every match and challenge. The three body types can be swapped at will, after (but not during) any match, assuming the body types have been unlocked.

**NOTE**

**When creating a new character, the "Medium" or "Normal" Body Type is your default. This can be changed, ideally after you become a more advanced player. The types of weaponry each body type can utilize are flagged in the Weapons chapter. For details on S.M.A.R.T. moves, consult the Gameplay chapter later in this guide.**

#### Heavy

| Statistic | Rating | Notes |
|---|---|---|
| Hit Points | ★★★ | By default, the Heavy Body Type has more hit points (180) than the Medium Body Type. |
| Speed | ★ | The big guy is of course the slowest character (Run speed: 120, Sprint speed: 200). |
| Climbing | ★ | The big body type can only attempt vaulting. He can't climb by jumping up walls at all. |

Notes: Heavy Body Types can carry any weapon (including heavy assault types) as their primary weapon, and for a secondary, they can use anything up to a standard assault sized weapon, making them very powerful.

#### Medium

| Statistic | Rating | Notes |
|---|---|---|
| Hit Points | ★★ | Medium Body Type has the default Hit Points (140). |
| Speed | ★★ | Medium also has the default speed (Run speed: 150, Sprint speed: 230). |
| Climbing | ★★ | The Medium Body Type can vault over obstacles around one meter high, AND can also jump and pull up onto obstacles that are not above head height. |

Notes: Medium Body Types can carry use any size weapon, up to and including standard assault types as his primary weapon, and for a secondary, can use anything up to a SMG sized weapon.

### Light

| Statistic | Rating | Notes |
|---|---|---|
| Hit Points | ★ | Light Body Type has fewer hit points than normal (120). |
| Speed | ★★★ | This guy is incredibly quick. (Run speed: 180, Sprint speed: 270) |
| Climbing | ★★★ | The Light Body Type can press the jump button just as he hits a wall to Wall-jump even higher (or alternately, he can hold the S.M.A.R.T. button when connecting with walls), letting him pull up to ledges that other characters simply cannot reach. |

Notes: Light Body Types use SMGs or rifle-sized weapons as their primary, but are limited to only pistols as their secondary. They can inflict sizable damage with a knife, however.

## Character Builds

Perhaps you'd like to tailor your character to a specific set of abilities and weapons, with a loadout that helps you perform certain tasks spectacularly, to the admiration of your teammates and the stunned astonishment of your enemies? Then try these meticulously crafted character builds, designed to give you the very best class of fighter available. Don't settle for a mediocre Ark dweller with no specializations; the plan here is extreme and battle-tested proficiency!

**The character's faction and outfits are not indicative of the build, but an example of how each build might dress.**

 NOTE

**You can obviously choose more abilities than are listed with each build, but the ones indicated are most important. Afterward, pick universal and class-specific abilities until you run out.**

 TIP

### The Hacker

Class: Operative

Specialization: Disruption and disarray

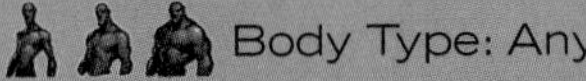 Body Type: Any

- [Universal] Supply Max Increase
- [Operative] Firewall Command Post
- [Operative] Hack Turret
- [Operative] Control Turret
- [Operative] EMP Grenades
- [Weapon Preference] Mossington w/ Silencer, Tampa w/ Silencer and a Pistol w/ Silencer (for knife kills)

### The Wall

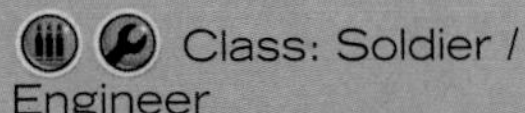 Class: Soldier / Engineer

Specialization: Defending strategic points with heavy hardware

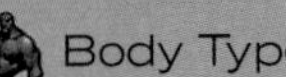 Body Type: Heavy

- [Universal] Resupply Rate Increase
- [Soldier] Grenade Mastery
- [Soldier] Satchel Charges
- [Engineer] Gatling Turret
- [Engineer] Extra Landmine
- [Weapon Preference] Lobster Grenade Launcher and Gotlung Minigun

### The Speed

Class: Operative

Specialization: Hit and fade attack on enemy strongholds

Body Type: Light

- [Universal] Resupply Rate Increase
- [Universal] Sprinting Reload
- [Universal] Sprinting Grenade
- [Universal] Silent Running
- [Operative] Sticky Bomb
- [Operative] Caltrop
- [Weapon Preference] Ritchie Revolver pistol with Side-Vent Muzzle Brake/Speed Holster/ Rapid Fire/YeoTek Red Dot Sight and Tampa/ CARB-9 SMG with Muzzle Brake/Speed Sling/ High-Capacity Magazine/YeoTek Red Dot Sight

## The Deadeye

Class: Soldier

Specialization: Sniping from afar

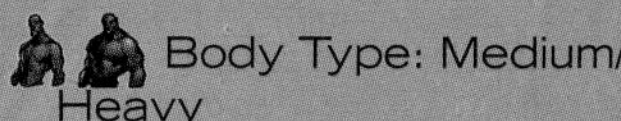

Body Type: Medium/ Heavy

- [Universal] Silent Running
- [Soldier] Extra Magazine
- [Soldier] Armor Piercing Ammo
- [Weapon Preference] Drogonav or Barnett w/ Snoop-R Scope, Rockstedi w/ COGA Scope, Tampa w/ Drum Magazine or Pistol sidearm w/ Rapid Fire attachment

## The Demolition Man

Class: Soldier

Specialization: Blowing things up

Body Type: Medium/ Heavy

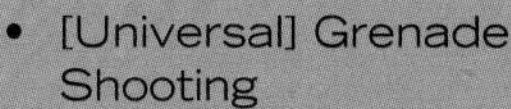

- [Universal] Grenade Shooting
- [Soldier] Grenade Mastery
- [Soldier] Grenade Damage
- [Soldier] Frag Blast
- [Soldier] Kevlar Vest
- [Soldier] Satchel Charges
- [Weapon Preference] Mossington, Lobster, EZ-Nade

## The Tank

Class: Medic

Specialization: Bullet sponge

Body Type: Heavy

- [Universal] Battle Hardened
- [Universal] Resupply Rate Increase
- [Universal] Downed Fire
- [Medic] Self Resurrection
- [Medic] Increase Supplies
- [Medic] Improved Increase Supplies
- [Weapon Preference] Euston & Galactic w/ Drum Mag

## The Doctor

Class: Medic

Specialization: The Hippocratic Oath

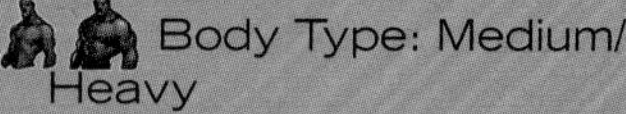

Body Type: Medium/ Heavy

- [Universal] Resupply Rate Increase
- [Medic] Improved Life Buff
- [Medic] Increase Supplies
- [Medic] Improved Increase Supplies
- [Medic] Metabolism
- [Medic] Lazarus Grenade
- [Weapon Preference] Gerund & Galactic w/ Drum Mag

## The Smoking Barrel

Class: Soldier

Specialization: Bullets... lots of bullets

Body Type: Heavy

- [Universal] Battle Hardened
- [Universal] Combat Intuition
- [Universal] Downed Fire
- [Soldier] Extra Magazine
- [Soldier] Kevlar Vest
- [Soldier] Armor Piercing Ammo
- [Weapon Preference] Gotlung Minigun, Chinzor MG, and Maximus MG
- [Attachment Preference] Extended/Drum Magazine and Front Grip

## The Little Tinker

Class: Engineer

Specialization: Execution through machinery

Body Type: Light

- [Universal] Resupply Rate Increase
- [Engineer] Gear Head
- [Engineer] Improved Weapon Buff
- [Engineer] Command Post Upgrade
- [Engineer] Gatling Turret
- [Engineer] Extra Landmine
- [Weapon Preference] Ritchie Revolver pistol with Side-Vent Muzzle Brake/Speed Holster/ Rapid Fire/YeoTek Red Dot Sight and Tampa/ CARB-9 SMG with Muzzle Brake/Speed Sling/ High-Capacity Magazine/YeoTek Red Dot Sight

HISTORY OF THE ARK
CHARACTER CREATION
GAMEPLAY
WEAPONS DETAIL
CAMPAIGN & FREEPLAY MAPS
CHALLENGES
APPENDICES

# GAMEPLAY

## Brinktroduction

This chapter serves as a reminder of the most important facets of this game. It goes over, and adds advanced maneuvering, to S.M.A.R.T. moves. It reminds you of the basics of cover and the leaning system you can employ. It introduces you to melee attacks, gives some advanced strategies for keeping the enemy on the defensive (even when they're supposed to be on the offensive), and looks at classes and the types of objectives, radar, and supplying. Finally, there's a quick primer on how to play *Brink* more proficiently. This is all required reading before you embark on the Ark!

**Stop! Before continuing, it is worthwhile (for the XP alone) accessing the Dossier ↘ Training menu, then watching (and re-watching) the Training videos that bring you up to speed on game Basics, Objectives, the Heads Up Display, General Gameplay, Classes, and Hazards information. You receive some free XP for your troubles, as well as an increased knowledge of how everything works. Watch these videos again after your first match, and a third time after your fourth or fifth match; this significantly reduces your learning curve. The following tactical information pre-supposes the knowledge contained within these videos.**

TIP

## Character Classes and Objectives

In *Brink*, you can choose to play as one of four classes, each of which can help your team in different ways. You can change class at any time during a mission at a Command Post (these can be the ones inside your deployment zone, or neutral posts you've captured that also give you health or supply bonuses). Always pay attention to what your team is doing, and don't hesitate to switch roles if it will help the overall mission.

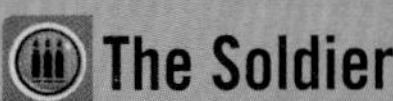

### The Soldier

Soldiers are masters of destruction. They can plant Heavy Explosive Charges to complete destruction objectives. In addition to the standard Frag Grenade, they also come equipped with a Molotov Cocktail (and when purchased in abilities, a Flashbang and a Satchel Charge), so they have twice as much grenade power as any other class. And they can refill their teammates ammo as well as their own, making them incredibly valuable to have on a squad.

#### ↘ The Tools of a Soldier

Ammo Pack

### Medic

Medics keep everyone alive, including teammates and occasional Mission Objective VIPs. They can use their Health Syringes to heal and boost their and their teammate's health, and can also toss Revive Syringes to downed teammates so they can get back up to continue the fight, instead of having to join reinforcement waves. Later, they can purchase abilities to increase a team's supplies, and even purchase an experimental Lazarus Grenade, which can revive all incapacitated teammates within its healing cloud!

#### ↘ The Tools of a Soldier

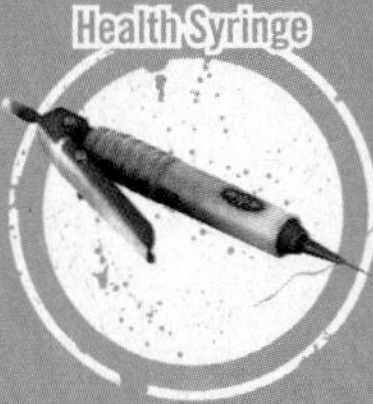

## Engineer

Engineers are a versatile class, concerned primarily with building, repairing, and upgrading things on the battlefield with their trusty Blow Torch. They are often called upon to construct Primary and Secondary Objectives, as well as build Machine Gun Nests for defense. They can upgrade their or their teammate's weapons to increase their damage, and put down landmines to surprise unwary enemies.

### The Tools of an Engineer

## Operative

Operatives are the spies of *Brink*. They can disguise themselves to hide in plain sight among the enemy, waiting for the opportune moment to strike. They're also the only class that can see enemy landmines, and are able to "spot" them (by looking at them while Iron Sighting) to ensure that their teammates won't be caught unawares. Additionally, they can hack computer systems using their PDAs to complete certain mission objectives to ensure victory for their team. They can also purchase (via abilities) Caltrop Grenades to slow down pursuers, and EMP Grenades to slow down anything with an electrical pulse.

### The Tools of an Operative

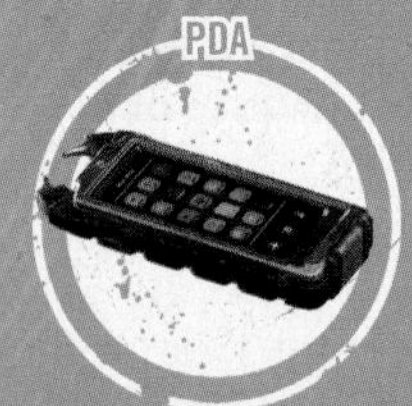

**Check out the Character Creation chapter for a full run-down of all the different class abilities.**

TIP

### Mission Objectives

### Core Objectives

These objectives, also sometimes known as Primary Objectives, must be completed for a team to win, and are always listed as the highest priority on the Objective Wheel. There is only one Primary Objective active at any time. The following lists the general Core Objectives you'll encounter. The Campaign and Freeplay chapter deals in specifics.

#### Soldier: Destroy Core Objective

Some missions require a Soldier to plant an HE (High Explosive) Charge on a key structure. Once this is done, it must be protected from enemy Engineers trying to defuse it, until it can detonate.

### Engineer: Build/Repair Core Objective

Often, key pieces of equipment vital for success must be repaired or even constructed by Engineers for a team to win. In these cases, the Engineer must approach the object (or location where the object will be built), and use his build/repair tool for an extended time. During this period, the Engineer is defenseless, so it's wise to wait for some teammates to provide cover.

### Medic: Revive Primary VIP

In some missions, VIPs must be escorted, and if the enemy incapacitates them, a Medic must revive them to get them moving again.

### Operative: Hack Core Objective

When a computer system needs to be compromised, Operatives can use their PDAs to get the job done. They must first plant a "Hack Box" on the computer in question to start the hack. While hacking, they are free to move around and find good defensive positions. However, the farther away they are from their hack target, the longer the hack will take. Also, enemy Engineers can remove the Hack Box to undo all the progress made, so the Hack Box must be protected.

### Escort Primary VIP/Vehicle

Sometimes a mission's Core Objective is to ensure that a person or vehicle gets from point A to point B. In these cases, someone has to stay close to them for them to move. As long as they do so, they'll be earning a steady stream of XP.

Simultaneously, the opposing team will have objectives to stop the VIP or vehicle.

### Deliver Primary Objective Data

Some missions require a team to transport small items from point A to point B. To achieve this, someone must first pick it up by touching it, and then travel to a specific location and interact with an object in the world to deliver it. The enemy team will have objectives to prevent this delivery, which they can do by killing the carrier, and then interacting with the object to return it to its origin.

## Secondary Objectives

These are objectives that are very important to the mission's completion, but aren't required to win. The list below contains some of the more common ones in the game.

### Stand Guard at Objective

Staying near the location of any objective will result in a steady stream of XP for "standing guard." This XP is earned regardless of whether enemies are present or not, so this is a great way to earn XP with relatively little effort, and also to be at the right place at the right time.

### Escort Teammate

Whenever a team member is completing a Core Objective, their teammates can choose to "Escort" them. While on this mission, as long as they stay close to the target, they'll be earning a steady stream of XP, as long as the target is still alive.

### Change Class

If a team does not have enough of its members as the class required to complete the current Primary Objective, a new objective will be created to prompt team members to become that class.

It's very important for someone to answer this call, or there's very little chance of success. The Campaign and Freeplay chapters of this guide help you gauge how many of each class are needed for every Core Objective.

### Help Teammates

Medics, Soldiers, and Engineers all have ways they can boost certain properties of their teammates (such as health, ammo, armor, revival, damage potential). As such, there's usually an objective available to help nearby team members. This nets not only XP but also the gratitude of that teammate.

### Capture Command Post

This objective leads to the nearest neutral or enemy Command Post, which can be captured for XP as well as a global bonus for the entire team.

### Find Nearest Team Command Post

This is a special entry that's always on the Objective Wheel and will lead to the nearest Command Post. No XP is awarded for this, because it's not really a mission critical objective, but if you're ever lost, this can come in handy.

**Audio Chatter: Be sure you're listening to the voices of your teammates and also Brother Chen (Resistance) or Captain Mokoena (Security). They aren't barking orders just for the fun of it. These are important instructions you must (and should) react to!**

 TIP

## Command Posts

There are four different types of Command Post that can be encountered:

**Faction Command Posts (friendly):** These are always inside your deployment zone, steps away from your spawn point, and never change sides.

**Faction Command Posts (enemy):** These are always inside the enemy's deployment zone. Thanks to their invulnerable turret defenses, and the lack of interactivity, these can never be accessed by your team.

**Neutral Command Posts:** For each map, there is a deactivated Command Post (picture 1). These can be captured by any class of teammate for your team, and display your faction's logo when successfully captured (picture 2). If the enemy captures the Command Post, it changes to your enemy's logo (picture 3). There are two types of neutral Command Posts: Health and Supply.

**Some missions take place over two maps, and therefore you should expect a second Health or Supply Command Post later in your mission. But you can never go back to the previous map, or earlier Command Post, because each map is self-contained and sealed.**

 NOTE

## Health and Supply

The two neutral Command Posts grant a bonus when taken for your team: Health Command Posts buff each member of your team an additional pip on their Health meter, allowing them to absorb more damage. Supply Command Posts buff each member of your team an additional pip on their Supply meter, allowing them to utilize more special abilities.

HISTORY OF THE ARK
CHARACTER CREATION
GAMEPLAY
WEAPONS DETAIL
CAMPAIGN & FREEPLAY MAPS
CHALLENGES
APPENDICES

**The trick here is to learn where the two neutral Command Posts are on a map, hand over capture duties to a teammate, take and hold onto them for as long as possible, but without stretching yourselves so thinly that the enemy can complete an objective, or prevent you from completing one. Generally, always try to capture and recapture any and all available Command Posts—they'll give your entire team a boost. But be aware, the more alert enemy players will be trying to do the same thing.**

 **TIP**

## Upgrades and Firewalls

It is wise to give Command Post duties over to your Engineers and Operatives, because they have an additional ability (when purchased) that adds to the overall impact a post brings to your team. The Engineer can Upgrade, doubling the effect of a Command Post. The Operative can Firewall, lengthening the time the enemy must wait during their retake of that post. These obvious benefits should be employed.

**The default time that a Supply meter recharges is 30 seconds per pip, so bear that in mind when using up your special abilities.**

**CAUTION**

**Try not to place turrets too near the doorway they're covering, so they can't be taken out by grenades thrown through or into that doorway. Turrets make good defenders of Command Posts, if they're hidden well.**

 **TIP**

**Obviously, place mines, Sticky Bombs, or Satchel Charges on or close to the objective locations, main route doorways, and on each and every Command Post. But bear in mind that mines only detonate when the victim steps off them, so you want the enemy to move over them, not stop on them: place the mines just in front of where they'll stop and stand at the Command Post, for instance, not at the Command Post itself.**

 **TIP**

# The Radar

## The Knowledge

The radar (shown in the bottom-right corner of your HUD screen) is an often-overlooked advantage. Rectify that problem by utilizing all the capabilities it offers you and your team.

If you see an enemy on screen, he appears on your radar. If you aim your gun at an enemy, your character automatically shouts "enemy spotted!" into his radio, and then the enemy will appear on the radar of your teammates.

Also, if you hear the enemy (that is, you're within a certain distance when he moves or shoots), he will appear on your radar, even if neither you nor your teammates know where he is. However, if the enemy puts a silencer on his weapon, then his position won't be given away by gunfire, and if he has the Silent Running Ability, his footsteps won't give him away either.

There is an Operative ability called "Comms Hack." If an Operative on your team uses this on an incapacitated enemy, then every enemy will appear on your entire team's radar for the next few seconds.

Once an enemy appears on your radar, he'll stay on there for a few seconds, but will then disappear if you "lose track of him." Keep him on your radar consistently by continuing to keep him on screen; he also stays on if he continues to make noise.

It is important to note that while the radar is incredibly powerful, it doesn't show any of the environment, so you can at best get a rough idea of where enemies are (you can't tell if someone is hiding in the left corner of the room ahead, because no landscape is shown). But good players are definitely aware of it, both of what's on it, and when they're on the enemies' radar.

# S.M.A.R.T. Movement

**This section goes through the important points of S.M.A.R.T. movement. Be sure to test out any techniques presented here using a Light Body Type character; Heavier Body Types are severely limited in the S.M.A.R.T. moves they can attempt.**

CAUTION

**The areas in every mission where S.M.A.R.T. moves are possible, along with the body types that can successfully attempt them, are shown throughout the Campaign and Freeplay Chapters.**

NOTE

## Getting S.M.A.R.T.

### Basic Techniques

The following S.M.A.R.T. moves from the available missions detail the different basic moves, so you know what you're doing, and how you're doing them.

**Sprinting:** You must be running at speed when you approach an area you need to S.M.A.R.T. move over. Jumping while moving at slower speeds means you won't leap as far, and may grab and have to pull yourself over an obstacle, instead of landing on top of it.

**Tap the Sprint button to shift into a full sprint. You can keep sprinting as long as you're moving forward, but firing, reloading, or throwing a grenade will take you out of sprint (unless you purchase an ability to negate this). When you hold Sprint, you stay in S.M.A.R.T. mode and will thus attempt to climb every obstacle in your path. So release this button if you don't want to climb or grab (when falling through a hole, for example).**

TIP

**Climbing:** Avoid this whenever possible. Stopping at a vertical obstacle, and then jumping vertically so you grab the top and pull yourself up, is extremely slow.

**Mantling:** Instead, use this technique, which is to approach the same obstacle at speed, and then climb and jump up and over it in one fluid technique known as mantling. Increase your speed, and obstacles become almost invisible to you!

**Vaulting:** A lower obstacle that is usually less than half your height, or one that you can jump to without grabbing onto it, can be vaulted over, which is an excellent way to quickly maneuver over low-lying objects. Vaulting keeps your sprint speed up, too.

**The differences between a mantle and a vault? The mantle requires you to grab and pull yourself up onto an obstacle. The vault enables you to land with your feet on that same obstacle.**

TIP

**Sliding:** Aside from the combat benefits of slide tackling a foe (see the Advanced Combat section later in this chapter for more information), sliding under an object is another way to maneuver through it. However, if you have a choice, it is better to leap over an object because your speed doesn't decrease, which it does after a slide.

**Wall-Jumping:** Also known as wall-hopping, this technique (available to Light Body Types) is one of the most important maneuvers to master; as it allows you to circumvent large troughs or lower areas, and master shortcuts. You simply sprint, leap, hit the Jump button as you reach the wall you want to jump off, and you're propelled across in the direction you're facing!

## Diagrammatic Evidence

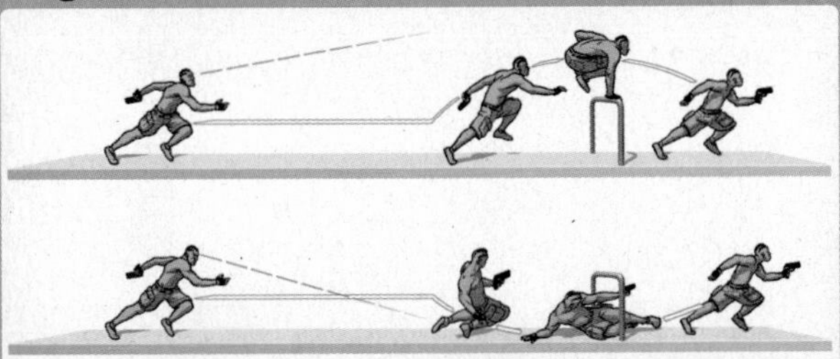

**Look before you leap:** S.M.A.R.T. movement is very intuitive, and as well as depending on your speed, it also depends on your viewpoint. In this diagram, the runner looks forward and up slightly while running and holding the Sprint/S.M.A.R.T. button. He will **vault over** the obstacle. However, if he looks forward and down slightly, he will **slide under** the obstacle.

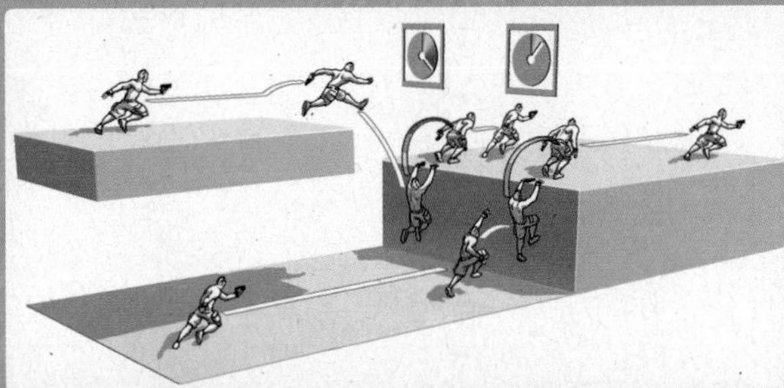

**Ascending, not Descending:** Dropping kills your sprinting inertia, as the clock icons demonstrate on the adjacent diagram. Notice the run-up the right-hand runner demonstrates, which allows him to mantle over the obstacle. Whereas the left-hand runner leaps and falls, must grab the top of the obstacle to pull himself up, and wastes time. Try to land any jumps you make, instead of falling short!

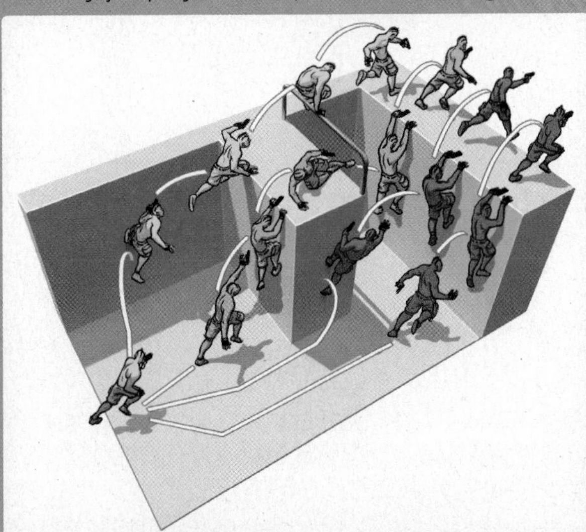

**Spatial Awareness:** Know your surroundings, and you can significantly lessen the time it takes to get over an obstacle, or in this case, a group of obstacles. The faster techniques are shown in yellow. The slower techniques are shown in red. As you can see, the height the yellow runner gained from an initial wall-jump allowed him to reach the top of the obstacle, and the momentum propelled him over a bar without any loss in speed.

However, whenever you have to grab the lip of an obstacle, stop, and climb instead of mantling, or (to a lesser extent) slide under an object, you lose speed. Learn this, and you can take full advantage of the topography of the maps!

## ↘ Making All the Right Moves

Now for the advanced master-class! All S.M.A.R.T. moves are executed faster if you run into them faster (up to a limit in the case of vaults or mantles). Your exit velocity will be the same as your entry velocity, but slightly redirected. Slides always bring your speed down lower than normal, but have a push at the beginning, and inherit current velocity.

### Building Speed

Chaining S.M.A.R.T. moves (especially vaults, wall-jumps, jumps, and slides) together is a great way to increase your travel speed. Try to figure out routes in maps that let you vault into wall-hop into landing slide. Slides inherit velocity, so building speed by chaining vaults and wall-hops together is a good way to extend the range of your slide tackles.

If you are touching the ground, your speed will always be pulled back to pedestrian amounts—hit jump before you touch the ground to "skip," maintaining your momentum. Note that overdoing this results in diminishing returns, so only use it once or twice at the most.

Your sprinting speed increases slightly the longer you do it. Not by much, but enough to make the difference in a tricky jump. Don't stop and start, though; keep moving.

### Vaulting versus Mantling

Vaulting is always quicker than mantling (though mantling has a few other uses).

Vaults and mantles occur in response to the height of a ledge relative to your height. If you see a ledge at about eye height, you'll normally mantle if you rely just on S.M.A.R.T. or jump too late. If you hold the S.M.A.R.T. button, sprint at the ledge, and hit Jump just before you'd normally mantle, you have a good change of converting the mantle into a much quicker vault. You can do the same without S.M.A.R.T. by **holding**, rather than tapping, Jump. However, this prevents you from moving your head and aiming at the next obstacle you want to S.M.A.R.T. move over, which is a problem.

### Avoiding Falling Damage

Landing into a slide (hold S.M.A.R.T. and crouch) will reduce any falling damage, and generally make you look like a cool dude.

## ↘ Hop to It: Wall-Jumping

Firstly, remember there are two ways to complete a wall-jump:

Press Jump when you're in the air and touching a wall. Or,

Hold S.M.A.R.T. when you're in the air and push your left analog stick **away** from the wall you're touching.

### Wall-Hopping Nuances

The direction you hold your movement has a noticeable impact on the resulting wall-jump.

Jumping **toward** the wall you're wall-jumping off, will only gain you a small amount of height—enough to mantle a high ledge (if it's reachable).

Jumping **away** from a wall (on a console, this involves pulling the left stick away from the wall you're touching when you jump) gives you significantly more height than jumping straight up the wall.

If in doubt, **reflect** your wall-jumps (push your movement directly away from the wall). It will almost always give more benefit.

You can perform as many wall-jumps in a row as you like, but you cannot perform a wall-jump on the same wall twice in a row—you must either wall-hop from a perpendicular or opposite-facing wall, or touch the ground to wall-hop off the same wall direction again.

The wall jump has a "cooldown" period so that you can't bounce between two walls forever. This cooldown resets as soon as you touch the ground.

**Xbox 360 and Playstation 3 only:** Immediately after a wall-jump (or mantle), you can turn away from the wall you're facing faster than normal. This is so that you can use wall-jumps to bounce and grab ledges opposite the wall you jumped off. This is tricky but satisfying, and also useful for combat.

## ↘ Using Wall-Jumps for Distance

### 1. Using S.M.A.R.T. and Controlling Your Aim

Hold S.M.A.R.T., and run off a ledge at an angle, so that you touch a wall mid-flight.

As soon as you jump, push your left analog stick **away** from the wall. Let the momentum of the jump collide you with the wall. As soon as you touch, you'll execute a wall-jump away. This gets you the most vertical and lateral distance from a jump.

For example, if you have a wall to your left, with a drop just ahead:

Hold S.M.A.R.T., move left and up on your left analog stick, and wait for your character to automatically jump off the ledge, then immediately move the left analog stick to the right, and hit the wall due to your momentum.

### 2. Attempting This Manually

Move toward a wall. Double-tap Jump. This ensures that a wall-jump occurs.

Immediately after the jump, try to move your left analog stick **away** from the wall before you hit it, to ensure you get the biggest (or farthest) wall-jump possible.

For example, if you have a wall to your left:

On your left analog stick, press Left and Jump at the same time. Then as you're about to hit the wall, on your left analog stick, press Right and Jump once more.

3. The Hybrid of Both

Hold Sprint, jump toward a wall. Immediately pull away. Let S.M.A.R.T. automatically reflect you away from the wall.

For example, if you have a wall to your left:

Hold S.M.A.R.T., then pull away on your left analog stick by pressing Left and Jump, then after you hit the wall, press Jump and you're automatically reflected.

## ↘ Using Wall-Jumps for Height

The easiest way to use a wall-jump to get you up over high ledges is to run straight at it, and let the wall-jump automatically hop you into mantle range. However, if there is a perpendicular wall to the wall you want to mantle up, you can do a wall-hop from **that wall** to increase your height higher than a straight wall-jump, and potentially convert what would be a mantle into a vault. The Spatial Awareness diagram earlier in this chapter shows these different possibilities.

## ↘ Mantles (Advanced Shenanigans)

### Mantle Jumping Away

You can "cancel" a mantle by releasing S.M.A.R.T., and pulling away from the mantle (this is normally down on your left analog stick).

**Light Body Types:** You can break out of a mantle into a wall-jump by holding "backward" on your left analog stick (that is, the direction opposite to where you're going) while holding S.M.A.R.T. and mantling. This can **very, very, occasionally** be used to jump backward over pursuer's heads, or at least make you a difficult target if you're caught mid-mantle.

### The 180-Degree Mantle Jump Away

This is a chained-together technique involving a mantle, turn, and wall-jump in quick succession.

During a mantle or wall-jump, you can turn around faster than normal. This is to allow you to break out of mantle using a wall-jump, straight into another mantle on an opposing wall.

Hold S.M.A.R.T. and go for a mantle. When you see the mantle animation start, begin turning, but let go of your left analog stick. When you have turned around 120 degrees, push forward on your left analog stick, and you'll break out of the mantle using a wall-jump. Because the wall-jump is **away** from the wall, you'll get a huge jump out of it, and can get to higher, opposite facing ledges.

For example, you have a ledge ahead of you, and a **higher** ledge behind you.

Hold S.M.A.R.T., press up on your left analog stick, start the mantle, let go and center your left analog stick, then turn right on your right analog stick so you're facing away from the wall, and finally press up on your left analog stick again.

### S.M.A.R.T. Combat Tips

S.M.A.R.T., combined with a pistol is a great way to rush down the enemy. Choose your moment: wait for them to be distracted, then close ground as fast as you can. Your pistols don't lose much accuracy from moving at speed, and closing in for a highly damaging knife attack is a great way to finish off. Try to get into the air before you start firing so that you don't break your speed. Punish people for moving slow. Only go for slides if you can't close for a knife slice before they gun you down—you'll do far less damage, and the knockdown could give them a chance to fight back.

Hedge your bets on knocked down enemies. Shoot at knocked down enemies, but close in on them in a spiral to give yourself a chance at an instant melee finisher if they decide to stay down and shoot, or a follow up melee if they stand up. Only if you're already very close to an enemy during a knockdown, and aware of their position, and have decent health, should you really go for the finishing move above all else.

**Xbox 360 and Playstation 3 only: Aim Adhesion ("Sticky Aim") is more noticeable when moving at higher speeds, so don't be afraid to build speed and use the adhesion to your advantage.**

 **TIP**

## Combat and Formations

Winning the missions and defeating the enemy team takes more than simple combat prowess, or blustering hubris. In this section, there's advice on creating a synergic team that can dynamically react to enemy incursions, the types of team maneuvers that work well in these environments, and more information on combat moves you may not have utilized as often as you should. As before, the Dossier [[>]] Training menu videos help you through knowledge of primary and secondary weapons, and the like.

### The Ultimate Team

#### The Concept of Teamwork

The first plan when engaging the enemy is to have already figured out what each teammate is going to do beforehand. That means choosing classes and weapons before you spawn, moving to locations immediately to gain the upper hand, and keeping in constant radio contact with your brethren. Playing to your class strengths (for example, Soldiers are better at charging enemy strongholds, while Medics are more adept at helping others complete objectives) is vital.

#### Chokepoints

You'd expect a high propensity for violence to occur at the intersections of thoroughfares, chambers adjacent to Core Objective rooms, and other high-traffic areas. This obviously depends upon the map and what your objectives are, so consult the Campaign and Freeplay chapters for specific help and coverage. Generally, it is vital to know where you're likely to get snarled up, and the routes or combat to take to mitigate these problem areas.

### Multiple Lines of Fire

Each team must immediately recognize whether they're on offense or defense; then offensive and defensive lines can be attempted.

**Offensive Lines:** If you're on the attack, plot a route that your opposition isn't expecting. Time incursions into their defensive line simultaneously, and from multiple directions. Or, if the chokepoint is large enough, a barrage from one direction. Vary your attacks so the enemy never knows how many you are, and when you'll attack.

**Be sure to fully buff your team, and attack in groups. Single enemies with little augmentation, and without a captured Command Post, are easy pickings for dug-in defenders.**

**CAUTION**

**Defensive Lines:** If you know the enemy is about to descend on your location, attempt to create a tight shield of teammates, turrets, and explosive devices. Know the number of possible incursion points, lace them with traps (such as mines, Satchel Charges, and turrets that can pivot between locations), and react quickly if the enemy breaks through. Be sure one of your team has readied more defenses farther back and closer to the Core Objective you're defending.

> **The trick during matches is to keep a steady offensive line pushing forward, or a water-tight defensive line that holds, while at the same time completing Secondary Objectives (such as claiming Command Posts) without your line crumbling.**
>
> **CAUTION**

## Outflanking

Your lines of offense or defense are your primary paths to success, but what about teammates, such as the Operative, who is also adept at going it alone? These are more suited to flanking maneuvers (although parts of, or indeed your whole team, can also attempt these moves). This involves exploiting a weak defensive line such as: a location the enemy has forgotten about, a lightly-defended location, or one that can be assaulted using trickery such as the Operative's Disguise Ability.

If you manage to move around and behind the enemy line, attacking from behind is an obvious choice. Less obvious, but more cunning, are setting traps yourself, or taking over enemy turrets using Operative abilities.

> **Distraction: A variation on this plan involves creating a disturbance to distract the enemy; usually the retaking of a Command Post. If foes peel off to deal with a problem, you can exploit the weakness in their line and punch through to a more important Core Objective.**
>
>  **TIP**

## Enfilade and Defilade Fire

**Enfilade Fire:** Try to line yourself up so you have multiple enemies on the same (or very similar) bearing to you, so that even your misses will hit. If you can do so from a defilade position (from behind their angle of advance, so you're protected and hidden by cover until they're past you), your strikes will become even more devastating.

## Wedge Formations

Having a wedge or "spear" formation when taking down an enemy's defensive line is great for breaching a gap, and having the teammates behind the "tip of the spear" widen the gap. Use this technique when facing a defensive line, and place your most battle-hardened veteran Soldier first, backed up by Medics and more Soldiers or Engineers on the flanks.

> **Send in the Clones: Does dressing in dark clothing help you in the shadows? What about all dressing in exactly the same clothing, so the enemy can't immediately distinguish you? These plans help only very marginally, but are still worth thinking about.**
>
>  **TIP**

## Additional Combat Techniques

### Leaning

Leaning, also known as "peeking," allows you to use cover to look and shoot while remaining a small target. From a regular stance (picture 1), utilize Iron Sighting, then use your directional pad (or keyboard command) to peek left and right (picture 2). This is very useful when defending or covering corners.

> **Are you using a COGA Scope for leaning or zooming? Some teammates dislike the bulk of the device's casing; it can shield your peripheral vision to a greater extent compared to other types of top attachments. Generally, the less space your weapon takes up on-screen, the more you'll notice.**
>
>  **TIP**

### Melee Strikes: Gun Butts

Melee attacks are extremely effective when at very close range or when you're low on ammo. When enemies are knocked down by a melee attack you can follow up with a finishing blow to finish them off for good by standing close, looking directly at them, and pressing the Melee Attack button. You can also finish them off from a distance with gunfire, but that takes a lot of ammo unless you're aiming for the head.

### Melee Strikes: Knives for a Pro

All teammates who have a pistol equipped also hold a knife in their left hand. They can use the knife for a higher damage melee attack, but only when they're holding their pistol. If you see an enemy with a pistol, it's likely they've either run out of ammo for their primary weapon, or have switched to their pistol specifically to use their knife. Knife attacks do more damage than a normal melee attack, but do not knock the enemy down.

### Melee Strikes: Sliding Knockdown

To slide, press crouch while sprinting in the direction you are moving. Sliding is a great way to evade enemy fire. You can still fire while sliding, but with a significant accuracy penalty. Sliding into an enemy will knock them down, just as you will be knocked down if an enemy slides into you.

### Other Advice

**Falling Damage:** If you fall too far, you'll take damage when you land. To negate falling damage, slide at the moment of impact. This requires precise timing.

**Knock-Downs:** Explosions or melee attacks will knock you down. You can still fire at enemies while knocked down, but with a considerable accuracy penalty. Hold up on your left analog stick, or move in any direction to get back up. If an enemy melees you while you're knocked down, they'll kill you.

**Spotting:** Whenever you hear a teammate announce they've spotted an enemy, that enemy's position is now displayed on the radar of every player on your team. Whenever you aim directly at an enemy, you automatically spot and announce their presence to your teammates.

**Mid-Level Cinematics:** When the attacking team completes a Primary Objective that will result in everyone restarting combat in a new part of the map, you're shown a mid-level cinematic. During these cinematics you can use the Spawn menu to change class and ready yourself for the next part of the mission. For instance, if the next objective takes place in an enclosed or very open area you may want to change your primary and secondary weapons to maximize short or long range firepower.

## Experience (XP)

Throughout your missions, you are constantly being awarded Experience Points (XP), which allow you to reach higher levels (up to 20) and ranks (up to 5 at Level 20, with each rank awarded every 5 levels). Outfits and important abilities unlock as you progress, and these are your prizes for leveling up. If you want to know exactly how many XP you receive for completing any and every action, consult the Appendices.

**Ranking up:** When you gain enough levels, you are promoted to a higher rank. This gives you access to entirely new and more versatile abilities, so you can no longer play in rank-restricted matches that are below your rank.

**Objective Wheel:** Access the wheel to choose objectives and communicate what you're going to do to your team. You earn more XP for completing objectives if you do this. If you're in a hurry, tap instead of holding the button that accesses this menu, and you'll immediately be given the most important available objective, based on the current tactical situation.

**Playing *Brink* Better:** If you're experiencing difficulty playing the game, try adjusting your controls in Menu > Options > Controls. You may want to try inverting your controller's Y axis. Tactically, try moving more than you shoot. The Iron Sight or Crouch both increase your accuracy. Fire only in short bursts. If you start getting shot by the enemy, don't stop and duel with them, run away, find cover, and let your health recharge. Never stop in doorways; you're too easy a target. Watch out for enemy grenades. Stick with friendly teammates. If you're firing and missing a lot, you may just be firing from too far away to be effective. Sneak up closer until the enemy fills your crosshairs before opening fire. If you see a group of enemies but they don't see you, don't open fire if you're outnumbered. Wait till the time is right to strike. And reload your weapon often. Good luck!

# WEAPONS DETAIL

## Brinktroduction

Firepower: A character's weapons are the mainstays of his offensive capabilities. In this chapter, we reveal all the weapons you can carry, and present an exhaustive and highly accurate chart with every minute difference between each of the weapons, so you can choose the one best-suited to the objectives you're tasked with. Welcome to the Ark's gun club.

> You may notice that some weaponry is locked; this is because you haven't completed the necessary Challenges to allow access to this armament. You are encouraged to do this first, prior to any intensive Campaign or Freeplay Matches. For a complete list of what is unlocked, consult the Appendices at the back of this guide.
>
> **NOTE**

## Weapon Availability

### Where to Reload and Rearm

You can select weapons from two different locations. The first, where you can also customize your weapon, is in the Weapon Selection menu. You can view each weapon, see some general statistics (which change when attachments are placed on a weapon), and choose a default Primary and a Secondary Weapon that you will begin each match with.

The second location to select a weapon from is any Command Post that your team owns (including Health and Supply Command Posts). Although you can't customize weapons here, you can reload them with ammo, or swap either weapon for a new one. This is yet another reason why Command Posts are so vital during combat.

### Weapons by Body Type

The type of weapons available to you depend upon your body type. While Light Body Types can fling themselves around the scenery using a variety of S.M.A.R.T. moves, their weapon choices are curtailed due to weight. Conversely, the Heavy Body Types can't climb at all well, but they make up for it by having every single armament available to them. This is how the weapons availability breaks down:

> Light Body Types can only wield pistols and SMGs. This may seem like a limitation, but they compensate with their speed and agility. This is handy for successful knife attacks, for example.
>
>  **TIP**

#### Pistols

| Weapon | Body Type: Light | Body Type: Medium | Body Type: Heavy |
|---|---|---|---|
| Kalt | Secondary | Secondary | Secondary |
| Tokmak | Secondary | Secondary | Secondary |
| Belgo MP | Secondary | Secondary | Secondary |
| Sea Eagle | Secondary | Secondary | Secondary |
| Hockler MP (Special Item) | Secondary | Secondary | Secondary |

#### Submachineguns

| Weapon | Body Type: Light | Body Type: Medium | Body Type: Heavy |
|---|---|---|---|
| Kross | Primary | Primary or Secondary | Primary or Secondary |
| Galactic | Primary | Primary or Secondary | Primary or Secondary |
| Bulpdaun | Primary | Primary or Secondary | Primary or Secondary |
| Carb 9 | Primary | Primary or Secondary | Primary or Secondary |
| Tampa | Primary | Primary or Secondary | Primary or Secondary |

HISTORY OF THE ARK
CHARACTER CREATION
GAMEPLAY
WEAPONS DETAIL
CAMPAIGN & FREEPLAY MAPS
CHALLENGES
APPENDICES

### Rifles

| Weapon | Body Type: Light | Body Type: Medium | Body Type: Heavy |
|---|---|---|---|
| Gerund | Not Available | Primary | Primary or Secondary |
| Euston | Not Available | Primary | Primary or Secondary |
| Rhett | Not Available | Primary | Primary or Secondary |
| Rokstedi | Not Available | Primary | Primary or Secondary |
| FRKN-3K | Not Available | Primary | Primary or Secondary |

### Heavy Machineguns

| Weapon | Body Type: Light | Body Type: Medium | Body Type: Heavy |
|---|---|---|---|
| Maximus | Not Available | Not Available | Primary |
| Chinzor | Not Available | Not Available | Primary |
| Gotlung Minigun | Not Available | Not Available | Primary |

### Revolvers

| Weapon | Body Type: Light | Body Type: Medium | Body Type: Heavy |
|---|---|---|---|
| Ritchie | Secondary | Secondary | Secondary |
| Caesar (Special Item) | Secondary | Secondary | Secondary |

### Long Rifles

| Weapon | Body Type: Light | Body Type: Medium | Body Type: Heavy |
|---|---|---|---|
| Drognav | Primary | Primary or Secondary | Primary or Secondary |
| Barnett | Primary | Primary or Secondary | Primary or Secondary |

### Grenade Launchers

| Weapon | Body Type: Light | Body Type: Medium | Body Type: Heavy |
|---|---|---|---|
| Lobster | Not Available | Primary | Primary or Secondary |
| EZ-Nade | Not Available | Not Available | Primary |

### Shotguns

| Weapon | Body Type: Light | Body Type: Medium | Body Type: Heavy |
|---|---|---|---|
| Mossington | Not Available | Primary | Primary or Secondary |
| Hjammerdeim | Not Available | Not Available | Primary |

## Weapon Selection Checklist

The following checklist shows a visual representation of every weapon, in both Resistance and Security colors. If the weapon requires a specific unlock, this is mentioned. "Special Unlock" indicates the item is a pre-order, or otherwise specific unlock normally unavailable through regular gameplay.

### Pistols

All pistols are available as Secondary weapons.

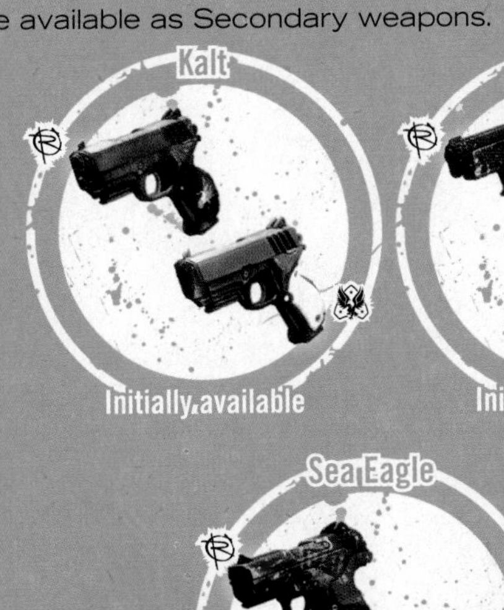

Kalt
Initially available

Sea Eagle
Initially available

Tokmak
Initially available

Belgo MP
Challenge: Complete Level ★★ of Parkour This

Hockler MP
Special Unlock

## ↘ Submachineguns

These are Primary weapons for Light Body Types, and can be either Primary or Secondary for Medium and Heavy Body Types.

**Kross**

Initially available

**Galactic**

Initially available

**Bulpdaun**

Challenge: Complete Level ★★ of Be More Objective

**Bulpdaun (DOOM)**

Special Unlock–Stats are unchanged.

**CARB-9**

Initially available

**CARB-9 (Fallout)**

Special Unlock–Stats are unchanged.

**Tampa**

Initially available

## ↘ Rifles

These are Primary weapons for Medium Body Types, and can be either Primary or Secondary for Heavy Body Types.

**Gerund**

Initially available

**Euston**

Initially available

**Rhett**

Initially available

**Rokstedi**

Initially available

**FRKN-3K**

Challenge: Complete Level ★ of Tower Defense

## ↘ Heavy Machineguns

These are Primary weapons for Heavy Body Types, and cannot be used by other body types.

**Maximus**

Initially available

**Chinzor**

Initially available

**Gotlung Minigun**

Challenge: Complete Level ★★ of Tower Defense

## Revolvers

These are Secondary weapons for any body type.

Ritchie

Challenge: Complete Level ★ of Be More Objective

Caesar

Special Unlock.

## Long Rifles

These are Primary weapons for Light Body Types, and either Primary or Secondary weapons for Medium and Heavy Body Types.

Drognav

Initially available

Barnett

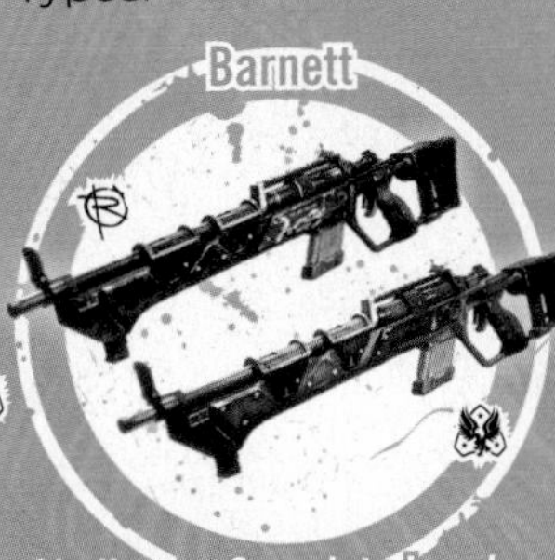

Challenge: Complete Level ★ of Parkour This

## Grenade Launchers

The EZ-Nade is a Primary weapon for Heavy Body Types, and cannot be used by anyone else. The Lobster is a Primary or Secondary weapon for Heavy Body Types, Primary for Medium Body Types, and cannot be used by Light Body Types.

Lobster

Challenge: Complete Level ★ of Be More Objective

EZ-Nade

Challenge: Complete Level ★★ of Escort Duty

## Shotguns

The Mossington is a Primary weapon for Heavy Body Types, and cannot be used by anyone else. The Hjammerdeim is a Primary or Secondary weapon for Heavy Body Types, Primary for Medium Body Types, and cannot be used by Light Body Types.

Mossington

Initially available

Hjammerdeim

Initially available

# Attachments

With the exception of the Gotlung Minigun and the two Grenade Launchers, every weapon can be augmented. You can see a rough approximation of how the attachments you've fitted onto your weapon have changed your weapon by checking the statistical bar in the Weapon Selection screen. But what does each attachment actually do? Consult the following chart for a breakdown of the problems and benefits of each attachment, and whether the attachment is available for the weapon you're using.

**Although you may see "Problems" with many attachments, the shortfalls they present are usually very slight, and have an obvious benefit to compensate for these issues. Try a match using the original weapon. Then add one attachment, and play again to compare. Continue tweaking until you're happy with the results.**

TIP

## Attachment Problems and Benefits

### Silencer
**Problem:** Range
**Benefit:** Invisible to Radar

### Suppressor*
**Benefit:** Invisible to Radar

### Four-Vent Muzzle Brake
**Problem:** Range
**Benefit:** Aim Stability

### Six-Vent Muzzle Brake
**Problem:** Range
**Benefit:** Aim Stability

### Up-Vent Muzzle Brake
**Problem:** Range
**Benefit:** Aim Stability

### Down-Vent Muzzle Brake
**Problem:** Range
**Benefit:** Aim Stability

### Side-Vent Muzzle Brake
**Problem:** Range
**Benefit:** Aim Stability

### Dual-Vent Muzzle Brake
**Problem:** Range
**Benefit:** Aim Stability

### Adjusted Iron Sights
**Benefit:** Accurate Aiming with wider field of view

### Green Eye Scope*
**Problem:** Equip Speed
**Benefit:** Accurate Aiming

### COGA Scope
**Problem:** Equip Speed
**Benefit:** Accurate and Zoom-Aiming

### D-Flex Red Dot Sight
**Problem:** Equip Speed
**Benefit:** Accurate Aiming

** Special pre-order unlock*

HISTORY OF THE ARK
CHARACTER CREATION
GAMEPLAY
WEAPONS DETAIL
CAMPAIGN & FREEPLAY MAPS
CHALLENGES
APPENDICES

### C-U-Gone Red Dot Sight

**Problem:** Equip Speed

**Benefit:** Accurate Aiming

### YeoTek Red Dot Sight

**Problem:** Equip Speed

**Benefit:** Accurate Aiming

### Snoop-R Scope

**Problem:** Equip Speed

**Benefit:** Accurate and Extreme Zoom-Aiming

### Speed Sling

**Problem:** Stability

**Benefit:** Equip Speed

### Underslung Grenade Launcher

**Problem:** Accuracy and Equip Speed

**Benefit:** Additional Weapon, fires grenades that detonate on impact

### Front Grip

**Problem:** Equip Speed

**Benefit:** Stability

### Speed Holster

**Problem:** Stability

**Benefit:** Equip Speed

### High-Capacity Magazine

**Problem:** Accuracy, Reload Speed, Equip Speed

**Benefit:** More Ammunition

### Duct-Taped Magazine

**Problem:** Accuracy, Equip Speed”

**Benefit:** Reload Speed, More Ammunition

### AR Drum Magazine

**Problem:** Accuracy, Reload Speed, Equip Speed

**Benefit:** More Ammunition

### SMG Drum Magazine

**Problem:** Accuracy, Reload Speed, Equip Speed

**Benefit:** More Ammunition

### Rapid Fire

**Problem:** Stability

**Benefit:** Increased Rate of Fire

| | Silencer | Suppressor | Four-Vent Muzzle Brake | Six-Vent Muzzle Brake | Up-Vent Muzzle Brake | Down-Vent Muzzle Brake | Side-Vent Muzzle Brake | Dual-Vent Muzzle Brake | Adjusted Iron Sights | Green Eye Scope | COGA Scope | D-Flex Red Dot Sight | C-U-Gone Red Dot Sight | YeoTek Red Dot Sight | Snoop-R Scope | Speed Sling | Underslung Grenade Launcher | Front Grip | Speed Holster | High-Capacity Magazine | Duct-Taped Magazine | AR Drum Magazine | SMG Drum Magazine | Rapid Fire |
|---|---|---|---|---|---|---|---|---|---|---|---|---|---|---|---|---|---|---|---|---|---|---|---|---|
| **Pistols** | | | | | | | | | | | | | | | | | | | | | | | | |
| Kalt | • | • | | | • | | | | • | • | • | • | | • | | | | | • | • | | | | • |
| Tokmak | • | • | | | • | | | | • | • | • | • | | • | | | | | • | • | | | | • |
| Belgo MP | • | • | | | • | | | | • | • | • | • | | • | | | | | • | • | | | | |
| Sea Eagle | • | • | | | • | | | | • | • | • | • | | • | | | | | • | • | | | | • |
| Hockler MP (Special Unlock) | • | • | | | • | | | | • | • | • | • | | • | | | | | • | • | | | | |
| **Submachineguns** | | | | | | | | | | | | | | | | | | | | | | | | |
| Kross | • | • | • | • | | • | | • | • | • | • | • | | • | | • | | • | | • | • | | • | |
| Galactic | • | • | • | • | | • | | • | • | • | • | • | | • | | • | | • | | • | • | | • | |
| Bulpdaun | • | • | • | • | | • | | • | • | • | • | • | | • | | • | | • | | • | • | | • | |
| CARB-9 | • | • | • | • | | • | | • | • | • | • | • | | • | | • | | • | | • | • | | • | |
| Tampa | • | • | • | • | | • | | • | • | • | • | • | | • | | • | | • | | • | • | | • | |
| **Rifles** | | | | | | | | | | | | | | | | | | | | | | | | |
| Gerund | • | • | • | • | | • | | • | • | • | • | • | • | • | | • | • | • | | • | • | • | | |
| Euston | • | • | • | • | | • | | • | • | • | • | • | • | • | | • | • | • | | • | • | • | | |
| Rhett | • | • | • | • | | • | | • | • | • | • | • | • | • | | • | • | • | | • | • | • | | |
| Rokstedi | • | • | • | • | | • | | • | • | • | • | • | • | • | | • | • | | | • | • | • | | • |
| FRKN-3K | • | • | • | • | | • | | • | • | • | • | • | • | • | | • | • | • | | • | • | | | |
| **Heavy Machineguns** | | | | | | | | | | | | | | | | | | | | | | | | |
| Maximus | • | | • | • | | • | | • | • | • | • | • | • | • | | | | | | • | | | | |
| Chinzor | • | | • | • | | • | | • | | | | | | | | | | | | • | | | | |
| Gotlung Minigun | | | | | | | | | | | | | | | | | | | | | | | | |
| **Revolvers** | | | | | | | | | | | | | | | | | | | | | | | | |
| Ritchie | • | • | | | | | • | | • | • | • | • | | • | | | | | • | | | | | • |
| Caesar (Special Unlock) | • | • | | | | | • | | • | • | • | • | | • | | | | | • | | | | | • |
| **Long Rifles** | | | | | | | | | | | | | | | | | | | | | | | | |
| Drognav | • | • | | | • | | • | | | • | • | • | • | • | | • | | | | | | | | • |
| Barnett | • | • | | | • | | • | | | • | • | • | • | • | • | • | | | | | | | | |
| **Grenade Launchers** | | | | | | | | | | | | | | | | | | | | | | | | |
| Lobster | | | | | | | | | | | | | | | | | | | | | | | | |
| EZ-Nade | | | | | | | | | | | | | | | | | | | | | | | | |
| **Shotguns** | | | | | | | | | | | | | | | | | | | | | | | | |
| Mossington | • | | | | | | | | • | | | • | • | • | | • | | | | | | | | |
| Hjammerdeim | • | | | | | | | | • | | | • | • | • | | • | | | | | | | | |

## Weapon Statistics

Need to know which weapon is intrinsically "best," or more proficient than the rest? Want to figure out how each type of weapon compares to all the others? Desperate for the knowledge on the delay between reloads of every firearm to the nearest 0.1 of a second? Well, even if you don't, this chart is here to reveal that information! Think of it as a highly accurate version of the bar charts you see in the Weapons menu.

**CAUTION**

This chart was accurate at time of guide release. Accuracy may fade over time, if the game is balanced over the coming months.

| Higher or Lower Value is Better? | | Higher | Lower | - | Lower | Higher | Higher | Lower | Lower | Lower |
|---|---|---|---|---|---|---|---|---|---|---|
| | Weapon Role | Damage (Projectiles) | Rate of Fire (secs per bullet) | Fire rate mode | Delay between bursts(secs ) | Clip Size | Ammo Reserves (total) | Reload (secs) | Equip Speed (s) | Dequip Speed (s) |
| **Pistols** | | | | | | | | | | |
| P1 - Kalt | Comfortable choice | 30 | 0.16 | Semi | n/a | 12 | 60 | 1.2 | 0.15 | 0.125 |
| P2 - Tokmak | Fast firing rate; for gunslingers | 24 | 0.128 | Semi | 0.4 | 18 | 60 | 1.6 | 0.2 | 0.125 |
| P3 - Belgo MP | Panic weapon | 18 | 0.064 | Auto | n/a | 20 | 60 | 1.6 | 0.3 | 0.125 |
| P4 - Sea Eagle | Packs a punch | 55 | 0.24 | Semi | n/a | 10 | 60 | 1.6 | 0.2 | 0.125 |
| P5 - Hockler MP (Special Unlock) | Panic weapon | 18 | 0.064 | Auto | 0.69 | 20 | 60 | 1.6 | 0.3 | 0.125 |
| **Submachineguns** | | | | | | | | | | |
| SMG1 - Kross | Comfortable choice | 18 | 0.064 | Auto | n/a | 35 | 200 | 1.75 | 0.3 | 0.125 |
| SMG2 - Galactic | Ammo, suppressing fire | 17 | 0.064 | Auto | n/a | 45 | 200 | 2 | 0.325 | 0.125 |
| SMG3 - Bulpdaun | The closest thing the Light Body Type can get to a rifle | 20 | 0.064 | Auto | n/a | 27 | 200 | 2.32 | 0.4 | 0.125 |
| SMG4 - CARB-9 | Burst fire, high damage | 23 | 0.064 | Auto | 0.5 | 30 | 200 | 1.89 | 0.275 | 0.125 |
| SMG5 - Tampa | Short range spray | 22 | 0.064 | Auto | n/a | 30 | 200 | 1.2 | 0.2 | 0.125 |
| **Rifles** | | | | | | | | | | |
| R1 - Gerund | Comfortable choice | 30 | 0.096 | Auto | n/a | 30 | 150 | 1.9 | 0.4 | 0.125 |
| R2 - Euston | Rifle with some similarities to an SMG | 25 | 0.064 | Auto | n/a | 28 | 150 | 1.6 | 0.425 | 0.225 |
| R3 - Rhett | Stable, punching shots with a chunky feel | 32 | 0.096 | Auto | n/a | 25 | 150 | 2 | 0.55 | 0.225 |
| R4 - Rokstedi | Single shot, semi accurate with hefty damage | 54 | 0.256 | Semi | n/a | 15 | 150 | 2.2 | 0.45 | 0.325 |
| R5 - FRKN-3K | Burst fire - aim for the chest | 30 | 0.096 | x3 | 0.375 | 24 | 150 | 2 | 0.483 | 0.225 |
| **Heavy Machineguns** | | | | | | | | | | |
| HMG1 - Maximus | Accurate option (burst fire) | 30 | 0.096 | Auto | n/a | 75 | 200 | 4 | 1.1 | 0.25 |
| HMG2 - Chinzor | Stable option (maintain fire) | 24 | 0.064 | Auto | n/a | 100 | 300 | 4 | 0.8 | 0.3 |
| HMG3 - Gotlung Minigun | Spam option (suppressing fire) | 24 | 0.066 | Auto | n/a | 200 | 400 | 5 | 0.6 | 0.25 |
| **Revolvers** | | | | | | | | | | |
| Rev1 - Ritchie | Accurate, powerful beast with too much kick | 80 | 0.325 | Semi | n/a | 6 | 30 | 2.15 | 0.375 | 0.125 |
| Rev2 - Caesar (Special Unlock) | Accurate, powerful beast with too much kick | 80 | 0.325 | Semi | n/a | 6 | 30 | 2.15 | 0.375 | 0.125 |
| **Long Rifles** | | | | | | | | | | |
| SR1 - Drognav | Bodyshots are OK too! | 80 | 0.3 | Semi | n/a | 6 | 20 | 3 | 0.5 | 0.325 |
| SR2 - Barnett | One shot one kill mentality | 125 | 2.25 | Single | n/a | 4 | 20 | 4.5 | 0.7 | 0.325 |
| **Grenade Launchers** | | | | | | | | | | |
| GL1 - Lobster | Powerful & predictible | 110 | N/A | Single | n/a | 1 | 10 | 2.8 | 0.35 | 0.125 |
| GL2 - EZ-Nade | Area denial; Horribly innaccurate if spammed | 75 | 0.48 | Auto | 1.9 | 6 | 18 | 5.4 | 0.9 | 0.225 |
| **Shotguns** | | | | | | | | | | |
| SG1 - Mossington | Anyone close will die | 22 | 0.93 | Semi | n/a | 6 | 36 | 0.6 | 0.475 | 0.225 |
| SG2 - Hjammerdeim | A more tactical choice with funnelled shots | 16 | 0.256 | x2 | 0.6 | 8 | 36 | 2.25 | 0.45 | 0.125 |

# CAMPAIGN AND FREEPLAY

## Brinktroduction

The vast majority of this guide provides meticulous descriptions and tactics for the entire Campaign and Freeplay experience. Here's how to utilize this mission information to the fullest extent.

### How to Use this Chapter

#### Campaign and Freeplay Access

In the game, you can select whether to play a match as part of an ongoing (single or multiplayer) Campaign, or in Freeplay mode. The key difference is the active story and the faction you appear on. Depending on the Campaign mission you choose, you'll be working with either the Resistance or the Security forces. During Freeplay, this is less important, and can be randomly determined.

The information is presented in Campaign format. All eight of the Resistance Campaign missions are presented. Then all eight of the Security Campaign missions are shown. But all of the information is still applicable to Freeplay mode; just reference the name of the map, find the chapter that relates to it based on the faction you're part of, and read on! The following table shows where the faction maps are located:

| Faction | Mission Name | Map Name | Pg. # |
|---|---|---|---|
| Resistance | Day 1: Getting Answers | Aquarium | 45 |
| Resistance | Day 2: Breakout | Security Tower | 62 |
| Resistance | Day 3: Chen's Plans | Terminal | 77 |
| Resistance | Day 6: Black Box | Resort | 92 |
| Resistance | Day 7: Attack on CCity | Container City | 111 |
| Resistance | Day 8: Airborne | Refuel | 132 |
| Resistance | What-If: Operation Babel | Shipyard | 146 |
| Resistance | What-If: Critical Reaction | Reactor | 165 |
| Security | Day 1: Hostage Rescue | Aquarium | 181 |
| Security | Day 3: Smash and Grab | Terminal | 198 |
| Security | Day 4: Dirty Bomb | Container City | 212 |
| Security | Day 5: Prison Break | Security Tower | 232 |
| Security | Day 6: Early Launch | Shipyard | 248 |
| Security | Day 8: Fallout | Reactor | 267 |
| Security | What-If: Chopper Down | Resort | 285 |
| Security | What-If: Grand Theft Aero | Refuel | 305 |

#### Information Overview

**Maps:** Each Campaign mission begins with a map of the zone you're fighting in. Locations, places where you can attempt a S.M.A.R.T. move, Engineer mine and turret placements, camping spots, deployment zone turrets, and objectives (both Core and Secondary) are all shown on these maps.

**Briefing:** You then receive briefing information from your commander (Brother Chen or Captain Mokoena). Then, for each Core Objective (COb), the optimal numbers of each class are shown, followed by a list of all the objectives to attempt.

**Important Locations:** Every map is segmented into locations. The topography, cover opportunities, entrances and exits, and other pertinent information is detailed here. This should help you understand the maps, and situate yourself within them. Also included are the most helpful S.M.A.R.T. moves for each location; this is where you can Vault, Mantle, Slide, or Wall-jump to gain an advantage.

**Objective Tactics:** After the tour of locations, battle-tested tactics to complete every Core Objective, and then every Secondary Objective, are shown. This includes lines of defense to try, routes to take, and maneuvers to attempt. This continues to the end of each mission strategy section.

**Calculating Time:** Listed with every objective is an approximate time; usually how long it takes to reach the location from your nearest deployment zone (based on a Light Body Type using shortcuts); and how long each task within an objective takes, where appropriate. For example, how long it takes to fix a Crane. This assumes one Engineer; it is quicker if more than one teammate of the same class (Engineers and Operatives) join during certain tasks (repairing and hacking).

**Automated Ordnance:** This reveals the optimal locations for an Engineer to place a turret, and a mine. These are numerous and optional. If your character isn't an Engineer, this information is still beneficial, because you can learn (by reading the enemy's mission) where to expect these so you can avoid them. Other classes can benefit too because the locations also work for Satchel Charges (Soldier) and Caltrop Grenades (Operatives).

**Sniper's Ally: Camping Spots:** Camping spots, vantage points, or sniping locations are all flagged and detailed here, so you can cover your team as they defend or advance on a target.

**Solo Tactics and Mission Completion:** The information concludes with advice on tackling the match in single-player, as well as the mission's victory and defeat conditions.

> **Notes, Tips, and Cautions dot the pages, providing copious amounts of helpful information. For example, make sure you read both the Resistance and Security versions of each map so you know what your team and your enemies should be planning!**
>
> TIP

### FOR THE ARK!

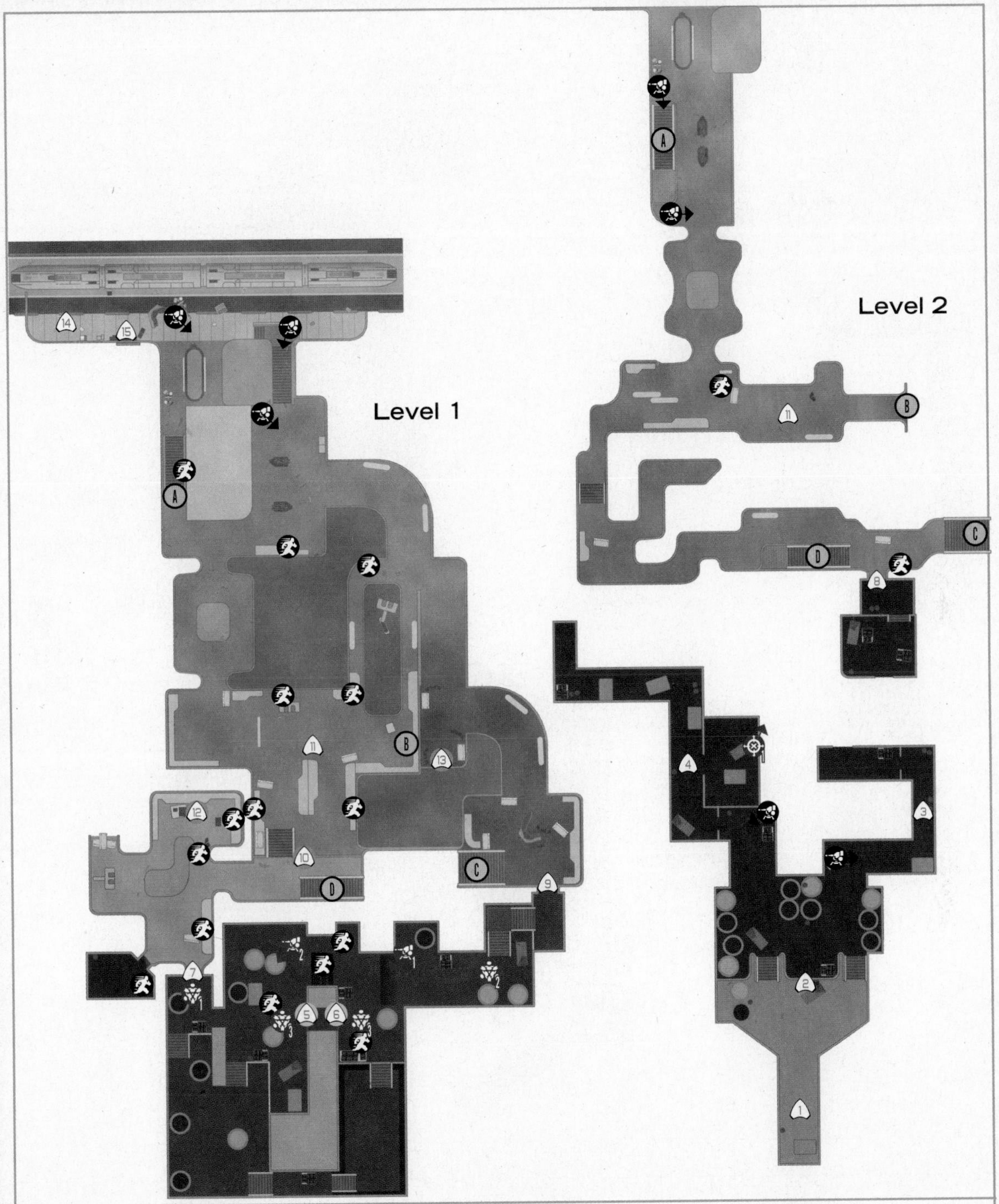

## MAP LEGEND

**Aquarium: Core Objective 1**

1: Resistance Deployment Zone (Pt. 1): Maintenance Bay (Lvl. 2)
2: Resistance Command Post (Pt. 1) (Lvl. 2)
3: Maintenance Bay Conduits (1) (Lvls. 1 & 2)
4: Maintenance Bay Conduits (2) (Lvl. 2)
5: Storage Room (Side 1) (Lvls. 1 & 2)
6: Storage Room (Side 2) (Lvls. 1 & 2)
7: Ark Water Treatment Access (1) (Lvl. 1)
8: Ark Water Treatment Access (2) (Lvl. 2)
9: Ark Water Treatment Access (3) (Lvl. 1)
10: Atrium & MG Nest (Lvl. 1)
11: Atrium Floor & Upper Balconies (Lvl. 2)
12: Supply Command Post (Lvl. 1)
13: Health Command Post (Lvl. 1)
14: Security Deployment Zone (Pt. 1): Monorail (Lvl. 2)
15: Security Command Post (Pt. 1) (Lvl. 2)

**Aquarium: Core Objective 2**

16: Resistance Deployment Zone (Pt. 2): Vat Chamber (Lvls. 1 & 2)
17: Resistance Command Post (Pt. 2) (Lvl. 2)
18: Mattress Alley to the Mezzanine Lobby (Lvls. 2 & 3)
19: The Long Ramp & MG Nest (Lvls. 1 & 2)
20: The Long Ramp Entrance (Lvl. 1)

BRINK | Aquarium: Overview Map

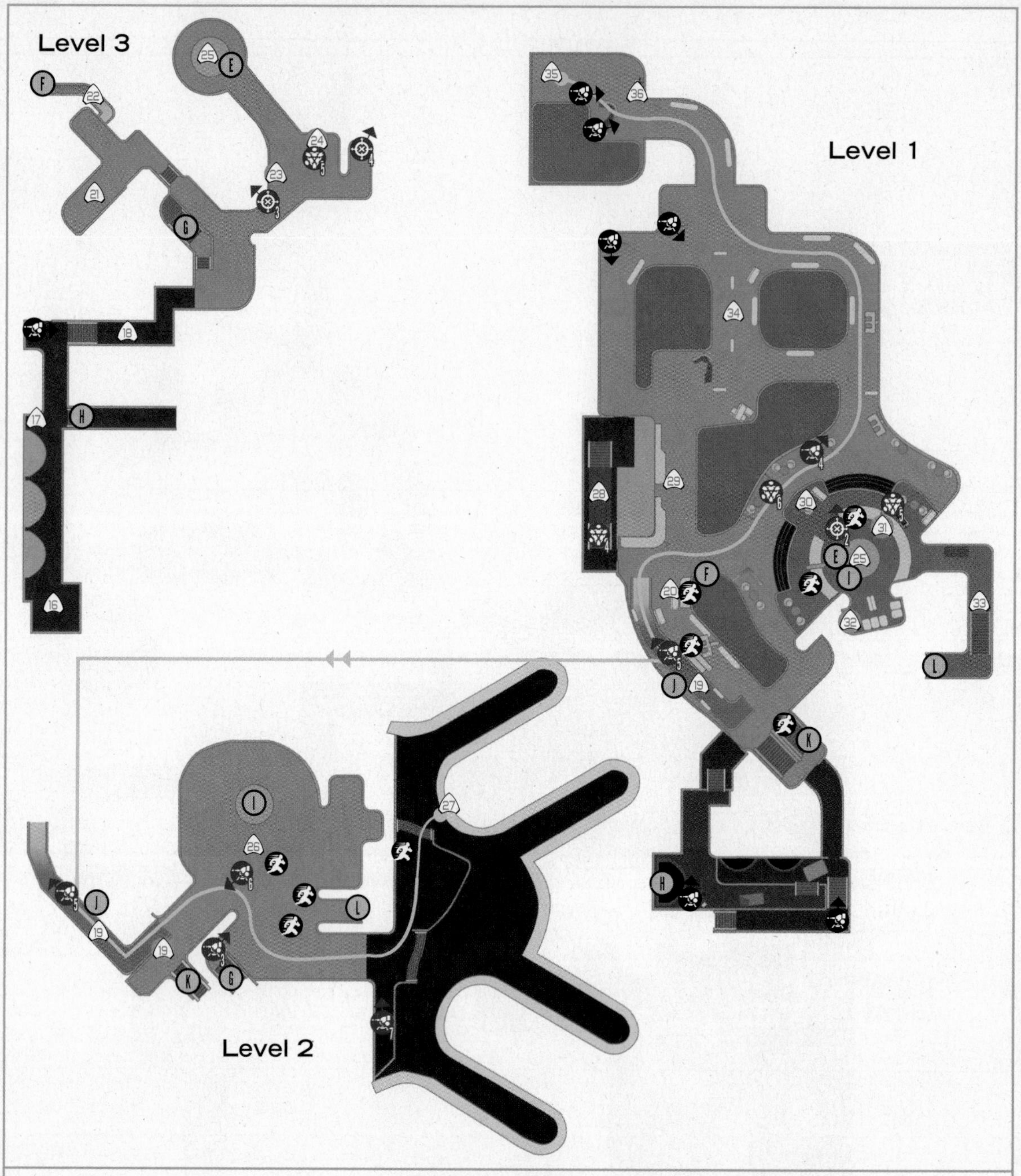

Level 3

Level 1

Level 2

## MAP LEGEND (continued)

21: Upper Balcony (Lvl. 3)
22: Air Conditioning Duct (Lvl. 3)
23: The Ark Lobby: Overlook Balcony & MG Nest (Lvl. 3)
24: The Ark Lobby: Health Command Post (Lvl. 3)
25: The Ark Lobby: Elevator (from Kyuden Restaurant) (Lvls. 1 & 3)
26: The Ark Lobby: Main Floor (Lvl. 2)
27: The Ark Lobby: Marina Docks (Lvl. 2)
28: Water Treatment: Pipe Pressure Corridor (Lvl. 1)
29: Aquarium Alley (Lvl. 1)
30: Kyuden Restaurant (Lvl. 1)
31: Supply Command Post (Lvl. 1)
32: Lift Generator (Lvl. 1)
33: The Side Stairs (Lvls. 1 & 2)
34: Undersea Corridors (Lvl. 1)
35: Security Deployment Zone (Pt. 1): Undersea Hall (Lvl. 2)
36: Security Command Post (Pt. 1) (Lvl. 2)

S.M.A.R.T. Move
Engineer Mine (Optimal Placement)
Engineer Turret (Optimal Placement)
Camping Spot
Deployment Zone Turret (Invulnerable)
Core Objective Location
Secondary Objective Location
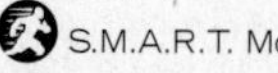
Critical Path (Route)
Level Link

BRINK ↘ Aquarium: Overview Map

# DAY 1: GETTING ANSWERS

FREEPLAY: AQUARIUM SECURITY CAMPAIGN—DAY 1: HOSTAGE RESCUE

## 10:19 Aquarium Exhibition Area and Maintenance Bay

MISSION TIME (COb 1): 08:00

MISSION TIME (COb 2): +12:00

### Brother Chen: Briefing

Brothers! For months now, we've had an agent in the Founder's council. Now it's time to pull him out. On my orders, he liberated some very specific intel, and made his way to your safe house in the old Visitors Center. We're debriefing him now, but Mokoena's men are hot on his tail. I've sent a boat to extract you all you must protect him until we get all the intel. He knows too much; don't let them take him alive! Mokoena's men will shoot to kill! Hold out until the boat gets there!

### Objectives (Resistance)

#### First Part

- Defend the Door
- Escort Core Objective Class Teammate
- Capture the Health Command Post
- Capture the Supply Command Post
- Construct the Atrium MG Nest

#### Second Part

- Stop the Agent
- Defend Lift Generator
- Capture the Health Command Post
- Capture the Supply Command Post
- Construct the Ramp MG Nest
- Construct the Lobby MG Nest

### Optimal Class Numbers

| | COb 1 | COb 2 |
|---|---|---|
| Soldier | [2] | [3] |
| Medic | [2] | [2] |
| Engineer | [3] | [2] |
| Operative | [1] | [1] |

## Important Locations (Core Objective 1)

### 1 Resistance Deployment Zone (Pt. 1): Maintenance Bay (Lvl. 2)

This is a large, cylindrically roofed chamber with a Command Post between two sets of stairs. Enemies usually stay away from here (due to the automatic turrets that cut them down). Use this area to wait for spawning teammates and buff other players before splitting into groups to tackle specific objectives.

**CAUTION**

**It is possible for suicidal Security forces to breach this deployment zone, dodging the turrets and taking a stand on the raised area behind the Command Post or behind your spawning point. Exercise extreme prejudice when attacking these annoyances.**

## Resistance Command Post (Pt. 1) (Lvl. 2)

You are quite safe (but well away from the action) at this initial Command Post within your deployment zone. Use this Command Post to change to a different class or swap weapons.

 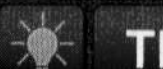

**TIP**

It wastes far less time if you've already chosen the appropriate pair of weapons (with associated attachments), based on your body type and the class you spawn as, before the match begins. Otherwise, make a quick check at the post and spawn a class your team is low on (using the numbers next to the names of each class in the Command wheel).

## Maintenance Bay Conduits (1) (Lvls. 1 & 2)

Head along the left passage to access two important areas within these connecting corridors, drops, and balconies. The first (picture 1) is the open balcony overlooking the Storage Room area (Side 1). This is a prime location for defending the door, and the balcony offers a lot of protection. It can be climbed up from below though, so watch for foes.

Follow the passage around to the left to drop down (picture 2) into a small waste-containment area with medium-sized cylindrical vats around the lower alcove below. This is occasionally accessed from the ground by the enemy (see below), but for the Resistance, this offers the quickest route to the Supply Command Post. Use it mainly for this purpose.

### S.M.A.R.T. Moves

In the Vat Chamber, leap on the propped lid of a container, and up to the balcony. Warning! This balcony leads into the enemy spawn area.

Stand on the slightly askew vat lid, and ascend to this balcony to gain some height, if you're on the Storage Room floor.

## Maintenance Bay Conduits (2) (Lvl. 2)

Head along the right passage, which winds around to a balcony directly above the Storage Room area (Side 2). This is less of a thoroughfare than the previous conduit corridors, because it doesn't lead to as many important locations, but you can clamber back up (Light Body Type, Resistance only). You can also aim at enemies through the horizontal pipes as they flood onto the balcony opposite, from Ark Water Treatment Access 2. You can also watch the foot traffic near the Storage Room door, and drop grenades (or yourself) to execute an ambush.

### S.M.A.R.T. Moves

You can climb back up into the conduit, although that offers little advantage.

##  Storage Room (Side 1) (Lvls. 1 & 2)

Expect mayhem on both sides of this central connecting chamber. The Resistance Agent is being debriefed here before being extracted. Security are trying to capture him before he gives up their secrets. On the upper floor, a balcony accessed via the first Resistance Conduit is a fine place to rain fire down on foes below. The area adjacent to the first Storage Room door **(picture 1)** is accessed by the Ark Water Treatment Access Point 1, and via the jutting pipe that separates each side of the Storage Room. There is an occasionally used U-shaped connecting conduit **(picture 2)** to the other side of the Storage Room, too.

**It can be helpful to hold the Sprint / S.M.A.R.T. button as you constantly move and jump around the Storage Room, especially if you're a smaller body type. Use it in conjunction with jumping, and leap over barriers or onto the numerous pipes on the walls.**

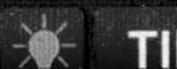 TIP

 **S.M.A.R.T. Moves** 

Tuck yourself onto the pipe above the red valve, but watch for enemies sliding under you!

## 6 Storage Room (Side 2) (Lvls. 1 & 2)

The most frantic combat takes place in this location, which is accessed by the U-shaped connecting conduit (ground floor) that is the less-used section of this chamber; by the jutting pipe that separates each side of the Storage Room; and by two Ark Water Treatment Access Points (2 and 3), which offers the enemy routes via the Upper Balcony (which you can S.M.A.R.T. climb to) or the ground corridor. Be ever mindful that you're likely to be overrun, and make plans accordingly (which are detailed in the next section of this guide).

 **S.M.A.R.T. Moves**

Climb the white cylindrical vat up onto the Upper Balcony to thwart foes attempting to infiltrate from here.

Climb up onto the pipe that runs above the Storage Room, and set up camp overlooking the balcony and most of the room, in the darkened corner.

## 7 Ark Water Treatment Access (1) (Lvl. 1)

An excellent defensive point for the Resistance forces, this is the first of three Access Points into the Maintenance Bay that the enemy must use; they cannot reach the Storage Room by any other route. This ground-level Access Point can be fortified and guarded by a few of your team. It's near the Supply Command Post, which can be guarded at the same time.

There are two doors; the Access Point is under the red banner and leads directly into an adjoining entrance area and Side 1 of the Storage Room. This is a well-trafficked chokepoint, but watch for the occasional lightweight enemy scaling the alcove of vats, and up into the Maintenance Bay Conduits (1).

## S.M.A.R.T. Moves

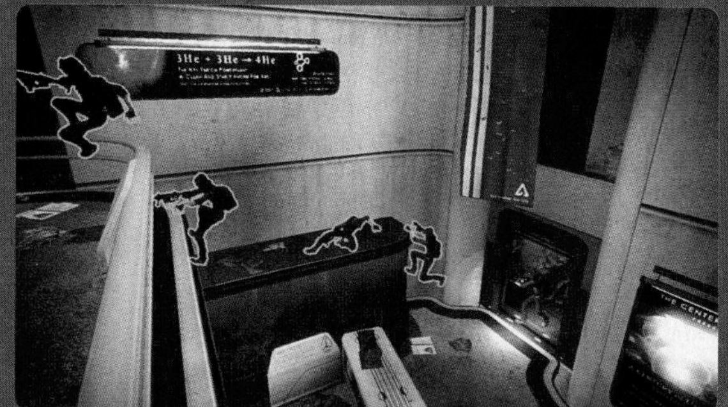

If the need arises, you can climb onto the Aquarium exhibit, and onto the Upper Balcony across from the Atrium and above the Supply Command Post.

## 8 Ark Water Treatment Access (2) (Lvl. 2)

The middle Access Point leads directly into the Storage Room (Side 2), and the balcony overlooking one of the doors itself. The enemy usually storms this via the stairs leading up from the MG Nest, or up the steps from Access Point 3. Stopping foes by reinforcing the MG Nest area, or halting them as they reach the Storage Room (Side 2) is of paramount importance.

## S.M.A.R.T. Moves

Climbing atop the exhibit tank by the door affords you an excellent view of the Atrium, and stairs down to the MG Nest.

## 9 Ark Water Treatment Access (3) (Lvl. 1)

The third Access Point is a longer, ground-level corridor leading from the meeting of two corridors out from the Atrium, MG Nest, and the Health Command Post. It's a favored rush spot for the enemy, so expect congregations of them pushing up into the Storage Room (Side 2). There are a vat and crates to hide behind as foes enter the Storage Room, so keep a presence here (with the doorway and scenery to protect you), and make intermittent dashes to the Health Command Post to retake it.

**CAUTION**

**Watch for foes standing atop the white sign or exhibit tank on either side of the exit on the Atrium side.**

## 10 Atrium & MG Nest (Lvl. 1)

## 11 Atrium Floor & Upper Balconies (Lvl. 2)

Expect the main battle during the initial stages of combat to be fought here, before you're forced back into the Storage Room. Flood this area via any of the three Access Points. Combat usually occurs around the MG Nest **(picture 1)**, and the lower Atrium with the two floating shark exhibits hanging from the ceiling. Be aware of enemies storming up the stairs near Access Point 3, as well as through the Atrium; that MG Nest is there for a reason!

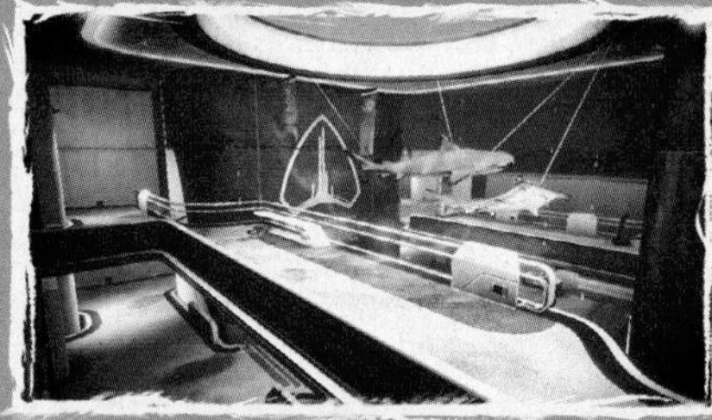

The Upper Balconies and walkways **(picture 2)** are usually the domain of the Security forces, as they are more easily reached from their deployment zone. Although stairs lead to the Upper Balconies on either side (and above the MG Nest), S.M.A.R.T. movement across the Atrium is another option. It is usually advisable to venture no farther into Security territory than the MG Nest, or you risk being overrun.

## S.M.A.R.T. Moves

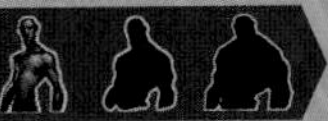

A skilled wall-runner can use either side wall to reach the opposite Upper Balcony. The enemy also likes to climb onto the exhibit tanks, and use the two stacked crates to reach the balcony above the MG Nest.

## 12 Supply Command Post (Lvl. 1)

Located below a hammerhead shark exhibit, this area is more difficult for the enemy to reach, and is the better bet for taking a Command Post during the initial action. The enemy can reach it either by dropping from the Upper Balcony (and a circling, counterclockwise corridor route), or via the MG Nest thoroughfare from the Atrium. A direct route for the Resistance is to drop down to Access Point 1, take the post, and use S.M.A.R.T. movement to guard the nearby balconies.

## S.M.A.R.T. Moves

Aside from leaping onto the balcony above the Supply Command Post (or crouching on the tank behind it), you can also climb up the man-sized barrier, and onto the Upper Balcony below the entrance to this area.

## 13 Health Command Post (Lvl. 1)

On a section of ramped walkway between an access doorway and the Atrium Upper Balconies, this is within easy reach of the Security forces. They are likely to commandeer it first unless you bring it back up. The immediate area allows access back to the Security Deployment Zone, both floors of the Atrium, and around to the map's central spine where the three Access Points are. Crouch on top of or behind the scenery and use it as an ambush point or cover.

## S.M.A.R.T. Moves

Climb onto the top of the signpost, crouching and ambushing foes below at the doorway.

Utilize the buttress foundations in the corner of the Atrium to fire on foes all around you.

## 14 Security Deployment Zone (Pt. 1): Monorail (Lvl. 2)

The Security forces stream down the steps and along the upper walkways from this point, which is well-defended by invulnerable turrets, making a Resistance strike here inadvisable. Optionally mine or place turrets, focusing on the doorways and corridors here, but don't venture farther than the glass-walled foyer. You have ground and upper access to the Atrium and Health Command Post, and more direct upper access to the Supply Command Post, if you're maneuvering in from the Security Deployment Zone.

### 15 Security Command Post (Pt. 1) (Lvl. 2)

Close to the spawning point for the Security forces, this initial Command Post is within the enemy deployment zone, and cannot be captured. The enemy uses this to change to a different class or swap weapons.

## Important Locations
(Core Objective 2)

**NOTE**

This section of the Aquarium is not connected to the first part.

### 16 Resistance Deployment Zone (Pt. 2): Vat Chamber (Lvls. 1 & 2)

This giant L-shaped chamber with half-filled vats of water is where you begin the action if you failed to keep the Agent inside the Storage Room, and the Security forces now have him. They are escorting him from the opposite end of this second section of the Aquarium. Meanwhile you must set up blockades to hold the Agent back. Exit this location via one of two lower stairwell exits; each leads to the floor of the Long Ramp chamber. Or, choose to run up Mattress Alley to reach the Mezzanine Lobby, near the Marina where the Agent's journey ends.

### 17 Resistance Command Post (Pt. 2) (Lvl. 2)

You're on defense at this point, so the Engineer is a good choice. You can change class or weapons here.

### 18 Mattress Alley to the Mezzanine Lobby (Lvls. 2 & 3)

Race along the Upper Balcony inside the Resistance spawn point to reach some stairs and a corridor up and out into the Mezzanine Lobby of the Ark's main entrance. From here, you can set up final defenses, or locate the Side Stairs down to the Kyuden Restaurant and Lift Generator.

### 19 The Long Ramp & MG Nest (Lvls. 1 & 2)

### 20 The Long Ramp Entrance (Lvl. 1)

The Long Ramp is the second of the three main locations where you'll try to hold the Agent and the enemy forces back. It is also the one that's quickest to reach from your spawn point. Race down here to reach the Kyuden Restaurant (where the first main fight occurs), but as the enemy progresses, you have the height and firepower advantage, as the Agent must climb the ramp to reach the foyer.

The MG Nest is an excellent addition to your team's firepower, as long as you realize the limited movement it has. Reach the low wall with the nest via the orange-ceiling stairwell that links to your deployment zone. Take a defensive posture here.

The ground level is where the enemy storms in from. Note the two main entrances: the marked one at the base of the ramp, and the side one connecting to the Restaurant. Use the numerous crates and scattered scenery as cover and stand midway up the ramp to drop foes heading down any of the connecting corridors.

## S.M.A.R.T. Moves

You can assault the Long Ramp by clambering up the Aquarium cleaner and exhibit. Climb the box at the lower area.

Stand atop the crates under the stairs to fire on foes coming in from the Kyuden Restaurant or Long Ramp, then hide behind them.

Don't forget to ascend the crate and exhibit, haul yourself into the Air Conditioning Duct, and use that as an ambush point!

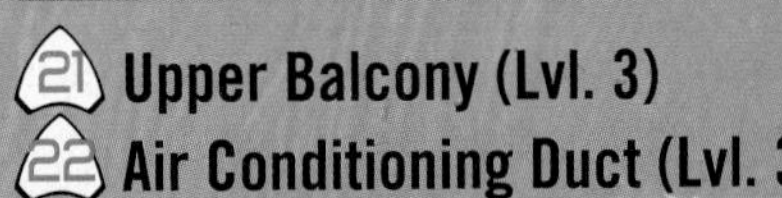

## 21 Upper Balcony (Lvl. 3)
## 22 Air Conditioning Duct (Lvl. 3)

There's an even higher balcony directly above the MG Nest facing the Long Ramp, and it's accessed via a small set of steps near your spawn point exit in the Ark Lobby. The L-shaped Upper Balcony allows you to peer down and drop behind the enemies as they reach the top of the ramp. The main draw to this location though is the entrance to an Air Conditioning Duct that allows access to an excellent ambush spot at the opposite end of the Air Conditioning Duct, above the Long Ramp. Just be careful enemies don't climb in from the Long Ramp, climb through the Air Conditioning Duct, and fire down from the Upper Balcony.

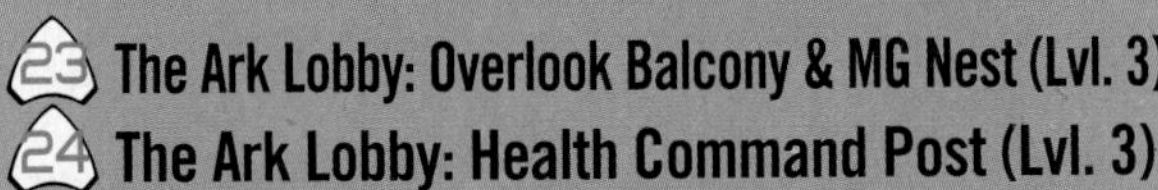

## 23 The Ark Lobby: Overlook Balcony & MG Nest (Lvl. 3)
## 24 The Ark Lobby: Health Command Post (Lvl. 3)

This giant domed enclosure is an architectural wonder, and the third (and final) concentrated chokepoint during the Agent's slow trek to freedom. From your deployment zone exit, there are stairs down to the Main Floor, across to the Upper Balcony, or around to the main Overlook Balcony. Around the curve in the Overlook Balcony, you'll spot an MG Nest with a Health Command Post close by. Your team's proximity to this location makes it handy to take and prep the MG Nest for the final assault. Beware of its limited aiming movement though.

Just to the side of the Health Command Post is a balcony overlooking the Marina. This is a good last spot to fire on the Agent before he escapes. At the other side of the balcony is the Elevator down to the Kyuden Restaurant, which the enemy tries to fix. Look over the balcony below the Health Command Post for the Side Stairs, another quick way to reach the Restaurant (if you don't drop down the lift shaft).

**TIP**

**This is a tactically advantageous position during the late stages of this mission, and worth maintaining a presence in; just don't get swamped if the enemy gets the Elevator working!**

## S.M.A.R.T. Moves

Leap from this balcony and onto the main Aquarium exhibit, then down to the Main Floor of the Lobby.

## 25 The Ark Lobby: Elevator (from Kyuden Restaurant) (Lvls. 1 & 3)

The Elevator is currently offline, and the shaft is accessible from the Overlook Balcony. The entrance to the Elevator offers excellent line-of-sight to the top of the Long Ramp, too. But the main benefit of this elevator (or lift) is to drop down it early in the mission, set up defensive lines in the Restaurant directly below, and stop the enemy from mending the generator.

If you leave the enemy to it, the doors close, and Security can stream out of this upper exit, overwhelming the Lobby area.

## 26 The Ark Lobby: Main Floor (Lvl. 2)

This large expanse of carpet, glass, and metal is the final stage in the fight to keep the Agent from leaving. Take some time to learn all the exits: the stairs with the "Fossil Discovery" sign leading up to your spawn point, the entrance to the top of the Long Ramp where the Agent staggers in from, the Side Stairs down to the Kyuden Restaurant, and the exterior entrance to the Marina Docks.

Around the elevator shaft (which can't be entered from this level) is a bar and reclining area; use the cover here when fighting the foes if they appear from the Long Ramp or out of the lift.

 S.M.A.R.T. Moves 

Hop on a planter (as shown), or a sign, or the central Aquarium exhibit, and then grab the railing of the Overlook Balcony to gain some height.

## 27 The Ark Lobby: Marina Docks (Lvl. 2)

This is the mission's only exterior location, and if you're fighting near here, hope is almost lost. The Agent stumbles across to the waiting Ark Guard boat, while Resistance forces use the cover and fortify the ground entrance in the Lobby.

S.M.A.R.T. Moves 

Drag yourself up onto the white sign, and the balcony overlooking the docks, which also allows you into the Lobby.

## 28 Water Treatment: Pipe Pressure Corridor (Lvl. 1)

## 29 Aquarium Alley (Lvl. 1)

These two parallel corridors mark the quickest route to and from the Long Ramp area, and it's your team's job to defend them with whatever armaments you have. Start at the far end of the corridor closest to the Undersea Corridors, then retreat as the enemy advances. The straight corridors make long-range weapons a must, although usually these corridors are fired through, rather than from.

> **TIP**
>
> The small stack of metal boxes to the side of Aquarium Alley in the Undersea Corridors offers a long-range shot straight into the exit of the Security Deployment Zone. Firing from the "Ark Facts" sign is a great way to annoy your foes!

## 30 Kyuden Restaurant (Lvl. 1)

## 31 Supply Command Post (Lvl. 1)

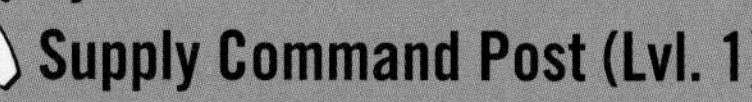

## 32 Lift Generator (Lvl. 1)

This is the location of the first major confron-tation between forces, as the enemy must

chaperone the Agent through this area, and into the Long Ramp location. Racing here first should be a matter of preference, as the circular bar area, metal boxes, and even the lift shaft provide good cover, with an excellent field-of-vision into the Undersea Corridors.

That isn't the only entrance into this area though; enemies can flank you from the two corridors and low end of the Long Ramp, or run through the Long Ramp area and attack from the side entrance here. You have the drinks machines at the end of the Side Stairs to guard, too. The drinks machines can be stood on, or hidden behind, as you fire into the Restaurant to good effect.

Both the Supply Command Post and Lift Generator are in this area too, and should be guarded down to the last man. If you can keep the enemy from mending the generator, you can keep them from ascending onto the Lobby Overlook Balcony and outflanking your team. Be sure to use the shaft to drop down into this area though.

### S.M.A.R.T. Moves

Remember to climb the balconies and vault over the bar surface to quickly reach a defensive position here.

### 33 The Side Stairs (Lvls. 1 & 2)

Don't overlook these Side Stairs because the enemies certainly don't; they can outflank you by moving to the left of the Supply Command Post and up the steps into the Ark Lobby area. Meanwhile, you can pour into the Kyuden Restaurant (and claim the Supply Command Post) at the beginning of the battle before the enemy reaches the area.

### 34 Undersea Corridors (Lvl. 1)

The "figure-8" shaped corridors that lie between the Security spawn point and the entrances to the Kyuden Restaurant, Pipe Pressure Corridor, and Aquarium Alley are teeming with foes, and it isn't wise to venture too far into this area. Sentry guns are active, and there are always more enemies. You can keep moving around the corners, back and forth, strafing foes to preoccupy the enemy while your brethren reinforce tactical strongholds.

### 35 Security Deployment Zone (Pt. 1): Undersea Hall (Lvl. 2)

Security begins here at the shark exhibit, with the Agent, who must be constantly attended to with Medical supplies.

The Undersea Hall is large and well-guarded, and the Resistance shouldn't venture here due to the superior firepower.

### 36 Security Command Post (Pt. 1) (Lvl. 2)

This post is never accessed by the Resistance, and will not function for your team.

**TIP**

**Remember to consult the opposing team's strategy elsewhere in this Walkthrough, so you know what the enemy is planning and can react accordingly!**

# Objective Tactics: Core Objective 1

## Defend the Door

Spawn Point to Storage Door: 00:12

Time to Disarm Explosives: 00:05

Time to Plant Explosives: 00:07

Countdown to Explosion: 00:30

### General Tactics

Your number-one task is to defend the door in the Storage Room at all costs. There are two sides to the door, and a number of directions from which the enemy can attack, so ensure that you and your team are patrolling both of them effectively. The doors can be opened only via an explosive charge affixed to either of the doors by an enemy Soldier (and only that class). Therefore, enemies closing in on the door with the Soldier icon above their heads in your target reticle are your primary targets. Your secondary targets are enemies backing up Soldiers, especially Medics.

If an explosive is clamped to one of the doors, you are informed verbally, and have around 30 seconds to pry the explosive off the door as an Engineer (and only that class). Seek back-up from your teammates, and remove the device as quickly as you can, which takes around five seconds to complete.

**Remember, you don't have to keep the entire Security team dead at all times; just delay and distract them from the Core Objective. If you can get them to chase and duel with you, you're winning, because then they're not completing the Storage Room detonation!**

TIP

### Lines of Defense

For this overall objective, cohesive tactical guarding with all teammates working in unison is the key to success. React to where the enemy is going, rather than grouping in a couple of places and hoping the enemy meets you *en masse*.

You may elect to take a stand as close to the enemy's spawn point as is feasible: In the Atrium from the Ark Water Treatment Access 1—while claiming the Supply Command Post during a lull, and using the MG Nest. Fierce fighting will occur here; watch for foes attacking from the Upper Balcony as well as pushing up from the Atrium floor and the Health Command Post **(picture 3)**. This covers all the major enemy routes.

If the enemy breaches the Atrium (and they will), or your teammates become unfocussed, retreat to the three Ark Water Treatment Access entrances, just inside the doorways until the enemies swarm you, and then back into the Storage Room, or the Upper Balconies, or the connecting Pipe Room.

The battle culminates in the Storage Room. The balcony above the Storage Room (Side 1) is a great place to stand your ground, cutting foes down below, and watching for them scaling the balcony itself. Your Engineers can jump down, quickly disarm the explosive charge, and scoot back up again. But this isn't the best place for a turret.

Make sure you're covering both the Storage Room doors, as the L-shaped room (Side 2) has enemies dropping in from the balcony, as well as the stairs from Ark Water Treatment Access (3). Lurk in the darkened side areas, corners, and behind the main corridor and also try running between the each side of the Storage Room via the connecting passage with the leaky pipes; you can shoot longer distances from here.

## Automated Ordnance

This turret location cuts down foes as they drop down from the balcony above. Guard Access 3 with your own weapons, though.

Prime a mine inside the doorway of Access 1 to soften up the foes while you guard the inner Storage Room entrance.

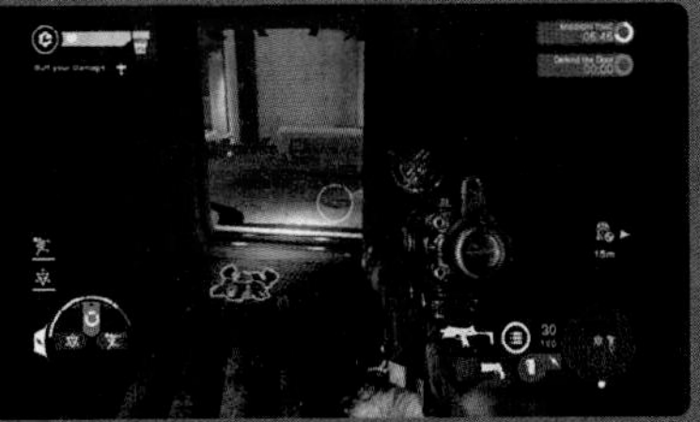

As long as you're covering the other side, a turret in this general area cuts down foes streaming in from the doorway.

Drop a mine at the base of the steps, and another in the dark to the side where foes like to hide.

Place a mine in front of the Storage Room door (one on each side) to thwart Soldiers planting the explosives.

> These are examples of the best placements for these weapons. Follow this advice before picking other, less optimal areas.
>
>  NOTE

## Sniper's Ally: Camping Spots

The balcony above the Storage Room foor (Side 1).

## Secondary Objectives

(First Map)

### Escort Core Objective Class Teammate

Official Escort Info: Shadow a teammate (color-coded yellow on your screen and easy to spot) as he sets off to defend the Core Objective. Your teammate will be an Engineer--they are the only ones who can defuse the enemy's HE Charges--so back him up as a Soldier or a Medic. Alternatively, as an Engineer you can take over bomb-disposal duties should he fall. You receive XP when you're near your teammate, so stay close.

###  Capture the Health Command Post

 Engineer & Operative Advantage!

Spawn Point to Command Post: 00:22

Time to Claim Command Post: 00:10 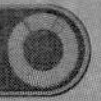

Expect a sizable enemy presence at this location, which is close to the Security forces' Aquarium thoroughfares, especially early in the match. Security forces can reach this location more easily, but you usually have a height advantage if you're defending here, plus the pedestrian barricades nearby to use as cover. Keep two teammates here because you have excellent line-of-sight across the Atrium (and balcony above), and can retreat back into the glass corridor if you're overwhelmed.

### Capture the Supply Command Post

 Engineer & Operative Advantage!

Spawn Point to Command Post: 00:16

Time to Claim Command Post: 00:10

Attempt to secure this as early as possible, so you aren't running into a nest of Security snipers on the upper walkways surrounding this post. That way you can claim the Command Post, upgrade it (using an Engineer), leave a mine on the Command Post (also using an Engineer), and then guard it from the relative safety of the Access 1 door, near the Storage Room, which offers a good view of foes trying to reclaim it.

### Construct the Atrium MG Nest

 Engineer

Spawn Point to MG Nest: 00:23

Time to Construct: 00:04

Unless you're fighting an incompetent enemy, this MG Nest is a little too far from effective cover (especially because you can be out-flanked on both sides). It makes for an entertaining diversion and can net some useful XP, but be sure to retreat once Security forces overwhelm you.

## Objective Tactics: Core Objective 2 (Second Map)

### Stop the Agent

#### General Tactics

As with the previous Core Objective, your main task is to follow or predict where the enemy will be, and then fight them at that location, which gradually becomes a series of nasty chokepoints along the Agent's staggering route out of the Ark. Your overriding plan is to distract, annoy, and delay. Try everything you can to stop Security from moving that Agent. Your priority is the Agent; focus on him and cut him down to a crouch. Your next-most-important targets are enemy Medics. Halt them from healing the Agent and he'll stay put (which in turn allows your team to fortify the areas ahead).

Despite all the talk of Light Body Type fighters with amazing climbing abilities, don't underestimate the advantages your Heavies bring to this fight. Heavies provide supporting fire, and the weapons only they can carry (such as the belt-fed MG or Gotlung) are key to your team's victory. Wound foes down to between 30 to 50 percent of their health, and let teammates finish them off; this assist is the key to effective team play.

> **Your defending doesn't need to be static. Maneuver aggressively to disrupt enemy attacks and split their team into ones and twos. Also encourage Security foes to run toward you while you back up—you'll probably do more damage to them while you jog backward than they can do sprinting toward you.**
>
> 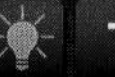 TIP

#### Lines of Defense

The first line of defense is the Kyuden Restaurant, where the bar, furniture, and lack of other entrances (except the two parallel passages merging into the Long Ramp area) make this a prime spot to defend. There's a lot to defend as well: this chokepoint, the Lift Generator, and the Supply Command Post. Keep the enemy at bay here for as long as you can.

Redeploy on the Long Ramp, moving from the base of it to the top as the enemy becomes more brash or successful. The distance you can see (and aim) makes the firefight long and brutal. You benefit from an MG Nest and a height advantage. Don't forget the Upper Balcony, where foes can drop grenades or themselves down on your defenses. Fire down from the Air Conditioning Duct.

You're pushed back into the giant Ark Lobby. Gain a height advantage from the balconies and top of the central exhibit tank, and place as many turrets and mines as you can to waylay the enemy. Although most attacks are directed at the top of the Long Ramp and the Agent's entrance, watch your backs. The enemy can outflank you here, especially around the Elevator and the Side Stairs.

The last line of defense is out in the Marina, where you have some corners, scenery, and a balcony to use as cover and vantage points, and the benefit of spawning slightly closer than the enemy. Send all attacks against the Agent or enemy Medics because your cause is almost lost.

## Automated Ordnance

1 Close to your deployment zone, this turret is partially hidden and focuses on the Agent's route, while defending you.

2 Place this by the comfy chair at the entrance to the Restaurant, to waylay your foes from the very beginning.

3 Set a turret halfway up the Long Ramp to catch foes and the Agent as they try to ascend, then replace it farther up as they advance.

4 Putting the turret here makes it more difficult to hit, and covers the final push into the Ark Lobby. Stay by the turret to cover the lift area.

5 Cutting down the Agent or a foe during the last frantic seconds of battle can be very demoralizing for the enemy.

4 On the steps of this thoroughfare, or anywhere down this corridor (or one like it), a mine can be deadly.

5 Always place a mine close to a Command Post to thwart foes as they try to reclaim it.

6 Put mines all along the path of the Agent, especially in narrow areas such as the Long Ramp.

These are examples of the best placements for these weapons. Follow this advice before picking other, less optimal areas.

 NOTE

Don't forget about turrets and mines. These need constant replacing as they're hit or removed by the enemy. It may be worth putting down a new turret a little farther down the route rather than having to keep going back to repair your previous turret.

 TIP

## Sniper's Ally: Camping Spots

2 Set up behind the Restaurant bar, covering the Agent's route.

3 Control the Balcony Overlook, and you control the Ark Lobby.

4 Attacking from the outer balcony is the final time to stop the Agent, during the final push.

# Secondary Objectives (Second Map)

### Defend Lift Generator

Spawn Point to Generator: 00:12

Time to Repair Lift Generator: 00:20

Time to Plant Explosives: 00:05

Time to Disarm Explosive: 00:05

Countdown to Explosion: 00:20

The Lift Generator is behind the cylindrical Elevator shaft at the back of the Kyuden Restaurant, and one or two of your team may elect to stick around after the first line of defense has been breached to stop enemy Engineers from fixing the generator. If you let Security complete this, they have direct access up the elevator shaft into the Lobby, and can easily outflank you. Placing mines near the generator with a turret close by and taking cover behind the drinks machines in the Side Stairs area allows one team member to run interference and cover both the Lift Generator area and the Command Post. If the Lift Generator has been fixed by the time you reach there, a Soldier on your team must set an explosive to detonate, restarting the Objective for the enemy.

### Construct the Ramp MG Nest

### Construct the Lobby MG Nest

Spawn Point to Ramp MG Nest: 00:10 

Spawn Point to Lobby MG Nest: 00:11 

Time to Construct: 00:04

The Ramp MG Nest is far more useful than the one back in the Atrium, and it's close to your spawn point, if you use the exit up the stairs. Construct this once the Agent has managed to stagger away from the Kyuden Restaurant and into the Long Ramp hallway. Then blast away at him, and any nearby enemies.

Across from the Health Command Post, this MG Nest is used by either team during the mission's later stages. It provides excellent firepower along the Agent's route, cutting him down in seconds. If Security forces have fixed the elevator, they can easily take this over and wreak havoc, so watch the Upper Balcony.

### Capture the Health Command Post

 Engineer & Operative Advantage!

Spawn Point to Command Post: 00:12 

Time to Claim Command Post: 00:10

This is slightly closer to your starting point than the enemy's, so elect a teammate to immediately rush to this location, and then watch for foes sneaking around (via the Side Stairs or Elevator) during the match, while you're mostly preoccupied with the Agent's route on the Long Ramp. As you're pushed back, stay on the balconies to keep this safe.

### Capture the Supply Command Post

Engineer & Operative Advantage!

Spawn Point to Command Post: 00:14

Time to Claim Command Post: 00:10

This is located in the Kyuden Restaurant, which is likely to be in a constant state of combat as the Lift Generator and Agent routes are both nearby. You can approach this post from the front or the back to claim it (which is handy because you can use the bar for cover). Have your team cover this as well as the Lift Generator, fortifying the entire area with mines, turrets, and men.

### Solo Tactics

With teammates you can't directly call on, take a more central role in keeping the enemies away from both Storage Room doors. The Engineer is the recommended class, so you can remove any explosives from either door. Mix up your door guarding by sprinting to either of the Command Posts and claiming it for the Resistance (you usually have enough time to make it back and disarm an explosive if necessary), before returning to your Storage Room door patrol.

During Core Objective 2, head to the Supply Command Post to claim it, and try to keep the Agent from moving forward into the Kyuden Restaurant area, before backing up the ramp and continuing to focus on the Agent problem. Listen for foes trying to repair the Lift Generator, then peel off and intercept them.

## Mission Completion Conditions

### Core Objective 1

#### Completed!

The match ends if the Resistance successfully defends the Storage Room door, and the Agent isn't captured by the Security forces.

#### Continuation...

The match continues if the Resistance fails to defend the Storage Room door, and the Agent is extricated by the Security forces. Part 2 of this mission now commences....

### Core Objective 2

#### Completed!

The match completes if you successfully keep the Agent from reaching the Ark Guard Boat in the Marina, outside the Lobby.

#### Unsuccessful!

Resistance forces lose if the Agent reaches the Ark Guard Boat in the Marina before the timer reaches zero.

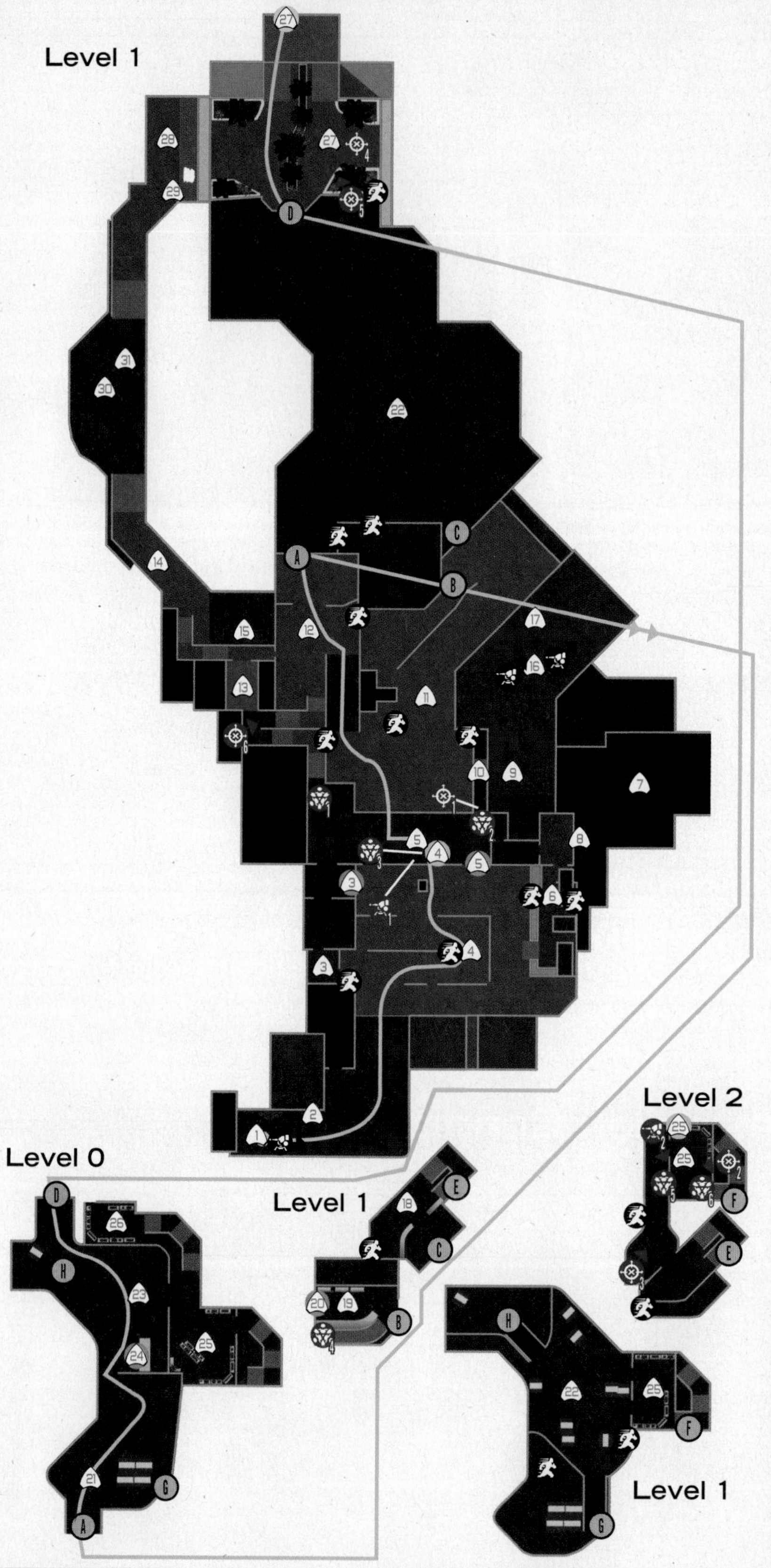

Level 1

Level 0

Level 1

Level 2

Level 1

## MAP LEGEND

### Security Tower: Core Objectives 1 and 4

1: Resistance Deployment Zone (Pt. 1): Outskirts (Lvl. 1)
2: Resistance Command Post (Pt. 1) (Lvl. 1)
3: Side Guardhouse Thoroughfare and MG Nest (Lvl. 2)
4: Security Checkpoint and Guard Tower (Lvl. 1)
5: Guard Tower Battlements and MG Nest (Lvl. 2)
6: Sewer Tunnel and Side Battlements (Lvls. 0, 1, and 2)
7: Security Deployment Zone (Pt. 4): Warehouse (Lvl. 2)
8: Security Command Post (Pt. 4) (Lvl. 2)
9: Sewer Exit and Storage Room Thoroughfare (Lvls. 0 and 1)
10: Forecourt and Security Checkpoint Stairs (Lvl. 2)
11: Forecourt Road (Lvl. 1)
12: Sunken Forecourt (Lvl. 0)
13: Maintenance Bot Garage and Side Access (Lvl. 2)
14: Security Deployment Zone (Pt. 1): Security Corridor (Lvl. 2)
15: Security Command Post (Pt. 1) (Lvl. 2)

### Security Tower: Core Objectives 2, 3, and 4

16: Resistance Deployment Zone (Parts 2 & 3): Storage Room (Lvl. 1)
17: Resistance Command Post (Parts 2 & 3) (Lvl. 1)
18: Ark Security and Staircase (Lvls. 1 and 2)
19: Ark Service Rooms and Staircase (Lvls. 0 and 1)
20: Health Command Post (Lvl. 1)
21: Sec 05 Service Entrance (Lvl. 0)
22: Sec 05 Headquarters (Lvls. 1 and 2)
23: Sec 05 High Security and Storage Area (Lvl. 0)
24: Supply Command Post (Lvl. 0)
25: Police and Warden's Offices, and Central Stairwell (Lvls. 0, 1, and 2)
26: Side Controls (Lvls. 0 and 1)
27: Sec 04 Exterior Plaza and Infirmary (Lvl. 0)
28: Resistance Deployment Zone (Pt. 4): Sec 04 Security Roof (Lvl. 1)
29: Resistance Command Post (Pt. 4) (Lvl. 1)
30: Security Deployment Zone (Parts 2 & 3): Security Corridor (Lvl. 2)
31: Security Command Post (Parts 2 & 3) (Lvl. 2)

- S.M.A.R.T. Move
- Engineer Mine (Optimal Placement)
- Engineer Turret (Optimal Placement)
- Camping Spot
- Deployment Zone Turret (Invulnerable)
- Core Objective Location
- Secondary Objective Location
- Critical Path (Route)
- Level Link

# DAY 2: BREAKOUT

FREEPLAY: SECURITY TOWER ↘ SECURITY CAMPAIGN—DAY 5: PRISON BREAK

## 14:42 ↘ Safehouse 12, Guest Pelgo Near Main Security Tower Checkpoint

MISSION TIME (COb 1): 07:00

MISSION TIME (COb 2): +07:00

MISSION TIME (COb 3): +07:00

MISSION TIME (COb 4): +07:00

### Brother Chen: Briefing

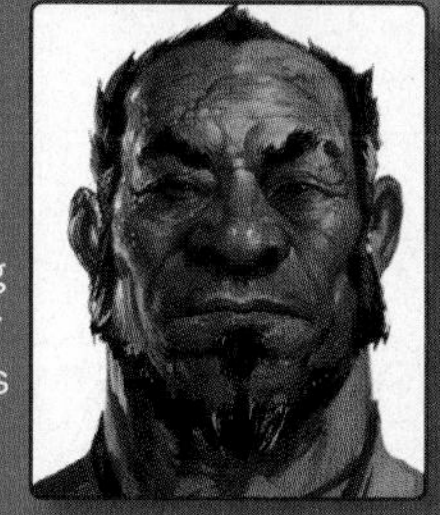

Our spy in the Founder's Council has given us the intel we need. Now we must act on it! The fascists are holding our only reliable pilot, Brother Nechayev, in Sec Tower. He's in the Infirmary. You all know what that means. Mokoena will break him and kill him! We need Nechayev to reach the outside world. He must be rescued!

### Optimal Class Numbers

| | COb 1 | COb 2 | COb 3 | COb 4 |
|---|---|---|---|---|
| Soldier | [4] | [1] | [4] | [2] |
| Medic | [2] | [2] | [2] | [4] |
| Engineer | [1] | [1] | [1] | [1] |
| Operative | [1] | [4] | [1] | [1] |

### Objectives (Resistance)

- Core Objective 1: Destroy the Conduit
- Core Objective 2: Hack the Safe
- Core Objective 3: Deliver the Passcode
- Core Objective 4: Escort Nechayev
- Escort Core Objective Class Teammate
- Capture the Health Command Post
- Capture the Supply Command Post
- Construct the Guardhouse MG Nest
- Construct the Wall MG Nest

## Important Locations (Core Objective 1 and 4)

**NOTE**

Once the initial Conduit has been removed (Core Objective 1), all these locations are accessible during each part of the mission.

### 1 Resistance Deployment Zone (Pt. 1): Outskirts (Lvl. 1)

Across the bridge from Container City (which you can see if you look to the right), this windswept promontory also serves as the final part of the escape route during the last frantic moments of the fourth Core Objective. To begin with though, your team uses this area to reach the Security Checkpoint via the ramp. Don't forget to check the Command Post (because one of you must be a Soldier to prime the explosive for the Conduit destruction), as well as the often-overlooked side doorway in the left wall, just before the corner, which leads to the Side Guardhouse.

### 2 Resistance Command Post (Pt. 1) (Lvl. 1)

This post can be easily accessed from your deployment area, allowing quick changes to your class or weaponry if you began this mission without properly planning these attributes.

### 3 Side Guardhouse Thoroughfare & MG Nest (Lvl. 2)

The lower, and seemingly dead-end section of this corridor is accessed via the Resistance Deployment Zone, and allows access to a ground-level balcony inside the Security Checkpoint. Use S.M.A.R.T. moves to climb to a second balcony directly above it. This balcony leads into a Side Guardhouse overlook, where enemies are to be expected. There's an MG Nest to commandeer (or take out), which offers firing opportunities over the Security Checkpoint. Continue around to the Guard Tower Battlements.

#### S.M.A.R.T. Moves

From the lower corridor, leap to the concrete barrier, then up onto the wall-mounted fuse box, and up onto the balcony directly above.

### 4 Security Checkpoint & Guard Tower (Lvl. 1)

The large Checkpoint and Guard Tower marked with the phrase "The Ark. United," and the graffiti underneath "Ishtar" is the main battleground for the first Core Objective, and the last stand for the enemy as you escort Nechayev back to your initial deployment zone (Core Objective 4). Aside from the Side Guardhouse balcony you can clamber up on, there are many routes to check out; although most of the high ones are likely to have enemies firing at you.

From the entrance ramp, follow the gaps in the concrete security fencing and across the labeled tarmac to the Conduit (Core Objective 1) in the right inside wall of the Guard Tower, optionally using the barricade winch box as cover. Or, hide from enemy fire in the algae-filled sewer outlet section as you move around the perimeter. Scale (or dash under) the Guard Tower in the Sewer Tunnel area, too.

Beware of the MG Nests; there's one up on the left Side Guardhouse, and another just right of the Conduit up on the Battlements. Either build and hold them, or prevent foes from doing the same. For the opposite side of the Security Checkpoint, check the location marked "Sewer Tunnel and Side Battlements."

> **"The Ark. United": Look for this sign atop the Guard Tower gate during the latter stages of Core Objective 4, so you know you're almost out of this complex with your pilot Nechayev in tow.**
>
> TIP

#### S.M.A.R.T. Moves

This is one of the few areas where S.M.A.R.T. moves aren't really an advantage; although scaling any of the "Secboard" signs and running across the tops of the mesh fences can cause a distraction.

### 5 Guard Tower Battlements & MG Nest (Lvl. 2)

It is important to remember that the main Guard Tower Battlements must have the Conduit blown apart, allowing access via a gate that opens, and activates the second Core Objective. Just as important are the numerous routes you can take to reach the battlements. From the Security Checkpoint, you can head up the Side Guardhouse area, or via the pipes above the Sewer Tunnel.

From the opposite side, using the Security Checkpoint Stairs allows anyone in the Forecourt to reach the MG Nest, which should be nullified during Core Objectives 1 and 4; otherwise this is a key defense for the Security forces. Stairs running from the Maintenance Bot Garage and Side Access meet up at the Side Guardhouse.

The actual Battlements are three small sections of broken concrete wall. One is near the Guardhouse. The next has the MG Nest. The third is at the top of the sewer pipes you can climb. The obvious point of reaching here (during Core Objectives 1, 2, and 4) is to provide supporting fire and to spot enemies below, while nullifying any defenses up here.

Once the Conduit has been destroyed, the gate under the Battlements opens, allowing access to and from the Forecourt.

##  6 Sewer Tunnel & Side Battlements (Lvls. 0, 1, & 2)

The wet and green-tinged path under the Battlements provides access under the gate and Battlements, which is vital for the first and fourth Core Objective, as it allows teammates to reach and command areas beyond the current objective. The sewer ends with a hole in the left wall, which allows access into the Sewer Exit.

Above the Sewer Tunnel are pipes with reinforced metal surrounding them. These offer a series of "steps" that (providing you jump the gaps) enables you to reach the Battlements and other side of the gate. Moving here prevents the enemy from doing the same and raining fire on your forces down below.

Utilize S.M.A.R.T. movement to reach the Side Battlements, a quiet area (during Core Objective 1, but an enemy exit during Objective 4) where you can provide long-range covering fire to your teammates.

###  S.M.A.R.T. Moves 

Utilize the concrete blocks with rebar sticking out of them as steps, and leap to cling on the second set of pipes.

From the edge of the highest pipes, you can leap and climb up onto the Side Battlements leading to Security Deployment Zone 3.

## 7 Security Deployment Zone (Pt. 4): Warehouse (Lvl. 2)

The Security team uses this deployment zone during the last Core Objective. Otherwise, this warehouse is empty. It can be used as a path down and into the Storage Room Thoroughfare (and Forecourt beyond), but can be accessed only via S.M.A.R.T. jumps from the highest Sewer Tunnel pipe section.

Once you drop down to the Storage Room Thoroughfare, you can't climb back up.

 CAUTION

## 8 Security Command Post (Pt. 4) (Lvl. 2)

Offering the Security forces a change of class or weapon, this is never accessible to Resistance forces.

## 9 Sewer Exit & Storage Room Thoroughfare (Lvls. 0 & 1)

Although the enemy uses this empty Storage Room with a hole in one side to drop down from during Core Objective 4, this is still a viable thoroughfare, and allows you to move between the Sewer Tunnel near the Security Checkpoint and the Forecourt.

This is one of a few locations that's specifically useful: Your team can move to and hold a location farther ahead of the objective (such as the Power Conduit of Core Objective 1) to speed up mission success.

CAUTION

## 10 Forecourt & Security Checkpoint Stairs (Lvl. 2)
## 11 Forecourt Road (Lvl. 1)
## 12 Sunken Forecourt (Lvl. 0)

The battle across this expanse of exterior tarmac rages throughout Core Objective 4. It is also well-trafficked as your team picks a route up to the Warden's Office during Core Objective 2, inside the Security Tower. To the side of the main gate and under the Sewer Exit is a balcony and set of stairs up to the Guard Tower Battlements; use this to drop down into the Forecourt during Core Objective 1, and use the stack of crates to reach the balcony during Objective 4. This makes a good vantage point to spot or fire on enemies.

The upper level Forecourt Road starts with a "CLEAR" sign on the tarmac, and runs as a four-lane road past a security check-in with a mesh fence, and down to the second Resistance Deployment Zone, plus two entrances into the Security Tower itself, making the far end a well-trafficked route to reach the safe in the Warden's Office (Core Objective 2). Also note the barriers and signage to use as cover.

Separated by a wall and a large set of stairs, the Sunken Forecourt area is the best way to reach the Sec 05 Service Entrance and Tower interior, and where you'll stall in your escort battle during Core Objective 3. The Side Access up to the Battlements, and the Maintenance Bot Garage is adjacent here, and Security streams down from this point, too.

**Use the ground markings on the tarmac to figure out the position within this area; especially the painted arrows, lines, and "CLEAR" sign.**

**TIP**

### S.M.A.R.T. Moves

Clamber onto the pile of metal boxes to reach the balcony above the Sewer Exit, and up to the Battlements.

Use the Secboard with the Monorail map to climb up and leap onto the security booth, offering a good (but exposed) vantage point.

At the top of the stairs, use the (locked) weapon cabinets to climb up and onto the Side Access stairs.

At the top of the stairs, jump on the wall railing, and run across to take an ambush spot above the Sec 05 Service Entrance.

## 13 Maintenance Bot Garage & Side Access (Lvl. 2)

The one-room interior building above the Maintenance Bot Garage is a route that Security forces use to reach the stepped Side Access, which allows movement between the Guard Tower Battlements and the Sunken Forecourt areas. Although the Side Access is available, the garage route (leading from the Security spawn point to a small dead-end balcony you drop from) is inaccessible until you approach it from the security corridor during Core Objective 4 in the latter stages of this mission.

## 14 Security Deployment Zone (Pt. 1): Security Corridor (Lvl. 2)

Although away from the Conduit, Security forces begin their sortie with a height advantage, and an easy route onto the Side Access area to reach the Battlements. The garage door to the security corridor behind them opens up only after Core Objective 1 is complete. Your team also uses this route past the Maintenance Bot Garage during Core Objective 4, if they take the Security Corridor route from Resistance Deployment Zone 3.

### 15 Security Command Post (Pt. 1) (Lvl. 2)

Security forces use this during the early stages of this mission; your team can't access it.

## Important Locations

(Core Objectives 2, 3, and 4)

**The remaining locations unlock only after the Conduit has been destroyed, and Core Objective 1 has been completed. Glass doors or garage shutters prevent access before this point.**

NOTE

### 16 Resistance Deployment Zone (Parts 2 & 3): Storage Room (Lvl. 1)

This is actually the other side of the warehouse from where the Security forces spawn during Core Objective 4, but the shelves prevent you from reaching that location. This offers quick access across the Forecourt and into the Security Tower. You continue to spawn here until Nechayev has been freed (the end of Core Objective 3).

### 17 Resistance Command Post (Parts 2 & 3) (Lvl. 1)

Offering a quick class-change or weapon swap, this is close to the deployment zone exit and easily accessible.

### 18 Ark Security & Staircase (Lvls. 1 & 2)

The entrance with "Ark Security" etched onto the glass wall offers quick access up to the Warden's Office. The flashing orange lights make this chamber easy to spot and race through. Use the stairs to reach the landing on the upper floor, which leads straight onto an upper walkway inside Sec 05 Headquarters. This chamber (approached from inside the Security Tower) is sometimes used as an alternate route when chaperoning Nechayev during Core Objective 4.

**S.M.A.R.T. Moves**

A quicker way is to ignore the stairs, and instead clamber up the metal containers on the shelving behind the security desk.

### 19 Ark Service Rooms & Staircase (Lvls. 0 & 1)

### 20 Health Command Post (Lvl. 1)

The entrance is to the left of the one marked "Ark Security" and offers a small Service Room with a Health Command Post inside. This is relatively easy to claim while the rest of the team storms the Warden's Office during Core Objective 2. The stairs lead down to the Sec 05 Service Entrance, and offer a change of direction if you're trying to outflank the enemy. This is also true if you take the stairs up from Sec 05, and out onto the Forecourt to attack the enemy from above and behind during Nechayev's escort.

### 21 Sec 05 Service Entrance (Lvl. 0)

This initially bewildering area offers another main path up and into the Sec 05 Headquarters from the Sunken Forecourt. When assaulting the Warden's Office, this area is a thoroughfare; choose the



HISTORY OF THE ARK
CHARACTER CREATION
GAMEPLAY
WEAPONS DETAIL
CAMPAIGN
Getting Answers
Breakout
Chen's Plans
Black Box
Attack on CCity
Airborne
Operation Babel
Critical Reaction
CHALLENGES
APPENDICES

stacked benches or ramp to reach the Sec 05 Headquarters. You can also enter the High Security and Storage Area below, either to work ahead of your team or claim the Supply Command Post.

During Nechayev's escort, the place is usually packed with foes at the security terminals and milling around by the glass doors into the Forecourt. This is a key chokepoint to clear out during the chaperoning, and the climbable scenery is mainly used for cover.

### S.M.A.R.T. Moves

Ascend the large stack of metal boxes and leap the gap to the Headquarters of the cellblock.

Don't forget you can slide across the gap in the wall between the security terminals and the glass entrance doors.

### Sec 05 Headquarters (Lvls. 1 & 2)

The main interior of the Security Tower is the cellblock-lined Headquarters, the scene of a recent riot. This enables access from the Sunken Forecourt, or one of the entrances from the upper Forecourt, into the cellblock or the High Security and Storage Area underneath. At the opposite end of the cellblock (near the wall marked "Sec 01"), close to a trio of corpses inside body bags, is a set of stairs leading down to a couple more corpses, the Sec 04 Exterior Plaza, and back around into the High Security area. A balcony overlooks the Exterior Plaza entrance.

Between these two exits are the Police and Warden's Offices, which are on two floors of the Central Stairwell. During Core Objective 2, this is where much of the fighting takes place, as you attempt to scale the chamber to reach the Warden's safe. Afterward, this becomes an alternate route to and from Nechayev's location.

### S.M.A.R.T. Moves

A jumble of stacked containers, benches, and other scenery allows you to ascend to the walkway by the Warden's Office, without the need for stairs.

### Sec 05 High Security & Storage Area (Lvl. 0)
### Supply Command Post (Lvl. 0)

The security fencing and entrance underneath the Headquarters cellblock reveals a High Security location leading into a Storage Area, which meets at the staircase at the opposite side of the Headquarters, allowing access out into the Exterior Plaza in Sec 04. Midway through the Storage Area is the entrance to the Central Stairwell. Close by is the Supply Command Post; secure it as quickly as possible. Although it can be taken during the initial stages of Core Objective 2, it becomes a priority during Core Objective 3.

This provides an alternate route up to the Warden's Office, but is mainly the battleground while escorting Nechayev during Core Objective 4. A frantic back-and-forth battle occurs as you try to push Nechayev forward through this location, so learn how the corridor weaves.

### Police & Warden's Offices, & Central Stairwell (Lvls. 0, 1, & 2)

Midway along the Headquarters cellblock is a large Central Stairwell, which runs from the High

Security Area under the cellblock all the way up three floors to the Warden's Office itself. The bottom two floors consist of Police Offices, with desks and computer terminals. Expect enemies to storm this stairwell during Core Objective 2. The Warden's Office contains the safe that must be hacked to get the Passcode, which must be taken to the Prison Infirmary, so be sure you know all the ways to reach and leave this room.

You can arrive by:

Heading up the staircase from the Ark Security.

Climbing up the stacked crates from the Headquarters cellblock area.

Scaling the Central Stairwell from the High Security area.

This is where you should expect enemy incursions too. You can leave by:

Heading out onto the balcony walkway, and leaping through either gap in the mesh security fence.

Descending the staircase to the Ark Security area, although this is away from Core Objective 3.

Racing down the Central Stairwell. Alternately you can hop over the banister and drop down.

**Need to know where the Warden's Office is? Aside from the guide map, look for flashing orange lights, and follow the signposts inside the Headquarters cellblock.**

 TIP

## 26 Side Controls (Lvls. 0 & 1)

At the base of the Central Stairwell, across from the Supply Command Post, is an alternate exit to and from the Exterior Plaza: two control room offices, one directly above the other. Use the stairs to reach the upper one; both have exits out onto the Exterior Plaza, which is useful if you're carrying the Passcode during Core Objective 3 (this is an alternate route to reach the Infirmary door). The upper balcony here is good for providing supporting fire over the Plaza itself.

 S.M.A.R.T. Moves 

With a Wall Run, you can launch yourself off the upper balcony, and land close to the steps up to the Infirmary, which is great if you're carrying the Passcode.

## 27 Sec 04 Exterior Plaza & Infirmary (Lvl. 0)

The end of Core Objective 3 and the start of Core Objective 4 occurs in this Exterior Plaza, which is separated into two areas by a long planter and glass fencing. The two exits are from the Security Tower and the Side Controls. During Objective 3, expect a large number of enemies dropping down from the roof and out of Sec 04 Security (after dropping from the hole in the roof). Across the Plaza are steps up to a terminal next to the Infirmary doors. Inserting the Passcode opens the doors, freeing Nechayev. The Infirmary cannot be entered.

## 28 Resistance Deployment Zone (Pt. 4): Sec 04 Security Roof (Lvl. 1)

You begin Core Objective 4 from this point. When escorting Nechayev, the location of the pilot determines which route you'll take: If the pilot isn't almost out of the Security Tower (that is, close to the Sunken Forecourt), it is usually best to drop down or leap over the wall, into the Exterior Plaza. If Nechayev is in the Forecourt or closer to the exit, it is quicker to run past the Security Deployment Zone (Parts 2 & 3), and out by the Maintenance Bot Garage. You can also stand on the wall and use it as a vantage point to take down enemies during the initial stages of Core Objective 4.

## 29 Resistance Command Post (Pt. 4) (Lvl. 1)

This is the Command Post for the remainder of the mission once Nechayev has been freed. You can't return to it once you've dropped down, so choose your weapon or class immediately, if necessary. Medics are recommended at this point.

HISTORY OF THE ARK
CHARACTER CREATION
GAMEPLAY
WEAPONS DETAIL
CAMPAIGN
Getting Answers
Breakout
Chen's Plans
Black Box
Attack on CCity
Airborne
Operation Babel
Critical Reaction
CHALLENGES
APPENDICES

### 30 Security Deployment Zone (Parts 2 & 3): Security Corridor (Lvl. 2)

Security forces spawn here during the time the Resistance is securing the Passcode and taking it to the Infirmary. You can't actually access this Corridor until Core Objective 4, after which it becomes a quicker route to reach the Sunken Plaza, via the Maintenance Bot Garage and another old Security spawn point.

### 31 Security Command Post (Parts 2 & 3) (Lvl. 2)

This doesn't appear to Resistance teammates during this mission; it is only used by Security forces.

## Objective Tactics: Core Objective 1

### Destroy the Conduit

Spawn Point to Conduit: 00:12

Time to Open the Conduit: 00:10

Time to Plant Explosives: 00:07

Time to Disarm Explosives: 00:05

Countdown to Explosion: 00:40

### General Tactics

**Destroying the Conduit is your Core Objective, but remember that the Conduit panel needs to be opened, first! Any class can do this, so prior to the match starting, choose a (Light Body Type) teammate to race over the gaps in the Checkpoint barricades and open the panel. Do this before the Security even shows up, for an advantage straight away!**

TIP

Milling about on the Checkpoint ground is a surefire way to waste time, although maintaining a presence and using the lower concrete barriers as cover is always effective. Two or three Soldiers should stay in this location, preventing enemy Engineers from prying the explosive charge off the Conduit. Make sure these teammates pick off Engineers as primary targets for just this reason.

Your other teammates should take up positions on and around the upper Battlements and side balconies that surround the Checkpoint. The enemy is streaming up to the Side Guardhouse before moving across the Battlements too, so a fracas here is mandatory to ensure that the rest of the team keeps that explosive ticking.

**Standing in front of the Conduit isn't necessary once the explosive is ticking down; in fact, a friendly Engineer can (optionally) drop a mine by the Conduit, and your entire team can take defensive sniping positions, all covering the Conduit itself.**

TIP

### Other Conduits

**Location A:** The firing bay accessed via the doorway just left of your deployment zone is a great place to hold up in, because it overlooks the gate and covers the Wall MG Nest, and the pipes and upper balcony the enemy uses. This is a good defilade position for enfilade fire on any foolhardy Security trying to defend too far forward. After some S.M.A.R.T. jumping, you can also reach the balcony above, and cover the Guardhouse MG Nest and repel enemies climbing the stairs on the other side of the Battlements.

**Location B:** The lichen-stained sewer outflow, just to the right of the spawn area, is another place to defend from. Although you may face grenades being lobbed down by foes, the bays give you the option of using the concrete edge with the railing, the rim in the middle of the two bays, or the barrier ramp on the right as cover, and fire at the gate's Battlements. If the Wall MG Nest (or a turret) fires down at you, simply duck back into cover.

Location C: Light and Medium Body Types can scale the end ramp of the sewer outflow

area and vault up the pipe stacks, allowing lithe team members to interrupt the enemy or shoot them all the way across the Forecourt to their spawning point.

**Operatives, if you can steal an enemy disguise and head into the Sewer Tunnel and through the base of the wall, you can get right in among the Security defenders and really annoy them!**

TIP

## Automated Ordnance

Because you're the attacking team, there's much less time to set up defenses. Check Security's section for ideas, and areas to avoid or watch for.

1 Turrets are easily removed by the swarm of enemies, but anything to waylay them during their bomb removal is worth attempting, such as this turret guarding the Conduit.

1 2 Stop enemies from rushing up their side stairs with a mine at the top (location 1 shown).

3 Partner with a Soldier, and drop a mine below the Conduit after the explosive is planted.

## Sniper's Ally: Camping Spots

1 From this covered side Battlement opening, you can see (and shoot) enemies swarming both side staircases, and the Battlement wall itself.

# Objective Tactics: Core Objective 2

### Hack the Safe

Spawn Point to Safe: 00:17

Time to Hack the Safe: 01:00

### General Tactics

Much of this mission is about pre-planning during the previous Core Objective; be sure you have at least two or three Operatives ready as the Conduit is detonated. Another option is to find (using the map or Mission Wheel) the Health Command Post, and then capture it immediately. Then switch your classes (and weapons to closer assault firearms if needed), and maneuver up into the Warden's Office from every different direction you possibly can (see below).

When you reach the Warden's Office, make sure one or more Operatives are hacking, and as many other teammates as possible are guarding the exterior balcony and stairwell as a last line of defense. Make sure one Operative is hacking and shrugging off enemy fire, while the other(s) can stop and retaliate. Charging in groups instead of individually also helps more of you reach the Warden's Office, and survive for longer.

HISTORY OF THE ARK
CHARACTER CREATION
GAMEPLAY
WEAPONS DETAIL
CAMPAIGN
Getting Answers
Breakout
Chen's Plans
Black Box
Attack on CCity
Airborne
Operation Babel
Critical Reaction
CHALLENGES
APPENDICES

⚠ CAUTION

If Security Engineers put down turrets, flank them and grenade them. Operatives should spot enemy mines. Expect most of your enemies to be Engineers in order to remove the Hack Box from the safe, and to lace the area with explosives and defensives.

## Warden Office Rampage

**Route A:** Entering via the lower Sec Tower (Sec 05 Service Entrance), you can dash up the interior ramp in the Headquarters (or climb the stacked scenery), and then climb the second stack of crates and furniture to a gap in the fence and onto the outside balcony, or head through the Police Offices and up the stairwell from this middle floor.

**Route B:** Or, you can head into the Headquarters and then remain on the lowest level, running past the body bags into Sec 05 High Security and Storage Area, passing the Supply Command Post, and then ascend up through the Police Offices and all the way up the stairwell from this lower floor.

TIP

Remember you can use the Ark Service Rooms and Staircase (where the Health Command Post is), which links the Service Entrance to the Ark Security and Staircase, and double-back if you spot a congregation of enemies or defenses blocking one path.

**Route C:** Or, you can rush in from your deployment zone, into the Ark Security and Staircase, and utilize the crates or the stairs to reach the upper balcony outside the Warden's Office. This is the quickest route, and Light Body Types may be able to get there (and perhaps set up a turret or mine) before the majority of foes arrive.

## Automated Ordnance

2 Cover the top of the stairs and the entire balcony with this strategically placed turret. When placed near the glass wall, an Engineer can repair it from cover.

4 If you decide to storm the Warden's Office from the Ark Security entrance, place a mine on the stairs up to the Health Command Post, which helps defend the post, too.

5 6 The enemy won't be able to cut your Operative down if the Warden's Office is mined at both entrances (location 5 shown).

## Sniper's Ally: Camping Spots

2 Patrol the stairwell moving up and down one floor between the Police and Warden's Offices; you can retreat if you're swarmed from below.

3 Cover the opposite side of the Warden's Office from here; protective glass allows you to see (but not feel the wrath of) the enemy coming up the stairs. The gaps in the fence are covered, too.

# Objective Tactics: Core Objective 3

## Deliver the Passcode

Spawn Point to Warden's Office: 00:12

Warden's Office to Infirmary: 00:14

Time to Deliver Passcode: 00:05

### General Tactics

Fleeing the Warden's Office with the Passcode requires more than just a few dodging maneuvers and route-knowledge. Any class can attempt this (so Operatives who opened the safe can hand this off to another teammate). More important are the team members following the Passcode carrier; make sure at least one of them is an attentive attending Medic, and more are helpful. Prep for this plan during Core Objective 2; have two or three Medics guard the Operative during the latter stages of his hacking.

Then pick a route, with the knowledge that more than one is available (see below). Once you're out of the Sec Tower building and into the Exterior Plaza, sprint to the Infirmary door at the top of the steps, with most enemy attacks coming from the security structure and inaccessible roof on your left. Use cover! Don't just stand there, even if you're firing, because you're making yourself an easier target. Let two or three teammates out first to soak up the damage and provide supporting fire and a distraction.

### Accessing the Infirmary

**Route A:** From the Warden's Office, dash onto the interior balcony overlooking the cellblock, and leap the gap in the mesh fencing, before sprinting down and out of the main exit.

**Route B:** If the Central Stairwell down to the Police Offices and Supply Command Post is more or less free of foes (which isn't usually the case), descend the stairs (or drop down over the banisters with haste). Then dash across and out of the main exit.

Route C: Use the Central Stairwell descent, but utilize the Side Controls room (on either floor) to the right of the main exit. Not only do you appear on the right side of the large glass wall and planter (which you can use as cover), but you can Wall-jump from the upper Controls room, landing close to the edge of the Infirmary steps without even touching the Plaza ground!

Watch out for those glass panels, and don't get stuck behind them: Figure out which are doorways to step through, and which result in an embarrassing face-plant!

CAUTION

The central planter that divides the Exterior Plaza is only climbable where there's a gap between the glass sections, so S.M.A.R.T. moves are of limited help here. However, it can provide vital cover while your health recharges (so you can complete the final sprint to the Infirmary entrance).

TIP

## Sniper's Ally: Camping Spots

4 Crouch on these boxes behind the glass planter to cover the Passcode carrier and check for foes coming in from both directions.

5 The Side Controls upper level is a great location to snipe from, covering the Passcode carrier.

# Objective Tactics: Core Objective 4

## Escort Nechayev

Infirmary to Deployment Zone: 00:38

### General Tactics

The logical choice here is to change classes to a Medic for the remainder of this mission. Nechayev needs to stay alive, and for this to occur, he needs to keep moving and have a steady supply of syringes. As the pilot only moves along one route (which the enemy should already have learned), it is useful to move ahead, flanking their prepared defenses, and maneuvering around to tackle them from behind or the side. Keep them guessing, and keep that pilot upright and moving!

### The Pilot's Flight

**Chokepoint 1 (Entrance to Sec 05 High Security and Storage Area):** Enemies really begin to mass

after you head into the Sec Tower and try to push through the winding corridor below the cellblock. Have two of your beefier teammates tackle foes on the stairs while you rush Nechayev under them. When you're by the Supply Command Post, cover the exit doorway and push onward.

**Chokepoint 2 (Exit from Sec 05 High Security and Storage Area):** The enemies use the desk (and have usually taken the Health Command Post nearby, making them harder to kill) in this location, before retreating into the Forecourt. Keep a teammate checking behind Nechayev, and have two or three of your team fighting on the path, but the rest circling around (use the Security Corridor or Warden's Office to head outside, and outflank the enemy from behind). This solves a stalemate!

**Chokepoint 3 (Forecourt to Battlements):** The enemy used the passage above the Maintenance Bot Garage to reach the Guardhouse, and some of your team should do the same; that way they can snipe at foes rushing to the Forecourt stairs.

If you're just bunched together at the Sec 05 exit and Sunken Forecourt, you'll never get any farther. Scale the right side of the Forecourt and attack from above, as well as below! Also remember you can flank around from the upper Forecourt too.

**Chokepoint 4 (Checkpoint and freedom!):** As long as your Medics are fighting on the ground and coaxing Nechayev along, your snipers and long-range takedown experts are manning the Side Guardhouse, and you optionally have a lunatic causing enemy distractions away from both groups, Nechayev may stand a fighting chance at freedom!

### Sniper's Ally: Camping Spots

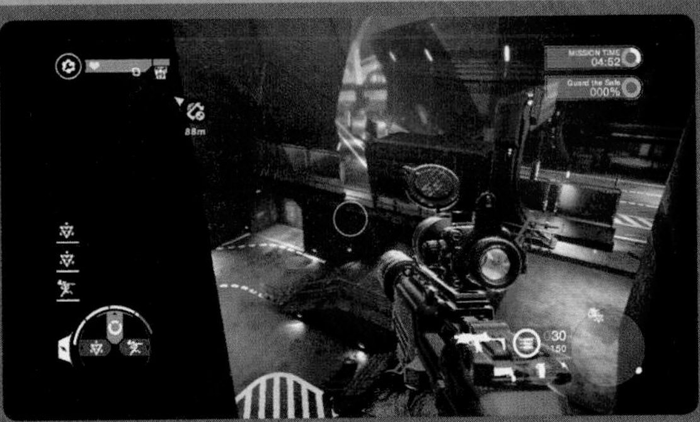

6 Now that you have access to the balcony above the Maintenance Bot Garage, use it to lob grenades down and cover your Medics as Nechayev's death march continues.

## Objective Tactics: Secondary Objectives

### Escort Core Objective Class Teammate

**Official Escort Info:** During Core Objective 1, choose a Medic (or a second Soldier) to shadow the Soldier attempting to destroy the Conduit, and keep the enemy's fire away from him. For Core Objective 2, help the Operative with the Warden's hacking by either covering the Operative (using a Soldier or Engineer) or helping with the hack (as a Medic or additional Operative). During Core Objective 3, guard the Passcode carrier (a tough Soldier is a good choice here), and pick up the item if the carrier falls. Finally, you can add yourself to the Medics helping Nechayev.

**Unofficial Escort Info:** Ignore this Objective selection, but team up with a second player to run interference, especially during Core Objective 4.

### Capture the Health Command Post

Engineer & Operative Advantage!

Spawn Point to Command Post: 00:16

Time to Claim Command Post: 00:10

Located in the Ark Service Rooms and Staircase, this isn't available until Core Objective 2 is

accessible. Pre-plan with your team, choosing an Engineer to race to the upper entrance, and dive in just as the doors open as the Conduit is destroyed. Then keep the Health Command Post by trapping it with a mine or a turret placed across at the second Resistance spawn point. As the match progresses, have the Engineer periodically return if the Command Post is under threat, staying in the vicinity as Nechayev reaches the Sec Tower exit. Then continue to capture it depending on the pilot's progress.

 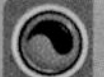

### Capture the Supply Command Post

 Engineer & Operative Advantage!

Spawn Point to Command Post: 00:19

Time to Claim Command Post: 00:10

This post, tucked away inside the Sec 05 High Security and Storage Area, is also inaccessible until Core Objective 2 has started. You may wish to employ the same Engineer to run to this Command Post from the Health one, and secure that, although there's far more fighting in this area, because it's part of the route Nechayev takes once he's freed. Learn to use the surrounding shelving as cover (sliding under and staying by the glass to avoid fire).

### Construct the Guardhouse MG Nest

### Construct the Wall MG Nest

 Engineer

Spawn Point to Guardhouse MG Nest: 00:14

Spawn Point to Wall MG Nest: 00:17

Time to Construct: 00:04

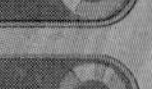

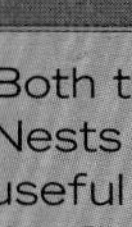

Both the MG Nests are useful during the first and fourth Core Objectives, because they offer covering fire to your teammates on the ground, whether removing the Conduit or helping Nechayev out of this hell-hole. Beware of enemies—especially on the Wall MG side because it's close to the final Security Deployment Zone—rushing you from the sides, as well as the inherent aiming difficulties that all MG Nests have; they don't aim with the flexibility of a firearm.

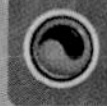

### Solo Tactics

**No friends? Then sprint to the Conduit as a Soldier, and handle the first Core Objective yourself. Once the Conduit is open, dash to the nearest Command Post to change to an Operative, before battling up to the Warden's Office, which becomes incredibly difficult to defend on your own. You may wish to prowl the area and remove threats first. With the Passcode, sprint via one of the previously described routes to the Infirmary, and while chaperoning Nechayev, pick the Medic so you can keep the pilot moving.**

## Mission Completion Conditions

### Continuation...

**Core Objective 1:** Your team succeeds in destroying the Conduit at the Checkpoint. Part 2 of this mission now commences....

**Core Objective 2:** You successfully hack the Warden's safe and obtain the Passcode. Part 3 of this mission now begins....

**Core Objective 3:** You free Nechayev at the terminal by the Infirmary door. Part 4 of this mission now begins....

### Completed!

The match completes if you successfully escort Nechayev all the way through the Sec Tower, past the Checkpoint, to your original deployment zone, before the timer ticks down.

### Unsuccessful!

Resistance forces lose if the enemy stops you from completing any Core Objective by the time the timer reaches zero.

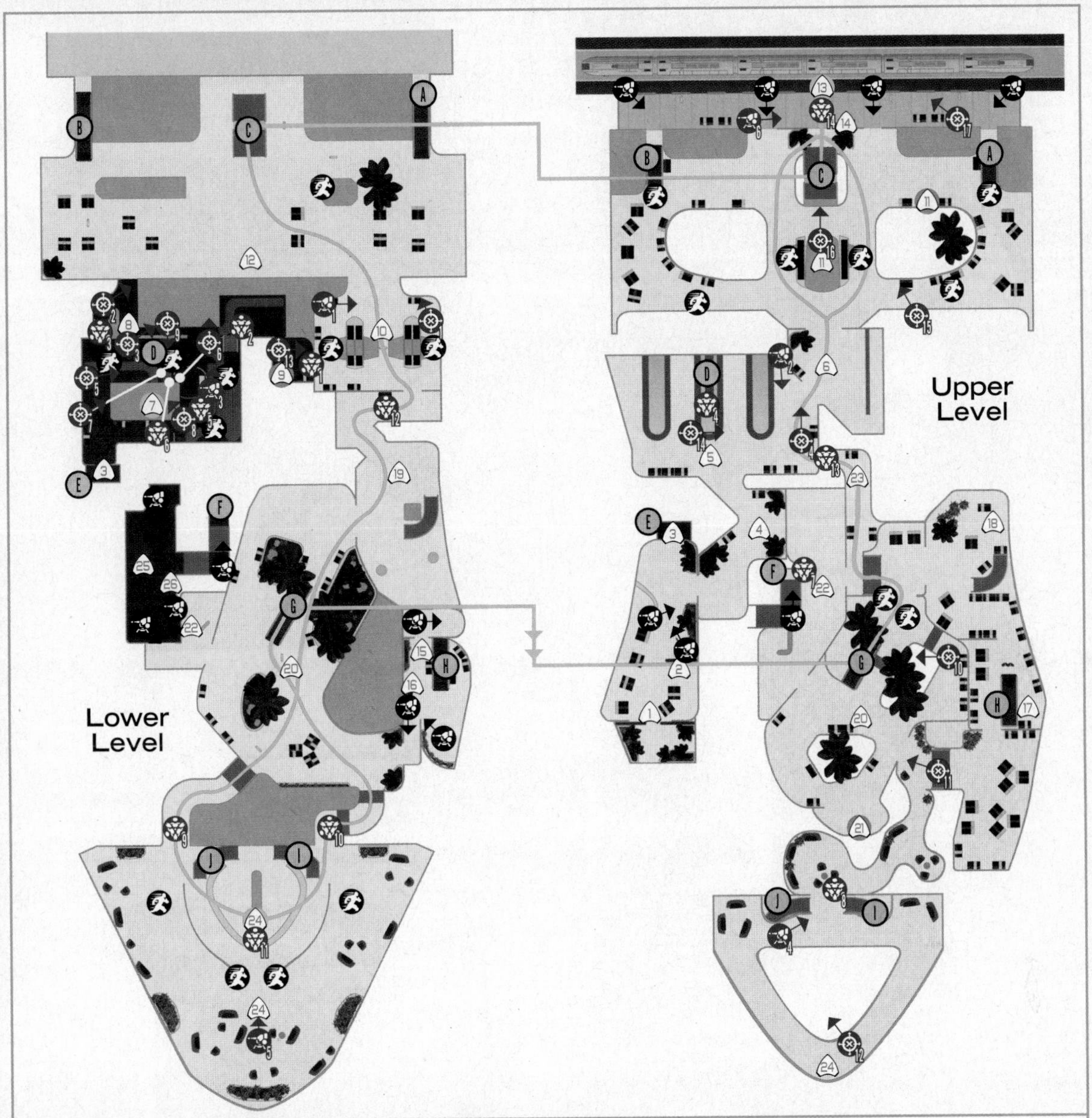

Lower Level

Upper Level

## MAP LEGEND

**↘ Terminal: Core Objective 1 (& 3)**

1: Resistance Deployment Zone (Pt. 1): Gate A1 (Upper)
2: Resistance Command Post (Pt. 1) (Upper)
3: Elevator Shaft (Upper and Lower)
4: Airport Corridor: Resistance (Upper)
5: Baggage Claim (Upper)
6: Airport Cashier Corridor (Upper)
7: Conveyor Control Point: Mainframe (Lower)
8: Baggage Chutes (Lower)
9: Health Command Post (Lower)
10: Security Scanners (Lower)
11: Airport Mezzanine: Security and Check-In MG Nest (Upper)
12: Airport Mezzanine: Tickets and Information (Lower)
13: Security Deployment Zone (Pt. 1): Monorail (Upper)
14: Security Command Post (Pt. 1) (Upper)

**↘ Terminal: Core Objective 2 (& 3)**

15: Resistance Deployment Zone (Pts. 2 & 3): Gate B5 (Lower)
16: Gate A5 (Upper)
17: Gate A6 and Curved Stairs (Upper)
18: Resistance Command Post (Pts. 2 & 3) (Lower)
19: Tihjin Moon and Gaccie (Lower)
20: Central Shopping Plaza Mezzanine (Upper and Lower)
21: Supply Command Post (Upper)
22: Blossum (Upper and Lower)
23: Airport Corridor: Plaza to Baggage Claim (Upper)
24: Fra Diavolo Lounge & Restaurant with Safe (Upper and Lower)
25: Security Deployment Zone (Pts. 2 & 3): Baggage Maintenance Office (Lower)
26: Security Command Post (Pts. 2 & 3) (Lower)

- S.M.A.R.T. Move
- Engineer Mine (Optimal Placement)
- Engineer Turret (Optimal Placement)
- Camping Spot
- Deployment Zone Turret (Invulnerable)
- Core Objective Location
- Secondary Objective Location
- Critical Path (Route)
- Level Link

BRINK

↘ Terminal: Overview Map

# DAY 3: CHEN'S PLANS

FREEPLAY: TERMINAL | SECURITY CAMPAIGN—DAY 3: SMASH AND GRAB

## 16:24 Abandoned Executive Lounge, Airport

MISSION TIME (COb 1): 08:00

MISSION TIME (COb 2): +06:00

MISSION TIME (COb 3): +06:00

### Brother Chen: Briefing

Our pilot brother Nechayev is hurt. He needs time to recover, and we need to figure out a way to get our hands on a NavComputer. Meanwhile, I need you to guard our plans. They're encrypted on a Datakey cached in the old airport terminal. If we are compromised, a data-bomb will activate, deleting everything! But if Security do come knocking, you have to hold out long enough for the Datakey to delete itself. We are a direct threat to Mokoena's power now; he's turning the Ark upside down looking for us. Everyone lie low, stay alert! Guard the Datakey with your lives!

### Optimal Class Numbers

| | COb 1 | COb 2 | COb 3 |
|---|---|---|---|
| Soldier | [2] | [3] | [3] |
| Medic | [2] | [2] | [2] |
| Engineer | [3] | [2] | [1] |
| Operative | [1] | [1] | [1] |

### Objectives (Resistance)

- Core Objective 1: Defend the Mainframe
- Core Objective 2: Defend the Safe
- Core Objective 3: Defend the Datakey
- Escort Core Objective Class Teammate
- Capture the Health Command Post
- Capture the Supply Command Post
- Construct the Check-In MG Nest

## Important Locations (Core Objective 1 and 3)

**NOTE**

**These locations are accessible during Core Objective 1. They are also accessible afterward, but are only really traversed during Core Objective 3.**

### 1 Resistance Deployment Zone (Pt. 1): Gate A1 (Upper)

You begin on the upper level of this two-floored Airport, in a boarding lounge for Gate A1 (which is to your left, through the inaccessible glass windows). Because you're only concerned with reaching the Mainframe, seek the Elevator Shaft or the Airport Corridor as soon as possible; both are by the gate kiosk.

### 2 Resistance Command Post (Pt. 1) (Upper)

Swap out your weapons or choose a different class at this Command Post, located within your deployment zone. This is only available during Part 1 of this three-part mission; it switches to a standby mode afterward and cannot be accessed.

### 3 Elevator Shaft (Upper and Lower)

This is the quickest way into the Conveyor Control Point where the Mainframe is located; simply drop down the open shaft to a T-junction corridor, and rush down either passage to reach the Control Point itself. Unless enemy forces are guarding this thoroughfare, this is usually the optimal path to reach the target you're defending if your foes are already there.

### 4 Airport Corridor: Resistance (Upper)

Pass a couple of sealed-up stores to get from the Resistance Deployment Zone (Part 1) to the Baggage Claim chamber. This is another method of reaching the Conveyor Control Point, although you're likely to engage the enemy inside Baggage Claim itself. Use this route to waylay enemies while other teammates increase the defenses in the Conveyor Control Point.

###  Baggage Claim (Upper)

Directly above the Conveyor Control Point, the Baggage Claim consists of two entrances: one from the Resistance spawn point and the other from the Airport Mezzanine Security area (Upper). Carousel #2, currently open for maintenance, is another main arterial route that the enemy uses to reach the Mainframe. Guarding this conveyor belt is of paramount importance, either from this location or at the Mainframe chamber below. Note the red light illuminating the entrance below it. This is also part of a possible escape route during Part 3 of this mission.

> **NOTE**
>
> Note that the door marked with the red emergency exit sign (the man running to a door) is sealed during Part 1 of this mission, but opens during Parts 2 and 3.

### 6 Airport Cashier Corridor (Upper)

Providing a wide (and dangerous) route from the Airport's Upper Mezzanine (and the Security forces' spawn point) into Baggage Claim, this triangular room with a long cashier's desk along one wall is likely to be an initial line of defense. Although it isn't accessible, the Health Command Post is underneath this area, along with baggage chutes into the Conveyor Control Point. This is also part of a possible escape route during Part 3 of this mission.

> **TIP**
>
> Spot the sparking safe behind the cashier counter? Use that as a reference point so you know where you are, and what locations are adjacent to your position.

### 7 Conveyor Control Point: Mainframe (Lower)

This vital area during Part 1 of your mission is directly underneath Baggage Claim. Although anyone can use the variety of entrances to reach the Mainframe, Resistance forces usually reach this point by dropping down the Elevator Shaft, or heading down the chute from Baggage Claim. Security forces use the corridor from the Health Command Post, and either of the two exits from the Baggage Chutes area adjacent to the Tickets and Information area of the Airport Mezzanine. Security also utilize the chute from Baggage Claim.

Although numerous baggage conveyor belts crisscross the Control Center, the Mainframe itself can be accessed only via one of three doorways cut into the glass wall surrounding it.

> **NOTE**
>
> Note that the sealed door marked with the red emergency exit sign (the man running to a door) is sealed during all parts of this mission. The room you can see through the glass is the Security forces' second spawn point. Don't confuse this with the open doorway leading from here to the Mezzanine.

## S.M.A.R.T. Moves

By clambering on any of the containers or crates on the ground, you can climb onto any conveyor belt, even the one up into Baggage Claim.

Climbing up onto the conveyor belts allows you to gain height (but not movement) advantage over your enemies.

## 8 Baggage Chutes (Lower)

Most of your offensive firepower is generated toward this area connecting the Health Command Post at one end to the Security forces' entrance just right of the Ticket Gates in the Airport Mezzanine. The enemy may find the parallel conveyor belt to be beneficial when attempting to push through one of the three exits, and into the Conveyor Control Point itself.

## 9 Health Command Post (Lower)

Just around the corner from the Baggage Chutes is the Health Command Post, where concentrated fighting is likely to occur during Part 1 of this mission. This area provides access to the Conveyor Control Point, and is an ideal location to fortify before the Security forces reach it and do the same. If the mission continues to Part 2 or 3, many teammates forget that this Health Command Post is still accessible; claim it throughout the match.

**The Supply Command Post is in the upper Plaza area, behind doorways that are sealed during Part 1 of this mission, making this the only neutral Command Post you can claim.**

NOTE

## 10 Security Scanners (Lower)

This is ideally the first line of defense for the Resistance forces. Venturing through the wide exit and any farther into the Airport Mezzanine usually results in you being overwhelmed, or shot at from the MG Nest overlooking the Check-In area. This area is also adjacent to the Tihjin Moon, and the associated door only unlocks during Parts 2 and 3 of this mission. During Part 3, this area is a viable escape route for the Security forces.

**Notice the sparking light fixture in this area? Use that, and the red glowing "Tihjin Moon" sign behind the glass doors, as reference points.**

TIP

## S.M.A.R.T. Moves

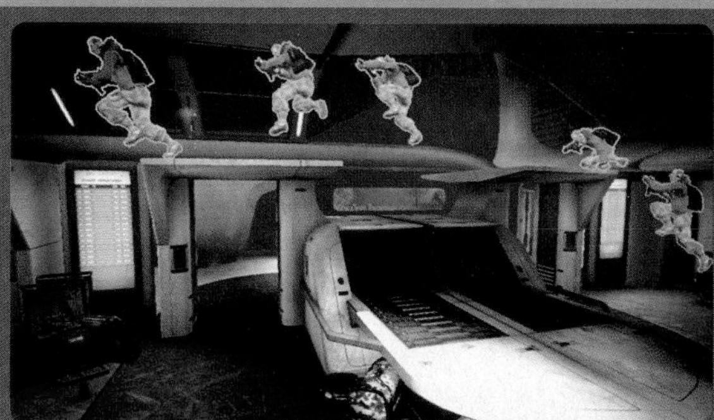

You can leap atop the security machines and conveyor belts as you secure this area or fend off attackers.

## 11 Airport Mezzanine: Security and Check-In MG Nest (Upper)

## 12 Airport Mezzanine: Tickets and Information (Lower)

The vast Airport Mezzanine is a two-floor area running the entire width of the structure, and the domain of Security forces. During Part 1 of this mission, this area isn't usually explored to

any great degree due to the number of enemies streaming down from the Monorail deployment zone. However, during Part 3, this location becomes a critical last line of defense to stop the Security forces from an ultimate victory. For this reason alone, this area is worth exploring.

The upper floor is accessed by the Airport Cashier Corridor via normal movement, or from the lower level via S.M.A.R.T. Moves or the staircases (although the stairs are too close to the Security spawn point to be of any use during Part 1). A circle of empty (and inaccessible) stores surrounds three main areas. There are two large holes: One allows access down to a visitor information center kiosk, overlooked by the MG Nest. The other has a scale model of the original Ark. In the middle is a security checkpoint. Behind that are the main steps up to the Monorail.

The lower floor is accessed via the connecting corridor into the Baggage Chute area and Mainframe, or the wide entrance into the Security Scanners. This large floor houses some scattered seating and boarding terminals, and the base of the scale model of the Ark (which is impossible to climb). Nearby is a side escalator. A similar space occupies the opposite side, although a visitor information center is under the open Mezzanine balcony, which can be climbed on. Close to that is a second escalator on the opposite edge of this area. Check the escalators for enemies streaming in during Part 1, or as an excellent alternative to the main stairs to sprint up when reaching and defend the last line of defense during Part 3. In the middle of the lower level is the main ticket gate and stairs.

**Use the two-story, dead palm tree near the visitor information center to situate yourself when maneuvering about in this initially confusing area.**

TIP

### S.M.A.R.T. Moves

Climb atop the visitor information center and jump from the narrow edge of the roof, grabbing the upper floor wall and ascending.

You can also climb atop the security checkpoint on the top floor, and then onto the roof of the checkpoint itself.

If you're running down the main steps or escalators, you can leap and grab the low wall ahead, if you decide to stay on the upper floor instead.

### S.M.A.R.T. Moves

Upper floor: The white concrete pillars, as well as the flight departure terminals, can be climbed on or hidden behind.

Upper floor: Use the pillars and terminals to leap to the roofs of the vacant stores on either side of the Airport Cashier Corridor entrance.

### 13 Security Deployment Zone (Pt. 1): Monorail (Upper)

Although in Part 1 this is a deadly location for the Resistance, and where the enemies stream down from (via the upper Airport Mezzanine, or down the steps or escalators to the lower level), the gun emplacements disappear during Part 3, when you must prevent the enemy from returning to this area with a Datakey suitcase. This provides a last line of defense between your team and mission failure, so learn the locations of the departure terminal consoles, benches, and three entrances so you know how to get (and defend) here.

### 14 Security Command Post (Pt. 1) (Upper)

This Command Post is well-guarded by spawning enemies and sentry guns. The enemy uses this terminal during Part 1. It cannot be brought online for the Resistance. Ignore it.

## Important Locations
(Core Objective 2 (and 3))

**These locations are inaccessible during Core Objective 1, but unlock if Core Objective 2 occurs, and are also available during Core Objective 3. All of the previous locations are also accessible.**

NOTE

## 15 Resistance Deployment Zone (Parts 2 & 3): Gate B5 (Lower)

## 16 Gate A5 (Upper)

## 17 Gate A6 and Curved Stairs (Upper)

If you failed to prevent the Security forces from accessing the Mainframe, the action moves farther into the Airport. Resistance forces begin at this location for the rest of the match, which is close to the (inaccessible) Gate B5, as well as two ground exits and an escalator. During Part 2, rush past Gate B5, around and into the lower level Plaza area, and straight into the Fra Diavolo Lounge & Restaurant where the safe with the Datakey is located. As Part 3 progresses, rush through the opposite doorway, into the Tihjin Moon and Gaccie store area, so you can catch the enemy with the Datakey before he reaches the Monorail Station.

The escalator leads up to Gate A5, directly above the deployment zone. The gate itself isn't as important as the two upper thoroughfares. The first allows upper access into the Plaza and Fra Diavolo. The other way (directly ahead if you're running up the escalator) leads to Gate A6, the Curved Stairs, and another Plaza entrance. This latter route is useful when retreating toward the Airport Mezzanine during Part 3. Gate A6 isn't accessible, but the Curved Stairs are a great way to reach the Tihjin Moon and Gaccie to head off a suitcase-carrying foe scrambling through the Plaza.

> Although you can clamber over seating and hide behind pillars during firefights, there are few S.M.A.R.T. opportunities here.
>
>  **NOTE**

## 18 Resistance Command Post (Parts 2 & 3) (Lower)

Change weapons or pick a different class at this Command Post, which is adjacent to your deployment area. This post is used during Parts 2 and 3 of this mission.

## 19 Tihjin Moon and Gaccie (Lower)

Think of this location as a lower level junction, allowing access to several adjacent areas. Resistance teammates can quickly reach here from their spawn point. This also marks the end of the lower-level section of Plaza. The Curved Stairs allow access to and from Gate A6 and the upper Plaza. Finally—once you pass the Gaccie store—you exit into the Security Scanners area, making this a well-trafficked route during Part 3.

## 20 Central Shopping Plaza Mezzanine (Upper and Lower)

## 21 Supply Command Post (Upper)

The central hub during Parts 2 and 3, this two-floor Plaza Mezzanine is easily accessed from the Resistance spawn point via a door and short corridor, or a door and a quick step through the Tihjin Moon location. Expect both constant fighting and maneuvering along here as teams race to the safe or the suitcase during the latter stages of this mission. The two-story store called Blossum on the opposite side of the Plaza is where the Security forces swarm out from. The rest of the lower floor offers an inaccessible coffee shop ("In a Cup"), and the entrance to Gate B5, as well as the two lower entrances to the Fra Diavolo Lounge & Restaurant. The middle of the Plaza offers escalator access to the walkways above.

The upper floor of the Plaza offers an initially confusing series of shallow steps close to the top of the escalator, and access via the main walkway toward the Airport Corridor leading to Baggage Claim. The rest of the top floor consists of linked walkways around three large openings you can drop (or fire) down, leading to the lower level. There's an enemy-filled entrance to Blossum here, too. At the far end are entrances back to Gate A5, and the upper entrances to the Fra Diavolo, through the orange-padded walls of the lounge.

The alcove at the far end of this Plaza holds the Supply Command Post, which is accessible during Parts 2 and 3 of this mission. Don't forget to claim it while battling the streams of foes storming across from the Blossum entrance.

### S.M.A.R.T. Moves

Surprisingly, there isn't a way to reach the upper Plaza walkway from below, save for the escalator. However, you can stand atop the flight departure signs.

On the upper floor, you can edge along the top of the railing by the glass wall and Blossum store to gain protection from behind, a sniping point, and a commanding view across and down.

## 22 Blossum (Upper and Lower)

Unless you're completely overwhelming the opposition, it usually isn't wise to linger in the remains of this two-floor boutique. The lower section is linked to the larger one above only by stairs that the Security forces use to exit their deployment zone, so exercise extreme caution. The dark corners of either floor can be used as an ambush point though, and the front glass wall allows you to spot enemies before they reach the Plaza. The upper exits from Blossum place the enemy at the Airport Corridor junction, and close to the Supply Command Post.

## 23 Airport Corridor: Plaza to Baggage Claim(Upper)

Featuring a sunken area with a few chairs that leads to Gate A6 and the Curved Stairs, this is the other main opening into the Plaza. Glass walls on either side allow you to see, but not fire on, your enemies. Expect heavy enemy traffic from the Blossum entrance atop the stairs. The upper corridor leads around and into Baggage Claim, via a door that opens only once Part 2 of the mission occurs.

## 24 Fra Diavolo Lounge & Restaurant with Safe (Upper and Lower)

This fancy lounge and restaurant is the main location for Part 2, and the starting locale for Part 3 of this mission. The lounge is accessed via one of three entrances, all from the Plaza area. On the lower level, there's a small winding corridor and a few steps close to Gate B5 (the quickest route from your spawn point). A second corridor on the opposite side (frequented by the enemy) allows access up steps and a corridor and into the other side of the restaurant. On the upper floor, access is through the orange-padded walls of the lounge, near Gate A5 and the Supply Command Post.

Once inside this triangular floorplan, you have two levels to defend from. The upper area consists of a triangular balcony, which you can hop over at any time to reach a sunken bar area below. Or use either of the curved staircases. The lower floor is composed of the sunken bar with the safe (containing the Datakey suitcase), and a raised ground area with scattered seating and a segmenting wall on each side; mainly used as cover.

### S.M.A.R.T. Moves

Climb on the sunken bar and access the balcony above, near the upper exit.

Climb the sliver of wall on each side of the sunken bar and grab and vault onto the balcony. You can also run up the ramped support columns and stand atop them under the balcony floor for increased height and visibility.

### 25 Security Deployment Zone (Parts 2 & 3): Baggage Maintenance Office (Lower)

This darkened chamber is guarded by a number of sentry guns, and offers a side entrance straight into Blossum and the Plaza, and a set of stairs to the upper level of Blossum. The enemy spawns here, so avoid this location, but arm yourself with the knowledge that this is where the enemy runs out from.

### 26 Security Command Post (Parts 2 & 3) (Lower)

You might see this Command Post when you switch sides. It's inside the Security Deployment Zone, guarded by sentry guns.

## Objective Tactics: Core Objective 1

###   Defend the Mainframe

Spawn Point to Mainframe: 00:12

Time to Disarm Hack Box: 00:05

Time to Plant Hack Box: 00:02

### General Tactics

The enemy approaches the Mainframe room (Conveyor Control Point) via the Baggage Claim (and down the luggage conveyor chute), through the Security Scanners and past the Health Command Post, or by using one of the Baggage Chutes from the lower Mezzanine entrance. Due to the enemy's proximity to the Mainframe, and their ease in attacking the Mainframe from multiple entrances, there's little time to launch a stand much closer to their spawn point (although recommended defensive lines are mentioned below), but sending one or two of your team to run a recon and communicate where the enemy is massing helps you prepare for the main attack.

Resistance forces should take the right-hand doorway and intercept Security personnel trying to descend into the luggage conveyor chute in Baggage Claim; Resistance can also drop down the Elevator Shaft to the Mainframe room. You may find that the Mainframe room is difficult to defend because the enemy can easily lob grenades into it. However, dodging these blasts is worthwhile, especially if you're an Engineer standing ready to remove any of the enemy's Hack Boxes that Operatives plant on the Mainframe itself. Between attacks, reinforce this area with mines in the doorways and on the conveyor belts, and position turrets so that attackers can't easily knock them out with grenades.

### Lines of Defense

**Preparation:** Split your team up so each chamber adjacent to the Conveyor Control Point is defended. Augment the areas with mines and turrets. Hide behind corners, scenery, and walls to defend. Expect combat (and defend from) the Security Scanner room near the Health Command Post, and the Baggage Chutes entrance on the lower levels. Prepare for altercations in Baggage Claim on the upper floor.

**Split your teams into pairs, with two teammates guarding each of the following lines of defense, but all ready to move quickly back into the Mainframe area, and out to one of the three adjacent chambers if the enemy concentrates their attack at a single chokepoint. You can choose which side of the Core Objective you want to come out in front of: Mix it up to keep the enemy guessing.**

 TIP

**Security Scanners:** Claim the Health Command Post, then clamber onto the wall overhang above the entrance to the Baggage Chutes on this side, or on the security machines, or stand on either side of the large entrance from the Mezzanine and ambush foes from each side. Turrets are an option, along with mines at the narrow entrances. Advance and recon the Mezzanine if no threats appear. Fall back when the area is compromised.

**Baggage Chutes:** Stand by the doorway (which should be mined, with additional explosives primed in the connecting passages inside this location), which offers views of the Ark model and Mezzanine stairs. Mill around in the Mezzanine, retreating to this door if enemy firepower is overwhelming. Advance and recon the Mezzanine if no threats are present. Keep this area for as long as you can, then fall back.

**Baggage Claim:** Begin with snipers or turrets aiming through the Cashier Corridor into the Mezzanine, and then fall back into cover positions around the baggage conveyor belt below carousel #2. There are numerous pillars and walls to hide behind, and the large open room makes turrets a good bet. Mine the conveyor belt before the enemy arrives, and then fall back (remember you can use the Elevator Shaft near your spawn point).

**Conveyor Control Point:** If you can't hold the foes off at the previous locations, fall back and take cover inside the room with the Mainframe. Make sure you have a large number of Engineers to augment your defenses. Stand on the conveyors so the enemy has less chance of hitting you with a grenade. Learn the ambush spots listed below, and make sure at least one Engineer is always ready to deactivate any Hack Boxes that are set (and the rest of you are covering him).

> Choose one teammate to become a "spotter" who shouts the location of the latest enemy incursion. Come up with proper descriptions of the four openings the foes can attack from ("Baggage Claim chute," "Left door," "Middle chute," or "Health Command Post," for example).
>
> 
>
> **TIP**

## Automated Ordnance

There are many locations where Engineer weaponry can make a difference. Here are some of the more optimal examples:

1 (Security Scanners): Catch foes from the side as they head through the wide doorway at the Security Scanners.

2 (Baggage Claim): Back up your sniper with a turret around the corner of the entrance, near carousel #1.

3 (Conveyor Control Point): Mow down enemies as they stagger in from the mine-ridden Health Command Post corridor.

1 (Security Scanners): Place a mine just inside the doorway, by the Health Command Post.

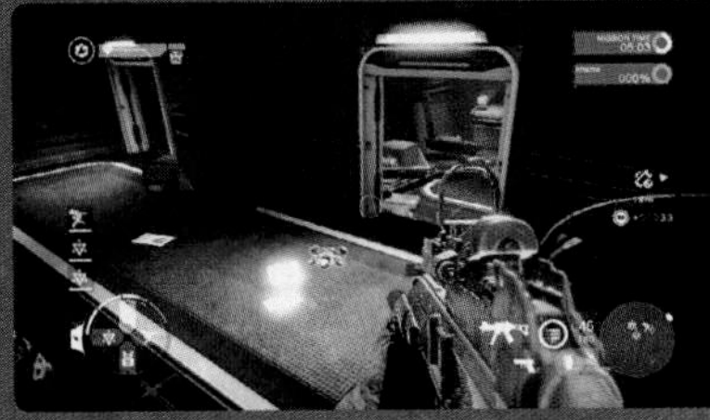

2 (Baggage Chutes): Then set another in the connecting corridor between the Command Post and the Conveyor Control Point.

3 (Baggage Chutes): Place a mine by any doorway leading into the room with the Mainframe.

## Automated Ordnance (continued)

4 (Baggage Claim): Be sure the enemy doesn't enter the conveyor chute at carousel #2 unscathed.

5 (Conveyor Control Room): Set mines on the well-trafficked conveyor belts, especially to the sides or rear of where you're defending.

6 (Conveyor Control Room): Mine the Mainframe to add insult to injury.

## Sniper's Ally: Camping Spots

1 (Security Scanners): Stand under the x-ray scanner and train your weapon toward the Mezzanine stairs.

2 (Baggage Chutes): Snipe all the way to the Mezzanine stairs from inside this connecting room.

3 (Baggage Chutes): Crouch on the R-134a generator for a view of the entire Baggage Chutes area.

4 (Baggage Claim): You have excellent views through the Cashier Corridor into the Mezzanine.

5 (Security Scanners): Ambush your foes from this corridor cover as they try to drop into the conveyor belt chute.

6 (Conveyor Control Point): Cover three of the four entrances from this cubbyhole.

7 (Conveyor Control Point): Catch foes running into the Mainframe area from this doorway alcove.

8 (Conveyor Control Point): Fire through the window above and behind the Mainframe, taking down hackers with ease.

9 (Conveyor Control Point): Position yourself above the middle chute entrance, and cover the Mainframe.

# Objective Tactics: Core Objective 2

##  Defend the Safe

Spawn Point to Safe: 00:10

Time to Crack the Safe: 01:00

### General Tactics

It can get confusing during this part of the mission, so trust your Command Wheel and keep an eye on your radar (for foes).

TIP

With so many routes to the Fra Diavolo Core Objective, it's wise to try and cover more than one of them. With around half of your teammates defending the actual safe, you may wish to interrupt or distract the attackers before they get there, because anything you do to waylay them means less time for them to open the safe. Prowl in a pair (or trio) and patrol the approaches listed below. Then play a nasty trick on them:

Attackers usually expect to see you in front of them, with your back to the objective. Instead, learn the routes to the objective, stay out of sight, and then rush after the foes and attack them from behind. When the Fra Diavolo is breached (enemies can enter via three openings), try to utilize both floors of this location, splitting up so the enemy is forced to widen their firing on both a horizontal and vertical plane, again with the plan of distracting them. Your foes will waste time switching between targets and do less damage your team.

### Exits and Entrances

**Bloodshed at Blossum:** The enemy spawns close to the Mainframe they successfully hacked, and moves into the Plaza via the Blossum store. The stairwell at the back of the store is the exit, and your first line of defense could be the exit chokepoint on either floor. The upper floor Blossum store has two glass exits and the enemy can choose either from their stairwell. The lower floor has a single exit. Block this area with gunfire and other ordnance. Split into three teams; the main one moving to the Fra Diavolo, and the other two guarding either floor.

A great route to try when patrolling the Plaza is to head up the escalator from your spawn point, before swinging back into the Plaza's upper floor. Peering across (or down) allows you to see all three exit points for the enemy, after which you can disrupt their attack routes (capturing the Supply Command Post while you're at it).

 TIP

**Firestorm in the Fra Diavolo:** The map legend (earlier in this section) shows the two lower entrance corridors and the upper lounge entrance into the Fra Diavolo. Spread your team out so the enemy must assault your team and turrets from a variety of angles (decreasing the chance that you'll all die). Learn the ambush positions shown below, and keep that safe intact!

## Automated Ordnance

4 (Fra Diavolo): Cover the upper lounge entrance and both stairwells. Back these emplacements up with gunfire.

5 (Fra Diavolo): Cover the safe, but from far enough away that enemy grenades won't hit the turret.

7 (Blossum Store): If you have the time, place a mine at the top of the enemy stairwell, then gun down foes as they try to escape! Try the same downstairs, too!

8 9 10 (Fra Diavolo): The narrow corridors leading into the Fra Diavolo restaurant or through the upper lounge are great locations for mine placement (mine 8 shown).

11 (Fra Diavolo): The most important location for a mine is under the safe; under fire, enemies almost always step on it!

## Sniper's Ally: Camping Spots

10 (Plaza Mezzanine): Stand here on the upper balcony, and cover all three enemy exits.

11 (Gate A5): Lurk at the steps leading up from Gate A5 and cover the enemy's upper exit, the Supply Command Post, and the Fra Diavolo restaurant's upper entrance.

12 (Fra Diavolo): Patrol the upper balcony, which offers great views of all entrances, as well as the safe.

# Objective Tactics: Core Objective 3

## Defend the Datakey

Safe to Monorail: 00:33 

### General Tactics

Although the enemies may have the Datakey briefcase, they must traverse the entire length of this map to reach the Monorail to achieve victory. Your orders are to fall back and defend the platform itself, and this is your ultimate goal. However, it is always better to block the enemy en route, so they drop the Datakey and you can return it.

Engineers are an excellent choice here, because they can lay down defenses (mines and other explosives in particular) as you retreat. The enemy can fake you out by moving up and down floors in the Plaza, but they have only two exits to take when reaching the Airport check-in Mezzanine (see below). If the foes break through either of these, the situation becomes dire, and the entire team should pull back to the Monorail, where some of your squad should be finishing a final layer of defenses. If everything is going wrong, linger and lurk by the Monorail platform. The enemy will be heading your way soon enough!

If you manage to down the objective carrier in a particularly easy-to-cover spot, don't return the Datakey to the safe. Let it stay where it is and pick off enemies as they come to pick it up—they won't be as familiar with its location, may not be able to use their favorite route.

**TIP**

Beware! Mines and turrets won't fight the enemy for you, but they can distract and damage your foes, leaving them vulnerable so you can shoot them. Remember, when your mines detonate, or your turrets are hit with grenades, you need to replace them. Keep your defenses active; don't delegate everything to their firepower.

**CAUTION**

## Lines of Defense

**Final stand in the Fra Diavolo:** To begin with, keep the tight ring of protection around the safe just like you did during Core Objective 2. Obviously, something went terribly wrong last time, so tighten that cordon! Don't let the enemy out of the restaurant with the briefcase! If you have at least four members (and turrets) in here, this plan can seriously waylay your foes.

**Choking in the Tihjin Moon:** Ignore the double-back antics the enemy may try in the Plaza; once the foes are out of the restaurant with the briefcase, make sure one of your team keeps a constant visual on the Datakey and tells your team where it is. Then split into three squads; the one at the Tihjin Moon (lower floor) can set up traps and stop the foes where possible.

**Excess Baggage:** The second squad should be trapping the Baggage Claim area and upper entrance to the Mezzanine. Your "spotter" should quickly relay which route the briefcase-carrier is attempting, and foes can peel off to reinforce that position. As soon as the enemy is about to break through either chokepoint, retreat one final time.

**Platform Games:** This is where your third squad (of Engineers, ideally) should have set up their remaining traps. With a spotter in the Mezzanine, figure out which staircase or doorway the foes are coming from, and concentrate all firepower on the briefcase-carrier. Don't be swayed into chasing a foe trying to coax you away; that's your team's tactic!

## Automated Ordnance

6 Place a turret here to cover the final capture point, and back it up with regular gunfire.

12 Place mines along the route of the Datakey thief. They may double-back a number of times, so put mines down where they have to travel, like the Tihjin Moon corridor...

## Automated Ordnance (continued)

13 ...or just around the corridor leading into Baggage Claim.

14 Be sure to have a last-ditch mine planted at the capture point!

## Sniper's Ally: Camping Spots

13 Hide by the Health Command Post, cut down foes as they pour out of Tihjin Moon, and keep the post for your team.

14 Step behind the support pillar by carousel #2, and cut down foes heading through the newly opened door.

15 Remember the tops of the stores on either side of the entrance into the Cashier's Corridor; clamber up here and snipe foes from behind, too!

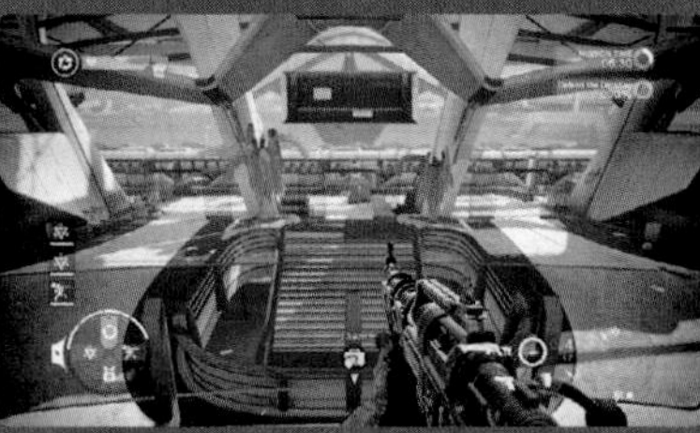

16 Stand atop the security booth in the middle of the Mezzanine, giving you partial cover and a 360-degree view of every single exit, including the escalators, stairs, and exit from the Cashier's Corridor.

17 Cover the capture point from behind these support pillars.

# Objective Tactics: Secondary Objectives

###  Escort Core Objective Class Teammate

**Official Escort Info:** Pair up with an Engineer (as a Medic for health, or as a Soldier to cover him) who can remove the enemy's Hackboxes during Core Objective 1. After that, your team is on the defensive; ignore this objective in favor of stopping the safe being cracked and the Datakey removed.

**Unofficial Escort Info:** Ignore this objective selection, but team up with two Engineers who work well together, replacing mines and mending each other's turrets. Also try a Soldier and a Medic together. You receive XP when you're near your teammate.

###   Capture the Health Command Post

Engineer & Operative Advantage!

Spawn Point to Command Post: 00:18 

Time to Claim Command Post: 00:10

Finding and upgrading the Health Command Post is the first job one of your Engineers should accomplish.

This post is in a chokepoint, so you should already be defending it pretty heavily, although it will change hands multiple times. Don't forget this during later Core Objectives; the enemy may be preoccupied with rushing the restaurant and torching open the safe, so employ one Engineer to flit between both posts, claiming them while leaving a mine below each.

###   Capture the Supply Command Post

 Engineer & Operative Advantage!

Spawn Point to Command Post: 00:19

Time to Claim Command Post: 00:10

This isn't accessible until the beginning of Core Objective 2. As your team dashes back to defend the Fra Diavolo and safe, have one of your Engineers peel off and claim this, and then upgrade it. Following that, be sure one of your team is dedicated to defending the upper Plaza and lounge area and keeping an eye on the post. This is close to the enemy's spawn point for the rest of the match, so only ignore this completely when the briefcase is in the check-in area close to the Monorail.

###  Construct the Check-In MG Nest

 Engineer

Spawn Point to MG Nest: 00:17

Time to Construct: 00:04

This is usually already constructed by the enemy team, because it rests above the information center. It shouldn't get much use during Core Objective 1, but is well worth fixing during Core Objective 3, when you can strafe the briefcase-carrier and his protectors as they emerge from the Security Scanners. Once the foes pass under you, ignore this MG Nest and push back to the Monorail.

###  Solo Tactics

On your own? Then choose an Engineer during Core Objective 1, so you can remove any enemy hacking devices on the Mainframe, and defend the location with more than just firearms and grenades. Defend close to the Health Command Post so you can keep claiming it for your team.

You may wish to continue as an Engineer during Core Objectives 2 and 3. Set up defenses inside the Fra Diavolo Restaurant before obtaining the Supply Command Post, and then roam the far end of the restaurant behind the pillars and walls, ensuring no one cracks the safe. If they do though, target all your attention on the briefcase-carrier, retreating all the way to (and then fortifying) the Monorail once the foes reach the Security Scanners.

##  Mission Completion Conditions

###  Continuation...

**Core Objective 1:** The enemy succeeds in hacking the Mainframe. Part 2 of this mission now commences....

**Core Objective 2:** The enemy unlocks the safe, exposing the Datakey. Part 3 of this mission now begins....

###  Completed!

The match completes if you successfully stop the enemy from hacking the Mainframe, opening the safe, or reaching the Monorail with the briefcase once the timer ticks down.

###  Unsuccessful!

Resistance forces lose if the enemy succeeds in bringing the briefcase to the rendezvous point on the Monorail.

Level 2

## MAP LEGEND

**↘Resort Pelgo: Shopping and Cuisine**

1: Resistance Deployment Zone (Pt. 1): Plaza Insertion Point (Lvl. 1)
2: Resistance Command Post (Pt. 1) (Lvl. 1)
3: Pelgo Shopping Mezzanine & MG Nest (Lvl. 1 & 2)
4: Shop Door to Eco Nom & Escalators (Lvl. 1)
5: Health Command Post (Eco Nom) (Lvl. 1)
6: Fashionista Store & Supply Command Post (Lvl. 2)
7: Side Storage (Lvls. 2 & 3)
8: Krill Co Store (Lvl. 2)
9: GUUD Store & MG Nest (Lvl. 2)
10: Hennesea Lounge & MG Nest (Lvl. 2)
11: Pelgo Support Pillar, Balcony, & MG Nest (Lvls. 1, 2, & 3)
12: Velouté Soup & Salad Bar (Lvls. 2 & 3)
13: Security Deployment Zone (Pt. 1): Plaza Helipad & Access Walkway (Lvl. 3)
14: Security Command Post (Pt. 1) (Lvl. 3)

**↘Resort Pelgo: Living Quarters**

15: Resistance Deployment Zone (Pt. 2): Organdy Casual Wear (Lvls. 1 & 2)
16: Carrier Bot: Starting Location (Lvl. 1)
17: Resistance Command Post (Pt. 2) (Lvl. 1)

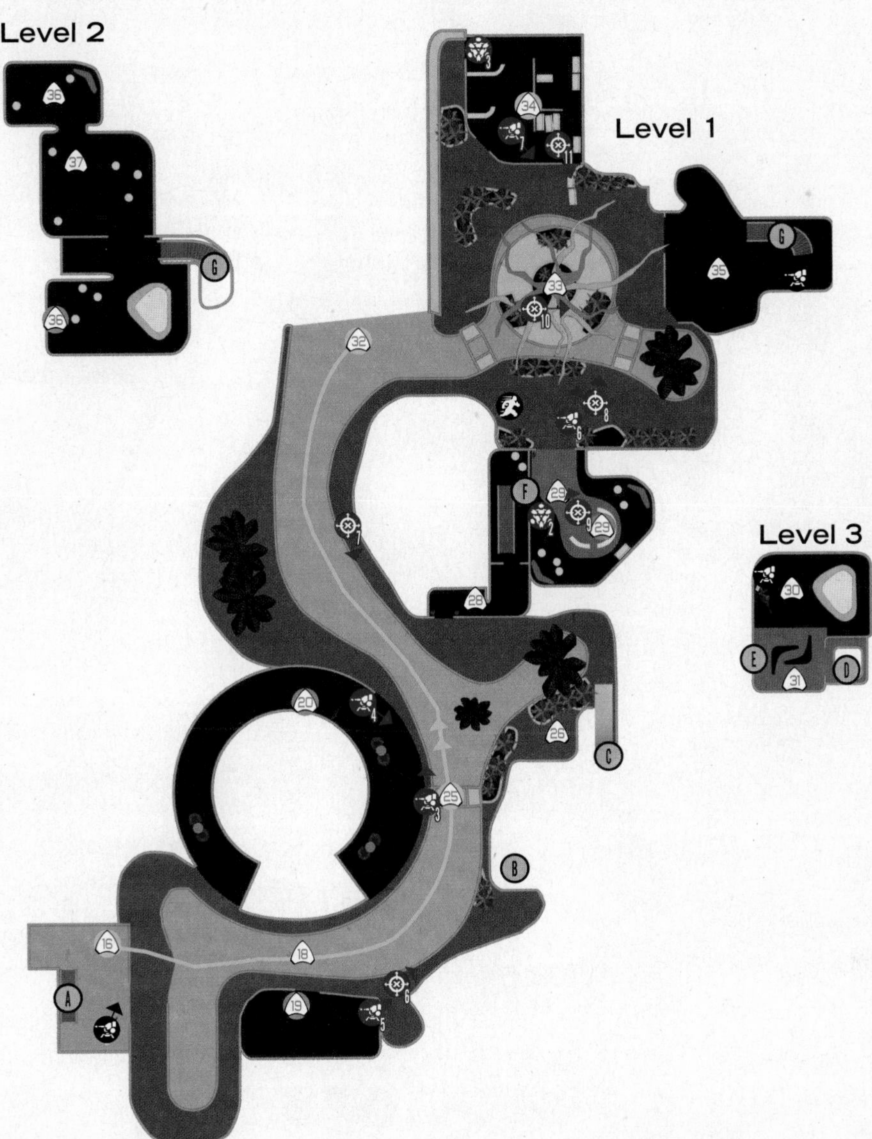


## MAP LEGEND (continued)

18: Pelgo Central Canal Mezzanine (Lvls. 1 & 2)
19: In a Cup Coffee House & MG Nest (Lvl. 1) & The Mozno Club (Lvl. 2)
20: The Circular Foyer & Supply Command Post (Lvl. 1)
21: Executive Suite 1 (Lvl. 2)
22: Resistance Deployment Zone (Pt. 3): Executive Suite 2 (Lvl. 2)
23: Resistance Command Post (Pt. 3) (Lvl. 2)
24: The Upper Promenade (Lvl. 2)
25: Canal Bridge (Lvl. 1)
26: Forecourt, Ramps, & Bridge with MG Nest (Lvls. 1 & 2)
27: Split Bridge & Le Flow Balcony with MG Nest (Lvl. 2)
28: Executive Suite 3 (Lvls. 1 & 2)
29: Le Flow Foyer & Health Command Post (Lvl. 1)
30: Security Deployment Zone (Pt. 2): Executive Suite 3 Bathroom (Lvl. 3)
31: Security Command Post (Pt. 2) (Lvl. 3)
32: Outer Canal & SeaGate (Lvl. 1)
33: Neon Tree Courtyard (Lvl. 1)
34: RMS SeaGate Controls (Lvl. 1)
35: Executive Suite 4 (Lvl. 1)
36: Security Deployment Zone (Pt. 3) & MG Nest: Executive Suite 4 Upstairs (Lvl. 2)
37: Security Command Post (Pt. 3) (Lvl. 2)

S.M.A.R.T. Move
Engineer Mine (Optimal Placement)
Engineer Turret (Optimal Placement)
Camping Spot
Deployment Zone Turret (Invulnerable)
Core Objective Location
Secondary Objective Location
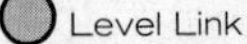
Critical Path (Route)
Level Link

BRINK ↘ Resort: Overview Map

# DAY 6: BLACK BOX

FREEPLAY: RESORT · SECURITY CAMPAIGN—WHAT IF: CHOPPER DOWN

## 19:48 Approaching Resort Marina Wall

MISSION TIME (COb 1): 10:00

MISSION TIME (COb 2): 00:00

MISSION TIME (COb 3): +06:00

MISSION TIME (COb 4): +05:00

### Brother Chen: Briefing

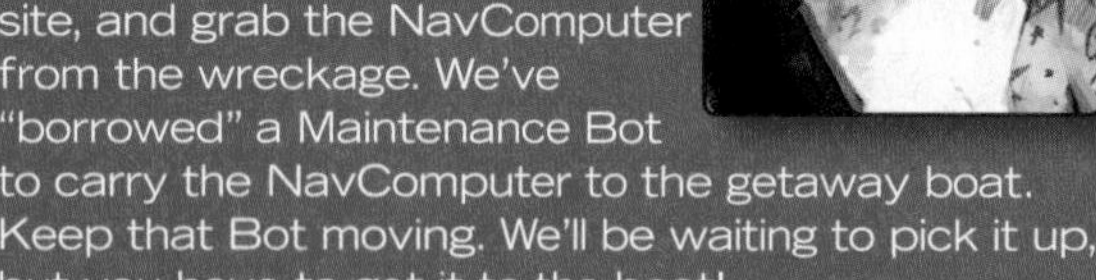

We have a pilot, a destination, and a plane. All we need is a NavComputer, and now we have the chance to get one! Our missile shot down a Security gunship with its NavComputer still intact. We must beat Security to the crash site, and grab the NavComputer from the wreckage. We've "borrowed" a Maintenance Bot to carry the NavComputer to the getaway boat. Keep that Bot moving. We'll be waiting to pick it up, but you have to get it to the boat!

### Objectives (Resistance)

- Core Objective 1: Destroy the Pillar
- Core Objective 2: Escort the Bot
- Core Objective 3: Destroy the Bridge
- Core Objective 4: Hack the Gate Controls
- Escort Core Objective Class Teammate
- Hack the Shop Door
- Capture the Health Command Post
- Capture the Supply Command Post
- Construct the Entrance MG Nest
- Construct the Shop MG Nest
- Construct the Lounge MG Nest
- Construct the Crash Site MG Nest
- Construct the Cafe MG Nest
- Construct the Balcony MG Nest
- Construct the Hotel Balcony MG Nest
- Construct the Apartment Balcony MG Nest

### Optimal Class Numbers

| | COb 1 | COb 2 | COb 3 | COb 4 |
|---|---|---|---|---|
| Soldier | [4] | [2] | [4] | [2] |
| Medic | [2] | [2] | [2] | [2] |
| Engineer | [1] | [3] | [2] | [1] |
| Operative | [1] | [1] | [0] | [3] |

## Important Locations

Resort Pelgo: Shopping & Cuisine

### 1 Resistance Deployment Zone (Pt. 1): Plaza Insertion Point (Lvl. 1)

After breaching the Resort's outer wall with a boat, Resistance forces are gathered at the far end of the Pelgo Shopping Mezzanine, in front of a pair of escalators. The only way onward is through the Mezzanine using either floor to reach the Support Pillar. You aren't likely to be attacked this far back, so leave the vicinity quickly.

### 2 Resistance Command Post (Pt. 1) (Lvl. 1)

Set up at the foot of the escalators, this Command Post offers new weaponry or class-swapping if needed.

Unlike many Command Posts, this isn't positioned against a wall. Therefore, you can run behind it, and access the Command Post from 360 degrees around it, which helps during the initial jostling with your teammates.

TIP

## 3 Pelgo Shopping Mezzanine & MG Nest (Lvls. 1 & 2)

The two-level Shopping Mezzanine consists of a few stores on each side that you can't enter; this is a main pathway toward the Support Pillar location. The MG Nest at the top of the stairs is worth building for some XP, but is usually only used if you're being pushed back to your spawn point. On the upper floor, you can access the Fashionista Store, which also offers a second exit across an adjacent bridge to the GUUD Store; a winding route toward your goal. On the ground floor, there are two information terminals to climb, and a locked Shop Door that an Operative must hack to reach the Escalator area and Health Command Post.

## S.M.A.R.T. Moves

To reach the upper floor from the ground level, clamber up onto either information terminal and onto the balcony.

There are three shortcuts across the low walls of the upper level; stand on them to navigate past the front windows of Fashionista to the adjacent bridge.

Do the same to reach either of the openings into Hennesea, and both are quicker than moving through the stores. The narrow pebble-filled planter with grass between the two Hennesea openings can also be traversed, too.

## 4 Shop Door to Eco Nom & Escalators (Lvl. 1)

## 5 Health Command Post (Eco Nom) (Lvl. 1)

The enemy has a slight advantage over you, because they can easily access this area via the escalators that lead up to the Support Pillar. Counteract this, and unlock the Shop Door by hacking the panel next to it; an Operative must undertake this Secondary Objective. Behind the glass doors is a Health Command Post, and another route up to your target.

You may elect to leave this door locked, so the enemy can't easily spill out into the Shopping Mezzanine, although this removes the ground-level access to the Core Objective.

TIP

## 6 Fashionista Store & Supply Command Post (Lvl. 2)

Although enemies may attack via the Side Storage that links this store to their spawn point, this is still a worthwhile location to race through, because it leads (after a long right turn) right into the Support Pillar location. After entering via the upper Mezzanine, you can immediately exit and head toward the GUUD Store, or stay and take the Supply Command Post before pushing on to your target.

## 7 Side Storage (Lvls. 2 & 3)

The small Side Storage area with the stack of cardboard boxes to the rear of Fashionista is more dangerous than you think, because enemies can drop down from the ceiling here, which is adjacent to their deployment zone. You may wish to rethink an assault on the Krill Co Store from this direction. Otherwise, this is another path to the Support Pillar.

HISTORY OF THE ARK
CHARACTER CREATION
GAMEPLAY
WEAPONS DETAIL
CAMPAIGN
Getting Answers
Breakout
Chen's Plans
Black Box
Attack on CCity
Airborne
Operation Babel
Critical Reaction
CHALLENGES
APPENDICES

## S.M.A.R.T. Moves

Of course, you can climb on top of the cardboard boxes and ambush enemies dropped down off the balcony above.

## 8 Krill Co Store (Lvl. 2)

This small store with a glowing sea-tree spindle is adjacent to your target location and accessed from the Fashionista Side Storage area. Enemies are more likely to be here than in the other stores surrounding the Support Pillar.

## 9 GUUD Store & MG Nest (Lvl. 2)

This is a simple thorough-fare into the Hennesea Lounge, and is worth taking to build an MG Nest, which offers a straight shot into the Support Pillar area. This is useful for covering those rushing the Core Objective, or keeping the enemy from encroaching too far into your turf.

## 10 Hennesea Lounge & MG Nest (Lvl. 2)

This offers a bar to hide behind and two exits out to the Pelgo Support Pillar area. This is the focus of some fraught fighting as you try to push into the target chamber. One concern is the MG Nest facing the Shopping Mezzanine; the enemy can use this, so avoid its fire or guard it so it isn't used. Then choose either exit to encroach out of.

## 11 Pelgo Support Pillar, Balcony, & MG Nest (Lvls. 1, 2, & 3)

This is the hub of activity during Core Objective 1. Look up, and you'll see a Security helicopter gunship that has crashed into the resort's main Support Pillar. Removing the pillar is your main plan. You can access this chamber from multiple locations and directions:

Escalators up from the locked corridor and Health Command Post.

Two doorways at either end of the Hennesea lounge.

One doorway from the Fashionista Store.

One doorway from the Krill Co Store.

The enemy is likely to have come in from the Krill Co Store, the balcony with the MG Nest, or the entrance below the balcony (both the balcony and the entrance below it lead from the Velouté Soup and Salad Bar).

Although Security forces are likely to offer considerable defensive threats as you approach this location, they are also likely to be raining fiery death down from the balcony above, which is accessed via the stairs (or from inside Velouté). Enemies can stand on the seating and shoot down, using the reinforced plastic wall as cover. An MG Nest is a particular problem, because it can be constructed to one side of the stairs.

## S.M.A.R.T. Moves

You can stand on the lip of the low balcony wall directly above the escalator, and ambush foes moving up from the Health Command Post and locked corridor.

## 12 Velouté Soup & Salad Bar (Lvls. 2 & 3)

This two-story eatery offers a lot of protection to the Security forces. They fire out from the interior

because the location offers a good view of the Support Pillar. The lower level offers a swanky restaurant, with a number of shadowy cubbyholes to hide in, if you go "rogue" and try to cause a distraction while your team tries to tag the target.

Continue your death-wish upstairs, which is where many foes are heading from; you can see (and be cut down by) the Security sentry gun turrets. It isn't wise to head into these parts, unless you're completely routing the enemy.

### 13 Security Deployment Zone (Pt. 1): Plaza Helipad & Access Walkway (Lvl. 3)

Security forces head down from their chopper from this location, which is off-limits to Resistance fighters. They have two entrances to pick: the Side Storage inside Fashionista, or the Velouté (and a drop down to the lower floor of the Soup and Salad Bar as they enter, if they don't mind the gap).

### 14 Security Command Post (Pt. 1) (Lvl. 3)

This is always in-accessible to Resistance troops; you'd be cut down before you reached it anyway.

## Important Locations

Resort Pelgo: Living Quarters

### 15 Resistance Deployment Zone (Pt. 2): Organdy Casual Wear (Lvls. 1 & 2)

### 16 Carrier Bot: Starting Location (Lvl. 1)

This is your spawn point until the Carrier Bot (Core Objective 2) has passed the destroyed remains of the Canal Bridge (Core Objective 3). Ignore the handbags and instead focus on the two exits; one leading to the balconies overlooking the Canal Mezzanine and the Mozno Club, while the other leads downstairs to your waiting Carrier Bot, which must be chaperoned to the Canal Bridge and beyond.

### 17 Resistance Command Post (Pt. 2) (Lvl. 1)

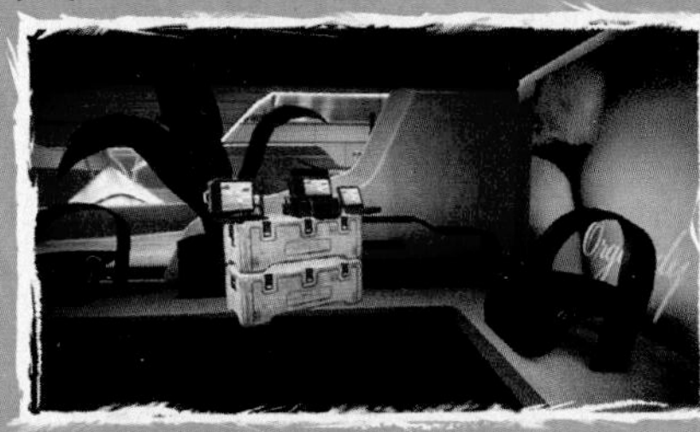

Change your weapons or class here. Remember that Soldiers are needed immediately to place a bomb on the Canal Bridge.

### 18 Pelgo Central Canal Mezzanine (Lvls. 1 & 2)

This initial, open-air canal section features a number of routes you can take to reach (or guard) the bridge. By the canal, a couple of low walls (and dead-end cubbyholes) provide good cover and easy access into the In a Cup Coffee House as well as the Circular Foyer, where you should quickly commandeer the Supply Command Post. The only shortfall is that you can't easily ascend to the upper floor unless you reach the Canal Bridge area, or retreat to your spawn point.

On the upper balcony, you have immediate access to the Mozno Club, and Executive Suite 1. Take both and use them as cover while you protect the Soldiers attempting to destroy the Canal Bridge. You can reach the second bridge between the Mozno and Suite exits, which is great for locating enemies and firing at them. Use the low walls as cover, too.

### S.M.A.R.T. Moves

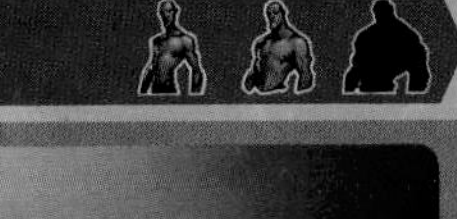

Leap the gap over the canal between the Organdy and Executive Suite 1 balconies for quick access to the opposite side of the canal.

## 19 In a Cup Coffee House & MG Nest (Lvl. 1) & The Mozno Club (Lvl. 2)

Mozno and the bridge connecting to the Executive Suite and exit into the Promenade serves as cover and a place to spot incoming enemies from. Focus on reinforcing the far end close to the bridge. One level below is the In a Cup Coffee House, entered via the canal pathway and offering great cover as well as an MG Nest that provides supporting fire across to the Canal Bridge.

## 20 The Circular Foyer & Supply Command Post (Lvl. 1)

This curved passage allows easy (and covered) access from your spawn point around to the Canal Bridge, and some scenery to hide behind during the inevitable firefighting. The Supply Command Post is important because you can easily take and hold it during the initial stages of combat. Keep an eye on this throughout the rest of the mission; your next spawn point is just above here.

##  21 Executive Suite 1 (Lvl. 2)

Leap across to the balcony connected to this upper suite and you can traverse the interior and reach the bridge connected to Mozno and the Promenade, as well as a curved corridor to the Split Bridge, which is used later in the mission. It's a quick thoroughfare to the bridge from which you can provide supporting fire.

**The Executive Suite's glass doors open once the Carrier Bot passes the destroyed Canal Bridge, allowing access out of the third Resistance Deployment Zone.**

 **NOTE**

## 22 Resistance Deployment Zone (Pt. 3): Executive Suite 2 (Lvl. 2)

This is the base for the remainder of the mission as you attempt to take the Carrier Bot to the end of the canal and hack the SeaGate. The two exits lead into the Executive Suite 1 or out to the Split Bridge.

## 23 Resistance Command Post (Pt. 3) (Lvl. 2)

Choose your class from this terminal, and swap out your weapons. Remember your team needs at least one Operative to complete Core Objective 4 and hack the SeaGate.

## 24 The Upper Promenade (Lvl. 2)

This covered area provides a thoroughfare between the Mozno Club and the upper bridge and the Forecourt, Ramps, and Bridge with the MG Nest that overlooks the Canal Bridge from the opposite side. Combat takes place only at either end.

##  25 Canal Bridge (Lvl. 1)

This low bridge spans the canal and is surrounded by upper balconies and a bridge where both sides usually fire from. The bridge must be destroyed by a Soldier's timed explosives, after which the Carrier Bot trundles through. This triggers the move from Deployment Zone 2 to 3 for both sides.

### Forecourt, Ramps, & Bridge with MG Nest (Lvls. 1 & 2)

Learn the position of both Ramps because they provide the only means of ascending to the balconies and straight bridge above, from the canal path near the In a Cup Coffee House, and via the Forecourt and Ramp with the Tihjin Moon poster. The enemies are usually dug in around the MG Nest, because Executive Suite 3 (and the enemy spawn point) is in this building. This is an alternative route into Executive Suite 3. The MG Nest itself is likely to be in enemy hands, and therefore a focus of your attacks.

### S.M.A.R.T. Moves

Leap across the gaps in the low walls of the upper balcony. This one allows access to and from the Tihjin Moon Ramp and straight bridge.

This one provides a helpful extra route to the Split Bridge (and back again) from the MG Nest area, or the blue bench.

You can also stand atop the curved awning near the In a Cup Ramp area, and access over the glass wall onto the straight bridge, or leap over the Canal to the bridge that spans the Mozno and Executive Suite 2.

You can forgo the Ramps and stand on the low wall below the "Ocean Retreat" sign, and climb up that to assault the MG Nest directly.

Take a similar climb up the second Tihjin Moon sign above the canal, and up onto the Split Bridge by the blue bench.

### Split Bridge & Le Flow Balcony with MG Nest (Lvl. 2)

Remember you can climb up here from the Tihjin Moon signage over the low wall by the blue bench, or leap across from the MG Nest on the balcony. Otherwise, this is the route the Resistance uses when rushing from the third spawn point. The short, wide bridge section leads into Executive Suite 3. The long, narrow bridge section curves around to overlook the Outer Canal, SeaGate, and Neon Tree Courtyard, and also allows access into Executive Suite 3. Use the MG Nest here to provide covering fire across the Courtyard to the RMS SeaGate Controls.

### Executive Suite 3 (Lvls. 1 & 2)

This is a four-room, two-story interior attached to the Le Flow Foyer. The single, canal-level entrance is under the MG Nest balcony, and allows access into the Foyer and Health Command Post when the glass doors unlock (after the Carrier Bot reaches the destroyed Canal Bridge). Reach the upstairs via the staircase.

Level 2 is accessible via doorways from either of the sections of the Split Bridge, and a doorway leading out onto the MG Nest and Straight Bridge. This thoroughfare is mostly a Security team hotspot, because their second deployment zone is up through the ceiling above the green couch, near the straight bridge exit. They can also drop down toward the Split Bridge entrances, so watch for incoming fire or grenades from this spawn point.

### Le Flow Foyer & Health Command Post (Lvl. 1)

This opens up once Core Objective 4 is under way, and the circular desk houses the Health Command Post. Access this via Executive Suite 3, or the exterior Outer Canal and SeaGate area and the Courtyard.

### Security Deployment Zone (Pt. 2): Executive Suite 3 Bathroom (Lvl. 3)

The top floor of Executive Suite 3, which is mainly a bathroom, is where the enemies spawn prior to the destruction of the Canal Bridge and Carrier Bot infiltration. You cannot climb up to this level, which is teeming with foes anyway. Watch for gunfire and grenades from either gap in the ceiling from Level 2 of the suites.

## 31 Security Command Post (Pt. 2) (Lvl. 3)

This post is never accessed by the Resistance, and cannot be climbed to.

## 32 Outer Canal & SeaGate (Lvl. 1)

This is traversed during the final stages of escorting the Carrier Bot to the SeaGate itself, which is the arched canopied structure with two orange lights opposite the Le Flow resort hotel entrance. The palm-tree planter with the overhang and shuttered windows offers good protection, as does the canal path on the opposite side by the exterior wall of Executive Suite 3. Head under the Split Bridge and into the Neon Tree Courtyard.

### S.M.A.R.T. Moves

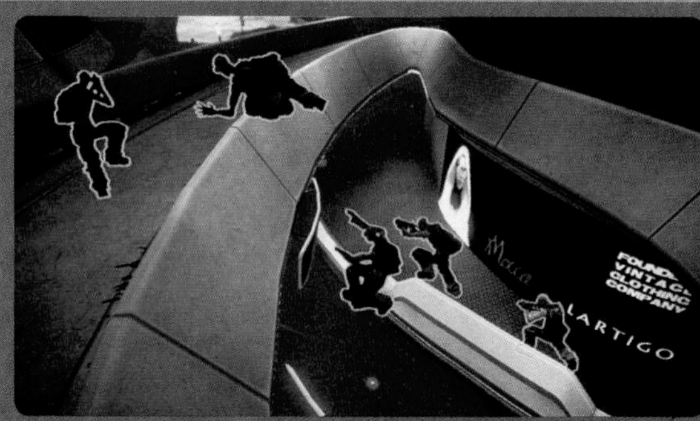

Climb up onto the wall on the right canal path by the wall advert for the resort shops, and use the Fashionista sign to climb up and onto the Split Bridge.

Attempt the same maneuver from the canal itself, under the MG Nest on the Split Bridge near the Le Flow entrance; climb on the Tihjin Moon signage.

## 33 Neon Tree Courtyard (Lvl. 1)

The glowing strands of neon in the middle of this circular courtyard provide the landmark for the final battle, which pits the Resistance (as they flee to the RMS SeaGate Controls) against the Security (streaming out of Executive Suite 4).

Notice the two footbridges and various planters or support columns that you (or the enemy) can use as cover. The Resistance forces should be holed up inside the RMS SeaGate Controls; spending time here isn't as necessary as fortifying the Controls area. There are also three doorways into the Control room, two into Executive Suites 4, and one into the Le Flow Foyer.

### S.M.A.R.T. Moves

You can grab and pull yourself onto the awning above Le Flow entrance, and then leap to the MG Nest and balcony to the right.

## 34 RMS Seagate Controls (Lvl. 1)

Although compact, this final stand (during which Core Objective 4 is completed by an Operative or two) allows a good deal of fortification, although you must be aware of the three entrances—two at the front, and one at the side—which can result in your team being outflanked. Seek cover behind desks or storage boxes.

## 35 Executive Suite 4 (Lvl. 1)

The ground floor of the Executive Suites to the left of the Controls room has enemies streaming from it. You can enter through either of the doors, but at your peril. However, knowing enemies are using these doorways, or the balcony above with the MG Nest, allows you to focus your fire.

### 36 Security Deployment Zone (Pt. 3) & MG Nest: Executive Suite 4 Upstairs (Lvl. 2)

A set of curved stairs guarded by a sentry turret, and a lavish suite with an MG Nest balcony is the final spawning grounds for your opposition. It is wise to remain at a distance, but train your weapons on the ground level doorways the enemy must come through, if they don't drop down from the balcony. The MG Nest is a problem, so stay out of its range.

The more cunning Resistance members play this mission as Security, build the MG Nest here (or indeed, at any location throughout a mission), and then learn the horizontal limits of the turret's movement. Then they stand just outside these limits when playing as Resistance forces when taking out this emplacement.

TIP

### 37 Security Command Post (Pt. 3) (Lvl. 2)

This is another Security Command Post that Resistance forces can't usually reach, or interact with.

## Objective Tactics: Core Objective 1

### Destroy the Pillar

Spawn Point to Pillar: 00:19

Time to Plant Explosives: 00:07

Time to Disarm Explosives: 00:05

Countdown to Explosion: 00:40

Enemy Engineers are the only ones who can pry the explosives off the pillar once they are set. So target them, then Medics as a priority: It doesn't matter if there are enemy Soldiers or Operatives milling about if the bomb is about to go off!

TIP

### General Tactics

Charging the Support Pillar isn't easy, because the enemy is likely to be here in high numbers, with additional turrets and explosives planted to weaken and thwart your team. Thus, it is better to take a direct approach, with at least three of your team being Soldiers (backed up by a couple of Medics), and going for the Support Pillar head-on. Unless the enemy's defenses are impenetrable, it's always better to send out one or two Soldiers to clamp the explosives, rather than sitting back and letting the time tick by.

With the enemy spawn point so close, Hit and Fade attacks from one of the five entrances are a good way to annoy and whittle your opponents down. Peek out of a doorway, inflict as much damage as possible, and then hide again to replenish your health. When you believe there's an opportunity, sprint and slide to the pillar (position yourself, for example, between the pillar and the MG Nest on the balcony so fewer attacks strike you), and plant the bomb. Then retreat, and have your entire team covering it from the numerous entrances.

### Incursion Points

**Escalators (one exit):** This is only accessible after the Shop Door is opened by an Operative. You lack height advantages, and this area is likely to be thoroughly mined and patrolled, so this might be a good place to distract the enemy; coax them down the escalator while your main force runs in from an upper entrance.

**Hennesea (two exits):** This is arguably the safest way in to the Support Pillar, because the enemy spawn isn't close by, and you're very near the Support Pillar itself. The two exits mean that you can provide supporting fire from both; although it is better to have two (or more Soldiers) rushing in from different directions at the same time, so the foes don't know who to tag. Remember there are longer-range sniping points from the GUUD Store, too.

**Fashionista (one exit) and Krill Co (one exit):** One bonus of arriving at the Fashionista doorway is that the glass doesn't crack, meaning you can see the enemy emplacements and yell out where they are, without being hit by longer ranged fire. Krill Co is another entrance, but it's behind the Side Storage area where the enemies drop in from, which is much more dangerous.

**You can also try to thoroughly annoy the enemies by dashing into Velouté on a suicide run. If the foes follow you in, the rest of the team can plant the bomb and guard it. If they don't follow you in, attack them!**

TIP

## Automated Ordnance

Your forces are more likely to be moving for the objective, and not creating defenses. So check the Security mission for more emplacements to locate or avoid.

During a lull in the battle, place a turret here to cover all of the enemy's entrances.

2 This covers the Support Pillar, stopping enemy Engineers from removing the explosives. You're away from enemy entrances, and can fix the turret more easily, too.

1 This can help slow enemies heading out of the Krill Co exit, and alerts you if you're at Camping Spot 3.

## Sniper's Ally: Camping Spots

1 Hang back between the GUUD Store MG Nest and the Hennesea exit, and cover the enemy's lower exit from Velouté and the Support Pillar explosive.

2 This is another reasonable spot to tag foes as they run along the ground exit of Velouté, although watch for attacks from behind.

3 Once you venture into the bomb site, stand on this rock and guard all the enemy entrances.

# Secondary Objectives (First Map)

##  Escort Core Objective Class Teammate

**Official Escort Info:** Support your Soldiers as they make their assault and place HE Charges on the Support Pillar. Bolster your main Soldier's performance with either with a Medic or another Soldier. Cover the Pillar while the Soldier clamps the explosive to it.

**Unofficial Escort Info:** Or, don't attempt this by the book, but split into teams of two. Along the way, think about hacking the Side Door; one of you guards, or both of you hack to speed up the process. Or, head into the Support Pillar chamber from two different directions, creating crossfire opportunities.

##   Hack the Shop Door

Spawn Point to Shop Door: 00:08

Time to Hack Door Controls: 00:45

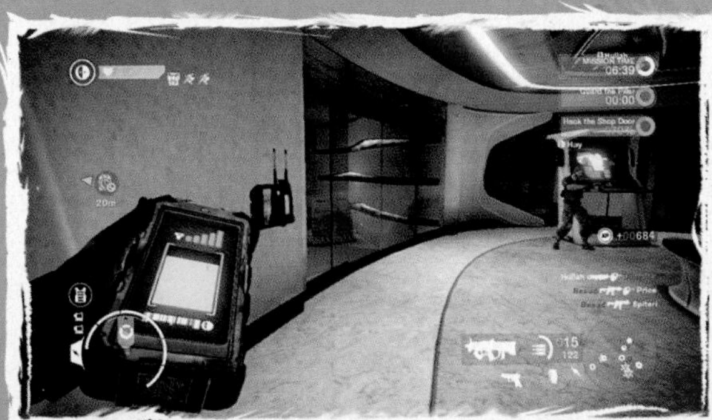

Opening up the lower Shopping Mezzanine and Support Pillar chamber (via the escalators) involves some hacking, and weakens your team during this process because you don't have full manpower to assault the Support Pillar. However, the minimal time it takes is worth it to allow your team another access point (enabling you to split into squads and attack from opposite directions into the Support Pillar room at the same time). Plus, the enemy has less chance of keeping the Health Command Post indefinitely. Finally, just the threat of another intrusion point makes the enemy try to cover more entrances, spreading them more thinly.

##  Capture the Health Command Post

Engineer & Operative Advantage!

Spawn Point to Command Post: 00:08

Time to Claim Command Post: 00:10

This post is likely to be taken early by the enemy, and kept by them, because there's a glass (but impenetrable) door between your team and the post. You can hack the Shop Door (and watch through the glass to see whether the enemy is taking the post, or has left a trap for you) and take the post, risking attacks from the escalator above. Or, you can storm the Support Pillar Chamber, drop down the escalator, fight off any foes, and claim the post, which is a reasonable plan because it takes the enemy away from guarding the Pillar. A better bet though, is to push through the door.

##   Capture the Supply Command Post

Engineer & Operative Advantage!

Spawn Point to Command Post: 00:10

Time to Claim Command Post: 00:10

Your team should be able to capture (and keep) this post, inside the Fashionista Store, relatively easily despite its being close to the Side Storage where the enemy drops from. This is close to the route you'll take to get to the Support Pillar, so a teammate can quickly peel off and deal with threats to take the post while still maintaining a relatively true course to the Core Objective. This is even easier if you're using the Fashionista route to the Support Pillar. Leave a mine here, too.

### Construct the Entrance MG Nest

### Construct the Shop MG Nest

### Construct the Lounge MG Nest

### Construct the Crash Site MG Nest

Engineer

Spawn Point to Entrance MG Nest: 00:06

Spawn Point to Shop MG Nest: 00:09

Spawn Point to Lounge MG Nest: 00:15

Spawn Point to Crash Site MG Nest: 00:21

Time to Construct: 00:04

You can construct and use four MG Nests. The first, by your deployment zone, is only necessary if the enemy is pushing extremely far into your territory. Otherwise, this is just for those wanting the extra XP (hopefully not at the expense of your team's tactics).

The Shop MG Nest is inside the GUUD Store. This is a good strategic location to hold and fire from, whether you're using the MG or not. This is useful when covering teammates trekking toward the Support Pillar, and to stop those trying to access the Lounge MG Nest or take up position inside Hennesea.

This MG Nest is more useful to the enemy than your team (which means you shouldn't build it so the enemy can just waltz in and take it over!), because it overlooks the balcony, GUUD Store, and the lower Shopping Mezzanine at the place where your team goes to hack the Shop Door. Nullify any foes attempting to use this.

The last MG Nest is up on the balcony by the upper exit from Velouté, and the enemy uses this to cut down your forces as you try to reach the Support Pillar. Lob a grenade up here, or keep the pillar between you and the MG Nest. The MG Nest has good views of the Hennesea and Fashionista exits, and covers the balcony stairs too.

## Objective Tactics: Core Objective 2

### Escort the Bot

Spawn Point to Bot: 00:03

Spawn Point to Canal Bridge (with Bot): 00:45

Canal Bridge to Seagate (with Bot): 01:08

### General Tactics

There are no subtle tactics to learn here; brute force is the only way you're going to get this tracked robot past the bridge. Time your chaperoning so the Bot doesn't trundle around the bend and under the first bridge until your Soldiers have successfully destroyed the Canal Bridge, because the Bridge is covered by an MG Nest and Executive Suite 3, where Security spawns (and can therefore constantly strike the Bot, forcing lengthy fixing). Chaperone the Bot with at least two Engineers, so there's always one on hand to mend it.

Once you're past the Canal Bridge, the enemy's deployment zone is all the way at the far end of the Neon Tree Courtyard, in Executive Suite 4, close to the SeaGate controls that need hacking. This makes guarding the Bot much easier because you're always closer to the Bot and can drop down from your new spawn point. The enemy usually gives up and fortifies for the final battle.

## Escort Route

**Deployment Zone and Canal Bridge:** This initial run is the trickiest, because the enemy is grouped above you (making them more difficult to hit), and they spawn just above a balcony overlooking the canal you're moving through. However, as long as your team picks multiple routes and distracts as many foes as possible, two Engineers with the Bot can crawl past the exploded bridge.

**TIP**

Your life is worth less than the Maintenance Bot. Don't hide behind it and take cover; instead try to beckon the enemy into killing you, so the minimal amount of weaponry is aimed at the Bot. If you die, but the Bot trundles a few more feet forward, this is a small tactical victory; a moving Bot is better than one sitting and being fixed.

**Canal Bridge and Seagate:** For the rest of the journey, the enemy is too far back to offer any significant problems, while your team can swarm the Split Bridge over the canal and offer covering fire to the Bot. Only one Engineer needs to accompany the Bot; the rest should be sprinting to the SeaGate Controls.

## Automated Ordnance

3 Place this turret to cover the Soldier while he clamps the explosives to the Canal Bridge.

4 This is a good spot to cover the Canal Bridge, because you have protection from the outer wall.

5 The same benefit applies here; the glass wall covers the turret, and Engineers escorting the Bot are nearby to help mend either turret.

## Sniper's Ally: Camping Spots

4 There are few better locations to cover the Canal Bridge than this upper bridge structure connected to the Mozno Club.

5 The top of this Ramp enables you to run up and fire at the enemy balcony, then retreat back into the cover the Ramp provides.

## Sniper's Ally: Camping Spots (continued)

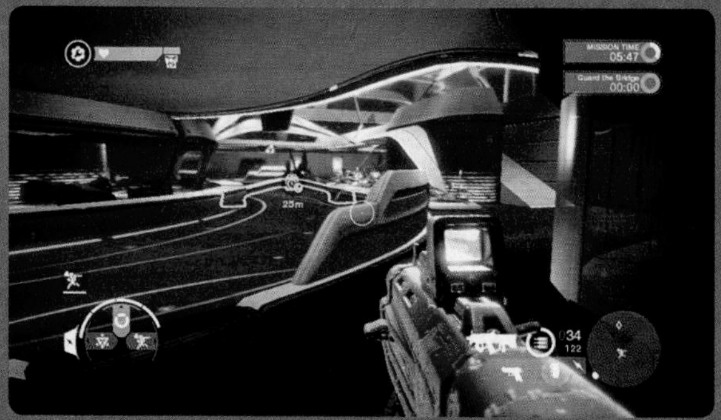

6 This alcove just in front of In a Cup covers the Canal Bridge, and you can spot foes coming down the Ramp to the right.

7 Circumvent the enemy completely and set up to cover the Canal Bridge from under the Split Bridge, well ahead of the objective.

# Objective Tactics: Core Objective 3

### Destroy the Bridge

Time to Plant Explosives: 00:07

Time to Disarm Explosives: 00:05

Countdown to Explosion: 00:40

### General Tactics

Enemies expect you to run along the canal pathways, in front of the trundling Bot, only to be cut down by withering MG Nest fire and enemy gunshots from the balcony attached to Executive Suite 3. But this is only one possible route. Vary the route throughout to keep your foes guessing. A far better route is to dash through the upper floor of your spawn point, through the Mozno Club, and into the covered Promenade.

The Promenade has some great cover and long-range sniping opportunities, and allows you to fight on the same vertical level as your foes, so they have no height advantage. Control this area by pushing the enemy back into their spawn point while a Soldier detaches from your team to plant the bomb. Once the explosive is clamped, an enemy Engineer must rush to defuse it; this is extremely tricky if you're covering the area with all your troops, from every vantage point.

**TIP:** Remember you can plant the charge on either side of the bridge; choose the one closest to your deployment zone, so your team can more easily kill enemy Engineers trying to disarm it.

### Other Route Options

**TIP:** Pair off or form squads of three or four and swarm the enemy from all angles. Moving as a single mass just makes it easier to hit you. Make the enemies change direction and look around for their next kill; a second wasted by the enemy is a second you have to take out that Bridge!

**Down and Out:** The canal-level is the most dangerous, because you're below most of the enemies (which are thus more difficult to hit), and you're right in the gaze of the MG Nest defender. Use the cover from the Circular Foyer, especially if you've taken the Supply Command Post inside here, and are goading the enemy to take it, which means fewer foes guarding the bridge. Otherwise, dash along the right side to the Ramp, which allows your more tank-like soldiers to rush the enemy balcony, or step around into Promenade cover.

**TIP:** Doing something crazy, like leaping on the wall section directly below the Balcony MG Nest, climbing up the sign, and cutting down the defenders with pistols and knifing is a great way to distract your foes. If you survive!

**Circular and Peeking:** From the upper bridge spanning across from Mozno to the outer curved path of Executive Suite 1, you can support your ground troops. Better yet, run to the other side of the path to the Split Bridge.

**Split Bridge Slaughter:** The classic outflank maneuver is on the cards if you head to the start of the Split Bridge. From here, look right, and attack defenders on the MG Nest balcony from the side. Or run across and enter the enemy's Executive Suite (3), looking right and up at the lip of the opening they drop from. Wound them, lob grenades up here, and generally annoy and distract. Do the same by running amok on the ground floor of their building!

> The MG Nest is a problem. Aside from grenades to soften up the MG user, learning the perimeter of the MG's firing range is a must. Play as Security, learn the pivoting limits of the MG, and then stand outside these limits, making the weapon far less effective.
>
>  TIP

## Objective Tactics: Core Objective 4

### Hack the Gate Controls

Spawn Point to Controls: 00:18

Time to Hack the Controls: 01:00

### General Tactics

You have two main goals: one is straightforward, and the other can turn the tide of battle but is more subtle. The former involves locating and fortifying the SeaGate Controls building, adjacent to the Neon Tree Courtyard. Gather your forces here as quickly as possible, ensuring that at least two of your team are Operatives; one focusing on hacking and the other helping, but stopping to defend the Gate Controls more quickly so that the hack progresses continuously.

The other goal is the control of the Health Command Post, in the foyer of Le Flow Hotel. Controlling this room (which is just as important as the Command Post itself) allows you to look out across Executive Suite 4, basically the enemy's entire final deployment zone. Wound them as they exit from there, while causing as much distraction as possible; do anything to prevent your foes from taking down your Operatives completing the hack.

### Defensive Positions

> This is the first time you've had to move to a location and keep it under your control during this mission, so consult the Automated Ordnance and Sniper's Ally sections for more detailed placement of ambush spots and explosives.
>
>  NOTE

**Le Foyer Fracas:** A mixture of smooth jazz and long-range firepower is the order of the day at this location. Remember you can get here through the interior of Executive Suite 3, with almost no enemy contact during this objective. With the Health Command Post, you have the bonus of a healthy team. Take the Supply Command Post too (under your spawn point) and your advantage is even more significant.

**Le Flow Firepower:** Check the sniping positions below for the best views around; these should encompass locations up on the Hotel Balcony (with or without the MG Nest), rifle-fire through the doorway, and other locations (see Sniper's Ally below). Cross to SeaGate Controls via the Neon Tree Courtyard, using the low circular wall as cover, then sprint for the SeaGate Controls building.

**SeaGate Controls:** As you launch salvos against the embattled Security teams, strengthen your defenses. Operatives, a Medic, and Engineers should congregate in here, placing mines at entrances and turrets with good open distances to fire at. The desks and storage boxes are excellent places to seek cover. Remember there are three entrances; head around the alley to enter the third one (which is handy if enemies are inside the building as you try to clear them out).

## Automated Ordnance

6 Sit a turret on Le Flow's awning (it covers the enemy's exits, and is harder to hit with grenades). Cover it from the MG Hotel Balcony.

2 Guard the side entrance from infrequent flanking attacks with a mine at the Le Flow Foyer threshold.

7 Place the last turret here, to cover your Operatives hacking the panel.

3 The enemy likes to enter the SeaGate Controls room and use the rear doorway. Mine it to stop foes from flanking your Operatives.

## Sniper's Ally: Camping Spots

8 Lurk by Le Flow's front pillar, using it to take all the enemy damage. If the foes are firing at you, they aren't firing at the Operatives!

9 Inside Le Flow's Foyer, you have even more protection, and can keep the Health Command Post for your team, too.

10 As long as you stay behind the Neon Tree, this is a good spot to watch all three enemy exits, and take cover. Watch for flanking foes, though.

11 Just inside the SeaGate Controls building, you can watch foes dash across from their spawn point; and bring them down.

# Secondary Objectives (Second Map)

## Escort Core Objective Class Teammate

**Official Escort Info:** In Core Objective 2, back up your Engineers to keep that Bot moving--have two Engineers on each side of the Bot to cover and mend it! For Core Objective 3, cover your Soldiers (from both sides of the balcony) to ensure the bridge is destroyed, and target enemy Engineers to halt a bomb defusal. For the final Core Objective, shield your Operatives with covering fire, and target enemy Engineers who can pry off the Hackboxes on the Seagate Controls. Remember; two Operatives can hack more quickly while watching for each other.

**Unofficial Escort Info:** Team up with a second player of any Class to interfere and annoy; divert the enemy fire away from those engaged in Core Objectives. During Core Objective 4, partner up and take up opposing sniping positions.

## Capture the Health Command Post

Engineer & Operative Advantage!

Spawn Point to Command Post: 00:14

Time to Claim Command Post: 00:10

This is locked behind the glass doors in Le Flow Hotel's foyer, and only accessible once the Canal Bridge is removed and the Bot crosses the remains of it. When the enemy spawns over in their last deployment zone, both teams are around the same distance, so make sure you head through and claim it, and then cover it with snipers from both sides of the Neon Tree Courtyard (inside Le Flow covering the SeaGate Controls, and from the Controls side alley across to the Hotel door).

## Capture the Supply Command Post

Engineer & Operative Advantage!

Spawn Point to Command Post: 00:16

Time to Claim Command Post: 00:10

This is located within the Circular Foyer, and is easily accessed from either team's spawn point, although your team has the advantage because they can use the cover of the Foyer to reach it, while still moving toward the Canal Bridge. This is worth taking and defending (usually with an Engineer to upgrade, lay mines, and place a turret). During the last objective, this is under your final deployment zone and much easier to take and keep because the enemy are well away.

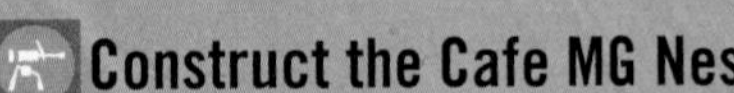

## Construct the Cafe MG Nest

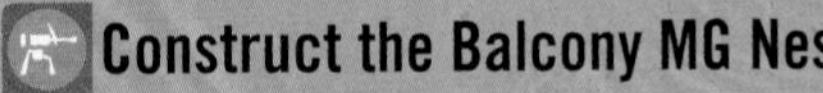

## Construct the Balcony MG Nest

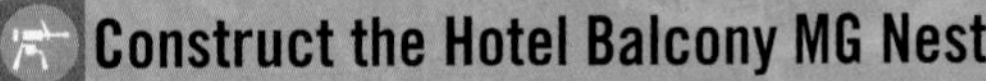

## Construct the Hotel Balcony MG Nest

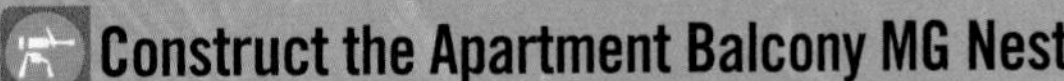

## Construct the Apartment Balcony MG Nest

Engineer

Spawn Point to Cafe MG Nest: 00:08

Spawn Point to Balcony MG Nest: 00:18

Spawn Point to Hotel Balcony MG Nest: 00:10

Spawn Point to Apt. Balcony MG Nest: 00:20

Time to Construct: 00:04

The MG Nest inside In a Cup offers a reasonable amount of covering fire to your team as they progress toward the Canal Bridge. It can't hit the enemy's Balcony MG Nest, only those on the side of the balcony near the Ramps. However, it becomes a valuable extra piece of killing equipment when aimed at enemy Engineers trying to disarm the Canal Bridge after a bomb is planted. Ready it for that purpose alone.

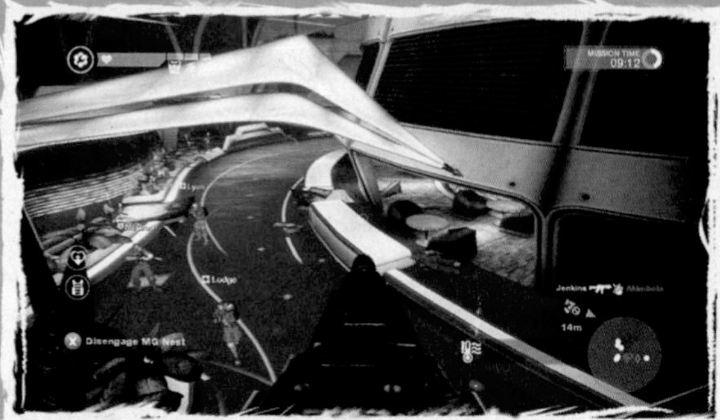

This is usually taken over by the enemy, because it's right outside one of their spawn points. It covers the Canal Bridge and exits in that area (the Circular Foyer and Promenade). Remember this when you're assaulting the Bridge; it's almost worth rushing forward under the gun's aiming to lob a grenade up here. Your team doesn't usually take this objective.

This looks over the end of the canal and where the Bot finally parks by the SeaGate, and the Neon Tree Courtyard. The balcony shields your team from the fire; the MG Nest can hit your team only as you race toward the SeaGate Controls. This is worth taking because you can use it on the enemies heading out of the three exits from Executive Suite 4 and their final spawn point, and it offers a good view of this entire Courtyard.

The Apartment Balcony MG Nest is part of the enemy's deployment zone, and cannot be built. Even if you can somehow reach this area, the MG Nest isn't accessible. Dodge its fire on your way to the SeaGate Controls.

## Solo Tactics

With no one but computer friends, you'll need to take a central role. Rushing the Support Pillar as a Soldier is a great plan, stepping back to claim both Command Posts if your initial attempt fails, before slowly pushing back again. The map changes, but keep your class, and try to set the second charge on the Canal Bridge before backing up into In a Cup cover. Then switch to an Engineer, escort the Bot, and as soon as it reaches the SeaGate, switch to an Operative and begin a hack. If you're overwhelmed, change to an Engineer and begin to defend the SeaGate Controls, and wait for a teammate Operative to finish the hack job.

# Mission Completion Conditions

### Continuation...

**Core Objective 1:** Your team succeeds in destroying the Support Pillar. Part 2 of this mission now commences....

**Core Objective 2:** Your team succeeds in destroying the Canal Bridge. Part 3 of this mission is running concurrently....

**Core Objective 3:** Your team successfully escorts the Maintenance Bot to the Seagate. Part 4 of this mission commences....

### Completed!

The match is won if you successfully hack the SeaGate Controls before the timer ticks down.

### Unsuccessful!

Resistance forces lose if the enemy stops you from completing any Core Objective by the time the timer reaches zero.

## MAP LEGEND

### Container City: General Icons

1: Resistance Deployment Zone (Pts. 1 & 2): Bow of the *Hope* (Lvl. 2)
2: Resistance Command Post (Pts. 1 & 2) (Lvl. 2)
3: Maintenance Bot Start: Jetty (Lvl. 0)
4: Security Deployment Zone (Pts. 1 & 2): Jetty (Lvl. 1)
5: Security Command Post (Pts. 1 & 2) (Lvl. 0)
6: Container City Harbor Entrance (Lvl. 1)
7: Entrance Gate (Lvl. 1)
8: Side Door (Lvl. 2)
9: Exterior Stairwell Scramble Point (Lvl. 2)
10: Container City Thoroughfare (Lvl. 1)
11: Decaying *Hope*: Starboard MG Nest & Balcony (Lvl. 2)
12: The Rusty Bridge (Lvl. 2)
13: Decaying *Hope*: Interior Hold & Health Command Post (Lvl. 1)
14: Decaying *Hope*: Interior Passageways & MG Nest (Lvl. 2)
15: Decaying *Hope*: Lower Hold Road (Lvl. 1)
16: Container Clearing (Lvl. 1)
17: Rusting Hull to Side Stairs (Lvls. 0, 1, & 2)
18: Container Crossing (Lvl. 2)
19: Crane Yard Vantage Point (Lvl. 2)
20: Free Ark Rooftop Alley (Lvl. 3)
21: Crane & Decaying *Hope*: Port Balcony (Lvls. 1, 2, & 3)
22: Extraction Point (Lvl. 2)
23: Security Deployment Zone (Pts. 3 & 4): Decaying *Hope* (Lvl. 2)
24: Security Command Post (Pts. 3 & 4) (Lvl. 2)
25: Crane Yard Bridge & Dry Dock (Lvls. 0, 1, & 2)
26: Crane Magnet & MG Nest (Lvl. 2)
27: Circumventing Passage & Stairs (Lvl. 2)
28: Mini-Pipe Passage to Crane Scaffold Overlooks (Lvls. 2 & 3)
29: Market Passage (Lvl. 2)
30: Market Thoroughfare (First Street) (Lvl. 2)
31: Mop's Pawn Shop Balcony (Lvl. 3)
32: Market Thoroughfare (Beer & Babes) (Lvl. 2)
33: Market Thoroughfare (Kebabs) (Lvl. 2)
34: Market Alley & Supply Command Post (Lvl. 2)
35: Gantry Overlook (Lvl. 2)
36: Resistance Laboratory Garage & Dirty Bomb (Lvl. 1)
37: Resistance Laboratory: Water Tank Balcony (Lvl. 2)
38: Resistance Laboratory: Interior Passageway (Lvl. 2)
39: The Mighty Pipe Courtyard (Lvl. 2)
40: Flickering Light Passage to Container Overlook (Lvl. 2)
41: Comfy Couch Stairs to Lab Parapet (Lvls. 2 & 3)
42: Resistance Deployment Zone (Pts. 3): Container City Hideout (Lvl. 2)
43: Resistance Command Post (Pts. 3) (Lvl. 2)

S.M.A.R.T. Move
Engineer Mine (Optimal Placement)
Engineer Turret (Optimal Placement)
Camping Spot
Deployment Zone Turret (Invulnerable)
Core Objective Location
Secondary Objective Location
Critical Path (Route)

BRINK | Container City: Overview Map

# DAY 7: ATTACK ON CCITY

FREEPLAY: CONTAINER CITY  SECURITY CAMPAIGN—DAY 4: DIRTY BOMB

## 18:58 Container Shack Formerly Known as Clinic 14, Container City

MISSION TIME (COb 1): 08:00

MISSION TIME (COb 2, Part 1): +04:00

MISSION TIME (COb 3): +06:00

MISSION TIME (COb 2, Part 2): +06:00

MISSION TIME (COb 4): +06:00

### Brother Chen: Briefing

Brothers. The sickness continues to spread through the guest Pelgos. Until we get help from the outside world, we're on our own. So, we've had to help ourselves. We've stripped the medical equipment from the *Hope*, and synthesized the vaccine. For now, whoever controls this vaccine, controls the Ark! No surprise; Mokoena will kill to take it from us. The vaccine must reach the people! We can't let Mokoena steal it, and ration it for priority personnel. Hold Security off long enough for us to move the vaccine to safety. Do not let Mokoena's men steal it: Drive them back into the sea!

### Optimal Class Numbers

| | COb 1 | COb 2 | COb 3 | COb 4 |
|---|---|---|---|---|
| Soldier | [2] | [3] | [3] | [3] |
| Medic | [2] | [2] | [1] | [1] |
| Engineer | [3] | [2] | [3] | [3] |
| Operative | [1] | [1] | [1] | [1] |

### Objectives (Resistance)

- Core Objective 1: Defend the Gate
- Core Objective 2: Disable the Maintenance Bot
- Core Objective 3: Defend the Crane
- Core Objective 4: Defend the Sample
- Escort Core Objective Teammate
- Defend the Side Door
- Defend Side Stairs
- Construct Market Barricade
- Capture the Health Command Post
- Capture the Supply Command Post
- Construct the Gate MG Nest
- Construct the Ship MG Nest
- Construct the Crane MG Nest

## Important Locations

**"Decaying *Hope*" refers to a rusting medical frigate, currently sunken into the detritus between the Harbor and the Dry Dock. Both the Resistance and Security forces take turns spawning in this long-abandoned vessel.**

**NOTE**

## 1 Resistance Deployment Zone (Pts. 1 & 2): Bow of the *Hope* (Lvl. 2)

This is your starting point until the enemy manages to repair the Crane in Core Objective 3. You're inside the bow section of the *Hope* ship; drop down and head left during the initial enemy interception, and to the right as the Maintenance Bot nears the Crane. Note the lack of sentry turrets, meaning you can be attacked as you drop to the exterior alley.

## 2 Resistance Command Post (Pts. 1 & 2) (Lvl. 2)

This is inside the *Hope*'s bow, right in front of your spawn point. Change weapons and classes here.

## 3 Maintenance Bot Start: Jetty (Lvl. 0)

The Security Maintenance Bot begins its slow journey under enemy protection from this roughly constructed jetty. You'll be cut down by enemy sentry turrets before you reach this point, so wait for the Bot to arrive in the Harbor area.

## 4 Security Deployment Zone (Pts. 1 & 2): Jetty (Lvl. 1)

Security forces appear from this location up until they fix the Crane, and the Maintenance Bot is carried over into the Market area. They rush down this metal gantry, and have a choice of two different paths to reach the Harbor. Be sure your team is covering both of them.

## 5 Security Command Post (Pts. 1 & 2) (Lvl. 0)

This is inaccessible to your team. It's guarded by turrets, and offline to Resistance personnel.

## 6 Container City Harbor Entrance (Lvl. 1)

## 7 Entrance Gate (Lvl. 1)

## 8 Side Door (Lvl. 2)

The first major attack occurs at this point, because you complete the mission if you hold the Entrance Gate, and prevent the enemy from pushing through to the other side. The grounds of this location slowly rise up to the Gate itself, with a number of hiding spots, cover points, and a Scramble Point that allows the enemy over and behind the Entrance Gate. Be sure you are defending this area appropriately from the enemy appearing from one of two Harbor alleys.

The Entrance Gate itself is your focus, because any explosives must be removed. You can slide under the gap in the Entrance Gate, but the enemy can too, so defend this area with vicious attacks. The Side Door passage is another place the enemy tries to infiltrate; hold up here yourself, because you can climb up into two upper doorways, and an opening allows you to fire into the Thoroughfare below.

The following are some areas to hide or fire from:

You can stand on the metal container by the wooden ship's mast by the lower of the two alleys to create a distraction, although you'll be out-gunned near the enemy spawn point.

Stand on or under a set of steps to a small balcony overlooking the farther alley from the Entrance Gate.

Partial cover is available from the outside near the water tank you can step on to reach the Scramble Point.

The steps and walkway to the Side Door are good places to fire from, or you can hide behind the concrete barrier, under the walkway. You can also climb on the metal awning roof over the sealed door to the left of the Entrance Gate.

 **S.M.A.R.T. Moves** 

Look up and behind you at the Side Door to see two doorways above this location. The one directly above the Side Door leads down to the platform and side of the *Hope*, and the main Thoroughfare.

The one behind and above the Side Door (if you're facing the *Hope*) allows access to a passage directly above the Entrance Gate, where you can fire down and lob grenades on enemies with excellent cover protection.

###  Exterior Stairwell Scramble Point (Lvl. 2)

This allows you to maneuver to and from the Harbor Entrance and Thoroughfare via a series of stairs and containers. This is accessed from the Thoroughfare as well as the Rusty Bridge on the Resistance side, and via climbing a water tanker on the Harbor side. Whether the enemy is on either side, this is a good place to fire down from, using the metal scenery as cover. Also note the passage through a container that leads right to the Resistance side of the Entrance Gate.

###  Container City Thoroughfare (Lvl. 1)

This is where the second major battle occurs, as you attempt to stop the Maintenance Bot from reaching the Lower Hold Road after the Entrance Gate is breached. This road is narrow with the *Hope* on one side (and its Balcony you can move along, as well as the ground-level Interior Hold you can access via two adjacent entrances), and the Exterior Stairwell and containers to scramble onto on the other.

**Aside from the concrete barrier under the MG Nest stairs, remain on the sides and above ground level while traversing this location, so you can fire down on foes hiding behind the Maintenance Bot.**

 **TIP**

 **S.M.A.R.T. Moves** 

Leap and climb onto the platform near the Side Door.

Jump from the Exterior Stairwell and land on the metal roof on the inside corner of the Thoroughfare.

###  Decaying *Hope*: Starboard MG Nest & Balcony (Lvl. 2)

Build this MG Nest before the enemy breaks through the Entrance Gate, and train it on the Gate or the Exterior Stairwell. The Balcony that this MG Nest sits on allows access into the *Hope*'s Interior Passageways (but not the lower-level Interior Hold).

###  The Rusty Bridge (Lvl. 2)

One of the first locations you can reach, this offers a quick route up and onto the Exterior Stairwell en route to the initial Harbor chokepoint. Enter the Bridge via pulling yourself up from the concrete barriers by the *Hope*. Then fire on the enemies in the Thoroughfare from the gaps in the structure. Use the concrete barriers on either side below the Bridge as cover.

## 13 Decaying *Hope*: Interior Hold & Health Command Post (Lvl. 1)

The two doorways at ground-level near the Rusty Bridge let you enter the remains of the *Hope*'s hold. The small, L-shaped passage allows access to and from the Lower Hold Road. The other lets you enter the main Hold room, which houses a Health Command Post, and links to the Crane Yard on the other side, below the Container Crossing. Use these routes to reach the Crane Yard, too.

**Neither of the ground-level Interior Hold locations provides direct access to the Interior Passageways, MG Nests, and second Security Deployment Zone on the level above.**

**CAUTION**

## 14 Decaying *Hope*: Interior Passageways & MG Nest (Lvl. 2)

Another optional route to the Crane Yard (indeed some Security may take this shortcut before the Maintenance Bot reaches the Crane), the Balcony and MG Nest on the Thoroughfare side of the *Hope* has a second balcony on the opposite deck, after the "H"-shaped connecting passageway has been navigated. This second MG Nest overlooks (and offers quick access into) the Container Crossing and Crane Yard.

##  15 Decaying *Hope*: Lower Hold Road (Lvl. 1)

This ground-level road with an opening into the Interior Hold allows the Maintenance Bot direct access through into the Container Clearing. Correct positioning of teammates and other ordnance slows this maneuver down.

## 16 Container Clearing (Lvl. 1)

This opens to a various locations: the Resistance spawn point, the Lower Hold Road, into the lower Rusting Hull, and the Crane Yard Vantage Point. Climbing to the nearby promontories helps you guard the area and stops the death march of the Maintenance Bot. The nearby spawn alley helps ambush enemies, too.

###  S.M.A.R.T. Moves 

Jump up onto the blue metal container that's holding the Container Crossing structure, and climb to the knife-edge top of the structure itself.

##  17 Rusting Hull to Side Stairs (Lvls. 0, 1, & 2)

In one corner of the Container Clearing (under the washing line) is a hole in the ground leading to an underground passage. Once you enter, if you turn left, the passage brings you out in the Dry Dock under the Crane Yard Bridge, after passing a tiny, rusty restroom you can hide in. Turn right, and you reach the Side Stairs, which must be built by an enemy Engineer as part of the Secondary Objectives. Once constructed, these stairs allow your opponents (or you) quicker access up onto the Market Thoroughfare (First Street).

## S.M.A.R.T. Moves

Ignore the stairs building and simply Wall-jump up the gap instead.

## 18 Container Crossing (Lvl. 2)

Crossing above the yard between the Crane and the Hold exit is a blue container open to the elements. The nearby ramp doesn't actually attach to the container (it leads to the Crane Yard Vantage Point); this structure must be climbed, or accessed from the *Hope* Balcony near the MG Nest. You can fire from this precarious location, both before and after the Maintenance Bot passes underneath. This is also the only way to reach the Free Ark Rooftop Alley.

## S.M.A.R.T. Moves

Wall-jump and Mantle onto the lip of the container, cross it, and jump up and into the Free Ark Rooftop Alley.

As well as the blue container, you can climb up the metal lean-to on the Crane Yard side to reach the lip of the container wall.

You can also leap from the top of the ramp, grab the AC fan box, and haul yourself up onto the orange container at the base of the Rooftop Alley entrance.

## 19 Crane Yard Vantage Point (Lvl. 2)

Directly above the Dry Dock and Rusting Hull that leads to the Side Stairs, this location is reached via the ramp next to the Container Crossing. This offers commanding views of the Crane Yard, which is excellent for camping (no matter what the nearby sign may say), both as the Bot is transported across the Yard and during the late stages when a foe is attempting to reach the Extraction Point.

## S.M.A.R.T. Moves

Grab the AC fan box, and pull yourself up onto the edge of the Vantage Point instead of using the ramped passage.

## 20 Free Ark Rooftop Alley (Lvl. 3)

The enemy may not need to build the Side Stairs if you don't guard this shortcut, which requires some scrambling to reach. This offers a vantage point over the Container Clearing to snipe from, and an overview of the Market Thoroughfare and Alley, and around to the "Bar" signage. You can also climb up onto the Rooftop Alley from the street below, where the "FREE ARK" graffiti is displayed.

## Crane & Decaying *Hope*: Port Balcony (Lvls. 1, 2, & 3)

The main focus of Security Engineers during the third Core Objective for your enemies, this massive blue Crane with its giant magnet dominates the Crane Yard. Reach the Crane's control booth by climbing it, either from the Yard or the nearby Port Balcony of the *Hope*. The Balcony itself connects to the Interior Passageways and MG Nest. Use the area underneath, with the concrete barriers and containers, as cover or ambush points. Once the Maintenance Bot reaches the Crane, the Port Balcony door swings back, revealing the second Security Deployment Zone. Beware of a huge enemy presence, and think about retreating at this point.

## Extraction Point (Lvl. 2)

This is the last location from where you can save this mission for Resistance forces, because the mesh gate is where Security forces attempt to take the Sample from your Laboratory. Remember you can stand on the container below the Crane booth, leap the concrete barriers to reach the Extraction Point, and hide in and around this location to dodge incoming enemy fire, usually emanating from the last deployment zone aboard the *Hope*.

## Security Deployment Zone (Pts. 3 & 4): Decaying *Hope* (Lvl. 2)

As soon as an enemy Engineer fixes the Crane, your deployment zone—and your enemies'—changes. Security forces head out of the starboard end of the *Hope*; so watch for an influx of foes at the balcony and near the Crane. Don't venture onto this section of balcony; turrets are there to mow you down.

## Security Command Post (Pts. 3 & 4) (Lvl. 2)

Inside the hull of the *Hope*, this Command Post is inaccessible.

## Crane Yard Bridge & Dry Dock (Lvls. 0, 1, & 2)

## Crane Magnet & MG Nest (Lvl. 2)

Although the Maintenance Bot is carried over the Crane Yard Bridge by the Crane (if your team lets this happen!), the bridge itself should be the focus of your defensive plans (the MG Nest is effective and should be used). You'll be surprised at how effortlessly some of the more lithe enemies can reach the MG Nest area, so be sure to cover the Dry Dock and the Market Thoroughfare, holding out for as long as possible before you're swamped. There are exits out of the Dry Dock via the Circumventing Passage, or the lower-ground passage to the Side Stairs.

### S.M.A.R.T. Moves

Either side of the Dry Dock can be climbed up, but the taller edge under the MG Nest can be Wall-jumped.

Failing that, you can Wall-jump the side of the bridge, and climb to the top of the pipe to reach the far side of the Dry Dock.

## 27 Circumventing Passage & Stairs (Lvl. 2)

This is usually the route the enemy takes when scurrying to the Extraction Point with the Sample, but it also offers a less-trafficked route into Resistance territory, and various upper vantage points overlooking the Laboratory. Race along the zigzag Circumventing Passage, and up into the Mighty Pipe Courtyard, or back again.

The "Mighty Pipe" is a useful landmark for the Resistance forces, because you can follow it to a container stack just across from the green neon cross, and Laboratory. A second, "Mini-Pipe" also weaves through here; follow that to the next location.

TIP

S.M.A.R.T. Moves

You can Wall-jump the metal girders and water tank along the left side, and into the Circumventing Passage.

## 28 Mini-Pipe Passage to Crane Scaffold Overlooks (Lvls. 2 & 3)

There are two entrances to this two-tier vantage point: The first is to follow the mini-pipe from the Mighty Pipe Courtyard. The mini-pipe winds through a container stack passage, leading you to a walkway balcony behind the Crane Magnet (which you can also walk along). Here, you can blast enemies below you, or turn and climb up again to a sniper's nest directly above the passage exit.

S.M.A.R.T. Moves

The other way up here is to Wall-jump off the ship's mast and water tank and onto the blue Crane Magnet crossbeam.

## 29 Market Passage (Lvl. 2)

Behind the Crane Magnet is sloping ground into a tight passageway that leads out into the Laboratory Garage area. Seal this obvious shortcut as a matter of urgency, or the enemy can swarm the Market and Lab with ease.

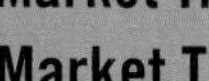

## 30 Market Thoroughfare (First Street) (Lvl. 2)
## 31 Mop's Pawn Shop Balcony (Lvl. 3)
## 32 Market Thoroughfare (Beer & Babes) (Lvl. 2)
## 33 Market Thoroughfare (Kebabs) (Lvl. 2)

This large, U-shaped street runs through Container City's Market district, and is the last line of defense before the chaperoned Maintenance Bot reaches the Resistance Laboratory. The initial Thoroughfare has the alley opening (which you can fight from because it has more cover), and the Rooftop and Side Stairs exits.

Around the corner is the main Market area itself. Enter and take cover in the Bar and Souvenir store, the Pawn Shop, and the bedroom inside the Triple-X store. Upstairs from the Pawn Shop is a balcony, offering advantageous height and cover. On the inside of the route is the Market Alley area, offering narrower passage to and from the Laboratory. Once the enemies pass the Kebab place, they are almost at the Laboratory, and you must push your defenses back again.

## S.M.A.R.T. Moves

You can climb onto the Pawn Shop balcony via the container with the "Bar" sign on it.

You can also clamber atop the lean-to awning by the "Mobile" sign on the inside corner.

## 34 Market Alley & Supply Command Post (Lvl. 2)

This offers quicker access to and from the Laboratory via the Gantry Overlook, and two exits onto the Market Thoroughfare. The big draw here is the Supply Command Post; keep this in your possession as you gradually retreat. It can be captured after Security has repaired the Crane.

## 35 Gantry Overlook (Lvl. 2)

As the match progresses, this should be a well defended area against those trying to enter via the Market Passage. Then use it to quickly reach the Market Thorough-fares via the alley and

Supply Command Post. Finally, use it to fire on the enemy trying to open the Laboratory Garage. Although elevated, this area is open, and you're likely to be outflanked if you stand around here.

**Echoing shouts can be heard throughout this area of the map; this cues you to where you are as you learn this map's layout.**

TIP

## 36 Resistance Laboratory Garage & Dirty Bomb (Lvl. 1)

This is permanently sealed until the Security forces manage to get the Maintenance Bot to this location, after which the Garage is spot-welded open. Prior to this, use the multiple vantage points to cover this location. Afterward, step inside the Garage to ambush a foe trying to take the Sample and focus everyone here! Note the multiple routes you can use to reach here.

## 37 Resistance Laboratory: Water Tank Balcony (Lvl. 2)

## 38 Resistance Laboratory: Interior Passageway (Lvl. 2)

Above the Garage is a balcony your team can fire from with relative safety; indeed a sniper has a great line-of-sight up the Market Thorough-fare and toward the Market Passage.

Climb up here from below, or enter via the Interior Passageway itself, which is entered via the doorway under the solar panels, and near the draped giant anchor.



HISTORY OF THE ARK
CHARACTER CREATION
GAMEPLAY
WEAPONS DETAIL
CAMPAIGN
Getting Answers
Breakout
Chen's Plans
Black Box
Attack on CCity
Airborne
Operation Babel
Critical Reaction
CHALLENGES
APPENDICES

### 39 The Mighty Pipe Courtyard (Lvl. 2)

This is a Resistance stronghold, because you're near the spawn point, but foes still use this route to reach the Laboratory, or flee with the Sample. Use the giant rusting pipe above as a marker, following it to the Garage if you become lost. Also check the two doorways leading up to vantage points, and Circumventing Passage and Stairs (guard this during the last part of the match to thwart a Sample carrier).

### 40 Flickering Light Passage to Container Overlook (Lvl. 2)

### 41 Comfy Couch Stairs to Lab Parapet (Levels 2 and 3)

Two of the most cunning vantage points when guarding the Garage are entered via doorways in the Mighty Pipe Courtyard. They are easy to distinguish: The doorway with a flickering light leads across to a container overlooking the Garage and Market Passage exit. You can reach this location from the ground below, too.

The other entrance has a comfy couch under the light, and leads up to the Lab Parapet near the green neon cross. There's a covered area at each end to dodge gunfire from, and a great view of the Market Thoroughfare and Garage. This is the only way to reach this location.

### 42 Resistance Deployment Zone (Pts. 3): Container City Hideout (Lvl. 2)

Amid the echoing shouts of the Resistance dwellers, your team continues the match from this point once the Crane has been activated. Be sure you know your surroundings; the spawn point is behind a half-buried container with a hazard symbol on it. Learn the different routes to the Dry Dock, Crane Yard, Market Passage, Thoroughfare, and Garage so you spend no time lost. The Mighty Pipe Courtyard is your adjacent location.

### 43 Resistance Command Post (Pts. 3) (Lvl. 2)

Engineers (and their mines and turrets) may be beneficial, so use this Command Post accordingly.

## Objective Tactics: Core Objective 1

### Defend the Gate

Spawn Point to Gate: 00:13

Time to Open the Conduit: 00:10

Time to Plant Explosives: 00:07

Time to Disarm Explosives: 00:05

Countdown to Explosion: 00:40

### General Tactics

As the action begins, it is important to cover the Harbor Entrance as an initial line of defense, retreating to the actual Entrance Gate as the enemy pushes through your outer skirmishes. The team should split into a couple of groups; the first can provide some fire from high camping spots atop the balconies, Scramble Point, and above the actual Gate itself. Meanwhile, around four Engineers can set up defenses on both sides of the Gate, to waylay enemies even after Core Objective 1 has been compromised.

But your main focus, what all of your team should be attempting, is the takedown of the bomb-planting Soldier. Obviously, targeting any enemy with a Soldier icon is a matter of priority. But if tagging them as they approach isn't working, sniping them through a hole in the Gate's door is a highly effective tactic. Choose from various spots (see the Sniper's Ally box below), but one of the best is accessed from the blue container at the base of the Scramble Point. Mantle onto the rusty overhang, and stand just behind the vertical pipe on the corner. You can tag the foe from here, without much enemy recourse.

## Targets Acquired

**Maintenance Bot Blasting:** From your vantage points around the Harbor, your priority targets are Soldiers. Next are enemies trying to climb over the Scramble Point to attack you from your own alleys by the *Hope*. Then are enemies trying to help the Soldiers, such as Medics. Finally comes the Maintenance Bot. Although a low priority target, the Bot is worth damaging (with grenades because it is easy to hit, as well as gunfire) as a precursor to Core Objective 2. If this helps divert enemies away from this Core Objective to fight you, so much the better.

**Harbor Takedowns:** Dashing around the Harbor is the enemy's plan; you're better off remaining in cover, using height, and locations you can quickly retreat from when you're overwhelmed. The most dangerous *and* beneficial location to be is flitting between the slide gap in the Gate and the concrete barrier under the Side Door stairs. Standing on the corner of the stairs, and up on the Scramble Point are other recommended defensive locations.

**At the Gate:** Your Engineers should be feverishly placing turrets and mines in the Thoroughfare and dotted around the defensive locations this alley has in abundance, ready for Core Objective 2. But spare some time to cover the Gate from this side. Whether you're manning the Gate MG Nest, guarding the Side Door passage and peering through the hole to cover the Gate, or standing around the *Hope*'s Balcony, train your weapons on the Gate, then fire and grenade it when the Soldiers come. The sliding gap is another incursion point; make the foes pay for trying to enter before the Gate is compromised.

**Remember that enemy Operatives may be trying to hack the Side Door (or climb over the gaps to your side of the Gate), allowing your foes to outflank you. Consult the Secondary Objective for repelling plans.**

 **NOTE**

**Turrets do not aim at the Maintenance Bot; only human enemies. Mines do not explode when a Bot moves over them, either.**

 **CAUTION**

##  Automated Ordnance

Because you're the defending team, use your Engineers to set up the following defenses:

Place a turret as an initial annoyance. An Engineer at Camping Spot 1 can quickly fix it.

You need a turret that can catch foes swarming the Scramble Point. Set one here, across the Balcony from the MG Nest.

Place a mine on the Harbor side of the Gate where the explosives are placed. It won't explode if it's on your side.

Set a mine on the other side of the slide point, stopping foes from swarming your defenses.

HISTORY OF THE ARK
CHARACTER CREATION
GAMEPLAY
WEAPONS DETAIL
CAMPAIGN
Getting Answers
Breakout
Chen's Plans
Black Box
Attack on CCity
Airborne
Operation Babel
Critical Reaction
CHALLENGES
APPENDICES

## Sniper's Ally: Camping Spots

1 Although you're easily overrun, you can hide here, wait for a team of enemies to pass, then ambush them from behind. This also provides good Bot takedown opportunities.

2 This is a great location, because you can see where the enemies are running up from, and can retreat if they swarm your Scramble Point.

3 Use the Side Door passage to climb up and into this vantage point above the Gate itself, which covers both Security attack routes.

4 Stay in the Side Door passage to guard against foes, and peer through the window hole, and aim through the gaps in the Gate.

5 Use the MG Nest, or stand with a preferred weapon to the right and behind (so you can use the *Hope*'s interior when you take cover). Both are great for shooting at enemies through the holes in the Gate.

6 Cover the Gate, and any foes trying to use the Side Door passage to flank you.

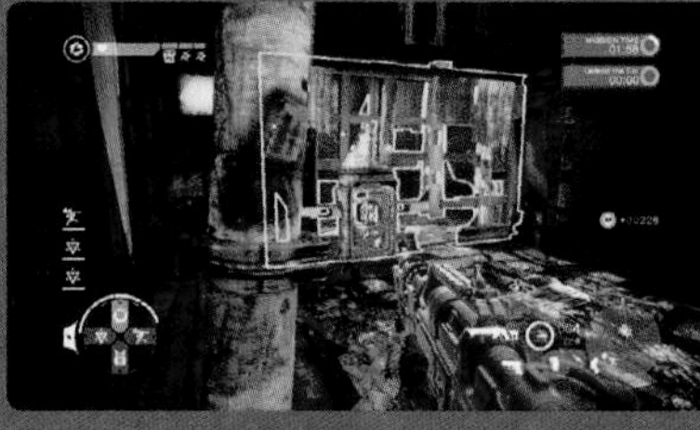

7 This is the optimal place to shoot enemies: on the overhang by the vertical pipe you Mantle onto. Note that Light Body Types can jump over from the MG Nest to here.

# Objective Tactics: Core Objective 2 (Part 1)

### Disable the Maintenance Bot

Time to Repair the Bot: 00:10

### General Tactics

**This Core Objective continues all the way from the Harbor Gate to the Garage and Laboratory deep in Container City. Slowing the Bot down is your major plan of attack throughout.**

**NOTE**

When the opposition sets out on the long road to the Garage, try everything you can to slow down and stop the Bot. Keep a core set of teammates focused on blasting the Bot, and a keen lookout for any Security Engineers, the only class that can repair the Bot once it stops moving. Try to disable the Bot when it reaches the U-turn of the Lower

Hold Road, and passes through the *Hope*. But even with ferocious gunfire, the Bot may eventually creep out into the Container Clearing, passing under the Container Crossing, and park under the Crane's girders. Should this occur, Core Objective 3 begins, while this objective continues.

### Taking Bot Shots, I

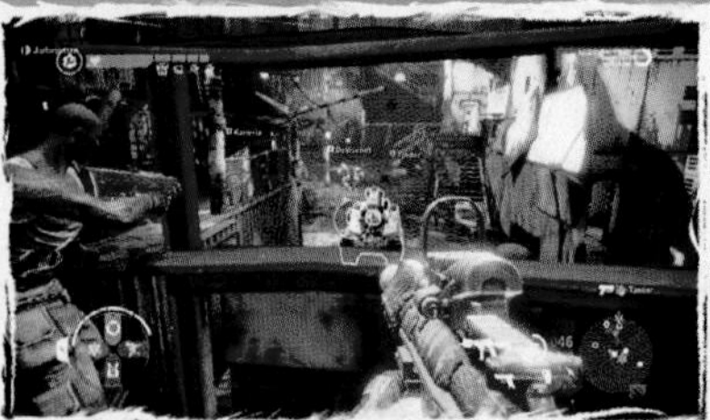

**Thoroughfare:** It isn't wise, and certainly isn't that helpful, to stay on the ground while the Bot and enemies are

pushing down this narrow alley because you can't really see the enemy. A better plan is to fire down from the *Hope* Balcony, Rusty Bridge, and Exterior Stairwell. Watch for foes leaping over this Scramble Point, as well as entering the *Hope*. As the Bot continues, prep the Crane with mines and turrets for Core Objective 3, before the Bot gets there.

**Lower Hold Road:** This is the most difficult place for Security to attack from, because it is both confined and right next to your spawn point. Try placing a turret directly facing the Robot, and a mine in front of it (to dissuade enemies moving around it). Then prime your sharpshooters to take down sneaky enemy Engineers trying a suicide run to repair it.

**Container Clearing:** At this point, the enemy may try to split up, with Light Body Types attempting to Wall-jump over the Side Stairs, while others race for the Crane. Don't fall for their trick and chase them when there's still time to waylay the Bot; it is better to keep most of your team battering the Bot than leaving it to reach its Crane Yard parking spot. Instead, blast from the camp spots shown below.

## Automated Ordnance

Place a turret on either side of the Thoroughfare under the Rusty Bridge, where the enemy has a hard time landing grenades, or on the Bridge itself (#3 shown).

At least one turret on the Container Clearing side of the Lower Hold Road helps demolish and demoralize the enemy.

Stop the Scramble Point from being used with a mine here. The turret placed on the *Hope* Balcony during Core Objective 1 is still effective, too.

Guard your teammates on the Rusty Bridge with a mine at the entrance.

Mines dotted throughout the Lower Hold Road help remove enemy Engineers trying to mend the Bot.

## Sniper's Ally: Camping Spots

Stand on the Rusty Bridge and cover the advancement of the Bot on the Thoroughfare below.

The corner of your deployment zone is extremely safe, and you can aim all the way up the Thoroughfare.

Guard the entrance to the Side Stairs, once Core Objective 3 is over and the enemy can build this, to stop foes using it and flanking you into the Dry Dock. Drop down if you come under fire.

## Sniper's Ally: Camping Spots (continued)

11 Snipe from the ramp at the far end of the Container Crossing; there's a great view of the Lower Hold Road.

12 Guarding the Container Clearing from the Free Ark Rooftop Alley means you have options to drop into the Container Crossing, or retreat to tackle foes heading farther into the city.

# Objective Tactics: Core Objective 3

### Defend the Crane

Spawn Point to Crane: 00:18

Time to Repair the Crane: 00:30

#### General Tactics

While Core Objective 2 still continues, the enemy now tries to break away from its Bot chaperoning to ready the Crane. Engineers are the only enemy type that can attempt this, so search them out among the foes, and drop them as a priority. Have your team retreat and take up defensive positions around the Crane Yard, as well as stopping enemies from ascending the Side Stairs (check the Secondary Objective for more information).

#### Routes to Crane Control

**Container Clearing:** Foes spread out from here, even before the Bot parks and the Crane controls become active. Split your team into those who are stopping the enemy from outflanking you via the Free Ark Rooftop Alley and Side Stairs, and those who are setting up defenses and camping spots in the Crane Yard itself.

***Hope*'s Interior Passageways:** Enemies (especially those re-spawning) usually use the *Hope*'s Interior Passageways to quickly reach the controls, so prepare some traps as they emerge, and watch for them trying out the Ship's MG Nest to delay or annoy you.

> **Both the Resistance and Security Deployment Zones change after this Core Objective starts, so prepare to appear much deeper in Container City. Note that all of these camping spots can be used during the last Core Objective, too. Once the Bot has been transported over the Dry Dock and bridge, the Side Stairs and Barricade can be constructed (Secondary Objective). Prior to that, the gap could only be Wall-jumped by Light Body Types.**
>
> **NOTE**

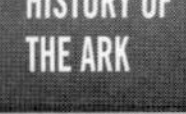

## Automated Ordnance

7 Set a turret on the lower gantry steps of the Crane, up from grenade explosions, and with a clear view of the Bot through the Container Crossing.

8 Set a turret here to catch Engineers running up to the Control room; but when the spawn points change, this is soon removed.

9 Place a turret on the Extraction Point container, to cut down foes crossing the Crane Yard.

6 Try to plant a mine at one of the two entrances into the Crane's control room; Engineers have to get in this way and will likely set it off.

7 Mine the entrance (or slightly inside around the corner) of the Circumventing Passage and Stairs.

## Sniper's Ally: Camping Spots

13 Drop into the Container Crossing, and sidestep to the end closest to the MG Nest. Lean out, and you have a fully protected and direct view of the control room!

14 The MG Nest on the upper edge of the Dry Dock is a fantastic place to cut the enemy down, from the Crane control room to the Extraction Point.

15 Oversee the entire area from the Crane Yard Vantage Point.

16 Long-range takedowns are possible from the Crane Scaffold Overlooks (lower balcony shown), and you can retreat to cover the Garage via the Mini-Pipe Passage behind you.

# Objective Tactics: Core Objective 2 (Part 2)

### Disable the Maintenance Bot

Time to Repair the Bot: 00:10

### General Tactics

The Maintenance Bot, once transferred over the bridge, takes a long path around the main Market Thoroughfare, before a final trundle down the slope to the Garage, when the objective is finally complete. Your team has a number of locations to worry about, and keeping the enemy from popping up all over the place is a constant problem. Don't worry about foes wandering into your final deployment zone at first; they're just one less foe guarding the Bot for you to worry about, and only the Bot is important here.

One of the best plans is to always keep the shortcut barrier in the Market Passage constructed. This way, your entire team can concentrate on the route through the Market Thoroughfare that the Bot is taking. You can cut down defenders and damage the Bot from height and cover at various locations (shown below). But the barricade is key; building that means the enemies are funneled into guarding the Bot, and you can mount an impressive series of defense lines, ending with a final disabling on the slope leading to the Laboratory itself, because there are many high defenses to snipe or construct turrets on.

## Taking Bot Shots, II

**Market Thoroughfare (First Street):** Don't hang on to the Side Stairs or Free Ark Rooftop; those are already compromised and it is better to keep the enemy guessing where you are from the initially bewildering Market Alley and Thoroughfare. Have an Engineer on constant watch to maintain the Market Passage barrier. Snipe from the Crane Scaffold Overlooks. And dart out of the side Alley and Thoroughfare corner.

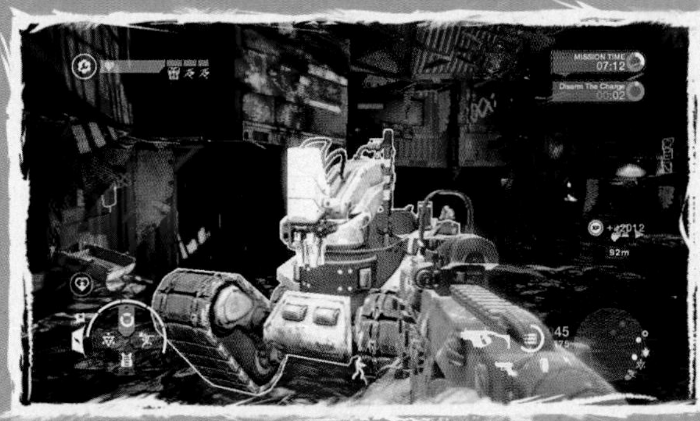

**Market Thoroughfare (Beers and Babes):** Attack from three sides to really slow the Bot down; guard the Alley and flank around to attack from behind once the Bot passes. Climb onto the balcony running from the Triple-X store, above the Pawn Shop, to the Bar. Dropping grenades and demolishing Bot armor from here is a great plan. Station a sharpshooter just behind the Triple-X store to snipe foes, and retreat to the final defenses.

**Resistance Laboratory (Garage):** Infuriate the enemy by lobbing grenades and blasting the Bot on the slope. With the timer ticking down, the frantic enemy must contend with your campers too; sit up above the Garage using the water containers as cover. Wall-jump between the two sides of the Market Passage exit, staying on the containers (and Gantry Overlook). Position teammates (and turrets) on the Container Overlook and Lab Parapet.

## Automated Ordnance

10 There are many crossfire opportunities with turrets, as long as you place them partially hidden from the enemy, such as on the other side of the "Bar" sign.

11 Set a turret to rattle off bullets at the enemies escorting the Bot, or milling about at the Garage door.

8 Place a mine to defend the Market Passage if building a barricade isn't possible, or to give you time to build the barricade.

9 Set a mine in the container connecting the Gantry Overlook to the Supply Command Post.

HISTORY OF THE ARK
CHARACTER CREATION
GAMEPLAY
WEAPONS DETAIL
CAMPAIGN
Getting Answers
Breakout
Chen's Plans
Black Box
Attack on CCity
Airborne
Operation Babel
Critical Reaction
CHALLENGES
APPENDICES

## Sniper's Ally: Camping Spots

17 Stand at the junction in the Market Alley to cover the Bot route and the Supply Command Post.

18 Prowl Mop's Pawn Shop Balcony along the Market Thoroughfare.

19 Crouch on the metal awning on the far corner of the Market Thoroughfare mid-section; you're less likely to be struck by mines if you're not on the ground.

20 21 Patrol both sides of the Gantry Overlook (Camping Spot 20 shown).

22 Sit atop the water tanks on the Garage in the Laboratory area and cover the Market Passage, flanking routes, and Market Thoroughfare to the Garage.

23 Race up the Comfy Couch Stairs to the Lab Parapet; another excellent place to snipe from.

## Objective Tactics: Core Objective 4

### Defend the Sample

Spawn Point to Garage & Sample: 00:12

Spawn Point to Extraction Point: 00:12

Garage to Extraction Point: 00:14

Time to Deliver the Sample: 00:05

### General Tactics

Once Core Objective 2 finally fails, and the enemy manages to get their Maintenance Bot to your Garage, its plasma cutter makes short work of the container, leaving an entrance and the Sample exposed. Your vantage points around the Laboratory become more important than ever. The enemy must now take the Sample (Dirty Bomb) and run through Container City to the Extraction Point. Forethought is vital here; the enemy's possible exit routes, and the exit itself, must be properly guarded (as detailed below).

The carrier is likely to be of Light Body Type (and thus faster), and have abilities to accentuate his speed. Tanks should have retreated and taken up sharpshooting positions in the locations detailed below. The rest should be on the higher side of the Crane Yard, across from the Dry Dock, because the enemy's spawn makes marauding around the Crane somewhat difficult. Then try to catch the carrier on his route back.

**If the carrier drops the Sample in an advantageous spot for your team, don't return it to the Garage (which may have enemies nearby waiting to take it again). Instead, wait at the location and cover it from all angles; perhaps even set traps so it becomes almost impossible for the enemy to retake it.**

TIP

**Match the carrier's abilities by choosing them for a Light Body Type rival, who can keep up and is built to counteract the enemy carrier, as well as these type of Core Objectives. Consult the "Builds" section of the Characters chapter earlier in this book. But think about a Medic with Sprinting Grenade, Sprinting Reload, Silent Running, Speed Boost (from a Medic), and Adrenaline Boost.**

TIP

## Exit Routes: Shutdown!

**Funnel your foes: This involves cutting off exits so there's a great chance the enemy will take one or two routes, which you can then fortify and guard with an increased presence.**

TIP

**Circumventing Passage:** Set up mines within the Passage itself, turrets around the Mighty Pipe, and a couple of teammates along the route; one in the Mini-Pipe Passage (so he can fire at the carrier, then head up to the Crane Scaffold Overlooks for some final sniping), and another below the exit of the Circumventing Passage, across from the Dry Dock, to ambush the carrier but also cover any of the other routes into the Crane Yard.

**Market Passage:** This straight shot is a lot harder if you've set up the barricade as a Secondary Objective! If that hasn't happened, you should mine the interior (keeping the Sample in here is excellent, because you can surround this area). Teammates should be on the ground near the Crane girders (guarding both this, and the Market Thoroughfare), and the camping spot at the Crane Yard Vantage Point, covering the enemy spawn and Extraction Point.

**Market Thoroughfare:** You can't be sure whether the carrier will use the Alleys near the Supply Command Post, so position a teammate guarding both entrances, and the upper entrance to the Side Stairs, so that isn't utilized. Turrets covering the Thoroughfare toward the Crane girders are also beneficial. Have a second teammate guarding the Free Ark Rooftop in case the carrier gets creative. This teammate can then quickly move to the Container Crossing to cover the exit.

**Crane Yard and Extraction Point:** You're fighting the enemy as they spawn, and also as they rush back from the Garage. Keep calm in all this chaos, and have one or two colleagues annoying the respawning enemies from the balcony, exit containers, or Crane Yard. The others are in the previous recommended positions so you have complete coverage of the Extraction Point, which should be mined, too!

**Check out Core Objective 3 for camping spots around the Crane Yard.**

NOTE

## Automated Ordnance

Turrets and mines are even more important during the carrier's rush. Most of these should have been placed just before the Garage was compromised.

12 Cover the Market Passage with a turret as the carrier exits.

13 Give any enemies a nasty surprise when they try to reach the Garage via the Laboratory passage.

10 Stop foes from sneaking into the Laboratory itself by setting a mine in the connecting corridor.

11 Mine the Extraction Point if you can, as a last desperate line of defense.

## Sniper's Ally: Camping Spots

24 Move up and down the Container Crossing to cover the Extraction Point, and distract the spawning enemies.

# Secondary Objectives

### Escort Core Objective Class Teammate

Official Escort Info: With Engineers swarming the Gate, shadow one of them as a Medic (to heal them), a Soldier (to cover them as they deploy traps or complete objectives), or another Engineer (so you can fix and place more turrets). While you're defending areas ranging from the Harbor to the Garage and Laboratory, having weapons trained from opposite sniping or camping points is also helpful. So is a spotter who can let you know where foes are in this rusting maze.

### Defend the Side Door

Spawn Point to Side Door: 00:09

Time to Hack the Side Door: 00:20

This occurs during Core Objective 1, and involves an Operative attempting to release a door so the enemy can outflank you around the Gate. Effectively halt this easily by looking for foes using the side stairs next to the Gate itself. If you can spot an Operative (the only enemy class who can hack), drop him in the Harbor exterior, ideally from the window above the Gate. If an Operative manages to enter the Side Door passage, he still needs time to hack; a friend in camping spot 3 can turn around and gun the Operative down from behind. You may find that the enemy ignores this in favor of using the Scramble Point.

### Defend Side Stairs

Advantage Soldier!

Spawn Point to Side Stairs: 00:10

Time to Build Side Stairs: 00:20

Time to Plant Explosives: 00:07

Time to Disarm Explosives: 00:05

Countdown to Explosion: 00:40

The Side Stairs are an important route for the enemy to take at around halfway through the mission, because it allows them to reach the Market Thoroughfare, and the Maintenance Bot (as well as the Supply Command Post) more quickly. Unless the enemy is a team of tanks, they may even ignore the stairs building completely, because the gap can be Wall-jumped! However, placing a mine at the top of the gap (or the stairs if you relent and the enemy builds them) makes them think twice about using this route. Don't fixate on keeping the stairs out-of-bounds; instead position a sharpshooter at the opposite end of the Market to tag foes as they emerge. This sniper is also much closer to more important objectives (the Garage, Supply Command Post, and Sample). Also remember you can (and should) destroy the Stairs using a Soldier's charge.

### Construct Market Barricade

Engineer

Spawn Point to Barricade: 00:18

Time to Build Barricade: 00:20

Time to Plant Explosives: 00:07

Time to Disarm Explosives: 00:05

Countdown to Explosion: 00:40

The zigzag connecting Market Passage behind and below the Crane Magnet girders sees constant battle during the last half of the mission. Leaving the barricade unmade is extremely dangerous, because it offers an excellent shortcut straight into the Resistance's inner sanctum, with the Garage and Lab straight ahead. Plan to seal this well ahead of time; if the enemy is about to fix the Crane Magnet, construct the barricade, after leaving a mine on the outer side first. If the enemy starts dismantling the barricade, leave a mine and/or a turret for them to run into as they exit. The Mini-Pipe Passage to Crane Scaffold Overlooks is the quickest way to reach the entrance if you want to lob in a grenade and halt the barricade's destruction. Keep an Engineer focused on mending this consistently; especially because the Sample carrier can use it to reach the Extraction Point much more quickly.

### Capture the Health Command Post

Engineer & Operative Advantage!

Spawn Point to Command Post: 00:11

Time to Claim Command Post: 00:10

This post is located in the bowels of the *Hope*, and as long as you enter the correct Interior Passageway, you should claim this within five seconds of starting the mission. It is likely to remain yours, but as the enemy encroaches, and the Maintenance Bot nears the Crane Magnet, it becomes increasingly more difficult to retake. Once the spawn points change, and the enemy appears in the same ship as this post, it may be better to simply let the enemies take it. Either that, or choose an Engineer whose job it is to interfere with the enemy's routes to the Garage and divert their attention, while also doing something beneficial for your team's health.

### Capture the Supply Command Post

Engineer & Operative Advantage!

Spawn Point to Command Post: 00:12

Time to Claim Command Post: 00:10

The Supply Command Post is in a narrow Market Alley, deep in Container City, and close to your Garage and Lab. Once Security has repaired the Crane, send an Engineer to claim and upgrade this post before rejoining your squad at the Harbor Gate. The enemy needs to take some considerable risks to dodge your spawning teammates before finding and taking this post; so utilize it for an early bonus. This becomes increasingly more contested the longer the mission lasts, so assign one or two Engineers to go from their tasks to retaking this post.

### Construct the Gate MG Nest

### Construct the Ship MG Nest

### Construct the Crane MG Nest

Engineer

Spawn Point to Gate MG Nest: 00:06 

Spawn Point to Ship MG Nest: 00:07 

Spawn Point to Crane MG Nest: 00:09 

Time to Construct: 00:04  

The Gate MG Nest is the most beneficial of the three you can build, simply because it can aim directly at the Harbor Gate, dropping enemies as long as you're aiming through the holes in the Gate. Even after the Gate has been removed, the MG Nest can rake the Maintenance Bot, causing it to slow and stop, which effectively traps it in the Thoroughfare. Then turn your attention to the Engineers trying to mend it. Only retreat from this MG Nest once the enemy uses grenades or shoots you from outside your aiming perimeter.

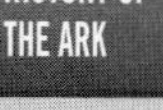

The Ship MG Nest is the least useful of the three, because it doesn't cover any important locations as well. True, you can use it to batter the Maintenance Bot as it passes through Container Crossing, but this is a tiny part of the overall mission. Dropping enemies as they try to climb to the Free Ark Rooftop Alley is another reasonable plan, but it's better to move to more important defendable locations, such as covering the Crane, Market Thoroughfare, or Garage. Ignore it once the enemy spawn point moves onto the *Hope*.

Although you need to have a second teammate covering the possible enemy attacks from outside your MG Nest's aiming perimeter (the Dry Dock, Market Thoroughfare, and bridge to your right), the Crane MG Nest is excellent for taking down the Maintenance Bot before it can be trundled into place below the Crane Magnet. Then cut down the Engineers trying to mend the machine or fix the Crane controls. Later on, you can even spawn-camp here, wounding enemies and slowing them down while your team fortifies the Garage and Lab. Finally, remember you can cut the Sample carrier down at the Extraction Point, too!

## Solo Tactics

Choose an Engineer and guard the Gate, watching for enemies using the Scramble Point. Drop Soldiers, and pry off the explosives as soon as you can. Then retreat and trap the Crane before helping your team waylay the Maintenance Bot. Find a camping spot to drop the enemy Engineer who accesses the Crane controls, but once the Bot has been transferred into the Market area, trap the shortcut path and construct the Market Barricade to keep the enemy from completely swarming your Garage and Laboratory. If the Bot cuts the Garage open, trap the Sample and guard it from the vantage points, then retreat to the Extraction Point instead of chasing down the carrier to take a final stand there.

## Mission Completion Conditions

### Continuation...

**Core Objective 1:** Your team fails to stop the enemy destroying the Gate at the Harbor Entrance. Part 2 of this mission now commences....

**Core Objective 2:** Your team fails to stop the enemy from escorting the Maintenance Bot to the Crane. Part 2 continues and Part 3 of this mission now begins....

**Core Objective 3:** Your team fails to stop the enemy repairing the Crane. Part 2 of this mission continues....

**Core Objective 2 (again):** Your team fails to stop the Maintenance Bot, and it successfully opens the Resistance Garage. Part 4 of this mission now begins....

### Completed!

The match completes if you stop the enemy from completing any Core Objective by the time the timer reaches zero.

### Unsuccessful!

Resistance forces lose if the enemy successfully delivers the Sample to the Extraction Point, before the timer ticks down.

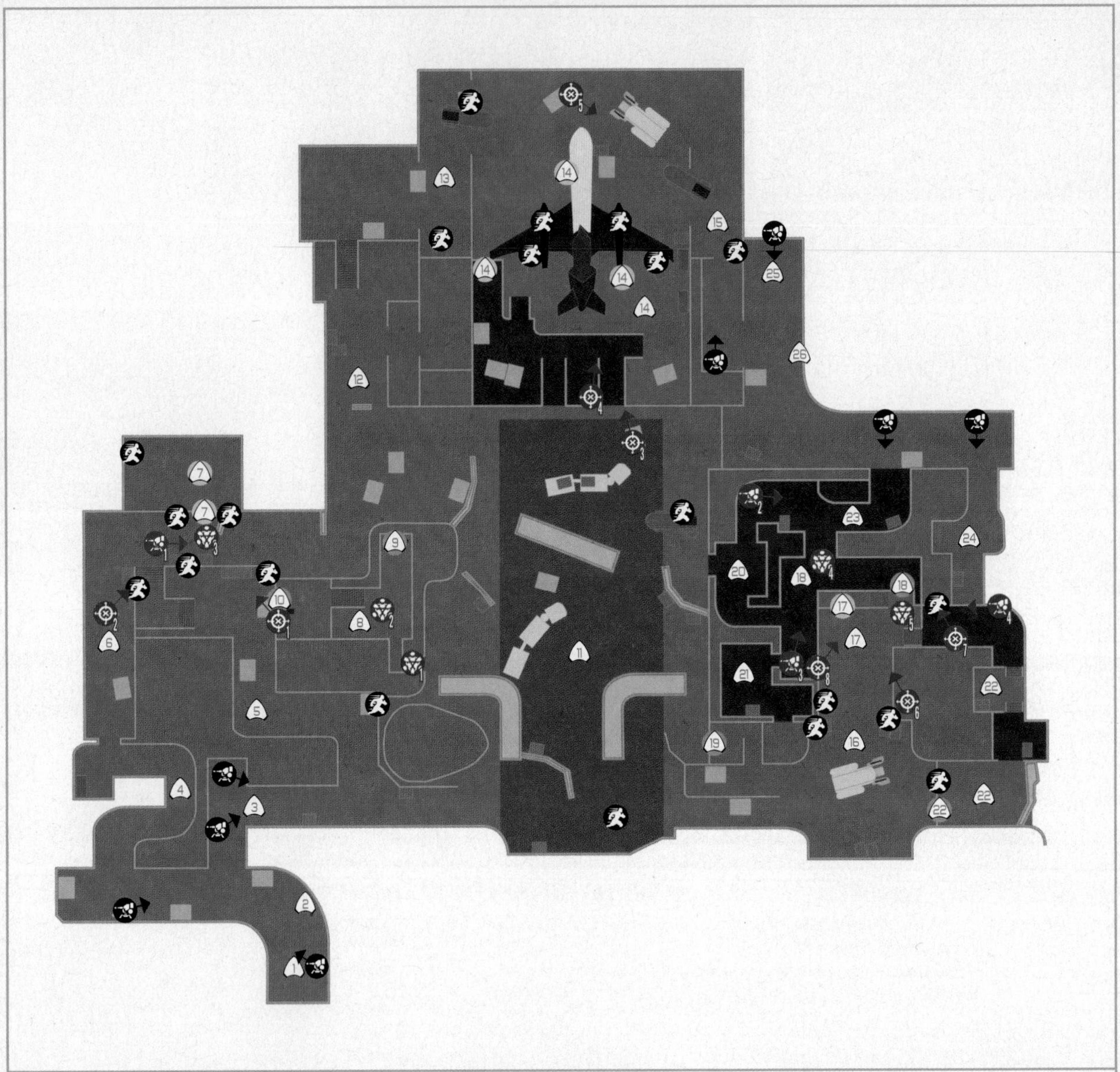

## MAP LEGEND

### ↘Refuel: Core Objective 1

1: Resistance Deployment Zone : West Jetty [F10] (Lvl. 1)
2: Resistance Command Post (Lvl. 1)
3: Storage Corridors F11 to F14 (Lvl. 1)
4: Storage Corridors F12 to F13 and Security Booth (Lvls. 1 & 2)
5: Sunken Storage Depot Road and Ramps (Lvls. 1 & 2)
6: Raised Storage Depot Road (Lvl. 2)
7: Storage Depot Door F31, Hydraulic Fluid, and Pathway (Lvl. 2)
8: Nimbus Airways Storage Building F40 to F41 (Lvls. 2 & 3)
9: Health Command Post (Lvl. 2)
10: MG Nest (Lvl. 3)
11: Maintenance Yard and Taxiway (Lvl. 2)
12: Main Cargo Corridor and Hangar Side Entrance (Lvls. 1 & 2)
13: Hangar 18: Petrol Truck Corridor F03 (Lvls. 1 & 2)
14: Hangar 18 F02 (Lvls. 1 & 2)
15: Hangar 18: Petrol Truck Corridor F01 (Lvls. 1 & 2)
16: ND Parcel Handling: Cargo Bay Entrance (Lvls. 1 & 2)
17: ND Parcel Handling: Warehouse and Robotic Arm F24 (Lvls. 1 & 2)
18: ND Parcel Handling: Warehouse Overlook and MG Nest (Lvl. 2)
19: Supply Command Post F23 (Lvl. 1)
20: ND Parcel Handling: Interior Corridor F25 (Lvl. 2)
21: ND Parcel Handling: Interior Corridor F22 (Lvl. 2)
22: ND Parcel Handling: Lower Corridor F25, Cordoned-off Bay, and MG Nest (Lvl. 1)
23: ND Parcel Handling: Interior Corridor F21 and Security Booth (Lvl. 2)
24: ND Parcel Handling: Interior Corridor and Drop F20 (Lvls. 1 & 2)
25: Security Deployment Zone: Security Station AP03 (Lvl. 2)
26: Security Command Post (Lvl. 2)

S.M.A.R.T. Move
Engineer Mine (Optimal Placement)
Engineer Turret (Optimal Placement)
Camping Spot
Deployment Zone Turret (Invulnerable)
Core Objective Location
Secondary Objective Location
Critical Path (Route)

BRINK

## ↘ Refuel: Overview Map

# DAY 8: AIRBORNE

FREEPLAY: REFUEL   SECURITY CAMPAIGN—WHAT-IF: GRAND THEFT AERO

## 22:46 Approaching Airport West Jetty

MISSION TIME (COb 1): 08:00
MISSION TIME (COb 2): +05:00
MISSION TIME (COb 3): +05:00
MISSION TIME (COb 4): +05:00
MISSION TIME (COb 5): +05:00

### Brother Chen: Briefing

This is it, brothers. Now we have a NavComputer, our destination, and our pilot. Our plane is nearly ready to fly! But Mokoena's learned of our plans, and a Security raid is incoming. Brothers, this is our final chance to escape the Ark, and contact the outside world: Get that plane in the air! All our efforts have led up to this—DON'T FAIL NOW!

### Optimal Class Numbers

| | COb 1 | COb 2 | COb 3 | COb 4 | COb 5 |
|---|---|---|---|---|---|
| Soldier | [4] | [3] | [1] | [3] | [2] |
| Medic | [2] | [2] | [2] | [2] | [1] |
| Engineer | [1] | [1] | [1] | [1] | [4] |
| Operative | [1] | [2] | [4] | [2] | [1] |

### Objectives (Resistance)

- Core Objective 1: Destroy the Storage Depot Door
- Core Objective 2: Deliver the Hydraulic Fluid
- Core Objective 3: Hack the Warehouse Controls
- Core Objective 4: Deliver the Avionics
- Core Objective 5: Repair the Fuel Pump
- Escort Core Objective Class Teammate
- Capture the Health Command Post
- Capture the Supply Command Post
- Construct the Nimbus MG Nest
- Construct the Warehouse MG Nest
- Construct the Fence MG Nest

## Important Locations

### 1 Resistance Deployment Zone: West Jetty [F10] (Lvl. 1)

This exterior, L-shaped dock has a Command Post ahead of your spawning location, and two entrances after the turn, along the far wall: storage corridors that allow your team to split up and head toward the first Core Objective at the Storage Depot, or onto the main Taxiway and Hangar 18 beyond.

**Learn the layout of this facility by eyeballing the numbers of each building's garage door. For example, the initial storage corridors are labeled "F11" and "F12." Remember these so you know immediately which route goes where.**

TIP

### 2 Resistance Command Post (Lvl. 1)

Change your weapons and your class type at this location. This is advisable later in the mission when other classes become more important.

### 3 Storage Corridors F11 to F14 (Lvl. 1)

This L-shaped corridor has two sentry guns to dissuade enemy intrusion, and an exit that leads to the Sunken Storage Depot Road and Ramps, as well as a ramp up onto the main Taxiway. This is the slower of the two routes to the Storage Depot, but it allows access to the fortified Nimbus Airways Storage Building.

### 4 Storage Corridors F12 to F13 & Security Booth (Lvls. 1 & 2)

The other accessible corridor from the Resistance deployment area winds past an inaccessible Security Booth, up some steps, around and then out onto the Raised Storage Depot Road. If you're attempting an early charge on the Storage Depot Door, this is the quickest route.

### 5 Sunken Storage Depot Road & Ramps (Lvls. 1 & 2)

This links the Storage Corridor at F14 to both the Taxiway Maintenance Yard and the Storage Depot area. This exterior road is enclosed on both sides, with the exception of some scattered crates you can jump on. It ends with a double ramp up to the Storage Depot Pathway and Core Objective. Beware of enemies in this area on the pathway, because they have a height advantage; there's also an MG Nest at the upper window of the Nimbus Airways Storage Building to contend with. Expect major fighting during the first part of this mission.

### S.M.A.R.T. Moves

Use this crate to clamber up onto the raised Taxiway, sneaking around between the silo and Nimbus building.

Use the crates to leap up and over the railing of the Storage Depot Pathway, or for a quick climb into the Nimbus doorway.

You can vault up over the railing and onto the Raised Storage Depot Road, too.

### 6 Raised Storage Depot Road (Lvl. 2)

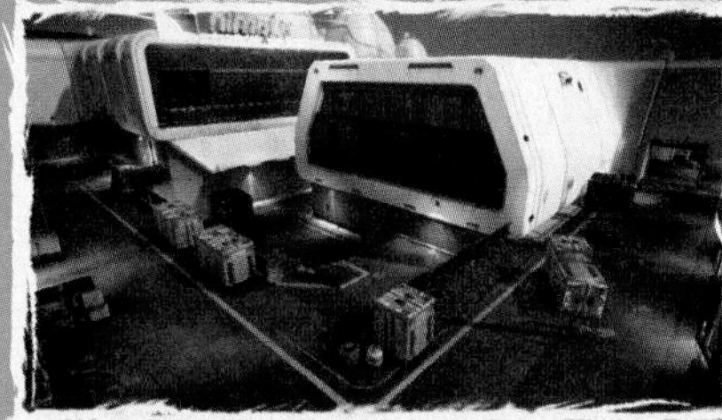

This leads from Storage Corridor F13 toward the Storage Depot Door. Climb the crates for extra height, or hide behind them during combat. This affords an excellent view of the Sunken Storage Depot Road and Ramps, and is a great location for mounting an attack on the Depot Door. Watch for a large-scale enemy presence in this area.

###  7 Storage Depot Door F31, Hydraulic Fluid, & Pathway (Lvl. 2)

The Industrial Liquid Storage Depot Building sits on a raised pathway above the Sunken Road and adjacent to the Nimbus Building. Surrounded by crates, the Depot Door is usually fortified by enemy forces almost immediately (foes don't usually fortify areas farther away because there are so many routes to reach this location), so expect a constant battle at this point. A Soldier needs to set an explosive charge at this door to complete the first Core Objective. Once the door has been blown off, the second Core Objective—the Hydraulic Fluid—is inside the one-room building itself.

## S.M.A.R.T. Moves

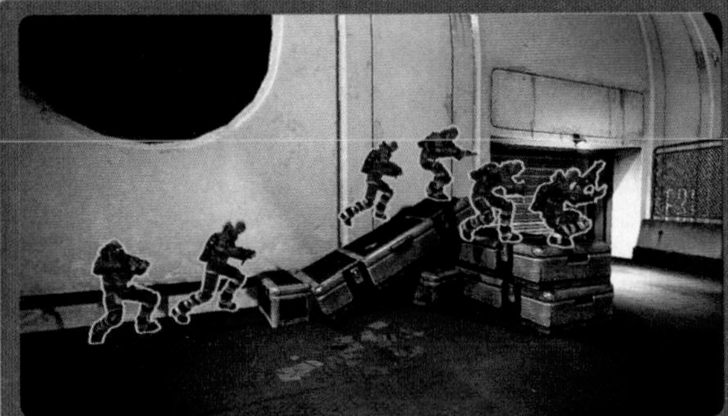

Hide behind the metal crates scattered around the outside of the door or climb atop them for a better view.

Do the same on the single fence section above the concrete barrier just to the right of the door.

The barrels inside the Storage Room are good to hide behind (for friends and foes), as is the shelving on the far wall.

## 8 Nimbus Airways Storage Building F40 to F41 (Lvls. 2 & 3)

## 9 Health Command Post (Lvl. 2)

## 10 MG Nest (Lvl. 3)

This important structure has a Nimbus Airways logo affixed to the roof so you can tell where it is. Not only does it offer you protection during the first and second Core Objectives (as an alternate route toward the Storage Depot or Hangar 18), but it houses a Health Command Post and MG Nest, both of which are extremely helpful to your team. The building is a simple zigzagging corridor, with a stairwell in the middle up to the MG Nest. Doorway F40 is accessed via the Taxiway (around from the silo if you're sneaking in). Doorway F41 is on the Storage Depot Pathway.

The Health Command Post is tucked into a cubbyhole near the staircase. Use the nearby stack of metal containers as an ambush point, or to cover a teammate hacking the post.

The MG Nest is at the top of the steps, and once built, it provides excellent covering fire over the Storage Depot and routes to reach it, including the Sunken Road and Ramps. Just watch for foes attacking from behind, and note that you can fire regular weapons just as effectively from this vantage point, or drop out of the window if necessary.

## 11 Maintenance Yard & Taxiway (Lvl. 2)

The largest open-air location, and the main hub of the Depot, this cluttered Taxiway provides ongoing opportunities for combat, and for lining up defenses to keep the enemy at bay or push them back as the mission progresses. There are access routes everywhere; the ramp (and sneaky crate entrance via the broken railing) at one end of the Sunken Storage Depot Road; the Nimbus building; the Main Cargo Corridor and Hangar front entrance; two of the ND Parcel building entrances (F25 and F22) and a second ramp leading down to the ND Parcel Cargo Bay Entrance. The many scattered vehicles, concrete barriers, and larger white-and-red barricades are excellent places to hide and attack from.

## S.M.A.R.T. Moves

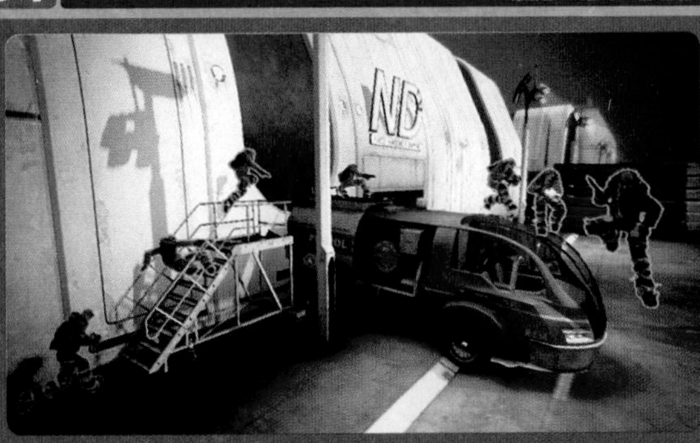


Climb the yellow steps and petrol truck for a better view inside Hangar 18.

Climb on the overturned aircraft docking steps for a better view of the Cargo Bay entrance.

## 12 Main Cargo Corridor & Hangar Side Entrance (Lvls. 1 & 2)

When your team attempts to outflank the enemy guarding the Hangar, this is the route to take. It is also a thoroughfare when the enemy tries to stop the breach of the Storage Depot earlier in this mission. Running from the Nimbus building and Storage

Depot Pathway alongside Hangar 18, this has two access doors (F03, and a half-open garage door to slide under), with a lower loading bay at the base of the steps. The numerous concrete barriers and crates make good cover.

## 13 Hangar 18: Petrol Truck Corridor F03 (Lvls. 1 & 2)

This is also used to outflank the enemy inside the Hangar. It is a two-level side corridor with a top entrance (F03) leading to the Main Cargo Corridor, and a bottom garage door to slide under, which is adjacent to a parked petrol truck and access into the Hangar itself. Don't overlook this access point!

 **S.M.A.R.T. Moves** 

Use the blue, unextended cherry picker to leap from the lower part of the corridor to the upper part.

Take cover at the crate pallet next to the petrol truck, or climb on it, then onto the truck itself.

##  Hangar 18 F02 (Lvls. 1 & 2)

The Hangar becomes an important location during Part 3, and for the rest of the mission. This large chamber houses a plane in which the Resistance is set to make its escape. Surrounding the plane are all manner of containers, crates, and refueling couplings. The main stepped entrance to Hangar 18 (F02) is off the Taxiway and likely to be heavily guarded. Two side entrances to the Hangar's rear each lead to a Petrol Truck Corridor (F03 and F01). Expect constant enemy incursions in this room, emanating from the F01 Corridor accessed via the two open garage doors to the right and rear of the chamber.

The Hydraulic Fluid is delivered to a pumping tank just right of the rear of the plane (Part 3). Once the Avionics Computer has been hacked (Part 4) over inside the ND Parcel Warehouse where the Robotic Arm is located, the Avionics are brought back into Hangar 18 (Part 5), and inserted into a side panel near the yellow steps on the left side of the plane, near the cockpit. Finally (Part 6), the nearby Fuel Pumps are repaired to complete this mission.

 **S.M.A.R.T. Moves** 

The two blue cherry pickers are both accessible from the wings of the plane, and offer a good vantage point, although you're prone.

The fuselage of the plane can't be leapt up, but the side storage shelving can, as well as the number of container pallets.

##  Hangar 18: Petrol Truck Corridor F01 (Lvls. 1 & 2)

This is a highly dangerous area for Resistance forces. The upper section is inaccessible, and enemies drop down from this point, adjacent to the Security Deployment Zone. Avoid or trap this area.

##  ND Parcel Handling: Cargo Bay Entrance (Lvls. 1 & 2)

This is one of two main routes to reach the Warehouse and Robotic Arm inside the ND Parcel Handling and Shipping building. Accessed via a ramp from the Taxiway (or a rarely used Cordoned-off Bay and MG Nest), this area sees fierce resistance during Parts 3 and 4, when the Avionics Computer is hacked and the components stolen. Drop down from the doorway of Interior Corridor F22, which is a good place to fire down from. You can also access the Supply Command Post corridor (F23) at the base of the ramp. Although you can't climb the white fire suppressant vehicle outside, it makes good cover.

HISTORY OF THE ARK
CHARACTER CREATION
GAMEPLAY
WEAPONS DETAIL
CAMPAIGN
Getting Answers
Breakout
Chen's Plans
Black Box
Attack on CCity
Airborne
Operation Babel
Critical Reaction
CHALLENGES
APPENDICES

### S.M.A.R.T. Moves

Leap on the container pallet below the ramp, grab the side railings of the ramp, and vault over.

Use the metal boxes on the left side of the cargo warehouse door as stepping stones up to the F22 corridor entrance.

The mesh fence with the MG Nest on the other side (near the inaccessible F55 door) is easily scrambled over.

## 17 ND Parcel Handling: Warehouse & Robotic Arm F24 (Lvls. 1 & 2)

## 18 ND Parcel Handling: Warehouse Overlook & MG Nest (Lvl. 2)

This interior chamber has a sloping floor leading to a computer terminal on a raised stepped area. This terminal (hacked during Part 4) controls the release of a Robotic Arm holding an Avionics Computer, which must be carried to the plane in Hangar 18 (Part 5). The arm is attached to the ceiling of this chamber, which is a confluence of passageways. No fewer than five routes reach this location: The first is via the exterior cargo bay and doorway F24.

Above the Warehouse and Robotic Arm floor is an L-shaped Overlook balcony with three separate entrances, all leading to different Interior Corridors within the ND Parcel Handling structure. Beware the MG Nest on the balcony during Parts 4 and 5 of the mission. Security forces approach from behind it, and it provides no line of site for you to cover your teammate at the objective. Steps to the side of the Warehouse lead to a hole in the ceiling, and a wrap-around passageway that leads outside to the Cordoned-off Bay and MG Nest; this is an alternate route into the Warehouse, too.

Fighting occurs on both floors, although usually most foes drop down from the Interior Corridor and Drop F20 that leads from Security's second deployment zone.

### S.M.A.R.T. Moves

Climbing between the floors is encouraged; step on the boxes and up onto a narrow balcony to the right of the main entrance.

Use the refueling trolley to reach the wall of storage containers, and climb up onto the balcony Overlook.

Stand atop the cabinet between the two sets of stairs, and wait to ambush an enemy dropping in from above or using the stairs.

## 19 Supply Command Post F23 (Lvl. 1)

This L-shaped lower-level corridor ends at the Supply Command Post. This location can be accessed at any time (and is usually overrun by the enemies first). It's particularly helpful if you need to switch classes to become an Operative, prior to hacking the computer inside the adjacent Warehouse during Part 4. Don't overlook this dead-end location, which can also be a reasonable hiding place unless you're overwhelmed.

## 20 ND Parcel Handling: Interior Corridor F25 (Lvl. 2)

Accessed via the open Maintenance Yard and Taxiway, look for the ND Parcel sign above the door, and the number (F25) to the right. Inside is a passage to the right, leading almost directly to the Warehouse Overlook and MG Nest. To the left, the corridor connects to the Interior Corridor F21 and Security Booth, which is dangerously close to the enemy's deployment zone. Use this corridor to quickly reach the Warehouse, or to head from there to the Hangar.

### ND Parcel Handling: Interior Corridor F22 (Lvl. 2)

This slightly safer, U-shaped corridor runs from the upper part of the Cargo Bay above the Supply Command Post, around and into the Warehouse Overlook and MG Nest. It provides another escape route to or from the Warehouse.

### ND Parcel Handling: Lower Corridor F25, Cordoned-off Bay, & MG Nest (Lvl. 1)

Not to be confused with the other doorway marked "F25," this area consists of an interior corridor that wraps around and into the Warehouse, and an exterior courtyard with a mesh fence, adjacent to the Cargo Bay. You can build the MG Nest to defend the Warehouse attackers, and this is another optional route into the Warehouse. However, the MG Nest is not defensively useful for Resistance because Security have no reason to leave the Warehouse, and they can easily sneak up behind anyone using it. The connecting corridor has a hole in the roof that enemies drop in from, making this a high-trafficked area during the latter parts of this mission.

### ND Parcel Handling: Interior Corridor F21 & Security Booth (Lvl. 2)

You'll know when you've run too far into enemy territory; the inaccessible Security Booth with the Ark logo on it is just around the corner from the Security Deployment Zone and a sentry gun that can cut you down in seconds. Foes use this corridor to reach the Warehouse, so keep them at bay at the Overlook entrance or the connecting Corridor F25.

### ND Parcel Handling: Interior Corridor & Drop F20 (Lvls. 1 & 2)

This is an inaccessible corridor (unless you reach the Security Deployment Zone and somehow enter the doorway marked "F20"). Enemies use it to quickly reach the Warehouse or as a route across to the Taxiway. It features a hole that foes drop down, which cannot be climbed by Resistance forces.

### Security Deployment Zone: Security Station AP03 (Lvl. 2)

Enemy forces spawn in this location, and have a choice of three doorways to maneuver through en route to whichever hotspot is most active. You can stumble into this area via the ND Parcel Handling Corridors, which isn't recommended, because you'll be cut to ribbons. But study the map to see the various routes the enemies are likely to take.

### Security Command Post (Lvl. 2)

This Command Post is utilized by enemy forces, and should be ignored by Resistance personnel.

## Objective Tactics: Core Objective 1

### Destroy the Storage Depot Door

Spawn Point to Door: 00:18

Time to Open the Door: 00:10

Time to Plant Explosives: 00:07

Time to Disarm Explosives: 00:05

Countdown to Explosion: 00:40

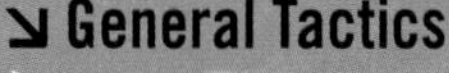

### General Tactics

Speed and a thorough knowledge of the map are needed for this Depot Door destruction. There are three possible routes to the Storage Depot Door F31

and Pathway, and splitting your team to run in from two directions not only causes the enemy to try to tackle both teams, but gives one of your teams a fighting chance to reach the location. The optimal route is to send your fastest Soldier up Storage Corridor F12, across the Raised Storage Depot Road, and to the Depot Door.

After reaching the location, lob a Molotov so it explodes at the corner of the Main Cargo Corridor, deterring any enemy counter-rush. Do this as you arrive at the door, then instantly plant the explosives. At this point, team reinforcements should have arrived, ideally via the Nimbus Building, and the Main Cargo Corridor and Taxiway approaches should be bristling with mines and turrets. The rest of your team should have captured the Health Command Post, and be guarding from the MG Nest windows; Engineers are a good bet to hold the Nimbus building by placing mines and turrets.

**Shave off seconds with the Sprinting Grenade Universal Ability, which allows you to lob the Molotov while keeping your speed up. Also, don't worry about capturing the Supply Command Post at this time; it's too far from your deployment zone and easily re-captured; expend the manpower at the Depot, and if you need more ammunition, remember to choose Supply Max Increase and Resupply Rate Increase Abilities.**

TIP

## Routes to the Depot Door

**Raised Storage Depot Road:** This is much quicker than taking the Storage Corridor F11 from your spawn, and keeps you at the same height as the enemy. Soldiers should run down here with a Medic and Engineer backing them up.

**Sunken Storage Depot Road:** Choose this once the enemy is wise to this optimal plan, because this winding route brings you up to the ramped section under the Nimbus MG Nest much later; you may need to start a battle without a clamped explosive if your bomber chose this path.

**Nimbus Building:** Enter the building via the Taxiway entrance, and hold it with three or four of your teammates. The defenses around here should be bristling, with mines at the doorways, a turret guarding the Health Command Post, and the MG Nest under your supervision. Without height, health, and rapid-fire emplacements, the enemy will falter.

## Automated Ordnance

Remember the enemy has their own Engineer emplacements, which you should also read up on. The following are examples; feel free to figure out your own favorite locations.

Protect the bomb placement area, and cut down foes rushing you, by setting a turret here.

Mine the entrance doorways to the Nimbus building; especially this one from the Taxiway, because there aren't usually any teammates in this immediate area.

## Automated Ordnance (continued)

2 Set a mine at the base of the stairs, but on the corridor to the Health Command Post, so both are trapped, and no foes sneak in and up to the MG Nest.

3 During a lull in the fighting, drop a mine here so those trying to defuse the Depot Door are caught.

## Sniper's Ally: Camping Spots

1 Cover the bomb site and keep the enemy from using the MG Nest at this location.

2 You're never flanked, can see all the routes, and have a good shot at the Main Cargo Corridor exit. Stand atop the crates on the Raised Storage Depot Road.

# Objective Tactics: Core Objective 2

### Deliver the Hydraulic Fluid

Spawn Point to Storage Depot: 00:18

Storage Door to Fluid Receptacle: 00:14

Time to Deliver the Fluid: 00:05

### General Tactics

This task gets progressively trickier the longer you leave the enemy to their own devices, which is usually to set up some bristling defenses that are difficult to push through, especially when you're carrying the Hydraulic Fluid, or trying to pour it into the receptacle. For this reason, a Light Body Type teammate should grab the Hydraulic Fluid, rush the Hangar, and deliver it on your team's first attempt.

Normally though, it's a little trickier than that. The enemy can reach the Hangar twice as fast as you, so countering and cracking their defenses are your options. Tool up your Operatives and Engineers with sniper rifles, grenades, and fast-firing, high-capacity, and fully automatic guns. Operatives with EMP Grenades are a great choice to knock out the mines and turrets for long enough to rip a hole in the Security defenses. Follow up the EMPs with rapid-fire weaponry, and snipers on the high ground above the entrance, and Engineers dropping your own mines and turrets once the area is clear. Then bring in the runner to pour in the Hydraulic Fluid.

A final plan is to use the Hangar's side entrance, by rushing the Main Cargo Corridor, and through the Petrol Truck Corridor F03 to emerge in the rear of the Hangar. Either as a team, or splitting your forces and catching foes with this outflank, tear through to the fluid receptacle.

### Sniper's Ally: Camping Spots

3 Most of your long-range attacks are from cover behind the crates above the Hangar entrance.

### Sniper's Ally: Camping Spots (continued)

4 Creep forward for a more comprehensive view (and aiming) of the entire Hangar. Crouch behind the low metal walls atop the ramps and cover your carriers.

5 If the enemies don't take the side entrance seriously, take cover behind the crate in front of the plane, and drop enemies as they emerge from their spawn point.

## Objective Tactics: Core Objective 3

### Hack the Warehouse Controls

Spawn Point to Warehouse Controls: 00:13

Hangar 18 to Warehouse Controls: 00:16

Time to Hack the Controls: 00:48

### General Tactics

Secure the Warehouse with two levels of defense and cut enemy supply lines to complete this Core Objective. While not as tricky as Core Objective 2, this is still a hard-fought slog, and impossible if your team is disjointed. So shelve sniper weaponry in favor of suppression tactics; have Medics and Soldiers working in unison to ensure the team is well, and well-supplied with ammo, respectively. This helps negate the lengthy travel times to the Cargo Bay entrance. The exact plans for securing this area are shown below.

There is an easy way to complete this Core Objective, but only if you're confident that your team is set to complete Core Objective 2 and deliver the Hydraulic Fluid. Have an Operative race to the Warehouse controls, and start the hack the moment the Hydraulic Fluid has been delivered. It's challenging because of your proximity to the enemy deployment zone, but if you're lucky, you can finish the hack before the enemy regroups, or even realizes what you're up to!

### Route Suppression

**ND Parcel Shutdown:** The first part of your Security force shutdown is to take away their balcony overlooking the Warehouse. Use the Taxiway entrance to the ND Parcel building, or climb the containers inside the Warehouse, and set up a sizable array of turrets and mines in the connecting corridors and balcony itself. Leave two or three teammates (with a Medic) to tend to these defenses and fire on the foes.

**F20 Corridor Drop:** This leaves the side corridor and drop; the enemy should try to use this as their upper location is suppressed. Because the drop down is blind, your soldiers (or Engineer's automated weaponry) can rake them from either side of the drop. With both chokepoint routes suppressed, the enemy either presents less of a threat, or tries to rush around through the Hangar and into the ND Parcel building, or all the way around to the Cargo Bay. Either of these routes gives your Operative time to finish the hacking.

**Warehouse Overlook Flanking:** Light Body Types can Mantle over the fences where the MG Nest is stationed, and rush through Interior Corridor F25. This links to the Security's F20 Corridor Drop from their spawn and the side of the Warehouse interior, allowing you to set mines or turrets, or attack from this flanking location.

## Automated Ordnance

2 Drop a turret here to cover Interior Corridor F21 and Security Booth, forcing foes into a firefight as they leave their spawn. Back this turret up with your own weapons, and stay here to guard.

3 Try a second turret at this entrance to the Warehouse balcony, so the foes are mown down, but can't easily lob a grenade at this turret.

4 Set a turret in this side corridor under the enemy's drop, next to your camping spot; two blasts of automatic gunfire are better than one!

4 Back up the ND Parcel Building turrets with a mine at each balcony entrance. This should persuade them to pick a different incursion route!

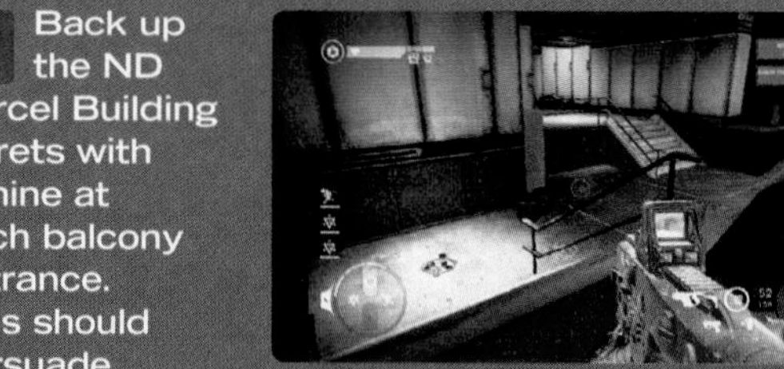

5 Drop a mine here near the Operative's hacking to provide a last line of defense in case a foe gets through.

## Sniper's Ally: Camping Spots

6 Wall-jump to the MG Nest area of the balcony after climbing up to this corner, where you can edge forward and cover the Operative.

7 Cut down foes as they drop through the hole above you; blasting from both directions catches them in a confused crossfire.

8 Stand at the balcony corner to catch foes dropping down the side corridor in crossfire, and anyone managing to stagger in from your ND Parcel defenses.

# Objective Tactics: Core Objective 4

## Deliver the Avionics

Spawn Point to Avionics: 00:23

Warehouse Controls to Avionics: 00:25

Time to Access Avionics: 00:05

### General Tactics

During the final seconds of the previous Core Objective, if your Operative is sure he'll be successful, charge toward Hangar 18, putting into practice all of the tactics you learned the first time you attacked this location. Consult Core Objective 2, because all the tactics apply here, too.

Because it takes a long time to get from your spawn point to the delivery location (on the side of the plane, toward the left rear side of the Hangar), try to push through on your first try. If not, teamwork and good communications are needed. The delivery point is on the other side of the plane, so you may wish to use the Main Cargo Corridor and side entrance into the Hangar, although this gives the enemy more time to prepare for your assault.

**Make sure one of your Medics has the Speed Boost Ability and he uses it on your Avionics carrier; if that carrier is a Light Body Type, he'll travel even faster!**

TIP

**The Automated Ordnance and Sniper's Ally: Camping Spots locations you utilized during Core Objective 2 apply here.**

NOTE

# Objective Tactics: Core Objective 5

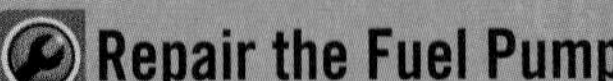

## Repair the Fuel Pump

Spawn Point to Fuel Pump: 00:22

Avionics to Fuel Pump: 00:03

Time to Repair: 00:10

### General Tactics

This objective is a little easier to accomplish than previous ones, and it requires a distinct lack of subtlety. Simply throw as many Engineers as your team can spawn into Hangar 18, and have them convene at the Fuel Pump attached to the low balcony. Repairing an object can't be "undone" (unlike hacking), which means that your Engineers can stay pinned to the objective, even while shrugging off enemy fire, before another Engineer continues the progress.

If your enemy is onto this less-than-cunning plan, try something involving actual teamwork. Back up your Engineers with some heavy-weapon Soldiers or Medics, and figure out an assault plan:

### Refuel Rampage

**Full Frontal Assault:** Attack the front of the Hangar with all of your team at more or less the same time; burst through enemy defenses with a combination of bravery and firepower. Have the meatier members of your team fight on the opposite side from the Fuel Pump, while the Engineers tinker away.

**Down the Front, Round the Back:** The other option is a two or three-pronged approach. Bring some firepower to bear via the front, but also send some troops down the Main Cargo Corridor and through the Petrol Truck Corridor F03, to outflank. Then have a single, annoying teammate creep to the deployment zone exit of Interior Corridor F21 to begin a spot of spawn-camping. Sneak Engineers through during the mayhem.

**NOTE**

The Automated Ordnance and Sniper's Ally: Camping Spots locations you utilized during Core Objective 2 apply here.

**CAUTION**

Engineers should be fixing the Fuel Pump over setting up defenses; the rest of your team should supply the firepower.

## Objective Tactics: Secondary Objectives

### Escort Core Objective Class Teammate

**Official Escort Info:** Follow a Soldier to back them up during the door removal in Part 1. For the remaining Core Objectives, use more general tactics to back up your teammates, as described in the other Objectives, and below.

**Unofficial Escort Info:** Taking a second player with you on a joint sortie allows you to try out the usual pairings (Soldier and Medic, two Engineers, Operative and Soldier, or Operative and Medic). During Part 1, you can approach from disparate routes, and quickly ascertain the enemy threats to relay back to the rest of your team while catching Security forces in your crossfire. In Part 2, follow the Hydraulic Fluid carrier, and pick up the item if he falls or heal him. At the Warehouse, cover the Operative, or double up to speed the hacking. During the final push, double Engineers with your team covering them are twice as likely to finish the fight in your favor.

###   Capture the Health Command Post

 Engineer & Operative Advantage!

Spawn Point to Command Post: 00:12 

Time to Claim Command Post: 00:10

This post is within the Nimbus building, which is accessed during the first Core Objective by the team wanting the MG Nest or a quick route to the Depot Door. During this time, the team that succeeds in capturing this usually holds the Command Post too. Try to take this and the MG Nest, but not at the expense of wasting time (or team members) detonating that door! During later Core Objectives, veer into this location en route to the Warehouse or Hangar, if you're an Engineer, and if the Command Post has fallen to the opposition.

###   Capture the Supply Command Post

 Engineer & Operative Advantage!

Spawn Point to Command Post: 00:16 

Time to Claim Command Post: 00:10 

Don't forget about this until you're entering the Cargo Bay and assaulting the Warehouse, because the enemy is likely to already be enjoying the post's benefits. Instead, while you're mainly engaged in combat at the Depot Door, have an Engineer separate and dash to this post, claiming (and upgrading) it, before setting a mine on the ground in front of the terminal, and a turret covering the door, if you can spare one. Then use this to change to Operatives when you require hacking inside the Warehouse.

### Construct the Nimbus MG Nest

### Construct the Warehouse MG Nest

### Construct the Fence MG Nest

| Engineer |
|---|
| Spawn Point to Nimbus MG Nest: 00:16 |
| Spawn Point to Warehouse MG Nest: 00:23 |
| Spawn Point to Fence MG Nest: 00:22 |
| Time to Construct: 00:04 |

The Nimbus MG Nest overlooks the Sunken Storage Depot Road and the Storage Depot Door; making it a prime site for both teams. Should this fall into enemy hands, your team is under fire and easily overrun while defending the Depot Door, so either deal with the gunner using sharpshooting or grenades, or station a couple of your teammates inside the Nimbus building to guard the MG Nest, use it on the opposition, and claim (and keep) the Health Command Post.

The shallow aiming pitch and yaw of the weapon means it's only suitable for wounding foes at the Warehouse door, and partway down into the Warehouse itself. If you're using that entrance, and the MG Nest is active, avoid this entrance, or lob a grenade to take out the gunner. You can also approach from the ND Parcel Interior Corridors and wipe the gunner out. This isn't to be fixed unless the foes are using this garage entrance too.

The main purpose of the Fence MG is to slaughter your own troops as they dash down the outside Cargo Bay ramp. Building this, aside from the XP, nets you little benefit, but allows the enemy instant access to a rapid-fire weapon that's quickly turned on you. Are the enemies using the ramp? Then fix this MG Nest. Otherwise, use the fenced wall and vehicle to hide behind and avoid the MG's bullets.

## Solo Tactics

If you're on your own, rush the Storage Door as a Light Body Type Soldier, clamp the explosives before the enemy arrives, and guard it from behind cover. Delivering the Hydraulic Fluid requires you to race around the map; use the Nimbus building and the Taxiway obstacles to recover your health, and remember that the side entrance is less well defended than the front. Switch to an Operative and prepare to assault the Warehouse, which is particularly tricky on higher difficulties, and you may need to switch back to the Engineer to lay defenses and cover a teammate instead. With the final push into Hangar 18, switch to an Engineer at either Command Post (be sure the Health Command Post is in your possession).

# Mission Completion Conditions

### Continuation...

**Core Objective 1:** Your team succeeds in destroying the Storage Depot Door. Part 2 of this mission now commences....

**Core Objective 2:** Your team succeeds in delivering the Hydraulic Fluid. Part 3 of this mission now commences....

**Core Objective 3:** Your team succeeds in hacking the Warehouse Controls. Part 4 of this mission now commences....

**Core Objective 4:** Your team succeeds in delivering the Avionics. Part 5 of this mission now commences....

### Completed!

The match completes if you successfully repair the Fuel Pump before the timer ticks down.

### Unsuccessful!

Resistance forces lose if the enemy stops you from completing any Core Objective by the time the timer reaches zero.

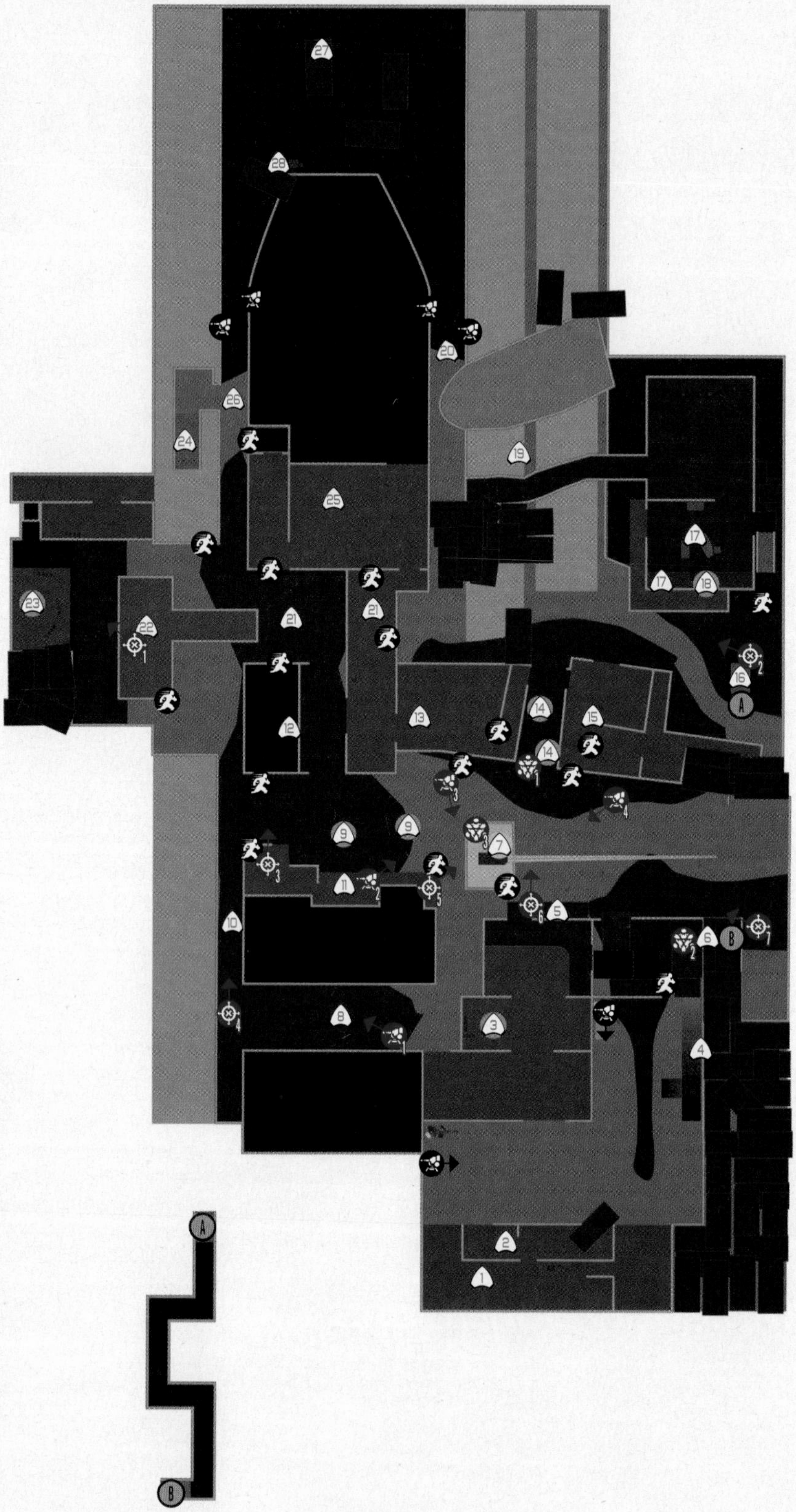

## MAP LEGEND

### Shipyard: Core Objective 1

1: Resistance Deployment Zone (Pt. 1): Rusting Shanty Hull (Lvl. 2)
2: Resistance Command Post (Pt. 1) (Lvl. 2)
3: Deano's Hull & MG Nest (Lvl. 1)
4: Metal Ramps & Low Road (Lvls. 1 & 2)
5: Pipe & Girder Overlook (Lvl. 2)
6: Subterranean Pipe Shortcut: Resistance Stairs (Lvl. 0)
7: Loading Crane Courtyard & Controls (Lvl. 1)
8: The Covered Alley (Lvls. 0 & 1)
9: The Central Alley & Side Barricade (Lvls. 0 & 1)
10: Below the Hull Thoroughfare (Lvl. 0)
11: Central Gantry Walk (Lvl. 2)
12: Main Gantry Walk (Lvl. 2)
13: Rusty Hull: Container Corridor & Barricade Overlook (Lvl. 2)
14: Rusty Hull: The Main Alley & Main Barricade (Lvl. 2)
15: Rusty Hull: Rusting Deck (Lvl. 2)
16: Subterranean Pipe Shortcut: Security Stairs (Lvl. 0)
17: Field Hospital & Lower Deck (Lvls. 1 & 3)
18: Health Command Post (Lvl. 3)
19: Drummond's Opening (Lvl. 1)
20: Drummond's Alley (Lvls. 0 & 1)
21: Anchor Chain Avenue & Gantry (Lvls. 0, 1, & 2)
22: Hull Hideout (Lvl. 1)
23: Supply Command Post Platform (Lvl. 0)
24: Cargo Railroad & Post Platform Access (Lvl. 0 & 1)
25: Tanker Quarters & Gantry Walk (Lvl. 2)
26: Tanker Alley & Quarters Entry Steps (Lvls. 0 & 1)
27: Security Deployment Zone (Pt. 1): Tanker Launch & Dock (Lvl. 0)
28: Security Command Post (Pt. 1) (Lvl. 0)

BRINK | Shipyard: Overview Map

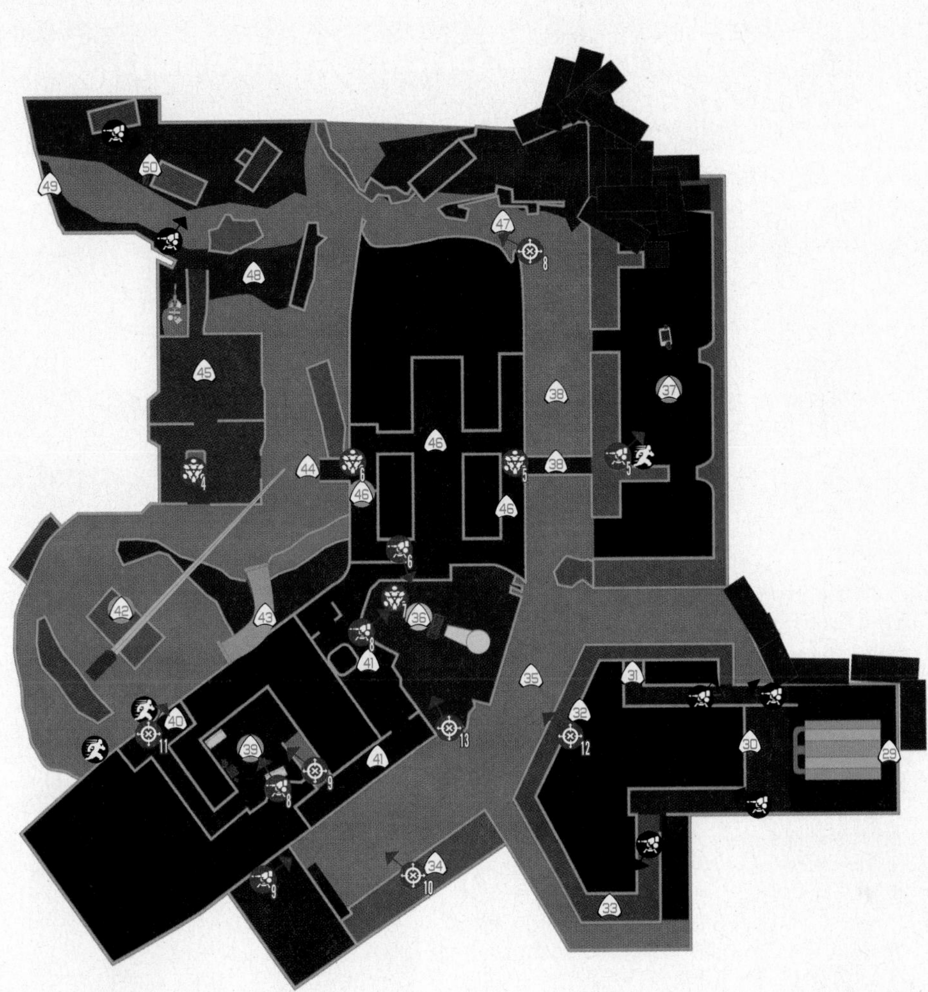

## MAP LEGEND (CONTINUED)

### Shipyard: Core Objective 2

29: Resistance Deployment Zone (Pt. 2): Hulk Turbine Room (Lvl. 1)
30: Resistance Command Post (Pt. 2) (Lvl. 1)
31: Resistance Hulk: Side Exit (Lvls. 1 & 0)
32: Resistance Hulk: Upper Gantry (Lvl. 2)
33: Resistance Hulk: Side Ramps (Lvls. 1 & 0)
34: Rusting Hull Overlook & Lower Dirt Side Path (Lvl. 1)
35: Air Defenses: Lower Dirt Path (Lvl. 0)
36: Air Defenses: Missile Courtyard (Lvl. 1)
37: Super Tanker Hold & Supply Command Post (Lvl. 1)
38: Super Tanker Bridge & Dirt Path (Port) (Lvl. 2)
39: Warship: Engine Room & Health Command Post (Lvl. 1)
40: Warship: Upper Starboard Overlook (Lvl. 2)
41: Warship: Port Overlook & Missile Courtyard Overlook (Lvl. 2)
42: Crane Controls & Yard (Lvl. 0)
43: Snaking Pipe (Lvl. 0)
44: Warship: Movable Bridge & Dirt Path (Starboard) (Lvls. 0 & 2)
45: Rusty Trawler Innards (Lvls. 1 & 2)
46: Warship: Storage Thoroughfare, MG Nest, & Port Deck (Lvl. 2)
47: Warship: Lower Dirt Path (Stern) (Lvl. 0)
48: Rusty Junk Junction (Lvl. 0)
49: Security Deployment Zone (Pt. 2): Lower Dirt Path (Lvl. 0)
50: Security Command Post (Pt. 2) (Lvl. 0)

S.M.A.R.T. Move
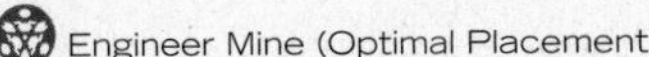
Engineer Mine (Optimal Placement)
Engineer Turret (Optimal Placement)
Camping Spot
Deployment Zone Turret (Invulnerable)
Core Objective Location
Secondary Objective Location
Critical Path (Route)
Level Link

BRINK | Shipyard: Overview Map

# WHAT-IF: OPERATION BABEL

FREEPLAY: SHIPYARD  SECURITY CAMPAIGN—DAY 6: EARLY LAUNCH

## 08:27 Secret Resistance Workshop, Breaking Yard Bay 3

MISSION TIME (COb 1): 10:00

MISSION TIME (COb 2): +10:00

### Brother Chen: Briefing

You know why the founders have never taken our demands seriously? Because we don't have a gun to their heads the way they have Security pointed at us! Well, now we do. We've secretly brought this old surface-to-surface missile system back online. Hah, this should focus the founders' minds! I've told them to disarm Security and end water rationing. If they try to take the missile from us, we'll use it. Founders' Tower is empty in any case, but its a symbol... While we have the missile, Security are powerless! Don't let them get anywhere near it!

### Optimal Class Numbers

| | COb 1 | COb 2 |
|---|---|---|
| Soldier | [3] | [3] |
| Medic | [2] | [2] |
| Engineer | [3] | [3] |
| Operative | [1] | [1] |

### Objectives (Resistance)

- Core Objective 1: Defend the Crane Controls
- Core Objective 2: Defend the Missile Controls
- Escort Core Objective Class Teammate
- Construct Main Barricade
- Construct Side Barricade
- Defend the Crane Controls
- Capture the Health Command Post
- Capture the Supply Command Post
- Construct the Crane MG Nest
- Construct the Bridge MG Nest

## Important Locations (Objective 1)

### 1 Resistance Deployment Zone (Pt. 1): Rusting Shanty Hull (Lvl. 2)

You're relatively close to the Core Objective that needs defending, as you move through and drop down from the Hull where you begin. There are a few entrances, so learn the ones that offer the most direct routes toward Deano's Hull and the Metal Ramps. Enemies are usually too preoccupied with the Crane to venture into this location, but there are turrets to see them off, if they do.

### 2 Resistance Command Post (Pt. 1) (Lvl. 2)

Your tasks are of a defensive nature, so more Engineers are necessary (to build the barriers as well as laying traps and turrets). Change here, and swap out weapons if you need to.

## 3 Deano's Hull & MG Nest (Lvl. 1)

Named for the graffiti artist who daubed his name across the wall near one exit, this is a handy defensive area, because you can fire on the enemies coming up along the Covered Alley, and rake them with MG fire. There's an exit to the alley too, or a scramble up to the Pipe and Girder Overlook next to the Crane itself. At least one or two of your team should be here, checking for foes.

## 4 Metal Ramps & Low Road (Lvls. 1 & 2)

The "other" route to take to reach the Pipe and Girder Overlook is via the Metal Ramp sections on the right side of the deployment zone. Run up, turn left, and leap the gap in the bridge to reach the Overlook itself. The Low Road running by the ramps gives easy access into the Loading Crane Courtyard, and there are sheets of metal and barrels to hide behind, if the enemy tries to advance on your spawn point.

### S.M.A.R.T. Moves

From the Low Road, climb the protruding girder and leap to the bridge to avoid using the ramp.

## 5 Pipe & Girder Overlook (Lvl. 2)

There are three different ways to reach this Overlook, which gives you excellent views of both barricades and the Crane you're defending: climb up from Deano's Hull, use the Metal Ramps and leap the bridge gap, or use the S.M.A.R.T. move shown below. Remember to step in and out of cover to avoid enemy fire, and use both balconies; the tiny one at the end of the bridge with the gap in it.

### S.M.A.R.T. Moves

Leap from the inside (or roof) of the Crane, and grab the balcony to pull yourself up and onto it.

## 6 Subterranean Pipe Shortcut: Resistance Stairs (Lvl. 0)

This shortcut allows you to venture deeper into enemy territory, because you appear in the open area near the Security forces' side of the Rusty Hull structure. More commonly, the enemy uses this shortcut to swarm into the Crane Courtyard, circumventing the barricades. Guard this area using teammates, turrets, or mines.

## 7 Loading Crane Courtyard & Controls (Lvl. 1)

This is the hub where your forces must congregate to halt the enemy from repairing the Loading Crane, and opening the giant gate (which is behind the Crane at the opposite end of the Courtyard). Expect attacks from the Main Alley and Barricade, the Central Alley and Side Barricade, and the Covered Alley, as well as sneakier infiltrations via the Subterranean Pipe Shortcut behind the Crane, close to your deployment zone.

More nimble enemies also jump the gaps between the Gantry Walks, and circumvent the barriers entirely. Watch for foes coming out of the cubbyhole to the left of the side barrier, and the Central Gantry Walk itself. Resistance forces can move up the wall to a toilet room and drop down into the Rusty Hull: Rusting Deck area to try an ambush.

Also remember the various cover options you have, ranging from the corners of the Crane and Hulk below the Pipe and Girder Overlook, the pipe section with barrels on top (which offers good coverage of the Crane and Side Barricade), and the corner under the Crane claw, where long-range sniping and ambushes can occur.

### 8 The Covered Alley (Lvls. 0 & 1)

Access the Covered Alley from the Crane Courtyard or Deano's Hull, staying at the upper end and covering the area with traps. The enemy gets frustrated if you hold them back here, because this access point is farthest from their spawn point. Push down to the Below the Hull Thoroughfare if your match is going well.

### 9 The Central Alley & Side Barricade (Lvls. 0 & 1)

Reaching this location and constructing a barricade in the fastest time is an excellent option, because the foes have a straight shot up to the Crane if you don't. Defend this area, optionally leaping up to the Central Gantry Walk to halt any of the more lithe infiltrators. Of course, you are lost if your team isn't reinforcing the Main Barricade too.

### 10 Below the Hull Thoroughfare (Lvl. 0)

This is one of the major routes the enemy takes to reach either of the two main alleys leading up and into the Crane Courtyard. It also offers access to Anchor Chain Avenue and the Supply Command Post, which is close to enemy territory (but worth having a teammate attempt to claim, while running interference). As you're defending, a long-range spotter at the far end of the Covered Alley, looking (and sniping) for foes and using the barrels as cover is a good option.

### 11 Central Gantry Walk (Lvl. 2)

### 12 Main Gantry Walk (Lvl. 2)

Scramble up near the blue barrel, on the corner of the Crane Courtyard next to the Crane itself, and you can access the Central Gantry Walk, using the rusting hull sides as cover, and shooting at the enemies attempting to enter the Central Alley.

The opposition likes to use the Main Gantry Walk as an attack point, so expect enemy activity in this area above Anchor Chain Avenue, where the toilets are. You can also reach all the nooks and crannies of the Rusty Hull, where more adept enemies tend to attack from.

#### S.M.A.R.T. Moves

Both you and the enemy can actually Wall-jump the gap between the Central and Main Gantry Walks; foes who succeed in this move can bypass the Side Barricade!

### 13 Rusty Hull: Container Corridor & Barricade Overlook (Lvl. 2)

The Resistance maneuvers into this area from the cubbyhole to the left of the Main Barricade in the Crane Courtyard. Security forces use the Main Gantry Walk area above Anchor Avenue near the toilets, and clamber up onto the container stack, and onto a balcony. From here, they can drop down into the cubbyhole, or look (and fire) into the Main Alley. Below the balcony is a side passage and exit out onto the Main Alley, too. Patrolling this area helps push back the more cunning enemies.

## S.M.A.R.T. Moves

Remember to leap or Wall-jump onto the large container and grab the balcony above, allowing access to the Barricade Overlook and Crane Yard itself! A tricky Wall-jump allows the lithe to clamber atop the platform overlooking the Crane Yard, and circumvent the Main Passage completely!

## 14 Rusty Hull: The Main Alley & Main Barricade (Lvl. 2)

At this point, your team should focus on building and guarding the barricade. Sealing this route means the enemy needs to either destroy the barricade, or use another route to reach the Crane. Be on your guard for foes circumventing the area by using the Container Corridor and Barricade Overlook to reach the cubbyhole in the Courtyard. Otherwise, don't stray too far into this Rusty Hull, because the enemy likes to congregate on the Rusting Deck.

## 15 Rusty Hull: Rusting Deck (Lvl. 2)

The enemy uses this area as a staging ground when waiting for the Main Barricade to explode. A couple of small chambers with connecting corridors lead to an exterior deck, all connecting to the Field Hospital area and Drummond's Opening, as well as Anchor Chain Avenue. You (but not the opposition) can access this area by climbing up the opening to the right of the Main Alley in the Crane Courtyard, then drop down from the toilet room at the top. Try the far end of the deck, overlooking the Subterranean Pipe Shortcut, as a sniper point.

## 16 Subterranean Pipe Shortcut: Security Stairs (Lvl. 0)

Located in the open area adjacent to the Rusting Deck, this is the exit to the Pipe Shortcut that is entered near the Metal Ramps by your deployment zone. Stand on the open hatch to gain height and cover. Remember to defend the area below from infiltrators.

## 17 Field Hospital & Lower Deck (Lvls. 1 & 3)

## 18 Health Command Post (Lvl. 3)

The enemy likes to use the severed bridge section of the Super Tanker to claim the Health Command Post inside, which is a little too far into enemy territory to be easily taken back (although one teammate can be assigned to try). The Field Hospital is accessed via an easily overlooked set of stairs near the Subterranean Pipe Hatch, although the enemy usually uses the ramp in Drummond's Opening. Check the balcony around the outside of the bridge, which foes tend to use for long-range sniping at the Rusty Hull and Main Alley. A ground-level Lower Deck route weaves under the bridge too, but doesn't connect to it.

## S.M.A.R.T. Moves

Use the edge of the Lower Deck doorway to reach the bent end of the balcony, and ascend to it.

## 19 Drummond's Opening (Lvl. 1)

## 20 Drummond's Alley (Lvls. 0 & 1)

This area's named for one of the ship sections that towers above this thoroughfare. The enemy uses this to reach both the Field Hospital (via the rickety ramp), Lower Deck (via the doorway to the left of the ramp), and the Rusty Hull area, where an assault on the Main Alley can begin. This is the farthest you need venture, because the enemy is out in force and can easily outflank you via Anchor Chain Alley. Drummond's Alley has an enemy turret, and leads directly to the enemy's spawn point.

##  21 Anchor Chain Avenue & Gantry (Lvls. 0, 1, & 2)

Look up as the path opens up to see the large rusting chain this avenue is named after. On the ground, this is a major arterial route for Security forces, because the lower end connects to Tanker Alley, the Hull Hideout, and the Below the Hull Thoroughfare. At the opposite end, Anchor Chain Avenue ascends past the chain, and a large stack of steel sheets, and opens up to the Rusty Hull and Alley.

Check out the upper Gantry too; enemies like to leap across the lower avenue from the Tanker Quarters, which allows access into the Main Gantry, the toilets area, and the Container Corridor with the Barricade Overlook. Both the Tanker and Anchor Gantries can also be accessed without leaping. Learn these initially confusing routes, because the enemy is likely to vary their tactics to make use of these upper pathways.

### S.M.A.R.T. Moves

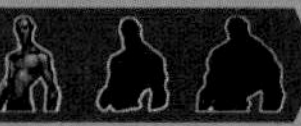

Clamber onto the steel sheet stack under the chain for a good view of the Main Alley and across to the Field Hospital.

You can expertly Wall-jump across Anchor Chain Avenue from the Main Gantry to the Tanker Gantry.

Climb the jutting pipe below the chain and ramp, and use it to climb up into the Anchor Chain Gantry and Tanker Gantry.

##  22 Hull Hideout (Lvl. 1)

At the intersection of the Tanker, Anchor Chain, and Below the Hull paths is a self-contained Hull Hideout. It features four entrances (slide under the one at the lower end of Anchor Chain Avenue). Three entrances are doorways you must climb to on each side of the structure. The upper interior simply links all four entrances. Use this area to ambush enemies, leap to the Cargo Railroad area, or provide covering fire over the Supply Command Post Platform.

> **TIP**
> The Hull Hideout is illuminated by two hanging lights, each illuminating some graffiti stencils featuring the silhouette of a monkey. Use these to situate yourself as you're finding your way about.

### S.M.A.R.T. Moves

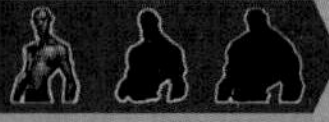

You can make the leap from the Cargo Railroad onto the metal wall with the red monkey on it, a possible ambush point. Stand on the metal lip overlooking the Below the Hull Thoroughfare for views of Anchor Chain and Central Alleys, another possible ambush spot.

### 23 Supply Command Post Platform (Lvl. 0)

This is likely to fall into enemy hands quickly, unless one of your team heads here directly. Difficult to keep, this can be accessed from the ground around the base of the Hull Hideout, as well as the Post Platform Access. Use the scenery (including the barriers) as cover, or attack from the Hull Hideout.

### 24 Cargo Railroad & Post Platform Access (Lvl. 0 & 1)

Security forces use this route as an alternative to the Tanker Alley, heading up the stairs and onto the Cargo Railroad before dropping into the Post Platform Access corridor, with a jump or a drop to reach the Supply Command Post. You might wish to lodge yourself against the cargo carriage and mow down enemies as they emerge from the stairs.

### 25 Tanker Quarters & Gantry Walk (Lvl. 2)

This is where the enemy enjoys mixing up its pathways to the Crane Courtyard. After entering this Tanker interior, you can maneuver down to Anchor Chain Avenue, or Wall-jump and land on the upper Main Gantry. You can access the Main Gantry via the toilets above the avenue, too. Don't forget you can climb up into the Tanker Quarter doorway from the lower ground area close to the Hull Hideout.

### 26 Tanker Alley & Quarters Entry Steps (Lvls. 0 & 1)

You're not likely to reach this area for long because the turrets easily dispatch you, and enemies use other routes or overwhelm you if you're pestering them from here. This long alley meets up at the Hull Hideout, but offers a scramble up into the Tanker Quarters as an alternate route. You can sidestep through the door and onto the Cargo Railroad too.

### S.M.A.R.T. Moves

Save some time and leap from the Quarters Entry Steps to the top of the Cargo Railroad.

### 27 Security Deployment Zone (Pt. 1): Tanker Launch & Dock (Lvl. 0)

The enemy has two main routes to take from the Dock: along Tanker Alley or Drummond's Alley, after which the routes split dramatically. You'll be cut down by enemy turrets before you reach here, so stay away.

### 28 Security Command Post (Pt. 1) (Lvl. 0)

This is an inaccessible Command Post, used only by Security forces.

## Important Locations
(Objective 2)

### 29 Resistance Deployment Zone (Pt. 2): Hulk Turbine Room (Lvl. 1)

Pass the giant turbine and then choose which of the three exits you want to take; this is governed by whether you're trying to hold a defensive line, going for a Command Post, or defending the Missile Controls.

## 30 Resistance Command Post (Pt. 2) (Lvl. 1)

Engineers are most beneficial when it comes to defending the Missile Controls, so plan accordingly before you leave the safety of this Hulk. Change weapons here, too.

## 31 Resistance Hulk: Side Exit (Lvls. 1 & 0)

## 32 Resistance Hulk: Upper Gantry (Lvl. 2)

## 33 Resistance Hulk: Side Ramps (Lvls. 1 & 0)

From the deployment zone, you have a choice of directions to take. Exit via the openings to your right via the ground level or a corridor directly above. This takes you quickly onto the Lower Dirt Path. Head left for a slightly longer route, past a side ramp and out onto the Lower Dirt Path near the Rusting Hull Overlook. Pick either of the gantry ramps if you wish to move to the Upper Gantry, which offers the best (and elevated) position over the Air Defenses area; a good sniping spot.

## 34 Rusting Hull Overlook & Lower Dirt Side Path (Lvl. 1)

This path allows you quick access into the Warship, and the Engine Room with the Health Command Post, as well as a route some foes try to take to reach the Missile Courtyard. The ramp and barrel platform at the far end is worth hiding near, because you can blast foes running toward the Courtyard. Or, you can cover the Engine Room from inside the Rusting Hull, which runs parallel to the dirt path, and allows you to blast away while in excellent cover. Fire from the doorway overlooking the Air Defenses area, too.

## 35 Air Defenses: Lower Dirt Path (Lvl. 0)

The lower sandy earth below the Missile Courtyard allows you to reach the Warship Engine Room to your left, or the Super Tanker Bridge and Dirt Path to the right. There's a clump of rusting defenses, and a doorway leading to a small corridor behind it that you can use as cover, but it is usually better to seek higher ground. Still, you can snipe from this cover.

## 36 Air Defenses: Missile Courtyard (Lvl. 1)

This is where your team takes its final stand: In this triangular platform, the enemy will try to hack into the Missile Controls, and you need to stop them. Knowing where the enemy appears from is a good start: Check the dirt paths on either side, and the segmented sections of Warship above and on either side of you. Foes pour out of the Storage Thoroughfare to your right, and the Missile Courtyard Overlook to your left. Remember you can ascend to these locations to try to stop the enemies overrunning the area.

Seeking cover is just as important as repelling enemies. Under both of the Warship's upper entrances is a small corridor you can hide in and ambush foes as they drop down or appear on the edge of the upper areas. The metal plates, barrels, and containers are all viable locations to hide behind, as is the missile system itself. A combination of mines, turrets, and snipers from the Resistance Hull finishes the job.

**Watch out if you're hiding below the Missile Courtyard Overlook (left side, if looking from the Resistance spawn point); there's a hole in the ceiling, and the enemy can drop a grenade in to halt your ambush.**

**CAUTION**

## 37 Super Tanker Hold & Supply Command Post (Lvl. 1)

## 38 Super Tanker Bridge & Dirt Path (Port) (Lvl. 2)

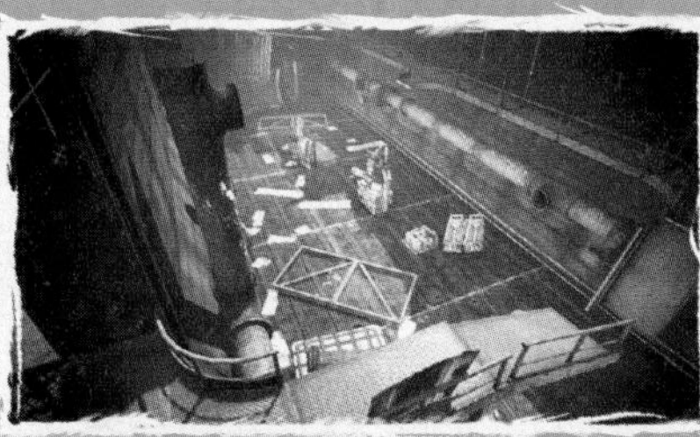

This is out of the way of the main areas of conflict, but is an important location to defend due to the Supply Command Post here. There are three entrances into this Super Tanker Hold: two via the Dirt Path and one from the Bridge above, which you can reach via the Storage Thoroughfare. Once inside, you can use the pipes and containers to clamber up to the Bridge point (if you need to fend off enemies nearby), or guard the doors by standing to one side and ambushing enemies. You can attack foes in the Dirt Path from here, too.

## 39 Warship: Engine Room & Health Command Post (Lvl. 1)

## 40 Warship: Upper Starboard Overlook (Lvl. 2)

The mangled remains of the Warship's Engine Room is a chokepoint with enemies rushing in from the Crane Yard and Snaking Pipe. Inside the location is a Health Command Post, a ramp up to the Port Overlook, and a gap to the Dirt Path where you're likely to be defending from. Try hiding in the cubbyhole on the starboard entrance behind the hull metal, across from the barrels.

There's also a ramped passage up to the Upper Starboard Overlook (hide at this entrance to ambush enemies). The Overlook itself offers protected shots down at the Crane Yard and the Snaking Pipe exit.

### S.M.A.R.T. Moves

The enemy can climb onto the balcony below the Upper Starboard Overlook, and then up into the Overlook itself, using this as an alternate route into the Engine Room.

## 41 Warship: Port Overlook & Missile Courtyard Overlook (Lvl. 2)

This is ostensibly a route for the enemy to take from the Engine Room to the Missile Courtyard, via the ramp in the Engine Room. The Overlook allows foes to drop down to the Missile Controls, into the small enclosed passage below, or across to the Storage Thoroughfare on the opposite side. Three open portholes along the way offer views down to the dirt road and into the Rusting Hull Overlook. Watch for attacks from here if you're inside the Rusting Hull; you're more exposed than you realize.

## 42 Crane Controls & Yard (Lvl. 0)

## 43 Snaking Pipe (Lvl. 0)

Outside the Engine Room is a secondary yard with a large Crane on a central platform. The Crane Controls, when repaired by an Engineer, allow the Security forces another (and closer) route into the Missile Courtyard, via a raised bridge into the Storage Thoroughfare. This is obviously to your team's detriment, so keep an eye on this area (from the Engine Room or Starboard Overlook). The rest of the yard offers protective scenery all the way around to the Rusty Trawler Innards, and a U-shaped Snaking Pipe; a quicker route from the Dirt Path below the Movable Bridge.

### 44 Warship: Movable Bridge & Dirt Path (Starboard) (Lvls. 0 & 2)

The bridge on the ground is attached to a Crane, which the enemy will attempt to raise. Stop this plan. The Dirt Path is an alternate route to the Snaking Pipe and Crane Yard if the Rusty Trawler Innards isn't utilized by the enemy. The Resistance doesn't usually prowl this close to the enemy spawn point.

### 45 Rusty Trawler Innards (Lvls. 1 & 2)

This two-floor interior is entered by the Security forces via a ramp, and offers two exits: down a hole and out into the Crane Yard, or onto the Movable Bridge (when raised) via an upper balcony. Hide behind the container inside this structure, beneath the hole, and ambush foes dropping down, or nearing the Yard or Snaking Pipe. You can also climb up the hole, and chase enemies into the Warship if necessary.

###  46 Warship: Storage Thoroughfare, MG Nest, & Port Deck (Lvl. 2)

Learn the visual cues in this initially confusing maze of metal; the entrance to the Movable Bridge is bathed in red light. The MG Nest is accessed via a passage close to the Missile Controls overlook, and the Port Deck is useful when locating the Supply Command Post in the Super Tanker across a second bridge. Remember to back into a corridor and use the metal walls as cover. This is another major route when reaching the Missile Courtyard. Also remember to fix and man the MG Nest, which can shoot at foes as they cross the bridge, but doesn't have the vertical movement to stop enemies running along the dirt path below.

### 47 Warship: Lower Dirt Path (Stern) (Lvl. 0)

### 48 Rusty Junk Junction (Lvl. 0)

Security forces split at these two locations when assaulting the area, but it isn't wise to head into either location; they're too far from important defensive points, and there are always more foes here, near their spawn point. Hide behind the different clusters of junk (such as the pipe alcove around the corner from their spawn point, near the ramp), then step out and shoot or ambush to annoy or slow down the opposition. Do this if the rest of your team is handling their allotted tasks with particular adeptness.

### 49 Security Deployment Zone (Pt. 2): Lower Dirt Path (Lvl. 0)

The enemy begins its second Core Objective from inside the broken hull of a massive rusting ship, just through the gate that was opened. The area is heavily fortified and shouldn't be attacked; you're wasting your energy as the turrets pick you off.

###  50 Security Command Post (Pt. 2) (Lvl. 0)

This Command Post is not accessible to Resistance forces. Please ignore it.

# Objective Tactics: Core Objective 1

## Defend the Crane Controls

Spawn Point to Crane Controls: 00:12

Time to Repair Crane Controls: 01:10

### General Tactics

The Locations section revealed all the different directions from the Security Deployment Zone to the Crane, and your team must decide how deep into enemy territory you wish to go. The farther back into the Crane Yard you sit or patrol, the more weapons you can bring to bear on the foes, and from more directions. However, there is little margin for error if all the enemies are massing right at the Crane.

The optimal plan is to stretch your team as far as the two barricades, ready to retreat to the Crane Yard if the foes try to usurp this initial line of defense. Keep on moving too; it's important to know the cracks the enemy can squeeze through even after the two barricades are up.

If you have time, dash forward and capture one of the neutral Command Posts. It boosts your entire team and diverts your enemy's attention: they have to expend time and effort recapturing it, or attack at a disadvantage. Continue capturing and recapturing the neutral posts whenever possible. This is a great spoiling move, and can often disrupt the Security team's rhythm and momentum.

### Lines of Defense

**For further plans on defending both barricades, check the Secondary Objectives, below.**

NOTE

**Main Barricade:** This shuts down the Main Alley and two major routes from the enemy's spawn, but the upper balconies and Barricade Overlook are still accessible to leaping and lithe foes. With that in mind, patrol the areas to the sides and above the Main Barricade, so enemies are dissuaded from trying to get into the Crane Yard via these narrow gaps.

**Side Barricade:** This seals the area from the Beyond the Hull Thoroughfare, but foes can still move around on the ground via the Covered Alley, or through the air by Wall-jumping across the gap onto the Central Gantry Walk. Be sure you have enough warm bodies to stop these more cunning (or flanking) incursions, as well as holding up the main force behind the barricade.

**Ideally you want to tie up the attackers continually trying to destroy your barricades. Don't worry if they do destroy a barricade, because you can always rebuild it. The overriding plan is to make them focus on the barricade, not the Core Objective it is protecting.**

TIP

**Crane Yard:** This area requires Engineers to bolster your defenses. Although mines and turrets aren't a match for a mobile humans defending the same area, they do buy you time and steal the attackers' attention away from the Crane while you bring them down, preferably in a crossfire, and from multiple directions. Cover the Subterranean Pipe Shortcut (at the edge of your deployment zone) with a mine too, but vary the location each time or the enemy gets wise to this delaying tactic.

## Automated Ordnance

Security has fewer ordnance positions to worry about, but checking their tactics certainly doesn't hinder your strategic know-how!

1 Stop the Security forces from flanking you with a turret in the Covered Alley.

2 Set a turret atop the Central Gantry Walk to cover the Crane objective.

3 Set a second turret to cover the Side Barricade and route along from the Covered Alley.

4 Variations on a theme; set a turret here with some wall cover, and a straight shot at both barricade entrances and the Crane.

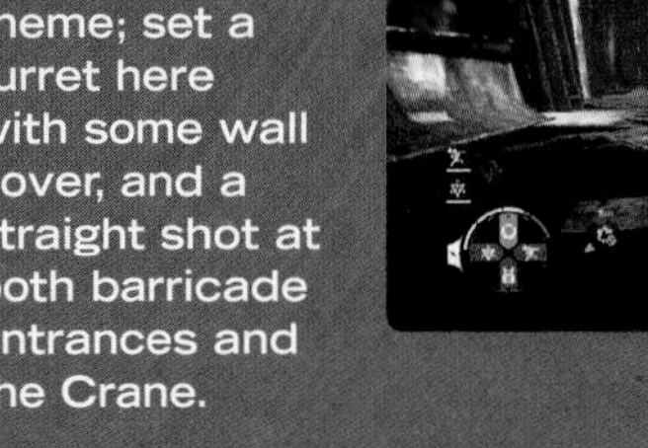

1 Has Security just broken through your Main Barricade? Then make sure you've set a mine as a thank you gift.

2 Drop a mine at the top of the Subterranean Pipe Shortcut to stop foes emerging near your spawn area. Vary the location so the enemy doesn't get wise to this.

3 Setting a mine on the Crane ensures the enemy Engineers won't be repairing this in a hurry.

## Sniper's Ally: Camping Spots

1 A bit of a lone wolf? Then cover either Command Post, such as the Supply one shown here, and help waylay the enemy while keeping your team bonus.

2 You're a little far from cover, but you can cover the Anchor Chain Avenue, Main Alley, Subterranean Pipe Entrance, and Health Command Post, and advance on any of these locations. Drop behind the pipe hatch for cover.

3 Watch the lower Below the Hull Thoroughfare, and almost the entire length of the Central and Main Gantry Walks from here.

4 Set up camp at the end of the Covered Alley, looking down the Below the Hull Thoroughfare, and tag foes rushing up.

5 Cover the Main Alley, and the Security Wall-jumping antics on this side of the barricade, as well as the cubbyhole down into the Crane Courtyard, all from here.

## Sniper's Ally: Camping Spots

6 The Pipe and Girder Overlook offers fantastic, pre-barricade sniping opportunities through the Main Alley, and is a great place to guard the Crane, too.

7 No one goes down to this gate. But with a long-range weapon, this is a great spot to tag Security punks milling around by the Crane itself.

# Secondary Objectives (First Map)

### Escort Core Objective Class Teammate

**Unofficial Escort Info:** This objective isn't usually available for a defending team, but some two-player tactics apply: Pair an Engineer with another teammate for a good partnership. Choose two Engineers (one to take over if the first falls under fire, or to fix each other's turrets, or to hasten barricade construction). Or, you can try an Engineer and a Soldier (to provide cover) or Medic (to heal). Two fast-moving teammates Wall-jumping and ambushing enemy patrols by attacking from different directions (and covering both Command Posts) is another option.

### Construct Main Barricade

Engineer

- Spawn Point to Main Barricade: 00:15
- Time to Build Barricade: 00:30
- Time to Disarm Explosives: 00:05
- Time to Plant Explosives: 00:07
- Countdown to Explosion: 00:40

Two main paths (from Drummond's Alley and the Anchor Chain Avenue) meet at this barricade, which should be first on your construction list. Be sure at least two teammates are covering the Engineer during the construction, otherwise the faster-moving enemies are likely to swamp you. With the barricade up, enemies can still cross into the Crane Yard via the Barricade Overlook and some adept Wall-jumping from the Rusting Deck; make sure you have defenders to help catch these more dexterous foes.

### Construct Side Barricade

Engineer

- Spawn Point to Side Barricade: 00:17
- Time to Build Barricade: 00:30
- Time to Disarm Explosives: 00:05
- Time to Plant Explosives: 00:07
- Countdown to Explosion: 00:40

This is certain to stop the heavier troops from entering the Crane Yard, but construction on the Side Barricade in front of the Crane is hampered by the time it takes, and the fact that Light enemies can Wall-jump across the gap and use the Central Gantry Walk to bypass the Barricade entirely. However, as long as you have teammates patrolling up here, you can seal this entrance, as well as watch for foes trying to race along and up the Covered Alley.

**On the plus side, as long as you don't wait more than ten seconds (after which the barricade resets), you can stop repair work on either barricade, and begin again without having to start from scratch. Once the barricade is constructed, watch for (and make priority targets of) enemy Soldiers, dropping them before they clamp a charge on the barricade. Should this happen, send an Engineer (plus a teammate to cover him) to disarm the charge on either barricade.**

**TIP**

### Capture the Health Command Post

Engineer & Operative Advantage!

Spawn Point to Command Post: 00:10 

Time to Claim Command Post: 00:10

This is located inside the Field Hospital of a rusting tanker bridge between Drummond's Alley and the Rusty Hull. It is likely to be sought after, but if you take the Subterranean Pipe Shortcut, you can claim this post. Then prowl the exterior balcony, which allows you to see the enemy coming here or heading for the Main Barricade. Snipe at both positions while keeping the post for as long as possible.

### Capture the Supply Command Post

 Engineer & Operative Advantage!

Spawn Point to Command Post: 00:11 

Time to Claim Command Post: 00:10

This is in a highly dangerous section away from the main action, but much closer to the enemy's spawn point. For this reason alone, the risk versus reward is worth it: Send a quick Engineer from your main defenses to take this post (hide to the side and behind it as partial cover as you claim it), and then quickly bound up into the Hull Hideout, where you can snipe enemies trying to reclaim the post. Bring a Soldier with you at first, to lock down the area, then send him back to your Crane defenses. Your Supply Command Post guard meanwhile, should be slowing the enemy down or keeping them from their main Core Objective.

### Construct the Crane MG Nest

 Engineer

Spawn Point to Crane MG Nest: 00:10 

Time to Construct: 00:10

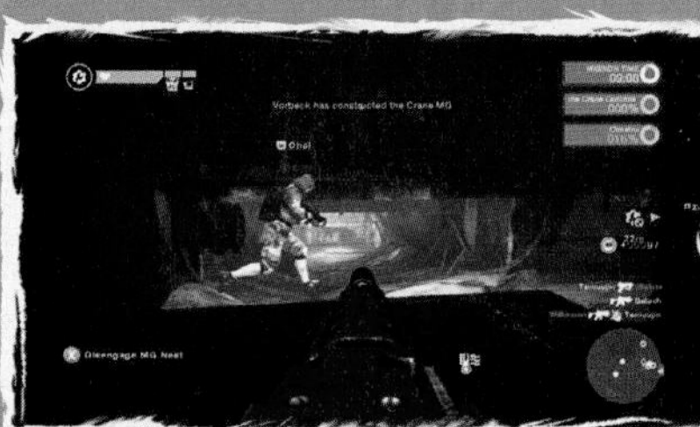

Situated inside Deano's Hull, with views out to the Covered Alley at the far end of the Below the Hull Thoroughfare, this MG Nest is excellent for cutting down foes storming the Covered Alley, but nowhere else. If the enemy uses this route, more fool them: Cut them down! Otherwise, ignore this MG Nest. Note that this MG Nest also takes longer (around 10 seconds) to build compared to other MG Nests.

## Objective Tactics: Core Objective 2

### Defend the Missile Controls

Spawn Point to Missile Controls: 00:08 

Time to Hack Missile Controls: 01:24 

#### General Tactics

If your team is composed of veterans, it becomes extremely difficult for the enemy to hack the Missile Controls in the Courtyard. This is due partly to your constant barraging of the area, but also to the demoralizing length of time it takes Security to reach this area (compared to your adjacent spawning grounds), especially if you've removed their Operatives multiple times. However, to achieve a stranglehold on the Missile Courtyard, you're going to need a competent crew and a clear set of defenses.

The actual defenses are detailed below, but sitting back and waiting for the enemy to come to you means they're likely to be tooled and buffed up, and have claimed one or both Command Posts. There must be no advantages given! So send a couple of your best fighters forward to thin out the enemy, lightening the pressure on your main defensive line. Then cement your line, moving to the Warship chambers on either side of the controls, which are your primary lines of defense; but remember that just as they provide perfect cover when you're defending the launch site, they are a perfect foothold from which the foes can hack the controls.

Be extra-vigilant for Operatives disguised as teammates. Because the enemy should be using them for most of their own team, expect many more sneak attacks. Perhaps develop a quick "tell" (such as a small jump or radio confirmation) that all your team does when passing each other, so doppelgangers are more easily spotted.

CAUTION

## Defensive Lines

**Engine Room and Health Command Post:** Place at least half of your team (with a couple checking the Missile Courtyard for enemy movement if necessary) at the Health Command Post. It is much easier to defend than the Storage Thoroughfare, but also has the benefit of the Crane Yard, allowing you to stop all movement into the Storage Thoroughfare; you're essentially covering two critical paths from one chokepoint! You can easily blow up the Crane Controls if the enemy somehow repairs them, you have the Engine Room interior, the Rusting Hull behind for snipers, and the Starboard Overlook above you to defend from. And let us not forget the ammo replenishment the Command Post provides!

**Storage Thoroughfare:** If the bridge is down, and this location can't be accessed by foes, keep a couple of teammates at the Missile Courtyard, and send the others to delay enemies along the Dirt Path that runs between the Warship and Super Tanker with the Supply Command Post in it. Because this is the only other incursion point, you can effectively block an increasingly furious set of foes with your turrets, mines, and lockdowns of the dangerous Dirt Road routes.

The situation changes if the Movable Bridge has been raised: The Storage Thoroughfare is now accessible, and it's a short dash to the open overlook and the Missile Courtyard itself.

**Missile Courtyard:** There are four enemy routes into this final destination: via the Storage Thoroughfare, the Overlook up the ramp from the Engine Room, and the two Dirt Paths on the Resistance side of the Warship. Learn the opposition's camp spots (by reading their Campaign chapter for this map), then check where they are and dispatch them. Remember though, that you're in no hurry to move from a good cover position; the enemy has the time problem. So only take chances if the Operative is attempting a hack.

Resistance defenders can stand on the Upper Gantry of your Resistance Hulk, and rain grenades on to the Missile Controls from relative safety. This is extremely effective, and can be made more so if you're using the Lobster or EZ-Nade.

TIP

## Automated Ordnance

If you can't be here to mow down enemies attempting to reach the Supply Command Post, leave a reminder of your prowess. Listen for the turret (or watch your XP increase) when it activates.

Cover the Missile Controls with a turret that can't be seen from the Storage Thoroughfare overlook.

Now set a turret to cover the Missile Controls that can't easily be seen from either overlook!

## Automated Ordnance (continued)

8 Stick a turret between the ramp and medical supplies in the Engine Room to annoy and slow the enemy.

9 Place a turret to tackle enemies using the Dirt Path to the rear of the Health Command Post. They must turn around to spot and destroy the turret, giving your team time to drop them.

4 A cheeky mine in the Rusty Trawler Innards annoys the heck out of foes escaping toward the Snaking Pipe.

5 Locked down the Engine Room? Then set a mine here just inside the Warship entrance of the Super Tanker Bridge, to stop the only other way into the Storage Thoroughfare.

6 Even if the enemy raises the Movable Bridge, a mine just inside the Warship entrance to the Storage Thoroughfare halts their rush.

7 Don't forget the obvious mine placement near the Missile Controls!

## Sniper's Ally: Camping Spots

8 You can drop a few enemies as they run in from their spawn point, before retreating down the Dirt Path.

9 Stand by the Health Command Post, drop foes, or ambush them from the narrow interior ramp up to the Starboard Overlook.

10 Use the Rusting Hull Overlook to tag foes in the Engine Room, and sidestep right to follow them from above, into the Missile Courtyard.

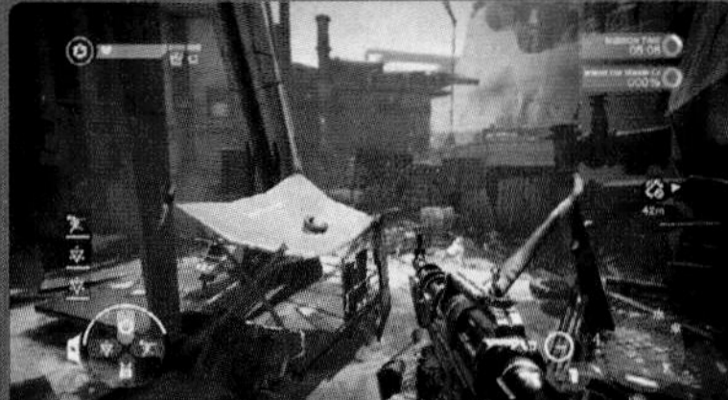

11 The Starboard Overlook itself offers good views of the Crane Yard, and foes crossing the Movable Bridge. Drop to a lower exterior balcony to tag foes coming out of the Snaking Pipe.

12 This is another spectacular camping spot; you can shoot or lob grenades right into the hack point, and really infuriate your foes!

13 Peer through the metal sheet partially welded to the Warship's hull, just below the Missile Courtyard. Peek through the gap and pick off Operatives at the hack point!

HISTORY OF THE ARK
CHARACTER CREATION
GAMEPLAY
WEAPONS DETAIL
CAMPAIGN
Getting Answers
Breakout
Chen's Plans
Black Box
Attack on CCity
Airborne
Operation Babel
Critical Reaction
CHALLENGES
APPENDICES

# Secondary Objectives (Second Map)

## Escort Core Objective Class Teammate

**Unofficial Escort Info:** This objective isn't usually available for a defending team, but some two-player tactics apply: Pair an Engineer with another teammate for a good partnership. Choose two Engineers (one to take over if the first falls under fire, to fix each other's turrets, or to hasten barricade construction). Or, use an Engineer and a Soldier (to provide cover) or Medic (to heal) . Two fast-moving teammates Wall-jumping and ambushing enemy patrols by attacking from different directions (and covering both Command Posts) is another option.

## Defend the Crane Controls

Soldier

Spawn Point to Crane Controls: 00:15

Time to Repair Crane Controls: 01:10

Time to Disarm Explosives: 00:05

Time to Plant Explosives: 00:07

Countdown to Explosion: 00:40

This takes place in and around the Upper Starboard Overlook, and the views below to the Crane Controls and Yard. Shutting down this repair option for the enemy means they can't raise the Movable Bridge and gain access to the Storage Thoroughfare, effectively cutting off one of the sides of attack at the Missile Courtyard. Also remember to set a charge to detonate, and drop the Movable Bridge at the controls, so Security has to repair it constantly. You must be a Soldier for this to occur, but do it as soon as the bridge is raised; pick a teammate with this as a main role.

## Capture the Health Command Post

Engineer & Operative Advantage!

Spawn Point to Command Post: 00:08

Time to Claim Command Post: 00:10

The good news is that the enemy almost always attacks this location from the Crane Controls and Yard. The bad news is that there's a constant stream of them to tackle. Early on, decide if this initial line of defense is going to receive enough teammates to defend properly, and then stick to this tactic because it's by far the best; waylaying the enemy here means fewer foes dropping in on the Missile Courtyard. Consult the Core Objective for a variety of excellent ambush spots to use instead of standing around on the gantry floor next to the post, waiting to die.

## Capture the Supply Command Post

Engineer & Operative Advantage!

Spawn Point to Command Post: 00:09

Time to Claim Command Post: 00:10

Unlike the Health Command Post, this is located in a rarely trafficked area (over inside the Super Tanker, and accessed via the Port Dirt Path or the Bridge from the Warship), making it much easier for you to take early on, and hold as the mission progresses. If you keep the Movable Bridge on the opposite side of the map grounded, the enemy finds it much more difficult to use the Super Tanker Bridge linking this area to the Warship. This means you can guard from the ground, up on the bridge, and race in from your spawn to tackle enemies when they take it back. Of course, this is beneficial because the foes aren't taking the Missile Courtyard.

###  Construct the Bridge MG Nest

 Engineer

Spawn Point to Bridge MG Nest: 00:11

Time to Construct: 00:04

This is perhaps the least helpful of the Secondary Objectives on your to-do list, because it is far more beneficial to spend time stopping the Movable Bridge (which this MG Nest covers) from being raised at all, instead of peering out of a porthole and firing on foes as they race past you. You are close to the Warship's Storage Thoroughfare though, and can detach yourself from the MG to attack enemies from the sides as they reach the Missile Courtyard.

###  Solo Tactics

**During Core Objective 1, perch between the two barricades, building one yourself as soon as you can, and then react to any enemies who try to break through. As an Engineer, setting up defenses trained on the Crane Controls allows you brief periods of time to take (or retake) a Command Post. But remaining adjacent to the Crane is most beneficial. Once Security moves toward the Warship, Engineers are the preferred choice here as well, mainly because they can strip away the Hack Box the enemy Operatives place on the Missile Controls. Lurk in the Missile Courtyard, and ensure that the timer ticks down to zero.**

## Mission Completion Conditions

###  Continuation...

**Core Objective 1:** Your team fails to stop the enemy repairing the Crane Controls. Part 2 of this mission now commences....

###  Completed!

The match completes if you successfully halt the enemy from completing any Core Objective by the time the timer reaches zero.

###  Unsuccessful!

Resistance forces lose if the enemy manages to hack the Missile Controls, before the timer ticks down.

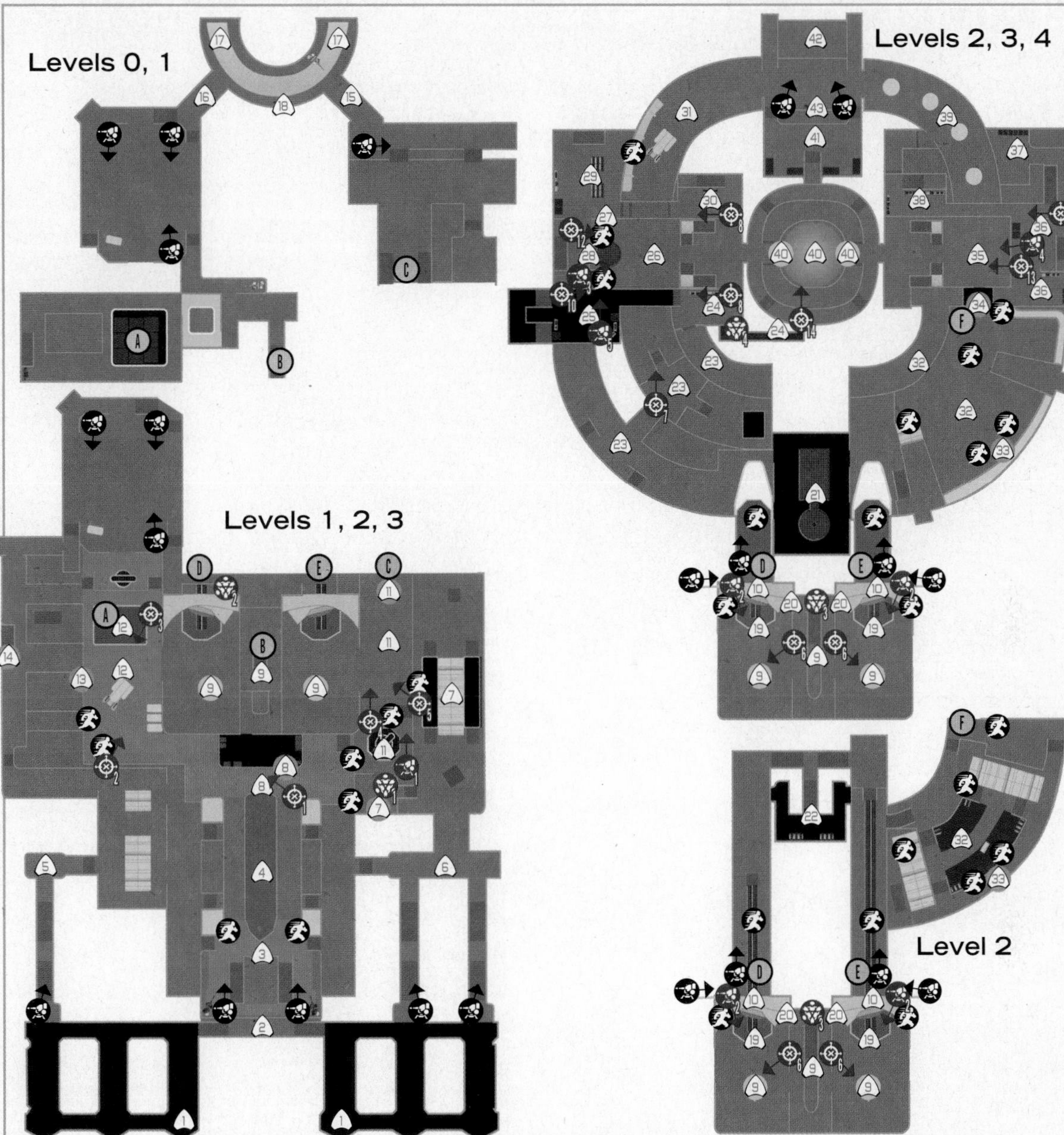


## MAP LEGEND

1: Resistance Deployment Zone (Pt. 1): Reactor Platform Lifeboats (Lvl. 0)
2: Resistance Command Post (Pt. 1) (Lvl. 1)
3: Power Plant Info Desk (Lvl. 2)
4: Scale Model Foyer & Vent Tower Entrance (Lvls. 2 & 3)
5: Starboard Service Stairs to Turbine Room (Lvls. 0, 1, & 2)
6: Port Service Stairs (2) (Lvls. 0, 1, & 2)
7: Health Command Post & Turbine Hall (Lvls. 2 & 3)
8: Bridge & Access Panel, & Control Room (Lvl. 3)
9: Vent Room, Airflow Controls, & Under Corridors (Lvls. 1, 2, & 3)
10: Ventilation Fans (Lvl. 2)
11: Steam Stack, Vent Room Entrance, & MG Nest (Lvl. 2)
12: Reactor Container Yard, Vent Room Entrance, & Cargo Bay (Lvls. 1 & 2)
13: Cargo Bay Control Room & MG Nest (Lvl. 3)
14: Starboard Deck & Supply Command Post (Lvls. 1 & 2)
15: Red Zone Passages (Lvl. 1)
16: Yellow Zone Passages (Lvl. 1)
17: Security Deployment Zone (Pt. 1): Reactor Server Room (Lvl. 0)
18: Security Command Post (Pt. 1) (Lvl. 0)
19: Resistance Deployment Zone (Pt. 2): Vent Fans Passages (2) (Lvls. 2 & 3)
20: Resistance Command Posts (2) (Pt. 2) (Lvl. 2)
21: Reactor Pool Chamber (Lvl. 3)
22: Stairwell to Small Server Room (Lvls. 2, 3, & 4)
23: Yellow Zone: Outer, Inner, & Upper Stepped Chambers (Lvls. 3 & 4)
24: Yellow Zone: Command Room & Vent Shaft to Reactor (Lvl. 4)
25: Yellow Zone: Computer Room & Vending Machines (Lvl. 4)
26: Yellow Zone: Containment Room & Reactor Access (Lvls. 2, 3, & 4)
27: Yellow Zone: MG Nest (Lvl. 3)
28: Yellow Zone: Supply Command Post (Lvl. 4)
29: Yellow Zone: Server Rooms (Lvls. 3 & 4)
30: Yellow Zone: Server Rooms & Maintenance Corridor (Lvls. 3 & 4)
31: Yellow Zone: Broken Vent Pipe Chamber (Lvls. 3 & 4)
32: Red Zone: Turbine Outer & Upper Chambers (Lvls. 2, 3 & 4)
33: Red Zone: Health Command Post (Lvl. 3)
34: Red Zone: Small Server Rooms & MG Nest Corridor (Lvl. 4)
35: Red Zone: Containment Room & Reactor Access (Lvls. 2, 3, & 4)
36: Red Zone: Computer Room & Vending Machines (Lvl. 4)
37: Red Zone: Server Room & Staircase Thoroughfare (Lvls. 3 & 4)
38: Red Zone: Server Room & Maintenance Corridor (Lvls. 3 & 4)
39: Red Zone: Power Conduit Chamber (Lvl. 3)
40: Reactor & Core (Lvls. 2 & 3)
41: Storage & Lower Reactor Core Access (Lvl. 2)
42: Security Deployment Zone (Pt. 2): Midway Balcony (Lvls. 3 & 4)
43: Security Command Post (Pt. 2) (Lvl. 3)

BRINK

Reactor: Overview Map

# WHAT-IF: CRITICAL REACTION

FREEPLAY: REACTOR  SECURITY CAMPAIGN—DAY 8: FALLOUT

## 10:38 Commandeered Resistance Barge WSW of Reactor Pelgo

MISSION TIME (COb 1): 10:00

MISSION TIME (COb 2): +10:00

### MAP LEGEND (CONTINUED)

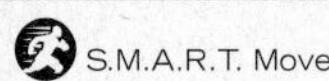
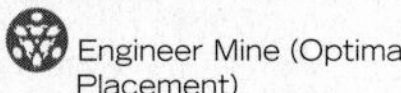
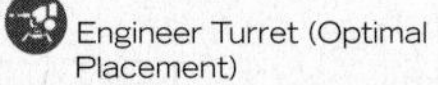
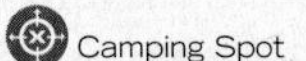
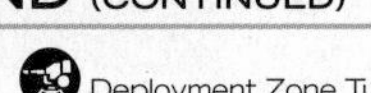
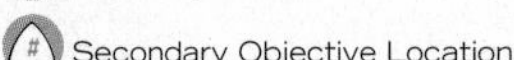
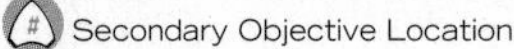
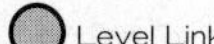

- S.M.A.R.T. Move
- Engineer Mine (Optimal Placement)
- Engineer Turret (Optimal Placement)
- Camping Spot
- Deployment Zone Turret (Invulnerable)
- Core Objective Location
- Secondary Objective Location
- Level Link

### Resistance Radio Transmission: Briefing

So far the Founders have chosen to ignore comrade Chen. We are the sword in his hand. The Founders have shown they only respect force. Then they'll respect this: In under one hour, our forces will seize control of the Reactor. Unless Security lay down their weapons and turn control of the Ark over to Brother Chen, we'll overload the Reactor, ejecting radioactive fallout and rendering the Ark as uninhabitable to the Founders as it is to the guests. Life on Ark will be fair and just. Or it will end within an hour. Our path is set.

### Optimal Class Numbers

| | COb 1 | COb 2 |
|---|---|---|
| Soldier | [2] | [4] |
| Medic | [2] | [2] |
| Engineer | [1] | [1] |
| Operative | [3] | [1] |

### Objectives (Resistance)

- Core Objective 1: Hack the Vent System
- Core Objective 2: Destroy the Reactor
- Escort Core Objective Class Teammate
- Repair the Bridge Access Panel
- Capture the Health Command Post
- Capture the Supply Command Post
- Construct the Office MG Nest
- Construct the Escalators MG Nest
- Construct the Doorway MG Nest
- Construct the Walkway MG Nest

## Important Locations

(Ventilation Deck)

### 1 Resistance Deployment Zone (Part 1): Reactor Platform Lifeboats (Lvl. 0)

Resistance forces begin evenly split in two parallel locations on either side of a staircase. Check the position of the staircase to determine which side you're on. The number of unlocked doors is also different; the starboard (left) side has a single door open at the far left side, while the port (right) side has two doors.

## 2 Resistance Command Post (Part 1) (Lvl. 1)

Be sure you have at least one Operative heading to the first Core Objective point; change class and weapons here if you need to. This post is at the top of the stairs, in the middle of the structure below the Power Plant Info Desk.

## 3 Power Plant Info Desk (Lvl. 2)

## 4 Scale Model Foyer & Vent Tower Entrance (Lvls. 2 & 3)

The entrance to the Reactor can be approached from three main locations: the Resistance Command Post stairs (or transparent middle), the Starboard Service Stairs to Turbine Room, or the Port Service Stairs. You can also retreat here from the Bridge and Access Panel inside the Control Room. This was the visitor foyer, prior to the recent hostilities.

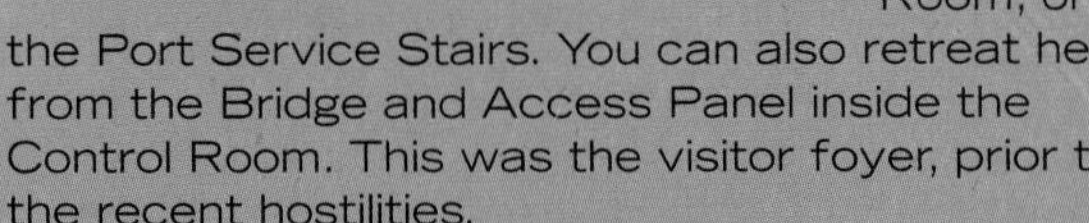

Once you reach the Info Desk, the connecting passages and doorways can be initially confusing; just remember there's an upper and lower entrance. The lower part has a scale model of the facility, an overturned drinks machine, two entrances on each side, and yellow flooring leading outside, under the bridge. The upper part (Vent Tower Entrance) has the bridge access, two balconies, and two entrances on each side. The side entrances lead down to passages that connect to the Service Stairs.

The sheer number of exits out of here means the enemy has a hard time containing you. If you're facing more than a single threat, and don't want to waste the time attacking, seek another route around to the Airflow Controls.

### S.M.A.R.T. Moves

Jump on the blue barrels on either side of the Info Desk and over the balcony to reach the Vent Tower Entrance.

**Throughout this map, pay close attention to the markers on the ground and walls, which are color-coded (areas marked yellow are to starboard, and red are port), and doorways have floor lines curved to the entrance, making them easy to spot.**

TIP

## 5 Starboard Service Stairs to Turbine Room (Lvls. 0, 1, & 2)

A set of steep stairs from one of the Resistance Deployment Zone areas, this joins a small turbine room with an exit in each corner: toward the outside area and Control Room, down to a connecting chamber near the Info Desk, or back around to the Starboard Deck. Learn which door is which! Climb on the turbine, using the height to peer out through the doorways, and drop behind it for cover.

## 6 Port Service Stairs (2) (Lvls. 0, 1, & 2)

On the opposite side are two parallel (and steep) stairs from the other Resistance Deployment Zone, which join a small connecting passageway at the top. This leads via a double doorway into the Turbine Hall, as well as across to a connecting chamber near the Info Desk.

## 7 Health Command Post & Turbine Hall (Lvls. 2 & 3)

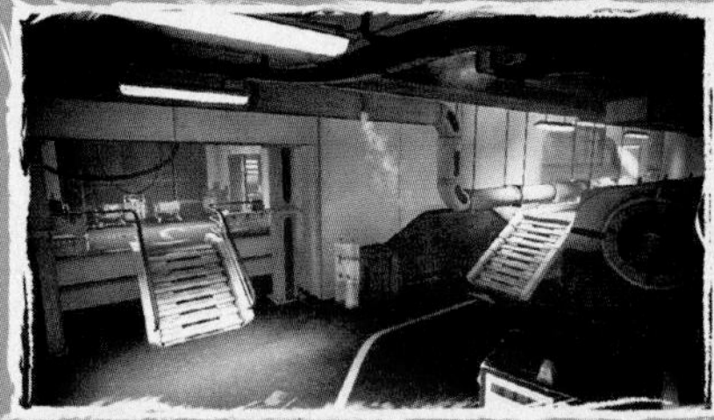

The Turbine Hall is a major connecting chamber between the Resistance and Security areas, and clashes are expected here. Stand on the raised steps on either side of the turbine to aim across, under the glass, across the Vent Room Entrance, and into the Airflow Control chamber.

The Health Command Post is visited by both teams, so leap on the medical cases in the corner near the door out to the Steam Stack, and ambush foes from both entrances as they try to take it.

### S.M.A.R.T. Moves

From the Vent Room Entrance, you can climb onto the water pipes under the schematic screen, and hop into the Turbine Hall.

## 8 Bridge & Access Panel, & Control Room (Lvl. 3)

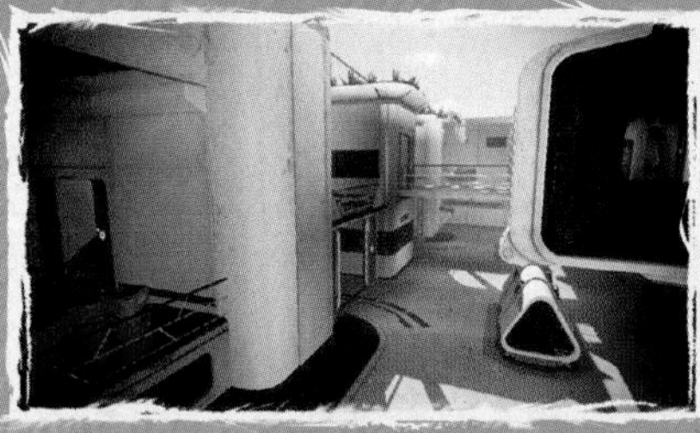

The yellow exterior floor allows swift movement between the starboard and port Vent Room Entrances. However, the bridge offers more immediate access into a Control Room, although the doors into the room at the far end of the bridge are locked. Overcome this by sending an Engineer to quickly sprint into the Vent Room, up onto the white "bridge" that holds the giant vent fans, and across into the Control Room, where the Access Panel can be repaired. Now you have a direct path into the Vent Room.

### S.M.A.R.T. Moves

Wall-jump the low balcony with the blue barrels on it, and scramble over the balcony opposite, by the Steam Stack.

## 9 Vent Room, Airflow Controls, & Under Corridors (Lvls. 1, 2, & 3)

## 10 Ventilation Fans (Lvl. 2)

The Resistance must focus almost all their attention on this two-level chamber, which has three separate areas of interest. On each side is an Airflow Control unit with a panel that must be hacked by one or more Operatives. Opposite the panels are giant Ventilation Fans that are your entrance deeper into this facility. You can climb the white slope and cross the "bridge" the fan motors and blades are connected to, or use the middle staircase (or the fuel cylinders on the starboard side) to reach a balcony overlooking both areas. You can fire down from the fan bridges, too.

The balcony leads to the Control Room (where you can repair an Access Panel to open the door, allowing quicker access from your spawn points. Behind the Airflow Controls are some vertical struts to hide behind, and a tiny passage connecting the Vent Rooms.

Descend the stairwell in the central area to reach the winding (and slightly confusing) underground passages. One leads to the Cargo Bay and Starboard Deck, while the other allows you to reach the yellow side of the Security Deployment Zone.

HISTORY OF THE ARK
CHARACTER CREATION
GAMEPLAY
WEAPONS DETAIL
CAMPAIGN
Getting Answers
Breakout
Chen's Plans
Black Box
Attack on CCity
Airborne
Operation Babel
Critical Reaction
CHALLENGES
APPENDICES

## 11 Steam Stack, Vent Room Entrance, & MG Nest (Lvl. 2)

This port side area has a large floor marking of the Reactor's symbol, and a schematic of the adjacent Turbine Hall. Dominating the exterior area and raised platform that leads to the Health Command Post is a large Steam Stack (a useful landmark), and an open area offering some barrels and boxes to hide behind. Beyond the floor symbol is an MG Nest that the enemy is likely to have working (if their presence is strong, seek other routes to the Vent Room).

**Note the red stripes along the walls of the rooms beyond this MG Nest; this is useful for finding your way around the latter chambers of this facility.**

TIP

## 12 Reactor Container Yard, Vent Room Entrance, & Cargo Bay (Lvls. 1 & 2)

The starboard side area adjacent to the Vent Room consists of a Container Yard bathed in sunlight, and some radioactive cylinders, one of which is in mid-transit. Clamber on these and the vehicle for protection and the height advantage. Of course, the main entrance to the Vent Room is of paramount importance, but there are other locations to reach (or head in from) too:

The Cargo Bay (or the two sets of steps on either side of the unused steam stack) at the far end of the Container Yard offers a way down to the enemy's spawn points, so watch for foes in this area. Descend past the bay's platform, and you can also reach the Starboard Deck, which loops around and up, and back into the yard. You can also look over the yard from the Control Room, which is great for cutting down Security forces en route to the Vent Room.

### S.M.A.R.T. Moves

This is more skillful than useful, but you can traverse this entire Container Yard without ever touching the ground. Practice it!

Find the locked door near the barrel, clamber onto the barrel, and shimmy into the open Control Room window.

## 13 Cargo Bay Control Room & MG Nest (Lvl. 3)

Although this may be taken by the enemy (who start closer to this location), the Control Room is still a handy chamber to commandeer. Use the staircases from either end of the Starboard Deck (or the barrel in the Container Yard) to reach this upper room, with three windows that offer excellent (sniping) views of the exterior facility and one of the Vent Rooms. Build and train the MG at the Control Room too; although if you're facing an enemy using this weapon, simply avoid the entrance, or stay in the shadows if you're in the yard, because the MG has limited vertical and horizontal movement.

## 14 Starboard Deck & Supply Command Post (Lvls. 1 & 2)

There are two reasons to visit the Starboard Deck: to claim the Supply Command Post under the stairs, and to outflank the enemy, because you can reach the spawn area corridors and Cargo Bay rather easily. Enter the Starboard Deck via the Starboard Service Stairs Turbine Room, which offers immediate access up into the Control Room, and a longer trek to the other Container Yard and yellow spawn corridors. Remember the Supply Command Post is under the middle stairwell, near the two short corridors that connect to the Cargo Bay.

## 15 Red Zone Passages (Lvl. 1)
## 16 Yellow Zone Passages (Lvl. 1)

The Security Deployment Zone offers two distinct routes to the exterior locations and Vent Room, each marked with a different wall stripe. The Red Zone Passages enable Security to reach the MG Nest and Turbine Hall. The slightly more maze-like Yellow Zone Passages lead past a large underground room with a blue floor and parked cargo vehicle, and three possible destinations: The Starboard Deck, the Cargo Bay (disused steam stack), and the stairwell below the Vent Room. Once you figure out these routes, you can plan to block them according to the enemy's flow.

## 17 Security Deployment Zone (Part 1): Reactor Server Room (Lvl. 0)

This curved chamber is deep in the bowels of the Reactor area (indeed, the Reactor is on the other side of the inside curve, although it isn't accessible). The enemy has a choice of two exits (the Yellow or Red Zones). The large number of turrets makes waltzing down here an inevitable death-trap.

**Although underneath some of the passageways in the main Reactor area, this Server Room is cut off from the Reactor section that is traversed during the latter part of this match.**

**NOTE**

## 18 Security Command Post (Part 1) (Lvl. 0)

Placed equidistant between the two exit corridors, this isn't used (or even seen) by the Resistance.

# Important Locations
## (Reactor Control)

## 19 Resistance Deployment Zone (Part 2): Vent Fans Passages (2) (Lvls. 2 & 3)

Your subsequent starting point is behind one of the two stopped fans on either side of the stair balcony in the Vent Room. You can quickly tell which side because the Command Post is on the chamber's inside corner. Now venture down your chosen Vent Fans Passage; remember you can climb atop the fan and access the upper passage, which offers a quicker infiltration of the Yellow Stepped Chambers (left) and Red Turbine Chambers. At the far end of each passage (lower level) are stairs up into the Small Server Room.

### S.M.A.R.T. Moves

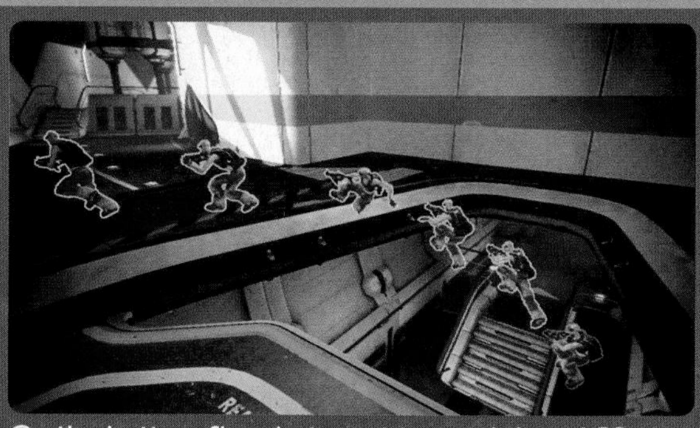

On the bottom floor but want to reach Level 3? Then move to the steps and grab the lip of the hole in the passage and pull yourself up. This means you can reach the Outer Stepped Chamber instead of the Inner one, to vary your routes.

## 20 Resistance Command Posts (2) (Part 2) (Lvl. 2)

Remember your team needs a Soldier to blow the Reactor, so change your team up accordingly.

## 21 Reactor Pool Chamber (Lvl. 3)

## 22 Stairwell to Small Server Room (Lvls. 2, 3, & 4)

Used as a thorough-fare between the Stepped and Turbine Chambers, the Reactor Pool Chamber is accessible from the upper Vent Fans Passage and your spawn point. This chamber is unique because it has both yellow and red wall stripes. It is also separate from the Stairwell to Small Server Room. Head up here if you want to reach the Upper Chambers, the inside curved corridors around the Reactor center.

## 23 Yellow Zone: Outer, Inner, & Upper Stepped Chambers (Lvls. 3 & 4)

Entered via the left Vent Fans Passage, these three, mostly separate curved chambers make up almost one quarter of the Reactor layout. Which chamber you traverse depends on how you got here; the Outer Chamber links to the upper floor of the left Vent Fans Passage. The Inner Chamber is maneuvered up and into via blue barrels along the lower floor of the left Vent Fans Passage, and the Upper Chamber is at the top of the Stairwell to Small Server Room, on the Yellow Zone side.

The Outer and Inner Chambers offer some leaky pipes and a small connecting passage with two doorways, in the middle. The machinery and doorways offer ample ambushing opportunities, although the enemy is usually farther into the facility. At the far end, the Outer Chamber leads to a staircase allowing you into the Computer Room with the Vending Machines. The Inner Chamber offers direct access into the Containment Room and Reactor; just follow the orange lights.

Meanwhile, the Upper Chamber (which is separate) offers a window into the Inner Chamber to fire from (but which is too small to head through), and a quick route to the Command Room that overlooks the Containment Room.

**Check the floor for orange lights; these lead you to the Reactor area. Also look for sparks in ceilings and water rushing from pipes; remembering where these are helps you situate yourself in this maze.**

TIP

## 24 Yellow Zone: Command Room & Vent Shaft to Reactor (Lvl. 4)

## 25 Yellow Zone: Computer Room & Vending Machines (Lvl. 4)

Aside from some servers you can tuck yourself behind to ambush enemies, this cramped Command Room (with the "18" marking on the wall) enables you to swiftly reach the Reactor. This can be via the bridge that you can leap off into the Containment Room, or via the Vent Shaft in the corner wall. After a crawl down a duct, you reach the Reactor itself, where you can sneak in, plant a bomb, or fire at foes, having outflanked them.

Across the bridge is a Computer Room with Vending Machines, and a window that Security forces like to fire from, which overlooks the Stepped Chamber. This simple linking chamber is important because the doorway leads straight to the Supply Command Post.

## 26 Yellow Zone: Containment Room & Reactor Access (Lvls. 2, 3, & 4)

## 27 Yellow Zone: MG Nest (Lvl. 3)

## 28 Yellow Zone: Supply Command Post (Lvl. 4)

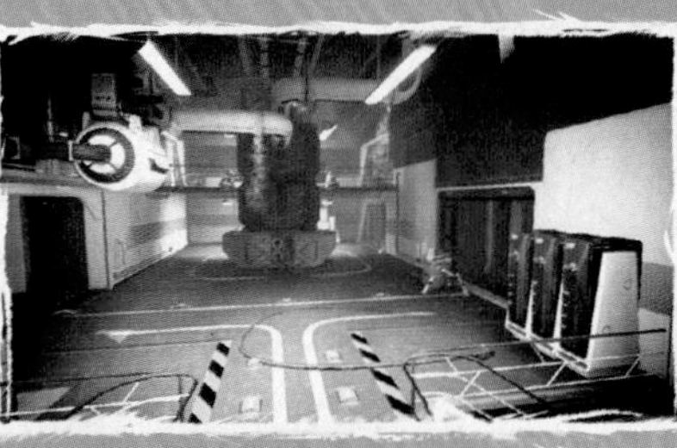

This Containment Room is not to be confused with the one in the middle of the Red Zone, which is directly opposite, through the Reactor Room. Expect a large amount of fighting in this area, which is accessed via the Stepped Chambers on one side, and the Maintenance Corridor and Broken Vent Pipe Chamber on the other. The "ground" is actually Level 3. Find cover behind a huge slab

HISTORY OF THE ARK
CHARACTER CREATION
GAMEPLAY
WEAPONS DETAIL
CAMPAIGN
Getting Answers
Breakout
Chen's Plans
Black Box
Attack on CCity
Airborne
Operation Babel
Critical Reaction
CHALLENGES
APPENDICES

cylinder of machinery; behind this are stairs up to the Supply Command Post, on the platform above. This platform is a thorough-fare between rooms, and difficult to defend, but it does offer snipers a good view of the Reactor.

Back on the ground is an MG Nest in front of a doorway alcove, which the enemy may have appropriated. But the main draws are the illuminated steps into the Reactor, and your final "Core" Objective. The door to the left takes you into a Maintenance Corridor—a favorite enemy hiding place, or location to draw enemies into. Finally, note the stairs leading down on either side; these allow you into the Core itself (which is useful for keeping the enemy guessing where you'll attack from).

**Lob grenades at foes manning the MG Nest, because they can't move any way except toward you.**

 TIP

### S.M.A.R.T. Moves

Use the slab cylinder to Wall-jump up and grab the railing of the upper balcony for a quick route between floors and to the Supply Command Post.

### 29 Yellow Zone: Server Rooms (Lvls. 3 & 4)

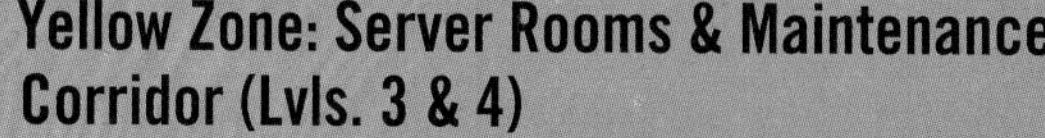

### 30 Yellow Zone: Server Rooms & Maintenance Corridor (Lvls. 3 & 4)

### 31 Yellow Zone: Broken Vent Pipe Chamber (Lvls. 3 & 4)

Across the Containment Room on the side of the chamber with the MG Nest are doorways at each

end of the wall. These lead into separate, two-floor Server Rooms that are linked by a passage on the upper level. The larger of the two Server Rooms, on the outer edge of the facility, offers a window out onto the Broken Vent Pipe Chamber beyond, and a more sedate opening on the lower floor.

The other, smaller Server Room has window access into the Containment Room (you can fire and fall down from here), stairs down, and an L-shaped Maintenance Corridor that leads out into the Broken Vent Pipe Chamber. There are plenty of dark corners, walls, and cubbyholes behind the server stacks to ambush from, and the enemy may try this.

Exit to the Broken Vent Pipe Chamber itself, to find a parked vehicle near a large pipe that is leaking what you hope is just steam. The Maintenance Corridor takes you straight into the enemy's deployment zone, as well as the important Storage and Lower Reactor Core Access.

### 32 Red Zone: Turbine Outer & Upper Chambers (Lvls. 2, 3, & 4)

### 33 Red Zone: Health Command Post (Lvl. 3)

Entered via the right Vent Fans Passage, this giant Turbine Outer Chamber, with its much smaller Upper Chamber on the inside of the curve, is the "other" main route to take to reach the opposite Containment Room, and then the central Reactor. This is arguably a better route to take than the Yellow Zone, because you can access the Upper Chamber, windows are easier to clamber through, and there are many more S.M.A.R.T. move opportunities.

The room has two giant turbines, with a raised platform in the middle that holds the Health Command Post. This is closer to your spawn point than the enemy's, so be sure one of your team claims it during the initial rush. Running along the outer edge is a low passage (allowing you to rush around without being easily spotted), and a duct directly above if you're faster and lighter. Just watch for enemy fire from the MG Nest. Also use the balconies above the two turbines to reach the duct and other locations, or to fire from. Step back into the alcove behind the balcony if you come under attack.

The Upper Chamber offers a quick route to the Containment Room from the Stairwell to Small Server Room. The only different between this and the route above the Stepped Chambers is that the windows are big enough to squeeze through.

### S.M.A.R.T. Moves

Grab the protruding turbine rod and climb into the window of the Upper Chamber. The other turbine has no rod, so leap the gap to or from the window.

Leap onto the single server towers by each support pillar to hop across from turbine to turbine.

Climb the snaking pipework near the lower exit, and clamber into the window of the Computer Room with the Vending Machines.

## 34 Red Zone: Small Server Rooms & MG Nest Corridor (Lvl. 4)

At the end of the curved Turbine Upper Chamber is a tiny, dark Server Room, a connecting passage, and a second small Server Room with a window overlooking the Containment Room. Enemies may ambush you here because the side of the server tower is a great hiding place. The window is good for firing down on enemies. Along the connecting passage is an MG Nest that's used mainly by the enemy on Resistance members rushing the Turbine Room.

## 35 Red Zone: Containment Room & Reactor Access (Lvls. 2, 3, & 4)

## 36 Red Zone: Computer Room & Vending Machines (Lvl. 4)

This Containment Room is not to be confused with the one in the middle of the Yellow Zone, which is directly opposite, through the Reactor Room. Expect the enemy to be out on force in this location, which is accessed via the Turbine Chamber on the ground, and the Computer Room on the upper floor.

The Computer Room leads directly to the MG Nest, and a two-story chamber that covers the rear of the Containment Room (hide behind the servers and fire on foes). Locate the entrance behind the servers, and stairs up. Drinks machines are in the connecting corridor, which leads to two side chambers (Server Rooms) that feed back into the main Containment Room. Snipe from the window next to the Vending Machines, or leap through it into the Containment Room floor.

The main draws are the illuminated steps into the Reactor, and your final "Core" Objective. A door to the left here takes you to a cubbyhole hiding spot. Also check the entrance and two windows on the right side leading to a Server Room, and a pair of half-opened double doors to the Power Conduit Chamber. Finally, note the stairs leading down on either side; these allow you into the Core itself (which is useful for keeping the enemy guessing where you'll attack from).

**Can't tell which Containment Room is which? The one in the Red Zone features a covered upper platform across from the Reactor, and no Command Post.**

TIP

HISTORY OF THE ARK
CHARACTER CREATION
GAMEPLAY
WEAPONS DETAIL
CAMPAIGN
Getting Answers
Breakout
Chen's Plans
Black Box
Attack on CCity
Airborne
Operation Babel
Critical Reaction
CHALLENGES
APPENDICES

## 37 Red Zone: Server Room & Staircase Thoroughfare (Lvls. 3 & 4)

## 38 Red Zone: Server Room & Maintenance Corridor (Lvls. 3 & 4)

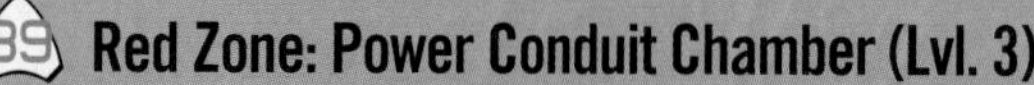

## 39 Red Zone: Power Conduit Chamber (Lvl. 3)

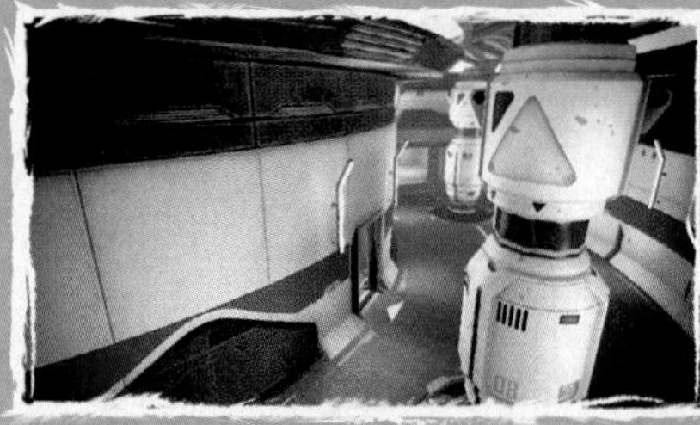

On the upper floor and right side of the Containment Room is a passage to a Server Room running parallel to the Containment Room, and a stairwell leading down near the vending machines. Follow the path around above the stairwell to a small Server Room and an escape window into the Power Conduit Chamber. At the bottom of the stairs is a thorough-fare out to the same chamber.

Head down the upper level passage instead, and you reach a second Server Room overlooking the Containment Room, with a window to leap (or fire) down from. Directly down the stairs is a room with a few barrels (ambush foes from under the stairs), and a doorway out to the Reactor. Opposite is an L-shaped Maintenance Corridor to the Power Conduit Chamber.

The Power Conduit Chamber itself has four huge couplings running the height of the curved corridor chamber, and access to the Security's spawn point. This room is dangerous to enter, and this entire area is used more by the opposition, so run interference or avoid this place.

## 40 Reactor & Core (Lvls. 2 & 3)

## 41 Storage & Lower Reactor Core Access (Lvl. 2)

The Reactor is in the center of this second section of the facility, and there are more ways to reach it than you may realize. The two obvious entrances are via the Yellow and Red Containment Rooms, where Soldiers on your team place their explosives (one set on either mainframe panel). The room itself is circular, with an outer and inner path that connects to the opposite panel. You can hide on the lower path and ambush foes (although you're usually spotted before this becomes beneficial).

The duct high on the Yellow Zone side is another way to head to and from here (or fight from). But down below, and accessed via the lower stairs in either Containment Room, or via the Storage area across from the Security spawn point, is the crackling Core itself. The door to the Yellow Zone is sealed here. Direct access to the Core isn't beneficial; you must move back and around to the panels to finish the Core Objective. The Storage Room itself is swarming with spawned foes, but worth ambushing.

## 42 Security Deployment Zone (Part 2): Midway Balcony (Lvls. 3 & 4)

Security forces enter via a platform that is too high to climb up, and has sentry turrets that stop you long before you reach this area. That is, unless you step into the dead-end passage on either side of the drop from the spawn point. Ambush foes (with the knowledge that you'll be slaughtered after one or two kills at the most) from here.

## 43 Security Command Post (Part 2) (Lvl. 3)

This Command Post is out of bounds to your team, and attempting to reach it ends badly for you.

# Objective Tactics: Core Objective 1

## Hack the Vent System

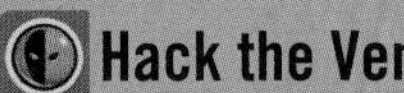

Spawn Point to Vent Room: 00:15

Time to Hack Airflow Controls: 01:00

### General Tactics

You attack the Vent Room, which is the central location in this initial zone of the Reactor, from a variety of entrances. There are two Airflow Controls (hack either, or both at the same time with two or more Operatives), and four incursion points. The exact routes to the points are shown below. Most of the fighting takes place in the adjacent locations surrounding the Vent Rooms. Think about splitting your team, and each taking a route (either splitting into forces of four to take two entrances, or two to take all four); not only can you let each other know where the enemy hotspots are, but attacking from all directions can seriously impede your opponents' competence. Of course, mixing up your plan, and all storming from one direction (especially if it's lightly guarded) is a good idea, too.

Once inside the Vent Room, try various ways to make the Airflow Controls hacking go more smoothly. There are two large Control units on each side of the Vent Room, split by a central balcony and staircase down to the Under Corridors. Having teams in both splits up the enemy. Having all your folks in one allows you to defend it more easily; choose either option depending on the strength of the Resistance. Do whatever you can to protect the Operative hacking; you may wish to have four or more Operatives on your team to minimize hacking time.

### Route Planning

**From the Sides (Container Yard):** Choose to pour in through the Starboard Service Stairs, Info Desk area, or Starboard Deck, and then through into the open Reactor Container Yard. Expect problems from the Cargo Bay Control Room, the Cargo Bay itself (where the enemy is likely to be heading up from), and defenders from the Vent Room entrance.

**From the Sides (Vent Room Entrance):** Maneuver through the Port Service Stairs, then into the Turbine Room and out of the gap in the left wall, or out via the opening near the Bridge and Info Desk. Engage the enemy by the Steam Stack and Vent Control Entrance with the Escalator MG Nest, and then repel defenders in the Vent Room itself.

**From the Front (Bridge and Control Room):** Assuming an Engineer has already run in the Vent Room and repaired the Access Panel (as a Secondary Objective), mass your troops above the Info Desk and into the Vent Tower Entrance, then head through the Control Room and into the Vent Room itself.

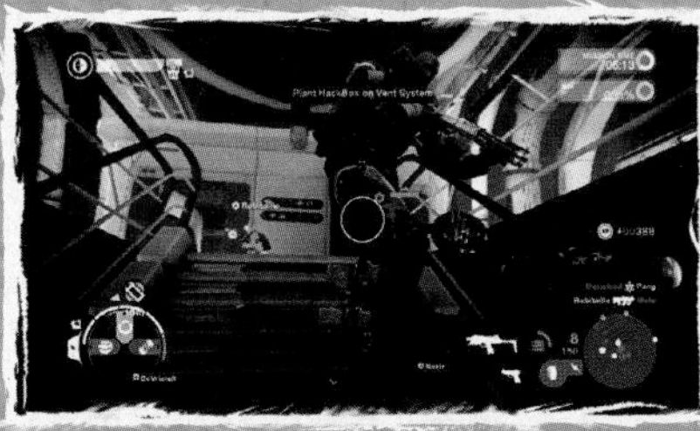

**From Below (Under Corridors):** A most cunning route is to use the Starboard Service Stairs, connecting to the Starboard Deck, down the exterior deck stairs (have an Engineer peel off to claim the Supply Command Post if you wish), and then along past the Cargo Bay, and up the Under Corridors into the center of the Vent Room.

**Vent Room Attack:** If you enter as a team, spread out around the room and on different floors so foes must aim everywhere to take each one of you down. Use the Airflow Controls as cover, and the passages connecting each side of the room. Climb on the ventilation fans, then cross to the central balcony, which allows you to guard both sides; of course the enemy is likely to be there. Remember they use three of the four entrances (they don't usually head through the Control Room and bridge you've opened the door to). From here, a mixture of hacking, covering the Operatives, and using all your weaponry (guns, grenades, and Engineer ordnance) is the order of the day.

## Automated Ordnance

Because you're the attacking team, there's much less time to set up defenses. Check the Security's placement for ideas, and areas to avoid or watch for.

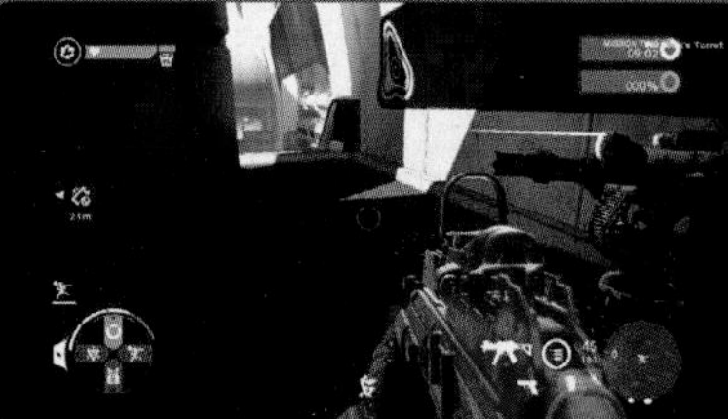

1 Place this by the Steam Stack, so it can fire down on the Vent Room Entrance area and guard the Health Command Post at the same time.

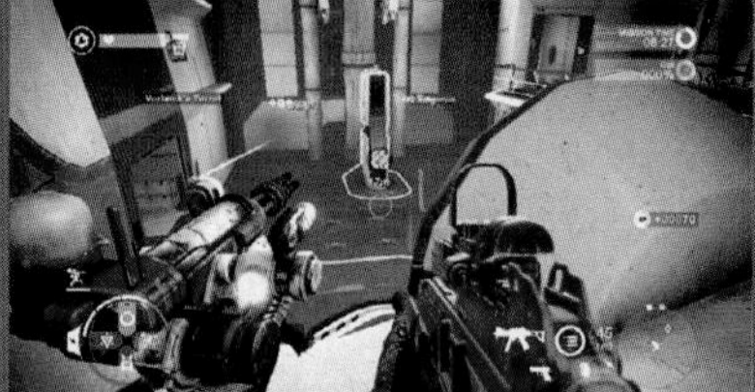

2 Defend your Operatives by placing turrets up on the fan supports. The enemy must turn around, away from the Operative, to deal with the turret. The height advantage means they are more difficult to hit.

1 Mine the Health Command Post; you have the time, and you should constantly check and re-trap the area.

2 Add insult to injury and prime a mine on the edge of the enemy deployment zone, in the Under Corridors.

3 Place mines in the narrow corridors and base of the stairs so foes running between the sides of the Vent Room receive a nasty surprise.

## Sniper's Ally: Camping Spots

1 The enemy doesn't usually know where this gunfire is coming from until too late; tag foes in the Cargo Bay Control room from here, near the closed bridge.

2 Hop on this Reactor cylinder and guard the Container Yard, tagging foes coming out of the Cargo Bay, in the Control Room, and the Vent Room.

3 Cover the Cargo Bay, all of the Container Yard, and into the Vent Room to stop foes from using this route. Watch for foes heading into this room via the stairs though.

4 Stand on the railing next to the Steam Stack for the extra height this affords you. Then fire on foes coming up into the Vent Room Entrance.

5 Hop on the pipe running along the inside opening of the Turbine Room; you can cover the Vent Room entrance, and the Security side of the Turbine Room too.

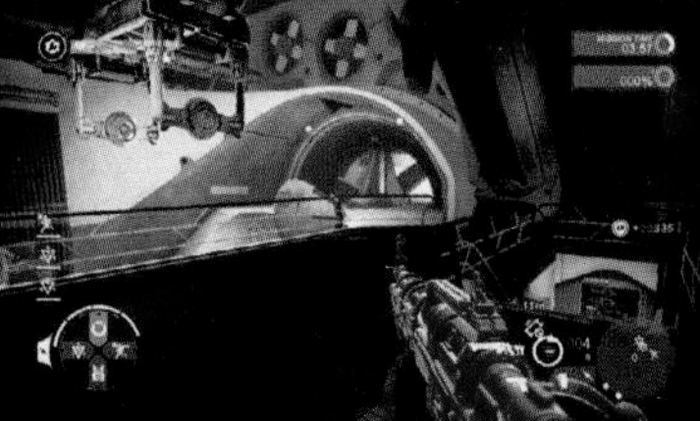

6 Both the Resistance and Security forces are at an advantage when patrolling back and forth to cover each side. Watch for foes coming up the stairs, too. Multiple guards here are a good idea.

# Objective Tactics: Secondary Objectives

## Escort Core Objective Class Teammate

**Official Escort Info:** The four different entrances are made for this objective; splitting into pairs allows you to each take a different entrance while keeping an eye on each other. Or, pair up but take an opposite entrance, so you can see where all your teammates are, and can attack from four directions simultaneously. Operatives backed up by Medics are an obvious and much-needed duo, or two Operatives covering each other with Caltrops and firearm fire.

**Unofficial Escort Info:** Use Soldiers and Medics to fight while the hacking is going on.

## Repair the Bridge Access Panel (First Section)

Spawn Point to Access Panel: 00:16

Time to Repair Panel: 00:10

This certainly isn't necessary, and may waste time and resources that could be better spent in the Vent Rooms warding off enemy incursions, but you may wish to have a single Engineer head into the Vent Room, and then up and into the Control Room containing the Access Panel (it can't be reached by any other route).

If you can combine this feat with coaxing one or two enemies away from guarding the Airflow Controls (allowing your teammates to start hacking earlier), you've more than done your job. Then figure out if this is a great way to enter the Vent Rooms. The open bridge may attract enemies watching the area, so the other option is to open the bridge access, but never use it!

## Capture the Health Command Post

Engineer & Operative Advantage!

Spawn Point to Command Post: 00:11

Time to Claim Command Post: 00:10

In a small room connected to the Resistance end of the Turbine room, this is easily overlooked in the rush to the Vent Room and your main objective. Have one Engineer responsible for capturing (and upgrading), and then trapping this Command Post, before joining the rest of your forces. They can then use the side doors in the Steam Stack area, returning quickly if Security wades in to retake it.

## Capture the Supply Command Post

Engineer & Operative Advantage!

Spawn Point to Command Post: 00:12

Time to Claim Command Post: 00:10

Tucked away under the lower stairs on the Starboard Deck, this is another post that's often overlooked in the race to the Vent Room. However, this is slightly closer to the enemy's deployment zone, and you need to memorize the route across the Reactor Container Yard and out onto the Starboard Deck to return to battle over it. Weigh up whether the manpower to do this is worth fewer of your team hacking the Airflow Controls; capture this once and lay a mine on your way to the Vent Room.

## Construct the Office MG Nest

## Construct the Escalators MG Nest

Engineer

Spawn Point to Office MG Nest: 00:17

Spawn Point to Escalators MG Nest: 00:15

Time to Construct: 00:04

This MG Nest in the Cargo Bay Control Room overlooks the Vent Room where one of the Airflow Controls is visible. The Control Room is accessed via the Reactor Container Yard, which means it's slightly closer to the enemy spawn point, and normally more useful to them, because your team is more likely to be storming the Vent Rooms from one of the four different entrances. It offers moderate suppressing fire, but a greater chance of being attacked by foes from behind if you man it.

This is at the Security end of the Steam Stack, Vent Room Entrance area. The Turbine Hall is on the left. Security forces use this MG Nest on your team, so it is important to know where this MG Nest is, but it isn't critical to use it.

## Objective Tactics: Core Objective 2

###   Destroy the Reactor

Spawn Point to Reactor Room: 00:25

Time to Disarm Explosives: 00:05

Time to Plant Explosives: 00:07

Countdown to Explosion: 00:40

### General Tactics

There are two major plans to consider when rampaging through this inner Reactor zone. You need to figure out a way through this maze without getting caught up in the outer rooms, and you need to reach either of the Containment Rooms as quickly as possible. Then you need to find a way to detonate the Reactor when the full might of the Security opposition is likely to be waiting for you. For this, a mixture of cunning and route planning is key.

The route planning is detailed below. The cunning involves when to attack: Storm both Containment Rooms and each Reactor entrance simultaneously, with snipers on the balconies at the far end of the Containment Room, and as many Soldiers as you can spawn. Or, become an Operative, disguise yourself as an enemy, and enter the Reactor Room before taking out most of their turrets and mines from behind enemy lines; your Soldiers then have an easier time of it. When the explosives are finally clamped, keep some teammates milling about, but others guarding the Lower Reactor Core Access. If you have an Engineer here, have him set up traps, because respawning Security forces almost always take this (quickest) route back from their deployment zone.

### Route Planning

**Yellow Zone:** Take a left up through the Vent Fans Passages, and storm through the Stepped Chambers. The orange floor lights show you the way... straight into an enemy MG Nest, so use these only if you're not situationally aware. Fight into the Containment Room from the stairs, or the Computer Rooms accessed via the Upper Stepped Chamber. Combat inside here is fierce, so although you're arriving in unison, make sure you're appearing via all the different Stepped Chamber paths. Then take the balcony (and the Supply Command Post) before attending to the Reactor.

**Red Zone:** Effect the same exact plan if you're coming in via the Turbine Room. Turn right from the Vent Fans Passages, race through the Turbine Room (stop to claim the Health Command Post, and watch for MG Nest fire), then storm into the Containment Room via every possible entrance (detailed in the Locations section, previously).

 TIP

For either route, all use the same path, or split into teams of four and storm from opposite Containment Rooms.

**End Zone:** When you reach the Containment Room, the enemy is likely to be defending this place with every single explosive, turret, and firearm they have. Whether you're attacking in waves, or better yet; at the same time from both zones, you have the option to sneak in via the Vent Shaft and attack foes from inside the Reactor gantry.

## Automated Ordnance

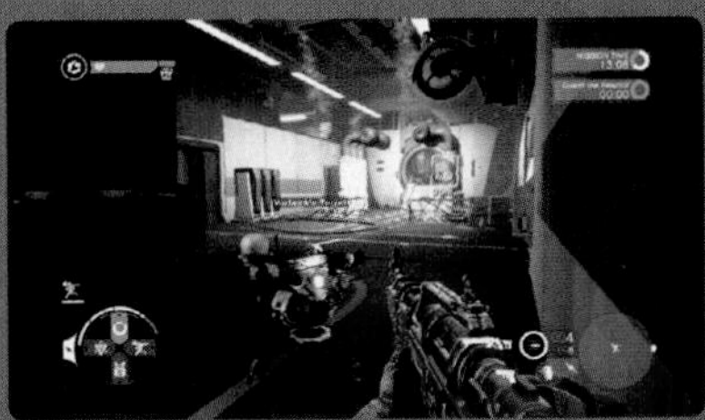

3 4 A turret to the side of the scenery in the rear of the Containment Room shields it from the enemy's entrances, and covers the Reactor Room.

3 Cover the Supply Command Post from the Computer Room with the Vending Machines.

4 Mine the entrance to the Vent Shaft so foes can't follow you in here.

## Sniper's Ally: Camping Spots

7 The doorway linking the Outer and Inner Stepped Chamber sections is a good place to snipe, check out the Containment Room, and report any movement or an active MG Nest.

8 9 Cover the Computer Rooms adjacent to the Containment Rooms on the upper floor; you can defend the passageways and shoot down through the window (Camping Spot 8 shown).

10 11 The back corner of this Containment Room allows you to view enemy movement from any doorway and the stairs, as well as covering the Reactor Room (Camping Spot 10 shown).

12 13 Stand atop the upper floor of the Containment Room, so you can cover your teammates as they push into the Reactor Room. Watch for attacks from your side (Camping Spot 12 shown).

14 15 Sitting at the Vent exit, you can bide your time before rushing to the Reactor to clamp your bomb, or shoot from here and duck into cover (Camping Spot 14 shown).

# Objective Tactics: Secondary Objectives

### Escort Core Objective Class Teammate

**Official Escort Info:** Team up with a Soldier, perhaps with a second Soldier or a Medic. Fighting through your opponents' fortifications is the key to victory. Perhaps you want a Soldier and an Operative; the latter interferes with your foe's turrets (with the Hack Turret and Control Turret Abilities), or disguises himself to create a diversion.

### Capture the Health Command Post

Engineer & Operative Advantage!

Spawn Point to Command Post: 00:12

Time to Claim Command Post: 00:10

With the enemies not usually venturing into the Red Zone Turbine chambers, you have an advantage of taking this post, leaving a mine on the path the enemy most travels, and continuing into either of the Containment Rooms. Remember you can climb up from the perimeter path, or drop down from the air duct above. Although it's a short hop from the Small Server Rooms and MG Nest, your foes should be coaxed into constant Reactor Room battles; usually your team wants to end this mission quickly.

###  Capture the Supply Command Post

Engineer & Operative Advantage!

Spawn Point to Command Post: 00:13

Time to Claim Command Post: 00:10

This is in the Yellow Zone Containment Room overlooking the Reactor access doorway, so if the walls are striped and red, you've gone the wrong way! Get here via the left route, along the Stepped Corridor, and you'll arrive at about the same time as the foes. They have the luxury of waiting you out, so give up fighting over this if you're about to lose the mission. Otherwise, take the post, and set up a turret or sniper in the Computer Room with the Vending Machines.

###  Construct the Doorway MG Nest

###  Construct the Walkway MG Nest

 Engineer

Spawn Point to Doorway MG Nest: 00:14

Spawn Point to Walkway MG Nest: 00:15

Time to Construct: 00:04

The Doorway MG Nest is in the Yellow Zone Containment Room, and is easy to find if you're following the orange floor lights. This MG Nest's main purpose is to gun down your troops as they follow these lights, and it can only really be aimed into the Stepped Chamber, so leave it alone. Let the enemy take the time to build this, while you take more important objectives. Be sure to take the gunner out with grenades, because he has nowhere to run.

The Walkway MG Nest is likely to be already manned by foes, because it covers the Turbine Room. This is a major thoroughfare for your team, so learn the limitations of the MG Nest's aiming zone. If this is manned by the enemy, approach in the Turbine Room via the low perimeter path, or the Upper Chambers so you aren't hit, and strike the gunner using grenades through the open window, or gunfire from the Small Server Room corridor.

###  Solo Tactics

**One human and a host of robots puts you center stage for this final Reactor explosion. This means Command Posts are more important; so you can begin as one type (so you can set turrets and mines as an Engineer, and upgrade posts), but change to a Soldier (ideally at the Supply Command Post) once you reach the Yellow Zone Containment Room. Breaching the Reactor via the Vent Shaft is a good plan, and if you're unable to clamp a bomb, change to an Engineer and force the foes back while a teammate (hopefully) does the job.**

## Mission Completion Conditions

###  Continuation...

**Core Objective 1:** Your team succeeds in destroying the Vent System. Part 2 of this mission now commences....

###  Completed!

The match completes if you successfully destroy the Reactor before the timer ticks down.

###  Unsuccessful!

Resistance forces lose if the enemy stops you from completing either Core Objective by the time the timer reaches zero.

Level 2

Level 1

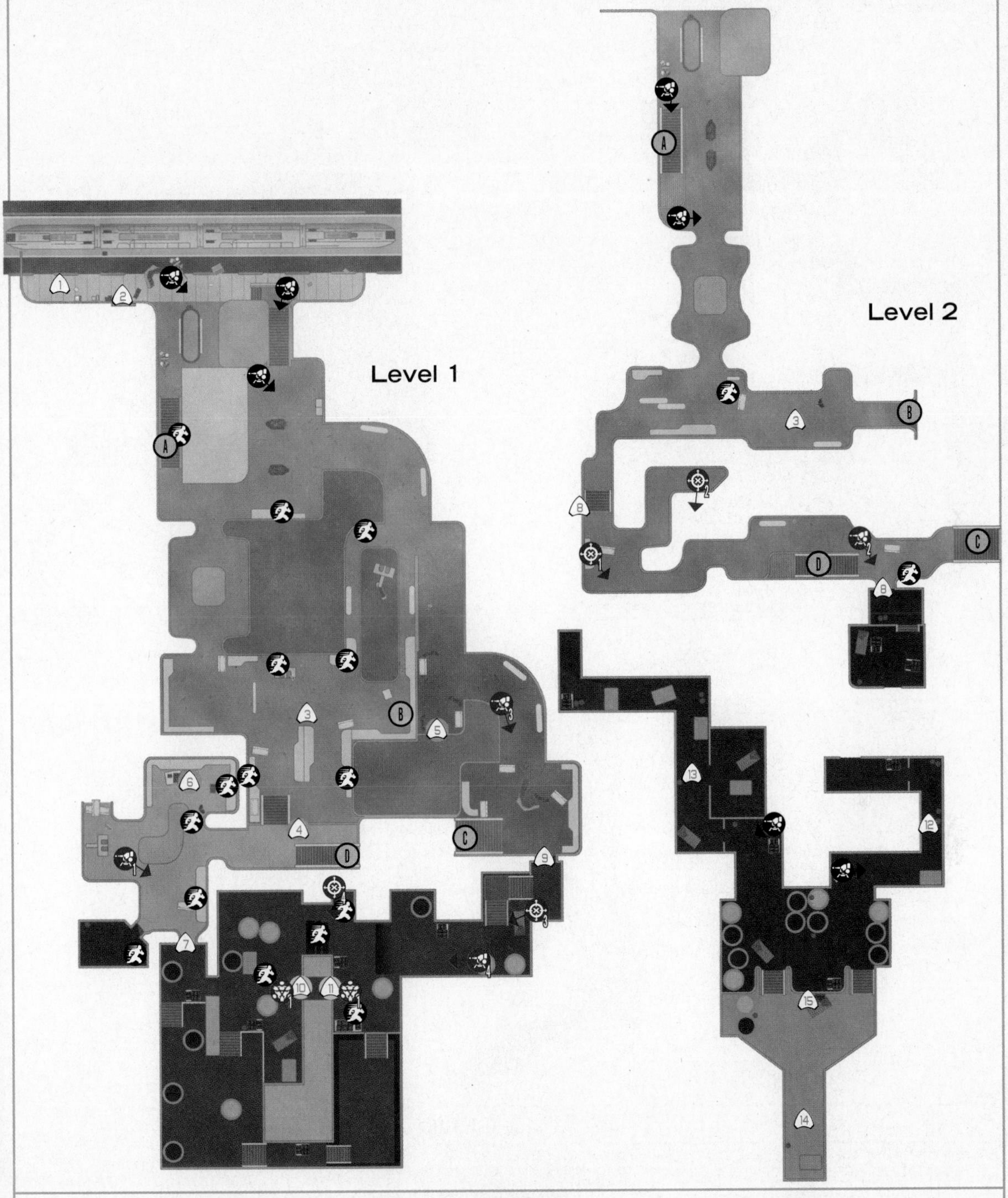

## MAP LEGEND

**↘Aquarium: Core Objective 1**

1: Security Deployment Zone (Pt. 1): Monorail (Lvl. 2)
2: Security Command Post (Pt. 1) (Lvl. 2)
3: Atrium Floor & Upper Balconies (Lvl. 2)
4: Atrium & MG Nest (Lvl. 1)
5: Health Command Post (Lvl. 1)
6: Supply Command Post (Lvl. 1)
7: Ark Water Treatment Access (1) (Lvl. 1)
8: Ark Water Treatment Access (2) (Lvl. 2)
9: Ark Water Treatment Access (3) (Lvl. 1)
10: Storage Room (Side 1) (Lvls. 1 & 2)
11: Storage Room (Side 2) (Lvls. 1 & 2)
12: Maintenance Bay Conduits (1) (Lvls. 1 & 2)
13: Maintenance Bay Conduits (2) (Lvl. 2)
14: Resistance Deployment Zone (Pt. 1): Maintenance Bay (Lvl. 2)
15: Resistance Command Post (Pt. 1) (Lvl. 2)

**↘Aquarium: Core Objective 2**

16: Security Deployment Zone (Pt. 1): Undersea Hall (Lvl. 2)
17: Security Command Post (Pt. 1) (Lvl. 2)
18: Undersea Corridors (Lvl. 1)
19: Aquarium Alley (Lvl. 1)
20: Water Treatment: Pipe Pressure Corridor (Lvl. 1)

BRINK

## ↘ Aquarium: Overview Map

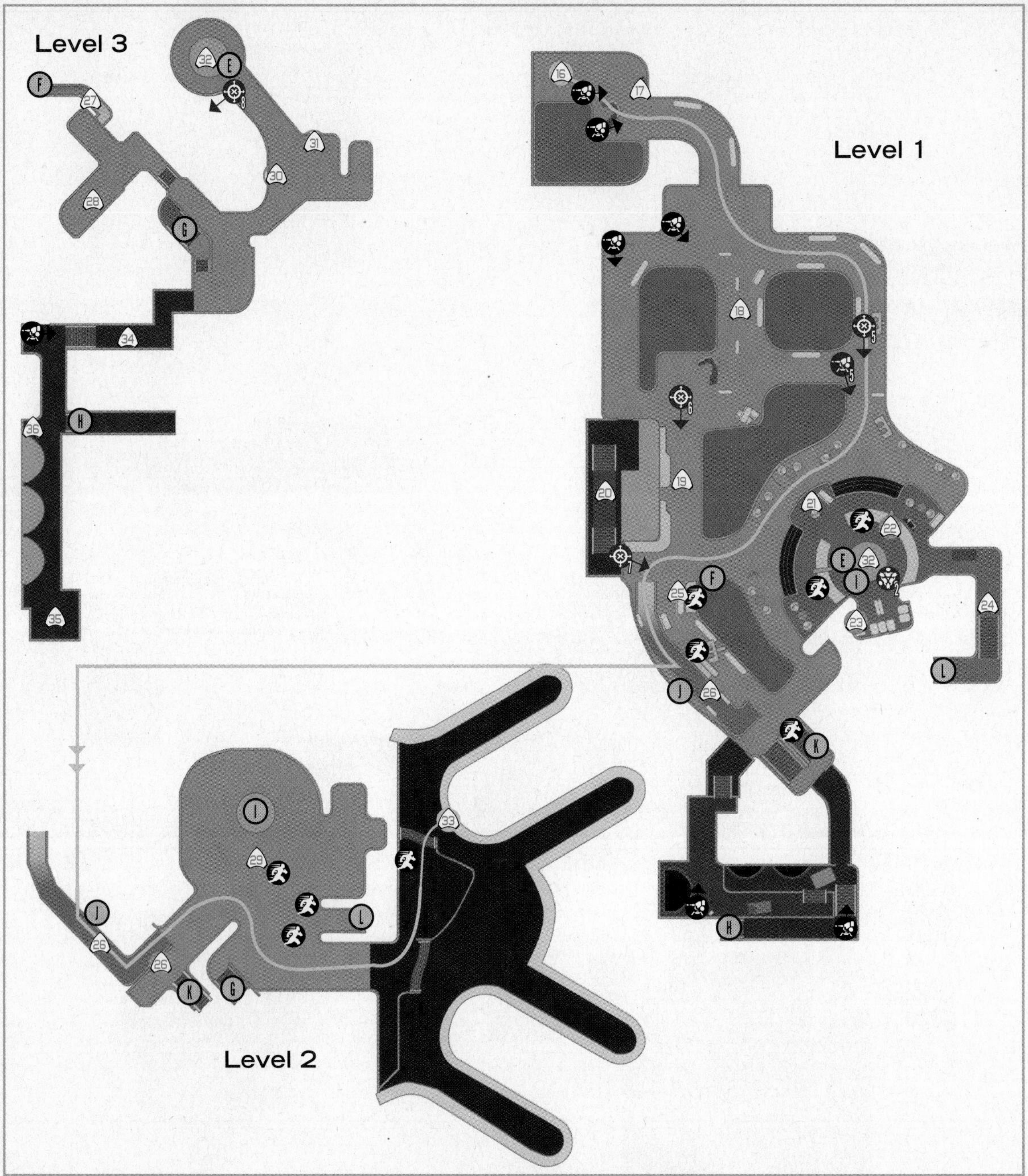

Level 3

Level 1

Level 2

## MAP LEGEND (continued)

21: Kyuden Restaurant (Lvl. 1)
22: Supply Command Post (Lvl. 1)
23: Lift Generator (Lvl. 1)
24: The Side Stairs (Lvls. 1 & 2)
25: The Long Ramp Entrance (Lvl. 1)
26: The Long Ramp & MG Nest (Lvls. 1, & 2)
27: Air Conditioning Duct (Lvl. 3)
28: Upper Balcony (Lvl. 3)
29: The Ark Lobby: Main Floor (Lvl. 2)
30: The Ark Lobby: Overlook Balcony & MG Nest (Lvl. 3)
31: The Ark Lobby: Health Command Post (Lvl. 3)
32: The Ark Lobby: Elevator 1 (from Kyuden Restaurant) (Lvls. 1 & 3)
33: The Ark Lobby: Marina Docks (Lvl. 2)
34: Mattress Alley to the Mezzanine Lobby (Lvls. 2 & 3)
35: Resistance Deployment Zone (Pt. 2): Vat Chamber (Lvls. 1 & 2)
36: Resistance Command Post (Pt. 2) (Lvl. 2)

S.M.A.R.T. Move
Engineer Mine (Optimal Placement)
Engineer Turret (Optimal Placement)
Camping Spot
Deployment Zone Turret (Invulnerable)
Core Objective Location
Secondary Objective Location
Critical Path (Route)
Level Link

# DAY 1: HOSTAGE RESCUE

FREEPLAY: AQUARIUM ↘ RESISTANCE CAMPAIGN–DAY 1: GETTING ANSWERS

## 10:23 ↘ Inner Loop Monorail approaching Aquarium Visitor Center

MISSION TIME (COb 1): 08:00

MISSION TIME (COb 2): +12:00

### Captain Mokoena: Briefing

Chen's terrorists have seized the Founder's council member. They're holding him in the old Aquarium's Visitors' Center. The clock's ticking! To force the council into action, Chen's injected the hostage with a neuro-toxin, and he'll be dead within the hour if we don't get him to medical. If you can't rescue him in time, don't stay for payback; cut your losses and pull out. We're on show here; if Chen sees we can't protect the Founder, there'll be more kidnappings. If the guests don't think we can protect them, we lose all legitimacy... and we lose the Ark! I'm counting on you to get in there, neutralize the terrorists, and get that man to safety: ASAP!

### Objectives (Security)

#### First Part

- Destroy Door
- Escort Core Objective Class Teammate
- Capture the Health Command Post
- Capture the Supply Command Post
- Construct the Atrium MG Nest

#### Second Part

- Escort the Hostage
- Repair Lift Generator
- Capture the Health Command Post
- Capture the Supply Command Post
- Construct the Ramp MG Nest
- Construct the Lobby MG Nest

### Optimal Class Numbers

| | COb 1 | COb 2 |
|---|---|---|
| Soldier | [4] | [2] |
| Medic | [2] | [4] |
| Engineer | [1] | [1] |
| Operative | [1] | [1] |

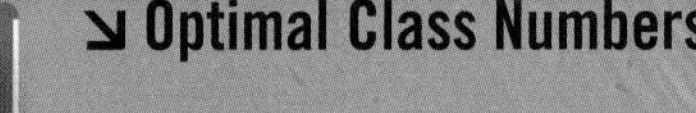

## Important Locations (Core Objective 1)

### 1 Security Deployment Zone (Pt. 1): Monorail (Lvl. 2)

Due to the automatic turrets guarding this platform, Resistance forces aren't to be expected in this spawning area. After optionally checking in at the Security Command Post, take one of the two exits. The nearer one leads to the Atrium Upper Walkway (and more direct access to the Supply Command Post), while the exit stairs allow access down to the Lower Corridors.

### 2 Security Command Post (Pt. 1) (Lvl. 2)

It's very safe to access this initial Command Post within your deployment zone, far from the action. Use it to swap to a different class (one that your team requires; check the numbers next to the names of each class in the menu wheel) or change your weaponry.

Talk with your team prior to the match about which class you should spawn as. That way you can sprint to a critical chokepoint without waiting around at this spawn point. Choose an appropriate body type and pair of weapons too. Then, as the situation dictates, check in at this Command Post.

 TIP

## 3 Atrium Floor and Upper Balconies (Lvl. 2)

## 4 Atrium and MG Nest (Lvl. 1)

Accessed via stairs from the Monorail Station, or next to the ground-level gift shop (which is closed), the Lower Corridors are an important couple of connecting chambers and passages. You can also access them by leaping off the initial balcony area to the left (on top of the gift shop roof).

The curved underwater passage to the left allows access into the area close to the Health Command Post. As you round the corner, you have an excellent line-of-sight up the ramp, toward the Command Post itself, and the ground foyer wraps around to the Atrium on the right.

The quickest way to the Atrium is directly through the gap on either side of the main support pillar, and around into the area under the Atrium's upper balcony. Here, you can use the exhibits, signs, and other scenery as cover; the enemy likes to take a stand at this chokepoint (especially at the MG Nest).

You can't easily reach the Supply Command Post if you choose to use the ground floor.

 CAUTION

Choose to remain (or climb up) on the gift shop balcony roof, and race to either side of the main support pillar (you can drop down to the Lower Corridor at this point if you wish) to reach the Atrium Floor and Upper Balconies. This is the quickest route to the Atrium.

One of the main paths your team takes is through this central Atrium, with the two hanging sharks and high ceilings. Watch for enemies at the MG Nest, and the far balcony above it. If you're being waylaid by foes, the information rack and tanks on both levels make good cover. You have easy access to the adjacent Health Command Post (on your left), and the Upper Balcony on your right continues around toward the Supply Command Post, which is the optimal path to take when attempting to claim it. The area with the MG Nest leads to one of the three Water Treatment Access Points.

### S.M.A.R.T. Moves

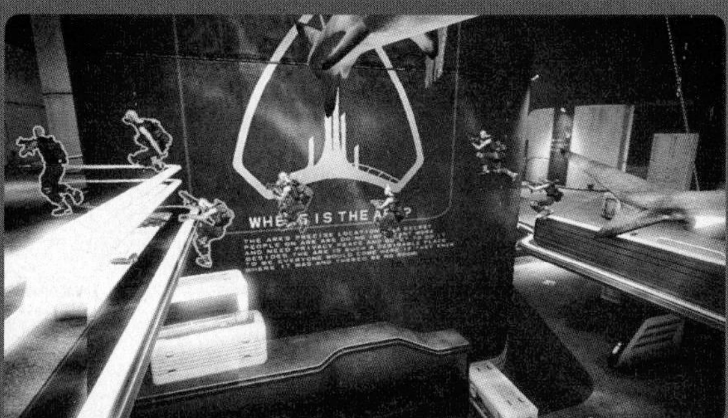

Atrium: Leap up the side wall with the Ark logo on it (from either the ground or balcony), and use the crates to clamber onto the balcony above the MG Nest.

Use the empty Aquarium exhibit under the coral reef banner to jump and climb up onto the gift shop balcony.

You can also turn while halfway up or down the stairs adjacent to the gift shop, and climb up onto the balcony.

Ground Floor: Climb on this exhibit and cover the ramps and Health Command Post across from you.

Leap on an Aquarium exhibit to cover the ramps and Health Command Post across from you.

Upper balconies: Climb on any of the Aquarium exhibits for cover or to gain height advantage.

Climb the "Shopping, Eating" signpost to gain height or to use as cover when firing on the MG Nest area.

Leap on this Aquarium exhibit to cover the ramps and Health Command Post across from you.

## 5 Health Command Post (Lvl. 1)

This is at the intersection of three different routes: the ramped balcony leading to the Atrium, the lower ramp from the Security's Atrium Lower Corridors, and the second underwater tunnel that allows you to reach the third Water Treatment Access Point. Such an open area makes spotting enemies easy but defending the Command Post more difficult.

**You can run along the outside of the ramp railing when closing in on the Health Command Post, in case enemies appear from the upper corridor, allowing you to drop down and take cover under the ramp bridge, or head into the Atrium.**

TIP

### S.M.A.R.T. Moves

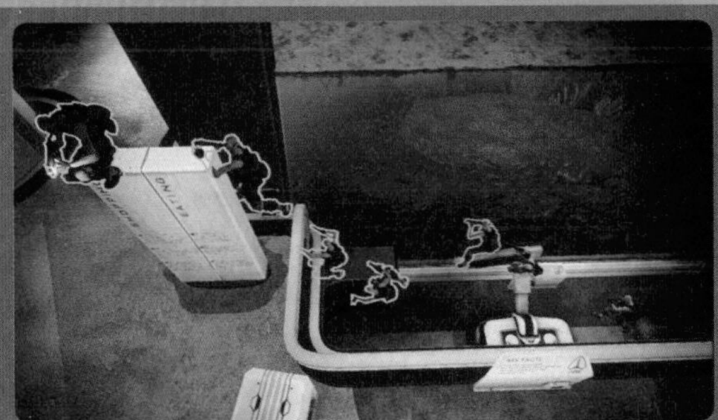

Use the Aquarium exhibits in the corner of the Atrium to fire on foes all around you.

Climb onto the top of the signpost, ambushing foes running in from the tunnel or balconies.

## 6 Supply Command Post (Lvl. 1)

Although the Resistance forces have an advantage in the direct route they can take to reach this location, Security forces have a usually secure route with a height advantage; simply use the upper balcony and weave around to the balcony above the Supply Command Post (or the end of the balcony above Water Treatment Access 1). Then drop down to reach it.

### S.M.A.R.T. Moves

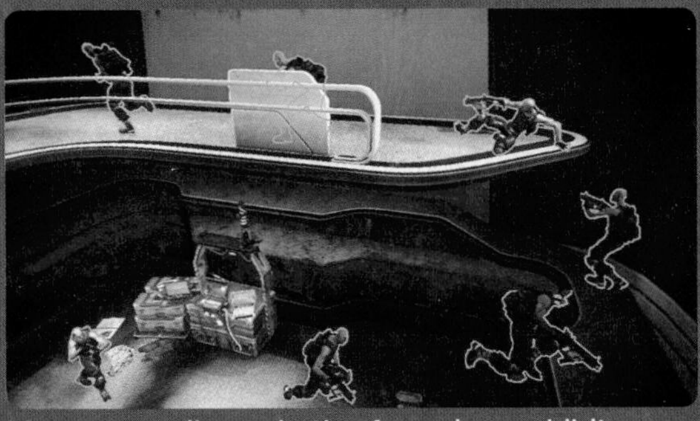

You can easily scale the Aquarium exhibit and hop back up to the balcony above this Command Post.

## 7 Ark Water Treatment Access (1) (Lvl. 1)

Expect fierce battles at this major chokepoint as you attempt to push into this narrow, ground-level doorway. If you're on the balcony, drop down when you see the red banner, which is directly above the entrance. You can also reach this location from the Upper Balcony above the MG Nest, or the Atrium itself. Your team has the height advantage, so use it: Shoot down and lob grenades from the balcony above.

If you manage to make it through the access doorway, expect a heavily mined and well-guarded small antechamber before a doorway on your left that leads into the Storage Room (Side 1). At the access doorway, a second entrance to your right leads to a small waste-containment area with vats. Use a S.M.A.R.T. move here.

### S.M.A.R.T. Moves

To quickly gain height, leap from this exhibit to the balcony above. If you have the dexterity, you can jump on the vat lid propped against the wall, and leap to grab the balcony rail, allowing you into the enemy's deployment area (and balcony overlooking the Storage Room).

### 8 Ark Water Treatment Access (2) (Lvl. 2)

This access is conveniently located at the top of the stairs that lead up from the MG Nest. Use these objects as scenic clues as you memorize the routes to reach this point. The direct path across the Atrium (by foot or S.M.A.R.T. route) is quick, but you can also reach it from the Upper Balcony that loops around from the Supply Command Post, or the steps up from Ark Water Treatment Access (3).

Once through the doorway, you're on a balcony directly above the Storage Room floor and can easily reach the door (and waiting enemies) down below. Because you're more difficult to hit until you drop into the Storage Room, this is a good route choice for a rush.

### 9 Ark Water Treatment Access (3) (Lvl. 1)

A little farther along the upper balcony above the MG Nest are steps down to a medium-sized open area with some scattered crates, two signs, and a couple of aquarium tanks. Because this area offers a route to and from the Health Command Post, expect heavy enemy activity here. The doorway leads down some steps and into a passage connected to the Storage Room; with the objective door spotted at the opposite end of this passage.

### 10 Storage Room (Side 1) (Lvls. 1 and 2)

Expect mayhem on both sides of this central connecting chamber where the Resistance Agent (Security's Hostage) is being held. On the upper floor is a balcony that you can climb to, but which has usually been taken over by the enemy. Clear that area so your Soldiers have a clear route to fix their explosives. You pin the bomb on the door on the far wall, having stormed the first Storage Room door accessed via the Ark Water Treatment Access Point 1, or by sliding under or around the jutting pipe that separates each side of the Storage Room. Beware of foes with longer-ranged weapons in the U-shaped connecting conduit to the right of the Storage Room door; run around there to coax foes into fighting with you, so they lose focus guarding the door itself.

**It can be helpful to hold the Sprint / S.M.A.R.T. button as you constantly move and jump around the Storage Room, especially if you're a smaller body type. Use it in conjunction with jumping, and leap over barriers or onto the numerous pipes on the walls.**

TIP

 **S.M.A.R.T. Moves** 

Remember you can slide under the jutting pipes instead of running around them; this is quicker.

Tuck yourself onto the pipe above the red valve, but watch for enemies sliding under you!

### 11 Storage Room (Side 2) (Lvls. 1 and 2)

The focus of combat occurs here. Reach this area via the U-shaped connecting conduit (ground floor), where you can hide and annoy the enemy. The jutting pipe that separates each side of the Storage Room is another access area, but you'll mainly converge on this point via the two Ark Water Treatment Access Points (2 and 3). Use the Upper Balcony to rain death down on the enemy, or the ground corridor for longer range attacks; and make sure you prepare for mines and turrets during the assault.

 **S.M.A.R.T. Moves** 

You can climb the white cylindrical vat and up onto the Upper Balcony as well as dropping down from it.

## 12 Maintenance Bay Conduits (1) (Lvls. 1 & 2)

To the right of Ark Water Treatment Access Point 1 is a small waste-containment area with medium-sized cylindrical vats around the lower alcove, and a balcony above. Use S.M.A.R.T. moves to leap onto the balcony, and storm the enemy's conduits. You can quickly overwhelm foes on the Storage Room balcony, and dodge the sentry turrets and cause havoc inside the enemy's deployment zone! This is a high-risk route, but one that can cause panic and draw attention away from the Storage Room, allowing your Core Objective to be met.

### S.M.A.R.T. Moves

Stand on the slightly askew vat lid, and ascend to this balcony to gain some height, if you're on the Storage Room floor.

In the vat room, leap on the propped lid of a container, and up to the balcony.

## 13 Maintenance Bay Conduits (2) (Lvl. 2)

This hole in the ceiling of the Storage Room (Side 2) actually leads to the Resistance force's other initial conduit passageways. Although you can stand just behind the area, in the U-shaped connecting passage of the Storage Room, and cut down enemies as they drop down, the conduit passage above isn't readily accessible.

## 14 Resistance Deployment Zone (Pt. 1): Maintenance Bay (Lvl. 2)

The Resistance forces spawn at this point, and utilize either of the two Maintenance Bay Conduits to reach the Storage Room area. Although the area is heavily guarded by both enemies and sentry turrets, it is possible to infiltrate this area.

**Infiltrate the area by leaping up onto the balcony inside Storage Room Side 1, or by jumping onto the vat lid, and then climb onto the conduit balcony: Both are adjacent to Ark Water Treatment Access Point 1. Then dash along the conduit and cause havoc before your inevitable demise. The conduit that leads to Storage Room Side 2 cannot be accessed by Security forces from the ground.**

TIP

## 15 Resistance Command Post (Pt. 1) (Lvl. 2)

Adjacent to the spawning point of the Resistance forces, this Command Post is inaccessible, even if you make it through the sentry guns. The enemy uses this to change to a different class or swap between ordnance.

## Important Locations

(Core Objective 2)

**The section of the Aquarium is not connected to the first part, and is completely self-contained.**

NOTE

## 16 Security Deployment Zone (Pt. 1): Undersea Hall (Lvl. 2)

Security begins here at the shark exhibit, with the Hostage, who must be constantly attended to with medical supplies.

The Undersea Hall is large and well-guarded, and it offers a single route into the Undersea Corridors. As your enemy is likely to be taking up positions inside the Restaurant, it isn't wise to dawdle, or hang around this area for longer than necessary. Pump the Hostage with medicine, and begin the chaperoning!

### 17 Security Command Post (Pt. 1) (Lvl. 2)

This easily spotted post enables you to quickly change both weapons and classes. Because the wounded Hostage requires constant care, Medic is one of the most important classes to switch to. Later on, ensure that at least one Engineer is tasked with upgrading Command Posts and fixing the Lift Generator.

### 18 Undersea Corridors (Lvl. 1)

The "figure-8" shaped corridors that lie between the Security spawn point, and the entrances to the Restaurant, Pipe Pressure Corridor, and Aquarium Alley should have few enemies to worry about, as your sentry guns take care of them. The long, straight distance down the corridors makes this an ideal area to snipe from. However, as the Hostage moves farther into this map, this is a simple thoroughfare to the Restaurant, Aquarium Alley, and the Pipe Pressure Corridor.

### 19 Aquarium Alley (Lvl. 1)

### 20 Water Treatment: Pipe Pressure Corridor (Lvl. 1)

These two parallel corridors mark the quickest route to and from the Long Ramp area, and are a good route to take to meet up with the Hostage if you're killed and respawn. The long-distance view of the Long Ramp area allows you to flank the enemy if they're holed up in the Restaurant area, or plant a turret to cut down foes across at the Long Ramp. Back up into either of these corridors to hide from withering enemy fire, too.

**This area is likely to be clad in explosives and turrets, which is one good reason to avoid (or mix up your routes through) these thoroughfares.**

**CAUTION**

### 21 Kyuden Restaurant (Lvl. 1)

### 22 Supply Command Post (Lvl. 1)

### 23 Lift Generator (Lvl. 1)

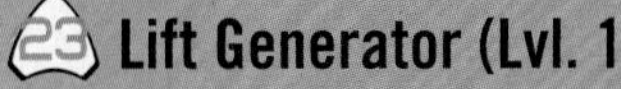

Expect the first major fracas to occur in the Kyuden Restaurant area, which also encompasses the Supply Command Post, and the Lift Generator behind it. An initial wave of teammates should rush here and clear the enemy from the circular bar area, and from behind the metal boxes and lift shaft so your team can take cover here. The Hostage must pass through this room, so you must hold the enemy at bay and move the Hostage into the Long Ramp location or the battle will turn into a stalemate.

Although you can fire in from Camping Spot 5 and cover the enemy, they're likely to be sniping you, so think about a couple of out-flanking maneuvers. Storm in from the side entrance at the Long Ramp location, or head under the Long Ramp and attack from the rear entrance, vaulting onto the raised bar area, or using the alcove as cover.

The drinks machine by the Side Stairs (you can double-back down from here, although that takes a little too long) is another place to lob in grenades and clear out foes, as is the usually heavily guarded Lift Generator. Elevator 1 is open at the start (and can be used as cover, although there's no way out). With an Engineer mending the Lift Generator, pour into Elevaror 1 and automatically ride it up and onto the Ark Lobby Balcony above; which is handy after the Hostage reaches the middle to top of the Long Ramp.

**The enemy usually isn't shy about planting explosives and turrets around the Lift Generator, the corners of the Side Stairs, or along the Hostage's route. Be careful out there!**

**CAUTION**

## S.M.A.R.T. Moves

Clamber over the railings and jump the bar to draw any attention you can away from the Hostage. Sacrifice for the greater good!

###  The Side Stairs (Lvls. 1 and 2)

This often-overlooked route lets you double back to claim the Supply Command Post or Lift Generator while your team is fighting up in the Ark Lobby. It also makes an excellent shortcut to reach the Lobby itself (during the last part of this mission). Try heading up here to the Health Command Post as early as you can.

###  The Long Ramp Entrance (Lvl. 1)

### 26 The Long Ramp and MG Nest (Lvls. 1 & 2)

This is the second major chokepoint for your team. You must guard the slow-moving Hostage up the ramp and force the enemy as they continuously pour out of their spawn point's connecting chambers, which are at the base and halfway up the stairs to the rear of the Long Ramp itself. While a frontal attack is mandatory, there are other ways to reach the top of the ramp. You can fix the Lift and pour out of the Ark Lobby and across to the top of the ramp, or access the same entrance via the Side Stairs. Another option is to use the Air Conditioning Duct (see below).

The Resistance forces also enjoy raking the Hostage with MG fire from the MG Nest atop the ramp, and firearms from behind the adjacent cover. Long-range sniping is one option, but another is to learn the outer limits of the MG's targeting system, and stay outside it until the threat is nullified. Also don't forget to use the stairwell under the MG Nest; although enemies constantly pour out, you can ascend to the exit and attack the MG Nest from behind.

##  S.M.A.R.T. Moves

Don't forget to ascend the crate, exhibit, and haul yourself into the Air Conditioning Duct, and use that as an ambush point!

You can assault the Long Ramp by clambering up the Aquarium cleaner and exhibit. Climb the box at the lower area.

### 27 Air Conditioning Duct (Lvl. 3)

### 28 Upper Balcony (Lvl. 3)

Scramble up the Air Conditioning Duct at the low end of the Long Ramp to reach an Upper Balcony directly above the MG Nest. You can also reach the Upper Balcony from a small set of steps near the enemy's spawn point in the Ark Lobby. Drop behind the Resistance and clear them from the top of the ramp, or lob grenades down. This is a great way to remove an otherwise dug-in enemy. The Air Conditioning Duct looking out onto the Long Ramp is a covered spot to fire from, too.

## 29 The Ark Lobby: Main Floor (Lvl. 2)

This large expanse of carpet, glass, and metal is the final stage in the fight to bundle the Hostage into the boat waiting in the adjacent Marina. Make sure you know every exit doorway: the stairs with the "Fossil Discovery" sign that leads up to the enemy's spawn point (and should be avoided), the entrance to the top of the Long Ramp where the Hostage stumbles up, the Side Stairs down to the Kyuden Restaurant (which is usually a quicker and safer route to get here), and the exterior exit into the Marina itself.

Surrounding the cylindrical elevator shaft (which is entered from the balcony above, and not this lower level) is a bar and reclining area; use the seating and other scenery as cover, and the shaft to hide and peek out from, when sniping.

### S.M.A.R.T. Moves

Hop on a planter, or a sign, or the central aquarium exhibit (as shown), and then grab the railing of the Overlook Balcony to gain some height.

## 30 The Ark Lobby: Overlook Balcony and MG Nest (Lvl. 3)

## 31 The Ark Lobby: Health Command Post (Lvl. 3)

## 32 The Ark Lobby: Elevator 1 (from Kyuden Restaurant) (Lvls. 1 and 3)

The upper levels of this giant domed enclosure hosts your final major battle to remove the Hostage from enemy hands. Because the enemy's deployment zone is close by, they have an advantage in this region, so use the Lobby's other locations to your advantage. Instead of using the high- trafficked enemy stairs

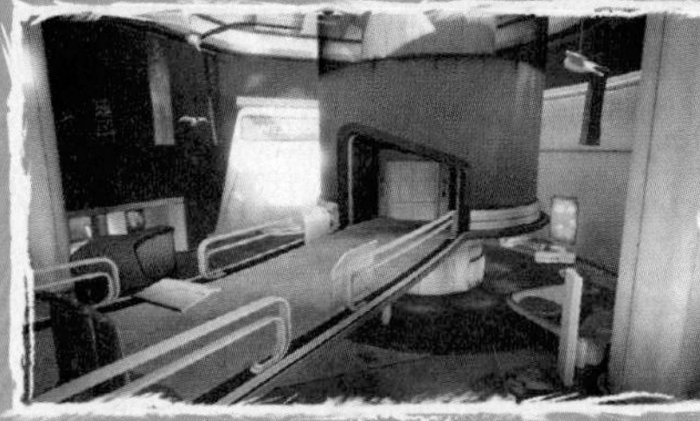

from the Main Floor (although hiding behind the exhibit tank and spawn-camping is always an option, especially with mines and turrets), clamber up to this Overlook Balcony using S.M.A.R.T. moves, or via Elevator 1 once you've fixed the Lift Generator.

Around the curve in the Upper Balcony, you'll spot an MG Nest with a Health Command Post close by. The enemy usually has these locations locked down early, so learn the perimeter of the MG Nest's aiming movement to dodge its fire, and try to capture these two areas during the mission's latter stages. Just to the side of the Health Command Post is a balcony overlooking the Marina. The enemy uses this balcony to fire on the Hostage during the very last stages, so train your weaponry or leave a mine up here to waylay them.

The lift (or elevator) is initially offline, and the enemy uses the open shaft here to quickly reach the Kyuden Restaurant. But not if you mine the bottom of it! However, when the Lift Generator is mended, stepping into Elevator 1 automatically scoots you up to the Overlook Balcony. Should an Engineer achieve this, storm and overrun the area, or use it as an additional method of getting to this place, so you can complete this lengthy escort. Otherwise, sprint up the Side Stairs to outflank the Resistance.

**This is a tactically advantageous position during the late stages of this mission, and worth maintaining a presence in. Just don't get swamped if the enemy sneaks up the Side Stairs or tries a concentrated attack!**

TIP

### S.M.A.R.T. Moves

Leap from this balcony and onto the main Aquarium exhibit, then down to the Main Floor of the Lobby.

### 33 The Ark Lobby: Marina Docks (Lvl. 2)

The Resistance will try a final line of explosives, turrets, and enemies as you try to reach the waiting Ark Guard boat. Should the Hostage stagger across to this craft within the allotted time, your mission is deemed successful. There are two entrances, both back into the Ark Lobby interior on different levels. Watch for final fortifications.

### S.M.A.R.T. Moves

Drag yourself up onto the white sign, and the balcony overlooking the Marina Docks, which also allows you into the Lobby.

### 34 Mattress Alley to the Mezzanine Lobby (Lvls. 2 and 3)

The Resistance uses this debris-strewn Mattress Alley to reach the Mezzanine Lobby inside the Ark's main Lobby. They usually set defenses up there for the final push, or rush the Side Stairs, Health Command Post, Kyuden Restaurant, or Lift Generator. Plug away at them if you're running interference while others chaperone the Hostage.

### 35 Resistance Deployment Zone (Pt. 2): Vat Chamber (Lvls. 1 and 2)

A sprawling L-shaped chamber with half-filled water vats is the Resistance spawning grounds. The two lower stairwells exit into the Long Ramp area, or the Mattress Alley leading up into the Ark Lobby. All are guarded by sentry turrets, making this a no-go area.

### 36 Resistance Command Post (Pt. 2) (Lvl. 2)

This is a Resistance Command Post, and off-limits to your team. Ignore it.

**TIP**

**Remember to consult the opposing team's strategy elsewhere in this Walkthrough, so you know what the enemy is planning, and react accordingly!**

## Objective Tactics: Core Objective 1

### Destroy Door

Spawn Point to Storage Door: 00:08 

Time to Disarm Explosives: 00:05 

Time to Plant Explosives: 00:07 

Countdown to Explosion: 00:30 

### General Tactics

Being on the offensive side requires focus and teamwork. You must reach the Storage Room (via any of the three Ark Water Treatment Access Points), clamp an explosive on either of the doors, and guard it until the device detonates. All other objectives are superfluous and should be attempted only if you have enough time, or the enemy isn't giving you a hard enough time in the Storage Room to allow for all of your team to battle there.

The enemy will be looking for Soldiers to cut down, so spawning a majority of your team as this class helps any of your team make a successful explosives clamp. Or, you can choose one or two of your side to perform this action, with others acting in a back-up capacity. Medics are more important than Engineers when you're attacking; your Soldiers need healing and covering fire, not turrets built or mines deployed (unless you've captured an area and you're holding it). The final tactic is to viciously defend an explosive device, from close or far range, depending on your location. There's no point in doing half the job—that explosive must be clamped *and* explode!

**Remember: The enemy will try to interfere, distract, or otherwise flummox your team, doing everything they can to distract you from the target. Ignore foes firing at you from ancillary locations and focus only on your Core Objective, completing it as early as possible. If that means ignoring Command Posts, so be it.**

 TIP

## Offensive Attack Routes

**Route 1: Predictable:** Storm down the gift shop stairs, and stream over the Atrium balcony or across the floor, and then up the stairs behind the MG Nest, and through Access Door 2 or down to 3. Your weight in numbers (with perhaps two teammates splitting off to capture and/or guard the Command Posts) allows you to push through into the Storage Room. The only problem? This is the shortest route to the target room, and therefore the one the enemy usually predicts that you will take: They will try to kill you *en masse* in the Atrium or at a doorway.

**Route 2: Unpredictable (Left):** Take the farthest route on your right from the Monorail, and move along the left side of the Atrium area, passing the Health Command Post, and moving directly toward Access Door 3. This offers a long view of the Storage Room (Side 2) door, and the steps down and corners are perfect for sniping, iron-sight aiming, and leaning out to fire. Cover enemies defusing the explosives with sniper fire from this doorway (Camping Spot 3)!

**Route 3: Unpredictable (Right):** Race along the gift shop roof, and at the Atrium platform, make a right so your entire team is past the small set of steps and on the balcony close and above the Supply Command Post. Stop at these steps, and fire on Access Door 1 *through* the steps, across from the balcony directly above the post, from Camping Spot 1, or by the balcony overlooking Access Door 1 itself.

## Offensive Attack Routes

**Two Places at Once:** Try to mix up the routes that your team takes, which requires good team communications. Split into two small squads and attack the Storage Room from both sides (and ideally at the same time), sending the enemy into a panic.

## Automated Ordnance

The attacking team usually doesn't stay in emplacements long, so there's less need for turrets and explosives. But there are still some areas to think about fortifying:

Turrets are handy if placed away from direct enemy fire, but at chokepoints such as outside any of the three Access doorways (Location 1 shown).

Back up teammates going in to clamp the explosives on the Storage Room door, or to cover the door itself; such as on a vat at the far end of this corridor, below Access Point 3.

Aside from the "regular" locations you should always use, dropping an explosive at the foot of the Storage Room door before or after you've clamped the device to the door hinders the enemy's progress in disarming it!

## Sniper's Ally: Camping Spots

1 Stand atop the Aquarium exhibit above the Supply Command Post to gain a sniper's eye view of Access 1, allowing you to cover both the access point and the post.

2 Crouch directly above the Supply Command Post, using the "Ark Facts" sign as partial cover, and fire through Access 1.

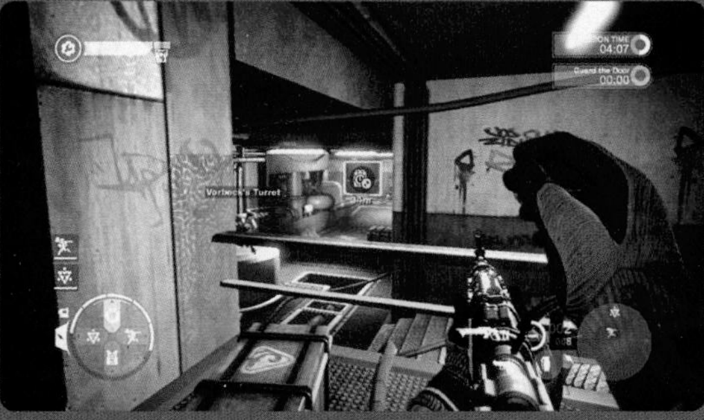

3 Crouch atop the steps just inside Access 3, and cover the Storage Room door from a long distance.

4 Climb up onto the pipe, or jump across from the balcony, and set up a camping spot overlooking the Storage Room balcony and most of the ground, in the darkened corner.

# Secondary Objectives (First Map)

##   Escort Core Objective Class Teammate

**Official Escort Info:** The teammate you're set to escort is a Soldier. The teammate is color-coded yellow on your screen and easy to spot. Simply shadow him (without straying too close to him, but near enough to receive a constant flow of XP), and back him up, especially as he reaches the Core Objective. Backing him up as a Soldier allows you to prime the explosives if he fails. Or become a Medic to buff and help him complete his main task.

##   Capture the Health Command Post

 Engineer & Operative Advantage!

Spawn Point to Command Post: 00:13

Time to Claim Command Post: 00:10

Send one or two teammates to capture this during your first rush, and keep one guarding it if you can spare the forces (because more health is better when assaulting). The enemy usually comes in from the curved tunnel, so plant the route with explosives, and remember that you can cover this post from the Atrium balcony, even across at the other side of the map.

##   Capture the Supply Command Post

Engineer & Operative Advantage!

Spawn Point to Command Post: 00:16

Time to Claim Command Post: 00:10

Have a teammate peel off from the rest of your assault squad to claim this (stay behind cover above or near the post to provide support fire). Upgrade it (using an Engineer), leave a mine on the floor by the Command Post (also an Engineer), and then guard it from above, shooting at foes who venture from the Access 1 door.

##   Construct the Atrium MG Nest

 Engineer

Spawn Point to Atrium MG Nest: 00:12

Time to Construct: 00:04 

Aside from netting some XP, this should be the last plan on your mind; the MG Nest faces the Atrium, which is where your team storms in from, and the opposition can easily outflank or attack an MG operator from behind.

# Objective Tactics: Core Objective 2 (Second Map)

##   Escort the Hostage

### General Tactics

Ready your syringes and spawn as a Medic, with the plan of keeping the Hostage both alive and moving. This obvious plan has other, more subtle components: If Resistance forces are shooting at you, they're diverting their attention away from the Hostage, and that is an excellent plan. Become a "bullet sponge" and coax foes into fighting you, and not blasting at the Hostage. This works less well when you're near the Hostage, so use different routes away from the Hostage's path to try to divide the defenders' fire.

## Outstanding Outflanking

Major hostilities occur at four chokepoints: the Kyuden Restaurant, the Long Ramp, the Lobby, and the final push into the Marina. The routes you take help keep the Hostage moving, and the Medics chaperoning him alive. Instead of simply following the Hostage route, peel off some of your team to any of the following locations where you can outflank your foes. The first is to the right, into the Pipe Pressure Corridor, and attack the defenders from the exit at the foot of the Long Ramp.

As the mission progresses, enter the Air Conditioning Duct from the base of the Long Ramp, and drop down onto the Upper Balcony, which offers routes into the Lobby and Marina, or down to the MG Nest. Outflank your enemies this way, while most of your team is engaged down in the Long Ramp area itself.

Using the Side Stairs after (re)capturing the Supply Command Post, watching for enemy turrets atop the stairs, and you'll appear close to the Marina exit. Now head toward the Hostage's location, cutting down foes preoccupied with the majority of your forces, and tackling foes from behind.

## Automated Ordnance

Because you're attacking, turret placement involves constantly moving and placing new turrets while discarding old ones. Place them to back up your team and the Hostage, or to cover a blind spot behind a sniper.

If you're sniping from a location, place a turret or mine to cover a blind spot or incursion point to the side or behind a sniper, to warn you of incoming foes. Place them at the Lift Generator, too.

**NOTE**

**These are examples of the best placements for these weapons. Follow this advice before picking other, less optimal areas.**

**TIP**

**Turrets and mines may be "fire and forget" weapons, but don't you forget about them. These expendable munitions need constant replacing as they're hit or removed by the enemy. It may be worth putting down a new turret a little farther down the route rather than having to keep going back to repair your previous turret.**

### Sniper's Ally: Camping Spots

5 Hide behind the cleaning machine in the Undersea Tunnels and snipe at foes at the Kyuden Restaurant bar.

6 From the Undersea Corridors end of Aquarium Alley, you have a great view of the Long Ramp area.

7 Snipe into the Kyuden Restaurant and up the Long Ramp from The Pipe Pressure Corridor exit.

8 On the Lobby Floor behind the Overlook Balcony, use the sign and side of the structure as cover, and aim down at the MG Nest. You can also see movement across the balcony and Health Command Post.

## Secondary Objectives (Second Map)

###   Repair Lift Generator

Spawn Point to Lift Generator: 00:12

Time to Repair Lift Generator: 00:20

Time to Plant/Disarm Explosives: 00:05

Countdown to Explosion: 00:20

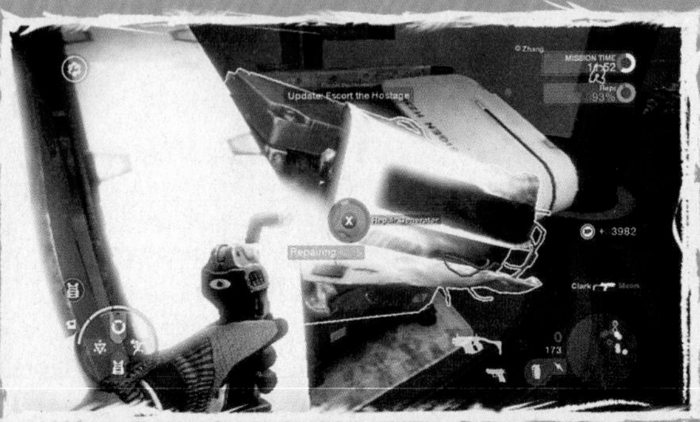

The generator powering the lift is behind the cylindrical lift shaft at the back-end of the Kyuden Restaurant, and fixing this (along with guarding the Supply Command Post) should be the remit of one or two of your team (unless the rest are having a terrible time keeping the Hostage moving). The only reason to fix the Lift Generator is so you can step into Elevator 1 and automatically ride it up to the Overlook Balcony in the Ark Lobby; which becomes increasingly helpful as the Hostage reaches the Long Ramp and Lobby itself. Pay more attention to this objective as the Hostage gets closer to these locations.

###   Capture the Health Command Post

Engineer & Operative Advantage!

Spawn Point to Command Post: 00:22 

Time to Claim Command Post: 00:10 

Forget about reaching this Command Post; this requires some maneuvering to reach unless the Elevator 1 is active. Instead, have an associate Engineer locate this point once you begin to use the Side Stairs and try to outflank the enemy in the Ark Lobby. The team that commands the Lobby Balcony Overlook commands this post!

### Capture the Supply Command Post

 Engineer & Operative Advantage!

Spawn Point to Command Post: 00:13

Time to Claim Command Post: 00:10

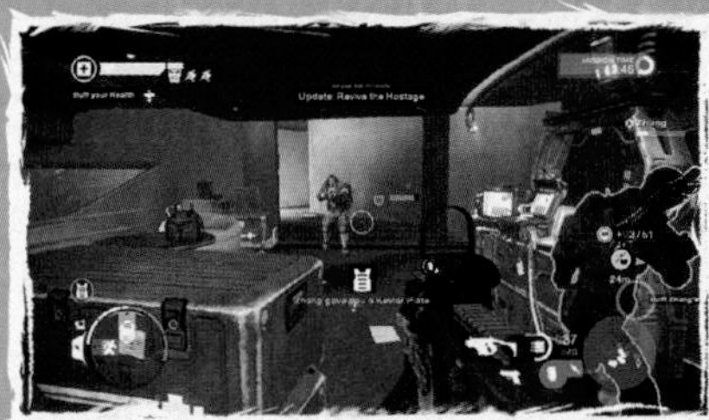

In the Kyuden Restaurant by the bar, expect enemies as you reach this post. This is also adjacent to the Lift Generator and Hostage route, and is worth securing after the initial restaurant fight, at the same time your Engineer is tinkering with the Lift Generator. It is worth expending a man or two to guard both these areas. Remember you can approach this post from the front or the back to claim it (which is handy because you can use the bar for cover). Place a mine at the controls to dissuade the enemy from reaching it.

### Construct the Ramp MG Nest

 Engineer

Spawn Point to MG Nest: 00:25

Time to Construct: 00:04

This MG Nest is only slightly more useful than the one you ignored in the Atrium. It has usually been constructed by the Resistance because it is so close to their spawn point. You're likely to be overrun by foes who take this over, so ignore this in favor of more important objectives. Or build it early, and cut down enemies milling about below.

### Construct the Lobby MG Nest

 Engineer

Spawn Point to MG Nest: 00:25

Time to Construct: 00:04

The enemy is likely to have built the Lobby MG Nest with the express intention of using it on the Hostage as he stumbles through the final interior section. Check that no one is manning this when the Hostage reaches the top of the Long Ramp, laying a mine to stop this being taken by the opposition. Or man the MG Nest yourself, and cut down foes on the move near the Hostage.

### Solo Tactics

**Without a cohesive fighting force you can bark orders to, take control of your own destiny by choosing the Soldier class at the start of this mission, and then rushing the Storage Room door as quickly as possible. Covering a second Soldier is another option, but finding a lull in the fighting and clamping the explosive on the door (and then guarding it) is the best way to spend your time.**

**During Core Objective 2, switch between Medics and Engineers. Use the former class to keep the Hostage moving throughout the level, pausing to switch to the Engineer if the Lift Generator becomes a helpful objective to try. Guarding keeps the Hostage moving, which is the only way to win.**

## Mission Completion Conditions

### Core Objective 1

#### Continuation...

Detonate either of the Storage Room doors, and the Hostage is extricated by the Security forces. Part 2 of this mission now commences....

### Core Objective 2

#### Completed!

The match completes if you successfully move the Hostage through the Aquarium and into the Ark Guard Boat in the Marina, outside the Lobby.

#### Unsuccessful!

Security forces lose if the Hostage fails to reaches the Ark Guard Boat in the Marina before the timer reaches zero.

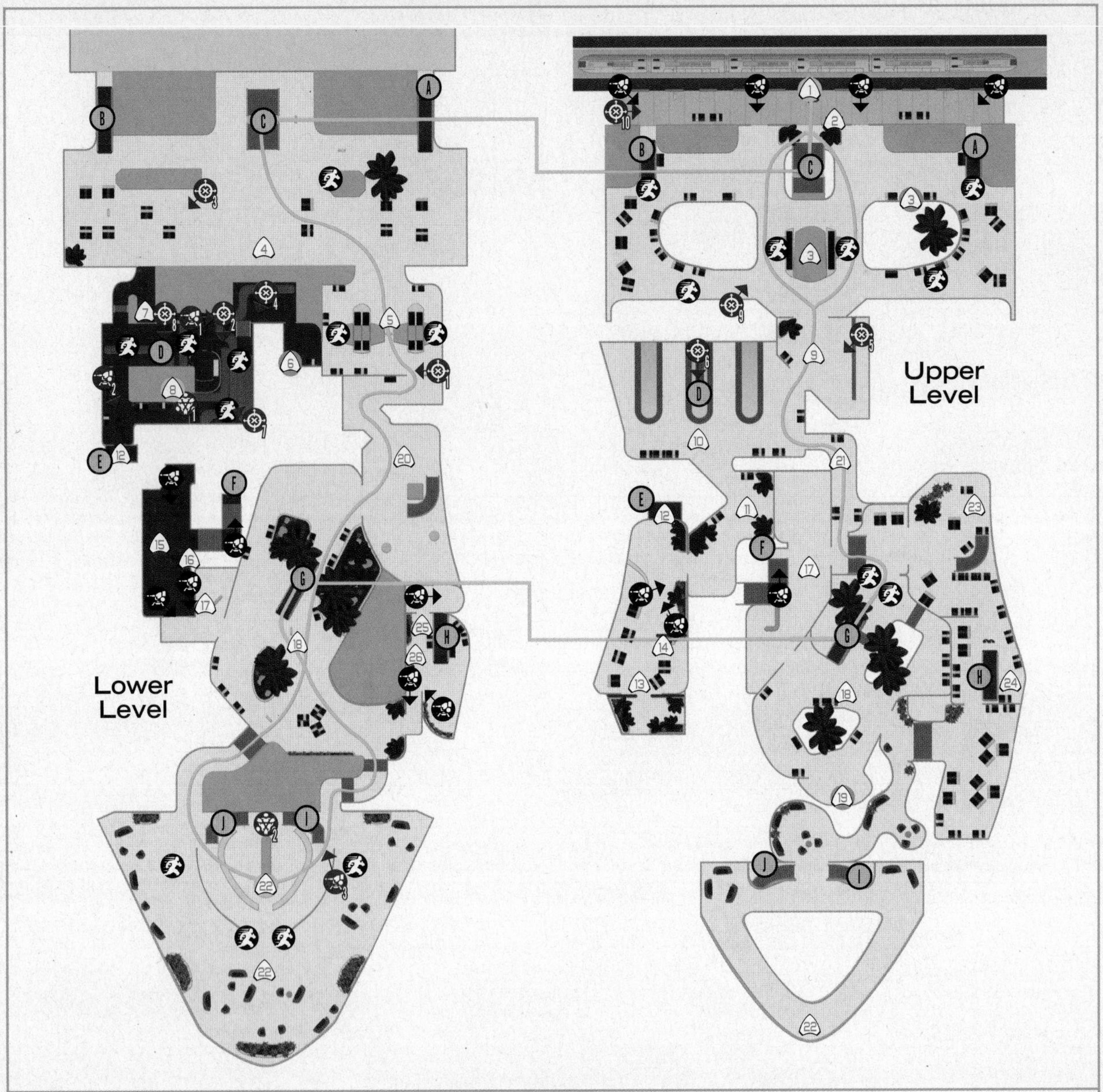

Upper Level

Lower Level

## MAP LEGEND

**Terminal: Core Objective 1 (& 3)**

1: Security Deployment Zone (Pt. 1): Monorail (Upper)
2: Security Command Post (Pt. 1) (Upper)
3: Airport Mezzanine: Security & Check-In MG Nest (Upper)
4: Airport Mezzanine: Tickets & Information (Lower)
5: Security Scanners (Lower)
6: Health Command Post (Lower)
7: Baggage Chutes (Lower)
8: Conveyor Control Point: Mainframe (Lower)
9: Airport Cashier Corridor (Upper)
10: Baggage Claim (Upper)
11: Airport Corridor: Resistance (Upper)
12: Elevator Shaft (Upper & Lower)
13: Resistance Deployment Zone (Pt. 1): Gate A1 (Upper)
14: Resistance Command Post (Pt. 1) (Upper)

**Terminal: Core Objective 2 (& 3)**

15: Security Deployment Zone (Parts 2 & 3): Baggage Maintenance Office (Lower)
16: Security Command Post (Parts 2 & 3) (Lower)
17: Blossum (Upper & Lower)
18: Central Shopping Plaza Mezzanine (Upper & Lower)
19: Supply Command Post (Upper)
20: Tihjin Moon & Gaccie (Lower)
21: Airport Corridor: Plaza to Baggage Claim (Upper)
22: Fra Diavolo Lounge & Restaurant with Safe (Upper & Lower)
23: Resistance Deployment Zone (Parts 2 & 3): Gate B5 (Lower)
24: Gate A5 (Upper)
25: Gate A6 & Curved Stairs (Upper)
26: Resistance Command Post (Parts 2 & 3) (Lower)

S.M.A.R.T. Move
Engineer Mine (Optimal Placement)
Engineer Turret (Optimal Placement)
Camping Spot
Deployment Zone Turret (Invulnerable)
Core Objective Location
Secondary Objective Location
Critical Path (Route)
Level Link

# DAY 3: SMASH AND GRAB

FREEPLAY: TERMINAL   RESISTANCE CAMPAIGN—DAY 3: CHEN'S PLANS

## 16:21 Monorail, Outer Loop, approaching Airport station

MISSION TIME (COb 1): 08:00

MISSION TIME (COb 2): +06:00

MISSION TIME (COb 3): +06:00

### Captain Mokoena: Briefing

We hit the motherlode! One of the terrorists you captured was Nechayev; Chen's number two. He's *co-operating*. He says Chen's been using the mainframe in the old airport terminal. We have to find out why. That terminal's been closed for years. They'll have had time to prepare defenses. You'll need to go in fast and hard, because we have to assume they'll trip an intel burn as soon as you show up. You won't have much time to find the Datakey, and upload it to HQ for decryption. Then we'll have Chen by the balls. He-heh!"

### Optimal Class Numbers

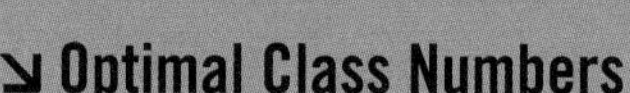

| | COb 1 | COb 2 | COb 3 |
|---|---|---|---|
| Soldier | [2] | [1] | [3] |
| Medic | [2] | [2] | [2] |
| Engineer | [1] | [4] | [1] |
| Operative | [3] | [1] | [2] |

### Objectives (Securty)

- Core Objective 1: Hack the Mainframe
- Core Objective 2: Crack the Safe
- Core Objective 3: Deliver Datakey
- Escort Core Objective Class Teammate
- Capture the Health Command Post
- Capture the Supply Command Post
- Construct the Check-In MG Nest

## Important Locations
(Core Objective 1 and 3)

**NOTE**

**These locations are accessible during Core Objective 1. They are also accessible afterward, but are only really traversed during Core Objective 3.**

### 1 Security Deployment Zone (Pt. 1): Monorail (Upper)

Until the first Core Objective is met, you commence your assault from this Monorail Station. Head down the steps or escalators into the Airport Mezzanine, or remain on the upper portion, en route to the Terminal Mainframe. The gun emplacements disappear from Core Objective 3 onward, because this becomes your team's final destination as you bring back the Datakey suitcase. The enemy likes to use this as their last line of defense, so learn the locations of the departure terminal consoles, benches, and three entrances so you know where your foes might be hiding.

##  Security Command Post (Pt. 1) (Upper)

The Mainframe requires an Operative (or three) to hack it, so choose your class carefully from this location. Swap out your weapons at the same time, if you need to.

## 3 Airport Mezzanine: Security and Check-In MG Nest (Upper)

## 4 Airport Mezzanine: Tickets and Information (Lower)

The vast Airport entrance Mezzanine is a two-floor area running the width of the entire structure, and the domain of your Security forces. During Core Objective 1, this area isn't usually the scene of too much fighting (unless the enemy is being extremely aggressive, which should result in you changing routes). However, during Core Objective 3, this is the final line of defense for your foes, as you push back into your previous deployment zone. Meticulously explore this area, because knowing it is critical to victory.

The upper floor is accessed by the Airport Cashier Corridor via normal movement, or from the lower level via S.M.A.R.T. moves or the staircases. A circle of empty (and inaccessible) stores surrounds three main areas. There are two large holes: One allows access down to a visitor information center kiosk overlooked by the MG Nest (which you should claim before the opposition later in this mission). The other has a scale model of the original Ark. In the middle is a security checkpoint. Behind the security checkpoint are the main steps up to the Monorail.

The lower floor accesses a connecting corridor into the Baggage Chute area and Mainframe, as well as the wide entrance into the Security Scanners. This large floor houses some scattered seating and boarding terminals, and the base of the scale model of the Ark (which is impossible to climb). Nearby is a side escalator. A similar space occupies the opposite side, although a visitor information center is under the open Mezzanine balcony, which can be climbed on. Close to that is a second escalator on the opposite edge of this area. Beware of foes hiding here to watch which route your team takes to reach the Mainframe. The escalators are also an excellent alternative to the main stairs when reaching the final mission exit.

**Use the two-story, dead palm tree near the visitor information center to situate yourself when maneuvering about in this initially confusing area.**

 TIP

 S.M.A.R.T. Moves 

Climb atop the security checkpoint on the top floor, and then onto the roof of the checkpoint itself.

You can also climb atop the visitor information center and jump from the narrow edge of the roof, grabbing the upper floor wall and ascending.

If you're running down the main steps or escalators, you can leap and grab the low wall ahead, if you decide to stay on the upper floor instead.

 S.M.A.R.T. Moves  

Upper floor: Climb on or hide behind the white concrete pillars and the flight departure terminals.

Upper floor: Use the pillars and terminals to leap to the roofs of the vacant stores on either side of the Cashier Corridor entrance (see picture for a good sniping spot).

## 5 Security Scanners (Lower)

This is usually the first line of defense for the Resistance forces; they tend not to venture through the wide exit and any farther into the Airport Mezzanine for fear of being overwhelmed or shot at from the MG Nest overlooking the check-in area. Use this to launch a concentrated attack past the Health Command Post, and into the Mainframe chamber. This area is also adjacent to the Tihjin Moon, and the associated door unlocks only during Parts 2 and 3 of this mission. During Part 3, this area is a viable escape route for the Security forces.

> **Notice the sparking light fixture in this area? Use that, and the red glowing "Tihjin Moon" sign behind the glass doors, as reference points.**
>
>  TIP

### S.M.A.R.T. Moves

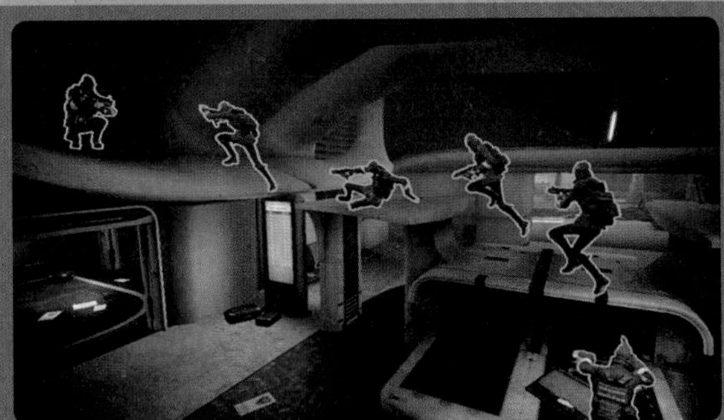

You can leap atop the security machines and conveyor belts as you secure this area or fend off the Resistance.

## 6 Health Command Post (Lower)

> **The Supply Command Post is located in the upper Plaza area, behind doorways that are sealed during Core Objective 1 of this mission, making this the only neutral Command Post you can initially claim.**
>
>  NOTE

As you enter the Baggage Chute access points from the Security Scanners, you run across the Health Command Post, where concentrated fighting is likely to occur during Core Objective 1. This area accesses the Conveyor Control Point and is an ideal location to race in from. Attempt to fortify it before the Resistance forces attempt the same. If the mission continues to Part 2 or 3, many teammates forget that this Health Command Post is still accessible; claim it throughout the match.

## 7 Baggage Chutes (Lower)

This area connects the Health Command Post at one end to the Security forces' entrance just right of the Ticket Gates in the Airport Mezzanine. Most of the team should seek progress through this area, and expect formidable enemy retaliation. Locate the parallel conveyor belt to increase the chances of pushing through one of the three exits, and into the Conveyor Control Point itself.

## 8 Conveyor Control Point: Mainframe (Lower)

This vital area during Core Objective 1 is directly underneath Baggage Claim. Although anyone can use the variety of entrances to reach the Mainframe, Resistance forces usually reach this point by dropping down the Elevator Shaft, or heading down the chute from Baggage Claim. Security forces use the corridor from the Health Command Post, and either of the two exits from the Baggage Chutes area adjacent to the Tickets and Information area of the Airport Mezzanine. Also use the chute from Baggage Claim.

Although numerous baggage conveyor belts crisscross the Control Center, the Mainframe itself can be accessed only via one of three doorways cut into the glass wall surrounding it.

> **Note that the door marked with the red emergency exit sign (the man running to a door) is sealed during all parts of this mission. The room you can see through the glass is your second spawn point. Don't confuse this with the open doorway leading from here to the Mezzanine.**
>
>  NOTE

## S.M.A.R.T. Moves

Climbing up onto the conveyor belts allows you to gain height (but not movement) advantage over your enemies.

By clambering on any of the containers or crates on the ground, you can climb onto any conveyor belt; even the one up into Baggage Claim.

## 9 Airport Cashier Corridor (Upper)

Providing a wide (and dangerous) route from the Airport's upper Mezzanine (and your spawn point) into Baggage Claim, this triangular room with a long cashier's desk along one wall is likely to be an initial line of defense for the Resistance. Although it isn't accessible from here, the Health Command Post is underneath this area, along with chutes into the Conveyor Control Point. This is also part of a possible escape route during Core Objective 3.

Spot the sparking safe behind the cashier counter? Use that as a reference point so you know where you are, and what locations are adjacent to your position.

TIP

## 10 Baggage Claim (Upper)

Directly above the Conveyor Control Point, the Baggage Claim consists of two entrances: one from the Resistance spawn point and the other from the Airport Mezzanine Security area (Upper). Carousel #2, currently open for maintenance, is another main arterial route that you should use to reach the Mainframe (although don't expect this to be free from enemy explosives or gunfire). Expect foes to guard this conveyor belt from this location or at the Mainframe chamber below. Note the red light illuminating the entrance below it. This is also part of a possible escape route during Core Objective 3.

Note that the door marked with the red emergency exit sign (the man running to a door) is sealed during Core Objective 1, but opens once the Mainframe is hacked.

NOTE

## 11 Airport Corridor: Resistance (Upper)

The Resistance forces use this corridor that passes a couple of sealed-up stores to get from their spawn point to the Baggage Claim chamber. The enemy uses the route to meet your forces in the Baggage Claim, and to interfere with your route down to the Conveyor Control Point, so their brethren can create further defenses.

## 12 Elevator Shaft (Upper and Lower)

This is one reason the enemy appears inside the Conveyor Control Point with alarming regularity: they simply drop down the open shaft at the edge of their spawn point, into the T-junction below, and rush to reach the Mainframe area. You may wish to lay explosives or a turret to catch those who favor this drop.

## 13 Resistance Deployment Zone (Pt. 1): Gate A1 (Upper)

The Resistance appears in this boarding lounge for Gate A1 (through the adjacent inaccessible glass windows). The only exits are via the Airport Corridor or Elevator Shaft. Enemy turrets make this a deadly place to visit.

## 14 Resistance Command Post (Pt. 1) (Upper)

You cannot activate the Command Post because it only responds to enemy input.

# Important Locations

(Core Objective 2 (and 3))

**These locations are inaccessible during Core Objective 1, but unlock if Core Objective 2 occurs, and are also available during Core Objective 3. All of the previous locations are also accessible, too.**

NOTE

## 15 Security Deployment Zone (Pts. 2 & 3): Baggage Maintenance Office (Lower)

This darkened chamber is guarded by a number of sentry guns, and offers a side entrance straight into Blossum and the Plaza, and a set of stairs to the upper level of Blossum. Vary the exit you take based on where the enemy is, and what objective you are undertaking.

## 16 Security Command Post (Pts. 2 & 3) (Lower)

For Core Objective 2, be sure at least two of you are Engineers with a safe-opening ability. When fleeing back to the Monorail in Core Objective 3, Soldiers and Medics are also helpful. Change here.

**Operatives! You cannot use disguise while carrying the Datakey. You will drop the Datakey if you enter your deployment zone to use this Command Post.**

CAUTION

## 17 Blossum (Upper and Lower)

This two-floor boutique store is where your team spills out from, and recognizing the different adjacent locations helps you plan routes to and from the Fra Diavolo Lounge & Restaurant. The lower section is linked to the larger one above only by stairs that the Security forces use to exit their deployment zone; remember this when figuring out which floor of the Plaza you want to step out onto. The dark corners of either floor can be used as an ambush point though, and the front glass wall allows you to spot enemies milling around the Plaza. The upper exits from Blossum place you at the Airport Corridor junction, or close to the Supply Command Post.

## 18 Central Shopping Plaza Mezzanine (Upper and Lower)

## 19 Supply Command Post (Upper)

This two-floor Plaza Mezzanine is the central hub during Parts 2 and 3. Your foes easily access this area from the Resistance spawn point via a door and short corridor, or a door and a quick step through the Tihjin Moon location. Expect both constant fighting and maneuvering along here as teams race to the safe or the suitcase during the latter stages of this mission. The two-floor store called Blossum is on the opposite side of the Plaza, where your team heads out from. The rest of the lower floor offers an inaccessible coffee shop ("In a Cup"), and the entrance to Gate B5 (which is part of the enemy's domain), as well as the two lower entrances to the Fra Diavolo Lounge & Restaurant. The middle of the Plaza offers escalator access to the walkways above.

The upper floor of the Plaza offers an initially confusing series of shallow steps close to the top of the escalator, and access via the main walkway toward the Airport Corridor leading to Baggage Claim. The rest of the top floor has linked walkways around three large openings you can drop (or fire) down, leading to the lower level, including another exit from your spawn point within Blossum. At the far end are doorways into the Resistance area of Gate A5, and the upper entrances to the Fra Diavolo, through the orange-padded walls of the lounge.

The alcove at the far end of this Plaza holds the Supply Command Post, which is accessible during Parts 2 and 3 of this mission. Don't forget to claim it before storming into the lounge to claim the Datakey suitcase within the safe.

### S.M.A.R.T. Moves

On the upper floor, you can edge along the top of the railing by the glass wall and Blossum store to gain protection from behind, a sniping point, and a commanding view across and down.

Surprisingly, there isn't a way to reach the upper Plaza walkway from below, save for the escalator. However, you can stand atop the flight departure signs.

## 20 Tihjin Moon and Gaccie (Lower)

Think of this location as a lower level junction, allowing access to several adjacent areas. Be careful, because Resistance teammates can quickly reach here from their spawn point. This also marks the end of the lower-level section of Plaza. The Curved Stairs allow access to and from Gate A6 and the upper Plaza (but this is likely to be overrun by enemies heading from their deployment zone). Finally—once you pass the Gaccie store—you exit into the Security Scanners area, making this a well-trafficked route during Part 3.

## 21 Airport Corridor: Plaza to Baggage Claim (Upper)

Featuring a sunken area with a few chairs that leads to Gate A6 and the Curved Stairs, this is the other main opening into the Plaza. Glass walls on either side let you see, but not fire on, your enemies. Expect heavy enemy traffic from Gate A6 and the Curved Stairs, but reinforcements come in from the Blossum entrance atop the stairs. The upper corridor leads around and into Baggage Claim, via a door that opens only once Core Objective 2 occurs.

## 22 Fra Diavolo Lounge & Restaurant with Safe (Upper and Lower)

This fancy lounge and restaurant is the main location for Core Objective 2, and the starting locale for Core Objective 3. The lounge is accessed via one of three entrances, all from the Plaza area. On the lower level, there's a small winding corridor and a few steps close to Gate B5 (the quickest route from the enemy spawn point). A second corridor on the opposite side (which offers the quickest access from your deployment zone) allows access up steps and a corridor and into the other side of the restaurant. On the upper floor, access is through the orange-padded walls of the lounge, near Gate A5 and the Supply Command Post.

Once inside this triangular restaurant floorplan, expect the enemy to defend on two vertical levels. The upper area is composed of a triangular balcony, which you can hop over at any time to reach a sunken bar area below. Or either of the curved staircases can be used. The lower floor consists of the sunken bar with the safe (containing the Datakey suitcase), and a raised ground area with scattered seating and a segmenting wall on each side; mainly used as cover.

### S.M.A.R.T. Moves

Climb the sliver of wall on each side of the sunken bar, and grab and vault onto the balcony.

Climb on the sunken bar, and access the balcony above, near the upper exit.

You can also run up the ramped support columns and stand atop them under the balcony floor for increased height and visibility.

team. The connecting chambers allow the Resistance a quick route past Gate B5, into the Plaza, and straight into the Fra Diavolo Lounge & Restaurant, where the safe with the Datakey is. When Core Objective 3 begins, the enemies rush in the opposite direction, through connecting chambers, past the Tihjin Moon and Gaccie stores, and out toward the Monorail.

Directly above your foes' spawning ground is Gate A5, and two (more important) thoroughfares, which enable the opposition to reach the Plaza (and Fra Diavolo), or toward Gate A6, the Curved Stairs, and the other Plaza entrance; vary your route to avoid this area when ferrying the suitcase back to the Monorail.

### 23 Resistance Deployment Zone (Pts. 2 & 3): Gate B5 (Lower)

### 24 Gate A5 (Upper)

### 25 Gate A6 and Curved Stairs (Upper)

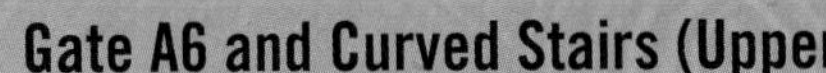

If you succeeded in hacking into the Mainframe, the action moves farther into the Airport, and the Resistance forces congregate in this location, on the opposite side of the Plaza from your

**Although you can clamber over seating and hide behind pillars during firefights, there are few S.M.A.R.T. opportunities here.**

NOTE

### 26 Resistance Command Post (Pts. 2 & 3) (Lower)

Sentry turrets will kill you before you reach this terminal. Seek the neutral Command Posts instead.

## Objective Tactics: Core Objective 1

### Hack the Mainframe

Spawn Point to Mainframe: 00:13

Time to Disarm Hack Box: 00:05

Time to Plant Hack Box: 00:02

### General Tactics

The enemy seemingly has the advantage as you begin your first Core Objective; they are likely to be controlling all three of the routes into the Conveyor Control Point where the Mainframe is located. The plan here is to dominate at least two of these three locations; ideally the Security Scanners and one other, because the Health Command Post is a much-needed bonus in the passage close to the Scanners chamber.

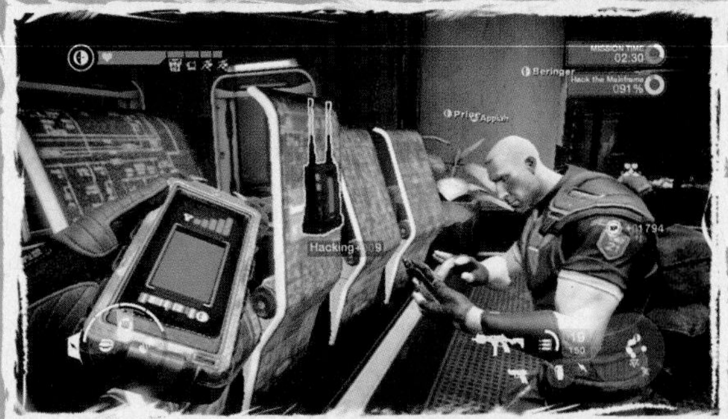

Heading into the Baggage Chutes location on the lower floor, to the left of the Security Scanners room, is your second option. This place is narrow and dangerous, but claiming both areas is easier because your team can quickly switch between locations; this is more difficult and takes a lot longer if you're attacking from up on the Baggage Claim. Of course, being unpredictable (but choosing the two main insert points beforehand) is the mark of a winning team. Choosing the bottom two locations means you fight the enemy more or less inside the Mainframe area, whereas attacking from Baggage Claim often leads to a fracas on the floor above, which limits your hacking chances.

## Attack Plans

**Security Scanners:** Drop into the lower Mezzanine near the MG Nest and rush to the Security Scanners room, and into the connecting passage with the Health Command Post. Do this immediately, and the enemy won't have claimed it first. Make a stand here; this is arguably the best place to take and hold.

**Baggage Chutes:** Drop down onto the lower Mezzanine but peel off to the right, by the Ark model, and sprint into the chutes. The fighting is close and chaotic; grenades become helpful. Remember the connecting conveyor linking the Health Command Post area to this location.

**Baggage Claim:** Foes sometimes stream into here, making this a problem area because you want to be fighting closer to your intended objective. However, having one or two teammates preoccupying the enemy at their entrance corridor is a worthwhile plan. This is also one of the few places where Security turrets can help out, if you have time to plant them.

**Conveyor Control Point:** You must have at least one Operative (and normally two or three) to have any chance of hacking this Mainframe. Remember the more teammates help, the quicker the hacking is done (but the more prone to attacks you are). Also remember the Operative can disguise himself as an enemy. This is handy if you want to move into the Mainframe room undiscovered, before gunning down foes who thought you were part of the Resistance.

**The Mainframe room is glass, but not walled off entirely. Learn which parts are glass, and where you can actually fire through.**

 **TIP**

**Cooked grenades thrown into a confined space equals a large amount of damage inflicted. Any of the grenade types work extremely well, including Flashbangs. Learn to throw them through the Mainframe room's window or doors.**

 **TIP**

## Automated Ordnance

Your team is advancing, so turrets and mines are less important. Although there are some optimal examples to come, check the Resistance section for many more examples:

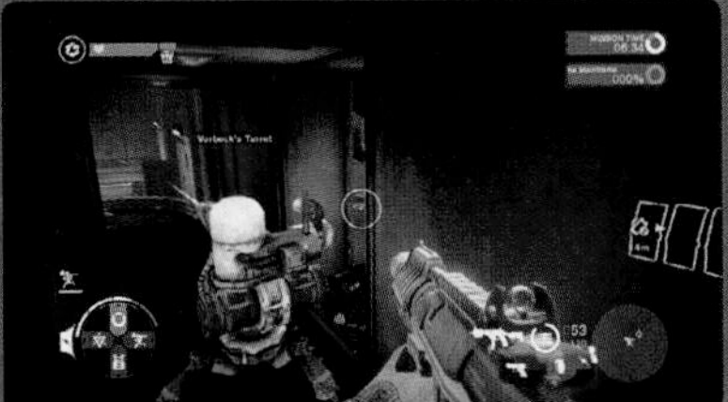

1 (Baggage Chutes): If you're crouching and firing on foes, but can't cover all directions, plant a turret to tackle enemies behind or to your sides.

2 (Conveyor Control Point): Place a turret (and perhaps mines) at the bottom of the Elevator Shaft to cut off one route the enemy takes to reach the Mainframe.

1 (Conveyor Control Point): If you manage to get inside the Mainframe area, quickly place a mine on a conveyor belt around a corner from you, to remove an enemy that may be moving toward you.

## Sniper's Ally: Camping Spots

1 (Security Scanners): Stand at the glass door by Tihjin Moon, and snipe enemies trying to claim the Health Command Post.

2 (Baggage Chutes): You have a great view of the Health Command Post, doorway to the Conveyor Control Point, and a good view inside. Snipe away!

3 (Baggage Chutes): Crouch by the Ark model sign, and tag foes in the Baggage Claim as you cover and then follow your team in.

4 (Baggage Chutes): Snipe from this midway point in the chutes, watching both sides for enemies.

If you can get your teammates to watch either side (guarding the doorways), at Camp Spot 4 so much the better. Watch out for grenades, and don't lean because you're easily attacked; stay mobile.

5 (Baggage Claim): Behind the Cashier's Corridor counter, you have a great sniping view of the enemy's initial corridor.

6 (Baggage Claim): Stand at the top of the conveyor belt at carousel #2; you can snipe foes coming out of the entrance corridor, and anyone heading up the belt from below.

## Sniper's Ally: Camping Spots (continued)

7 (Conveyor Control Point): Take a stand (or rather, a crouch) under the conveyor belt in the far corner, tagging enemies as they run in from the Elevator Shaft.

8 (Conveyor Control Point): Jam yourself into the cubbyhole directly above the middle exit of the Baggage Chute area, and you can (just) lob grenades into the Mainframe room.

# Objective Tactics: Core Objective 2

### Crack the Safe

Spawn Point to Safe: 00:14 

Time to Crack Safe: 01:00 

 **TIP**

**Have one Engineer with a single-minded purpose: to crack the safe. Other Engineers do the same, but break away and defend the primary Engineer when under fire.**

### General Tactics

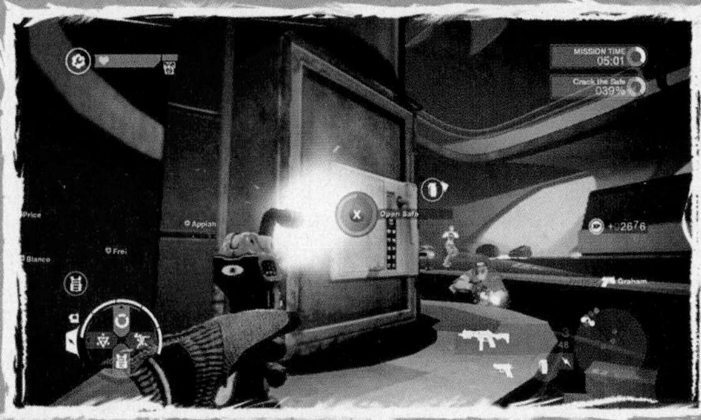

Fighting into the Fra Diavolo Lounge & Restaurant is no easy task if the enemy is defending the location properly. The easiest way to get killed is to rush in on your own, from a location the enemy knows you're coming from. There are two exits from your spawn stairwell (and three openings from the Blossum store); use them all. Your overriding plan is to be unpredictable in your routes, run directly to the restaurant without being detained, and get there in a group of at least two, so you can fight the foes instead of being killed in their crossfire.

When you reach the restaurant, wait in the corridor (in cover) for your teammates, and attack as a group. Going in there alone results in a quick death. Remember you have three restaurant entrances to appear from, so your group attack doesn't have to be from the same place; indeed, it is better if you split your groups up, but attack simultaneously. Then attack and try to draw the enemy's fire, and coax the foes out of cover so your friends can strike them too. Then have one (or more) Engineers peel off and torch the safe; the more Engineers attempt this, the faster it opens, but the fewer teammates there are to beat back the enemy.

### Attack Plans

**In Blossum:** The enemy can't be everywhere at once, but they can annoy you with mines and other entrapments en route to the safe. So use the slightly maze-like qualities of the Plaza to your advantage. Study the map and leap down off the balconies to enter via either of the lower entrances. Double-back around and perhaps choose a teammate whose job is just to coax foes away from the restaurant.

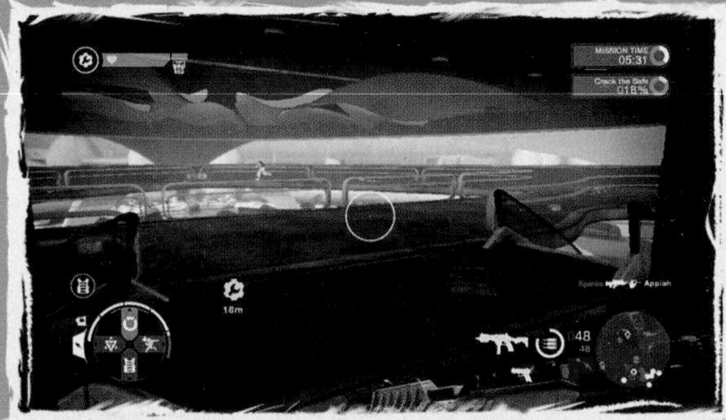

**Lounging Around:** The restaurant is entered via the top-floor lounge and bottom-floor side entrances. As before, wait for a group of you to arrive at any entrance, and then charge in. Where you charge is important: Split into around three groups, with one squad primarily focused on

lobbing grenades at turrets or finding mines. The second should focus on human foes, while the third heads to the safe (either directly, or in a long circle-strafe behind the walls by the lounge chairs). Have one teammate torching the safe at all times.

**A Crack Team:** Draw the enemy's fire and make them move around out of cover. You can always move backward to use the doorway or corridor as cover and try to pin them down so your teammates can flank them via another route. Then have at least one Engineer focus on the safe: Unless you've chosen the Sense of Perspective ability, you can still move around the objective while you're doing it. So Engineers, while you're cutting open the safe, don't be a static target, move around! You may be able to take cover from enemy fire while still completing this objective.

### Automated Ordnance

If you can get into the restaurant and mow down the enemies, make sure you place a turret (or two) covering each of the three entrances.

The same goes for mines; with six mines along the entrances, you can keep foes at bay during the safe cracking.

## Objective Tactics: Core Objective 3

### Deliver Datakey

Safe to Monorail: 00:33

### General Tactics

As soon as the safe springs open, any of your team can take the Datakey briefcase. Make sure it's someone who knows the route back to the Monorail, and can throw the enemy off along the way. After taking the Datakey, flee the restaurant via the exit with the least number of enemies (to the left, close to your spawn point is a good option). Then use the Plaza to lose any foes, but on your first run, attempt to get as close to the Monorail as you can; the enemy has less time to reach there and start defending.

### Checking the Chokepoints

**Dine and Dash:** There tend to be a lot of defenders on the stairs, so unless you see that the way is clear, don't use the higher routes. Instead, keep inside the horseshoe shape of the bar, run toward the back wall, and then break suddenly for the side exit on the left side of the lower floor.

Duck under the downcurve of that left staircase, head into the exit corridor, and keep on going. This way you're protected from enemy fire almost all of the way out of the room, and can quickly put a curved corridor between you and any pursuers. Cook a grenade and bounce it off a wall behind you as you go, as a little present for your foes.

**Lost Luggage:** When you're in the Plaza, note (on this guide's map) the two different exits; via Tihjin Moon and Gaccie (lower) and Baggage Claim (upper). Trying feints is a possibility (running for the Baggage Claim, and then dropping down or using the Curved Stairs to reach the Tihjin Moon at the last second, for example), but you're usually under heavy attack when you reach either chokepoint. Send in your heavy Soldiers first to clear out the foes, if you aren't being attacked from behind.

Shadow the briefcase runner with a couple of Light Body Types sprinting along the same route. That way, if the front-runner falls (to mines or gunfire), the second can quickly take the briefcase and continue the run. You may also wish to be a Medic, or run close to the teammate with the briefcase as a Medic, and take the Health Command Post for the obvious health benefits.

 TIP

**Terminal Velocity:** When you reach the Ark Mezzanine, you have a slight advantage because there are two escalators, the central stairs, and various balconies to maneuver between instead of taking a direct route to the Terminal (AKA Capture Point). As the doorways and Terminal are likely to be mined, send in Operatives first, and Soldiers to soak up the damage. Flit between floors and use cover. If that means running back into the Mainframe room and out again, so be it.

Even if you know the route and move fast, the chances are that by the time you get the Datakey near the Monorail, the Resistance will already have a couple of men defending it, with mines down in the doorways or by the upload terminal itself.

CAUTION

### S.M.A.R.T. Moves

It may be wise to lose a bit of weight if you're hoping to carry the Datakey briefcase all the way to the capture point at the Monorail. Light Body Types can dodge, climb, and maneuver with greater dexterity. Of course, they can die quicker, too.

### Sniper's Ally: Camping Spots

9 Clamber up to the rooftops above the storefronts on either side of the Cashier's Corridor entrance. Then you can cover your teammates, and fire across to the Monorail platform.

10 If you get to the Monorail platform but aren't carrying the briefcase, use the escalator entrance and head to either end of the platform. Use the signs as cover, and cut down anyone you see.

## Objective Tactics: Secondary Objectives

###   Escort Core Objective Class Teammate

**Official Escort Info:** This is an excellent Secondary Objective to undertake. During Core Objective 1, you cover the Operatives while they hack the Mainframe. During the Second Objective, partner with an Engineer and keep the foes at bay in the Restaurant while your mate cracks open the Safe. Obviously, chaperoning the briefcase carrier afterwards is yet another fine plan: You're likely to be doing this anyway, so why not earn additional XP for it? In each case, choose a class that complements your teammate.

###   Capture the Health Command Post

 Engineer & Operative Advantage!

Spawn Point to Command Post: 00:12 

Time to Claim Command Post: 00:10 

The enemy keeps this location under heavy guard, but it is important to obtain the post due to the health benefits it bestows on your team. If you have additional health, your Operatives can hack for longer. If the Resistance has this, they take more bullets to bring down. If you can keep an Engineer in this entrance corridor by the post, adding a mine or turrets to cover the post, this helps your team overall.

### Capture the Supply Command Post

Engineer & Operative Advantage!

Spawn Point to Command Post: 00:12

Time to Claim Command Post: 00:10

Tackle this Command Post, accessed during Core Objectives 2 and 3, once you push the enemy back into the restaurant; remember that you can leap down to the lower Plaza if you're attacked, but also take the upper exit from the stairs above your spawn point to reach this without delay. If you have one teammate running interference at this post, this is one less defender in the Fra Diavolo, although you must weigh whether that teammate is more effective torching the safe.

### Construct the Check-In MG Nest

Engineer

Spawn Point to MG Nest: 00:04

Time to Construct: 00:04

The only MG Nest on this map is not an imperative objective because the enemy doesn't usually venture this far into the Airport Mezzanine. Of course, there are XP to be gathered for such an undertaking. Another point to remember is that building the MG Nest means the enemy can access it instantly during Core Objective 3, turning it against your forces as you return to the Monorail. Therefore, this task is of limited help.

### Solo Tactics

Without fellow human beings to yell out, you must take a more central role in fulfilling the three Core Objectives. Begin as an Operative, dashing into the Mainframe area quickly to hack it as soon as possible. Take the Health Command Post so you have more health to absorb the enemy's incoming fire. Switch to the Engineer during Core Objective 2, so you can start torching the safe instead of waiting around for a fellow teammate to get around to it. For the final Core Objective, you may find a Light Body Type suits you, so you can double-back and move as quickly as possible back to the Monorail.

## Mission Completion Conditions

### Continuation...

**Core Objective 1:** Hack the Mainframe. Part 2 of this mission now commences....

**Core Objective 2:** Unlock the safe, exposing the Datakey. Part 3 of this mission now begins....

### Completed!

The match completes if you successfully reach the Monorail with the briefcase before the timer ticks down.

### Unsuccessful!

Security forces lose if the enemy prevents you from hacking the Mainframe, unlocking the safe, or reaching the Monorail with the briefcase, and the timer ticks down to zero.

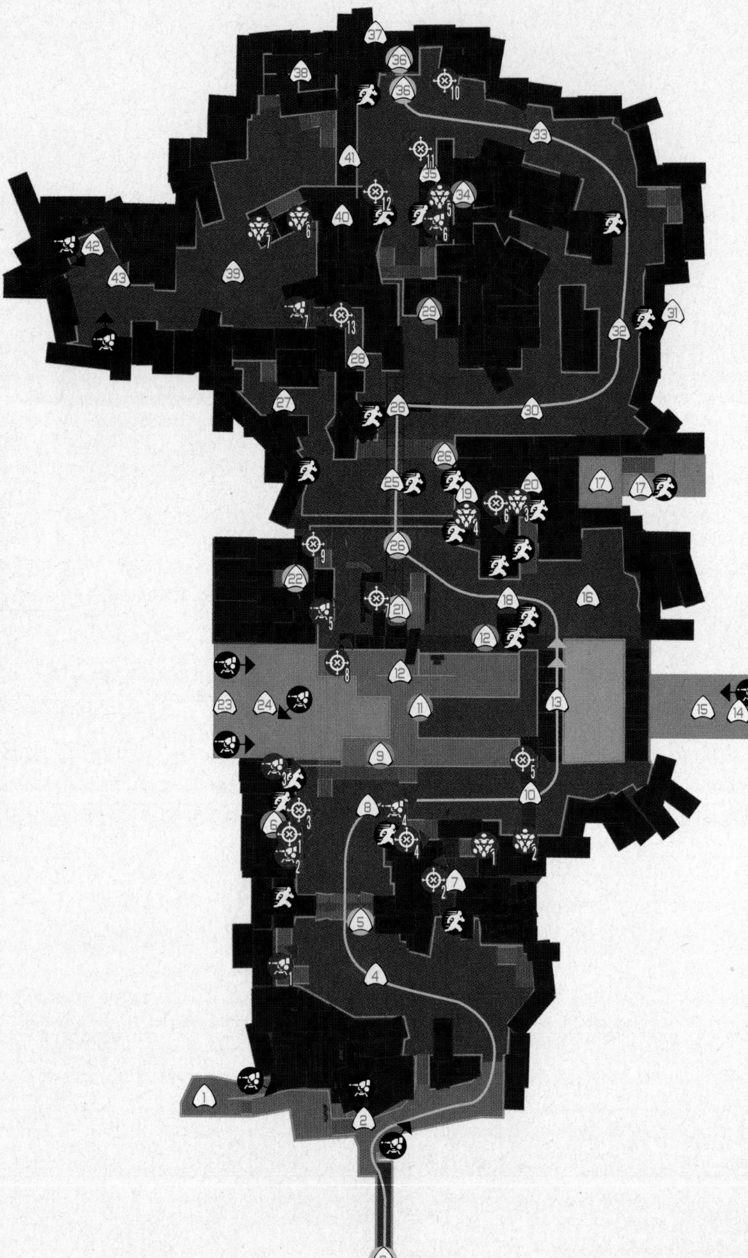

## MAP LEGEND

### Container City: General Icons

1: Security Deployment Zone (Pts. 1 & 2): Jetty (Lvl. 1)
2: Security Command Post (Pts. 1 & 2) (Lvl. 0)
3: Maintenance Bot Start: Jetty (Lvl. 0)
4: Container City Harbor Entrance (Lvl. 1)
5: Entrance Gate (Lvl. 1)
6: Side Door (Lvl. 2)
7: Exterior Stairwell Scramble Point (Lvl. 2)
8: Container City Thoroughfare (Lvl. 1)
9: Decaying *Hope*: Starboard MG Nest & Balcony (Lvl. 2)
10: The Rusty Bridge (Lvl. 2)
11: Decaying *Hope*: Interior Hold & Health Command Post (Lvl. 1)
12: Decaying *Hope*: Interior Passageways & MG Nest (Lvl. 2)
13: Decaying *Hope*: Lower Hold Road (Lvl. 1)
14: Resistance Deployment Zone (Pts. 1 & 2): Bow of the *Hope* (Lvl. 2)
15: Resistance Command Post (Pts. 1 & 2) (Lvl. 2)
16: Container Clearing (Lvl. 1)
17: Rusting Hull to Side Stairs (Lvls. 0, 1, & 2)
18: Container Crossing (Lvl. 2)
19: Crane Yard Vantage Point (Lvl. 2)
20: Free Ark Rooftop Alley (Lvl. 3)
21: Crane & Decaying *Hope*: Port Balcony (Lvls. 1, 2, & 3)
22: Extraction Point (Lvl. 2)
23: Security Deployment Zone (Pts. 3 & 4): Decaying *Hope* (Lvl. 2)
24: Security Command Post (Pts. 3 & 4) (Lvl. 2)
25: Crane Yard Bridge & Dry Dock (Lvls. 0, 1, & 2)
26: Crane Magnet & MG Nest (Lvl. 2)
27: Circumventing Passage & Stairs (Lvl. 2)
28: Mini-Pipe Passage to Crane Scaffold Overlooks (Lvls. 2 & 3)
29: Market Passage (Lvl. 2)
30: Market Thoroughfare (First Street) (Lvl. 2)
31: Mop's Pawn Shop Balcony (Lvl. 3)
32: Market Thoroughfare (Beer & Babes) (Lvl. 2)
33: Market Thoroughfare (Kebabs) (Lvl. 2)
34: Market Alley & Supply Command Post (Lvl. 2)
35: Gantry Overlook (Lvl. 2)
36: Resistance Laboratory Garage & Dirty Bomb (Lvl. 1)
37: Resistance Laboratory: Water Tank Balcony (Lvl. 2)
38: Resistance Laboratory: Interior Passageway (Lvl. 2)
39: The Mighty Pipe Courtyard (Lvl. 2)
40: Flickering Light Passage to Container Overlook (Lvl. 2)
41: Comfy Couch Stairs to Lab Parapet (Lvls. 2 & 3)
42: Resistance Deployment Zone (Pts. 3): Container City Hideout (Lvl. 2)
43: Resistance Command Post (Pts. 3) (Lvl. 2)

### Container City: General Icons

S.M.A.R.T. Move
Engineer Mine (Optimal Placement)
Engineer Turret (Optimal Placement)
Camping Spot
Deployment Zone Turret (Invulnerable)
Core Objective Location
Secondary Objective Location
Critical Path (Route)

BRINK — Container City: Overview Map

# DAY 4: DIRTY BOMB

FREEPLAY: CONTAINER CITY  RESISTANCE CAMPAIGN—DAY 7: ATTACK ON CCITY

## 17:34 Security Patrol Boat PB012, En Route to CCity Jetty 38

MISSION TIME (COb 1): 08:00
MISSION TIME (COb 2, Part 1): +04:00
MISSION TIME (COb 3): +06:00
MISSION TIME (COb 2, Part 2): +06:00
MISSION TIME (COb 4): +06:00

### Captain Mokoena: Briefing

The intel we recovered indicates Chen has been preparing operations against us for months. We've pinpointed a fortified vault in Container City. It's a bio-weapons lab. He must be developing a viral bomb. We can't destroy it from the air: Civilian casualties would be unacceptable. We need to recover a sample before Chen can weaponize it. Then, we can devise a counter-measure. We're sending you in with the Maintenance Bot that can cut its way into the lab. Keep that Bot moving. I know you didn't sign up to kick down the doors of civilians, but we have no choice here. Do your job.

### Optimal Class Numbers

| | COb 1 | COb 2 | COb 3 | COb 4 |
|---|---|---|---|---|
| Soldier | [3] | [2] | [2] | [3] |
| Medic | [2] | [2] | [2] | [2] |
| Engineer | [1] | [3] | [3] | [1] |
| Operative | [2] | [1] | [1] | [2] |

### Objectives (Security)

- Core Objective 1: Destroy the Gate
- Core Objective 2: Escort Maintenance Bot
- Core Objective 3: Repair the Crane
- Core Objective 4: Deliver Sample
- Escort Core Objective Class Teammate
- Hack the Side Door
- Construct Side Stairs
- Destroy Market Barricade
- Capture the Health Command Post
- Capture the Supply Command Post
- Construct the Gate MG Nest
- Construct the Ship MG Nest
- Construct the Crane MG Nest

## Important Locations

**"Decaying *Hope*" refers to a rusting medical frigate, currently sunken into the detritus between the Harbor and the Dry Dock. Both the Resistance and Security forces take turns spawning in this long-abandoned vessel.**

**NOTE**

### 1 Security Deployment Zone (Pts. 1 & 2): Jetty (Lvl. 1)

Until you mend the Crane arm and clamp the Maintenance Bot to it, this is your spawning area. Head down the metal gantry, and choose one of two paths up into the Harbor. Make sure some of your teammates move to the Maintenance Bot so it begins to move. Expect the enemy to cover both the near and far exits up the slope into the Entrance and Gate. The Bot always enters via the far path.

### 2 Security Command Post (Pts. 1 & 2) (Lvl. 0)

You require Engineers to fix the Maintenance Bot if it takes too much enemy damage. You need Soldiers to clamp an explosive to the Entrance Gate. You should have an Operative ready to hack the Side Door. Make these your class choices. Pick a weapon if you wish, too.

###  Maintenance Bot Start: Jetty (Lvl. 0)

When one of the Security forces moves into the Bot's activity field, it begins its slow trundle (under your protection) from this roughly constructed jetty. You don't face an enemy until you reach the Harbor Entrance. Note the route the Bot must take to reach its final objective: the Resistance force's Laboratory Garage deep in Container City.

### 4 Container City Harbor Entrance (Lvl. 1)

###  Entrance Gate (Lvl. 1)

###  Side Door (Lvl. 2)

The grounds near the Entrance Gate are the setting for the first major attack; you fail the mission if you don't remove the Entrance Gate as an obstacle, and push through into the Thoroughfare on the other side. The ground slowly rises up to the Gate itself, and the enemy is likely to be using various hiding spots while Security forces race out of either alley from their spawn point.

Focus mainly on the Gate, covering Soldiers as they clamp their explosives. Cause a distraction by sliding under the gap in the Gate, but watch for the enemy doing the same. Divert the enemy's attention by sprinting up and into the raised platform with the interior Side Door you can hack, and watch for the various openings you can scramble up, too. Fire on the enemy from a window here, too.

Expect the enemy to be hiding or firing from the following areas:

The metal container by the wooden ship's mast by the lower of the two initial alleys; these foes are too close to your spawn point and are easily out-gunned, but don't get distracted.

Foes can stand on or under a set of steps to a small balcony overlooking the farther alley from the Entrance Gate; shoot them if you spot them.

Watch for foes in partial cover near the water tank, which you can also use to scramble up and onto the Exterior Stairwell Scramble Point.

Expect foes firing from the steps and walkway to the Side Door, and behind the concrete barrier, under the walkway. Foes also climb the metal awning roof over the sealed door to the left of the Entrance Gate.

## S.M.A.R.T. Moves

The opening behind and above the Side Door (if you're facing the *Hope*) allows access to a passage directly above the Entrance Gate, where you can provide your teammates with excellent cover protection.

Look up and behind you at the Side Door; there are two doorways above this location. The one directly above the Side Door leads down to the platform and side of the *Hope*, and the main Thoroughfare.

### 7 Exterior Stairwell Scramble Point (Lvl. 2)

If you wish to distract the enemy, or swarm up and over the Exterior Stairwell and down into the Thoroughfare, climb the water tanker from the Harbor side and up across the Scramble Point. Then you have access down to the Rusty Bridge on the Resistance side, or the passage through a container that leads right to the Resistance side of the Entrance Gate. Use the height up here to offer covering fire as the Maintenance Bot creeps forward with the braver members of your team.

### 8 Container City Thoroughfare (Lvl. 1)

A second major attack occurs here as the Resistance forces desperately try to halt the Maintenance Bot by firing on it, or on your colleagues who are guarding it. You must push forward with the Bot in tow and reach the Lower Hold Road. This Thoroughfare is narrow, with the *Hope* to one side (move along its balcony, and access the ground-level Hold from two adjacent entrances), and the Scramble Point on the other.

Kee
the r
this l
concre

of your team close to the Bot, but move
m above ground level while traversing
can fire down on foes behind the
Ting to stop you.

S.M

## Moves

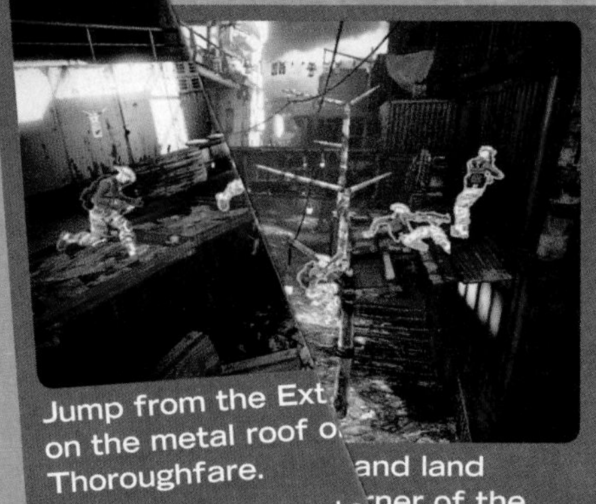

Jump from the Ext
on the metal roof o
Thoroughfare. and land

Leap and climb onto ner of the
Door.

ear the Side

### 9 Decaying *Hope*: Sta t & Balcony (Lvl. 2)

nce
to
s

train it on the Bot or your defende
Nest area allows you to enter the H
Passageways (but not the lower-leve
Hold). Man the MG Nest if you wish,
mainly an enemy fortification.

### 10 The Rusty Bridge (Lvl. 2)

Th
is n
ben
the e
becau
it offe
quick r
up and
the Exte
Stairwell
en route to the initial Harbor chokepoint. Enter the Rusty Bridge by pulling yourself up from the concrete barriers by the *Hope*. From up here, you can fire down on foes, which helps while the Bot moves down the Thoroughfare. However, this structure is more likely to have foes patrolling on it. The concrete barriers on either side below the Bridge also provide cover.

## 11 Decaying *Hope*: Interior Hold & He
## Command Post (Lvl. 1)

you
r the
s of
*ope*'s
ccess
er lets
Hold. The small, L-shaped pas es a
to and from the Lower Hold F ane Yard
you enter the main Hold roo rossing.
Health Command Post and rd, too.
on the other side, below the
Use these routes to reach

**Neither of the ground-level In ons provides**
**direct access to the Interior Nests, and**
**second Security Deploymen l above.**

**CAUTION**

ssageways &

## 12 Decaying *Ho*
## MG Nest (Lvl. 2)

Another optional route to the Crane Yard (indeed you should take this shortcut before the Maintenance Bot reaches
nd MG Nest on the
*Hope* has a second
the Cra deck, after you've
Thorou d connecting Passageway.
balcon verlooks (and offers quick
navig er Crossing and Crane Yard.
This
acc

## Lower Hold Road (Lvl. 1)

This ground-level road with an opening into the Interior Hold allows the Maintenance Bot direct access into
Clearing. Try to clear the area of
their explosive traps and turrets, or
slowing down.

## 14 Resistance Deployment Zone (Pts. 1 & 2): Bow of the *Hope* (Lvl. 2)

The enemy begins their mission at this point until you manage to complete Core Objective 3 (and Repair the Crane). Your foes have good access to either side of the decaying *Hope*. The lack of enemy sentry turrets means you can attack the enemy as they drop down to the exterior alley. Cover them with sniper fire if you can afford the manpower.

## 15 Resistance Command Post (Pts. 1 & 2) (Lvl. 2)

Inside the bow of the *Hope*, this terminal cannot be accessed by your team.

## 16 Container Clearing (Lvl. 1)

This has openings to a variety of locations; the Resistance spawn point, the Lower Hold Road, into the lower Rusting Hull, and the Crane Yard Vantage Point. Climbing to the nearby promontories helps you guard the area and cover the slow dawdle of the Maintenance Bot. The nearby spawn alley helps your opponents, so keep your team numbers up as the Bot moves through here.

### S.M.A.R.T. Moves

Jump up onto the blue metal container that's holding the Container Crossing structure, and climb to the knife-edge top of the structure itself.

##  Rusting Hull to Side Stairs (Lvls. 0, 1, & 2)

In one corner of the Container Clearing (under the washing line) is a hole in the ground leading to an underground passage. Once you enter, if you turn left, the passage brings you out in the Dry Dock under the Crane Yard Bridge, after passing a tiny, rusty restroom you can hide in. Turn right, and you reach the Side Stairs, which requires an Engineer to build them as part of your Secondary Objectives. Once constructed, the stairs allow your team quicker access up onto the Market Thoroughfare (First Street); a great advantage during the Maintenance Bot Market assault.

###  S.M.A.R.T. Moves 

Ignore the stairs building and simply Wall-jump up the gap instead.

##  Container Crossing (Lvl. 2)

Crossing above the yard between the Crane and the Hold exit is a blue container open to the elements. The nearby ramp doesn't actually attach to the container (it leads to the Crane Yard Vantage Point); this structure must be climbed, or accessed from the *Hope* Balcony near the MG Nest.
You can fire from this precarious location, both before and after the Maintenance Bot passes underneath. This is also the only way to reach the Free Ark Rooftop Alley.

###  S.M.A.R.T. Moves 

You can leap from the top of the ramp, grab the AC fan box, and haul yourself up onto the orange container at the base of the Rooftop Alley entrance.

As well as the blue container, you can climb up the metal lean-to on the Crane Yard side to reach the lip of the container wall.

Wall-jump and Mantle onto the lip of the Container, cross it, and jump up and into the Free Ark Rooftop Alley.

##  Crane Yard Vantage Point (Lvl. 2)

Reach this location, directly above the Dry Dock and Rusting Hull that leads to the Side Stairs, via the ramp next to the Container Crossing. This offers commanding views of the Crane Yard, which is excellent for camping (no matter what the nearby sign may say) as the Bot is transported across the Yard, or during the late stages when you're covering a teammate who is attempting to reach the Extraction Point.

###  S.M.A.R.T. Moves 

Grab the AC fan box, and pull yourself up onto the edge of the Crane Yard Vantage Point instead of using the ramped passage.

### 20 Free Ark Rooftop Alley (Lvl. 3)

If the enemy has made a competent (or explosive-filled) attempt to stop you from building the Side Stairs, and you wish to reach the Market Thoroughfare without using the Dry Dock bridge, scramble up here instead. This offers a vantage point over the Container Clearing to snipe from, and an overview of the Market Thoroughfare and Alley, and around to the "Bar" signage. You can also climb up onto the Rooftop Alley from the street below, where the "FREE ARK" graffiti is displayed.

### 21 Crane & Decaying *Hope*: Port Balcony (Lvls. 1, 2, & 3)

The Engineers in your team should attempt to reach the Crane as soon as possible; and certainly leave the Maintenance Bot with a light guard as it emerges into the Container Clearing. This massive blue Crane with its giant magnet dominates the Crane Yard. Reach the Crane's control booth by climbing it, either from the Yard or the nearby Port Balcony of the *Hope*. The Balcony itself connects back to the Interior Passageways and MG Nest. Use the area underneath, with the concrete barriers and containers, as cover or ambush points. Once the Maintenance Bot reaches the Crane, the Port Balcony door swings back, revealing the second Security Deployment Zone. The enemy usually retreats into the depths of Container City at this point.

### 22 Extraction Point (Lvl. 2)

This is the mission's ultimate location, where Security forces must deliver the Sample from the Laboratory. Remember you can stand on the container below the Crane booth, leap the concrete barriers to reach the Extraction Point, and hide in and around this location to dodge incoming enemy fire, usually emanating from behind you, around the MG Nest and far side of the Dry Dock.

### 23 Security Deployment Zone (Pts. 3 & 4): Decaying *Hope* (Lvl. 2)

As soon as the Crane is fixed by one of your team's Engineers, your deployment zone—and your enemies'—changes. Security forces head out of the starboard end of the *Hope*, and the Health Command Post is yours for the taking (because the enemy usually doesn't head back to try to claim it). Spread out from the *Hope*'s balcony and assault the Crane Yard.

### 24 Security Command Post (Pts. 3 & 4) (Lvl. 2)

Change class as the objectives progress, and reload or swap weapons as needed from this post.

### 25 Crane Yard Bridge & Dry Dock (Lvls. 0, 1, & 2)

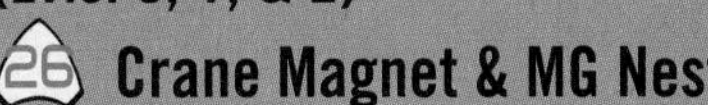

### 26 Crane Magnet & MG Nest (Lvl. 2)

During the time the Maintenance Bot is carried over the Bridge by the Crane, the enemy usually takes control of the opposite side of this Bridge above the Dry Dock, along with the MG Nest. Try your S.M.A.R.T. moves to reach the higher side of the Dock, or head up the Side Stairs or outflank from the Mini-Pipe Passage after heading up through the Circumventing Passage and Stairs. Then your Bot chaperoning along the Market Thoroughfare can begin.

## S.M.A.R.T. Moves

You can Wall-jump the side of the Bridge, and climb to the top of the pipe to reach the far side of the Dry Dock.

Failing that, climb either side of the Dry Dock, or Wall-jump the taller edge under the MG Nest.

## 27 Circumventing Passage & Stairs (Lvl. 2)

This is usually the route to try when scurrying to the Extraction Point with the Sample, but it also offers a less-trafficked route into Resistance territory, and the various upper vantage points overlooking the Laboratory. Race along the zigzag Passage and up into the Mighty Pipe Courtyard, or back again.

**The "Mighty Pipe" is a useful landmark for the Resistance forces, because they follow it to a container stack just across from the green neon cross, and Laboratory. A second "Mini-Pipe" also weaves through here; they follow that to the next location.**

TIP

## S.M.A.R.T. Moves

Wall-jump the metal girders and water tank along the left side, into the Circumventing Passage.

## 28 Mini-Pipe Passage to Crane Scaffold Overlooks (Lvls. 2 & 3)

There are two entrances to this two-tier vantage point: The first is to follow the mini-pipe from the Mighty Pipe Courtyard. The mini-pipe winds through a container stack passage, leading you to a walkway balcony behind the Crane Magnet (which you can also walk along). Usually a Resistance sniper is up here, blasting enemies while the Bot is moved by the Crane. Check the sniper's nest directly above the passage exit for a foe, too.

## S.M.A.R.T. Moves

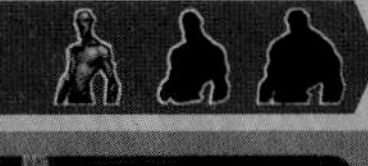

The other way up here is to Wall-jump off the ship's mast and water tank and onto the blue Crane Magnet crossbeam.

## 29 Market Passage (Lvl. 2)

Behind the Crane Magnet is sloping ground into a tight passageway that leads out into the Laboratory Garage area. This obvious shortcut is usually sealed by the enemy, but if you stop them you have an excellent advantage; you can swarm the Market area and Laboratory much faster.

###  Market Thoroughfare (First Street) (Lvl. 2)

###  Mop's Pawn Shop Balcony (Lvl. 3)

### Market Thoroughfare (Beer & Babes) (Lvl. 2)

###  Market Thoroughfare (Kebabs) (Lvl. 2)

This large, U-shaped street runs through Container City's Market district, and is the last line of defense of the Resistance forces before the chaperoned Maintenance Bot reaches their Laboratory. The initial Thoroughfare has the alley opening (which you can battle into or expect fire from because it has more cover), and the Rooftop and Side Steps exits.

Around the corner is the main Market area itself. Enter and take cover in the Bar and Souvenir store, the Pawn Shop, and the bedroom inside the Triple-X store. Upstairs from the Pawn Shop is a balcony, offering advantageous height and cover. On the inside of the route is the Market Alley area, offering narrower passage to and from the Laboratory. Once your team and the Bot pass the Kebab place, you are almost at the Laboratory, and the enemy must push their defenses back again.

 **S.M.A.R.T. Moves** 

Clamber atop the lean-to awning by the "Mobile" sign on the inside corner.

Climb onto the Pawn Shop balcony via the container with the "Bar" sign on it.

### Market Alley & Supply Command Post (Lvl. 2)

This offers quicker access to and from the Laboratory via the Gantry Overlook, and two exits onto the Market Thoroughfare. The big draw here is the Supply Command Post; keep this in your possession as you gradually push forward.

> **CAUTION**
>
> You may not be able to claim this Supply Command Post until much later into the match, so prepare to face foes with increased supplies. You can tag a particular teammate with the job of taking this, but only if you're making good progress.

### Gantry Overlook (Lvl. 2)

As the match progresses, this becomes an increasingly difficult area to traverse due to your foes defending this area, shooting those coming in from the Market Passage. This is an access point to reach the Market Thoroughfares via the Alley and Supply Command Post (which the enemy is likely to have taken). Also expect fire from here when you try to open the Garage. Try to outflank any foes here, because the location is reasonably open.

Echoing shouts can be heard throughout this area of the map; this cues you to where you are as you learn this map's layout.

TIP

## 36 Resistance Laboratory Garage & Dirty Bomb (Lvl. 1)

This is permanently sealed until your Security forces manage to get the Maintenance Bot to this location, after which the Garage is spot-welded open. Prior to this, the Resistance tends to employ the multiple vantage points to cover this location. Afterward, step inside the Garage for cover, and try to run with the Sample as quickly as possible; this Garage can become your tomb very easily thanks to incoming grenades or previously laid traps. Note the multiple routes you can take to reach here.

## 37 Resistance Laboratory: Water Tank Balcony (Lvl. 2)

## 38 Resistance Laboratory: Interior Passageway (Lvl. 2)

Unless the enemies have forgotten to secure this area, the balcony above the Garage is usually where the enemy likes to dig in and cover the Garage during your final assault. Beware of snipers hitting you as you emerge from the Market Passage. You can climb here from the ground, or enter via the Interior Passageway (locate the entrance via the doorway below the solar panels, and giant anchor).

## 39 The Mighty Pipe Courtyard (Lvl. 2)

This is a Resistance stronghold, because you're near their spawn point, but you can still take this route to reach the Laboratory, or flee back with the Sample. Follow the giant rusting pipe to the Garage if you become lost. Also check the two doorways leading up to vantage points, and Circumventing Passage and Stairs (beware of foes stepping out of these shadows to intercept a Security Sample carrier).

## 40 Flickering Light Passage to Container Overlook (Lvl. 2)

## 41 Comfy Couch Stairs to Lab Parapet (Lvls. 2 & 3)

Beware of these two passages; learn to lay traps here to catch foes before they use the routes to reach vantage points where they can fire on your Bot and troops over in the Lab Garage. Both vantage points are entered via doorways in the Mighty Pipe Courtyard. They are easy to distinguish: The doorway with a flickering light leads across to a container overlooking the Garage and Market Passage exit. You can reach this location from the ground below, too.

The other entrance has a comfy couch under the light, and leads up to the Lab Parapet near the green neon cross. There's a covered area at each end to dodge gunfire from, and a great view of the Market Thoroughfare and Garage. This is the only way to reach this location. Cover your team from here, but beware; the enemy loves using these positions.

### 42 Resistance Deployment Zone (Pts. 3): Container City Hideout (Lvl. 2)

If you hear the echoing shouts of Resistance dwellers, and feel the sentry turrets cutting into you, you know you've reached the last enemy spawn point, which is active only after the Crane has been repaired. Learn the surrounds so you don't venture up here on your way to or from the Laboratory. This location is behind a half-buried container with a hazard symbol on it. Learn the different routes to the Dry Dock, Crane Yard, Market Passage, Thoroughfare, and Garage so you spend no time lost. The Mighty Pipe Courtyard is your adjacent location.

### 43 Resistance Command Post (Pts. 3) (Lvl. 2)

Flee the area because this Command Post isn't activated by your hands.

## Objective Tactics: Core Objective 1

###   Destroy the Gate

Spawn Point to Gate: 00:13

Time to Plant Explosives: 00:07

Time to Disarm Explosives: 00:05

Countdown to Explosion: 00:40

#### General Tactics

This is all about timing, as in, don't waste any! If the Resistance locks this objective area down, it is fairly straightforward for them to continuously halt any and all attempts at planting the bomb, due to the large number of sniping spots on the far side of the Gate where they can shoot the bomb planter from (which are detailed in their campaign mission for this map). Prevent this by rushing a Light Body Type Soldier to the Gate the nanosecond this mission begins, and have him plant the bomb on the very first spawn.

Do this quickly enough, and it's planted before the enemy arrives. Now the Gate's many holes become an advantage for your forces; blast the enemy (and in particular, Engineers) trying to get out and to the bomb! If this doesn't work, try one of the plans outlined below, or locate the Maintenance Bot and move it up toward the Gate. Think of the Bot as a mobile wall of cover, and hide behind it before you make a dive for the bomb clamping.

#### Gaining Gate Control

**Scramble Point:** This is also used to reach the containers above the Thoroughfare during Core Objective 2, but for now it allows you to flank any foes at the Gate, and also intercept newly spawned enemies as they race across the Thoroughfare or Rusty Bridge to reinforce the area behind the Gate. Waylay these foes, and your Gate explosion becomes more certain!

**Side Door:** This isn't just for Operatives trying to open the left flank for you; there are openings out to the area behind the Gate, and all the way down the Thoroughfare if you stand atop the door. Even if your hacking isn't doing the job, firing through the openings in here helps distract your enemies. For more information, consult the Secondary Objective tactics.

**Harbor Gate:** If you can coordinate with teammates utilizing both the Scramble Point to the right of the Gate and the Side Door on the left, and have them engage the enemy in crossfire, you may be able to clamp an explosive on the Gate without succumbing to their bullets. Only the toughest tank-like Soldier with appropriately hardened abilities should try this.

> **Recommended abilities are Battle Hardened and Kevlar Vest.**
>
>  TIP

## Automated Ordnance

Because you're the attacking team, there's much less time to set up defenses. Check the Resistance's placement for ideas, and areas to avoid or watch for.

1 Sit a turret far from the Gate that enemy grenades don't hit it easily, but close enough to fire back through the holes at foes, as well as along the Side Door passage.

2 Cut down foes coming up the Thoroughfare or on the Balcony from the hole above the Side Door.

1 Set a mine at the base of these stairs if you can, so enemies are knocked back as they take to this side of the Thoroughfare.

## Sniper's Ally: Camping Spots

1 Tag enemies from inside the Side Door passage.

2 Stand atop the Scramble Point, and cover enemies as they spawn. Set a turret and mines to keep them from overrunning your position.

# Objective Tactics: Core Objective 2 (Part 1)

## Escort Maintenance Bot

Time to Repair the Bot: 00:10

### General Tactics

> **This Core Objective continues all the way from the Harbor Gate to the Garage and Laboratory deep in Container City. Keeping the Bot moving is your major plan of attack throughout.**
>
>  NOTE

The Maintenance Bot (which should have been activated and brought around to the Gate in time for the Gate destruction) must be taken on a slow and dangerous journey down the Thoroughfare, through the Lower Hold Road, and around to be parked under the giant Crane, for the start of Core Objective 3. During this time, it doesn't move on its own; there must be a teammate nearby so the Bot's proximity sensors activate and it starts to edge forward. The speed can be described as "leisurely."

Enemies are intent on destroying the Bot, and do so with gunfire. Because mines don't affect the Bot, watch for them underfoot as you maneuver around the Bot. Have one or two of your team helping the Bot move; ideally one should be in front, letting the Bot push him along so he can concentrate on enemies in vantage and ambush points throughout the path. If the Bot becomes too damaged, it stops. Mend it with an Engineer; ideally more than one.

### Critical Maintenance, I

**Thoroughfare and Lower Hold Road:** The end of the Thoroughfare and turn into the Lower Hold Road is the first problem area you'll come to, because the enemy is very close to their spawn, and it is easy for them to swarm to each end of the road to batter you from both angles. Help alleviate this roadblock by Mantling over the Scramble Point, and then use the Rusty Bridge or *Hope* Interior Passage to land in front of the Bot. The Resistance should be fighting off your brethren down the main Thoroughfare and may not notice you fixing the Bot. Then let it push you into the Container Clearing.

**Container Clearing:** Most of your team will need to be around the Maintenance Bot, coaxing it forward out of the Lower Hold Road, but if they reach an impasse, journey up and through the *Hope* at the entrance behind the Gate MG Nest, wind through to Container Crossing, and set up a camp spot and a turret up here to distract the enemy, help your team, and cut down foes blocking your path.

## Automated Ordnance

3 Set a turret facing the Rusty Bridge and Thoroughfare to cut down foes.

2 Set a mine at the exit from the Rusty Bridge, so you're not outflanked.

4 Place a turret up here to cover your team and fire on foes without being immediately hit with a grenade.

3 Fix a mine on the edge of the Rooftop Alley access, so foes are waylaid when reaching this area.

## Sniper's Ally: Camping Spots

3 Cover the Resistance approaches from this container corner, as the Bot moves down this Thoroughfare.

4 Crouch and sit on the metal roof awning, and cover the Bot's initial travels.

## Sniper's Ally: Camping Spots

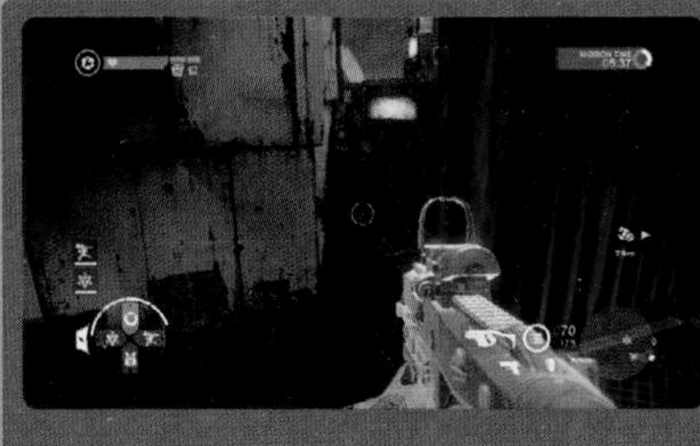

5 The end of the Rusty Bridge is helpful if your Bot is stuck here, because you can fire over it, into the corner of the spawn point.

6 The entrance to the Free Ark Rooftop Alley is the spot to drop a turret and snipe.

# Objective Tactics: Core Objective 3

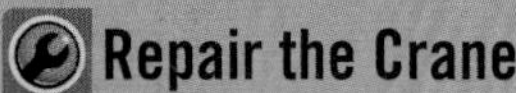

## Repair the Crane

Spawn Point to Crane: 00:18

Time to Repair the Crane: 00:30

### General Tactics

This intermediate task must be completed before the second part of Core Objective 2 takes place. Battle and climb into the open control room of the Crane, and start to repair the controls: They become active once the Maintenance Bot stops in front of the Crane. As with all repairs, the amount left to repair doesn't diminish if you take a break between fixing it. Once an Engineer finishes the repair, the Crane's giant magnet automatically scoops the Maintenance Bot from its parking place and deposits it over the Dry Dock.

**One of easiest ways to complete this is to ready yourself in the Crane control room as the rest of your team pushes the Bot into position. Then start repairs the second the Bot stops and the controls are accessible. The entire repair is possible before the Resistance can reach you from their final spawn position, so have your team cut down stragglers as this objective begins.**

TIP

### How to Gain a Crane

**Container Clearing Push:** You should be battling the Resistance for control of various vantage points surrounding the Crane Yard (as detailed below), but it is also imperative to give your Engineer enough unimpeded time to fix the controls. Cover him from whatever enemies are

still in the area; cutting them down so they have to respawn deep in Container City. Remember to begin to infiltrate farther into Container City at this point too; fixing the Side Stairs once Core Objective 3 is over, or clambering across the Free Ark Rooftop Alley.

**Heading from *Hope*'s Interior:** Your new spawning area is within the *Hope*. Previously, you could use the ship's Interior Passages to get to the Crane as early as possible. Now the Crane is extremely close to your deployment zone, and the balcony overlooking the Crane Yard is a great place to fire on your foes and cover teammates as they advance to the Market area of Container City.

**Both the Resistance and Security Deployment Zones change after this Core Objective starts. You appear inside the *Hope* for the rest of the mission. Note that all of these camp spots can be used during the last Core Objective, too. Once the Bot has been transported over the Dry Dock and bridge, the Side Stairs and Barricade can be constructed (Secondary Objectives). Prior to that, the gap could only be Wall-jumped by Light Body Types.**

NOTE

## Automated Ordnance

3 Set a turret to cover the Circumventing Passage, and your carrier during Core Objective 4.

4 Mine any of the camp spots the enemy tries to use, such as the Crane Yard Vantage Point.

## Sniper's Ally: Camping Spots

7 Stand on the Crane controls for great views of the enemy's favored vantage points.

8 Your spawn point balcony is a safe place to unload on the opposition.

9 This balcony is great for aiming out toward the Crane Yard Vantage Point, Market Thoroughfare, and Circumventing Passage.

# Objective Tactics: Core Objective 2 (Part 2)

##   Escort Maintenance Bot

Time to Repair the Bot: 00:10

### General Tactics

The rest of Container City is now available to investigate, and the various routes to the Garage are revealed (in reverse) during Core Objective 4. But your Maintenance Bot is keeping to the right, and on the main Thoroughfare that runs in a long counterclockwise semicircle around the Market, before reaching a slope and the Garage where the Bot's plasma-cutter is finally put to some good (and automatic) use.

Split your team into those who are actively escorting the Bot, and those who are interfering with the enemy. The latter should be taking the Market Passage and removing the barricade, spawn-camping, taking the Supply Command Post repeatedly, and generally annoying the enemy deep in their own territory, around their Laboratory. Any problems you can give the Resistance quickens your Bot's progress around the map.

### Critical Maintenance, II

**Maintenance-Free Camping:** There's an ideal place if you Mantle up the blue girders of the Crane Magnet, and climb onto the Crane Scaffold Overlooks. Then follow the Mini-Pipe Passage to its entrance, into the Mighty Pipe Courtyard. Set up a turret and a mine here before venturing back to the entrance. This slows down (and freaks out) your enemies as they stumble and fall down from their spawn exit. This gives your team precious moments to keep the Bot moving (or, during Core Objective 4, take the Sample to the Extraction Point)!

**Extend your presence in the Mighty Pipe Courtyard by covering the entrances to the Flickering Light Passage and Comfy Couch Stairs, and prevent foes using these to reach the vantage points they both lead to, which overlook the Garage.**

**TIP**

**Market Thoroughfare:** With two Engineers firing at foes and mending the Bot, and a couple of additional Soldiers (plus a Medic) to patrol the area in front of the Bot, make slow and plodding progress around the Market, watching for enemies at the far end of the streets, up on the store balcony to the right of the "Bar" sign, and shooting from the Market Alley. But the biggest threats usually occur at the end of this objective.

On the final slope before the Garage, enemies are likely to be firing down from vantage points around the Laboratory. Try crouching immediately behind the Bot and following it into the Lab area. The Resistance defenders are often positioned in high-up sniping spots in front of the Bot, and may not have an angle to shoot you and (hopefully) not enough time to disable the Bot.

**Final Slope and Resistance Lab (Garage):** As the Bot gets more than halfway through the Market Thoroughfare, peel off a few of your team (Engineers are recommended) into the Market Alley or send them up through the Market Passage if it isn't barricaded, to hold the Supply Command Post. The connecting passage left of the post leads to the Gantry Overlook, which offers partial cover and views of the Laboratory. Rush about here (optionally Wall-jumping to the Container Overlook opposite) to distract the enemy enough for the Bot to be escorted to the Garage itself.

## Automated Ordnance

6 Sit a turret on the Gantry Overlook to catch enemies trying to fix the barricade, and stop them heading into the Supply Command Post area.

7 Mow down some respawning foes and guard the Circumventing Passage entrance at the same time.

5 Mine the entrance to the Supply Command Post.

6 7 Then do the same for the entrances to the Flickering Light Passage and Comfy Couch Stairs (mine 6 shown).

## Sniper's Ally: Camping Spots

10 The corrugated metal provides protection, and the small platform provides views of the enemy's vantage points surrounding the Lab.

11 Set a mine or turret to your left, and fight viciously from the Gantry Overlook.

## Sniper's Ally: Camping Spots (continued)

12 You won't survive a grenade, but you can tag foes on the Resistance vantage points, as well as enemies rushing the Market Passage and Gantry Overlook.

13 Sit at the entrance to the Mini-Pipe Passage and plug away at recently spawned foes.

# Objective Tactics: Core Objective 4

## Deliver Sample

Spawn Point to Garage & Sample: 00:18

Spawn Point to Extraction Point: 00:12

Garage to Extraction Point: 00:14

Time to Deliver the Sample: 00:05

### General Tactics

Getting in, and then getting out of the Laboratory area is the biggest problem during this final objective, mainly due to the proximity of the Resistance Deployment Zone, and the camp spots above the Lab Garage that the Bot has cut a section out of. The Laboratory may be laced with mines, so to cover the carrier, continue to claim the Supply Command Post and Gantry Overlook for Security; this is your only really elevated position where foes can be sniped. Lob grenades into the Laboratory to clear out any traps and foes stationed there.

One of the ways you can reach the Garage is through the Laboratory itself, accessed by following the Mighty Pipe from the Circumventing Passage. Once teammates have cleared the interior of traps, change to an Operative and disguise yourself; you may be able to bypass the entire defensive area, sneak into the Lab Garage, grab the Sample, and flee via one of the routes detailed below.

### Exit Routes: Extraction!

**Circumventing Passage:** You can flee through the Laboratory, or follow the Mighty Pipe all the way to the Circumventing Passage, and Wall-jump the gap over the Dry Dock. The route is quite short, but the enemy spawn makes it very dangerous, and dropping the Sample in this area with the enemy leaving it there is a real problem. If you've just spawned or retreated back into the Crane Yard, cover the Circumventing Passage from the Yard; Resistance forces usually use this to reach the Extraction Point, because it is closest to their spawn point.

**Market Passage:** This direct and dangerous path assumes the enemy hasn't constructed the barricade in the middle of the passage. However, this is the shortest path to the Extraction Point, under the Crane Magnet and across the Dry Dock Bridge. Mix up the routes by darting left into the Side Stairs or up and across the Free Ark Rooftop Alley if enemies are everywhere.

**Market Thoroughfare:** Flee up the slope, or Mantle up onto the Gantry Overlook, and disappear into the Market Alleys. Choose the Side Stairs (or Free Ark Rooftop Alley) over the Crane Yard, because it may be easier to reach the protective cover of the *Hope* before leaping up into the balcony where your team spawns.

**If you try to fake a run to the Extraction Point and attempt to take cover in your spawn point, the Sample returns to the Garage! Head close so your spawning teammates can help you, but don't enter or you'll lose the Sample.**

CAUTION

**Crane Yard and Extraction Point:** The Extraction Point is likely to be defended by sharpshooters from various vantage points. Because it takes a few seconds to deliver the Sample, have friends cover you, even blocking your body with their own, anything to complete this objective.

**Check out Core Objective 3 for the turrets, mines, and camp spots around the Crane Yard. Try erecting traps along the route the carrier chooses, and keep in radio contact so your team can clear a route prior to the Sample being grabbed.**

TIP

## Secondary Objectives

### Escort Core Objective Class Teammate

**Official Escort Info:** As you cover the Soldier planting the HE Charge on the Harbor Gate, use gunfire or medical supplies to help him (depending on your class), and watch for enemy Engineers. Since the Bot needs constant attention for most of this mission, two Engineers who can repair it and cover each other at the same time is helpful. During the final Core Objective, it is worth partnering the carrier with a similarly speedy Medic to keep him in syringes, and with previous knowledge of the likely routes the carrier will take.

### Hack the Side Door

Spawn Point to Side Door: 00:09

Time to Hack the Side Door: 00:20

The Side Door passage to the left of the Harbor Gate is likely to be guarded by a foe or two, so send in an Operative who is light enough to scramble up and check the area above the bridge or door and take care of enemies (a grenade lobbed in these spots does the trick). The hacking isn't essential—in fact the passage is more important because you can fire through the open window at the foes behind the Gate while in some considerable cover—but helps if you're trying to outflank the enemy. You can also climb over (and thus ignore) the door and exit if you're light enough. You can only hack it from the interior passage side.

### Construct Side Stairs

Engineer

Spawn Point to Side Stairs: 00:10

Time to Build Side Stairs: 00:20

Time to Plant Explosives: 00:07

Time to Disarm Explosives: 00:05

Countdown to Explosion: 00:40

The optimal time to try this is just as Core Objective 3 concludes, when the enemy isn't expecting you in this part of the map. It is worth a suicide rush to start the staircase construction, before returning again and again until the enemy gives in. The stairs are useful for the Heavy Body Types on your team to ascend, because they head into the Market to chaperone the Bot. Light Body Types can Wall-jump the gap in the staircase, so building it for them is unnecessary. Then listen for enemy Soldiers attempting to place a charge on the stairs, and intercept if necessary (or simply fall down the gap if you're on your way back from the Market).

### Destroy Market Barricade

Soldier

Spawn Point to Barricade: 00:18

Time to Build Barricade: 00:20

Time to Plant Explosives: 00:07

Time to Disarm Explosives: 00:05

Countdown to Explosion: 00:40

Expect enemy Engineers to have built this barricade almost immediately during Core Objective 3. If they didn't, expect at least a mine or a turret to contend with. The advantages of keeping the Market Passage open are numerous: you can flank around when the Bot is being escorted, reach the Supply Command Post more easily, and move to and (more importantly) from the Garage to the Crane Yard much more directly during the final Core Objective. Give this task to a Soldier who can quickly place an explosive on the barricade, and guard it until detonation.

### Capture the Health Command Post

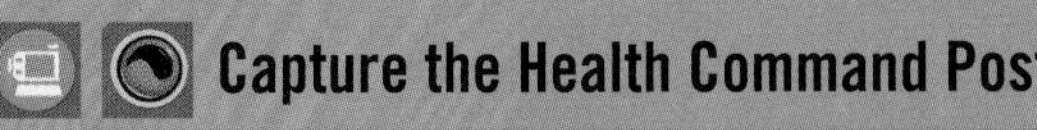
Engineer & Operative Advantage!

Spawn Point to Command Post: 00:11

Time to Claim Command Post: 00:10

Set into the hold of the *Hope*, this is usually claimed within the first few moments of the mission by the enemy. However, once Core Objective 1 is complete, it becomes increasingly easy to take for Security, so choose a teammate with this specific objective in mind. As your spawn point moves to the *Hope*'s interior, directly above this post, it becomes foolish *not* to take this immediately, and hold the enemy from retaking it; they'll be too preoccupied, anyway!

### Capture the Supply Command Post

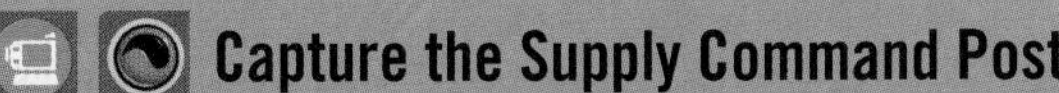
Engineer & Operative Advantage!

Spawn Point to Command Post: 00:12

Time to Claim Command Post: 00:10

Located deep within the enemy's territory, this post is a lengthy dash from your initial (and even your final) deployment zone. You can't capture this until the start of Core Objective 3, so prime your runners to storm this area at this time, or take a shortcut through the *Hope* earlier so they have already arrived as Core Objective 3 begins. Don't expect to hold this post for long,, because the enemy congregates around this area when they're defending the Garage. It is worth retaking the post and pushing the enemy back as the Bot arrives to cut open the Garage, and to give the edge to the Sample carrier.

### Construct the Gate MG Nest

### Construct the Ship MG Nest

### Construct the Crane MG Nest

Engineer

Spawn Point to Gate MG Nest: 00:06 

Spawn Point to Ship MG Nest: 00:07 

Spawn Point to Crane MG Nest: 00:09 

Time to Construct: 00:04 

The Gate MG Nest is utilized by the enemies to cut you down before and after you destroy the Harbor Gate. It isn't useful to your team in the slightest (aside from XP value, or if you scale the Side Door and try to turn it on the enemy, but that plan is almost never enacted).

The Ship MG Nest may be used by the enemy to shoot your Bot and teammates as you cross the Container Clearing to the Crane Yard. It should be appropriated by your forces during Core Objective 4, because it proves useful in strafing the far Crane Yard, Crane MG Nest, and enemies on the opposite side of the Crane Yard who are firing on your carrier.

The Crane MG Nest faces into the Crane Yard, and is utilized by the Resistance almost exclusively. There's no point in building this and the enemy has usually done it already. The meager XP isn't worth the use the enemy has when cutting you down as you emerge from your final deployment zone. Avoid this.

### Solo Tactics

**Throughout this mission, focus on the critical Objectives in case your team isn't pulling its weight. After a sprint to clamp explosives on the Gate (as a Soldier), guard and break through into the Thoroughfare. Then cover the Bot until you're slain, before respawning as an Engineer to help mend the Bot throughout its journey. Your class also helps you during the Crane fixing, and final trundle through the Market. Your Body Type is the final point to remember; a gifted Light Body Type with the abilities recommended earlier can deliver the Sample more easily than a tank.**

## Mission Completion Conditions

### Continuation...

**Core Objective 1:** Your team succeeds in destroying the Gate at the Harbor Entrance. Part 2 of this mission now commences....

**Core Objective 2:** You successfully escort the Maintenance Bot to the Crane. Part 2 continues and Part 3 of this mission now begins....

**Core Objective 3:** Your team succeeds in repairing the Crane. Part 2 of this mission continues....

**Core Objective 2 (again):** The Maintenance Bot successfully opens the Resistance Garage. Part 4 of this mission now begins....

### Completed!

The match completes if you successfully deliver the Sample to the Extraction Point, before the timer ticks down.

### Unsuccessful!

Security forces lose if the enemy stops you from completing any Core Objective by the time the timer reaches zero.

HISTORY OF THE ARK
CHARACTER CREATION
GAMEPLAY
WEAPONS DETAIL
CAMPAIGN
Hostage Rescue
Smash & Grab
Dirty Bomb
Prison Break
Early Launch
Fallout
Chopper Down
Grand Theft Aero
CHALLENGES
APPENDICES

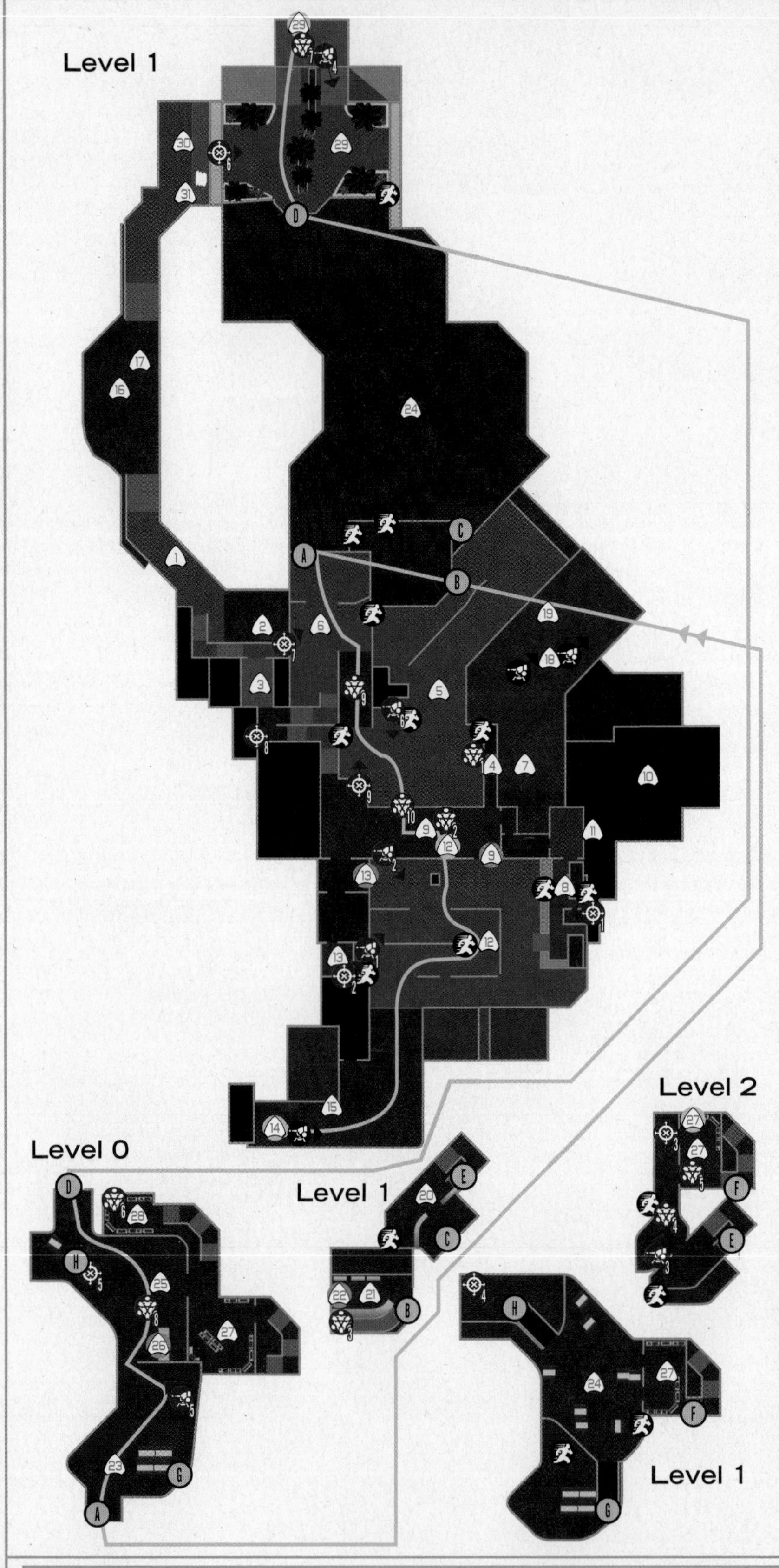

Level 1

Level 0

Level 1

Level 2

Level 1

## MAP LEGEND

### Security Tower: Core Objectives 1 and 4

1: Security Deployment Zone (Pt. 1): Security Corridor (Lvl. 2)
2: Security Command Post (Pt. 1) (Lvl. 2)
3: Maintenance Bot Garage & Side Access (Lvl. 2)
4: Forecourt & Security Checkpoint Stairs (Lvl. 2)
5: Forecourt Road (Lvl. 1)
6: Sunken Forecourt (Lvl. 0)
7: Sewer Exit & Storage Room Thoroughfare (Lvls. 0 & 1)
8: Sewer Tunnel & Side Battlements (Lvls. 0, 1, & 2)
9: Guard Tower Battlements & MG Nest (Lvl. 2)
10: Security Deployment Zone (Pt. 4): Warehouse (Lvl. 2)
11: Security Command Post (Pt. 4) (Lvl. 2)
12: Security Checkpoint & Guard Tower (Lvl. 1)
13: Side Guardhouse Thoroughfare & MG Nest (Lvl. 2)
14: Resistance Deployment Zone (Pt. 1): Outskirts (Lvl. 1)
15: Resistance Command Post (Pt. 1) (Lvl. 1)

### Security Tower: Core Objectives 2, 3, and 4

16: Security Deployment Zone (Pts. 2 & 3): Security Corridor (Lvl. 2)
17: Security Command Post (Pts. 2 & 3) (Lvl. 2)
18: Resistance Deployment Zone (Pts. 2 & 3): Storage Room (Lvl. 1)
19: Resistance Command Post (Pts. 2 & 3) (Lvl. 1)
20: Ark Security & Staircase (Lvls. 1 & 2)
21: Ark Service Rooms & Staircase (Lvls. 0 & 1)
22: Health Command Post (Lvl. 1)
23: Sec 05 Service Entrance (Lvl. 0)
24: Sec 05 Headquarters (Lvls. 1 & 2)
25: Sec 05 High Security & Storage Area (Lvl. 0)
26: Supply Command Post (Lvl. 0)
27: Police & Warden's Offices, & Central Stairwell (Lvls. 0, 1, & 2)
28: Side Controls (Lvls. 0 & 1)
29: Sec 04 Exterior Plaza & Infirmary (Lvl. 0)
30: Resistance Deployment Zone (Pt. 4): Sec 04 Security Roof (Lvl. 1)
31: Resistance Command Post (Pt. 4) (Lvl. 1)

S.M.A.R.T. Move
Engineer Mine (Optimal Placement)
Engineer Turret (Optimal Placement)
Camping Spot
Deployment Zone Turret (Invulnerable)
Core Objective Location
Secondary Objective Location
Critical Path (Route)
Level Link

BRINK — Security Tower: Overview Map

# DAY 5: PRISON BREAK

FREEPLAY: SECURITY TOWER   RESISTANCE CAMPAIGN—DAY 2: BREAKOUT

## 19:30 Barracks Area, Security Tower Garrison

MISSION TIME (COb 1): 07:00

MISSION TIME (COb 2): +07:00

MISSION TIME (COb 3): +07:00

MISSION TIME (COb 4): +07:00

### Captain Mokoena: Briefing

We've been holding Nechayev, the terrorist informant, in the Infirmary for his own protection. But he suddenly stopped talking. Chen must be planning a raid to free him. Double the guards! Expect trouble! Assume they've already compromised or can bypass our defenses. No prisoners must escape! Kill Nechayev if you must, but no one leaves!

### Optimal Class Numbers

| | COb 1 | COb 2 | COb 3 | COb 4 |
|---|---|---|---|---|
| Soldier | [2] | [2] | [3] | [3] |
| Medic | [2] | [2] | [2] | [1] |
| Engineer | [3] | [3] | [2] | [3] |
| Operative | [1] | [1] | [1] | [1] |

### Objectives (Resistance)

- Core Objective 1: Defend the Conduit
- Core Objective 2: Defend the Safe
- Core Objective 3: Defend the Pass Code
- Core Objective 4: Stop the Prisoner
- Escort Teammate
- Capture the Health Command Post
- Capture the Supply Command Post
- Construct the Guardhouse MG Nest
- Construct the Wall MG Nest

## Important Locations

(Core Objective 1 and 4)

Once the initial Conduit has been removed (Core Objective 1), all these locations are accessible during each part of the mission.

NOTE

### 1 Security Deployment Zone (Pt. 1): Security Corridor (Lvl. 2)

Your initial spawn point allows you to race along the Side Access area (or a drop down into the Forecourt) to reach the Guard Tower, Battlements, and the Power Conduit the enemy initially tries to detonate. Note the garage door behind your team, which connects to the rest of the Security Corridor and opens only after Core Objective 1 has been completed by the enemy; this is a heavily traveled road from your subsequent spawn point.

## 2 Security Command Post (Pt. 1) (Lvl. 2)

Playing a defensive game means setting up explosives and turrets as well as finding vantage points to shoot from. Weight your team with Engineers to help add firepower to known enemy thoroughfares. Change weapons here, too.

## 3 Maintenance Bot Garage & Side Access (Lvl. 2)

The one-room interior building above the Maintenance Bot Garage is a route that Security forces use to reach the stepped Side Access, which allows movement between the Guard Tower Battlements and the Sunken Forecourt areas. You have the advantage of using the route above the Maintenance Bot Garage, which leads from the Security spawn point to a small, dead-end balcony you can snipe or drop from. This is inaccessible to the enemy until they approach it from the Security Corridor during Core Objective 4.

## 4 Forecourt & Security Checkpoint Stairs (Lvl. 2)

## 5 Forecourt Road (Lvl. 1)

## 6 Sunken Forecourt (Lvl. 0)

The battle across this expanse of exterior tarmac rages throughout Core Objective 4. It is also well-trafficked as you try to stop the Resistance from entering the Security Tower during Core Objective 2 (although most of your defending should take place closer to the Warden's Office).

To the side of the main gate and under the Sewer Exit is a balcony and set of stairs up to the Guard Tower Battlements; use this to drop down into the Forecourt during Core Objective 1, and use the stack of crates to reach the balcony during Objective 4. The height afforded here makes this a good vantage point to spot or fire on enemies.

The upper level Forecourt Road starts with a "CLEAR" sign on the tarmac, and runs as a four-lane road past a security check-in with a mesh fence, and down to the second Resistance Deployment Zone, plus two entrances into the Security Tower itself, making the far end a frequently used route for the enemy to reach the safe in the Warden's Office (Core Objective 2). Also note the barriers and signage to use as cover; stalling the enemy wherever you can.

Separated by a wall and a large set of stairs, the Sunken Forecourt area is the best way to reach the Sec 05 Service Entrance and Tower interior, and where you'll want to stall the enemy as they escort their pilot during Core Objective 3. The Side Access up to the Battlements and the Maintenance Bot Garage is adjacent here. Your team streams down from this point, too.

**Use the ground markings on the tarmac to figure out the position within this area; especially the painted arrows, lines, and "CLEAR" sign.**

TIP

### S.M.A.R.T. Moves

Use the Secboard with the Monorail map to climb up and leap onto the security booth, offering a good (but exposed) vantage point.

Clamber onto the pile of metal boxes to reach the balcony above the Sewer Exit, and up to the Battlements.

At the top of the stairs, use the (locked) weapon cabinets to climb up and onto the Side Access stairs.

At the top of the stairs, jump on the wall railing, and run across to take an ambush spot above the Sec 05 Service Entrance.

## 7 Sewer Exit & Storage Room Thoroughfare (Lvls. 0 & 1)

This Storage Room is used to drop from when you spawn during Core Objective 4. The enemy uses the Sewer Exit as a thoroughfare between the Sewer and the Security Checkpoint in the Forecourt, and heads back again later in the mission.

**The access to and from the Sewers means that your team can move ahead of where the majority of the enemy is fighting, to hold a location (such as the Side Battlements or Checkpoint area during Core Objective 4) prior to the enemy arriving. This makes it even more difficult for the Resistance to punch through and achieve victory.**

TIP

## 8 Sewer Tunnel & Side Battlements (Lvls. 0, 1, & 2)

Expect enemies to scurry along the green-tinged path during the first and fourth Core Objectives. During initial combat, you can move from the Storage Room Thoroughfare, and out under the Battlements to waylay foes (although attacking from height is a better plan). Don't think your Battlements are solid; this is one way foes can sneak away from you!

Above the Sewer Tunnel on the Checkpoint side are pipes with reinforced metal surrounding them. These offer a series of "steps" that (providing you Wall-jump correctly) allow you to reach the Battlements and the other side of the gate. From here, you have a perfect place to rain fire down on the enemy, and stall their progress.

The Side Battlements become much more important during Core Objective 4, because they are an exit from your final deployment zone, and are used to provide long-range death over the Checkpoint area to stop the pilot's escape.

### S.M.A.R.T. Moves

From the edge of the highest pipes, you can leap and climb up onto the Side Battlements leading to Security Deployment Zone 3.

Use the concrete blocks with rebar sticking out of them as steps, and leap to cling on the second set of pipes.

## 9 Guard Tower Battlements & MG Nest (Lvl. 2)

Preventing the enemy from destroying the Conduit at the base of this Guard Tower is your first Core Objective. If you're successful, you win the match without needing to defend the rest of the map. Various routes lead to these main Battlements. From the Security Checkpoint below, the enemy likes to head up the Side Guardhouse, or climb the pipes above the Sewer Tunnel.

Security forces are better positioned to reach this location more quickly. A run up the stairs close to the Maintenance Bot Garage, using the Side Access (both routes meet at the Side Guardhouse) enables you to overlook the Checkpoint and fire on foes. Bounding up the Security Checkpoint Stairs means those in the Forecourt can reach the MG Nest up here, which is a great weapon to fix and use during Core Objectives 1 and 4.

When you're patrolling the Battlements, remember they are three small sections of concrete wall in disrepair. One portion is near the top of the sewer pipes the enemy likes to climb. One is next to the MG Nest. And one is near the Guardhouse. During Core Objectives 1, 2, and 4, fire on the foes on the ground, and prevent them from using this location for themselves. Once the Power Conduit has been destroyed (Core Objective 1), the gate under the Battlements opens, allowing access to and from the Forecourt.

### 10 Security Deployment Zone (Pt. 4): Warehouse (Lvl. 2)

This is the third and final location where your team spawns, and this begins during the last Core Objective (4). It offers great access onto the Battlements, Guard Tower, and into the Forecourt. Prior to this, the location is empty, but it can be used as a path down and into the Storage Room Thoroughfare (and Forecourt beyond), but can only be accessed via S.M.A.R.T. jumps from the highest Sewer Tunnel pipe section.

> **Once you drop down to the Storage Room Thoroughfare, you can't climb back up.**
>
>  CAUTION

### 11 Security Command Post (Pt. 4) (Lvl. 2)

During the last Core Objective, stopping the pilot is your overriding plan, so spawn Engineers to add turrets and explosives to an already difficult escape route. Swap your weapons here, too.

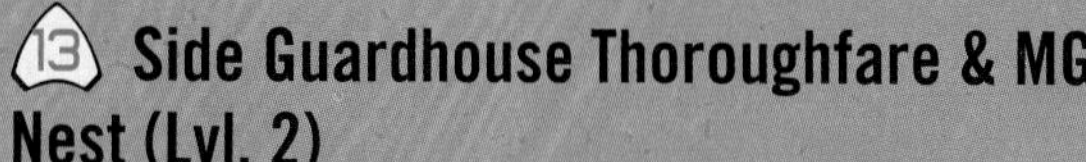

### 12 Security Checkpoint & Guard Tower (Lvl. 1)

### 13 Side Guardhouse Thoroughfare & MG Nest (Lvl. 2)

The large Checkpoint and Tower marked with the phrase "The Ark. United," and the graffiti underneath "Ishtar" is the main battleground for the first Core Objective. It also becomes the frantic last stand if the

enemy has managed to bring Nechayev back to this initial deployment zone (Core Objective 4). Make sure you know all of the routes from and to this area.

The Side Guardhouse is accessible from your enemy's first deployment zone; they usually access the ground-level balcony inside the Security Checkpoint, and bound up to the second balcony directly above it (via a S.M.A.R.T. move). This upper parapet leads to the Side Guardhouse, where you can overlook the Checkpoint and build an MG Nest to strafe the foes on their way in and back out again.

On the ground in the Checkpoint area itself, be mindful of the gaps in the fencing that your foes vault over; cover these locations with firepower from above. You may elect to guard the Power Conduit, using the barricade winch box as cover, but it is safer to lob in grenades or place explosives to waylay the enemy. The algae-covered sewer outlet at the opposite side of the Checkpoint is another place to launch a surprise attack from; especially during Core Objective 4.

Finally, remember that your foes can scale the Guard Tower via the sewer pipes, or head under via the Tunnel. But the two MG Nests in this area (the other is just right of the Conduit up on the Battlements) are worth manning and gunning from.

> **"The Ark. United": Look for this signage atop the Guard Tower gate during the latter stages of Core Objective 4. If the enemy reaches this landmark, you know they're about to escape with Nechayev.**
>
>  TIP

 **S.M.A.R.T. Moves** 

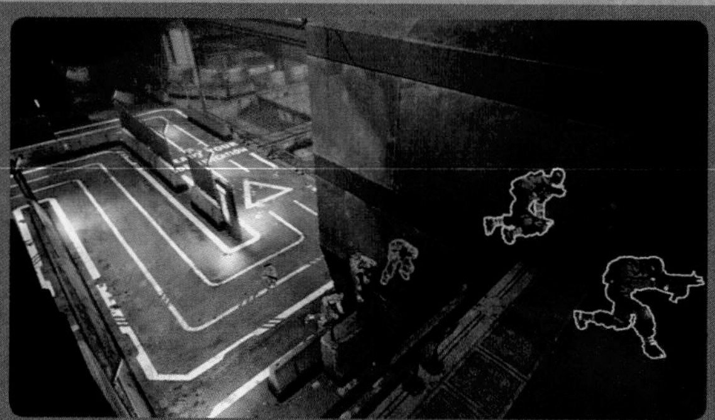

From the lower corridor, leap to the concrete barrier, then up onto the wall-mounted fuse box, and up onto the balcony directly above.

Scaling any of the "Secboard" signs and skipping across the top of the mesh fences causes a distraction, but little else.

### 14 Resistance Deployment Zone (Pt. 1): Outskirts (Lvl. 1)

This is both the Resistance force's initial spawning grounds and the final location during their attempt at moving their pilot Nechayev. The sentry turrets provide too much firepower for you to stay in this area; let the enemy come to you from this location early on, and give up hope if the pilot manages to stagger here at the end of the mission. Note the side doorway, which the foes sometimes use to reach the Side Guardhouse.

### 15 Resistance Command Post (Pt. 1) (Lvl. 1)

Forget this Command Post; the enemy utilizes it exclusively.

## Security Tower

(Core Objectives 2, 3, & 4)

> **NOTE**
>
> **The remaining locations unlock only after the Power Conduit has been destroyed, ending Core Objective 1. Glass doors or garage shutters prevent access before this point.**

### 16 Security Deployment Zone (Pts. 2 & 3): Security Corridor (Lvl. 2)

This spawning point is farther up the Security Corridor from your first spawning grounds, and allows your team to head in one of two directions. Either head down to the Maintenance Bot Garage and the old spawn point, and then into the Security Tower to fend foes off between here and the Warden's Office, or drop into the Exterior Plaza and Infirmary to create defenses between the Warden's Office and the Infirmary itself.

### 17 Security Command Post (Pts. 2 & 3) (Lvl. 2)

During the time the enemy attempts to hack the Warden's safe and free Nechayev, you should be setting up defenses throughout the Security Tower and out into the Plaza. Engineers are helpful in this regard.

### 18 Resistance Deployment Zone (Pts. 2 & 3): Storage Room (Lvl. 1)

This is on the other side of the warehouse from where your forces spawn during Core Objective 4, but the shelves separate you from reaching that location. The enemy has access across the Forecourt and into the Security Tower. They continue to spawn here until Nechayev has been freed (the end of Core Objective 3), or you stop them.

### 19 Resistance Command Post (Pts. 2 & 3) (Lvl. 1)

This Resistance replenishment terminal is out of bounds to your team.

### 20 Ark Security & Staircase (Lvls. 1 & 2)

The Resistance spawns close to this entrance, with "Ark Security" etched into the glass, and uses the door and stairs to access the Warden's Office. The flashing orange lights make this chamber easy to place, but your team starts on the opposite side of the Forecourt, so you may wish to attempt another route into the Security Tower. The stairs (or metal containers you can clamber up) lead straight onto an upper walkway inside Sec 05 Headquarters. Also keep in mind this offers a fast path back into the Forecourt, which you can use during the enemy's attempt to escort Nechayev.

### S.M.A.R.T. Moves

A quicker way is to ignore the stairs, and instead clamber up the metal containers on the shelving behind the security desk.

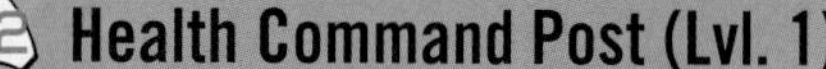

## Ark Service Rooms & Staircase (Lvls. 0 & 1)

## Health Command Post (Lvl. 1)

From Sec 05 Service Entrance, you can watch for foes streaming down here instead of using the Ark Security and Staircase to access the interior of this building. This entrance leads to stairs and a small Service Room with the Health Command Post. Battle here to own this post because the enemy is racing against time, and won't expend quite as much manpower to obtain or defend this terminal. The upper exit brings you out into the Forecourt next to the "Ark Security" doorway.

## Sec 05 Service Entrance (Lvl. 0)

This initially bewildering area offers another main thoroughfare up and into the Sec 05 Headquarters from the Sunken Forecourt. When assaulting the Warden's Office, this area is a thoroughfare; choose the stacked benches or ramp to reach the Sec 05 Headquarters. You can also enter the High Security and Storage Area below, either to work ahead of your team or to claim the Supply Command Post.

During Nechayev's escort, the place is usually packed with foes at the security terminals and milling around by the glass doors into the Forecourt. Clear out this key chokepoint during the chaperoning, and use the climbable scenery mainly for cover.

### S.M.A.R.T. Moves

Don't forget that you can slide across the gap in the wall between the security terminals and the glass entrance doors.

Climb the large stack of metal boxes and leap the gap to the Headquarters cellblock.

## Sec 05 Headquarters (Lvls. 1 & 2)

The main interior of the Security Tower is the cellblock-lined Headquarters, the scene of a recent riot. This enables access from the Sunken Forecourt, or one of the entrances from the upper Forecourt, into the cellblock or the High Security and Storage Area underneath. At the opposite end of the cellblock (near the wall marked "Sec 01"), close to a trio of corpses inside body bags, are stairs leading down to a couple more corpses, the Sec 04 Exterior Plaza, and back around into the High Security area. A balcony overlooks the Exterior Plaza entrance, too.

Between these two exits are the Police and Warden's Offices, which are on two floors of the Central Stairwell. During Core Objective 2, much of the fighting takes place here, as you attempt to thwart the Resistance in their attempts to scale the chamber to reach the Warden's safe. Afterward, this becomes an alternate route to take to and from Nechayev's location, although fewer defenses should be placed here, because the pilot takes the route below, through the Sec 05 High Security and Storage Area.

### S.M.A.R.T. Moves

A jumble of stacked containers, benches, and other scenery allows you to ascend to the walkway by the Warden's Office, without the need for stairs.

## 25 Sec 05 High Security & Storage Area (Lvl. 0)

## 26 Supply Command Post (Lvl. 0)

The security fencing and entrance underneath the Headquarters cellblock reveals a High Security location leading into a Storage Area, which meets at the staircase at the opposite side of the Headquarters, allowing access out into the Exterior Plaza in Sec 04. Midway through the Storage Area is the entrance to the Central Stairwell. Close by is the Supply Command Post, which should be secured as quickly as possible; don't ignore it during the initial stages of Core Objective 2.

This is an alternate route up to the Warden's Office, but is mainly the battleground as the enemy tries to escort Nechayev during Core Objective 4. A frantic back-and-forth battle occurs as you try to wound the pilot and keep the enemy from proceeding through this location. Placing defensive mines, charges, and turrets, and positioning friends in defensive positions, is imperative. Fortunately, you can claim and keep the Supply Command Post, giving you an advantage until the enemies overwhelm you. If you let them!

## 27 Police & Warden's Offices, & Central Stairwell (Lvls. 0, 1, & 2)

Midway along the Headquarters cellblock is a large Central Stairwell, which runs from the High Security Area under the cellblock all the way up three floors to the Warden's Office itself. The bottom two floors consist of Police Offices, with desks and computer terminals. Swarm the stairwell to reach the Warden's Office and impede the safe hacking during Core Objective 2. The office itself has the safe, so fortify that with every spare man, turret, and explosive you have. Be sure you know all the ways to reach and leave this room. You can arrive by:

Heading up the staircase from the Ark Security.

Climbing up the stacked crates from the Headquarters cellblock area.

Scaling the Central Stairwell from the High Security area.

You should expect the enemy to use these routes too. You can leave by:

Heading out onto the balcony walkway, and leaping through either gap in the mesh security fence.

Descending the staircase to the Ark Security area, although this is away from Core Objective 3.

Or race down the Central Stairwell. Alternately you can hop over the banister and drop down.

**Need to know where the Warden's Office is? Aside from the guide map, look for flashing orange lights, and follow the signposts inside the Headquarters cellblock.**

 TIP

## 28 Side Controls (Lvls. 0 & 1)

This is beneficial to the enemy rather than your team (unless you use this route to outflank and attack the enemy from behind once Nechayev is inside the Security Tower). Enter this from the base of the Exterior Plaza. It offers access into the Central Stairwell and Supply Command Post. Fire on foes in the Plaza from the balcony up here, or use it as an alternate route if the main path is too crowded.

S.M.A.R.T. Moves

With a Wall Run, you can launch yourself off the upper balcony, and land close to the steps up to the Infirmary; which is great if you're chasing a foe carrying the Passcode.

## 25 Sec 04 Exterior Plaza & Infirmary (Lvl. 0)

This becomes a major defensive position during the latter stages of Core Objective 3, and if Nechayev is freed at the start of Core Objective 4. The Exterior Plaza is separated by a long planter and glass fencing. Remember there are two exits from the Security Tower and the Side Controls area (so guard against foes coming from or into all these locations). The enemy is likely to be expecting you as you drop down from the roof and out of Sec 04 Security building, so you may wish to snipe from the balcony above this structure. Otherwise, set up defenses between the Tower and the Infirmary doors. You cannot enter the Infirmary itself.

## 30 Resistance Deployment Zone (Pt. 4): Sec 04 Security Roof (Lvl. 1)

This is where the enemy begins Core Objective 4 from, and they usually head in to help Nechayev through the facility, while others try to coax you into fighting away from the pilot's escape route. Note the two possible paths they take (and which you took during earlier objectives): down the hole or over the wall into the Exterior Plaza, or down the Security Corridor and out by the Maintenance Bot Garage.

## 31 Resistance Command Post (Pt. 4) (Lvl. 1)

This is shut down if you attempt to use it. Ignore this post and concentrate on the Supply and Health terminals.

# Objective Tactics: Core Objective 1

## Defend the Conduit

Engineer Advantage!

Spawn Point to Conduit: 00:14

Time to Disarm Explosives: 00:05

Time to Plant Explosives: 00:07

Countdown to Explosion: 00:30

### General Tactics

Aside from stopping the Conduit detonation, creating crossfire opportunities is an important goal during this Core Objective. Set up a pair of teammates on either side, with one of you drawing the enemy's attention while the other plants an accurate, unhurried headshot into the back of his cranium. That's the plan here. To get to these crossfire positions, split the locations where your team heads up from: bounding up the Forecourt

and Security Checkpoint Stairs or maneuvering through the Sewer on the left side, and ascending the steps around from the Maintenance Bot Garage and Side Access on the right side.

While you're fighting from the parapets of the Guard Tower Battlements, build the MG Nests overlooking the gate area and put down turrets in the gaps in the Battlements, but be aware you're very visible up here. Use that to your advantage; pop out of hiding and blast some shots, then dodge back behind cover and pop out somewhere

else (but not the same place every time; the enemy shouldn't be able to predict your next appearance). Keep enemy attackers staring at where you just were, not firing at anyone else, and not making any progress on the objective.

## Crossfire Ops

**Look Left:** Clambering up the pile of containers and the Security Checkpoint Stairs allows you quick access to the Wall MG Nest, and the top of the pipe stacks on the left side of the Checkpoint. Or, head through the Sewer Exit, but expect lighter enemies to be attempting this route, too. Waylaying them is good, but bearing down on the Conduit, so the enemies don't ever get out of the Checkpoint, is better.

**Look Right:** Choose the right side of the Forecourt, and the stairs up the side to the Guardhouse and a second MG Nest, and you can catch foes scrambling up the side of the structure to the upper balcony, which is normally a great sniping position (Camping Spot 1). Have one teammate patrol the Forecourt side of the Battlements in case a sneaky enemy tries to outflank you by taking the same routes you did, or is waiting for the glass doors of the Security Tower to open.

**Look Out:** Now that you're up here, coordinate your firing with anyone not standing directly next to you. Fire down from three separate directions: the corner and Wall MG Nest near the pipe stacks, all along the Battlements above the Conduit, and from the Side Guardhouse. If the enemy manages to clamp explosives on the Conduit, be sure one teammate already knows it's his job to drop down and remove it, while being covered by withering support fire from above.

**Don't forget that grenades work well; especially when lobbed at the Conduit while a hapless foe is planting the bomb.**

TIP

## Automated Ordnance

Check the Resistance section for more trap placement ideas, and try new locations out for yourself.

1 Place a turret in this alcove, which works for both Core Objective 1 and 4.

2 Set a turret on the gaps in the Battlement parapet.

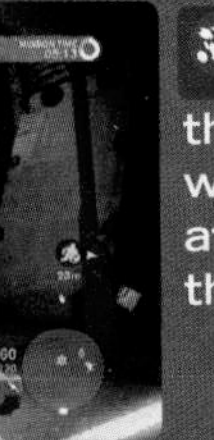

1 Stop foes from using the Sewer Exit with a mine at the top of these stairs.

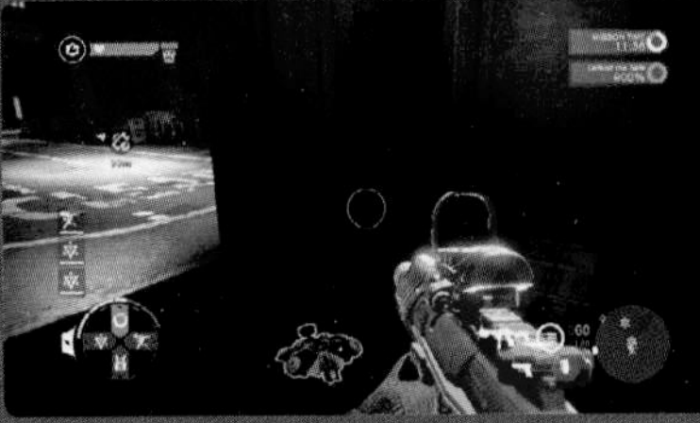

2 If there's time, drop a mine close to the Conduit, or inside the narrow opening in the gate once the explosion occurs.

## Sniper's Ally: Camping Spots

1 This high balcony above the side pipes is a great place to snipe during Core Objectives 1 and 4.

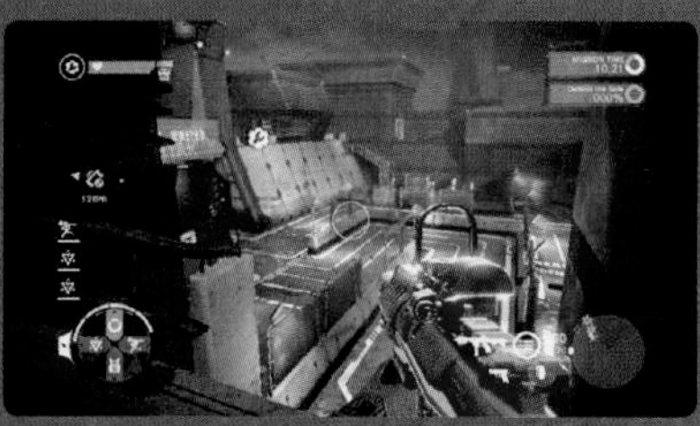

2 The upper balcony on the opposite side of the Checkpoint walls is a great spot too, close to the Guardhouse MG Nest. Watch for enemies climbing up here.

# Objective Tactics: Core Objective 2

## Defend the Safe

Spawn Point to Safe: 00:18

Time to Hack the Safe: 01:00

Time to Disarm Hackbox: 00:05

### General Tactics

At this point, the most important class becomes the Engineer, and at least half your team should be laying down mines and turrets covering the approaches to the Warden's Office. Engineers can also remove the Hack Boxes the Resistance manages to plant on the safe. Remember to make life extremely difficult for enemy Operatives too, from shouting that they've stolen your identity after you die (if you spot them attempting this), to aiming at every foe with an Operative icon above their heads.

The Health Command Post is an important trinket to wave in the faces of your foes. Be sure to capture and defend it during this objective in particular. Aside from the team benefit, the Resistance is likely to try to take it from you. This is a tactical victory because meanwhile they aren't massing and taking over the Warden's Office. If they realize you're coaxing them away and flee, run after and cut them down. If they're ignoring the area, rush to back up your team.

### Infiltration Chokepoints

**From Sunken Forecourt:** Foes heading into the Headquarters cellblock area can choose to climb the stack of scenery leading up to a gap in the mesh fence, or head to the base of the central stairwell to climb up. Station traps and men to cover both locations.

**From Ark Security:** The side stairwell from Ark Security is the second location where foes stream up from. You can interrupt their running from the Health Command Post as previously described, but also from the top of the stairs where mines, grenades, and gunfire are an excellent plan.

**Warden's Office:** Don't cram yourself into this room. Cover the adjacent thoroughfares with your team backed up by a large number of traps, courtesy of your Engineers. Engineers must also be on hand here to pry off the Operative's hacking equipment.

## Automated Ordnance

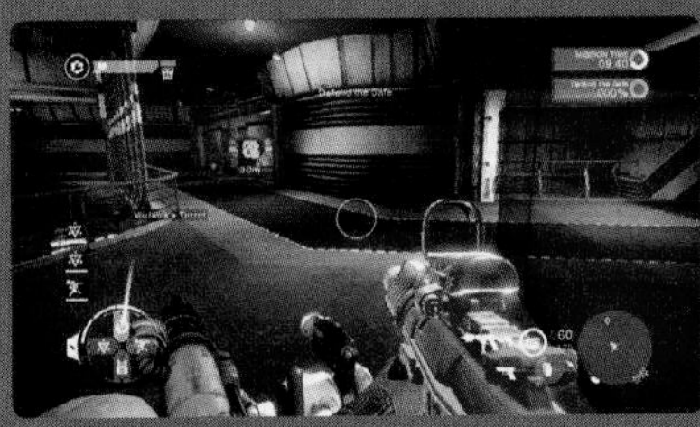

3 Cover the stairs from the Ark Security and the open balcony in the mesh wall from here; you're close to the Engineers guarding the safe if the turret needs fixing, too.

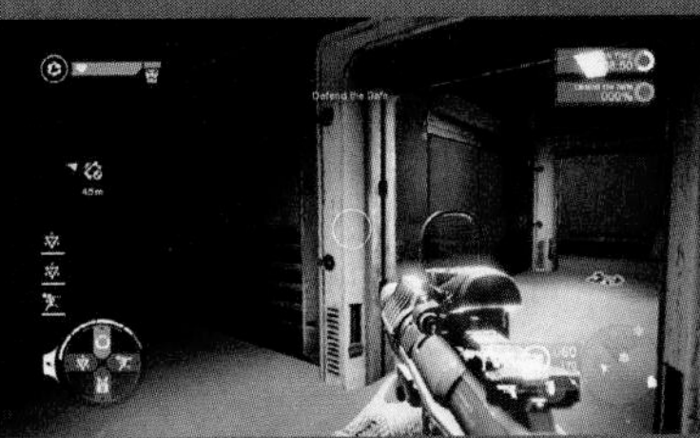

3 As well as trapping the Health Command Post, place a mine on the stairwell to catch foes moving between floors.

4 Place a mine here after the bend in the floor so enemies climbing over the railing and coming up the stairs are all caught.

5 Top of the stairs is the best place for a mine if you're engaging the enemy in a gunfight as well.

## Sniper's Ally: Camping Spots

3 Standing above the far exit enables you to snipe foes throughout the Headquarters and up on the Warden's balcony, then drop down to retreat (and fortify the Infirmary) during Core Objective 3.

4 Back up the turret on this balcony, with the bonus of sniping foes running in from the lower entrance.

# Objective Tactics: Core Objective 3

## Defend the Passcode

Spawn Point to Warden's Office: 00:18 

Warden's Office to Infirmary: 00:14 

Time to Deliver Passcode: 00:05 

### General Tactics

As soon as the Warden's safe is pried open, make sure your team splits into two distinct teams who already know their roles. Approximately half (and this varies based on where your team is, and the competence of the enemy) should retreat and start crafting a variety of nasty explosive and turret surprises at the far end of the Headquarters location, as well as the Exterior Plaza.

Meanwhile, the other teammates (perhaps anyone who isn't an Engineer) should try to stop the Passcode thief and return the item to the safe instead. Flick your Mission Wheel so the thief is always highlighted, and utilize your radar so you always know where the chief troublemaker is. Head him off because any attack is a tactical victory, even firefights you know you're going to lose.

When you jump over the upper wall after spawning, watch out for the central plant divider in the Exterior Plaza. You can only climb over it where there's a gap between the glass bits, and that gap isn't the same on both sides. Once you've learned where the gaps are, you can S.M.A.R.T. straight across, as long as you aim yourself obliquely.

TIP

## Plaza Lockdown

**Security Tower Main Exit:** The Passcode carrier's choice of exits includes the Security Tower, which is advantageous because it's easier to snipe the enemy from this point, or the Security Building under your spawn point. A mine at this exit helps stagger your foes, too.

**Side Controls Exit:** The enemy sometimes takes this more cunning route, via the upper or lower exits from the Side Controls rooms. These are less straightforward to aim at from range, so position your team behind the boxes or glass-walled planter to repel the enemy.

**Infirmary:** However, while other teammates try to return the Passcode to the safe and prevent the carrier from heading out to this side of the map, your Engineers should create a gauntlet of traps between the exit and the Infirmary. A couple of turrets, a mine at the door terminal, and more mines on the steps can stop the enemy, even if all other defenses haven't. Just be here to cover your traps, and fire on the foes too.

## Automated Ordnance

4 A turret on each side of the glass wall planter by the Infirmary (along with teammates guarding) reinforces this area.

6 Drop a mine here to kill a Passcode carrier who tries the fancy way out of the Sec Tower.

7 Place a mine by the door terminal at the Infirmary as a last line of defense.

## Sniper's Ally: Camping Spots

5 Hide below the stairwell near the exit to the Exterior Plaza to catch foes running by.

6 The balcony by your spawn point is excellent for tagging foes, and you can easily hide from their fire.

## Objective Tactics: Core Objective 4

### Stop the Prisoner

Infirmary to Deployment Zone: 00:38 

#### General Tactics

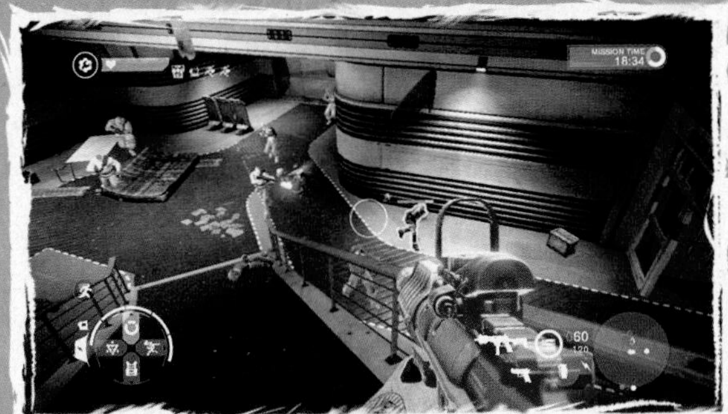

Your team's overriding priority is to target and down the pilot—Nechayev—who is framed in yellow and falls to his knees when cut down by your gunfire. He's down, but never out, and so keeping the enemy from reviving him is your second-most important plan. For this, you must target enemy Medics before any other foe. Once those two plans have been completed, your tasks include delaying, distracting, and annoying the enemy to such an extent that they fight with you, rather than healing and chaperoning Nechayev.

Make the enemy pay dearly for every inch they creep closer to the Checkpoint, and the exit (their initial spawning point). Be sure you know the route, and the chokepoints where you can really hammer the opposition. At the same time, draft in a couple of Engineers (at the very least) to lay mines along the narrow parts of the routes (shown below), and construct turrets to make Nechayev's departure next to impossible.

#### Fight, Not Flight

**Sec 05 High Security and Storage Area:** As soon as the Passcode goes into the Infirmary, swarm the Headquarters, and attack from the top of the stairs as well as the doorway below that leads into the High Security area and Supply Command Post. While your initial squad holds this area, have as many Engineers as you can spare lay mines along the narrow route to the building exit. The enemy only really attacks in one direction at this point, so stand firm, and take that pilot down!

**Sunken Forecourt:** You can annoy the opposition into a stalemate at this point, by the Headquarters exit. Seek cover behind the desk, lob grenades at the doorway the foes come out of, and gradually retreat into the Sunken and upper Forecourt before taking either staircase up to the Guard Tower Battlements and blasting from longer range. Turrets out of grenade range are a great plan, too.

**Security Checkpoint:** As Nechayev climbs the steps (which should be booby-trapped and heavily guarded), plant mines and turrets so the pilot's access through the gates is a violent one. Patrol the Checkpoint area to stop foes heading in from the Sewer Exit or climbing the walls; take the same positions you did during Core Objective 1. Optionally have snipers tagging foes as they run out of the Security Corridor, and either Sec Tower exit.

## Automated Ordnance

7 Position a turret near the body bags close to Nechayev's exit from High Security.

8 This offers good cover, and catches Nechayev after his death climb up the Forecourt ramp.

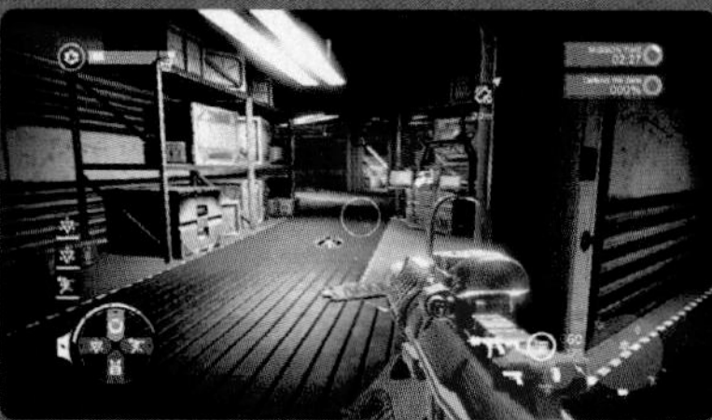
8 The pilot will succumb to this during his staggering exit, inside the High Security area near the Supply Command Post.

9 Place mines on the ramp connecting the Sunken to upper Forecourts.

10 Place mines inside the gate between the Forecourt and Checkpoint (marked with "CLEAR" on the tarmac).

## Sniper's Ally: Camping Spots

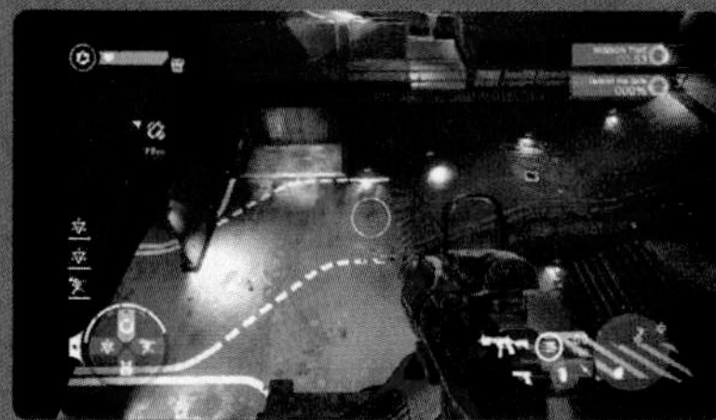
7 This is a particularly good place to snipe; tag the enemies if they use the Security Corridor from their spawn point, and cover the entire Forecourt, too.

8 Farther along, this dead-end balcony allows you to use cover and cut down foes on the Forecourt. Watch for enemies coming up via the Maintenance Bot Garage, though.

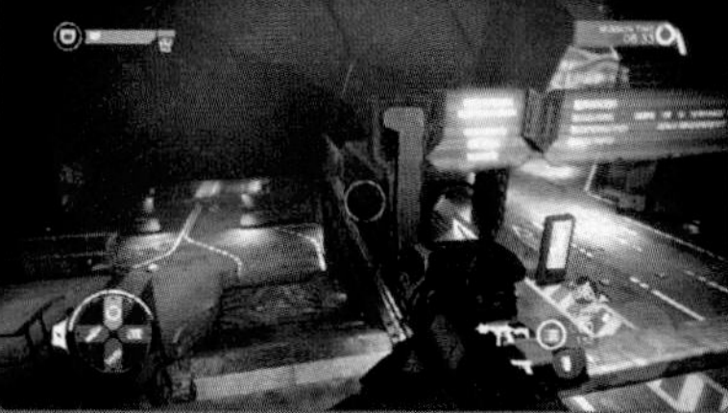
9 From your view atop the stairs on the Battlements, you can watch for enemies trying to outflank, and track Nechayev all the way from the High Security exit to the extraction point!

# Objective Tactics: Secondary Objectives

### Escort Core Objective Class Teammate

**Official Escort Info:** Two heads (and sets of firearms) are better than one! Partner with an Engineer during Core Objective 1 so you can quickly disarm enemy HE Charges. However, as you're on the defensive for most of this Mission, this Objective becomes less important, and usually isn't accessible.

**Unofficial Escort Info:** During Core Objective 2 onwards, try to catch foes in crossfire, and patrol areas together while earning XP. Help an Engineer defend the Warden's Office and Infirmary steps, and plant mines and turrets along Nechayev's route. Covering an Engineer (while setting up defenses as an Engineer) helps bolster the Security's defenses.

### Capture the Health Command Post

Engineer & Operative Advantage!

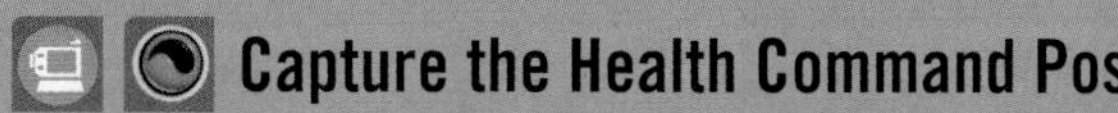
Spawn Point to Command Post: 00:16

Time to Claim Command Post: 00:10

Pick an Engineer whose job it is to sprint up to the Health Command Post at the start of Core

Objective 2, hold and trap the location, and interfere with the Resistance team's rush up the Ark Security stairs adjacent to the post itself. Holding this post is difficult, because you're across from the enemy spawn point, but this becomes easier as the enemy focuses on freeing Nechayev. Split your time between this and the other post because they're relatively close to each other, but only during lulls in the fighting, and when your team can spare you.

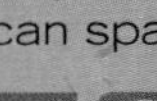

### Capture the Supply Command Post

Engineer & Operative Advantage!

Spawn Point to Command Post: 00:19

Time to Claim Command Post: 00:10

The Supply Command Post is deep in the bowels of the Sec Tower, and accessible only after Core Objective 1 has been completed. During your sprint up to the Warden's Office, have one of your team hang back to cut down foes as they enter this lower thoroughfare before they reach the stairwell. Lurk in the offices, Side Controls stairwell, or rear of the Headquarters cellblock before ambushing. Then return time and time again before and after Nechayev passes through.

### Construct the Guardhouse MG Nest

### Construct the Wall MG Nest

Engineer

Spawn Point to Guardhouse MG Nest: 00:14

Spawn Point to Wall MG Nest: 00:17

Time to Construct: 00:04

Both MG Nests overlook the Checkpoint area, and should be constructed during Core Objective 1, or prior to the end of Core Objective 4. Add up the benefits of building this (XP bonuses should be less important than team orders), compared to setting up traps or engaging the enemy rather than waiting for them to enter your aiming box. Place mines or turrets to cover your blind spots, so you know when you're being flanked.

### Solo Tactics

Without the benefit of human interaction, you must become the central force of the Security's defense. During Core Objective 1, cover the Conduit as an Engineer and immediately disarm the bomb if it is armed. In Core Objective 2, you may wish to strafe the cellblock with gunfire as a Soldier, or choose to be an Engineer and booby trap the enemy's routes, as well as cutting down foes in the Warden's Office area. Think about peeling off from the main fighting to take both Command Posts during a lull in the fighting from this point onward.

When the Passcode has been stolen, back up and prep the Infirmary with a turret and mines and prowl the area; this can be very effective because the end of the glass planter makes good cover. Then during the last objective, as the enemy tends not to outflank as quickly as human opponents, you have ample time as an Engineer to place mines on the route, and cut down Nechayev as your primary target. Fixate on the pilot and keep him stationary at all costs.

## Mission Completion Conditions

### Continuation...

**Core Objective 1:** Your team fails to stop the enemy destroying the Conduit at the Checkpoint. Part 2 of this mission now commences....

**Core Objective 2:** Your team fails to stop the Warden's safe being hacked, and the Passcode obtained. Part 3 of this mission now begins....

**Core Objective 3:** Your team fails to stop Nechayev being freed at the terminal by the Infirmary door. Part 4 of this mission now begins....

### Completed!

The match completes if you successfully stop the Resistance forces during any of the four Core Objectives and the timer ticks down.

### Unsuccessful!

**Core Objective 4:** Security forces lose if the enemy completes all four Core Objectives and Nechayev escapes before the timer reaches zero.

## MAP LEGEND

### Shipyard: Core Objective 1

1: Security Deployment Zone (Pt. 1): Tanker Launch & Dock (Lvl. 0)
2: Security Command Post (Pt. 1) (Lvl. 0)
3: Tanker Alley & Quarters Entry Steps (Lvls. 0 & 1)
4: Tanker Quarters & Gantry Walk (Lvl. 2)
5: Cargo Railroad & Post Platform Access (Lvl. 0 & 1)
6: Supply Command Post Platform (Lvl. 0)
7: Hull Hideout (Lvl. 1)
8: Anchor Chain Avenue & Gantry (Lvls. 0, 1, & 2)
9: Drummond's Alley (Lvls. 0 & 1)
10: Drummond's Opening (Lvl. 1)
11: Field Hospital & Lower Deck (Lvls. 1 & 3)
12: Health Command Post (Lvl. 3)
13: Subterranean Pipe Shortcut: Security Stairs (Lvl. 0)
14: Rusty Hull: Rusting Deck (Lvl. 2)
15: Rusty Hull: The Main Alley & Main Barricade (Lvl. 2)
16: Rusty Hull: Container Corridor & Barricade Overlook (Lvl. 2)
17: Main Gantry Walk (Lvl. 2)
18: Central Gantry Walk (Lvl. 2)
19: Below the Hull Thoroughfare (Lvl. 0)
20: The Central Alley & Side Barricade (Lvls. 0 & 1)
21: The Covered Alley (Lvls. 0 & 1)
22: Loading Crane Courtyard & Controls (Lvl. 1)
23: Subterranean Pipe Shortcut: Resistance Stairs (Lvl. 0)
24: Pipe & Girder Overlook (Lvl. 2)
25: Metal Ramps & Low Road (Lvls. 1 & 2)
26: Deano's Hull & MG Nest (Lvl. 1)
27: Resistance Deployment Zone (Pt. 1): Rusting Shanty Hull (Lvl. 2)
28: Resistance Command Post (Pt. 1) (Lvl. 2)

BRINK

## Shipyard: Overview Map

HISTORY OF THE ARK
CHARACTER CREATION
GAMEPLAY
WEAPONS DETAIL
CAMPAIGN
Hostage Rescue
Smash & Grab
Dirty Bomb
Prison Break
Early Launch
Fallout
Chopper Down
Grand Theft Aero
CHALLENGES
APPENDICES

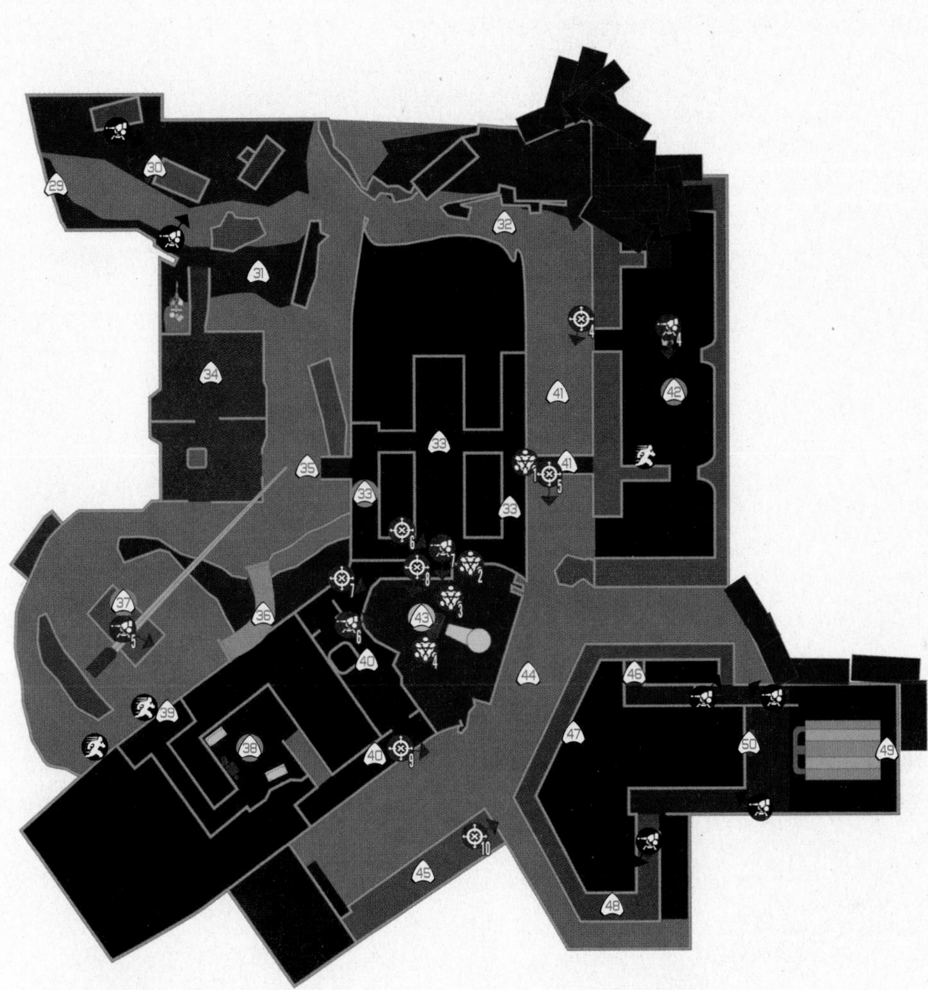

## MAP LEGEND (CONTINUED)

### Shipyard: Core Objective 2

29: Security Deployment Zone (Pt. 2): Lower Dirt Path (Lvl. 0)
30: Security Command Post (Pt. 2) (Lvl. 0)
31: Rusty Junk Junction (Lvl. 0)
32: Warship: Lower Dirt Path (Stern) (Lvl. 0)
33: Warship: Storage Thoroughfare, MG Nest, & Port Deck (Lvl. 2)
34: Rusty Trawler Innards (Lvls. 1 & 2)
35: Warship: Movable Bridge & Dirt Path (Starboard) (Lvls. 0 & 2)
36: Snaking Pipe (Lvl. 0)
37: Crane Controls & Yard (Lvl. 0)
38: Warship: Engine Room & Health Command Post (Lvl. 1)
39: Warship: Upper Starboard Overlook (Lvl. 2)
40: Warship: Port Overlook & Missile Courtyard Overlook (Lvl. 2)
41: Super Tanker Bridge & Dirt Path (Port) (Lvl. 2)
42: Super Tanker Hold & Supply Command Post (Lvl. 1)
43: Air Defenses: Missile Courtyard (Lvl. 1)
44: Air Defenses: Lower Dirt Path (Lvl. 0)
45: Rusting Hull Overlook & Lower Dirt Side Path (Lvl. 1)
46: Resistance Hulk: Side Exit (Lvls. 1 & 0)
47: Resistance Hulk: Upper Gantry (Lvl. 2)
48: Resistance Hulk: Side Ramps (Lvls. 1 & 0)
49: Resistance Deployment Zone (Pt. 2): Hulk Turbine Room (Lvl. 1)
50: Resistance Command Post (Pt. 2) (Lvl. 1)

S.M.A.R.T. Move
Engineer Mine (Optimal Placement)
Engineer Turret (Optimal Placement)
Camping Spot
Deployment Zone Turret (Invulnerable)
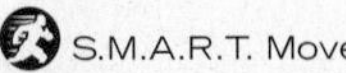
Core Objective Location
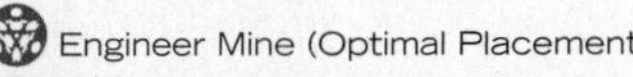
Secondary Objective Location
Critical Path (Route)
Level Link

BRINK | Shipyard: Overview Map

# DAY 6: EARLY LAUNCH

FREEPLAY: SHIPYARD   RESISTANCE CAMPAIGN—WHAT-IF: OPERATION BABEL

## 15:31 Security Patrol Boat PB012, En Route to Shipyard

MISSION TIME (COb 1): 10:00

MISSION TIME (COb 2): +10:00

### Captain Mokoena: Briefing

All units! Code Black! Chen has a surface-to-surface missile aimed right at the Founders' Tower! We're evacuating it as fast as we can, but thousands will die if you don't stop that missile! We have no margin for error here. If they know we're onto them, they'll launch. We'll insert you stealthily, by boat. Find a route to the Destroyer, and deactivate that missile; you must hack that thing before they fire it! SAVE FOUNDERS' TOWER!

### Optimal Class Numbers

| | COb 1 | COb 2 |
|---|---|---|
| Soldier | [1] | [1] |
| Medic | [2] | [2] |
| Engineer | [4] | [1] |
| Operative | [1] | [4] |

### Objectives (Security)

- Core Objective 1: Repair the Crane Controls
- Core Objective 2: Hack the Missile Controls
- Escort Core Objective Class Teammate
- Destroy Main Barricade
- Destroy Side Barricade
- Repair the Crane Controls
- Capture the Health Command Post
- Capture the Supply Command Post
- Construct the Crane MG Nest
- Construct the Bridge MG Nest

## Important Locations

### 1 Security Deployment Zone (Pt. 1): Tanker Launch & Dock (Lvl. 0)

From your position on a large Dock at the foot of a huge Super Tanker, you have two routes to take: along Tanker Alley to the right, or Drummond's Alley (on the left). The routes split dramatically, so check the map to figure out your favored way to the Loading Crane, and be sure your team backs you up.

## 2 Security Command Post (Pt. 1) (Lvl. 0)

Engineers (to fix the Crane) and Soldiers (to clamp explosives to any barricades) are indispensable during the first Core Objective; ensure they are on hand in good numbers. Change your class or weapon here.

## 3 Tanker Alley & Quarters Entry Steps (Lvls. 0 & 1)

Leading along the right side of the Super Tanker, this connects to the Hull Hideout, but offers a scramble up into the Tanker Quarters (if you're more nimble or want to use the higher and gap-filled routes) as an alternate route. You can also sidestep through the open door to the right, and up onto the Cargo Railroad, for a third possible route and shortcut to the Supply Command Post.

### S.M.A.R.T. Moves

Save some time and leap from the Quarters Entry Steps to the top of the Cargo Railroad.

## 4 Tanker Quarters & Gantry Walk (Lvl. 2)

Take some time to situate yourself among the few pathways on the way to the Crane Courtyard, not least of which are the different exits from this Tanker interior. You can maneuver down to Anchor Chain Avenue, or Wall-jump and land on the upper Main Gantry. You can access the Main Gantry via the toilets above the avenue, too. Don't forget you can climb up into the Tanker Quarters doorway from the lower ground area close to the Hull Hideout. Pick a favored thoroughfare to one of the Loading Crane Courtyard entrances from this point (above the ground path).

## 5 Cargo Railroad & Post Platform Access (Lvl. 0 & 1)

Use this route as an alternative to running down Tanker Alley. Instead, move up the stairs and onto the Cargo Railroad before dropping into the Post Platform Access corridor, with a jump or a drop to reach the Supply Command Post. Beware of the occasional enemy lodged against the cargo carriage, mowing your team down as you emerge from the stairs.

## 6 Supply Command Post Platform (Lvl. 0)

This is closer to your deployment zone, and with the shortcut passages you can take to reach the platform, make sure this falls into your hands as quickly as possible. Alas, this is difficult to keep, because it can be accessed from the ground around the base of the Hull Hideout, as well as the Post Platform Access. Use the scenery (including the barriers) as cover, or attack from the Hull Hideout.

## 7 Hull Hideout (Lvl. 1)

At the intersection of the Tanker, Anchor Chain, and Below the Hull paths is a self-contained Hull Hideout. It features four entrances (slide under the one at the lower end of Anchor Chain Avenue). Three entrances are doorways you must climb to on each side of the structure. The upper interior simply links all four entrances. Use this area to ambush enemies, leap to the Cargo Railroad area, or provide covering fire over the Supply Command Post Platform.

The Hull Hideout is illuminated by two hanging lights, each revealing some graffiti stencils featuring the silhouette of a monkey. Use these to situate yourself as you're finding your way about.

TIP

### S.M.A.R.T. Moves

Stand on the metal lip overlooking the Below the Hull Thoroughfare for views of Anchor Chain and Central Alleys, another possible ambush spot.

Leap from the Cargo Railroad onto the metal wall with the red monkey on it for a possible ambush point.

## 8 Anchor Chain Avenue & Gantry (Lvls. 0, 1, & 2)

Look up as the path opens to see the large rusting chain this avenue is named after. On the ground, this is a major arterial route, because the lower end of the avenue connects to Tanker Alley, the Hull Hideout, and the Below the Hull Thoroughfare. At the opposite end, the avenue ascends past the chain, and a large stack of steel sheets, and opens up to the Rusty Hull and Alley.

However, there's an upper Gantry to check out too; leap across the lower avenue from the Tanker Quarters, which allows access into the Main Gantry, the toilets area, and the Container Corridor with the Barricade Overlook. Both the Tanker and Anchor Gantries can be accessed without leaping. Learn these initially confusing routes, and vary your tactics to make use of these upper pathways.

### S.M.A.R.T. Moves

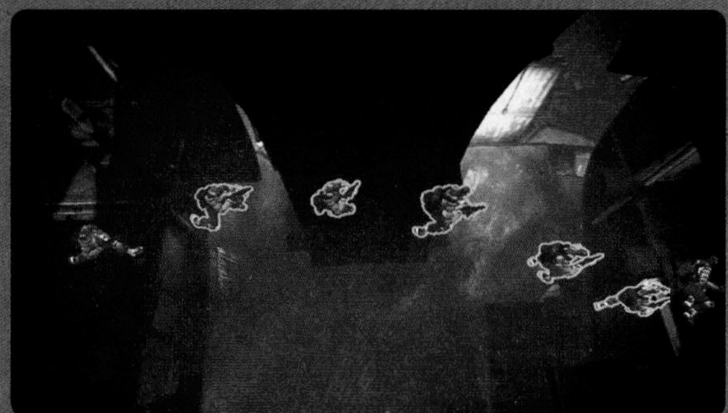

You can expertly Wall-jump across the avenue from the Main Gantry to the Tanker Gantry.

Clamber onto the steel sheet stack under the chain for a good view of the Main Alley and across to the Field Hospital.

Climb the jutting pipe below the chain and ramp, and up into the Anchor Chain Gantry and Tanker Gantry.

## 9 Drummond's Alley (Lvls. 0 & 1)

## 10 Drummond's Opening (Lvl. 1)

Use this path, named for one of the ship sections that towers above this thoroughfare, to reach the Field Hospital (via the rickety ramp), Lower Deck (via the doorway to the left of the ramp), and the Rusty Hull area, where an assault on the Main Alley can begin. You should begin to encounter enemy troops at this point, but splitting your forces and having some coming in from the Anchor Chain Alley can help nullify their presence.

## 11 Field Hospital & Lower Deck (Lvls. 1 & 3)

## 12 Health Command Post (Lvl. 3)

Use the severed bridge section of a Super Tanker to claim the Health Command Post inside,

which is a little too far from the enemy's spawning grounds to be easily taken back. The Field Hospital is accessed via the ramp in Drummond's Opening, but there's an entrance on the opposite side too: an easily overlooked set of stairs near the Subterranean Pipe Hatch. Check the balcony around the outside of the bridge, which you can use for long-range sniping at the Rusty Hull and Main Alley. The ground-level Lower Deck route weaves under the bridge, but doesn't connect to it.

### S.M.A.R.T. Moves

Use the edge of the Lower Deck doorway to reach the bent end of the balcony and ascend to it.

## 13 Subterranean Pipe Shortcut: Security Stairs (Lvl. 0)

Located in the open area adjacent to the Rusting Deck, this is the entrance to the Pipe Shortcut that exits near the Metal Ramps by the enemy's deployment zone. This provides an excellent way to outflank them if they aren't guarding this passage. Stand on the open hatch to gain height and cover. Remember to protect the area below from defenders.

## 14 Rusty Hull: Rusting Deck (Lvl. 2)

Utilize this as your main staging ground as you wait for reinforcements, push into the Loading Crane Courtyard, or wait for the Main Barricade to explode. A couple of small chambers with connecting corridors lead to an exterior deck, all connecting to the Field Hospital area and Drummond's Opening, as well as Anchor Chain Avenue. The enemy (but not Security forces unless you're in the Crane Courtyard) can access this area by climbing up the opening to the right of the Main Alley, in the Loading Crane Courtyard, then drop down from the toilet room at the top. Beware of enemies at the far end of the deck, overlooking the Subterranean Pipe Shortcut, using it as a sniper point.

### S.M.A.R.T. Moves

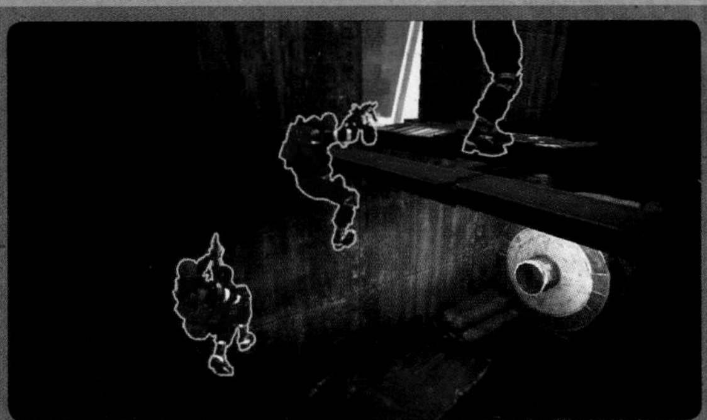

A tricky Wall-jump allows the lithe to clamber atop the platform overlooking the Crane Yard and circumvent the Main Passage completely! Remember to leap or Wall-jump onto the large container and grab the balcony above, allowing access to the Barricade Overlook and Crane Yard itself!

## 15 Rusty Hull: The Main Alley & Main Barricade (Lvl. 2)

The enemy team's focus should be on building and guarding of the barricade at this point. Sealing this route means you must either destroy the barricade, or use another route to reach the Crane. Of course, you can circumvent the barricade by using the Container Corridor and Barricade Overlook to reach the cubbyhole in the courtyard. Otherwise, blow the barricade apart by placing explosives on it, and guarding it during the countdown, so foes don't disarm it. Only Soldiers can plant the explosives.

## 16 Rusty Hull: Container Corridor & Barricade Overlook (Lvl. 2)

The Resistance maneuvers into this area from the cubbyhole to the left of the Main Barricade in the Crane Courtyard. Security forces use the Main Gantry Walk area above Anchor Avenue near the toilets, and clamber up onto the container stack, and onto a balcony. From here, you can drop into the cubbyhole, or look (and fire) into the Main Alley. Below the balcony is a side passage and exit to the Main Alley, too. Use these less-traveled routes so the enemy is constantly trying to plug different holes in their defenses.

### 17 Main Gantry Walk (Lvl. 2)

### 18 Central Gantry Walk (Lvl. 2)

Make sure you're on the upper Super Tanker interior above Anchor Chain Avenue (where the toilets are), and you can reach all the nooks and crannies of the Rusty Hull, where you can launch attacks and back up friends using the ground routes. When you're ready to assault the Central Gantry Walk, use the rusting hull sides as cover, Wall-jump across the Central Alley, and land on the opposite side. You can now rush into the Crane Courtyard, ignoring any barricades!

#### S.M.A.R.T. Moves

Both you and the enemy can actually Wall-jump the gap between the Main and Central Gantry Walks; succeed in this move and you can bypass the Side Barricade!

### 19 Below the Hull Thoroughfare (Lvl. 0)

This is one of the major routes to reach either of the two main Alleys leading up and into the Crane Courtyard. It also offers access to Anchor Chain Avenue, and the Supply Command Post. As you're attacking, watch for long-range snipers and other defenses at the far end of the Covered Alley. Use the barrels as cover.

### 20 The Central Alley & Side Barricade (Lvls. 0 & 1)

Resistance forces usually race to this location from their spawn point, and try to construct a barricade as quickly as possible. Because you have other routes, the more lithe members of your team can run interference to coax the enemy Engineer away from the construction job. Otherwise, fire on the Engineer from the alley, which is otherwise a chokepoint and focus of your team's attack into the Loading Crane Courtyard. Use the Central Gantry Walk to attack or maneuver above this alley; and direct your teammates to attack the Main Alley in unison to really overstretch your adversaries.

### 21 The Covered Alley (Lvls. 0 & 1)

The enemy accesses this Covered Alley from the Crane Courtyard or Deano's Hull, staying at the upper end and covering the area with traps. Because your foes can easily cover this route, it is worth exploring other route options (detailed earlier), but watch for foes encroaching down the Below the Hull Thoroughfare if you aren't putting up much of a fight.

### 22 Loading Crane Courtyard & Controls (Lvl. 1)

This is the hub where your forces must congregate to cover your Engineers as they attempt to repair the Loading Crane, and open the giant gate (which is behind the Crane at the opposite end of the Courtyard). Attack from the Main Alley and Barricade, the Central Alley and Side Barricade, and the Covered Alley, as well as sneakier infiltrations via the Subterranean Pipe Shortcut behind the Crane, close to the enemy deployment zone.

More nimble attackers also jump the gaps between the Gantry Walks, and circumvent the enemy barricades entirely. Head out of the cubbyhole to the left of the side barrier, and the Central Gantry Walk itself. Resistance forces can move up the wall to a toilet room and drop down into the Rusty Hull: Rusting Deck area to try to ambush your team.

Also remember the various cover options the Resistance has, ranging from the corners of the Crane and hulk below the Pipe and Girder Overlook, the pipe section with barrels on top, and the corner under the Crane claw, where long-range sniping and ambushes can occur.

### 23 Subterranean Pipe Shortcut: Resistance Stairs (Lvl. 0)

This shortcut allows you to venture deeper into enemy territory, because you appear here, adjacent to the Crane Courtyard and behind both the enemy barricades. Unfortunately, you're also in the enemy deployment zone, so move quickly toward the Crane, watching for mines, and reaching for the Crane Controls if it is safe to do so.

### 24 Pipe & Girder Overlook (Lvl. 2)

Expect the enemy to climb up to this Overlook (via Deano's Hull, the Metal Ramps, or by leaping the bridge) to view and fire on your incoming forces. Getting up here yourself is an option, although you're likely to be attacked by foes coming in from their spawn point behind you.

### 25 Metal Ramps & Low Road (Lvls. 1 & 2)

### 26 Deano's Hull & MG Nest (Lvl. 1)

The Metal Ramps and Low Road is a route the enemy takes to reach the Pipe and Girder Overlook, whereas Deano's Hull (named for the graffiti artist who daubed his name across the wall near one of the room's exits) is a handy defensive area for your opposition. Generally, avoid this area, especially the MG Nest, because it is too close to the enemy's deployment zone to be worth investigating. However, you can waylay the enemy by fighting them here while the rest of your team claims the Crane.

### 27 Resistance Deployment Zone (Pt. 1): Rusting Shanty Hull (Lvl. 2)

The distance between this deployment zone and the Core Objective gives the enemy an initial advantage. There's no way you'll survive the gun emplacements here, so avoid this location.

### 28 Resistance Command Post (Pt. 1) (Lvl. 2)

The enemy brings their own Command Posts with them; you can't reach this one, and it doesn't respond to your input commands.

## Important Locations
(Core Objective 2)

### 29 Security Deployment Zone (Pt. 2): Lower Dirt Path (Lvl. 0)

You begin under the broken hull of a massive ship, just through the gate that was opened during the previous Core Objective. The area offers two main pathways toward the Warship that dominates this map. Your starting grounds are heavily fortified; you shouldn't be attacked here until you venture onward.

## 30 Security Command Post (Pt. 2) (Lvl. 0)

With objectives requiring Engineers and Operatives to perform them, choosing a class from this Command Post is an imperative plan. Pick a new weapon from here if you need one.

##  31 Rusty Junk Junction (Lvl. 0)

##  32 Warship: Lower Dirt Path (Stern) (Lvl. 0)

These two routes allow you to split your forces when assaulting the area. Head straight on and around the hull of the Warship to hit the Dirt Path and Supply Command Post. Take the right-side route at the Rusty Junk Junction to access the Crane Yard, and a more convoluted (but hidden) route toward the Warship's Storage Thoroughfare, or the Engine Room. Back at the exterior below the ship's stern, hide behind clusters of debris if the enemy is coming too close to your initial spawn point.

## 33 Warship: Storage Thoroughfare, MG Nest, & Port Deck (Lvl. 2)

Learn the visual cues in this initially confusing maze of metal; the entrance from the Movable Bridge is bathed in red light. The MG Nest is accessed via a passage close to the Missile Controls overlook, and the Port Deck is useful when locating the Supply Command Post in the Super Tanker across a second bridge. Remember to back into a corridor and use the metal walls as cover. This is another major route when reaching the Missile Courtyard. Also remember that the enemy sometimes tries to fix and man the MG Nest. This allows them to shoot your team as they cross the bridge, but doesn't have the vertical movement to stop you if you're running along the dirt path below.

##  34 Rusty Trawler Innards (Lvls. 1 & 2)

This two-floor interior is entered by your team via a ramp, and offers two exits: down a hole and out into the Crane Yard, or onto the Movable Bridge (when raised) via an upper balcony. Occasionally, you may find foes hiding behind the container inside this structure, beneath the hole, waiting to ambush foes dropping down, or nearing the Yard or Snaking Pipe. You can also climb up the hole, and head into the Warship if necessary.

## 35 Warship: Movable Bridge & Dirt Path (Starboard) (Lvls. 0 & 2)

The bridge on the ground is attached to a Crane, which one of your Engineers should attempt to raise. The Dirt Path is an alternate route to the Snaking Pipe and Crane Yard if the Rusty Trawler Innards isn't utilized by the enemy. The Resistance doesn't usually prowl this close to the enemy spawn point.

##  36 Snaking Pipe (Lvl. 0)

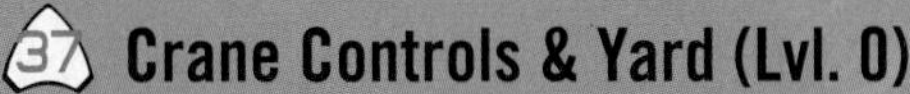

## 37 Crane Controls & Yard (Lvl. 0)

Between the Rusty Trawler Innards and the Engine Room is a secondary Yard with a large Crane on a central platform. The Crane Controls, when repaired by an Engineer, allow your forces another (and closer) route into the Missile Courtyard, via a raised bridge into the Storage Thoroughfare. This is recommended,

and should be done as quickly as possible (before the enemy has chance to mount a full attack), but watch for your foes moving the Crane back to its original position. The rest of the Crane Yard offers protective scenery all the way around to the Engine Room and a U-shaped Snaking Pipe; a quicker route from the Dirt Path below the Movable Bridge.

### 38 Warship: Engine Room & Health Command Post (Lvl. 1)

### 39 Warship: Upper Starboard Overlook (Lvl. 2)

The mangled remains of the Warship's Engine Room is a chokepoint to rush into from the Crane Yard and Snaking Pipe. Inside the location is a Health Command Post, and a ramp up to the Port Overlook, and a gap to the Dirt Path where the Resistance usually defends from. Also, try hiding in the cubbyhole on the starboard entrance behind the hull metal, across from the barrels.

There's also a ramped passage up to the Upper Starboard Overlook (take cover at this entrance to ambush enemies). The Overlook itself offers protected shots down at the Crane Yard and the Snaking Pipe exit, which is more useful to the enemy than your team.

#### S.M.A.R.T. Moves

An easily overlooked alternative route: Climb onto the balcony below the Upper Starboard Overlook, and then up into the Overlook itself, then into the Engine Room.

### 40 Warship: Port Overlook & Missile Courtyard Overlook (Lvl. 2)

Once you climb the Engine Room ramp, this is one of the main routes to take to reach the Missile Courtyard. When you reach the Overlook, you can drop down to the Missile Controls, into the small enclosed passage below, or across to the Storage Thoroughfare on the opposite side. Three open portholes along the way offer views down to the dirt road and into the Rusting Hull Overlook. Fire on any foes giving you trouble from inside the Rusting Hull.

### 41 Super Tanker Bridge & Dirt Path (Port) (Lvl. 2)

### 42 Super Tanker Hold & Supply Command Post (Lvl. 1)

This is out of the way of the main areas of conflict, but is an important location to defend due to the Supply Command Post here. There are three entrances into this Super Tanker Hold: two via the Dirt Path and one from the Bridge above, which you can reach via the Storage Thoroughfare. Once inside, you can use the pipes and containers to clamber up to the Bridge point (if you need to fend off enemies nearby), or guard the doors by standing to one side and ambushing enemies. You can attack foes in the Dirt Path from here, too.

## 43 Air Defenses: Missile Courtyard (Lvl. 1)

This is where the enemy takes its final stand: In this triangular platform, your forces need to hack into the Missile Controls, and you need to cover and help the Operatives attempting this heroic move. Knowing the routes to reach here helps: Use the dirt paths on either side, and the segmented sections of Warship above and either side of you. Maneuver out of the Storage Thoroughfare to your right, and the Missile Courtyard Overlook to your left. Remember you can stay at the top openings of these locations to shoot the milling foes below you, or engage them as they rise to meet you.

Seeking cover is just as important as covering your Operatives. Under both of the Warship's upper entrances is a small corridor you can hide in and ambush foes as they climb onto the platform the launcher sits on, or if they try to climb and defend the edge of the upper areas. The metal plates, barrels, and containers are all viable locations to hide behind, as is the Missile system itself. A combination of turrets, snipers, and outflanking from multiple locations can turn the tide of battle.

**Watch out if you're dropping down from the Missile Courtyard Overlook (on the right side, if you're looking toward the Resistance spawn point); there's a lower access corridor with a hole in the ceiling. Check if foes are in here, waiting to ambush you. If they are, drop a grenade to put a stop to their plan.**

**CAUTION**

## 44 Air Defenses: Lower Dirt Path (Lvl. 0)

This is the area of dirt between the Missile Courtyard and the Resistance Hulk. The Warship Engine Room and the continuation of the Dirt Path (which goes under the Super Tanker Bridge) meet up here. Beware of enemies rushing out constantly from the Hulk, and the debris-strewn defenses (which may be used by enemy snipers). Avoid this path and step quickly onto the Missile Courtyard.

## 45 Rusting Hull Overlook & Lower Dirt Side Path (Lvl. 1)

This path enables you to sprint down toward the Missile Courtyard from the Warship's Engine Room and Health Command Post. Because you're close to the enemy's deployment zone, expect fire along the path, but also from the Rusting Hull Overlook on the opposite side. Foes usually take cover and shoot into the Engine Room from here. Retaliate by moving around to the ramp and barrel platform, and firing through the Overlook toward the enemy, and creeping along here and using the structure to outflank and cover your teammates.

## 46 Resistance Hulk: Side Exit (Lvls. 1 & 0)

## 47 Resistance Hulk: Upper Gantry (Lvl. 2)

## 48 Resistance Hulk: Side Ramps (Lvls. 1 & 0)

The enemy has some choices in the pathway around their rusting Hulk. They can exit out to the sides and onto the Lower Dirt Path. Or, they can move onto the Upper Gantry, an elevated position over the Air Defenses area. Look for snipers from this general direction as you assault the Missile Controls.

## 49 Resistance Deployment Zone (Pt. 2): Hulk Turbine Room (Lvl. 1)

You'll be hard-pressed to reach this location without a complete enemy breakdown in competence. The alleys are still dangerous, and there's nothing but death at the hands of automated turrets in these parts.

## 50 Resistance Command Post (Pt. 2) (Lvl. 1)

This is hidden under a rusting overhang, and is of no use to your forces.

# Objective Tactics: Core Objective 1

## Repair the Crane Controls

Spawn Point to Crane Controls: 00:15

Time to Repair Controls: 01:10

### General Tactics

This race into enemy territory requires a large amount of teamwork, flanking, and firepower. The various pluses and minuses of the different routes into the Crane Yard are discussed below. But it is also important to remember to try to approach the Crane with some teammates covering you, ready to lob grenades at turrets and avoid mines, and try some advanced Parkour to exploit every narrow opening that heavier teammates can't reach.

Once you realize how pockmarked the entrances into the Crane Yard have become, you can keep your enemies guessing, splitting their firepower and having your faster members coaxing foes away from the Crane long enough for an Engineer (or three) to enact the repairs. Even if your fixing results in a suicide, any repairs you make to the Crane are beneficial, because they can't be undone. Have a constant supply of Engineers running for this objective instead of setting up traps—this wastes time and should be done only if you're having terrible problems punching through. Focus on mending the Crane. Your next biggest class? Soldiers, to clamp explosives on the barricades to remove the blockades.

> **You can always ban the bulk. Begin the mission without any Heavy or Medium Body Types, and ignore the barricades completely, whether they've been constructed or not. Use Wall-jumps and narrow gaps to enter the Crane Yard instead.**
>
> TIP

### Routes to the Crane Yard

**Drummond's Alley to Main Alley:** The favored route is to the left, up through Drummond's Alley, and out into the opening area where the Field Hospital is stationed, within the rusting skeleton of the Super Tanker Bridge. Have an Engineer peel off from the pack and claim this post, before trapping it with a mine and continuing to view the Main Alley, behind which is the Crane you need to repair.

If the Resistance is defending far forward, the walkways and ramps around that Super Tanker's Bridge aren't a bad place to snipe from: you can duck around corners for cover or drop down on particularly adventurous defenders. You're exposed to far less enemy fire than if you venture forward toward the Crane objective through the gaps in the Rusty Hull ahead.

Rushing forward into the Crane Yard is foolish, because the enemy is likely to be here (and erecting barricades) already. Plus, some of your team won't be able to travel as quickly, and therefore back you up. Build up an attacking force at the Main Alley, which is detailed in the Secondary Objective.

**Subterranean Pipe Shortcut:** Instead of fighting at the Main Alley, utilize the Subterranean Pipe Shortcut that brings you up and into the Crane Yard itself, but dangerously close to the enemy's deployment zone. This is usually defended with mines (so let an Operative go first to spot them, if possible), and the exit is often covered by an enemy turret. When you emerge from the tunnel, a left turn leads to the enemy deployment zone. Try not to mistakenly wander in there; focus on the Crane instead!

**Anchor Chain Alley:** There are other, less optimal routes to try, too. The Anchor Chain Avenue allows you to reach the Main Alley via the ground, passing under the chain itself.

**Light Body Type Insertion Points:** Climb onto the Main Gantry Walk, and a Wall-jump in the Container Corridor onto the Barricade Overlook (picture 1), which takes you via a dark drop into a cubbyhole overlooking the Crane itself! Or approach the Rusty Hull from the opposite side, close to the Subterranean Pipe hatch, and make a (difficult) Wall-jump (picture 2) to above the Rusting Deck, and out into the Yard.

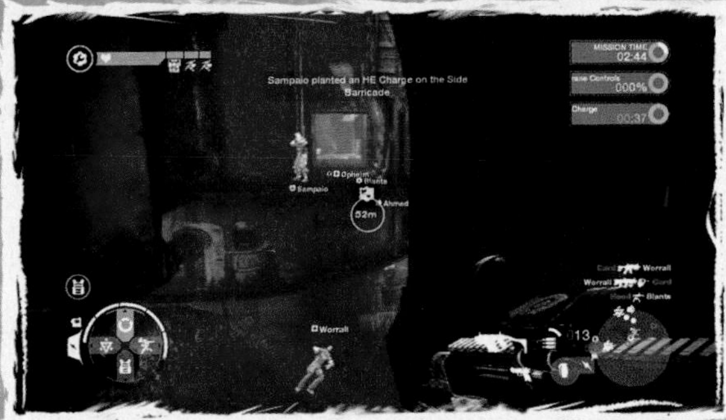

**Gantry Walk Wall-Jumps:** Or, you can try some amazing Wall-jumping to reach the Central Gantry Walk, where you can leap across and circumvent the Side Barricade (see the S.M.A.R.T. Moves earlier). Otherwise, this needs approaching from the Below the Hull Thoroughfare.

**Side Barricade and Covered Alley:** Or, you can jog along the Below the Hull Thoroughfare, to a probable battle at the Side Barricade, after which you're usually stuck trying to detonate with the enemy annoying you from the Central Gantry Walk above. It pays to be able to Wall-jump over here. Or you can try the least favorable route, up the Covered Alley, which usually has a turret and an MG Nest ready to repel visitors.

**Crane Yard Offense:** The large number of routes actually plays to your strengths. The enemy can't sit back and wait for you to appear because this could be from anywhere! However, you need team discipline so you attack in large numbers, and precisely at the same time. If you appear in the Crane Yard on your own, you won't stand a chance of repairing the Crane without the defenders overwhelming you.

Whether you appear without back-up or not, the non-Engineers in your party need to distract as much as possible; even clamping explosives on a barricade is good enough. But the gate at the opposite end of the yard from the Crane is a great place to taunt the enemy into charging; you can lean and fire, making defenders turn to face you (and shoot them if they don't), and even recharge your health.

## Automated Ordnance

Because you're the attacking team, there's much less time to set up defenses. Check the Resistance placement for ideas, and areas to avoid or watch for.

Place turrets by both of the barricades to cover those trying to remove them (1 shown).

Go "rogue" in this part of the Crane Yard by attacking from the gate end, laying a turret, and generally distracting the foes into a fight.

## Sniper's Ally: Camping Spots

1 Keep the Supply Command Post in your hands by covering it, the Hull Hideout, and the ground around it.

2 Stand on the Super Tanker Bridge balcony, in front of the Health Command Post, for a view of the Main Alley. Draw enemies away from their post by firing into the Barricade Overlook.

3 If you can Wall-jump up onto this balcony above the Rusty Hull's deck, you can cover the Resistance spawn area with devastating effectiveness!

# Secondary Objectives (First Map)

## Escort Core Objective Class Teammate

**Official Escort Info:** Engineers are vital to this task, and partnering them with a helpful teammate is an excellent idea: Two Engineers can double up on the Crane, with one taking the enemy fire more readily while the other concentrates on getting through as much of the repair as possible. A Medic can cover the Engineer while healing and firing back. Or a Soldier can provide devastating support fire to a Crane tinkerer.

## Destroy Main Barricade

Soldier

- Spawn Point to Main Barricade: 00:15
- Time to Build Barricade: 00:20
- Time to Disarm Explosives: 00:05
- Time to Plant Explosives: 00:07
- Countdown to Explosion: 00:40

This is likely to be heavily defended by enemies, and more difficult to attempt than seeking another way into the Crane Yard. But it is important for your tanks to gain access to the Crane Yard, so plant a charge on the barricade as soon as possible after it is erected. Fortify the area with brethren on either side of the Main Alley and up on the Overlooks, and set a turret or other traps to contain any enemy Engineers trying to pry the device off.

## Destroy Side Barricade

Soldier

Spawn Point to Side Barricade: 00:17

Time to Build Barricade: 00:20

Time to Disarm Explosives: 00:05

Time to Plant Explosives: 00:07

Countdown to Explosion: 00:40

If the enemy chooses to build the barricade in the Central Alley, your heavier Soldiers are ideal for removing the edifice, while lighter teammates Wall-jump the area above to ward off enemies using the Central Gantry Walk. Plant the charge and wait for the countdown, and guard the area so enemy Engineers don't remove the charge. Remember you can back off or cause a disturbance elsewhere to prevent the Resistance from stopping the explosion.

## Capture the Health Command Post

Engineer & Operative Advantage!

Spawn Point to Command Post: 00:11

Time to Claim Command Post: 00:10

Located on the Super Tanker Bridge just off the optimal route to the Main Alley and the Subterranean Pipe Shortcut, this is usually a stopping point for your team before they attempt to take one or both of these paths. This means it is simplicity itself to take the post for your team, and then keep a teammate guarding it, on the balcony in front. Change this tactic only if you're having real problems finishing the Core Objective.

## Capture the Supply Command Post

Engineer & Operative Advantage!

Spawn Point to Command Post: 00:10 

Time to Claim Command Post: 00:10 

Although this is located in a side area well away from the main action, it is still relatively close to your deployment zone, and should be taken immediately, and retaken each time the enemy tries to grab it back from you. Keep an Engineer on standby for this purpose, and have him take up residence near or in the Hull Hideout to cover the post, if he's not needed for the Crane Yard push.

## Construct the Crane MG Nest

Engineer

Spawn Point to Crane MG Nest: 00:10

Time to Construct: 00:04 

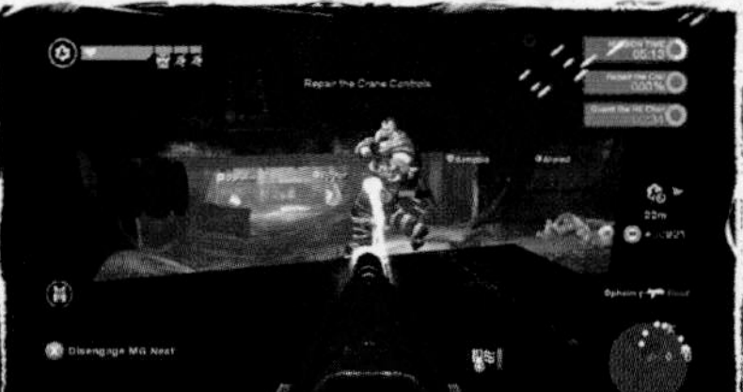

This MG Nest is technically within the confines of the Resistance Deployment Zone, and faces the Covered Alley. Therefore it is pointless to take, because you don't want to fire on your own team, or give the enemy an already-constructed MG Nest.

# Objective Tactics: Core Objective 2

## Hack the Missile Controls

Spawn Point to Missile Controls: 00:08

Time to Hack Missile Controls: 01:00

### General Tactics

Security forces are at a slight disadvantage during the final minutes of this mission. The defending Resistance force's deployment zone is extremely close to the Missile Courtyard, stretching your team out if you don't cluster together before trying to take over the area. Also, you have a very limited time to hack the Missile Controls before the enemy overruns you. If you're hacking and are interrupted, return to the Hackbox before enemy Engineers remove the device, otherwise the hack must begin again.

For this reason composing your team of at least three Operatives is a wise choice. Back them up with at least two engineers who can race to, and then hold the Missile Courtyard during the hack. Then push forward in unison, making the decision on whether to try to repair the Crane and raise the Movable Bridge ahead of time. The battle for Missile Control is arguably the most difficult to complete, and correct placement of your own team, as well as knowledge of where the enemy likes to stand, is vital to your success.

### Route Planning

**Dirt Road and Supply Command Post:** Don't ignore this possible route. It's the quickest way to reach the Missile Courtyard, and it is sometimes worth trying an immediate rush with all your team along the Dirt Path between the Warship and Super Tanker. The Supply Command Post is well worth taking, before one of you sets up on the Super Tanker Bridge to shoot at foes hiding in the Resistance Hulk. Create crossfire opportunities with a teammate who is firing from the Rusting Hull Overlook near the opposite Dirt Path. You can use the Super Tanker Bridge to reach the Storage Thoroughfare (and height advantage for covering the Missile Controls) without having to raise the Movable Bridge.

**Storage Thoroughfare:** Repairing the Crane (in the yard outside the Engine Room), which raises the Movable Bridge connecting the Rusty Trawler Innards to the Warship, opens up another, much faster route of attack, and a high platform overlooking the Missile that helps you pick and tag targets, as well as accessing the controls themselves. But be aware that the bridge is a huge bottleneck, and by raising it you also provide a route for the enemy to push forward and waylay you in the Crane Yard and Dirt Path area, keeping you from your task and fragmenting your forces.

**Engine Room and Health Command Post:** The enemy is most likely to be strongly defending this area, because the benefits of the Health Command Post (ammunition reloading, an extra Health Pip, the guarding of the Crane, and the closeness to the Resistance spawn point) are normally too numerous to ignore. It isn't worth getting tied up here for too long; sometimes rushing up the ramp into the Port Overlook and Missile Courtyard Overlook.

Remember you can also enter the area by climbing onto the balcony and up into the Starboard Overlook, before using the narrow passage down behind the Health Command Post. You can cross the interior of the Warship completely, and land on the exterior Lower Dirt Path on the other side, between the Warship and the Rusting Hull Overlook. Dive into this Hull and set up camp overlooking the no-man's land between the Resistance spawning area and the Missile Courtyard. Take advantage of this vantage and drop foes as they head toward the Missile.

**Missile Courtyard:** A cohesive strategy at this location is the most important factor here: Your Operatives need to drop down and hack with minimal enemy intrusion, while your Soldiers and Engineers cover them, and peer across the no-man's land to the Resistance Hulk to take down foes just after they spawn. Do this by knowing where the exits are on the Hulk (study the map, play as Resistance), and setting up the camp spots shown below. Try to clear the small rooms on either side of the Missile quickly—they provide a great foothold to both defend the area and hack the controls from.

> **Remember Operatives, utilize your Disguise Ability so you can get closer to the Missile or behind enemy fortifications!**
>
> 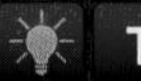 TIP

## Automated Ordnance

4 Set a turret behind the small barricades and cargo box to cover the Supply Command Post.

5 Stick a turret under the awning of the Crane in the yard; it can't be struck from above.

6 7 A turret in the cover of the lower rooms guarding the Missile Controls and Operative is a good plan (#6 shown).

1 Place a mine here to stop the enemy from crossing over into the Storage Thoroughfare part of the Warship.

2 Stop foes climbing the ramp up into the Storage Thoroughfare.

3 4 Try a mine on either side of the Missile to waylay enemies attempting to remove the Hack Box (#3 shown).

## Sniper's Ally: Camping Spots

4 The entrance into the Super Tanker near the Supply Command Post is a place to lean out and tag incoming foes or those rushing the Missile Courtyard.

5 The Super Tanker Bridge enables you to effectively shoot at the enemy's deployment zone.

6 The overlook from the Storage Thoroughfare provides complete coverage of the enemy's deployment zone, and the Missile Courtyard.

## Sniper's Ally: Camping Spots

7 The section of Warships still connected, at the Missile Courtyard Overlook, allows cover and coverage of the Courtyard too.

8 It is well worth using the cover of the Warship while guarding the Missile Courtyard from here, too.

9 Are the enemies dug in on the Resistance Hulk? Then tag them from a porthole in the Port Overlook.

10 Cut down enemies as they emerge from their spawn point and turn the battle from this covered location aboard the Rusting Hull Overlook.

# Secondary Objectives (Second Map)

### Escort Core Objective Class Teammate

**Official Escort Info:** Pairing up Operatives is of vital importance; you need an Engineer, Soldier, or Medic guardian to help fight off the enemies. A Medic is particularly useful, because you're not likely to survive the hacking if you aren't healed. Two Engineers covering the Missile Controls is another excellent plan, because they can set up turrets within the Missile Courtyard that can be repaired much more easily and quickly.

### Repair the Crane Controls

Engineer

Spawn Point to Crane Controls: 00:15

Time to Repair Crane Controls: 01:10

The enemies are likely to have a considerable presence here in the Crane Controls and Yard, with foes stationed in the Engine Room and Starboard Overlook. Tackle this if you've decided as a team that the Storage Thoroughfare is a route worth taking, and then send a squad of three or more into the fray; an Engineer to mend the Crane, with others attracting the enemy away from the Engineer. The awning above the Crane Controls offers some degree of protection. Then leave a mine at the controls, which infuriates enemy Soldiers trying to clamp their own explosives to lower the bridge! Expect to raise this a few times during a match, so choose an Engineer responsible for this task.

### Capture the Health Command Post

Engineer & Operative Advantage!

Spawn Point to Command Post: 00:09

Time to Claim Command Post: 00:10

This is always a hard-fought slog, but worth wrenching from enemy hands because hacking the Missile Controls is hard enough without the enemy being extra-healthy! Although you may not be assaulting your Core Objective by fighting here, if you can use this as a staging ground and effectively guard it with one or two hardy souls, the constant stream of your troops coming in from respawning makes this a place to wait for reinforcements, and then simultaneously attack the Missile Courtyard, spreading the final push out in multiple directions.

### Capture the Supply Command Post

 Engineer & Operative Advantage!

Spawn Point to Command Post: 00:08

Time to Claim Command Post: 00:10 

Although not as well-trafficked as the other Command Post, this is more important tactically for your team because the Super Tanker Bridge enables you to use the Storage Thoroughfare without the need to raise the Movable Bridge. Use that as an exit, after storming the Super Tanker interior and watching for both mines and turrets. Take this as a matter of importance, and then use the area as a staging ground: Position yourself on the Super Tanker Bridge to cover the team passing under you, on the Dirt Path toward the Resistance Hulk and Missile Courtyard.

###  Construct the Bridge MG Nest

 Engineer

Spawn Point to Bridge MG Nest: 00:10 

Time to Construct: 00:04 

This points out of the Warship's hull, and faces the Movable Bridge. The enemy likes to occasionally use this against you as you swarm the Storage Thoroughfare aboard the Warship. Aside from the XP, the value in building this is negative because enemies don't usually enter its aiming field.

###  Solo Tactics

In the first part of this mission, take a central role as an Engineer, attempting a mixture of Crane repairing and enemy distraction, lasting for as long as possible inside the Crane Yard. Once the Warship is accessible, it becomes extremely difficult to accomplish the final goal by running at the Missile Courtyard and expecting to hack the controls without being cut down. Instead, wait for a group and follow them in, building defenses and either waiting for an Operative to start the hack, or doing it yourself.

##  Mission Completion Conditions

###  Continuation...

**Core Objective 1:** Your team repairs the Crane Controls. Part 2 of this mission now commences....

###  Completed!

The match completes if you manage to hack the Missile Controls and stop the launch before the timer ticks down.

###  Unsuccessful!

Security forces lose if you are prevented from completing any Core Objective by the time the timer reaches zero.

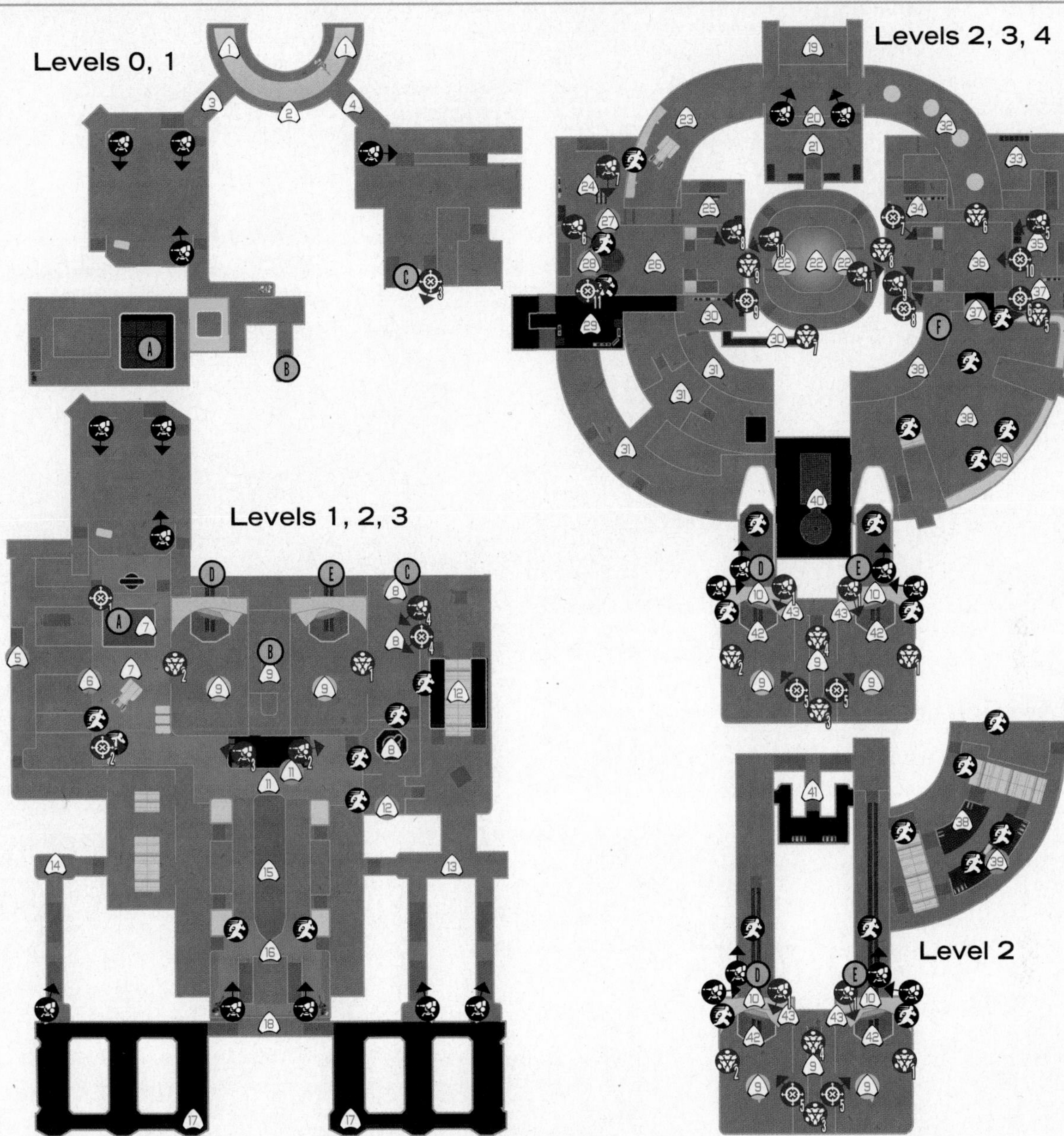


## MAP LEGEND

1: Security Deployment Zone (Pt. 1): Reactor Server Room (Lvl. 0)
2: Security Comm& Post (Pt. 1) (Lvl. 0)
3: Yellow Zone Passages (Lvl. 1)
4: Red Zone Passages (Lvl. 1)
5: Starboard Deck & Supply Comm& Post (Lvls. 1 & 2)
6: Cargo Bay Control Room & MG Nest (Lvl. 3)
7: Reactor Container Yard, Vent Room Entrance, & Cargo Bay (Lvls. 1 & 2)
8: Steam Stack, Vent Room Entrance, & MG Nest (Lvl. 2)
9: Vent Room, Airflow Controls, & Under Corridors (Lvls. 1, 2 & 3)
10: Ventilation Fans (Lvl. 2)
11: Bridge & Access Panel, & Control Room (Lvl. 3)
12: Health Comm& Post & Turbine Hall (Lvls. 2 & 3)
13: Port Service Stairs (2) (Lvls. 0, 1, & 2)
14: Starboard Service Stairs to Turbine Room (Lvls. 0, 1, & 2)
15: Scale Model Foyer & Vent Tower Entrance (Lvls. 2 & 3)
16: Power Plant Info Desk (Lvl. 2)
17: Resistance Deployment Zone (Pt. 1): Reactor Platform Lifeboats (Lvl. 0)
18: Resistance Comm& Post (Pt. 1) (Lvl. 1)
19: Security Deployment Zone (Pt. 2): Midway Balcony (Lvls. 3 & 4)
20: Security Comm& Post (Pt. 2) (Lvl. 3)
21: Storage & Lower Reactor Core Access (Lvl. 2)
22: Reactor & Core (Lvls. 2 & 3)
23: Yellow Zone: Broken Vent Pipe Chamber (Lvls. 3 & 4)
24: Yellow Zone: Server Rooms (Lvls. 3 & 4)
25: Yellow Zone: Server Rooms & Maintenance Corridor (Lvls. 3 & 4)
26: Yellow Zone: Containment Room & Reactor Access (Lvls. 2, 3, & 4)
27: Yellow Zone: MG Nest (Lvl. 3)
28: Yellow Zone: Supply Comm& Post (Lvl. 4)
29: Yellow Zone: Computer Room & Vending Machines (Lvl. 4)
30: Yellow Zone: Comm& Room & Vent Shaft to Reactor (Lvl. 4)
31: Yellow Zone: Outer, Inner, & Upper Stepped Chambers (Lvls. 3 & 4)
32: Red Zone: Power Conduit Chamber (Lvl. 3)
33: Red Zone: Server Room & Staircase Thoroughfare (Lvls. 3 & 4)
34: Red Zone: Server Room & Maintenance Corridor (Lvls. 3 & 4)
35: Red Zone: Computer Room & Vending Machines (Lvl. 4)
36: Red Zone: Containment Room & Reactor Access (Lvls. 2, 3, & 4)
37: Red Zone: Small Server Rooms & MG Nest Corridor (Lvl. 4)
38: Red Zone: Turbine Outer & Upper Chambers (Lvls. 2, 3 & 4)
39: Red Zone: Health Comm& Post (Lvl. 3)
40: Reactor Pool Chamber (Lvl. 3)
41: Stairwell to Small Server Room (Lvls. 2, 3, & 4)
42: Resistance Deployment Zone (Pt. 2): Vent Fans Passages (2) (Lvls. 2 & 3)
43: Resistance Comm& Posts (2) (Pt. 2) (Lvl. 2)

# DAY 8: FALLOUT

FREEPLAY: REACTOR   RESISTANCE CAMPAIGN—WHAT-IF: CRITICAL REACTION

## 11:06 Reactor Pelgo, Observation Deck 4

MISSION TIME (COb 1): 10:00

MISSION TIME (COb 2): +10:00

### MAP LEGEND (CONTINUED)

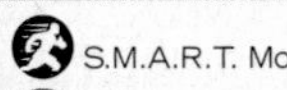
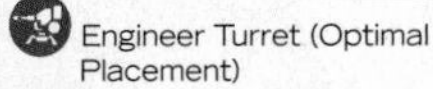
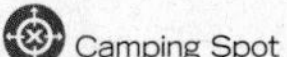
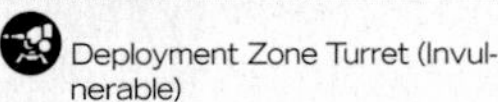
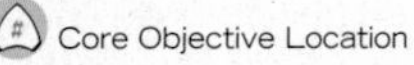
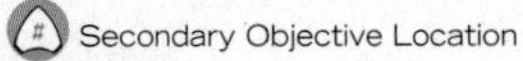
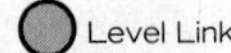

- S.M.A.R.T. Move
- Engineer Mine (Optimal Placement)
- Engineer Turret (Optimal Placement)
- Camping Spot
- Deployment Zone Turret (Invulnerable)
- Core Objective Location
- Secondary Objective Location
- Level Link

### Captain Mokoena: Briefing

We lost too many good men yesterday. But I need you to focus. We've just intercepted this Resistance message:

"So far the Founders have chosen to ignore comrade Chen. We are the sword in his hand. The Founders have shown they only respect force. Then they'll respect this: In under one hour, our forces will seize control of the Reactor. Unless Security lay down their weapons and turn control of the Ark over to Brother Chen, we'll overload the Reactor, ejecting radioactive fallout and rendering the Ark as uninhabitable to the Founders as it is to the guests. Life on Ark will be fair and just. Or it will end within an hour. Our path is set."

You heard him! They'll be with you any minute. Defend the Reactor with your lives!

### Optimal Class Numbers

| | COb 1 | COb 2 |
|---|---|---|
| Soldier | [2] | [1] |
| Medic | [2] | [2] |
| Engineer | [3] | [4] |
| Operative | [1] | [1] |

### Objectives (Securty)

- Core Objective 1: Defend the Vent System
- Core Objective 2: Defend the Reactor
- Escort Core Objective Class Teammate
- Defend the Bridge Access Panel
- Capture the Health Command Post
- Capture the Supply Command Post
- Construct the Office MG Nest
- Construct the Escalators MG Nest
- Construct the Doorway MG Nest
- Construct the Walkway MG Nest

## Important Locations
(Ventilation Deck)

### 1 Security Deployment Zone (Pt. 1): Reactor Server Room (Lvl. 0)

Although most of the fighting for the first Core Objective takes place outside, your squad begins inside this curved chamber deep in the bowels of the Reactor area (indeed, the Reactor is on the other side of the inside curve, although it isn't accessible). You have a choice of two available exits (the Yellow or Red Zones). The enemy doesn't venture down here, because the Security turrets would cut them down.

This Reactor (especially the locations you access during the second half of this mission) is split into halves, distinguishable due to the color-coded stripes and floor decals. The Yellow Zone is on the starboard side of the Reactor. The Red Zone is to the port side. If you're facing the Resistance Deployment Zone, the red areas are to your left, and the yellow to your right. Learn this so you don't get lost.

TIP

Although underneath some of the passageways in the main reactor area, this Server Room is cut off from the Reactor section that is traversed during the latter part of this match.

NOTE

## 2 Security Command Post (Pt. 1) (Lvl. 0)

Placed equidistant between the two exit corridors, this Command Post lets you change the class and weaponry of your team. You're defending this Reactor, so Engineers are a good choice to bolster your side.

## 3 Yellow Zone Passages (Lvl. 1)

## 4 Red Zone Passages (Lvl. 1)

The Security Deployment Zone offers two distinct routes to the exterior locations and Vent Room; each marked with a different wall stripe. The Red Zone Passages (entered via the left exit from your deployment zone) enable you to reach the MG Nest and Turbine Hall. The slightly more maze-like Yellow Zone Passages (entered via the right exit) lead past a large underground room with a blue floor and parked cargo vehicle, and three possible destinations: The Starboard Deck, the Cargo Bay (disused steam stack), and the stairwell below the Vent Room. Once you figure out these routes, you can plan to utilize them to halt the enemy before they reach the Vent Room itself.

## 5 Starboard Deck & Supply Command Post (Lvls. 1 & 2)

There are two reasons to visit the Starboard Deck from the yellow spawn corridors: to claim the Supply Command Post under the stairs, and to outflank the enemy, because you can reach the Starboard Service Stairs and Turbine Room, or the Control Room overlooking the Container Yard. Remember the Supply Command Post is under the middle stairwell, near the two short corridors that connect to the Cargo Bay.

## 6 Cargo Bay Control Room & MG Nest (Lvl. 3)

This is a good location to take early on, because it offers a good view of the Container Yard, and your team is closer to this location than the opposition. Use the staircases from either end of the Starboard Deck (or the barrel in the Container Yard) to reach this upper room, with three windows that offer excellent (sniping) views of the exterior facility and one of the Vent Rooms. Build and train the MG at the room too; although if you're facing an enemy using this weapon, simply avoid the entrance, or stay in the shadows if you're in the yard, because the MG has limited vertical and horizontal movement.

## 7 Reactor Container Yard, Vent Room Entrance, & Cargo Bay (Lvls. 1 & 2)

The starboard side area adjacent to the Vent Room consists of a Container Yard bathed in sunlight, and some radioactive cylinders, one of which is in mid-transit. Clamber on these and the vehicle for protection and the height advantage. Of course, the main entrance to the Vent Room is of paramount importance, but you can reach (or head in from) other locations too:

Your route to this location usually involves climbing up from the Cargo Bay (or the two sets of steps on either side of the unused steam stack) at one end of the Container Yard. If you use the Cargo Bay platform, you can also reach the Starboard Deck, which loops around and up, and back into the Container Yard. You can also look over the yard from the Control Room, which is great for cutting down Resistance forces as they attempt to swarm the nearer Vent Room.

### S.M.A.R.T. Moves

Find the locked door near the barrel, and clamber onto the barrel, and shimmy into the open Control Room window.

This is more skillful than useful, but you can traverse this entire Container Yard without ever touching the ground. Practice it!

## 8 Steam Stack, Vent Room Entrance, & MG Nest (Lvl. 2)

This port side area has a large floor marking of the Reactor's symbol, and a schematic of the adjacent Turbine Hall. Dominating the far end of the exterior area (and raised platform that leads to the Health Command Post) is a large Steam Stack (a useful landmark), and an open area offering some barrels and boxes to hide behind. At your team's entrance, close to the floor symbol, is an MG Nest that you should have working, so you can wound foes who enter the Vent Room via this location.

## 9 Vent Room, Airflow Controls, & Under Corridors (Lvls. 1, 2 & 3)

## 10 Ventilation Fans (Lvl. 2)

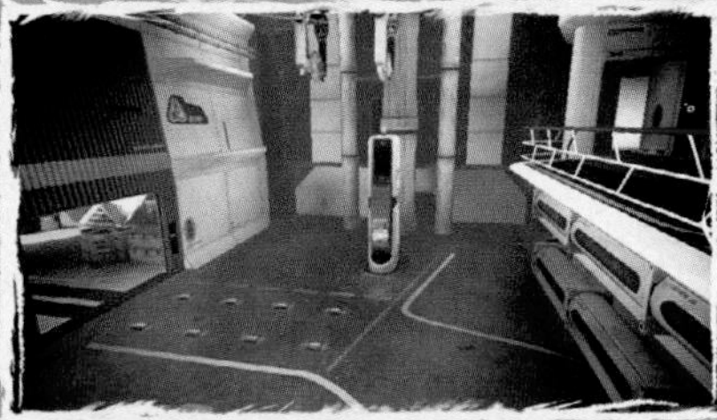

The Resistance must focus almost all their attention on this two-level chamber, which has three separate areas of interest. On each side is an Airflow Control unit with a panel that one or more enemy Operatives must hack. Opposite the panels are giant Ventilation Fans that mark the Resistance force's deployment zone when the action shifts to the second Core Objective. You can climb the white slope and cross the "bridge" the fan motors and blades are connected to, or use the middle staircase (or the fuel cylinders on the starboard side) to reach a balcony overlooking both areas (a great place to defend from). You can fire down from the fan bridges, too.

The balcony leads to the Control Room, where the enemy may try to repair a panel to open the adjacent door, allowing quicker access from their spawn points. Put a stop to that! Behind the Airflow Controls are some vertical struts to hide behind, and a tiny passage connecting the Vent Rooms.

Descend the stairwell in the central area to reach the winding (and slightly confusing) underground passages. One leads to the Cargo Bay and Starboard Deck, while the other allows you to reach the yellow side of your deployment zone.

## 11 Bridge & Access Panel, & Control Room (Lvl. 3)

The yellow exterior floor allows swift movement between the starboard and port Vent Room Entrances. However, the bridge offers the enemy forces more immediate access into a Control Room, although the doors into the room at the far end of the bridge are locked. This is overcome if your foes send an Engineer to quickly sprint into the Vent

Room, up onto the white "bridge" that holds the giant vent fans, and across into the Control Room, where the Access Panel can be repaired. Prevent this by ambushing the Engineer in the Vent Room, and periodically checking that the Access Panel isn't being fiddled with.

 S.M.A.R.T. Moves 

Wall-jump the low balcony with the blue barrels on it, and scramble over the balcony opposite, by the Steam Stack.

## 12 Health Command Post & Turbine Hall (Lvls. 2 & 3)

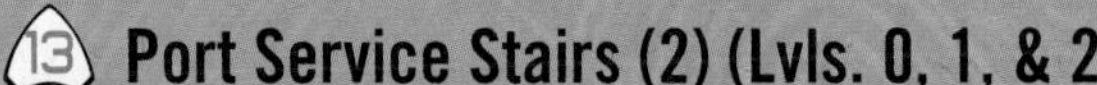

## 13 Port Service Stairs (2) (Lvls. 0, 1, & 2)

The Turbine Hall is a major connecting chamber between the Security and Resistance areas, and clashes are expected here. Stand on the raised steps on either side of the turbine and aim across, under the glass, across the Vent Room Entrance, and into the Airflow Control chamber.

At the far end of this chamber, the Health Command Post is visited by both teams, so leap on the medical cases in the corner near the door out to the Steam Stack, and ambush foes from both entrances as they try to take it.

On the opposite wall is a small connecting passageway leading (via a double doorway) from the Turbine Hall to a connecting chamber close to the Info Desk. Also off this passage are two parallel (and steep) stairs from one side of the Resistance Deployment Zone. It isn't wise to head down these stairs; let the enemy come to you.

S.M.A.R.T. Moves

From the Vent Room Entrance, you can climb onto the water pipes under the schematic screen, and hop into the Turbine Hall.

## 14 Starboard Service Stairs to Turbine Room (Lvls. 0, 1, & 2)

Follow the Starboard Deck around to the Turbine Room, which allows you into the exterior area, as well as a connecting chamber and the Info Desk. This also connects to a set of steep stairs, leading down to the other side of the Resistance spawn location. Learn which door is which! You can climb on the turbine, using the height to peer out through the doorways, and drop down behind it for cover.

## 15 Scale Model Foyer & Vent Tower Entrance (Lvls. 2 & 3)

## 16 Power Plant Info Desk (Lvl. 2)

You have little need to investigate the entrance to the reactor, because the enemy can easily outflank you and won't stick around to engage; they'll be heading for the Vent Room. The Foyer has two floors; the lower one (accessed from the yellow exterior floor) has a scale model of the facility, an overturned drinks machine, and two entrances.

The upper area (Vent Tower Entrance access from the closed bridge) has two balconies, and two entrances on each side. The side entrances on both floors lead to a connecting passage that link to the Service Stairs. At the far end of the lower floor is an Info Desk, which is connected to the Starboard Service Stairs Turbine Room and the Port Service Stairs, and leads down to the Resistance Command Post stairs.

### S.M.A.R.T. Moves

There are blue barrels in the corridor leading to the Resistance sentry guns. Wall-jump or climb over this railing to reach the Vent Tower Entrance.

### 17 Resistance Deployment Zone (Pt. 1): Reactor Platform Lifeboats (Lvl. 0)

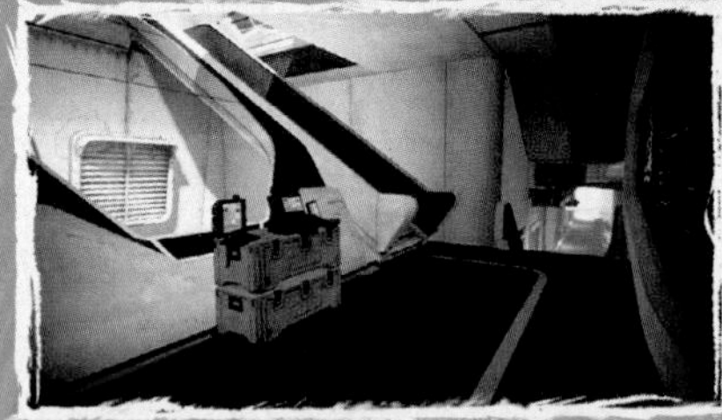

Resistance forces begin evenly split in two parallel locations on either side of a staircase. You're either seeking a quick death or are completely lost if you find yourself here.

### 18 Resistance Command Post (Pt. 1) (Lvl. 1)

This post is at the top of the stairs, in the middle of the structure below the Power Plant Info Desk. It cannot be used.

## Important Locations (Reactor Control)

### 19 Security Deployment Zone (Pt. 2): Midway Balcony (Lvls. 3 & 4)

Should the enemy hack the ventilation system, you begin the second (and final) Core Objective on this platform, which is too high for the enemy (or your team) to climb up once you drop off. Occasionally a foe may try to ambush you from the dead-end passage on either side of the drop. You're fortunate to be able to quickly reach the Reactor Core area from here; but try to spread out to chambers farther away, so it takes the enemy longer to reach their last objective.

### 20 Security Command Post (Pt. 2) (Lvl. 3)

Servicing your team defending the Reactor Core requires the skills (and mines) of Engineers, so be sure your team has some.

**The Yellow and Red Zones are in play in this part of the Reactor too. From your spawn point, turn left to reach the Yellow Zone, and right to head into the Red Zone.**

NOTE

### 21 Storage & Lower Reactor Core Access (Lvl. 2)

### 22 Reactor & Core (Lvls. 2 & 3)

The Reactor is in the center of this second section of the facility, and there are more ways to reach it than you may realize. The two obvious entrances the Resistance uses are via the Yellow and Red Containment Rooms, where enemy Soldiers place their explosives (one set on either mainframe panel), while your team waylays them, doing

everything possible to prevent this. The room itself is circular, with an outer and inner path that connects to the opposite panel. You can hide on the lower path and ambush foes (although you're usually spotted before this becomes beneficial).

The duct high on the Yellow Zone side is another way to head to and from here (or fight from). But down below (and accessed via the lower stairs in either Containment Room, or via the Storage area across from the Security spawn point) is the crackling Core itself. This offers a direct route via the Storage Room adjacent to your deployment zone. The door to the Yellow Zone is sealed here. You don't need to defend the lower chamber, just the upper area, and this is a great path to quickly reach the area.

### 23 Yellow Zone: Broken Vent Pipe Chamber (Lvls. 3 & 4)

### 24 Yellow Zone: Server Rooms (Lvls. 3 & 4)

### 25 Yellow Zone: Server Rooms & Maintenance Corridor (Lvls. 3 & 4)

The Broken Vent Pipe Chamber to the right takes you directly from your deployment zone past a parked vehicle near a large pipe that is leaking what you hope is steam. Openings on the side and end of this chamber, and the broken pipe in question, allow access into two nearby Server Rooms.

The smaller one has an L-shaped Maintenance Corridor, stairs up, and window views into the Containment Room (you can fire and fall down from here). Ambush foes from the dark corners, walls, and cubbyholes behind the server stacks. The larger of the two Server Rooms, on the outer edge of the facility, offers a window from the Broken Vent Pipe and a main opening on the lower floor. Each Server Room then connects to the Containment Room, through a doorway at each end, on the side with the MG Nest.

### 26 Yellow Zone: Containment Room & Reactor Access (Lvls. 2, 3, & 4)

### 27 Yellow Zone: MG Nest (Lvl. 3)

### 28 Yellow Zone: Supply Command Post (Lvl. 4)

Don't confuse this Containment Room with the one in the middle of the Red Zone, which is directly opposite, through the Reactor Room. Expect a large amount of fighting here, as the enemy storms in from a variety of outer locations. They can try entering via the Stepped Chambers to one side, while you (usually) come in from the Broken Vent Pipe Chamber on the other. At the far end of the lower floor of the Containment Room is a huge slab cylinder of machinery, offering cover opportunities and stairs up to the Supply Command Post on the platform above. This platform is a thoroughfare between rooms, and difficult to defend, but it does offer a good view of the reactor, which you or your foes can snipe from.

Back on the ground is an MG Nest in front of a doorway alcove, which you should fix. But the main draws are the illuminated steps into the Reactor, and the enemy's final "Core" Objective. The door to the left takes you into a Maintenance Corridor, which is a great place to hide and ambush from. Finally, note the stairs leading down on either side; these allow your squad out of the Core itself (which is useful for reaching the Reactor Room before your foes).

HISTORY OF THE ARK
CHARACTER CREATION
GAMEPLAY
WEAPONS DETAIL
CAMPAIGN
Hostage Rescue
Smash & Grab
Dirty Bomb
Prison Break
Early Launch
Fallout
Chopper Down
Grand Theft Aero
CHALLENGES
APPENDICES

Beware of foes throwing grenades at you if you're manning the MG Nest, because you can't move except toward your foes.

CAUTION

S.M.A.R.T. Moves

Utilize the slab cylinder to Wall-jump up, and grab the railing of the upper balcony, for a quick route between floors and to the Supply Command Post.

### 29 Yellow Zone: Computer Room & Vending Machines (Lvl. 4)

### 30 Yellow Zone: Command Room & Vent Shaft to Reactor (Lvl. 4)

Aside from some servers you can tuck yourself behind to ambush enemies, this cramped Command Room (with the "18" marking on the wall) is used by the Resistance to swiftly reach the Reactor. They tend leap off the bridge into the Containment Room, or enter via the Vent Shaft in the corner wall. After a crawl down a duct, you reach the Reactor Room itself, where foes have been known to sneak in, plant a bomb, or fire at your forces having outflanked them. Therefore, keep this duct route trapped and checked.

Across the bridge is a Computer Room with Vending Machines, and a window that offers excellent firing opportunities down into the Stepped Chamber. This is a simple linking chamber, but an important one because the doorway leads from the Supply Command Post.

### 31 Yellow Zone: Outer, Inner, & Upper Stepped Chambers (Lvls. 3 & 4)

Entered via the Command Room, these three, mostly separate curved chambers make up almost one quarter of the Reactor layout. The enemy heads into here from their spawning Vent Fans Passage; the Outer Chamber links to the upper floor of the left Vent Fans Passage. The Inner Chamber is maneuvered up and into via blue barrels along the lower floor of the left Vent Fans Passage, and the Upper Chamber is found at the top of the Stairwell to Small Server Room, on the Yellow Zone side.

The Outer and Inner Chambers offer some leaky pipes, and a small connecting passage with two doorways, in the middle. The machinery and doorways offer ample ambushing opportunities. Close to the Command Room is the Computer Room with the Vending Machines; a staircase here allows access down into the Outer Chamber. Just follow the orange lights if you want direct access from the Containment Room and Reactor into the Inner Chamber.

Meanwhile, the Command Room offers a quick route into the Upper Chamber (which is separate from the other parts of this location) with a window into the Inner Chamber to fire from (but which is too small to head through).

The orange illuminated floor lights lead to the Reactor area, and your team too (if you get confused by the Reactor's connecting chambers). Also look for sparks in ceilings and water rushing from pipes and remember where these are; this all helps you situate yourself in this maze.

NOTE

### 32 Red Zone: Power Conduit Chamber (Lvl. 3)

### 33 Red Zone: Server Room & Staircase Thoroughfare (Lvls. 3 & 4)

### 34 Red Zone: Server Room & Maintenance Corridor (Lvls. 3 & 4)

To the left of your deployment zone is the Power Conduit Chamber, with four huge couplings running the height of the curved corridor. At the opposite end are two Server Rooms. The first

features an entrance (from the Power Conduits) into an L-shaped Maintenance Corridor, and a small stairwell area with a few barrels (ambush Resistance forces from under the stairs), and a doorway out to the Reactor. Upstairs is the Server Room itself, overlooking the Containment Room, with a window to leap (or fire) down from.

Head down the connecting passage (upper floor) or into a Maintenance Corridor with floor markings (lower floor) to reach a connecting stairwell with some vending machines at the top of the stairs. This connects to the Containment Room server area at one end, and an upper Server Room with an escape window overlooking the Conduit Chamber on the other.

## 35 Red Zone: Computer Room & Vending Machines (Lvl. 4)

## 36 Red Zone: Containment Room & Reactor Access (Lvls. 2, 3, & 4)

This Containment Room is not to be confused with the one in the middle of the Yellow Zone, which is directly opposite, through the Reactor Room. You should be out in force in this location, which the enemy usually accesses via the Turbine Chamber on the ground, and the Computer Room on the upper floor. You can get here quickly via the half-opened double doors at the far end of the Power Conduit Chamber, or via the inner Core Chamber and up the stairs below the Reactor Access entrance.

The Computer Room leads directly to the MG Nest corridor overlooking the Turbine Room, and a two-story chamber that covers the rear of the Containment Room (hide behind the servers here and fire on foes). Locate the entrance behind the servers, and stairs up. Drinks machines are in the connecting corridor, which leads to two side chambers (Server Rooms) that feed back into the main Containment Room. Snipe from the window next to the vending machines, or leap through it into the Containment Room floor.

The main draws are the illuminated steps into the Reactor, and the enemy's final "Core" Objective. A door to the left here takes you to a cubbyhole hiding spot. Also check the entrance and two windows on the right side, leading to a Server Room.

**Can't tell which Containment Room is which? The one in the Red Zone features a covered upper platform across from the Reactor, and no Command Post.**

TIP

## 37 Red Zone: Small Server Rooms & MG Nest Corridor (Lvl. 4)

At the end of the curved Turbine Upper Chamber is a tiny, dark Server Room with a window overlooking the Containment Room. Try ambushing enemies here while hiding to the side of the server tower. The window is good for firing down on enemies. Along the connecting passage is an MG Nest; fix this and turn the weapon on foes rushing through the Turbine Room. If your team is competent enough, use this location as the first line of defense.

## 38 Red Zone: Turbine Outer & Upper Chambers (Lvls. 2, 3, & 4)

## 39 Red Zone: Health Command Post (Lvl. 3)

This giant Turbine Outer Chamber, with its much smaller Upper Chamber on the inside of the curve, is the "other" main route to take from the opposite Containment Room. This is arguably a better route for the enemy to take than the Yellow Zone, because they can access the Upper Chamber, the windows are easier to clamber through, and there are many more S.M.A.R.T. move opportunities.

This room features two giant Turbines, with a raised platform in the middle that holds the Health Command Post. This is closer to the enemy spawn point than yours, so you may need to concede it to the enemy for the good of the mission. Along the outer edge is a low passage (allowing you to rush around without being easily spotted); use a duct directly above if you're faster and lighter. Also use the balconies above the two turbines to reach the duct and other locations, or to fire from. Step back into the alcove behind the balcony if you come under attack. Support any of your teammates in this area by firing from the MG Nest up by the Small Server Room.

 S.M.A.R.T. Moves 

Climb the snaking pipework near the lower exit, and clamber into the window of the Computer Room with the Vending Machines.

Grab the protruding turbine rod and climb into the window of the Upper Chamber. The other turbine has no rod, so leap the gap to or from the window.

Leap onto the single server towers by each support pillar to hop across from turbine to turbine.

## 40 Reactor Pool Chamber (Lvl. 3)

## 41 Stairwell to Small Server Room (Lvls. 2, 3, & 4)

## 42 Resistance Deployment Zone (Pt. 2): Vent Fans Passages (2) (Lvls. 2 & 3)

The enemy begins their Reactor assault from the far end of the two stopped fans on either side of the stair balcony in the Vent Room. Each Fan Passage allows the enemy to reach either the Red Turbine Chambers (left), or the Yellow Stepped Chambers (right).

Between the Stepped and Turbine Chambers, the Reactor Pool Chamber (which has both yellow and red wall stripes) is used by the enemy from the Vent Fans Passages when they want to reach the Upper Chambers, which are the inside curved corridors around the Reactor center. Avoid these areas because you're simply too far from important defensive locations.

## 43 Resistance Command Posts (2) (Pt. 2) (Lvl. 2)

There's never any reason to head here, unless you're after a quick death.

HISTORY OF THE ARK
CHARACTER CREATION
GAMEPLAY
WEAPONS DETAIL
CAMPAIGN
Hostage Rescue
Smash & Grab
Dirty Bomb
Prison Break
Early Launch
Fallout
Chopper Down
Grand Theft Aero
CHALLENGES
APPENDICES

# Objective Tactics: Core Objective 1

## Defend the Vent System

Spawn Point to Vent Room: 00:12

Time to Hack Airflow: 01:00

### General Tactics

After you spawn, it is vitally important that you know where you're going (the Vent Room), how you're getting there (the quickest way possible), and which sections of the Vent Room you're covering (the doorways and then the Airflow Controls). The exact methods of holding the enemy back at these locations are detailed below. The enemy will likely split their teams up, so you should do the same; although it is usually best to keep a couple of Engineers back inside the Vent Room to set up an initial set of mines and turrets in readiness for the main combat to come.

Once this occurs, and your Airflow Controls are being threatened, the priority threats are enemy Operatives, closely followed by their Medic friends. Because hacking is involved, and leaving the hack points for a few moments causes the hacking to reset, you have a little more time to locate your enemies and drop them. The topography of the Vent Room helps; the central balcony and connecting passages between the Airflow Controls allow you to cover both room portions. Split your team into the two sub-chambers when the time comes to retreat and hold this critical location.

### Route Defense

**Container Yard Carnage:** Spread out around the shaded side of the Container Yard, and have a sharpshooter or two at the windows of the Control Room, as well as a teammate covering the Vent Room entrance. You can adequately cover foes attempting to gain entrance from the Vent Tower Entrance, Starboard Service Stairs or Deck, or via the Cargo Bay. Have an Engineer on standby to re-take the Supply Command Post if necessary, too.

**Vent Entrance Eviscerations:** Take control of the Red Zone and have teammates perched on the pipe in the Turbine Room under the schematic screen, behind crates (or the MG Nest) in the Vent Room Entrance, watching for enemies taking the Port Service Stairs, and of course, inside the Vent Room itself. Because you have fewer locations to cover, three teammates in this general area can hold back the enemy or raise the alarm, and keep the Health Command Post in Security hands, too.

**Bridge and Control Room Chaos:** Guarding this chamber is unnecessary, because the enemy has to maneuver through the Vent Room to reach and fix the Access Panel. But the Control Room itself is worth checking out, if only for the windows you can fire through, and watch enemy movements from, before radioing their locations, or cutting them down from this vantage point.

**Under Corridors Upheaval:** If the Resistance is using this route, be very careful because they can storm into the Vent Room while your team is covered everywhere else: A sure sign of the Resistance sneaking in this way is a severe lack of combat on the surface of the facility! A better plan is to place a couple of mines and/or a turret in the corridors the enemy uses (below the Cargo Bay is a good place) and listen for the explosions. Then retreat into the Vent Room and wait for the ruckus to begin.

**Vent Room Rampage:** One or two of your Engineers should be fitting this chamber out with traps from the moment the mission begins. If you know your enemy is extremely adept, you may wish to pull everyone back and create an impenetrable chamber of death. This involves turret and mine placement (examples below); full movement across the fan supports, middle balcony, linking corridors; and guarding the Under Corridor staircase.

**One of the best places to defend the Airflow Controls from is the small passage that links the two halves of the main Vent Room. From the middle of this, you can see both Airflow Controls simultaneously and keep an eye on them. Try taking a Gotlung in here and camping as a Soldier (thus infinite ammo) with the Minigun in constant "revved up" mode to rake hundreds of bullets into a hapless Operative or three!**

TIP

## Automated Ordnance

What has the Resistance got planned to trap you with? Check their turret, mine, and vantage point placements in their Reactor section of this guide.

1 A turret on the top of each Vent Fan support covers your Airflow Controls without being easy to take out with grenades.

2 3 A turret behind each triangular vent covers both the main exterior enemy routes (#2 shown).

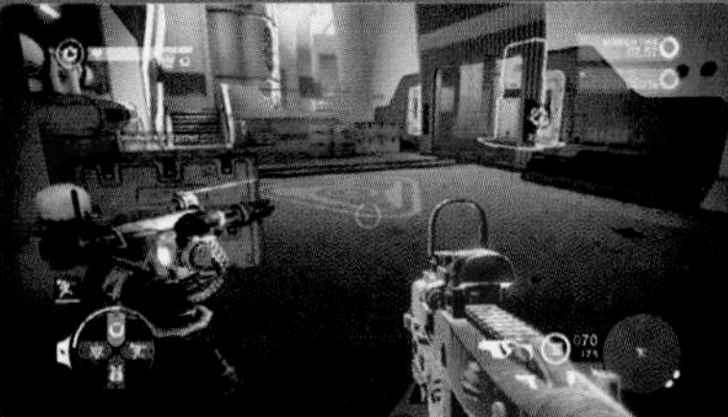

4 Set a turret here to cover the Airflow Controls, while being partially hidden by the crates.

1 2 A mine in either side doorway into the Vent Room is a recommended way to shorten the life of any enemy (#1 shown).

3 Lay a mine in the small corridor linking both sides of the Vent Room.

4 Stop the enemies from reaching the Control Room or taking over the central balcony by placing a mine atop the steps.

## Sniper's Ally: Camping Spots

1 Stand here, so you can see foes running past the Cargo Bay below, moving in the Control Room, and also across the Container Yard. Duck down the stairs if you come under fire.

2 Lurk near this radioactive container in the Container Yard, stepping to the left out of its cover to drop foes heading into the Vent Room. Check the Control Room for movement, too.

3 Cover the entire Vent Room Entrance at the escalator MG Nest, but shoot your own weapons, and use the entrance walls as cover.

4 Sit atop the pipes in the Turbine Room, under the schematic screen, and blast foes heading up from the Port Service Stairs, as well as Operatives at the Airflow Controls.

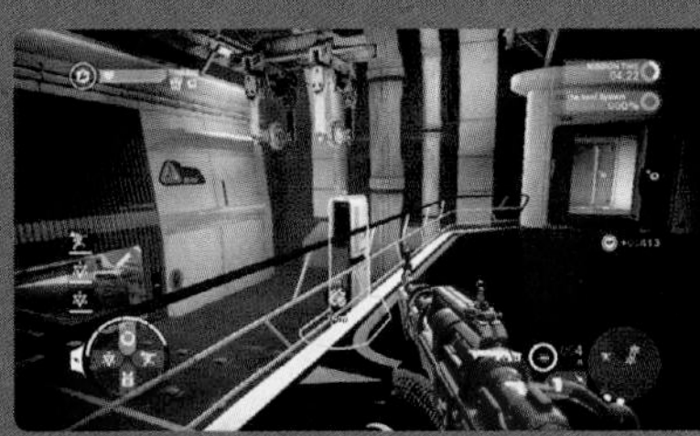

5 This is perhaps the most important balcony to patrol, because you can cover both Airflow Controls from here.

## Objective Tactics: Secondary Objectives

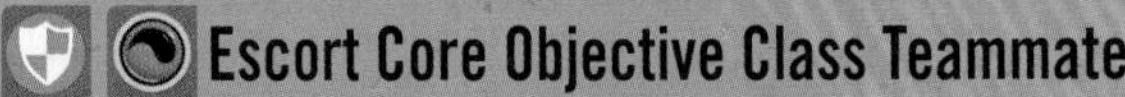

### Escort Core Objective Class Teammate

**Unofficial Escort Info:** As a defending team, this objective isn't usually available, but two-player tactics are an option: There are two sides to the Vent Room. There are two of you. Why not keep the team chatter down to a minimum and keep each other informed of enemies on the starboard and port sides of the facility? Two Engineers each fixing each other's turrets (and knowing where all the traps are) is another plan. Or a Medic healing up the Soldier tanks as they cover the Airflow Controls. All are viable within your team's main tactics.

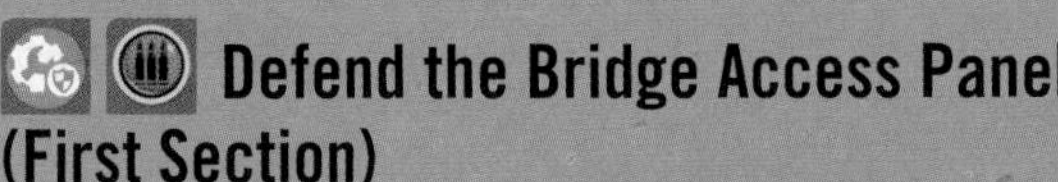

### Defend the Bridge Access Panel (First Section)

Spawn Point to Access Panel: 00:16

Time to Repair Panel: 00:10

This is low priority objective for the enemy, and an even lower one for your team. The Access Panel's location in the Control Room means the enemy must actually break into the Vent Room, then head up into the balcony partitioning the two sides of

the room, and into the Control Room itself, which is adjacent. Have troops on this partition to ensure that no enemy Engineer reaches the Control Room, and to perform defensive tasks inside the Vent Room.

### Capture the Health Command Post

Engineer & Operative Advantage!

Spawn Point to Command Post: 00:12

Time to Claim Command Post: 00:10

Located at the far end of the Turbine Hall, this is closer to the enemy than your deployment zone, and likely to have fallen into Resistance hands early on. Taking it back via the Steam Stack entrance, or Turbine Hall, means ignoring the main defense of the Vent Room, but if you can spare the time, you can then back up and sit on the pipe at Camp Spot 4, overlooking both post entrances, as well as the Airflow Controls on the port side of the Vent Room.

### Capture the Supply Command Post

Engineer & Operative Advantage!

Spawn Point to Command Post: 00:11

Time to Claim Command Post: 00:10

Tucked away under the steps of the Starboard Deck, this Command Post is accessed more quickly by your team: Exit the Yellow Zone corridors, and head around the Cargo Bay and down the narrow passage to reach it. Then drop down, blast any foe trying to claim it, and return to the Vent Rooms as soon as you hear that the post is being taken for the opposition. If you have brethren inside the Cargo Bay Control Room, they should be tasked with this plan.

### Construct the Office MG Nest

### Construct the Escalators MG Nest

Engineer

Spawn Point to Office MG Nest: 00:16

Spawn Point to Escalators MG Nest: 00:15

Time to Construct: 00:04

This MG Nest overlooks the yyxyy Vent Room from the window inside the Cargo Bay Control Room. Although it has a good field of vision to catch foes swarming in from the Vent Tower Entrance, and into the Vent Room itself, it can't shoot directly at the Airflow Controls, and more cunning foes either flank you and attack the gunner inside the Control Room, or avoid the area completely. Use this if the Vent Room is already filled with competent teammates.

This MG Nest is at the end of the Red Zone corridors, at the Vent Room Entrance. This is clearly an MG Nest positioned for your team, and using it is worthwhile if the enemy is milling about the Steam Stack, or heading out of the Health Command Post or through the gap in the Turbine Room wall.

## Objective Tactics: Core Objective 2

### Defend the Reactor

Spawn Point to Reactor Room: 00:16

Time to Disarm Explosives: 00:05

Time to Plant Explosives: 00:07

Countdown to Explosion: 00:40

### General Tactics

Setting up in the Reactor Room to create an impenetrable minefield (literally) is your first step; remember that you have a fast path from your spawn point via the Storage and Lower Reactor Core Access chambers. When you get to the Reactor chamber, place your defenses (as described below) and then move out to continue trap placement and locate the camping spots you'll use for the combat to come. Venturing out of the Reactor "thoroughfare"—the Red and Yellow Containment Rooms and the Reactor Room itself—is not recommended if your rivals are professionals. Don't go farther away than the Computer Rooms on the upper floor, adjacent to the Containment chambers.

Be ready for enemies at every entrance, and have your team on balconies to gain the height advantage and spot foes at a distance. Then engage, watching for enemies from the Stepped Chamber, Turbine Room, upper connecting Computer Rooms, plus the more cunning Soldiers dropping out of the Vent Shaft.

**Enemies have to pass through a Containment Room to reach the less-traveled sections of the map—the Broken Vent Pipe Chamber and Power Conduit Chamber—so as long as you have troops covering the Containment Room, you aren't likely to be attacked from the Maintenance Corridors and opposite side of the Containment Room.**

 NOTE

## Route Defense

**Seeing Yellow:** The Containment and Computer Rooms comprise the outer defensive line in this zone. Patrol the upper Computer Room and Vending Machines, and the Command Room with the Vent Shaft, to spot incoming foes in any of the Stepped Corridor chambers. Set a third teammate up at the balcony adjacent to the Supply Command Post, and have your fourth member guarding the Reactor Panel itself.

**Seeing Red:** The outer defenses in this zone are the Computer Room and the Small Server Rooms with the MG Nest Corridor. Begin by wounding as many enemies as you can in the Turbine Room by stationing a couple of sharpshooters here, with another teammate looking out of the window into the Containment Room. Your last teammate should be guarding the Reactor Panel facing into the Red Zone.

**The enemy sometimes heads down the steps that run underneath the Reactor Room. There's no need to follow them because they're usually trying to coax you away from guarding the Reactor. The passage leads to the opposite Containment Room, and as long as your team is guarding both sides, let the enemy come to you. After all, they're the ones with a time limit!**

 TIP

**Seething Reactor:** If one or both of the Containment Rooms are overrun, and shooting at the enemies from the upper windows isn't helping, retreat onto the ground of the Containment Room, and then into the Reactor Room itself. Remember all of the different mine, turret, and camp spots; and utilize both curved walkways between the Access Panels, cutting down Soldiers first and Medics second.

**Camp the Reactor Room using an Engineer, because his skills are extremely effective. With only two large entrances into this location (and the Vent Shaft), placing a mine in the shaft (not below it, because you can leap over that) stops foes from entering via the duct work. Set a turret pointing into one Containment Room, and defend the other yourself. All three incursion points are covered by a single person!**

 TIP

## Automated Ordnance

5 Stick a turret here to cover the main exit from the Turbine Room, in front of the servers so foes don't immediately see it when descending the stairs behind.

6 Between the MG Nest and the slab cylinder of machinery, a turret placed here watches the main ground entrance from the Stepped Corridor, and is partially hidden from foes coming down the stairs.

7 Set a turret in the upper Server Room across from the Supply Command Post to stop enemies from retaking it.

8 9 Place a turret in the Containment Room at this location to cover all entrances (#8 shown).

10 11 Stick a turret facing out into the Containment Room (#10 shown); every bit of firepower at the Resistance helps in the final seconds!

5 Stick a mine below the window to halt those scaling the air ducts for a way into the Small Server Room.

6 Place a mine between the two sets of half-closed doors just in case the enemy tries to outflank you via the Power Conduit Chamber.

7 Lay a mine in the Vent Shaft. Make sure it's at the far end just before the victim tries to exit into the Reactor Room; that way, he takes longer to find and hit the mine!

8 9 A mine at both the entrances to the Reactor Room on the doorway thresholds is an extremely good plan (#8 shown).

## Sniper's Ally: Camping Spots

6 The window by the MG Nest offers a better view than the one to the left, in the Small Server Room.

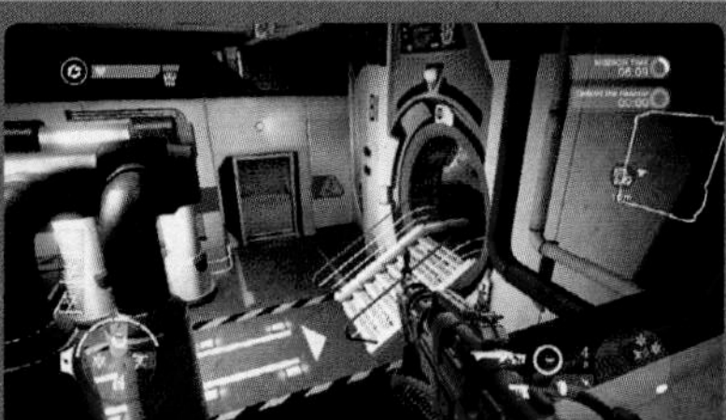

7 8 Stay at the window in the Server Room above the Maintenance Corridor, covering both the corridor and the Containment Room. Leap out of the window for a quick intercept (#7 shown).

## Sniper's Ally: Camping Spots (continued)

9 Sit next to the Vent Shaft in the Command Room, and watch the entrances down the long corridor.

10 11 Use the upper level of the Containment Room to cover the ground and the Reactor Room itself (#11 shown).

# Objective Tactics: Secondary Objectives

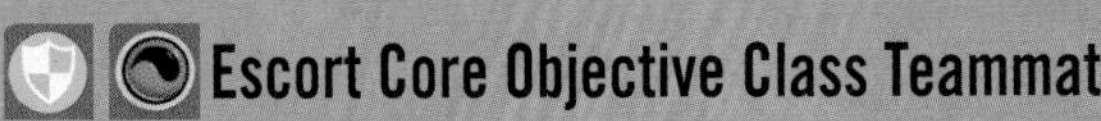

### Escort Core Objective Class Teammate

**Unofficial Escort Info:** As a defending team, this objective isn't usually available, but two player tactics are still worth remembering: Holding off the Reactor with a single Engineer is even more potent if you have a second teammate to help you (or heal if you swap to a Medic). Partnering up Soldiers at each Reactor panel, or two Medics responsible for the well-being of the entire team (and who can quickly yell for back up supplies) are all possibilities as the assault on the Reactor reaches a crescendo.

### Capture the Health Command Post

Engineer & Operative Advantage!

Spawn Point to Command Post: 00:13

Time to Claim Command Post: 00:10

If you can spare one (or two) teammates to race into the Turbine Room, without compromising your main defenses, then try to take this back, but be warned; the enemy uses this chamber constantly so you'll be constantly returning. The second teammate can stand on the duct work to cover the capture. Don't forget to trap this before you leave, and don't expect to keep it for long, unless you station a sniper at the upper windows or MG Nest nearby. However, turning up here and waylaying some enemies is reason enough to retake this post.

### Capture the Supply Command Post

Engineer & Operative Advantage!

Spawn Point to Command Post: 00:12

Time to Claim Command Post: 00:10

A quick reminder; this post is on the balcony above the Yellow Zone Containment Room, and you'll usually access it from the Broken Vent Pipe Chamber and Server Room en route to the Reactor. Take this on your first run, and then guard it well. You can camp in the Server Room, or cover the enemy from the balcony indefinitely, while your foes are under a timer. So guard both the Reactor Room and this post while the enemy wastes time trying to take it back. Remember that you can climb up the slab cylinder attached to the balcony as well as the stairs.

### Construct the Doorway MG Nest

### Construct the Walkway MG Nest

Engineer

Spawn Point to Doorway MG Nest: 00:15

Spawn Point to Walkway MG Nest: 00:14

Time to Construct: 00:04

The Doorway MG Nest is in the Yellow Zone Containment Room. Its alcove location means you won't be attacked from behind but don't have much room to dodge an incoming grenade. Also watch for enemies firing at you from the upper windows of the Computer Rooms on the opposite side of the room. This MG Nest cuts down enemies following the orange floor lights, but offers little additional help.

The Walkway MG Nest can annoy a multitude of Resistance troops as they cross the Turbine Room, and can cut down foes trying to take back the Health Command Post. For this reason (and the fact that only the enemy populates the Turbine Room in great numbers), this is worth building and manning; just watch for foes outflanking you from the passage on both sides.

## Solo Tactics

During the first Core Objective, your role is more central. Spawn as an Engineer with a weapon that can cut through Operatives with speed, then rush to the Vent Room, lay traps, and then quickly take either Command Post (or both) before returning. Take down any Operatives and the Medics who help them, ideally from partial cover between both Airflow Controls. During the Reactor strikes, follow the tactical advice about camping out in the Reactor Room, and single-handedly save the chamber as an Engineer, periodically rushing to take back the Supply Command Post. The Health one may be too far away to safely obtain.

## Mission Completion Conditions

### Continuation...

**Core Objective 1:** Your team allows the enemy to destroy the Vent System. Part 2 of this mission now commences....

### Completed!

The match completes if you stop the enemy from completing either Core Objective by the time the timer reaches zero.

### Unsuccessful!

Security forces lose if the enemy successfully destroys the Reactor before the timer ticks down.

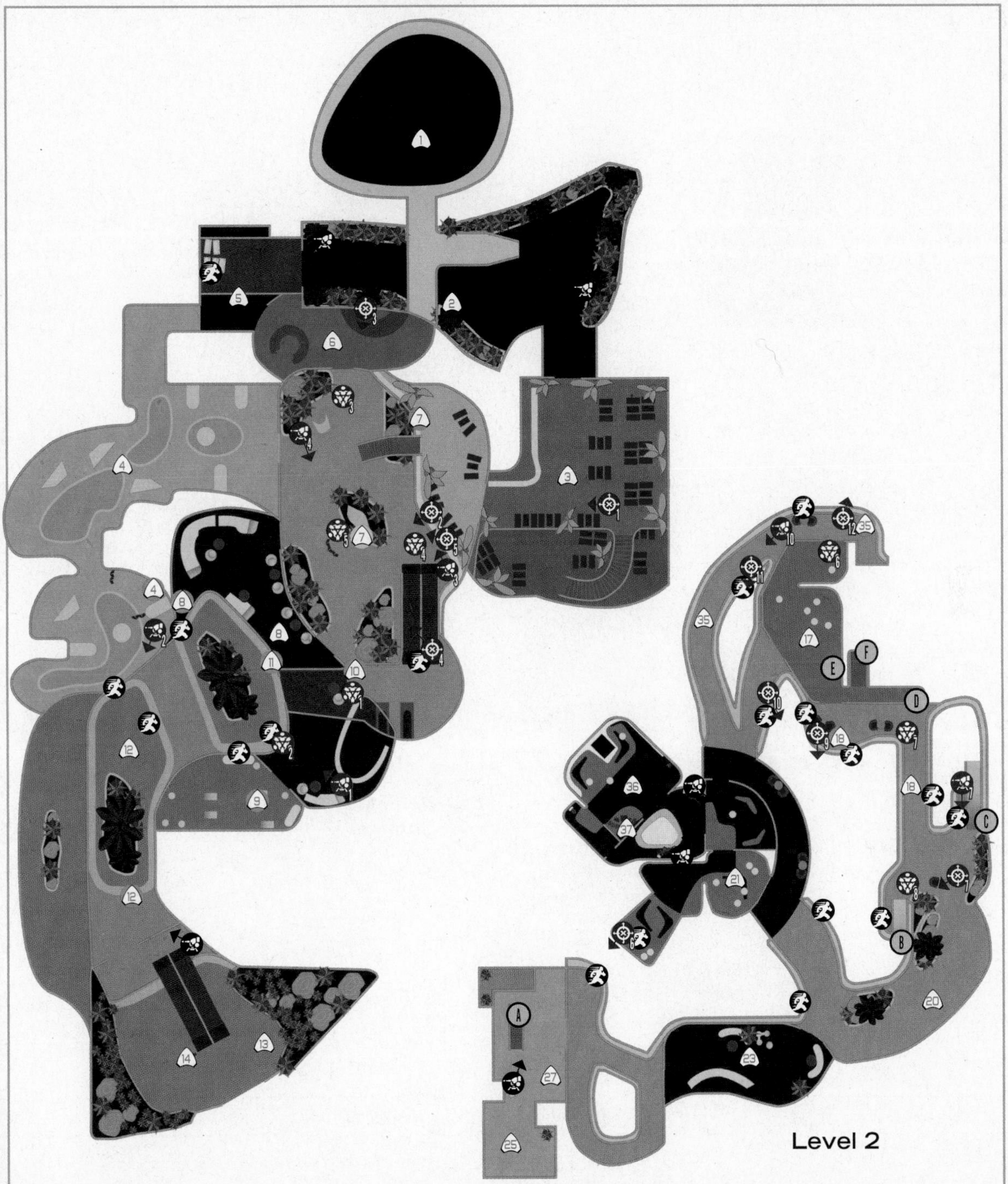

Level 2

## MAP LEGEND

**Resort Pelgo: Shopping & Cuisine**

1: Security Deployment Zone (Pt. 1): Plaza Helipad & Access Walkway (Lvl. 3)
2: Security Command Post (Pt. 1) (Lvl. 3)
3: Velouté Soup & Salad Bar (Lvls. 2 & 3)
4: Fashionista Store & Supply Command Post (Lvl. 2)
5: Side Storage (Lvls. 2 & 3)
6: Krill Co Store (Lvl. 2)
7: Pelgo Support Pillar, Balcony, & MG Nest (Lvls. 1, 2, & 3)
8: Hennesea Lounge & MG Nest (Lvl. 2)
9: GUUD Store & MG Nest (Lvl. 2)
10: Health Command Post (Eco Nom) (Lvl. 1)
11: Shop Door to Eco Nom & Escalators (Lvl. 1)
12: Pelgo Shopping Mezzanine & MG Nest (Lvl. 1 & 2)
13: Resistance Deployment Zone (Pt. 1): Plaza Insertion Point (Lvl. 1)
14: Resistance Command Post (Pt. 1) (Lvl. 1)

**Resort Pelgo: Living Quarters**

15: Security Deployment Zone (Pt. 2): Executive Suite 3 Bathroom (Lvl. 3)
16: Security Command Post (Pt. 2) (Lvl. 3)
17: Executive Suite 3 (Lvls. 1 & 2)

BRINK

**Resort: Overview Map**

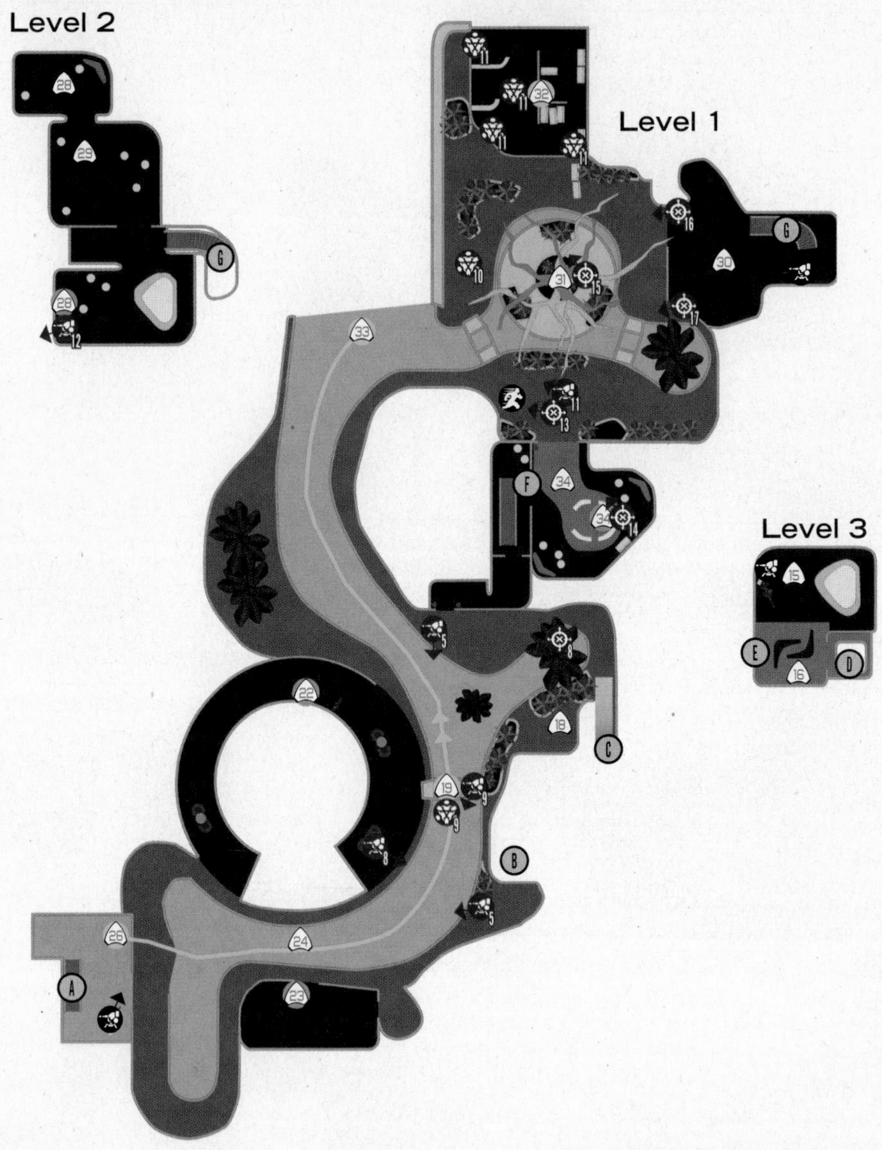


## MAP LEGEND (continued)

18: Forecourt, Ramps, & Bridge, with MG Nest (Lvls. 1 & 2)
19: Canal Bridge (Lvl. 1)
20: The Upper Promenade (Lvl. 2)
21: Executive Suite 1 (Lvl. 2)
22: The Circular Foyer & Supply Command Post (Lvl. 1)
23: In a Cup Coffee House & MG Nest (Lvl. 1) & The Mozno Club (Lvl. 2)
24: Pelgo Central Canal Mezzanine (Lvls. 1 & 2)
25: Resistance Deployment Zone (Pt. 2): Organdy Casual Wear (Lvls. 1 & 2)
26: Carrier Bot: Starting Location (Lvl. 1)
27: Resistance Command Post (Pt. 2) (Lvl. 1)
28: Security Deployment Zone (Pt. 3) & MG Nest: Executive Suite 4 Upstairs (Lvl. 2)
29: Security Command Post (Pt. 3) (Lvl. 2)
30: Executive Suite 4 (Lvl. 1)
31: Neon Tree Courtyard (Lvl. 1)
32: RMS SeaGate Controls (Lvl. 1)
33: Outer Canal & SeaGate (Lvl. 1)
34: Le Flow Foyer & Health Command Post (Lvl. 1)
35: Split Bridge & Le Flow Balcony with MG Nest (Lvl. 2)
36: Resistance Deployment Zone (Pt. 3): Executive Suite 2 (Lvl. 2)
37: Resistance Command Post (Pt. 3) (Lvl. 2)

S.M.A.R.T. Move
Engineer Mine (Optimal Placement)
Engineer Turret (Optimal Placement)
Camping Spot
Deployment Zone Turret (Invulnerable)
Core Objective Location
Secondary Objective Location
Critical Path (Route)
Level Link

BRINK ↘ Resort: Overview Map

# WHAT-IF: CHOPPER DOWN

FREEPLAY: RESORT — SECURITY CAMPAIGN—DAY 6: BLACK BOX

## 19:27 Helipad, AirResort North Tower

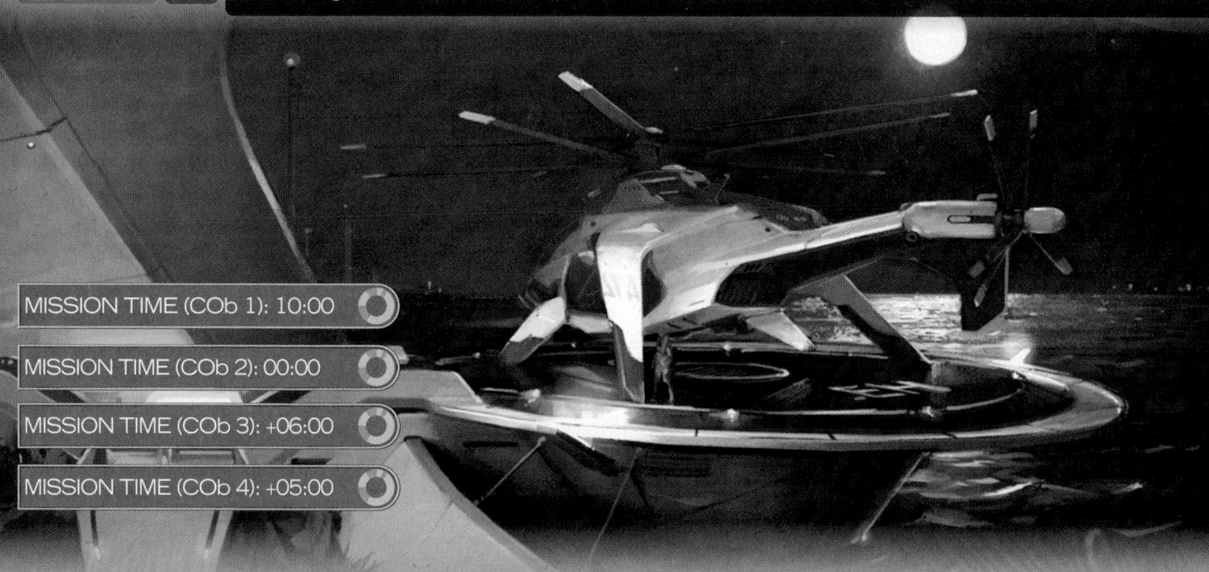

MISSION TIME (COb 1): 10:00

MISSION TIME (COb 2): 00:00

MISSION TIME (COb 3): +06:00

MISSION TIME (COb 4): +05:00

### Captain Mokoena: Briefing

The terrorists have downed one of our gunships. The pilot was forced to crash-land on the Founder Resort pelgo. Radio chatter indicates that a terrorist snatch squad and an armored extraction boat are already on their way to the crash site. Whatever they're after, they'll be using it to cause chaos. Don't let them touch the gunship crash site. Don't let them take anything from the chopper. DON'T LET ANYTHING OFF THAT PELGO!

### Optimal Class Numbers

| | COb 1 | COb 2 | COb 3 | COb 4 |
|---|---|---|---|---|
| Soldier | [2] | [3] | [2] | [1] |
| Medic | [2] | [2] | [2] | [2] |
| Engineer | [3] | [2] | [3] | [2] |
| Operative | [1] | [1] | [1] | [3] |

### Objectives (Security)

- Core Objective 1: Defend the Pillar
- Core Objective 2: Disable the Bot
- Core Objective 3: Defend the Bridge
- Core Objective 4: Defend the Gate Controls
- Escort Core Objective Class Teammate
- Defend the Shop Door
- Capture the Health Command Post
- Capture the Supply Command Post
- Construct the Entrance MG Nest
- Construct the Shop MG Nest
- Construct the Lounge MG Nest
- Construct the Crash Site MG Nest
- Construct the Cafe MG Nest
- Construct the Balcony MG Nest
- Construct the Hotel Balcony MG Nest
- Construct the Apartment Balcony MG Nest

## Important Locations

Resort Pelgo: Shopping & Cuisine

### 1 Security Deployment Zone (Pt. 1): Plaza Helipad & Access Walkway (Lvl. 3)

Don't get hung up at the sealed door directly ahead of your helipad spawn point; drop off the walkway to the left, which leads to a doorway into the Velouté (and a drop down to the lower floor of the Soup and Salad Bar as you enter, if you don't mind the gap). Or leap to the right, and enter the area via the Side Storage room inside Fashionista.

## 2 Security Command Post (Pt. 1) (Lvl. 3)

Because you're defending the Support Pillar, Engineers are the order of the day (to set up traps and turrets, and pry off explosives the enemy leaves on the Support Pillar). Choose your class or swap weapons here.

## 3 Velouté Soup & Salad Bar (Lvls. 2 & 3)

This two-story eatery, accessed from your spawn point, is the quickest way to the balcony and the Pelgo Shopping Mezzanine, where the majority of the bloodshed occurs. Leap the gap in the entrance doorway to avoid dropping to the lower ground, or fall down there to reach the lower Mezzanine more quickly. Velouté itself is usually just a thoroughfare, although the lower level of this swanky restaurant has some shadowy cubbyholes to hide in and snipe across at the Fashionista Store.

## 4 Fashionista Store & Supply Command Post (Lvl. 2)

## 5 Side Storage (Lvls. 2 & 3)

The enemies race through this store to reach you, but if your team is fast enough, you can reach (and fortify) the Supply Command Post, and begin combat as early as possible, blocking off a key enemy thoroughfare in the process. There is an exit to the Pelgo Support Pillar area, and sniping opportunities across to the GUUD Store.

Also be aware of the Side Storage with the stack of cardboard boxes, a major drop point from your spawning ground. Stay up here to tag foes as they pass below, although it is better to head down and fortify the Krill Co Store, or hide in it during the main combat.

### S.M.A.R.T. Moves

Of course, you can climb on top of the cardboard boxes and ambush foes running to and from the Krill Co Store.

## 6 Krill Co Store (Lvl. 2)

A compact store with a strange, luminescent sea-tree spindle, this is accessed from the Fashionista Side Storage, and the Pelgo Support Pillar area. Booby-trap this area and have a teammate (or two) guard the entrance, waylaying foes trying to enter from Fashionista or the Side Storage room.

## 7 Pelgo Support Pillar, Balcony, & MG Nest (Lvls. 1, 2, & 3)

Look above the Support Pillar you're defending, and you'll see why the enemy is so keen on blowing it up; one of your choppers has crashed into the Support Pillar, and the NavComputer is the prize they crave. The main battle occurs (or ends) at this location, and you can enter the area from:

The Velouté Soup and Salad Bar's lower entrance or upper balcony.

The doorway from the Krill Co Store.

The doorway from the Fashionista Store

One of two doorways at either side of the Hennesea Lounge.

Or the escalators up from the locked corridor and Health Command Post.

The enemy is likely to storm in from the last three areas, while you take up defensive positions on the balcony, by the MG Nest, or around the Support Pillar. You can stand on the balcony seating and shoot down, using the reinforced plastic wall as cover. Or man the MG Nest (after building it), because it offers a good view of the areas where enemies are active. Place mines, other explosives, and turrets while you mill about, checking where the foes are likely to attack from next.

## S.M.A.R.T. Moves

Stand on the lip of the low balcony wall directly above the escalator to ambush foes moving up from the Health Command Post and locked corridor.

## 8 Hennesea Lounge & MG Nest (Lvl. 2)

Think of this long, thin lounge as the first line of defense for the Pelgo Support Pillar area. In fact, it is unwise to venture any farther into the enemy's Shopping Mezzanine, where they spawn, for fear of being overrun. The two entrances, which lead to two openings overlooking the Mezzanine and a door into GUUD Store, are perfect for firing down on the enemy, and the MG Nest enhances this plan. Hide behind the bar, and remember you can also retreat but still fire into the Hennesea from the sniping location under the stairs by the Support Pillar.

## 9 GUUD Store & MG Nest (Lvl. 2)

Expect the enemy to rush in from this point, if they don't take the route through Fashionista or open the Shop Door. The MG Nest is trained on your area, so it's a good idea to stop them from building that. This is about as close to the enemy's spawn point as you need to get.

## 10 Health Command Post (Eco Nom) (Lvl. 1)

## 11 Shop Door to Eco Nom & Escalators (Lvl. 1)

The lower level access to the Support Pillar area and the Health Command Post is far more difficult for the enemy to reach than your team: Simply head down the escalators, and take the post as quickly as possible. You can also set up a turret or explosives in the area while the enemy watches, but can't do anything about it. Unfortunately, you can't access the Mezzanine where the Shop Door is located either, unless you fire down from Hennesea or GUUD stores. Listen for the announcement that the door is open; then you have an additional route to guard.

## 12 Pelgo Shopping Mezzanine & MG Nest (Lvl. 1 & 2)

The two-floor Shopping Mezzanine has a few locked stores on each side; the enemy uses the balcony and floor as a thoroughfare toward the Support Pillar. The MG Nest at the top of the stairs is only used if you plan on rampaging into the enemy's spawn point, which isn't wise. The upper floor provides access to the Fashionista Store (and its second exit across the adjacent bridge to the GUUD Store). On the ground, you can climb either information terminal if you fall down here. The only other reason to be here is to annoy an Operative hacking the Shop Door.

## S.M.A.R.T. Moves

There are three shortcuts across the low walls of the upper level; stand on them to navigate past the front windows of Fashionista to the adjacent bridge.

Do the same to reach either of the openings into Hennesea, and both are quicker than moving through the stores. The narrow pebble-filled planter with grass between the two Hennesea openings can also be traversed, too.

To reach the upper floor from the ground level, clamber up onto either information terminal and onto the balcony.

### 13 Resistance Deployment Zone (Pt. 1): Plaza Insertion Point (Lvl. 1)

A breach by a Resistance watercraft in the Resort's outer wall announces their arrival, in front of a pair of escalators. With many enemies approaching, heading down here isn't a viable option.

### 14 Resistance Command Post (Pt. 1) (Lvl. 1)

You cannot access this Command Post, because it belongs to the enemy. Ignore it.

## Important Locations

Resort Pelgo: Living Quarters

### 15 Security Deployment Zone (Pt. 2): Executive Suite 3 Bathroom (Lvl. 3)

The top floor of Executive Suite 3 holds a bath and a Command Post; access the latter before you drop down via either gap in the walls, because you can't climb back into this location. It also isn't worth waiting for foes to appear below you; drop down into Executive Suite 3 instead, and rush to meet the enemy. You spawn here prior to the destruction of the Canal Bridge and the Carrier Bot infiltration.

### 16 Security Command Post (Pt. 2) (Lvl. 3)

You're here to stop the Resistance from blowing up the Canal Bridge, so a mixture of combat-savvy Soldiers and Engineers to set up defenses is always a good option. Swap your classes and weapons here.

### 17 Executive Suite 3 (Lvls. 1 & 2)

Your team owns this building during the time the enemy tries to blast the Canal Bridge and bring the Carrier Bot down the canal. It is important to know the different routes out of this building: The doorways immediately under the gaps that you drop down from your spawn point allow you onto the MG Nest area and Straight Bridge. A third exit on this floor, leading out onto the Split Bridge, is mainly used by the enemy when you retreat to your third spawn point.

The stairs down grant you access to the canal-side pathway under the MG Nest balcony, but it's quicker to simply drop from the balcony instead. The glass door into Le Flow Foyer, behind which is a Health Command Post, doesn't open until the Canal Bridge has been blown up and the Carrier Bot reaches the bridge area.

## 18 Forecourt, Ramps, & Bridge, with MG Nest (Lvls. 1 & 2)

Stage your main defensive posture during the assault on the Canal Bridge, because you can see every possible enemy route onto the bridge itself, along with additional protection thanks to your upper-level vantage point. You needn't descend the Ramps (jump off instead), but learning where they are once you're on the ground is very important because you may need to retreat up them.

Get dug in around the MG Nest (which offers excellent takedown potential because of its prime position overlooking the Canal Bridge), but don't be afraid to leave the MG Nest if the enemies focus their attacks on you. Then cover the Promenade, the exit of the Circular Foyer, and the locations farther up the canal.

### S.M.A.R.T. Moves

Stand atop the curved awning near the In a Cup ramp area, and head over the glass wall onto the straight bridge, or leap over the canal to the bridge that spans the Mozno and Executive Suite 2.

Leap across the gaps in the low walls of the upper balcony. This one enables you to reach the Split Bridge (and back again) from the MG Nest area, or the blue bench.

Whereas this one allows access to and from the Tihjin Moon Ramp and straight bridge.

You can forgo the Ramps and stand on the low wall below the "Ocean Retreat" sign, and climb up that to assault the MG Nest directly.

Take a similar climb up the second Tihjin Moon sign above the canal, and up onto the Split Bridge by the blue bench.

## 19 Canal Bridge (Lvl. 1)

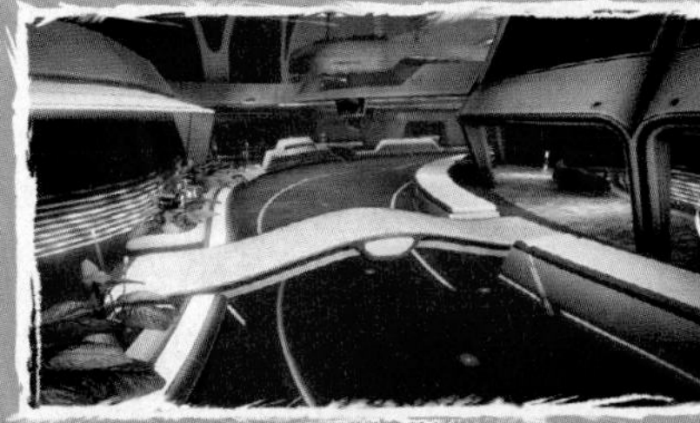

This low bridge spans the canal and is surrounded by upper balconies and a bridge where both sides usually fire from. The enemy is trying to destroy the bridge with a Soldier's timed explosives, after which the Carrier Bot trundles through (so train your weapons at enemies sporting the Soldier symbol). The bridge detonation and subsequent arrival of the Bot triggers the move from Deployment Zone 2 to 3 for both sides.

## 20 The Upper Promenade (Lvl. 2)

This covered area provides a thoroughfare between the upper bridge and MG Nest area, Forecourt, and the Mozno Club. Combat takes place only at either end.

## 21 Executive Suite 1 (Lvl. 2)

The bridge connected to Mozno and the Promenade leads into an upper suite; traverse the interior to reach a balcony overlooking the Resistance force's spawn point where the Carrier Bot starts. There is also a curved corridor to the Split Bridge, which the enemy uses. This is a quick thoroughfare, so train your weapons (or place explosives) at the entrance.

> **The Executive Suite's glass doors open once the Carrier Bot passes the destroyed Canal Bridge, and the enemy moves to this deployment zone.**
>
> NOTE

### 22 The Circular Foyer & Supply Command Post (Lvl. 1)

The enemy is likely to be moving into this ground-floor curved passage almost immediately, because it offers a covered path past a Supply Command Post, and an exit adjacent to the Canal Bridge itself. There's even scenery inside to hide behind as your team pushes into the area to stop the enemy Soldiers from breaching the bridge location. The enemy spawn point for the later part of this mission is above the Supply Command Post, so you can also use this to cut down and interfere with foes when they should be sprinting to the SeaGate.

### 23 In a Cup Coffee House & MG Nest (Lvl. 1) & The Mozno Club (Lvl. 2)

The Mozno Club is an upper-level location that the Resistance uses as a thorough-fare, with a bridge connecting to the Executive Suite, and an exit into the Promenade. Train your weapons from the MG Nest outside your spawn point at this area, and cut down foes venturing toward you. One level below is the In a Cup Coffee House, entered via the canal pathway. The MG Nest in here is a problem, so stay out of its range to stop your foes supporting their Soldiers at the Canal Bridge. It isn't necessary to maneuver into these areas unless you're trying to coax the enemy away from their proper objectives.

**The more cunning Security members play this mission as Resistance, build the MG Nest here (or indeed, at any location throughout a mission), and then learn the horizontal limits of the turret's movement. Then, when playing as Security, they stand just outside these limits when taking out or dodging this emplacement.**

 TIP

### 24 Pelgo Central Canal Mezzanine (Lvls. 1 & 2)

The area just outside the Resistance spawn area is dangerous, and not worth investigating too closely, due to the large number of enemy troops and sentry turrets. The enemy uses a number of routes to reach the bridge. They hide behind the low walls by the canal. They access the In a Cup Coffee House to take up defensive positions (and use the MG Nest). They sprint into the Circular Foyer to claim the Supply Command Post. On the upper balcony, they enter the Mozno Club and Executive Suite 1. Your team shouldn't send fighters here. Wait for the foes to come to you, because time is on your side.

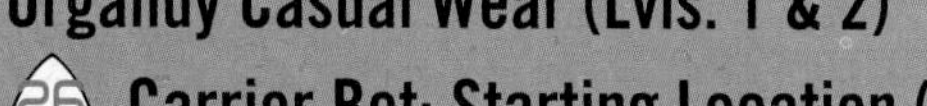

### 25 Resistance Deployment Zone (Pt. 2): Organdy Casual Wear (Lvls. 1 & 2)

### 26 Carrier Bot: Starting Location (Lvl. 1)

This two-story store is the spawn point from the time the Carrier Bot begins to move until it passes the destroyed remains of the Canal Bridge (Core Objective 3). The enemy has two exits, which you can spot from range. However, it isn't wise to venture too close to their sentry guns. Remain at the bridge connecting Mozno to Executive Suite 1 when opening fire.

### 27 Resistance Command Post (Pt. 2) (Lvl. 1)

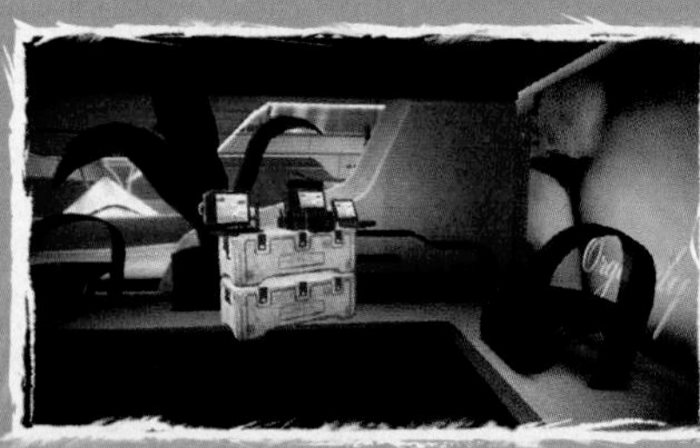

Avoid this terminal during your Resistance-hunting; it is too well-guarded, and can't be accessed by your team anyway.

## 28 Security Deployment Zone (Pt. 3) & MG Nest: Executive Suite 4 Upstairs (Lvl. 2)

You're fortunate to be quite close to the final Core Objective (the SeaGate Controls) when you spawn above the set of curved stairs, in a lavish suite with a balcony MG Nest. Fix the MG Nest to fire on the enemies as they try to reach the SeaGate Controls, while covering your own teammates streaming out of the lower doors or over the balcony. Weakening foes before they reach the SeaGate Controls allows your other colleagues to wear them down completely.

## 29 Security Command Post (Pt. 3) (Lvl. 2)

You're facing a persistent enemy who is using Operatives to hack the SeaGate. Respond with Engineers who can pepper the area with all kinds of defensive ordnance. Change weapons here if you need to, too.

## 30 Executive Suite 4 (Lvl. 1)

The ground floor from your team's final deployment zone is useful as a conduit into the Neon Tree Courtyard. Take cover in the doorways, and don't expect the Resistance to venture into here, because it is too heavily guarded.

## 31 Neon Tree Courtyard (Lvl. 1)

The final battle's most recognizable landmark, the glowing strands of neon in the middle of this circular courtyard mark the place to pass when you're keeping the SeaGate Controls out of enemy hands. With the enemy heading down the canal, keep away from the two footbridges, planters, and support columns and seek cover closer to the last Core Objective. Three entrances from this location lead into the Control Room; two allow you out of Executive Suites 4, and one into Le Flow Foyer if you're after the Health Command Post.

### S.M.A.R.T. Moves

Grab and pull yourself onto the awning above Le Flow entrance, and then optionally leap to an exposed location: the MG Nest and balcony to the right. Fire on the Resistance from either location.

## 32 RMS SeaGate Controls (Lvl. 1)

Get to this compact, two-chamber control room before the enemy does, or risk losing the entire match. If you can fortify this area with turrets, explosives, and warm bodies, you can push the enemy back so they're never able to hack the SeaGate. Remember there are three entrances (two at the front, one at the side) where the Resistance tries to outflank you (or where your team should try to outflank from if you let the enemy take command of this building).

## 33 Outer Canal & SeaGate (Lvl. 1)

The enemy floods in here during the last part of the mission, and you're less likely to push them back if you're in this area; it is better to fire from your fortified cover near the buildings. The enemies move the Carrier Bot to the SeaGate itself—the arched canopied structure with the two orange lights, opposite the Le Flow entrance—so you know when the final Core Objective is triggered.

Farther back along the canal, the palm-tree planter near the shuttered windows enables enemy snipers to seek cover, and the Resistance also stays out of the water by using the canal path under the Split Bridge, as they race into the Neon Tree Courtyard.

 **S.M.A.R.T. Moves** 

Climb up from the canal, under the MG Nest on the Split Bridge near the Le Flow entrance, and clamber on the Tihjin Moon sign.

Try the same maneuver by climbing up onto the wall on the right canal path by the wall advert for the resort shops, and using the Fashionista sign to climb up and onto the Split Bridge.

## 34 Le Flow Foyer & Health Command Post (Lvl. 1)

This opens up once Core Objective 4 is under way, and the circular desk houses the Health Command Post. Access this via Executive Suite 3, or the exterior Outer Canal and SeaGate area, and the Courtyard.

## 35 Split Bridge & Le Flow Balcony with MG Nest (Lvl. 2)

This is the main route the Resistance takes from their final spawn point. The short, wide section allows access into Executive Suite 3. The long, narrow section curves around to overlook the Outer Canal, SeaGate, and Neon Tree Courtyard, and also enables you to reach the first Security spawning ground. Use the MG Nest to shoot at enemies attempting to reach the SeaGate, but watch for foes pouring out of the Resistance Deployment Zone. Remember you can climb up here from the Tihjin Moon sign over the low wall by the blue bench, or leap across from the MG Nest on the balcony.

## 36 Resistance Deployment Zone (Pt. 3): Executive Suite 2 (Lvl. 2)

Your foes head out of here from the time they take the Carrier Bot to the end of the canal to when they storm and hack the SeaGate. You can opt to hide behind the Canal Bridge or inside the Circular Foyer to ambush foes, but not at the expense of weakening your main fighting teams.

## 37 Resistance Command Post (Pt. 3) (Lvl. 2)

You won't get to this enemy Command Post, and it never appears as a place to reach. Ignore it.

# Objective Tactics: Core Objective 1

## Defend the Pillar

Spawn Point to Pillar: 00:19

Time to Plant Explosives: 00:07

Time to Disarm Explosives: 00:05

Countdown to Explosion: 00:40

### General Tactics

Hunker down and protect the Support Pillar. Aside from intermittent rushes to either of the Command Posts, this is your only tactic. However, to minimize the enemy threats, push out from your spawn point in various directions rather than simply camping in the Support Pillar chamber. Moving your entire team into this confined location means an experienced enemy may well break your cordon of defense.

In fact, a two-tier defensive line is called for. Your team can stream quickly into Fashionista from the Side Storage to create a considerable threat and break the enemy's concentration for the Support Pillar. With a second squad fortifying the Hennesea lounge, or the bridge between Fashionista and GUUD Store, you can hold the Pelgo Shopping Mezzanine, even with the enemy's deployment zone nearby.

### Lines of Defense

**Front Line (Fashionista):** Rush to the Supply Command Post and quickly fortify it with turrets (that are trained almost on the enemy's spawning area!), mines, and general warm bodies. The glass walls allow you to see (but not be hit by) the enemy. Expand out onto the connecting bridge where you can rake foes running along the Mezzanine ground floor, trying to open the Side Door, or trying to win back the Supply Command Post.

**Front Line (Hennesea):** A second, slightly smaller squad should prowl the area between Hennesea and GUUD Store, catching the faster-moving foes if they leap the balcony edges into the MG Nest in Hennesea, or try for the Side Door hack. Use the MG Nest in Hennesea, but guard the one in GUUD, keeping it from the enemy for as long as possible.

**Last Line (Support Pillar):** Keep one or two Engineers from the front line to set up the recommended turrets and mines in the Support Pillar area and grab the Health Command Post to really give your side the advantage. If the Fashionista front line becomes overrun, retreat here, defending from the Krill Co, Velouté, and upper balcony locations. Spread your team out so you can hit foes from as many different angles as possible.

## Automated Ordnance

These are some of the more cunning placements of an Engineer's arsenal. Feel free to use your own judgment and locations too.

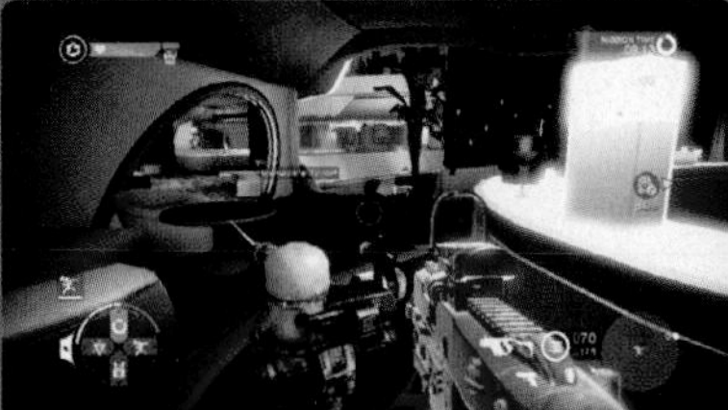

1 Position a turret inside Hennesea so the enemy can't easily lob a grenade at it. This catches foes running down from GUUD Store. Guard behind this turret.

2 Guarding the Supply Command Post with bristling defenses is a great first line of defense. The turret here takes advantage of the protective glass wall.

3 This is a great way to cover the enemy's entrance points, and the glass walls give a little more protection.

4 You have protection from grenades coming from Fashionista, and good coverage of the Core Objective.

1 A mine inside the Shop Door, or at the Health Command Post, delays the enemy from reaching its newly opened incursion point.

2 The enemy enjoys using the Mezzanine's information terminals—except when they climb onto a mine.

3 With friendlies on the bridge and in Fashionista, placing a mine between them prevents your foes from charging through. Any shop doorway is a good place for a mine.

4 This tends to stop enemies from charging up the escalators; place it only after the Shop Door is open. Any enemy entrance is an option, too.

5 There's a degree of satisfaction to seeing an enemy Soldier crumple as your mine beneath the Core Objective explodes.

## Sniper's Ally: Camping Spots

1 The additional cover the Velouté provides allows you to shoot foes over in the Fashionista, while others cover different entrances.

2 This is a long-range massacre point, enabling you to cut down foes all the way to GUUD Store. Have a teammate watch your right side though!

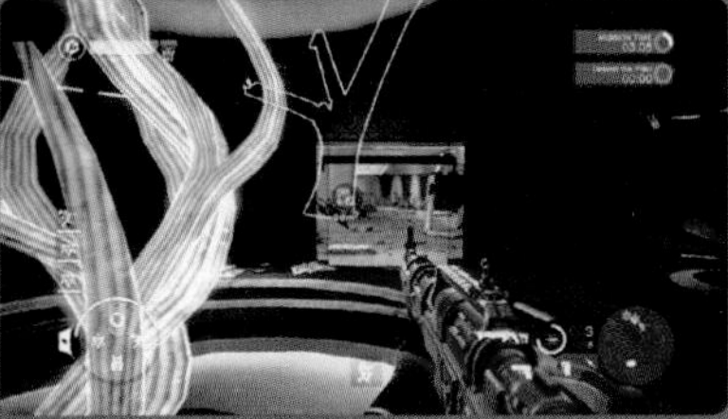

3 Stand by the neon tree inside Krill Co for a long-range shot at the Support Pillar. You can also cover the Side Storage entrance on your right.

## Sniper's Ally: Camping Spots (continued)

4 Crouch here, cover the exits, and cut down foes from behind as they climb the escalators. You can quickly retake the Health Command Post from here, too.

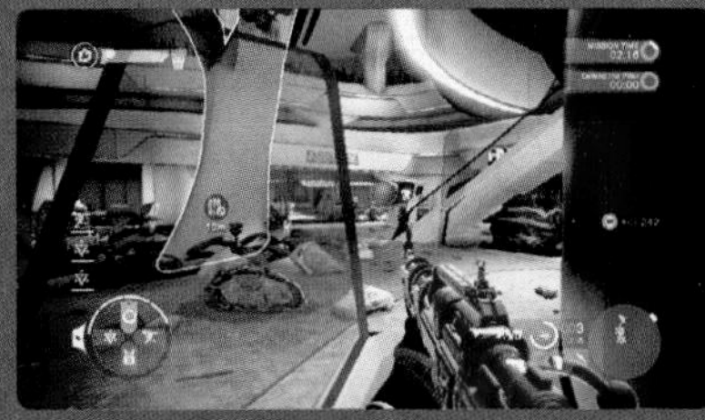

5 The glass wall here is great for absorbing enemy gunfire. Plus, you can see through this wall to every enemy incursion point!

# Secondary Objectives (First Map)

### Escort Core Objective Class Teammate

**Official Escort Info:** Your finest hour comes from covering an Engineer as they remove the enemy's HE Charges on the Support Pillar. But there are other options that aren't officially recognized, and won't garner you "Guard" XP.

**Unofficial Escort Info:** Cut through the chatter and noise of your teammates and team up with a like-minded individual to plan some enemy takedowns.Prowling the balcony (either outside Fashinonista in the enemy Mezzanine, or by the MG Nest in the Support Room) together is a great idea, with one of you armed to the teeth while the other supports and heals. Or take two Engineers down to the Support Pillar and continuously place mines and turrets (or repair each other's turrets). Taking charge of an MG Nest, while the other watches for enemies attacking from beyond the MG's aiming area is another possible plan.

### Defend the Shop Door

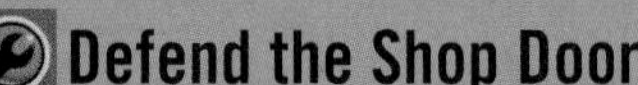

Spawn Point to Shop Door: 00:15

Time to Hack Door Controls: 00:10

The Resistance may try to hack the Shop Door leading to the Health Command Post and escalator. The problem with preventing this is that you have to attack from the side of the door where they are positioned. If you're quick, and have fortified the Supply Command Post, check the Side Door from the balcony above. If you haven't, you might as well retreat.

### Capture the Health Command Post

Engineer & Operative Advantage!

Spawn Point to Command Post: 00:14

Time to Claim Command Post: 00:10

Keep a couple of folks back in the Support Pillar room to set up defenses, and take this as soon as possible. The enemy can't reach it until the Shop Door is hacked, and other troops on the balcony and near the GUUD Store should be taking care of these enemy Operatives. Take the post, then ignore the area until the Resistance opens the door; then station a sharpshooter behind the grocery planters to guard both the post and the entrance, if you can spare a teammate.

### Capture the Supply Command Post

Engineer & Operative Advantage!

Spawn Point to Command Post: 00:15

Time to Claim Command Post: 00:10

You may think this is too close to the enemy's spawn point to be captured by your team. However, if you send a sizable force here, via the Side Storage route through Fashionista, you can claim the Command Post and use the surrounding location as a first line of defense. Make the Supply Command Post yours only after you can adequately cover the enemy's attacks: These will be plentiful, so don't be overrun trying to take the post instead of defending the area. It is better to guard a neutral post than to be killed while taking it.

### Construct the Entrance MG Nest

### Construct the Shop MG Nest

### Construct the Lounge MG Nest

### Construct the Crash Site MG Nest

Engineer

Spawn Point to Entrance MG Nest: 00:09

Spawn Point to Shop MG Nest: 00:06

Spawn Point to Lounge MG Nest: 00:10

Spawn Point to Crash Site MG Nest: 00:08

Time to Construct: 00:04

Of the four MG Nests, only two are useful to your cause. The Entrance MG Nest is right above the Resistance Deployment Zone, and impossible to fix.

The Shop MG Nest is inside GUUD Store. This faces the location you're defending, so your team shouldn't build it. Instead, guard it in this front line of your defenses, before abandoning it if the enemy pushes past you.

The Lounge MG Nest perched on the opening, inside Hennesea, is a good place to take shots at foes, backing up your teammates on the bridge and the entrance to Fashionista. You can cut down enemies trying to climb the information terminal, or moving to the Side Door (but not the wall terminal by the door itself).

This MG Nest gets the most use because it covers four of the five entrances into the Support Pillar room, but the explosive-clamping point and the escalator incursion point are hidden. Disconnect from the MG Nest once the enemies have moved into the room, but keep them at bay at the doorway entrances beforehand.

## Objective Tactics: Core Objective 2

### Disable the Bot

Enemy Spawn Point to Bot: 00:03

Enemy Spawn Point to Canal Bridge (with Bot): 00:45

Enemy Route: Canal Bridge to Seagate: 01:08

#### General Tactics

**While tackling the Maintenance Bot, there are a lot of overlapping tactics as Core Objective 3 takes place in the same area. So follow both sets of strategies concurrently.**

TIP

It is important to delay the Maintenance Bot for as long as possible, ideally so it never reaches the SeaGate. However, the concurrent Core Objective is to defend the Bridge from a Soldier's explosive device. The two are linked, but because the Bot can't move farther forward if the Canal Bridge is still intact, defending the Canal Bridge is preferable.

Attack the Bot by lobbing grenades or Molotovs; reducing its health with larger-damaging attacks that hit fewer times frees you up to move about, or help patrol the Canal Bridge. Bring out your big men and their big guns; the Chinzor MG, Hjammerdeim Shotgun, Maximus MG, or Lobster GL all work to keep this metal vehicle prone.

Once the Bot passes the bridge, your spawning grounds change to Executive Suite 4, across behind the Neon Tree Courtyard, and you're no longer at an effective range to easily reach the Bot. However, if you move quickly into Le Flow, through your old spawn building (Executive Suite 3), and out onto the Split Bridge, you can attack from here.

This objective spans Core Objectives 3 and 4. During 3, choose two teammates to primarily focus on the Bot, while the others defend the bridge. During 4, have two teammates do the same while the bulk of your team reinforces Le Flow and the SeaGate Controls building.

TIP

This objective can be tricky once the Bot moves past the bridge, because your spawn point moves a long way back to the hack area. Try dropping down from your final spawn area and heading into the command-post room on the left, then up the stairs on the right. At the top, take the middle exit and you will be on a balcony overlooking the canal. Try disabling the robot and its escorters from here, dropping Molotovs and grenades from above, then ducking back when you need health.

### Attack Points

Many of the locations your team uses in Core Objectives 3 and 4 are also locations to use when stopping the Bot. You're here to stall the Bot for as long as possible and every damaging attack helps!

TIP

**Before the Canal Bridge:** If you're focusing on the Bot, be as annoying as possible. Hit and run tactics are good, such as lobbing grenades or Molotovs from inside In a Cup or the bridge linking

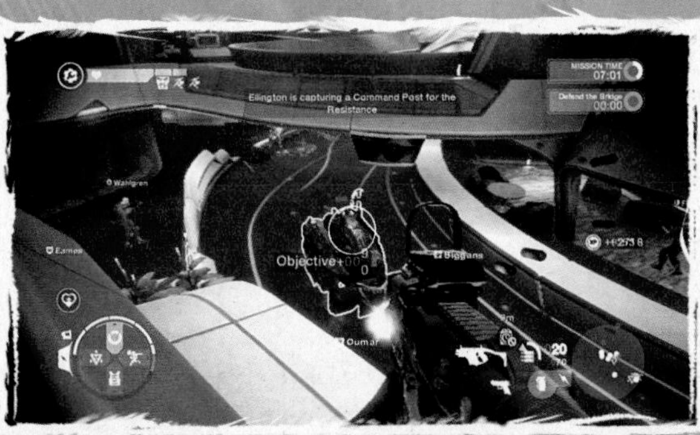

Mozno club to the Executive Suite. You can also run through the suite to the balcony overlooking the enemy spawn point after the Bot has already passed this point, and attack it (and any defenders) from behind.

You can't place mines in the water, meaning you can't stall the Bot with them, unless you place them on the Canal Bridge.

CAUTION

**After the Canal Bridge:** Attacks from the Split Bridge are recommended, ducking back into cover when you need health or grenade replenishment. The balcony with the MG Nest provides height and cover, and you can drop explosives on the Bot. The MG Nest itself cannot aim at the Bot due to its mounting position. Finally, if you have a teammate near the Canal Bridge (perhaps capturing the Supply Command Post), have him follow the Bot and strike from behind.

## Objective Tactics: Core Objective 3

### Defend the Bridge

Time to Plant Explosives: 00:07

Time to Disarm Explosives: 00:05

Countdown to Explosion: 00:40

### General Tactics

Elevated positions are the key to effectively defending this objective. With both the Maintenance Bot to worry about (which requires Engineers to keep fixing) and the Canal Bridge to remove (which requires Soldiers to place the explosives), your enemy may be short on Medics.

From the bristling balcony defenses outside your spawn point, cut down anything that moves (or tries to flank you on the upper left from the

Promenade, or lower right from the Circular Foyer). If it moves, and has a Soldier icon above its head, make that your primary target.

You have the upper hand prior to the explosive being planted. After that, the biggest problem is prying an explosive off the Canal Bridge once it is set. Prepare two or three of your more agile Engineers to rush the bridge, while the rest of you cover them.

**The Canal Bridge must not fall! Because the Maintenance Bot has to cross the exploded bridge anyway, pour all your offensive resources into defending this bridge; prioritize this over damaging the Bot.**

 TIP

### ↘ A Bridge Too Far

**From a Distance:** Make the ramped area and Promenade exit your domain. It usually isn't worth venturing too much farther forward than this (although a recon teammate to run interference up at Mozno or In a Cup is sometimes worthwhile). Stay here and fortify.

**Up Close and Personal:** The interior corner by the straight bridge covers the Canal, Bridge, Promenade, Ramps, lower Circular Foyer, and Split Bridge: That's every possible attack point. Spread out around this location, using the various camping spots detailed below.

## Automated Ordnance

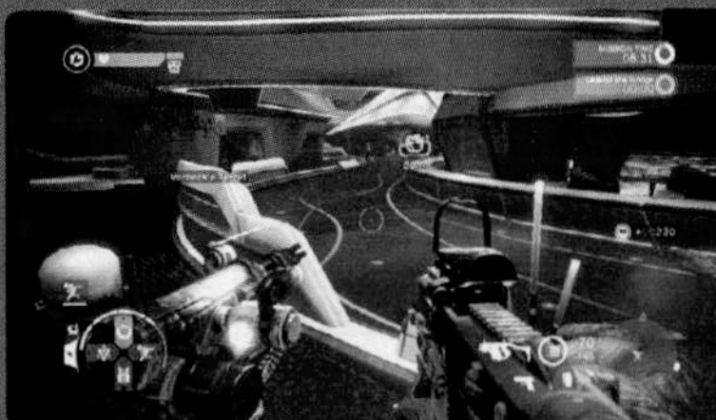

With the partial wall as cover, this turret can stop Soldiers and aim along most of the initial canal.

Set a second turret up here to cover the bridge, using the curved wall as protection.

A turret between the straight bridge and the Ramp catches foes coming from the Promenade, and is difficult to see if you're heading up the Ramp.

Place this turret so your foes must turn away from your teammates on the balconies above to tackle it, giving your team the opportunity to take them down.

Sit a turret on the bridge to give enemy Soldiers more than a headache.

Mine your spawn point exits (especially this one next to the Hotel Balcony MG Nest at the end of the Split Bridge). No one should outflank your first MG Nest.

## Automated Ordnance

7 Defend your balcony, especially from foes coming in from the Ramp or Promenade.

8 A mine at the top of either Ramp is certain to annoy, and keeps the enemy funneled away from your left flank.

9 Place a mine between both clamp points on the Canal Bridge.

## Sniper's Ally: Camping Spots

6 You can spawn camp on the balcony across from the Resistance Deployment Zone without the enemy's sentry turrets being able to hit you. Strike the Bot from here, too.

7 Stand close to the chair, and on it to spot foes rushing through Mozno, Promenade, or up the Ramp in front. Watch out behind you for an outflanker up the Ramp!

8 Lurk behind the palm tree at the base of the Ramp, and cover the Canal Bridge as well as the exit from the Circular Foyer.

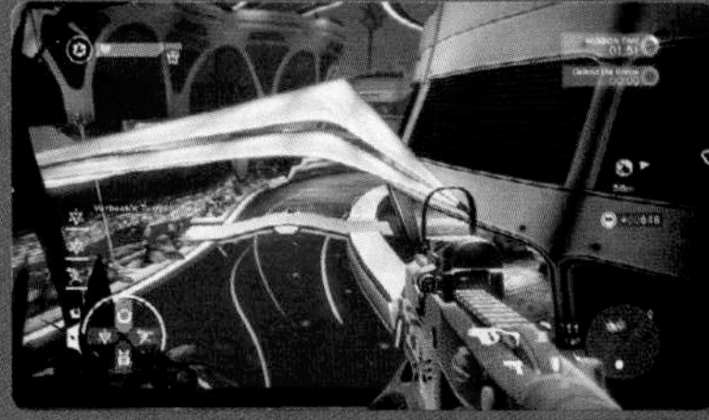

9 Aside from the MG Nest, this spawn balcony offers a great view of the Canal Bridge, Ramps, and the Promenade; all incursion points.

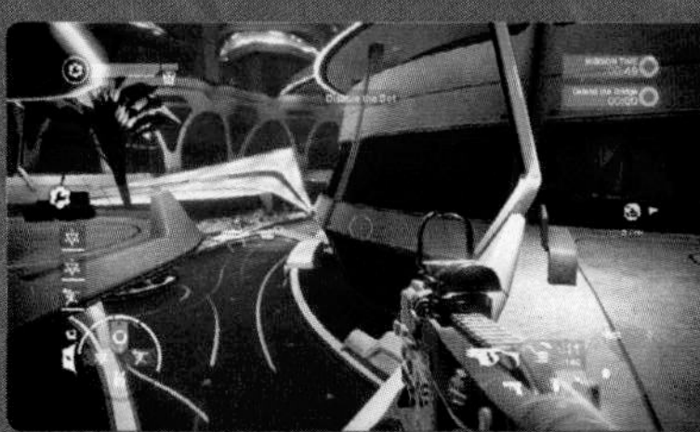

10 Aim at foes trying to tackle the MG Nest gunner, enemies heading out onto the Split Bridge, and the Canal Bridge from here.

#  Objective Tactics: Core Objective 4

### Defend the Gate Controls

Spawn Point to Controls: 00:10

Time to Hack the Controls: 01:00

#### General Tactics

For the final Core Objective, your team must change its overall tactics to be more offensive rather than defensive, but only after the SeaGate Controls building has been captured. Before then, try to set up an impenetrable cordon of death around the perimeter of the Neon Tree Courtyard. The courtyard is handy because it is open, and that's the only way enemies can reach the Controls, so you'll always see who's entered the final building.

The SeaGate Controls building offers close-quarter fighting. Remember your knife attacks

(especially if you're Light Body Type), sliding, and other advantageous techniques. Storm the entrance if you can, remembering there are two entrances at the front and one down a side alley. You can double-back around to attack the Operatives at the controls from both sides.

## Defense and Offense

**Outside Defense (Neon Tree Courtyard):** Prepare for the rush. You should have prepped the area and set up defenses the moment the Canal Bridge fell; peeling off your Engineers to set up turrets and defenses inside Le Flow, and mines throughout the SeaGate Controls. Your spawn point balcony (with the MG Nest) is an exceptional vantage point. Use that as the basis of your defensive attacks, splitting your team between here, Le Flow Foyer, and the Controls themselves.

**Interior Attacks (SeaGate Controls):** As the enemy proceeds farther toward, and eventually into, the SeaGate Controls room, your style of play must change to attacking. Take down Operatives before any other type of enemy. Assault the building with a mixture of speedy run-ins, distractions around both sides of the structure simultaneously, and a plethora of thrown grenades.

## Automated Ordnance

As you go from defenders to attackers, the number of places for mines and turrets diminishes.

10 Stick a turret behind the Balcony MG Nest to ward off flankers coming in from the Split Bridge or Executive Suite 3.

11 Place a turret covering the canal and SeaGate controls. Watch for foes in Le Flow, though.

13 Fortify the MG Apartment Balcony with a turret at one end, and a prowling sniper (or MG gunner or both) at the other.

10 Mines are less effective, except at this high-trafficked route to the Controls.

11 Also place mines at each doorway, and under the Controls themselves.

## Sniper's Ally: Camping Spots

11 Snipe foes as they rush out onto the Split Bridge from their spawn point. You can also see foes running along the canal below you.

12 The MG Nest on the Hotel Balcony is a great place to mow down those trying to reach the SeaGate Controls. Your regular weapon offers a better aiming radius though.

13 Cover the MG Nest on the Hotel Balcony with another sniper, who can wing foes down on the canal, and use the awning he's standing on as cover.

## Sniper's Ally: Camping Spots

14 Dive behind the curved desk surrounding the Health Command Post, guarding it, Le Flow's interior stairs, and the route to the SeaGate Controls.

15 Stand by the base of the Neon Tree (on the right, in case gunfire occurs from Le Flow); the enemy's route is completely open to your weapons. You may be able to tag the Operative hacking the Controls, too.

16 Stand behind the doorway inside the ground floor of Executive Suite 5. You're very safe, and can drop foes as they sprint to the SeaGate Controls door.

17 Cover the canal, pathway under the Split Bridge, MG Nest, and Le Flow Foyer from this ground level opening in your suite. Let your sentry gun deal with foes trying to attack you!

## Secondary Objectives (Second Map)

### Escort Core Objective Class Teammate

**Official Escort Info:** As you're on the defending team, this objective is less critical; just be sure to help those Engineers that should be removing the enemy's HE Charges and Hackboxes throughout Core Objectives 3 and 4.

**Unofficial Escort Info:** Buddying up with a cohort allows you to focus on tasks such as tackling the Bot (one of you demolishing it, while the other helps and heals). Try keeping one side of the MG Nest bridge clear, or standing on opposite sides and using crossfire on a single target at the same time. One of you can act as a spotter for a sniper holed up elsewhere, or hidden inside the Controls room, waiting for a target to appear before pouncing.

### Capture the Health Command Post

Engineer & Operative Advantage!

Spawn Point to Command Post: 00:15

Time to Claim Command Post: 00:10

This Command Post cannot be accessed until after the enemy Bot has crossed the destroyed Canal Bridge. After that, the doors to Le Flow's Foyer swing open. You're closest to the foyer doors, and the foyer is a tactical necessity for keeping the enemy away from the SeaGate Controls (because you cover their route from here). Plus, the desk surrounding the post is good cover. Beware of foes sneaking in via the staircase they access from the Split Bridge or other side of your old spawning grounds.

### Capture the Supply Command Post

Engineer & Operative Advantage!

Spawn Point to Command Post: 00:16

Time to Claim Command Post: 00:10

The Supply Command Post becomes trickier to reclaim the longer this mission lasts. At the start, you can send a teammate off to claim and set traps in the Circular Foyer, and use the foyer to coax

enemies away from guarding the Bot or taking the bridge. Later on when your spawn point moves, and the Resistance's Deployment Zone is literally a floor above the post, this is much more of a chore. If you can spare a single Engineer, have him claim it, then ambush foes from behind.

### Construct the Cafe MG Nest

### Construct the Balcony MG Nest

### Construct the Hotel Balcony MG Nest

### Construct the Apartment Balcony MG Nest

**Engineer & Operative Advantage!**

Spawn Point to Cafe MG Nest: 00:12

Spawn Point to Balcony MG Nest: 00:03

Spawn Point to Hotel Balcony MG Nest: 00:07

Spawn Point to Apartment Balcony MG Nest: 00:03

Time to Construct: 00:04

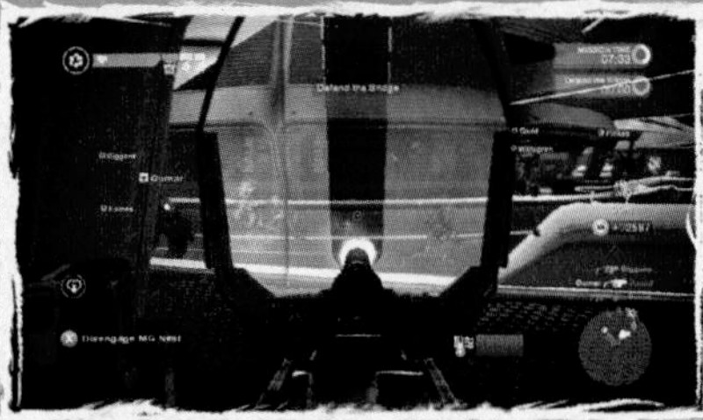

This is primarily a Resistance MG Nest, and it offers views across to the Canal Bridge. It is almost never used by your forces; although if you can sneak in here (perhaps in disguise as an Operative, assuming the MG Nest has already been constructed by the enemy), you can cover your Engineers as they defuse the bomb, or hit the Bot as it passes.

This is the central force in your defense of the Canal Bridge, and should be manned at all times. Watch for enemies outflanking you via the Split Bridge to your right; but your teammates should be covering your sides.

As long as someone is guarding the Split Bridge and doorway to your left and behind you, this is an excellent way to thin the Resistance herd as they charge up to the SeaGate Controls.

Only your team can access this Apartment MG Nest, which offers great views (and aiming) at the enemy as they cross into the SeaGate building.

## Solo Tactics

With no one to blame for a loss but yourself, you face one long defense of the Canal Bridge during Core Objectives 2 and 3. Be an Engineer to quickly claim the Supply Command Post, and defuse any bombs while keeping a high and covered position over the Canal Bridge. Once that plan is scuppered, run into the SeaGate Controls building immediately, and hold off the foes with a mixture of turrets, mines, and ambush fire.

## Mission Completion Conditions

### Continuation...

**Core Objective 1:** The enemy team succeeds in destroying the Support Pillar. Part 2 of this mission now commences....

**Core Objective 2:** The enemy succeeds in destroying the Canal Bridge. Part 3 of this mission is running concurrently....

**Core Objective 3:** The enemy successfully escorts the Maintenance Bot to the SeaGate. Part 4 of this mission commences....

### Completed!

Security forces win if you stop the enemy from completing any Core Objective by the time the timer reaches zero.

### Unsuccessful!

The match is lost if the enemy successfully hacks the SeaGate Controls before the timer ticks down.

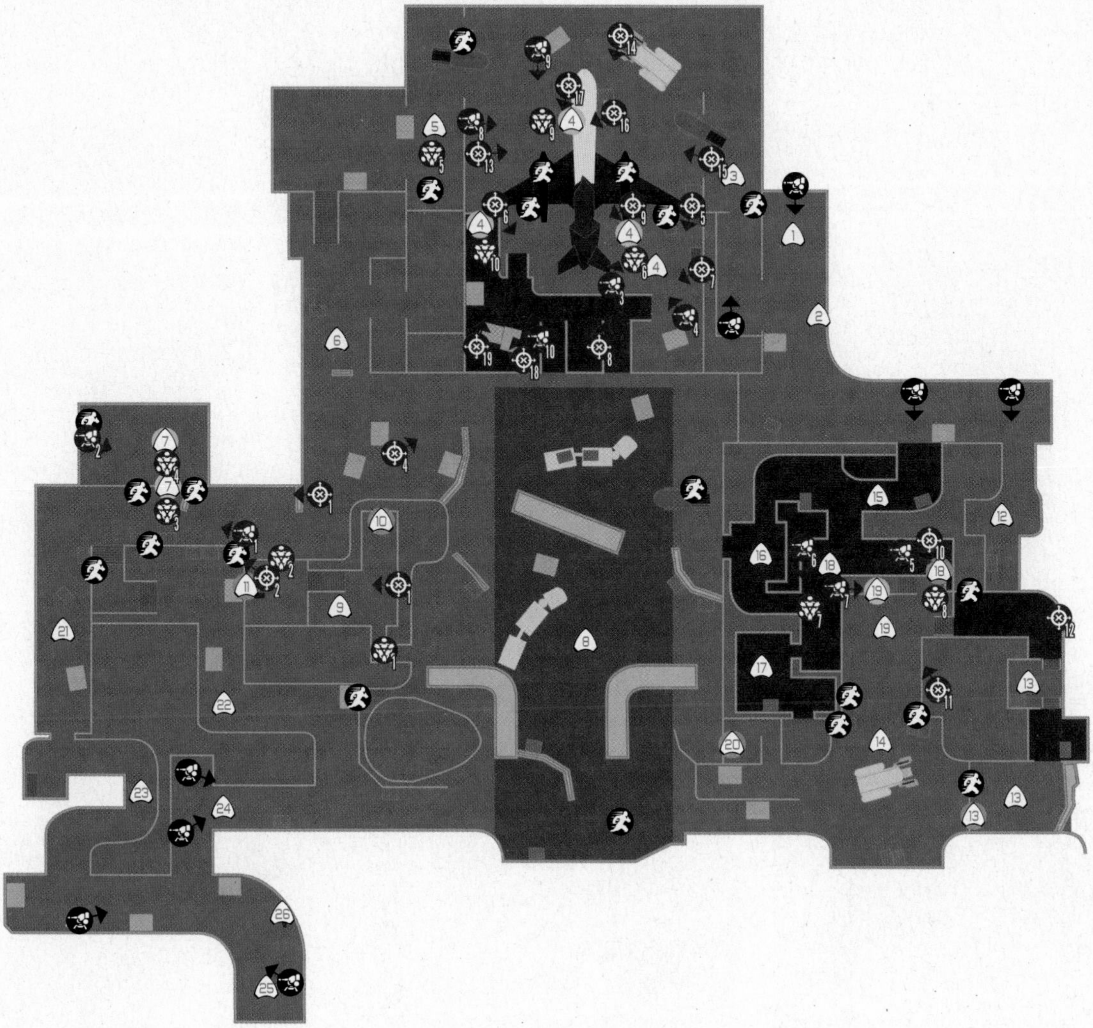

## MAP LEGEND

### ↘Refuel: Core Objective 1

1: Security Deployment Zone: Security Station AP03 (Lvl. 2)
2: Security Command Post (Lvl. 2)
3: Hangar 18: Petrol Truck Corridor F01 (Lvls. 1 & 2)
4: Hangar 18 F02 (Lvls. 1 & 2)
5: Hangar 18: Petrol Truck Corridor F03 (Lvls. 1 & 2)
6: Main Cargo Corridor & Hangar Side Entrance (Lvls. 1 & 2)
7: Storage Depot Door F31, Hydraulic Fluid, & Pathway (Lvl. 2)
8: Maintenance Yard & Taxiway (Lvl. 2)
9: Nimbus Airways Storage Building F40 to F41 (Lvls. 2 & 3)
10: Health Command Post (Lvl. 2)
11: MG Nest (Lvl. 3)
12: ND Parcel Handling: Interior Corridor & Drop F20 (Lvls. 1 & 2)
13: ND Parcel Handling: Lower Corridor F25, Cordoned-off Bay, & MG Nest (Lvl. 1)
14: ND Parcel Handling: Cargo Bay Entrance (Lvls. 1 & 2)
15: ND Parcel Handling: Interior Corridor F21 & Security Booth (Lvl. 2)
16: ND Parcel Handling: Interior Corridor F25 (Lvl. 2)
17: ND Parcel Handling: Interior Corridor F22 (Lvl. 2)
18: ND Parcel Handling: Warehouse Overlook & MG Nest (Lvl. 2)
19: ND Parcel Handling: Warehouse & Robotic Arm F24 (Lvls. 1 & 2)
20: Supply Command Post F23 (Lvl. 1)
21: Raised Storage Depot Road (Lvl. 2)
22: Sunken Storage Depot Road & Ramps (Lvls. 1 & 2)
23: Storage Corridors F12 to F13 & Security Booth (Lvls. 1 & 2)
24: Storage Corridors F11 to F14 (Lvl. 1)
25: Resistance Deployment Zone: West Jetty [F10] (Lvl. 1)
26: Resistance Command Post (Lvl. 1)

- S.M.A.R.T. Move
- Engineer Mine (Optimal Placement)
- Engineer Turret (Optimal Placement)
- Camping Spot
- Deployment Zone Turret (Invulnerable)
- Core Objective Location
- Secondary Objective Location
- Critical Path (Route)

BRINK

↘ Refuel: Overview Map

# WHAT-IF: GRAND THEFT AERO

FREEPLAY: REFUEL   RESISTANCE CAMPAIGN—DAY 8: AIRBORNE

## 22:51 Security Patrol Boat PB012, approaching Airport North Jetty

### Captain Mokoena: Briefing

Men. What I am about to tell you is classified. You are not to reveal this to anyone. There *is* an outside world. But it's in even worse shape than Ark. Thirteen years ago, we tried reestablishing contact. The team we sent was tortured to death to reveal our location. We had to move the entire Ark. We don't have the resources to move it again. We can't let Chen's fanatics reveal our coordinates. If the savages out there find us, they won't even leave our bones. You have to stop that plane from leaving!

### Optimal Class Numbers

| | COb 1 | COb 2 | COb 3 | COb 4 | COb 5 |
|---|---|---|---|---|---|
| Soldier | [2] | [3] | [2] | [3] | [2] |
| Medic | [2] | [2] | [2] | [2] | [2] |
| Engineer | [3] | [2] | [3] | [2] | [3] |
| Operative | [1] | [1] | [1] | [1] | [1] |

### Objectives (Security)

- Core Objective 1: Defend the Storage Depot Door
- Core Objective 2: Defend the Hydraulic Fluid
- Core Objective 3: Defend the Warehouse Controls
- Core Objective 4: Defend the Avionics
- Core Objective 5: Defend the Fuel Pump
- Escort Core Objective Class Teammate
- Capture the Health Command Post
- Capture the Supply Command Post
- Construct the Nimbus MG Nest
- Construct the Warehouse MG Nest
- Construct the Fence MG Nest

## Important Locations

### 1 Security Deployment Zone: Security Station AP03 (Lvl. 2)

Your forces begin their defense of Hangar 18 and the surrounding buildings from this L-shaped dock. You have a choice of three doorways to move through. To your right is the Petrol Truck Corridor (F01), leading down into the Hangar; this is a great route for defense or reaching the first Core Objective quickly. Ahead is the ND Parcel Handling: Interior

Corridor (F21) and Security Booth. This passage connects quickly to the Taxiway in the middle of the map, which is helpful when sprinting to any of the Core Objective locations. In the far left end of the dock is the ND Parcel Handling: Interior Corridor and Drop (F20). This is ideal for reaching the Cargo Bay area during Core Objectives 3 and 4.

**This facility has a number of interlocking corridors and buildings that are "tagged" with a particular number. Know which route goes where by learning these numbers: For example, the initial Petrol Truck Corridor is labeled "F01."**

TIP

## 2 Security Command Post (Lvl. 2)

Swap your class and repurpose your weaponry at this post. Because your team is defending, Engineers (with mines and turrets to position) make a good choice.

## 3 Hangar 18: Petrol Truck Corridor F01 (Lvls. 1 & 2)

Use this to reach the Hangar when you have to defend it from opposing forces. The Hangar's giant support column and the parked vehicles are good places to hide or snipe from, and they offer views of the Hangar entrance and the garage doors opposite (where foes like to outflank you).

## 4 Hangar 18 F02 (Lvls. 1 & 2)

## 5 Hangar 18: Petrol Truck Corridor F03 (Lvls. 1 & 2)

The Hangar is a vital location during Core Objectives 2 and 5, and for the rest of the mission, because the enemy is attempting to steal the plane parked in this large chamber. Surrounding the craft are a variety of containers, crates, and refueling

couplings. It is worth knowing which of these become Core Objectives to defend sooner, rather than later. The main stepped entrance leads up and onto the Taxiway. Always have a teammate or two patrolling this area. This offers quick access toward Core Objective 1 and the ND Parcel Building, making this a thoroughfare for your team early on, and a stronghold as the mission progresses.

There are two side garage corridors, each containing a parked petrol truck. The entrance chamber is a way to quickly reach the Hangar. The one opposite that (Corridor F03) is used by the Resistance to outflank you, after they enter one of the side garage doors inside the Hangar from the Main Cargo Corridor. You can slide under the partially closed garage door to head outside, too.

The Hydraulic Fluid is delivered to a pumping tank just right of the rear of the plane (Core Objective 3). Once the Avionics Computer has been hacked (Core Objective 4) over inside the ND Parcel Warehouse where the Robotic Arm is located, the Avionics are brought back into Hangar 18 (Core Objective 5), and inserted into a side panel near the yellow steps on the left side of the plane, near the cockpit. Finally (Core Objective 6), the nearby Fuel Pumps must be repaired. Stop the Resistance at any of these points, or face mission failure.

### S.M.A.R.T. Moves

The fuselage of the plane can't be leapt up, but the side storage shelving can, as well as the number of container pallets.

The two blue cherry pickers are both accessible from the wings of the plane, and offer a good vantage point, although you're prone to attack because of your high visibility.

## S.M.A.R.T. Moves

Take cover at the crate pallet next to the petrol truck, or climb on it, then onto the truck itself.

Use the blue, unextended cherry picker to leap from the lower part of the corridor to the upper part.

## 6 Main Cargo Corridor & Hangar Side Entrance (Lvls. 1 & 2)

Be ready as the first Core Objective falls, and the enemy departs with the Hydraulic Fluid from the Storage Depot Pathway and the Nimbus building; they enter Hangar 18 (where the Hydraulic Fluid is delivered) via the main entrance, but can also use this Main Cargo Corridor. The Corridor has two access doors (F03 and a half-open garage door to slide under), from the loading bay at the base of the steps. Climb the steps, use the numerous concrete barriers and crates as cover, and lay traps or force the enemy into the main Hangar entrance, where the rest of your team can cut them down. Don't let your foes use this area to outflank you.

## 7 Storage Depot Door F31, Hydraulic Fluid, & Pathway (Lvl. 2)

The Industrial Liquid Storage Depot Building sits on a raised pathway with the Sunken Road below it, adjacent to the Nimbus Building. With crates around the Depot Door, fortify this initial location in readiness for an almost instant enemy attack—this is Core Objective 1 territory. Expect heavy fighting, and do everything you can to prevent an explosive charge from being planted on the door. Core Objective 2 (the Hydraulic Fluid) is inside the one-room building itself.

## S.M.A.R.T. Moves

The barrels inside the Storage Room are good to hide behind (for friends and foes), as is the shelving on the far wall.

Hide behind the metal crates scattered around the outside of the door, or climb on top to gain a better view.

Do the same on the single fence section above the concrete barrier just to the right of the door.

## 8 Maintenance Yard & Taxiway (Lvl. 2)

Think of this large open-air location as the main "hub" of the Depot, with a variety of different sized clutter providing continuous hiding help during combat, and for helping with fortifications to quell the enemy's push deeper into your territory. There are access routes everywhere; the ramp (and sneaky crate entrance via the broken railing) at one end of the Sunken Storage Depot Road; the Nimbus Building; the Main Cargo Corridor and Hangar front entrance; two of the ND Parcel Building entrances (F25 and F22) and a second ramp leading down to the ND Parcel Cargo Bay Entrance. The large number of giant white-and-red barricades, concrete barriers, and scattered vehicles makes this a great locale to hide and attack from, especially if you can outflank foes as they try to enter the Hangar itself.

### S.M.A.R.T. Moves

Climb on the overturned aircraft docking steps for a better view of the Cargo Bay entrance.

Climb the yellow steps and petrol truck for a better view inside Hangar 18.

## 9 Nimbus Airways Storage Building F40 to F41 (Lvls. 2 & 3)

## 10 Health Command Post (Lvl. 2)

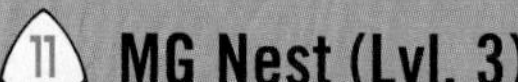

## 11 MG Nest (Lvl. 3)

This structure is important during the earlier part of this mission, but can be ignored afterward, apart from the important Health Command Post inside. This offers your forces protection from the enemy, and can be heavily fortified, stopping the Resistance from removing the door to the nearby Storage Depot. The enemy also uses this to reach the Taxiway because the building offers great cover.

Inside, the structure's corridor is a simple zigzagging passage, with a stairwell in the middle up to the MG Nest. Doorway F40 is accessed via the Taxiway. Doorway F41 is on the Storage Depot Pathway. The Health Command Post is tucked into a cubbyhole near the staircase. Use the nearby stack of metal containers as an ambush point, or to cover a teammate hacking the post.

The MG Nest is at the top of the steps, and once built, it provides excellent shots at foes running across to the Storage Depot and routes to reach it, including the Sunken Road and Ramps. Just watch for foes attacking from behind, and note that you can fire regular weapons just as effectively from this vantage point, or drop out of the window if necessary.

## 12 ND Parcel Handling: Interior Corridor & Drop F20 (Lvls. 1 & 2)

This debris-strewn corridor is a main route from your deployment zone, and used to quickly reach the Warehouse with the Robotic Arm, or to outflank the enemy by heading around and into the Cargo Bay via the Cordoned-off Bay. Look down and fire at foes from the balcony and drop (which you can't climb up onto).

## 13 ND Parcel Handling: Lower Corridor F25, Cordoned-off Bay, & MG Nest (Lvl. 1)

Don't confuse this with the other doorway marked "F25." This location is an interior corridor that wraps around and into the Warehouse, and an exterior courtyard complete with a mesh fence and MG Nest, adjacent to the Cargo Bay. Drop down from the balcony back on Corridor F20, and you can reach this area and fortify it, causing no end of headaches for the enemy as they try to access the Avionics Computer inside the Cargo Bay Warehouse. Expect high traffic during this part of the mission.

## 14 ND Parcel Handling: Cargo Bay Entrance (Lvls. 1 & 2)

This is the main route (of two) that allows access into the Warehouse and Robotic Arm inside the ND Parcel Handling building. The enemy sprints down the ramp from the Taxiway (and your forces can too, although it is quicker to use Corridor F20, or the ND Parcel building's interior corridors), so barricade yourselves in here beforehand, and do whatever you can to prevent the enemy from hacking the Avionics Computer, and stealing the components. The other way in here is via Interior Corridor F22 (patrol or fire from the balcony here). You can also head into the Supply Command Post corridor (F23) at the base of the exterior ramp, and use the fire suppressant vehicle as cover, or to lay turrets or traps.

 S.M.A.R.T. Moves 

Use the metal boxes on the left side of the cargo warehouse door as stepping stones up to the F22 corridor entrance.

Leap on the container pallet below the ramp, grab the side railings of the ramp, and vault over.

The mesh fence with the MG Nest on the other side (near the inaccessible F55 door) is easily scrambled over.

## 15 ND Parcel Handling: Interior Corridor F21 & Security Booth (Lvl. 2)

## 16 ND Parcel Handling: Interior Corridor F25 (Lvl. 2)

This is the other access corridor from your deployment zone. It leads past a Security Booth and connects with Corridor F25 inside the ND Parcel Handling building. This offers quick routes out onto the Taxiway (for the initial Core Objectives), as well as a way to reach the Overlook above the Warehouse with the Robotic Arm. Corridor F25 connects to Corridor F21 and is accessed via the Security Booth. Or, you can come in from the Maintenance Yard and Taxiway instead.

## 17 ND Parcel Handling: Interior Corridor F22 (Lvl. 2)

This U-shaped corridor runs from the upper part of the Cargo Bay above the Supply Command Post, around and into the Warehouse Overlook and MG Nest. It provides another route to or from the Warehouse.

## 18 ND Parcel Handling: Warehouse Overlook & MG Nest (Lvl. 2)

## 19 ND Parcel Handling: Warehouse & Robotic Arm F24 (Lvls. 1 & 2)

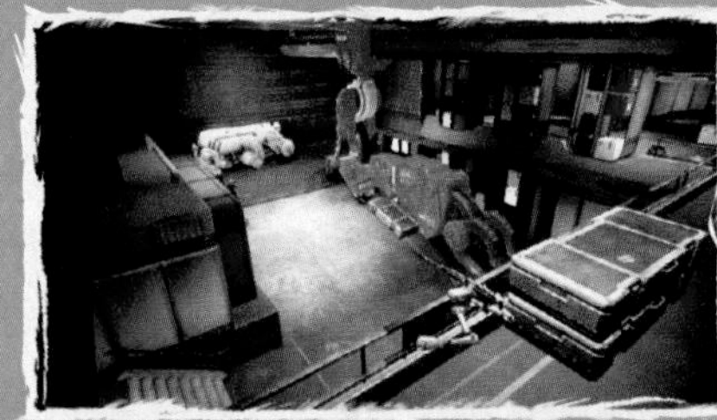

This sloping, interior room has a computer terminal on a raised stepped area at the opposite end. The enemy attempts to hack the terminal during Core Objective 4, releasing the Robotic Arm holding an Avionics Computer that is hanging from the ceiling. Your adversaries then try to carry this to the plane in Hangar 18 (Core Objective 5). This is a confluence of no less than five passages. The first is the enemy's preferred route: via the outside Cargo Bay and doorway F24,

Above the Robotic Arm is an L-shaped Overlook balcony with three entrances; all accessed from the ND Parcel Handling building. Constructing the MG Nest on this Overlook is an excellent plan, because you can cut down foes as they try to enter via the Cargo Bay (as long as someone is covering the upper entrances). You can also enter via the drop down from your spawn area Corridor F20, or via the wrap-around corridor that comes in from the exterior Cordoned-off Bay and MG Nest. Expect to defend this room viciously.

## S.M.A.R.T. Moves

Use the refueling trolley to reach the wall of storage containers, and climb up onto the balcony Overlook.

Climbing between the floors is encouraged; step on the boxes and up onto a narrow balcony to the right of the main entrance.

Stand atop the cabinet between the two sets of stairs, and wait to ambush an enemy dropping in from above, using the stairs, or heading down the ramp from outside.

## 20 Supply Command Post F23 (Lvl. 1)

This L-shaped, lower-level corridor ends at a Supply Command Post. You're closer to this post than your foes, so send a teammate here at the start of the mission to claim it (and lay traps here) first. This is also a reasonable hiding place; pop out and outflank foes trying to enter the Warehouse.

## 21 Raised Storage Depot Road (Lvl. 2)

The enemy runs across this road from their initial Storage Corridor (F13), and usually uses the crates here to gain height or cover. This offers good views of the Sunken Storage Depot Road and Ramps, and where the enemy launches an attack on the Depot Door. You're not likely to get here first, so attack the enemy in this location from the Nimbus building, especially the MG Nest.

## 22 Sunken Storage Depot Road & Ramps (Lvls. 1 & 2)

You overlook this location during Core Objective 1, as the enemy streams down this road and climbs the ramps (or over the crates and railings onto the Storage Depot Pathway). Because you have the height advantage, rain fire down on your foes, trap the ramps with explosives or a turret, and catch enemies with fire from atop the crates or up on the Nimbus building's MG Nest area. Preventing foes from leaving this location and heading to the Depot Door is your initial overriding plan.

## S.M.A.R.T. Moves

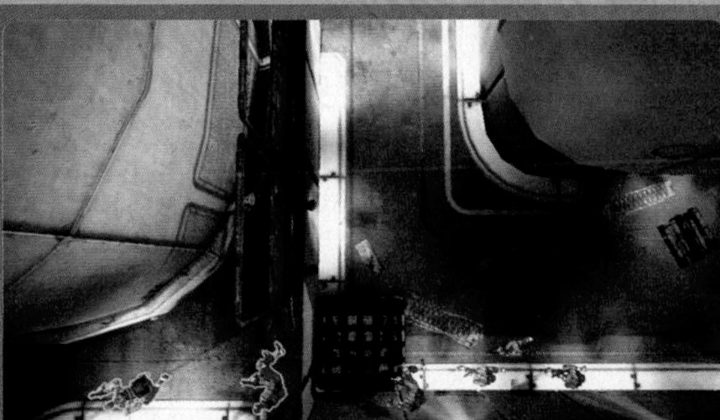

On the sunken ground? Use this crate to clamber up onto the raised Taxiway, sneaking around between the silo and Nimbus building.

Vault up over the railing and onto the Raised Storage Depot Road, if you drop down from the road or MG Nest.

You can use the crates to leap up and over the railing of the Storage Depot Pathway, or for a quick climb into the Nimbus doorway, too.

### 23 Storage Corridors F12 to F13 & Security Booth (Lvls. 1 & 2)

There isn't any point to rampaging through here because the sentry guns guarding the enemy spawn point are at the far end of this winding corridor from the Raised Storage Depot Road. Expect interaction here as the enemy tries to storm the Storage Depot Door, and utilize weapons (or turrets or mines) on the exit accordingly.

### 24 Storage Corridors F11 to F14 (Lvl. 1)

This L-shaped corridor connecting the enemy spawn point to the Sunken Storage Depot Road and Ramps, as well as the main Taxiway, is a possible route for the opposition to take during Core Objective 1, and becomes much more usable to head across the Taxiway and into the Cargo Bay or around to the Hangar. Hide behind the scenery in the Taxiway and snipe foes coming out of this location (or set turret or mine traps), if you can push up this far.

### 25 Resistance Deployment Zone: West Jetty [F10] (Lvl. 1)

Moving to this exterior, L-shaped dock gets you killed by sentry turrets positioned here by the Resistance team, or other enemy firepower. Although it is possible to place mines and turrets in the Storage Corridors to waylay the enemy, venturing into here is a death-sentence. The enemy chooses a corridor, and rushes to a Core Objective from this point.

### 26 Resistance Command Post (Lvl. 1)

This location lets your opposition change weapons and class. It cannot be interacted with by Security forces.

## Objective Tactics: Core Objective 1

### Defend the Storage Depot Door

Spawn Point to Door: 00:18

Time to Open the Door: 00:10

Time to Plant Explosives: 00:07

Time to Disarm Explosives: 00:05

Countdown to Explosion: 00:40

#### General Tactics

There's no time to lose; your enemies are likely to already be at the Depot Door when you arrive, leaving you at a slight disadvantage. Make up for that with squads that know their individual roles. First, be sure you have a large number of Engineers; you need one to defuse the bomb that's been planted. Next, figure out the quickest way to the Depot—via Petrol Truck Corridor F01, and out of the main Hangar ramps into the Taxiway.

From here, split your forces to head in from the Nimbus building, and the Storage Depot Pathway. Unless the enemy is well-defended and using the Taxiway for some reason, the Main Cargo Corridor is an option that takes slightly longer to traverse. Then break through enemy defenses and stop their Soldiers. Failing that, cover your own Engineers to stop the bomb.

## Defensive Posturing

**Nimbus Doors and Depot Pathway:** Shore up your defenses by dropping mines at the Nimbus Building's Taxiway entrance, and setting up snipers by the MG Nest. But the main forces are rushing in from this corner, by the Nimbus entrance F41. Tackle the foes up here by rushing, dodging behind the concrete barriers, and even dropping into the Sunken area and using the ramps to outflank.

**Grenade Prowess:** There are two insanely difficult grenade-lobbing possibilities to crush the enemy's morale if you pull them off: The first involves running up the Hangar ramp into the Taxiway, and looking up and right, at the narrow gap between the right edge of the Nimbus building, and the curved roof of the Main Cargo Corridor entrance and Depot building (picture 1). Cook a grenade as you race up the ramp and lob it in the gap. The grenade (or Molotov) passes between the buildings and lands on the Depot Door floor, killing the Soldier planting the bomb!

The other option is less crazy; as you reach the Storage Depot Pathway, try cooking and ricocheting a grenade or Molotov between the gap in the mesh fence and the side of the Depot building (picture 2), circumventing the protection the fence usually gives enemies.

**Yes, both grenade lobs require some practice! Have a "spotter" inform you where the grenades end up, so you can hone your aiming.**

TIP

## Automated Ordnance

You may wish to check the Resistance team's placement for ideas, and areas to avoid or watch for.

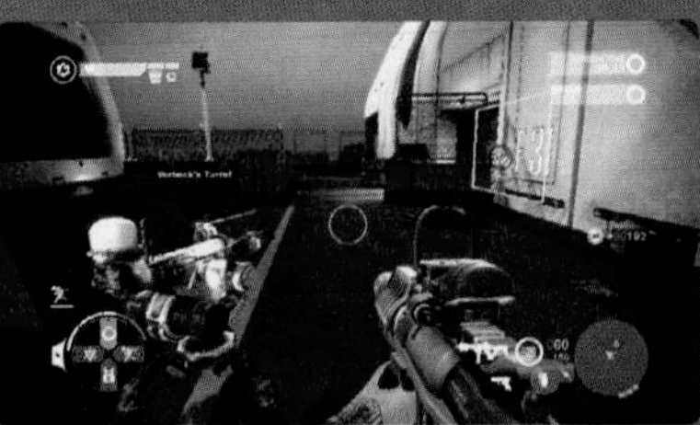

Stick a turret here, behind partial cover, but with an unimpeded view of the Depot Door.

1 Mines in the Nimbus building corridor entrance facing the Taxiway are recommended, so you don't need to watch for enemies ambushing you from behind.

2 Also place a mine around the corner at the Nimbus building exit (F41) to stop enemies outflanking you.

3 Don't forget to protect the Depot Door with a mine; even if it is spotted, it takes time to defuse.

## Sniper's Ally: Camping Spots

1 Hide behind the crates here, cutting down Resistance forces coming in from the Taxiway.

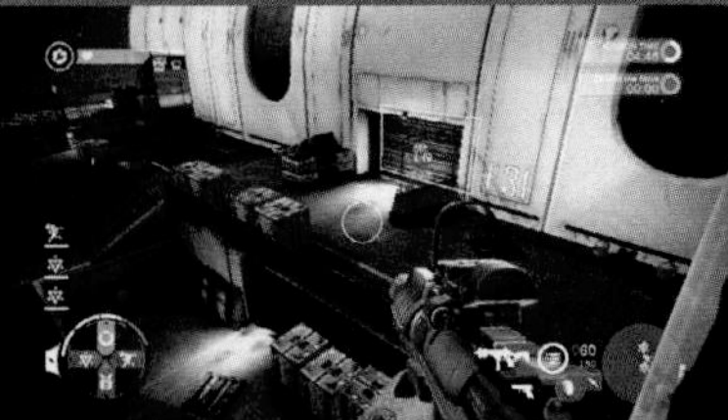

2 Commandeer the MG Nest, or guard it and use your own weapon to tag foes rushing along the routes to the Depot Door.

3 Standing at (or leaning around) the corner of the Main Cargo Corridor keeps you in cover, and enables you to fire at foes and the bomb-planter through the narrow gap between the mesh fence and wall.

# Objective Tactics: Core Objective 2

##   Defend the Hydraulic Fluid

Spawn Point to Storage Depot: 00:22

Storage Door to Fluid Receptacle: 00:14

Time to Deliver the Fluid: 00:05

### General Tactics

Even when the Depot Door is removed by the enemy, they must still locate, take, and carry the Hydraulic Fluid to the receptacle inside Hangar 18, and this is where your defending prowess must be displayed. To start with, shore up the defenses inside the Depot itself; get there before the enemy, and set up one of the more lethal turret traps available (shown in Automated Ordnance, below).

While some of your team try to keep the carrier at bay, interfering with their routes as much as possible, and forcing them (for example) back into the Sunken Storage Depot Road, and around to the Taxiway, the rest of your team should be fortifying the Hangar. There should be plenty of mines and turrets ready to tackle the enemy from either entrance. Perform a similar defensive posture during Core Objectives 4, and 5, both of which require the enemy to interact with machinery inside this Hangar.

### Hangar 18: Mega Death

**Main Entrance Massacre:** Have the majority of your team guarding the massive Hangar door, which is permanently open. Position your team in the various camp spots dotted around the Hangar, with Engineers setting up mines and turrets before taking their own cover spot (ideally close to a turret they can repair). Your primary target is the carrier. Secondary targets are Medics. Train your weapons on the entrance, then the Hydraulic Fluid receptacle if the carrier breaks through.

**A waiting mine, lobbed grenade, and turret fire in addition to your gunfire should occur as the Resistance reaches the receptacle! And if the Hydraulic Fluid is dropped in here, where you've expended time and energy setting up your defenses, leave it there, so the enemy keeps rushing to pick it up, and dying under your hail of bullets every time!**

 TIP

**Side Entrance Slaughter:** Position one or two of your team in covered positions in case the enemy decides to rush down the Main Cargo Corridor and in through Petrol Truck Corridor F03. If you place a mine or turret here, you can hear the discharge before you see the enemy, and react more quickly to stop the incursion.

## Automated Ordnance

2 *Enter the Storage Depot where the Hydraulic Fluid is, Mantle up the red shelving in the corner opposite the entrance, and set up this turret.

3 Cover the Hydraulic Fluid receptacle by placing a turret here, close to the crate so it protects the turret somewhat.

4 This is another recommended location for a turret, as the fencing protects it somewhat from enemy shots and grenades.

4 Set a mine over the Hydraulic Fluid, if the enemy isn't close enough to take it in time.

5 Set a mine in the Petrol Tank Corridor F03 so you can hear foes trying to outflank you.

6 Place a mine here, by the receptacle, as a final defense.

** This is one of the best turret spots on any map! This covers the only entrance and is immune to grenades hitting the floor, plus you can hide behind it while you repair it.*

## Sniper's Ally: Camping Spots

5 Use this open alcove, hiding by the crates and rattling off shots on the left side of the Taxiway at enemies trying to enter the Hangar.

5 Patrol either wing, jumping back and forth onto the cherry picker; you also have an unobstructed view of the receptacle and the ramps.

6 The top of this shelving enables you to see into the Taxiway, and blast foes heading over from the Nimbus building area.

## Sniper's Ally: Camping Spots (continued)

7 Ambush enemies coming down the ramp, and at the receptacle, which you can see through the railing.

8 Hide behind the actual receptacle, so you can dart out, dispatch, and return fire at foes incoming down the ramp.

# Objective Tactics: Core Objective 3

## Defend the Warehouse Controls

Spawn Point to Warehouse Controls: 00:13

Hangar 18 to Warehouse Controls: 00:16

Time to Hack the Controls: 00:48

### General Tactics

The enemy is on the march, but you have the advantage; you'll reach this chokepoint in half the time it will take the Resistance, you have the Overlook's height advantage, and the MG Nest over the foes streaming in from the Cargo Bay to utliize. Watch for enemy Operatives entering this location early. Have an Engineer prowling and setting up traps even before the Hydraulic Fluid is delivered, stopping any early-bird antics from the opposition.

When the action heats up properly, you have an outer set of defenses to man (see below) based off the enemy's proximity to each of them, and an inner defensive line, which is the small staircase leading to the hack point. Covering the steps to the hack point with mines and turrets is a sure-fire way of slowing or even completely stopping the enemy. Even if they realize the mines are there, they still have to take the time to remove them, and your snipers around the Overlook balcony, or re-spawned brethren running in quickly via the Interior Corridor and Drop F20, can help eradicate the Resistance menace.

### Incoming! Hold these Lines!

**Exterior Ramp and Cargo Bay:** Start your defenses off by heading down into the Warehouse and meeting the enemy on the outside Cargo Bay, taking the Supply Command Post, and laying some traps. If you can keep the enemy outside while your Engineers set up on the Overlook and cover the small stairs with mines and turrets leading to the hack point, you're well defended.

**ND Parcel Handling Corridors:** The enemy's major route is through the Interior Corridors, so take Interior Corridor F21 to the Taxiway outside, and have a spotter yell to you about where the majority of the enemies are heading. Meanwhile, cover the entrances to the Overlook so your foes can't easily take the area directly above your hack point.

**The Cordoned-off Bay:** The fence in the Cargo Bay leads (if you climb it) up and over to a Cordoned-off Bay and corridor that links to the interior of the Warehouse. The enemy enjoys flanking this, but not if you've left a few traps and a couple of teammates with their weapons at the ready. Be wary of dropping down the hole when you re-spawn and using Interior Corridor F20; enemies like to ambush you from here.

## Automated Ordnance

5 Place a turret atop the Overlook, and stop foes from taking over this upper area quite so easily.

6 A turret up here covers the Overlook without being immediately taken out with grenades.

A turret by the hack point is useful because it's difficult to remove from the other side with the screens in the way.

7 Cover the Overlook entrances with mines if you're constantly battling foes up here.

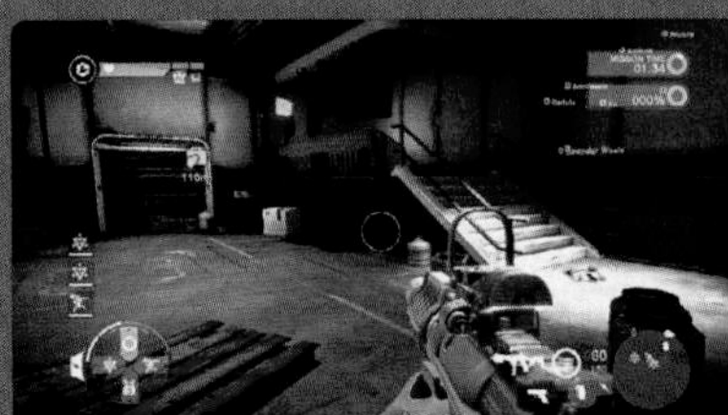

8 Multiple mines at this location help prevent Operatives from reaching the hack point.

## Sniper's Ally: Camping Spots

9 The MG Nest is in a good position on this Overlook but lacks aiming maneuver-ability. Instead, use your weapon to drop foes charging into the Warehouse.

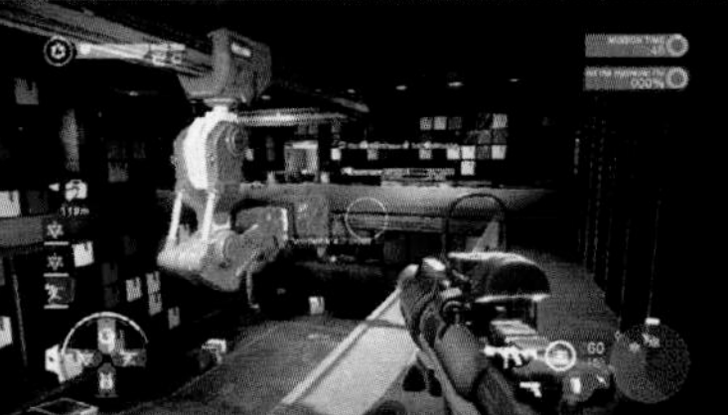

10 Cover the Cargo Bay entrance, the ramp down into the lower area, and the Overlook from this ambush point.

11 If the enemy is in disarray, you can command this corner of the flanking corridor leading from the Cordoned-off Bay, and cover friends dropping down from the hole above.

# Objective Tactics: Core Objective 4

## Defend the Avionics

Spawn Point to Avionics: 00:08

Warehouse Controls to Avionics: 00:25

Time to Access Avionics: 00:05

### General Tactics

When the Robotic Arm releases the Avionics, you can still utilize all of the defensive and camping positions you learned during Core Objective 3. But once any of the opposing team picks up the Avionics, have a couple of your team try to coax them into a ramble around the facility instead of a direct path, while the rest of your team—just like during Core Objective 2—reinforces the Hangar. And just like Core Objective 2, the enemy has two different incursion points: the main Hangar ramps and the Petrol Truck Corridor F03.

**The Automated Ordnance and Sniper's Ally locations you used during Core Objective 2 also apply here.**

NOTE

## Automated Ordnance

8 Surprise the Resistance somewhat by putting a turret here, hidden by the crates.

9 Cover the entire side of the Hangar, and have the crates act as partial cover.

9 A mine at the Avionics delivery point under the fuselage is your last line of defense, but the first place to put a mine during this objective.

## Sniper's Ally: Camping Spots

12 Locate the metal crates on the same wall as the Petrol Truck Corridor F03, and hide on either side of them, ideally on the opposite side from the way the enemy is approaching.

13 Sit by the vehicle that overlooks the Petrol Truck and front of the plane. You can cover both sides of the Hangar, the side entrance, and the Avionics delivery spot.

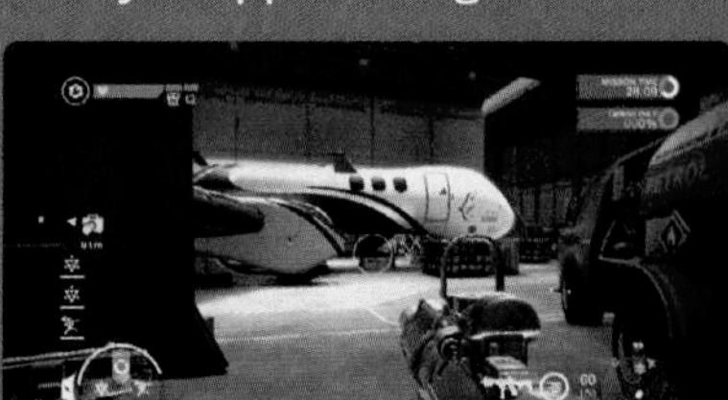

14 Stand between the Hangar structure and Petrol Truck for a covered ambush spot covering the Avionics delivery spot.

15 Crouch down by the plane's front wheel, for a closer ranged ambush attack location.

# Objective Tactics: Core Objective 5

## Defend the Fuel Pump

Spawn Point to Fuel Pump: 00:12

Avionics to Fuel Pump: 00:03

Time to Repair: 00:10

### General Tactics

The location remains unchanged, and the enemy routes remain just as they were. You are to defend Hangar 18 (with more competence than you displayed before), only this time the enemies are heading for the Fuel Pump on the elevated side platform, close to one of the wings. Be warned; this objective can be completed very quickly by one or two enemy Engineers, so denying them the area is most important. Cluster your mines and turrets in the area just in front of the repair point, place as many as possible, and have all your team take down Engineers as primary targets, and the Medics who heal them as secondary ones.

**The Automated Ordnance and Sniper's Ally locations you utilized during Core Objectives 2 and 4 also apply here.**

NOTE

## Automated Ordnance

10 Slot in a turret on the lower floor facing the Fuel Pump, with the railing and metal plates as cover.

10 The raised area the Fuel Pump is sitting on is a vital place to mine.

## Sniper's Ally: Camping Spots

16 Stand atop the yellow stairs by the plane's cockpit door, and Wall-jump to the wing for a closer takedown if your initial ranged shots don't do the job.

17 Crouch near one of the entrance ramps for a good view of the Fuel Pump, then ambush Engineers coming in to fix it.

18 Duck down on the other side of the crates near Camp Spot 19, which is another good place to pounce.

# Objective Tactics: Secondary Objectives

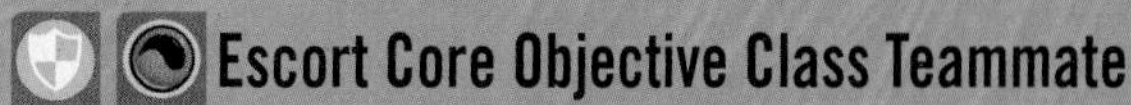

## Escort Core Objective Class Teammate

**Official Escort Info:** During Core Objectives 1 and 3, where Engineers can make a difference by removing enemy HE Charges and Hackboxes respectively, be sure you have covering fire as they wade into the ensuing firestorm. In general though, as a defending team, this objective isn't usually available, but two-player tactics are still worth remembering.

**Unofficial Escort Info:** Work with a teammate to secure the Nimbus building and defend it, or become a Medic and back up an Engineer attacking the bomb planters. When the foes deliver the Hydraulic Fluid or Avionics, or try to reach the Fuel Pump, setting up on opposite sides of the Hangar and catching enemies in the crossfire is always helpful. Doubling up as Engineers to set traps and fix turrets is a great option, too. In-between, defend the Warehouse Controls with a pair of Engineers who know where each other is placing turrets and mines.

## Capture the Health Command Post

Engineer & Operative Advantage!

Spawn Point to Command Post: 00:12

Time to Claim Command Post: 00:10

Fight over this sooner rather than later, because this location confers a tactical advantage during Core Objective 1, and it is worth claiming with the Nimbus MG Nest. Launch attacks on the Depot Door and Hangar from here. When the action moves to the opposite side of the map, this becomes much trickier to maintain, although there's some advantage to keeping an Engineer here, using the Nimbus building as cover when shooting foes from behind who are milling about the Taxiway and at the Hangar entrance.

## Capture the Supply Command Post

Engineer & Operative Advantage!

Spawn Point to Command Post: 00:14

Time to Claim Command Post: 00:10

Send an Engineer off to claim this at the mission's beginning, setting a mine and a turret to trap a foe jogging in to claim it for the opposition, and then rejoining your team to stop Core Objective 1 from failing. As the mission progresses, this becomes less and less tenable to keep, especially when the enemy rushes the Cargo Bay. However, it's a good ploy to have a spare Engineer constantly taking this away from the Resistance. The manpower they waste attempting to reclaim it means fewer foes engaged in more important objectives.

## Construct the Nimbus MG Nest

## Construct the Warehouse MG Nest

## Construct the Fence MG Nest

Engineer

Spawn Point to Nimbus MG Nest: 00:19 

Spawn Point to Warehouse MG Nest: 00:09 

Spawn Point to Fence MG Nest: 00:16 

Time to Construct: 00:04

Expect a fierce battle for control of the Nimbus MG Nest. If the enemy isn't there, then thank your deity of choice and man the MG as quickly as possible, after placing a mine at the base of the stairs and claiming the Health Command Post. You'll need help defending this MG Nest (the enemy usually storms this area), but if you can reach this window, you can easily cut down Soldiers trying to clamp a bomb on the Depot Door.

The enemies try their hardest to stop you even reaching the Overlook the Warehouse MG Nest sits on, never mind the MG Nest itself. If the Resistance is defending the ND Parcel Interior Corridors with vim and vigor, you may well wish to ignore this, especially because it doesn't cover the side entrance into the Warehouse, the lower part of the building under the crane, or the computer your rivals are hacking.

If the enemy hasn't realized, or isn't using the Cordoned-off Bay to reach the side incursion point, you can send a single Engineer off to mend and man this turret. Alas, although you can cut down foes on the exterior ramp, much of the MG's field of view is obscured by the vehicle. There are more important areas to defend.

### Solo Tactics

**With single-player heroics to master, take control of each Core Objective. Begin as an Engineer, build up your defenses, and stay by the Depot Door, ready to remove the bomb if it is planted. Fall back and set traps to ensure the Hydraulic Fluid isn't delivered, mining the Hangar and camping at a good angle to drop the enemy carrier. Then depart for the Warehouse, and cover the computer area with mines and a turret, before taking to the balcony to rain grenades and gunfire down. For the final two objectives, a similar plan is recommended as for Core Objective 2; rush to the Hangar, trap the area, and tag foes trying to reach the Avionics and Fuel Pump areas.**

# Mission Completion Conditions

## Continuation...

**Core Objective 1:** Your team fails to defend the Storage Depot Door. Part 2 of this mission now commences....

**Core Objective 2:** Your team fails to stop the delivery of the Hydraulic Fluid. Part 3 of this mission now commences....

**Core Objective 3:** Your team fails to halt the hacking of the Warehouse Controls. Part 4 of this mission now commences....

**Core Objective 4:** Your team fails to stop the delivery of the Avionics. Part 5 of this mission now commences....

## Completed!

The match completes if you successfully stop the enemy completing any Core Objective (1–5), and the timer ticks down.

## Unsuccessful!

Security forces lose if the enemy successfully repairs the Fuel Pump before the timer ticks down.

# CHALLENGES

## Brinktroduction

These four Challenges each take place in a different cube-shaped training maze, filled with obstacles and opponents on certain occasions. Each Challenge tests and teaches a different aspect of your natural abilities, whether that's completing objectives as different classes, using your Wall-jumping and S.M.A.R.T. move dexterity, learning to keep a Bot moving under fire, or keeping a Command Post from falling into enemy hands.

Complete these Challenges as early as possible, because they allow you to hone your skills and unlock some meaty armaments and other items. In fact, two Challenges (Escort Duty and Tower Defense) are significantly easier if perfected before you reach Level 1!

TIP

## Be More Objective

Challenge Time: 10:00

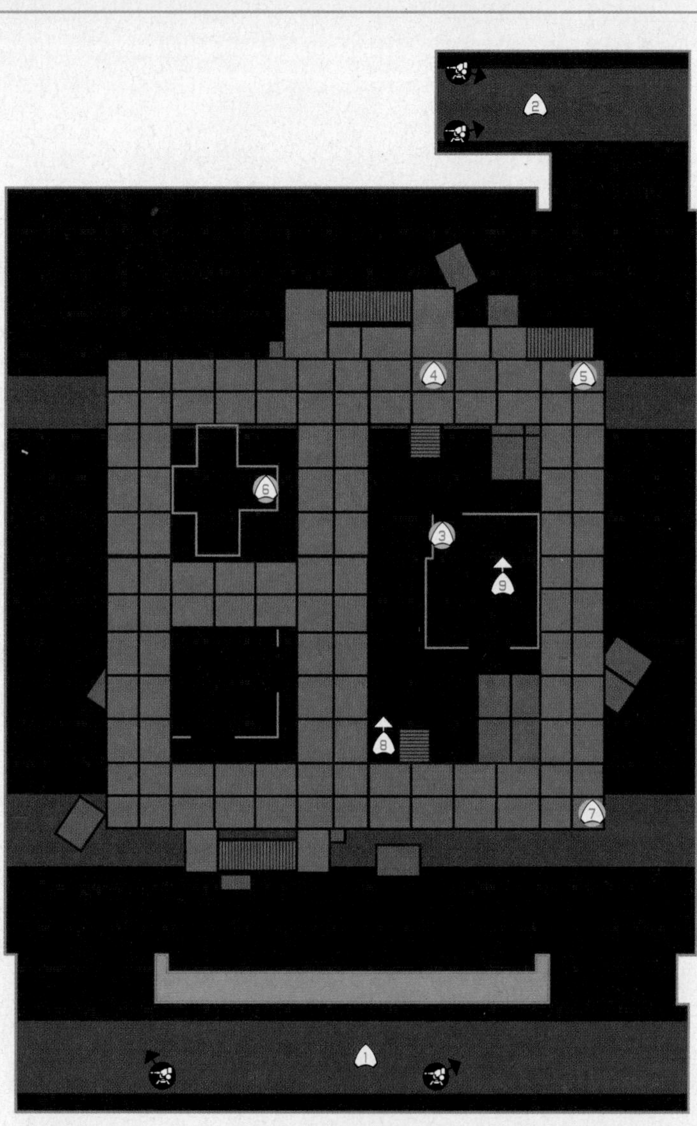


MAP LEGEND
(★★★ Difficulty Only)

1: Friendly Deployment Zone
2: Enemy Deployment Zone
3: First Objective: Bomb Site (Command Post)
4: Second Objective: Generator
5: Third Objective: Hacking Terminal
6: Third Objective: Intel
7: Final Objective: Delivery Box
8: Defensive Location 1
9: Defensive Location 2
Deployment Zone Turret (Invulnerable)

BRINK Be More Objective: Overview Map

## Briefing

Race to complete all the objectives while the rest of your team draws the enemy's fire. Bonus points are awarded for better time, not dying, getting headshots, and knocking down the enemy with Frag grenades. You unlock rewards for beating the three difficulty levels.

# Tactics

**The following tactics are for the hardest (★★★) difficulty: The position of each of the objectives differs for the easier versions of this Challenge. Because you cannot replay the less difficult versions unless you create a new character, the critical tactics are for the highest difficulty, shown on these pages.**

**A helpful tutorial voiceover is available if you play on ★ difficulty.**

**Remember you can play with human teammates, who may be a lot more proficient in covering and aiding you!**

**NOTE**

## First Objective

Bomb Placement: 00:05

Explosive Timer: 00:25

From your deployment zone, exit to the right, and then sprint directly to the "Bomb Plant" site. As you approach, ready a grenade (or Molotov) behind the stacked crates to distract the incoming enemies in the vicinity (picture 1). While your foes regroup, plant the bomb immediately, and then quickly retreat into the alley behind you (picture 2) to defend the bomb site as you wait for it to detonate. Then run to the Command Post (behind the door the explosives took out) and change class.

## Second Objective

Repair Generator: 00:16

The safest route to take as an Engineer is to double-back toward your deployment zone (turn right from the Command Post), and then rush the two sets of stairs on the raised platform (picture 1). Once you're on the upper gantry, cross to the other side, and use the stairs opposite to reach the generator (picture 2). Use the crates as cover if the enemy presence becomes troubling, although taking this route allows you to miss the majority of the fighting in the central part of this maze. When you begin the repair, keep facing the enemy's spawn point and quickly remove those who come too close.

**Remember that you can disconnect from your repair to cut enemies down, and then return where you left off.**

**TIP**

## Third Objective

Planting Hack Box: 00:03

Hacking: 00:16

As with the second objective, it is usually wise to double-back up the stairs nearest your spawn area. Follow exactly the same path from the Command Post as before to reach the upper gantry. With this route, you continue to maneuver without becoming involved in a mass battle, which is time-consuming and dangerous. Fight only when you have to!

Up here, the route offers plenty of cover as you approach (picture 1). When hacking this objective, use the adjacent stacked crates as cover from oncoming enemies; they mostly stream up and in from the stairs near the generator (picture 2).

### Final Objective

Upload Intel: 00:05

After the hacking, sprint down the gantry (stay on this upper platform) and turn left to the open hatch (picture 1), before dropping down to collect the intel. Exit left from the interior crates and double-back (again) toward your spawn area, moving counter-clockwise around the perimeter of this maze. Before you reach your deployment zone, Mantle up the crates shown (picture 2), and up to the gantry leaving only a short sprint to the delivery area (picture 3).

### Defensive Location 1

This location offers a good vantage point, if you're protecting a teammate engaged in the first and second objective. Placing a turret at this location is also beneficial.

### Defensive Location 2

From this vantage point, you can cover the second objective, and also prevent foes from attacking your teammate at the third objective (as shown). Quickly reach this location by Mantling some stacked crates near the Command Post.

**Splash Damage Score to Beat (Solo): 2,307,712**

**Splash Damage Score to Beat (2 Players): 1,800,771**

**Splash Damage Score to Beat (3 Players): 1,865,920**

**Splash Damage Score to Beat (4 Players): 2,011,108**

## Parkour This

Challenge Time: 01:00

### Briefing

As a Light Body Type, race around the environment, hitting all the checkpoints in any order as fast as you can. Bonus points for better time and passing through invisible markers in hard-to-reach places. For this Challenge only, you're given access to the Light Body Type. To use Light Body Type in regular gameplay, you must unlock it by earning XP to level up. You unlock rewards for beating the three difficulty levels.

## Tactics

### Beams of Light

As soon as you trigger the timer by stepping through the lit line, you begin. There are hundreds of different possible routes, but for the two lower difficulty settings, the actual time you take and score you receive don't matter. Your score on the ★★★ Difficulty is the one you can show off.

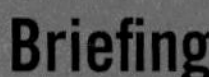

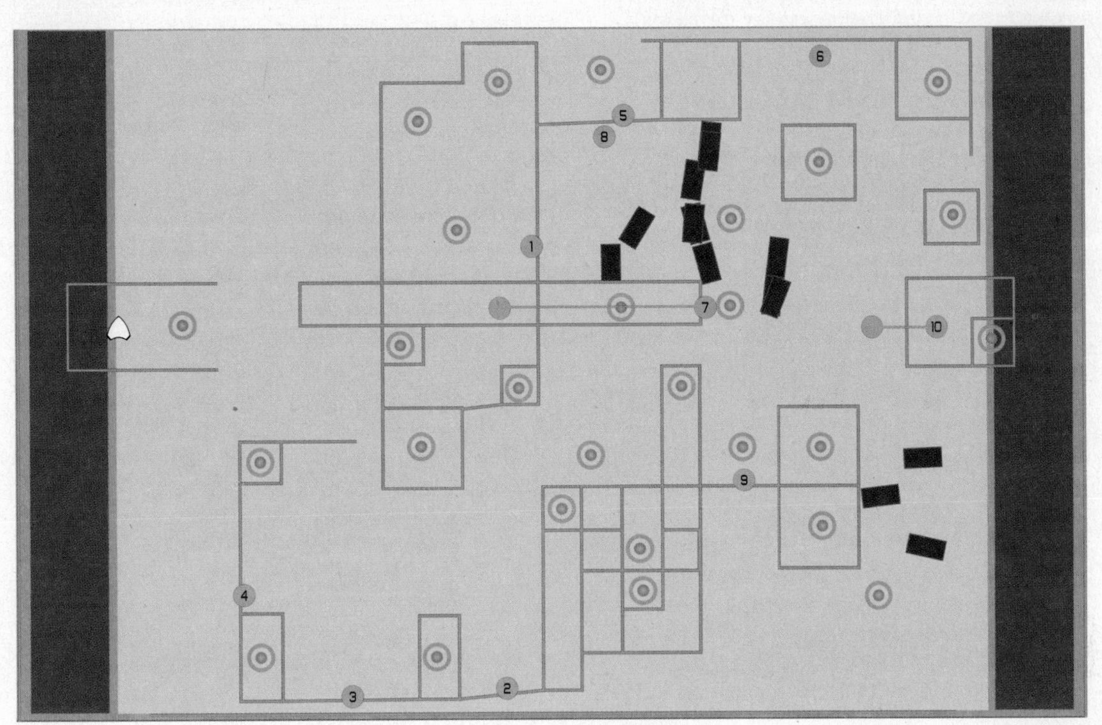


**MAP LEGEND** (All Difficulties)

- Friendly Deployment Zone / Completion Point
- Route Bonus Point

BRINK ↘ Parkour This: Overview Map

You can step over the beams of light in any order. Pass over them at any height; during a Wall-jump works just as well as stepping on them using your feet. Although the next beam of light appears on your radar (if you get lost, use it), the locations are better left to your planning; use this guide's map to see the locations, so you can visit them all as quickly as possible.

Now comes the part where your score skyrockets! To achieve the highest number of points, you need to combine completing the level (by hitting the final beam of light as shown), and collecting all of the route bonuses. The rest of this section reveals the locations of all 10!

> **NOTE**
> **Although these are numbered 1–10, you don't have to reach them in this order.**

## 1 Route Bonus

Wall-jump on this section.

## 2, 3, 4 Route Bonuses

Wall-jump on each section; there are three bonuses here.

## 5 Route Bonus

Wall-jump on this section.

## 6 Route Bonus

Wall-jump on this section, under the light fixture.

## 7 Route Bonus

Slide under this section, then Vault over this section for a single bonus.

## 8 Route Bonus

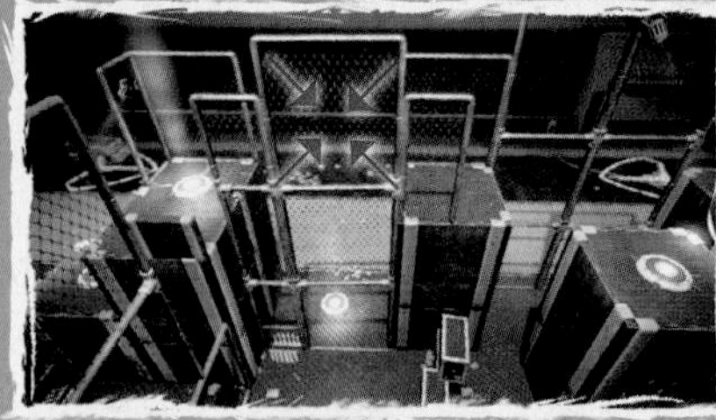

Wall-jump on this section.

## 9 Route Bonus

Wall-jump on this section.

## 10 Route Bonus

Slide under here; note the position of the crates so you know which side this is on.

**Combine all the advanced S.M.A.R.T. moves you've learned in the Gameplay chapter of this guide, use this guide map to trace the best path that covers all beams of light and route bonuses, and own the leaderboards!**

**TIP**

Splash Damage Score to Beat (Solo): 192,366

Splash Damage Score to Beat (2 Players): 246,002

Splash Damage Score to Beat (3 Players): 197,811

Splash Damage Score to Beat (4 Players): 125,705

# Escort Duty

Challenge Time: 10:00

Bot Repair Time: 00:10

Mine Deployment Time: 00:02

Turret Deployment Time: 00:03

### Briefing

Use your Engineering skills to keep the repair robot up and moving while you escort it to the end of the level amid incoming waves of enemies. Bonus points are awarded for better time, not dying, getting headshots, and knocking down the enemy with Frag grenades. You unlock rewards for beating the three difficulty levels.

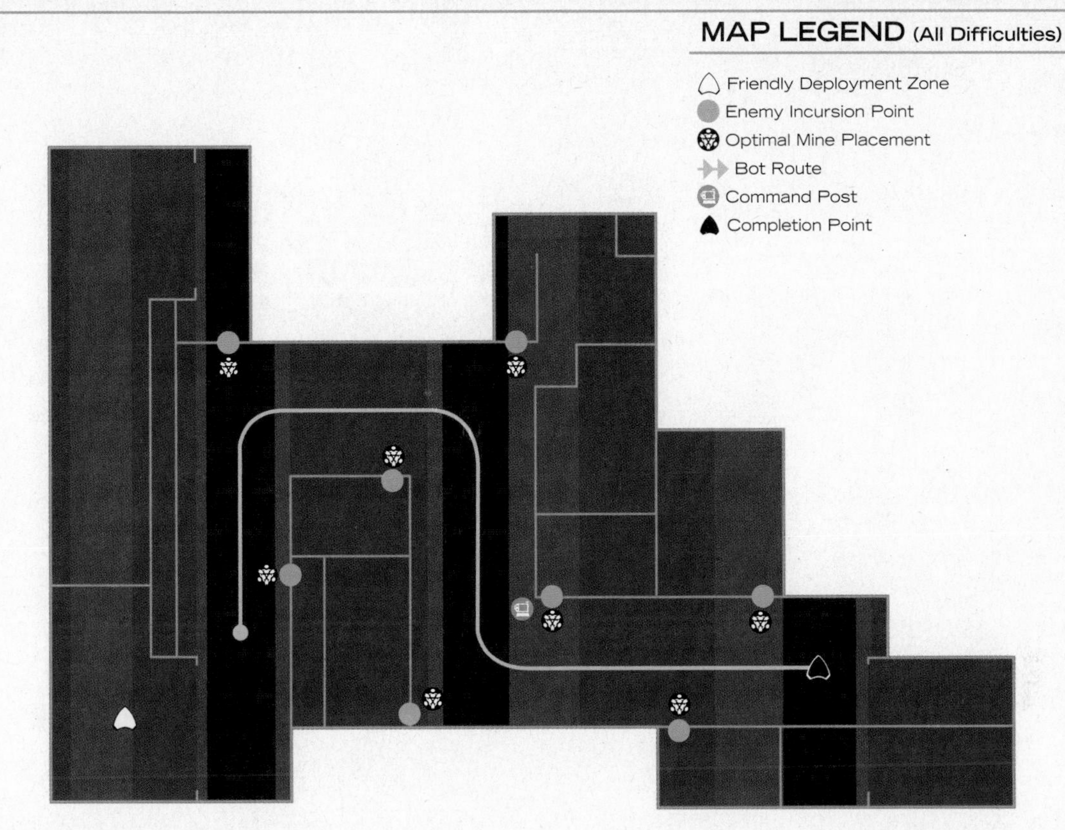


BRINK ↘ Escort Duty: Overview Map

## ↘ Tactics

### Enemy Incursion Points

The enemies in question rush out of Enemy Incursion Points, signified by an amber alarm light that flashes just before an incursion. Prep the area for these waves ahead of time, or risk being overrun! Note the bonuses you receive for headshots and knocking foes over with Frag grenades.

### Repairing and Reaping

As an Engineer, you have various powers at your disposal. To start with, you can buff your weapon's damage; do this immediately on spawning. Secondly, you can deploy mines and turrets. The former are extremely potent when placed in front of every Enemy Incursion Point. Turrets (as shown) can be effective (if placed at range, or with a lengthy aim, straight down a corridor at an Incursion Point), but the time you take placing (or constantly fixing) them could be better spent dodging enemy fire and cutting foes down with your regular weapon. Finally, you can (and must) repair the Bot you're chaperoning; where and when are detailed below.

Having trouble staying alive? Then sacrifice the speed of your Light Body Type and bulk up to a Heavy, with more health.

**TIP**

## Tactical Tips

As your Challenge begins, the enemies you face match you with the same quality of weaponry and type of abilities. Therefore, use a new character or complete this Challenge at the earliest possible time (prior to Level 1 is perfect, but the earlier the better) so the Challenge will be much easier.

Ammunition is a constant problem in this Challenge, because you run out of it with alarming frequency. Choose weapons with larger clip sizes and more total ammunition, such as the Kross and Galactic SMGs. Save a little time by grabbing your preferred weapon loadout and buffing your damage before you cross the start line.

As soon as you cross the start line, rush to capture the Command Post before you even think about repairing the Bot, because this splits the enemy's priorities throughout the Challenge (they'll be torn between taking the post back or fighting you). This also allows you to restock ammunition easily. Take out any enemies trying to recapture the post!

Capturing the Command Post not only allows you to quickly resupply your ammunition, but grants you an additional Health Pip, which is very useful when shrugging off the constant enemy fire.

**TIP**

One of the biggest problems—the constant stream of enemies coming from the highlighted doors—can be mitigated somewhat by placing mines outside the doors to knock the foes down, stop them from initially spreading out, and make them easier to dispatch. Optionally set up a turret to catch more foes streaming out, or better yet, lob in a grenade to explode as the foes pick themselves up.

As each wave of foes storms out into the corridors, your highest priority is dispatching them as fast as possible. The Bot should take as little damage as possible, and you shouldn't have to stop to repair it much. This isn't easy, especially on higher difficulties. When you've learned when the next wave is coming, try mowing down foes in their entrance corridors before they spread out.

You may think utilizing the Bot as cover is a great plan—after all, you're safe behind its bulk—but this simply draws more enemy fire, and you'll need to repair it much more often, making for a longer time and fewer bonuses. Instead, run ahead, use the scenery as cover, and split the foes so they can't fire on the Bot and you without completely changing direction.

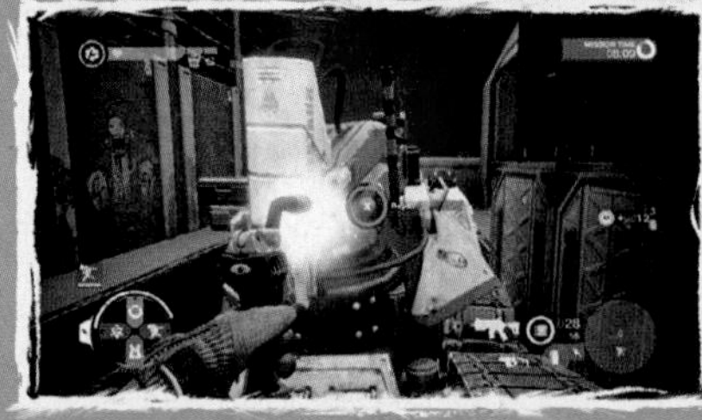

One very cunning plan is to halt your Bot repairing just before the machine reaches full health, and then fight off the current wave of enemies. The Bot is invincible in this state, and you can complete the repair while gaining more ground unabated after dispatching the current wave. Keep the Bot moving for as much of the Challenge as possible.

**CAUTION**

A stopped Bot equals a terrible Challenge score!

A hulking Heavy with a vicious-looking minigun might be an imposing threat, but enemy Medics are much more insidious, and should be targeted as a priority. You want to kill your enemies once, and not have them resuscitated and fighting you for a second time! Note the class icon next to the health bar above each enemy's head.

**Splash Damage Score to Beat (Solo): 1,805,896**

**Splash Damage Score to Beat (2 Players): 2,435,560**

**Splash Damage Score to Beat (3 Players): 2,211,671**

**Splash Damage Score to Beat (4 Players): 1,990,318**

# Tower Defense

Challenge Time: 15:00

Turret Deployment Time: 00:03

Mine Deployment Time: 00:02

**MAP LEGEND** (All Difficulties)

Friendly Deployment Zone

Enemy Incursion Point

Optimal Mine Placement

Command Post

BRINK

Parkour This: Overview Map

## Briefing

As an Engineer, you need to use all of your abilities to stop multiple waves of enemies from capturing your Command Post. Bonus points are awarded for better time, not dying, getting headshots, and knocking down the enemy with Frag grenades. You unlock rewards for beating the three difficulty levels.

The type of weapon you use is vitally important. A grenade launcher may seem to be an instant-kill mayhem-inducing device, but it has severely limited ammunition and you run out before you stop the later swarms. With this in mind, choose a weapon (and back-up) with large clip sizes and ammo reserves, such as the Kross and Galactic SMGs.

Watch for the amber lights to flash over the doors to signal an incoming enemy incursion. Focus your fire on those doors, and try (at least at the doors on the same level as you) to cut down foes as they run up the entrance corridor before heading out of the door; lob in Frag grenades to catch multiple foes and increase your bonus.

The Command Post is built to withstand regular ordnance, so use it as cover from enemy gunfire. This should only occur when you've failed to stop a wave, and foes have started to spread out from their Incursion Points due to multiple points opening at the same time. Stand your ground, and circle the Command Post to stay alive!

The Command Post also offers life-sustaining items, such as additional ammunition for your weapons. Check the post (to ensure it's in good shape), and reload your ammunition at the end of every wave, when you have the time. Doing this systematically means you may wish to swap out a weapon for one with more power, but fewer bullets (but one that still lasts for a wave).

## Tactics

**If you find yourself constantly low in health, switch to a Heavy body type.**

TIP

Attempt this Challenge before you level up your character because the waves of enemies keep pace with the weapons and abilities you've gathered thanks to unlocks, making them increasingly more difficult to battle. Try to finish all three Challenge levels before you reach Level 1 (so you gain the unlocks), before returning later in your character's life to try for fun and score improvement.

By now, you should know that the Engineer class buffs their weapon damage; apply this immediately before you cross the start line, and once more each time you re-spawn. Failure to buff simply wastes ammunition, because you aren't making the best use of every bullet. The deployment zone has two exits, so vary your movement to keep the enemy guessing.

You don't just have an itchy trigger-finger at your disposal; as an Engineer you can deploy turrets and mines. Turrets are useful, and should cover an Incursion Point (ideally an upper one with a straight aim so the turret doesn't take time to aim) while placed close to some cover, but don't waste time mending a turret until after a wave is over; you're better off using your firearms and not taking damage during a repair.

The other Engineer-employed device is the explosive mine. These are incredibly helpful in stopping the initial foe from a wave, and should be placed at the top of the stairs. Replenish them after each explosion as quickly as possible; mines are most helpful in taking out a foe from one direction while you focus on killing enemies coming in from a different route.

If the enemies have left their spawning tunnels and are fanning out from the Incursion Points, tackle any Medics as a priority, because they can bring back their brethren from the dead. You want to fight each enemy once, and not multiple times!

The electronic board on one of the side walls keeps track of what round you're on (out of three) and what wave you're on (each filled-in box signifies a completed wave). Check the picture for the total number of waves.

**Splash Damage Score to Beat (Solo): 10,244,400**

**Splash Damage Score to Beat (2 Players): 10,471,544**

**Splash Damage Score to Beat (3 Players): 7,159,613**

**Splash Damage Score to Beat (4 Players): 9,043,535**

# APPENDICES

## Brinktroduction

The following tables allow you to check your progress with a complete list of Achievements and Trophies; the necessary Experience (XP) needed for each Level and Rank; every single action that grants you XP (and how much); what the Challenge mode unlocks; and how all the Character Customizations are unlocked.

### Appendix I: Achievements and Trophies

| | Name of Reward | Description | Xbox 360 Points | Playstation 3 Trophy |
|---|---|---|---|---|
| | Time to sleep | Earn all other trophies | None | Platinum |
| | The start of something big | Win any mission, whether Campaign or What-If | 25 | Bronze |
| | You've saved the Ark | Win all main missions of the Security Campaign (not including What-If missions) | 60 | Bronze |
| | You've escaped the Ark | Win all main missions of the Resistance Campaign (not including What-If missions) | 60 | Bronze |
| | The story has just begun | Win both story Campaigns (not including What-If missions) | 100 | Silver |
| | Viva la revolution! | Win every Resistance Campaign mission, including bonuses | 75 | Silver |
| | To serve and protect | Win every Resistance Campaign mission, including What-If missions | 75 | Silver |
| | Tough as nails | Win all storyline Campaign missions (not including What-If missions) playing either Online Versus, or in Hard mode | 100 | Gold |
| | Use the wheel, earn more XP | Complete an objective after first selecting it on the Objective Wheel | 5 | Bronze |
| | I think I know a shortcut | Open a shortcut for your team | 10 | Silver |
| | Cut 'em off at the pass | Close an enemy team's shortcut | 10 | Silver |
| | Oh I'm sorry, was that yours? | Capture an enemy's Command Post | 5 | Bronze |
| | That's how you win a match | While on defense, take down an attacker who's completing a Primary Objective | 10 | Silver |
| | Not over till the fat lady sings! | Take down an enemy with gunfire while knocked down | 5 | Bronze |
| | Not so sneaky now, are you? | Reveal an enemy in disguise | 5 | Bronze |
| | Great shot kid! One in a million | Take down an enemy by shooting a grenade | 5 | Bronze |
| | You shall not pass! | While on defense, prevent the attackers from completing their first objective | 15 | Silver |
| | They never knew what hit them | While on offense, win the match in less than 30% of the time limit | 15 | Silver |
| | Was it the red or the blue wire? | Disarm an HE charge | 10 | Silver |
| | You can place another mine now | Take down an enemy with a mine | 5 | Bronze |
| | Pump up the volume! | Upgrade your team's Command Post | 5 | Bronze |
| | Smart decisions win battles | Attempt to Revive an objective-class teammate over a non-objective teammate near a Primary Objective | 10 | Silver |
| | Tis better to give than receive | As a Medic, using the Transfer Supplies ability, give the last of your Supplies away | 5 | Bronze |

| | Name of Reward | Description | Xbox 360 Points | Playstation 3 Trophy |
|---|---|---|---|---|
| | I live... again! | Revive yourself | 5 | Bronze |
| | That mine you found? Disarmed! | Spot a mine which is later defused by another Engineer | 10 | Silver |
| | Brinksmanship | Complete an Operative Primary Objective within 5 seconds of breaking disguise | 10 | Silver |
| | A bit of a headache | Take down an enemy with a Cortex Bomb | 5 | Bronze |
| | Boom! | Detonate an HE Charge | 10 | Silver |
| | No I insist, you take it | Use the last of your Supplies to refill a teammate's ammo rather than your own | 10 | Silver |
| | It's a trap! | Take down an enemy with a Satchel Charge | 5 | Bronze |
| | Well done! | Complete your first 1 Star Challenge | 10 | Silver |
| | Very well done indeed! | Complete your first 3 Star Challenge | 20 | Silver |
| | Who's bad? | Complete all 1 Star Challenges | 25 | Silver |
| | King of the world! | Complete all 3 Star Challenges | 100 | Gold |
| | Well that was educational | Collect all Audio Logs | 50 | Silver |
| | You're going places, kid! | Reach Rank 2 | 25 | Silver |
| | Time to start a new character | Reach Rank 5 | 100 | Gold |
| | Total (Xbox 360 and PC): | | 1,000 | |

## Appendix II: Required Experience for Ranking and Leveling

### Rank 1

| Level | XP Needed |
|---|---|
| Level 0 | 0 |
| Level 1 | + 1,000 |
| Level 2 | + 2,000 |
| Level 3 | + 3,000 |
| Level 4 | + 4,000 |

### Rank 2

| Level | XP Needed |
|---|---|
| Level 5 | + 5,250 |
| Level 6 | + 6,500 |
| Level 7 | + 7,750 |
| Level 8 | + 9,000 |
| Level 9 | + 10,250 |

### Rank 3

| Level | XP Needed |
|---|---|
| Level 10 | + 12,000 |
| Level 11 | + 13,750 |
| Level 12 | + 15,500 |
| Level 13 | + 17,250 |
| Level 14 | + 19,000 |

### Rank 4

| Level | XP Needed |
|---|---|
| Level 15 | + 21,750 |
| Level 16 | + 24,500 |
| Level 17 | + 27,250 |
| Level 18 | + 30,000 |
| Level 19 | + 32,750 |

### Rank 5

| Level | XP Needed |
|---|---|
| Level 20 | + 37,500 |

## Appendix III: Experience (XP) Rewards Breakdown

### General Actions

| Action | XP Reward |
|---|---|
| Damaging an enemy (per point of damage done) | 1 |
| Killing an enemy | 20 |
| Killing an enemy (melee attack) | 20 |
| Killing an enemy (melee attack with finish) | 20 |
| Killing an enemy (incapacitated enemy) | 2 |
| Killing an enemy (with teammates nearby) | 10 |
| Killing an enemy (while enemy disguised) | 10 |

| Action | XP Reward |
|---|---|
| Killing an enemy (while you are disguised) | 10 |
| Friendly fire (per point of damage done) | -1 |
| Being close to a killer (same team) | 1 |
| Removing a Sticky Bomb | 25 |
| Escorting an important VIP (per second) | 1 |
| Knocking down an enemy or VIP | 10 |
| Killing an enemy VIP | 20 |

## Gameplay

| Action | XP Reward |
|---|---|
| Hacking a Core Objective | 300 |
| Guarding a Core Objective (per second, 1 or no enemies present) | 1 |
| Guarding a Core Objective (per second, 2 or more enemies present) | 2 |
| Guarding a Secondary Objective (per second, 1 or no enemies present) | 1 |
| Guarding a Secondary Objective (per second, 2 or more enemies present) | 2 |
| Healing a VIP Escort | 5 |
| Completing a VIP Escort | 100 |
| Damaging a VIP Escort | 150 |
| Changing to class needed to complete Core Objective | 200 (30 secs. cooldown) |
| End of Match Bonus | 1 |
| Escort Bonus | 100 |

## Core Objectives

| Action | XP Reward |
|---|---|
| Repair a Core Objective (per second) | 10 |
| Complete a repair of Core Objective | 200 |
| Explosive destruction of Core Objective | 250 |
| Disarm explosive on Core Objective (per second) | 10 |
| Complete disarm explosive on Core Objective | 125 |
| Place explosive on Core Objective | 50 |
| Hack a Core Objective | 50 |
| Disarm a Hack Box (per second) | 10 |
| Completely disarm a Hack Box | 50 |
| Hack a Core Objective (per second) | 10 |
| Completely hack a Core Objective | 100 |
| Deliver package to Core Objective | 200 |
| Stop and return a package | 50 |
| Kill the carrier delivering a package | 75 |
| Picking up a dropped package | 20 |

## Secondary Objectives

| Action | XP Reward |
|---|---|
| Repair a Secondary Objective (per seconds) | 5 |
| Complete a repair of Secondary Objective | 100 |
| Explosive destruction of Secondary Objective | 100 |
| Disarm explosive on Secondary Objective (per second) | 5 |
| Complete disarm explosive on Secondary Objective | 75 |
| Place explosive on Secondary Objective | 25 |
| Hack a Secondary Objective | 25 |
| Disarm a Hack Box (per second) | 5 |
| Completely Disarm a Hack Box | 25 |
| Hack a Secondary Objective (per second) | 5 |
| Completely Hack a Secondary Objective | 50 |
| Capture a Command Post | 50 |
| Capture a Command Post (per second) | 5 |
| Deliver package to Secondary Objective | 100 |
| Picking up a dropped package | 10 |

## Soldier

| Action | XP Reward |
|---|---|
| Searching Bodies (Scavenge) | 40 |
| Flashbang Grenade (per use) | 30 |
| Resupplying Ammo (missing ammo/max ammo) | 150/100 |

## Medic

| Action | XP Reward |
|---|---|
| Reviving | 100 |
| Throwing a Syringe to teammate | 75 |
| Self Resurrection | 10 |
| Self Revival | 50 |
| Buffing Health | 75 |
| Buffing Metabolism | 75 |
| Buffing Health (Improved Life Buff) | 75 |
| Adrenaline Boost | 50 |
| Adrenaline Boost damage withstood (per point of damage) | 1 |
| Speed Boost | 75 |
| Reviving a VIP Escort | 50 |
| Reviving a VIP Escort (Improved Life Boost) | 75 |
| Lazarus Grenade reviving | 25 |

## Engineer

| Action | XP Reward |
|---|---|
| Buffing damage | 75 |
| Gave Extra Kevlar | 50 |
| Disarming an explosive charge | 100 |
| Constructing an objective (per second) | 5 |
| Constructed an objective | 60 |
| Enemy killed by mine | 20 |
| Enemy killed by turret (light) | 20 |
| Enemy killed by turret (medium) | 20 |
| Enemy killed by turret (Gatling) | 20 |
| Enemy killed by hacked turret | 20 |
| Enemy killed by controlled turret | 20 |
| Mine disarmed | 75 |
| Repairing a turret (per second) | 5 |
| Repaired a turret | 30 |
| Upgraded a Command Post | 50 |

## Operative

| Action | XP Reward |
|---|---|
| Spotting a mine | 75 |
| Spotting an enemy disguise | 150 |
| Homing Beacon (tagging a non-disguised enemy) | 50 |
| Successful disguise | 125 |
| Comms Hack success | 150 |
| Hacking a turret | 50 |
| Controlling a turret (per second) | 5 |
| Firewalled a Command Post | 30 |
| Successful Cortex Bomb damage against enemy | 40 |

## Appendix IV: Challenge Mode Unlocks

The following is unlocked as you progress through Challenge mode. Here's how it all breaks down:

| Challenge Name | Difficulty | Reward(s) |
|---|---|---|
| Be More Objective | * | Lobster Grenade Launcher, Ritchie Revolver, Duct-Taped Magazines |
| Be More Objective | ** | Bulpdaun Submachine Gun, Speed Slings, Speed Holsters |
| Be More Objective | *** | Your Top *** Score on Leaderboards |
| Parkour This | * | Barnett Light Rifle, Front Grips, Rapid Fire |
| Parkour This | ** | Belgo Machine Pistol, Silencers |
| Parkour This | *** | Your Top *** Score on Leaderboards |
| Escort Duty | * | High Powered Scopes, Red Dot Sights, Muzzle Brakes |
| Escort Duty | ** | EZ-Nade Auto Grenade Launcher, Drum Magazines |
| Escort Duty | *** | Your Top *** Score on Leaderboards |
| Tower Defense | * | FRKN-3K Assault Rifle, Underslung Grenade Launcher, Adjusted Iron Sights |
| Tower Defense | ** | Gotlung Minigun, High-Capacity Magazines |
| Tower Defense | *** | Your Top *** Score on Leaderboards |

## Appendix V: Appearance Customization Unlocks

The table below reflects what pieces of clothing are unlocked for each level the player hits.

| | Char. Lvl. | What Is Unlocked |
|---|---|---|
| | Level 0 | G Pants, Straps Jacket, Tattered Shirt, Forearm Bandages, Vest, White Skull Face Paint, Stubble, The Dude tied glasses |
| | Level 0 | The Good Cop Glasses, The Tank Jacket, The Tank Vest, Muscle Vest, Shirt and Sweatband, Muscle Shirt, Adhesive Bandages, The Tank Riot Helmet |
| | Level 0 | Hair: The Receding, The Buzz Cut, The Cropped, The Dreadlocks, The Tighten-Up, Facial Hair: The Stubble, all body and facial tattoos |
| | Level 1 | The Warrior Outfit |
| | Level 1 | The Bug Outfit |
| | Level 2 | The G Outfit |
| | Level 2 | The Unit Outfit |
| | Level 3 | The Mohawk, The Corn Rows, The Fin, The Tendril Afro |
| | Level 3 | The Flat Top |
| | Level 4 | The Wasted Outfit, Headshot Face Paint |
| | Level 4 | The Shield Outfit, The Scruff, War Paint |
| | Level 5 | Heavy Body Type (this ability must be purchased) |
| | Level 6 | The Firestarter Outfit |
| | Level 6 | The Jesse Outfit |
| | Level 7 | Light Body Type (this ability must be purchased) |
| | Level 8 | Facial Hair: The Beardy, The Chinny, The Goatee, The Plait, The P.I. |
| | Level 9 | The Boiler Suit Outfit, Hand Print Face Paint, The Hockey Mask |
| | Level 9 | The Good Cop Outfit, Broken Nose |
| | Level 10 | The Safety, The Rasta, The Stripes, The Natural, The Tattered Vest |

| | Char. Lvl. | What Is Unlocked |
|---|---|---|
| | Level 10 | The Flat Top, The Military Mohawk, The Ponytail |
| | Level 10 | Red tint for all hair |
| | Level 11 | The Dude Outfit, the Goggles |
| | Level 11 | The Look Outfit |
| | Level 12 | The Sweat, Tribal Face Paint |
| | Level 12 | Barbarian Face Paint, The Beret, The Cop Glasses |
| | Level 13 | The Lost Outfit, The Cannibal, String Vest |
| | Level 13 | The Eel Outfit, the Eel Vest |
| | Level 14 | The Dreads, The Spiky Big Hair, The Spiky Hair |
| | Level 14 | The Dreads and Cap, The Fashion |
| | Level 15 | The Voice Outfit |
| | Level 15 | The Bouncer Outfit, The Bouncer Shirt |
| | Level 16 | Voodoo Face Paint |
| | Level 16 | Camouflage Face Paint |
| | Level 16 | Facial Hair: The Chops, The Wrestler, The Beatnik, The Wolf, The Trimmed |
| | Level 17 | The Shemagh, The Spiky Helmet, The Disgrace |
| | Level 17 | The Cap, The Jesse shades |
| | Level 18 | The Fortress Outfit |
| | Level 18 | The Bomb Outfit |
| | Level 19 | Long-Sleeve Shirt, Clown Face Paint |
| | Level 19 | Stab Vest, Dirty Face |
| | Level 20 | The Anger Outfit |
| | Level 20 | The Freak Outfit |
| | Level 20 | Green tint for all hair |

# BRINK™

## OFFICIAL GAME GUIDE

WRITTEN BY DAVID S. J. HODGSON

Prima Games
An Imprint of Random House, Inc.

3000 Lava Ridge Court, St. 100
Roseville, CA 95661
www.primagames.com



Product Manager: Shaida Boroumand
Associate Product Manager: Jesse Anderson
Design & Layout: Jody Seltzer, Bryan Neff, Rick Wong, and Kari Keating
Manufacturing: Suzanne Goodwin
Maps: 99 Lives Design
Copy Editor: Asha Johnson
Technical Editor: André Fredrick



ISBN: 978-0-307-46997-7
Printed in the United States of America

11 12 13 14 LL 10 9 8 7 6 5 4 3 2 1

We want to hear from you! E-mail comments and feedback to **dhodgson@primagames.com**.

**Bethesda Softworks Credits**
Greg Hounsom
Ryan Wiltshire
Matt Grandstaff
Erin Losi
Paris Nourmohammadi
James Constantino

**Additional Content:**
Neil 'Exedore' Alphonso
Stephen 'Crispy' Etheridge
Steve 'badman' Hessel
Aubrey 'Bezzy' Hesselgren
Richard 'Fluffy_glMp' Jolly
Ed 'BongoBoy' Stern

**Special Thanks to:**
Steve 'Citrusy' Alves
Phil 'Pipster' Barnell
Simon 'Lianshi' Batty
Sean 'Poon' Francis
Pete 'Dusk777' Loveridge
Matt 'Anti' Lowe
Digby 'SirDigga' Murray
William 'Smooth' Richens
Everyone at Splash Damage

**David S. J. Hodgson**
Originally hailing from the English city of Manchester, David began his career in 1995, writing for numerous classic British gaming magazines from a rusting, condemned, bohemian dry-docked German fishing trawler floating on the River Thames. Fleeing the United Kingdom, he joined the crew at the part-fraternity, part-sanitarium known as GameFan magazine. David helped launch GameFan Books and form Gamers' Republic, was partly responsible for the wildly unsuccessful incite Video Gaming and Gamers.com. He began authoring guides for Prima in 2000. He has written over 80 strategy guides. He lives in the Pacific Northwest with his wife Melanie, and an eight-foot statue of Great Cthulhu.

**Author Thanks and Acknowledgements:**
To my loving wife Melanie; Mum, Dad, and Ian; The Moon Wiring Club, Boards of Canada, Laibach, and Kraftwerk; Ron & Fez; and J for poor Gustaf Johansen, A sailor from Oslo most sorely tried, Who survived pirates, R'lyeh and even Great Cthulhu, Then was hit by a bundle of papers and died. Extra special thanks to Shaida Boroumand at Prima for her dedication, help, and support on this project. Thanks too, to the cartographical skills of 99 Lives, the design prowess of Jody Seltzer and Bryan Neff; and all at Prima.
One thousand and one thanks to all at Bethesda Softworks, and Splash Damage; for their help, generosity, knowledge, and time on this project.